P9-AOW-528

WITHDRAWN

Acclaim for Carla Kaplan's

ZORA NEALE HURSTON

"This is a wonderful addition to what we need to understand about a spirited, extraordinary life." —Alice Walker

"[Hurston's] letters have a freshness, humor and immediacy that make you forget how long ago they were written."
—*Quarterly Black Review*

"The letters in Ms. Kaplan's collection tell a life story of exceptional interest." —*The Wall Street Journal*

"[An] epic collection. . . . The arrival of these letters is like a beacon cast on Hurston's life." —*The Orlando Sentinel*

"From her letters emerges an . . . articulate but qualitatively different voice, or better yet, chorus of voices, compounding the contradictions of an undeniably courageous life. We can finally see her . . . served up raw." —*Africana.com*

"Hurston's letters reveal an energetic writer. . . . Beautifully executed."
—*Publishers Weekly*

"Sublime and intimate. . . . An intriguing installment in the study of Hurston's work and life." —*Upscale*

"The Hurston we revered before this book was only an illusion. *Zora Neale Hurston: A Life in Letters* gives us a flesh and blood Hurston with sharp edges and dark corners and endless, enchanting layers."
—Emily Bernard, author of *Remember Me to Harlem: The Letters of Langston Hughes and Carl Van Vechten, 1925–1964*

WITHDRAW

CARLA KAPLAN

ZORA NEALE HURSTON

Carla Kaplan is Professor of English, Gender Studies, and American & Ethnic Studies at the University of Southern California and a noted Hurston scholar. She is the author of *The Erotics of Talk: Women's Writing and Feminist Paradigms,* and the editor of *Dark Symphony and Other Works* by Elizabeth Laura Adams, *Every Tongue Got to Confess: Negro Folk-Tales from the Gulf States* by Zora Neale Hurston, and *Passing* by Nella Larsen.

ALSO BY CARLA KAPLAN

The Erotics of Talk: Women's Writing and Feminist Paradigms

ZORA NEALE HURSTON

A Life in Letters

MONTGOMERY COLLEGE
ROCKVILLE CAMPUS LIBRARY
ROCKVILLE, MARYLAND

ZORA

A Life

NEALE

in Letters

HURSTON

Collected and Edited by

CARLA KAPLAN

ANCHOR BOOKS
A Division of Random House, Inc.
New York

308543

JUN 6 2005

FIRST ANCHOR BOOKS EDITION, DECEMBER 2003

Copyright © 2002 by Carla Kaplan
Letters copyright © The Estate of Zora Neale Hurston

All rights reserved under International and Pan-American Copyright Conventions. Published in the
United States by Anchor Books, a division of Random House, Inc., New York, and simultaneously in
Canada by Random House of Canada Limited, Toronto. Originally published in hardcover in the United
States by Doubleday, a division of Random House, Inc., New York, in 2002.

Anchor Books and colophon are registered trademarks of Random House, Inc.

The Library of Congress has cataloged the Doubleday edition as follows:
Hurston, Zora Neale.
Zora Neale Hurston : a life in letters / [edited by] Carla Kaplan.—1st ed.
p. cm.
Includes bibliographical references (p.) and index.
ISBN 0-385-49035-6
1. Hurston, Zora Neale—Correspondence.   2. Authors, American—20th century—Correspondence.
3. African American women authors—Correspondence.   4. Folklorists—United States—
Correspondence.   5. African American authors—Correspondence.   I. Kaplan, Carla.   II. Title.
PS3515.U789 Z48 2001
813'.52—dc21
[B]   00-065671

Anchor ISBN: 0-385-49036-4

Author photograph © Robin Hultgren
Book design by Jennifer Ann Daddio

www.anchorbooks.com

Printed in the United States of America
10 9 8 7 6 5 4 3 2 1

CONTENTS

CONTENTS

LIST OF
ILLUSTRATIONS

p. 701, Fragment of a burned letter from Hurston to William G. Nunn, editor of the *Pittsburgh Courier*. Courtesy of the Zora Neale Hurston Collection, George A. Smathers Libraries, University of Florida, Department of Special Collections.

p. 772, One of the last letters Hurston sent to a publisher, Harper Brothers, Jan. 16, 1959. Courtesy of the Zora Neale Hurston Collection, George A. Smathers Libraries, University of Florida, Department of Special Collections.

p. 838, Undated letter fragment. Courtesy of the Zora Neale Hurston Collection, George A. Smathers Libraries, University of Florida, Department of Special Collections.

ZORA NEALE HURSTON

A Life in Letters

FOREWORD

by Robert Hemenway

What joy it must have been to correspond with Zora Neale Hurston! The letter arrives, almost certainly with an unexpected postmark, probably without a return address, from a correspondent moving quickly across borders and through states, never long in one place, willfully in search of new experiences.

Open the envelope and Hurston's energy jumps off the page—a genie that cannot be suppressed. Like a good short story writer, she seizes attention with her very first words. "Well, the Negroes have been bitched again," she begins a letter to Walter White. Imagine Langston Hughes's quizzical smile as he opens a letter from Algiers, Louisiana: "Dear Langston, I have landed here in the kingdom of Marie Laveau and expect to wear the crown someday—Conjure Queen."

Two months later, Hughes receives another letter from Zora, postmarked New Orleans. She has been moving from room to room, using some of Langston's contacts, sleeping at 834 Orleans until "the bed bugs routed me," skipping over to Bogalusa to see a great Conjure doctor, collecting folklore in the "lap" of hoodoo, avoiding the effects of a police crackdown. She has collected "a marvelous dance ritual from the ceremony of death. Lots of thrilling things to make your heart glad." Hurston's enthusiasm bursts from the paper, a young, self-confident woman on her own in the land of goopher dust, black cat bones, and mysterious mojos.

Zora Neale Hurston lived a fascinating life and because she did, her letters fascinate as well. Whether telling about her latest Conjure conquest, gossiping about Harlem literary matters, or theorizing about the difference between white and black culture—"while white people strive to achieve restraint, we strive to pile beauty on beauty and magnificence on glory"—Hurston's letters reveal a thirst for experience and the courage to seek it. This self-confident quest, coupled with a God-given gift for narrative, helped make her one of the most famous American writers of the twentieth century.

This volume of letters presents Hurston in her full courage and complexity, a writer of genius, manipulating the language, using the idiom of the black South, sowing metaphors, unrestrained by the rules, with the sassiness to say things others avoid.

Who knows what Dr. Alain Locke, a Howard philosophy professor known for his manners and professional distance, must have thought when his former student responded to a plea for contact: "Dear Alain, I believe some monstrous old paper-eating ogre is grabbing my letters to you and swallowing them up tiddy-umpty." Whatever he thought, Locke would not win in an exchange with Zora over who wrote last. Six months later, she turns the tables: "I don't want to seem impatient Alain, but wrassle me out something and put it in the mail. I know that you lead a strenuous life, but my tongue is all lolled out, waiting to lap up that letter from you which is so long overdue."

What emerges most strongly from Hurston's letters is the force of her personality. She can be kind, and she can be tart; she can be full of joy and laid low by despair. She ends a letter to her "godmother," Mrs. R. Osgood Mason, "With high hopes for our venture and glory bulging from my pores, I am most lovingly and devotedly, Zora." Yet she also admitted Godmother could block her pores: "she ought not to supervise every little detail. It destroys my self-respect and demolishes me for weeks."

In the end, Hurston's complexity surfaces in almost every letter. She castigates African American leaders and white American politicians. She writes intimate, friendly letters to Hughes and yet delivers the full force of her fury when she feels he betrays her. She was a very complicated person and a very talented writer, and like most such figures, we approach her letters in search of the clue to her complexity, the magic key that can explain the contradictions of her career.

We often refer to letter writing as a lost art. As a culture, we do less and less of it, not because we are becoming a nation of bruted sensibility, but because letters have been rendered relatively unnecessary by the telecommunication revolution. Hurston's letters were written when correspondence was the dominant way for people to communicate, about matters both trivial and profound.

One sees here a writer's need to arrange meetings with friends and partisans, a friend's desire to share successes and failures, a rising star's intention to create an impression and market her talent. All of this, however, depended on one's mastery of the language. Zora's command of the writer's tools enabled her to establish intimacy with her correspondents. In person, Hurston was a dazzling personality, quick to impress and able to charm people to do her will. But she did not always have access on a face-to-face basis. There were many barriers to her person and her career that she overcame through letters.

Jook joints in Alabama mule camps offered blues singers and storytellers, but very few pay phones. In a turpentine camp in Loughman, Florida, she could not pick up the phone and call her New York agent. Telegrams were sometimes a possibility, but so expensive that one wrote in a kind of clipped pidgin English. E-mail and the fax machine existed somewhere beyond the limits of imagination. In this world, Zora's reports from the field became advertisements for her work.

So Zora used the U.S. Postal Service, a cheap, efficient federal agency, because there was often no other way to accomplish her need to reach out to others. Even if writing someone she had not met, she easily overcame the separation of distance and seduced her reader with the promise of friendship. Burton Rascoe's nomination of *Their Eyes Were Watching God* for the Book-of-the-Month contest enrolls him in the conspiracy: "It put my silver-singing trumpet to playing in my hand."

Surviving letters are always a caution. Inevitably a writer's biography is distorted by the extra-literary record left behind. Every author is known by his or her work, the written text that becomes the literary legacy. Letters provide a context for this textual achievement, but they are subordinate to it. Hurston's letters say relatively little about her published work. There is an interesting letter to James Weldon Johnson about the figure of the preacher in *Jonah's Gourd Vine* but not much at all about what she had in mind in her masterpiece, *Their Eyes Were Watching God.* Hurston does not pen long, thoughtful accounts of the literary influences on her work, ruminate about nuances of style, or offer advice on how a writer paints a canvas or sets a scene.

Hurston's letters really only began to be collected in the 1960s, and there are tantalizing references to what literary scavengers may have missed. Zora reports, "I am trying to find Helene Johnson who put a box of papers in storage for me." Apparently there was another suitcase of letters and manuscripts lost in storage in Jacksonville. Hundreds of letters may exist in dusty attics and basement trunks. The caution exists because we recognize the possibility of distortion, a skewing of the life because some of its most intimate moments go unrecorded while other relationships assume outsize importance. For example, we have many letters between Hurston and Hughes. They show much affection, at least in the twenties, during their youth; one wonders about an intimate relationship. By the same token, the many letters between Hurston and Mrs. Mason, her patron and "godmother," reveal a passionate intensity, despite a considerable difference in ages. And what do we make of the intense correspondence with Jane Belo?

But should we assume a sexual relationship? If so, what about her husbands? We know that Hurston was married several times, and had numerous liaisons, but there is virtually nothing in the letters about these relationships. What would change in our attitude toward her work, or how we interpret her life, if a cache of love letters were suddenly unearthed?

Skewed or not, Hurston's biography depends upon this extant epistolary record, and this first volume of her letters provides major themes for biographies of the future. Three major truths emerge from this volume, standing out amid the many new details that fill in the story of Zora's life.

First, folklore was the passion of her life and informs all of her work. She made incredible sacrifices and took extraordinary risks to collect it, record it, and broadcast it to a wide audience. Zora understood well how this folk artistry perpetuated itself. Whole letters become, primarily, reports on her fieldwork, especially if she writes to a fellow anthropologist. Her sensitivity to language had been awakened in Eatonville on Joe Clark's store porch, and it led to a lifelong study of the way Black folks turned daily communication into an art form. When she tells novelist Fannie Hurst that she should come to Barnard to attend Anthropology 110 because, "It is as full of things a writer could use as a dog is of fleas," Zora reveals her sense of herself as both participant and observer in the creation of African American art.

Second, Huston's career was a conscious struggle to obtain the economic means to release her artistic vision. If one were to do a content analysis of these letters, well over 50 percent of the content would have something to do with a lack of money—Zora's ever present companion and lifelong anxiety. "I had to come because I could not stay in New York until I made some more money"; "I have used up every available resource before appealing to you—even pawning my typewriter . . . I am now strapped and most desperate in mind."

From an early age, she knew that she would have to scramble economically, and she deliberately rejected the safe economic paths open to her. She could have settled into a black college; she taught at North Carolina Central College, and Bethune-Cookman, and lobbied for a job at Fisk. In the end, the classroom was too small a space for her talent or her temperament. The chances of employment were probably not helped when she told the Fisk president he ran his school "like a Georgia plantation," called North Carolina Central College a "one horse religious school," and referred to Mary McLeod Bethune as a "heifer."

She could have married for money and hidden her ambition. Her marriages, however, never were permitted to interfere with her career. She had the intelligence and the street smarts to establish a financial base, but she lacked both the will and ability to channel her brilliance to commercial goals. What she did do well was seek fellowships and patrons, and because granting agencies keep good records, we have a rather full account of her institutional funding. She spent an entire lifetime trying to buy time to create, to release what was inside, searching for the leisure to transfer to the page the stories she loved to tell: "I want peace and quiet to sit down and try to learn how to write in truth. I have always been too hurried before." In the end, the poverty she had dodged for a lifetime caught up with her and she died penniless.

Finally, Hurston's letters remind us well of the racial divide that is our American dilemma, and how self-conscious she was about making sure it did not limit her work or her life. She spoke frankly if not always consistently about race. She claimed early on that she didn't "know white psychology," and as a result she couldn't write about certain experiences: "I see white people do things, but I cannot grasp why they do them." Later, she wanted to break the "silly old rule about Negroes not writing about white people," and did so in her last novel. She staked out a conservative position on race that grew from her fierce pride in black institutions and her suspicion of any mask unless it were her own. As she told Eslanda Robeson, wife of Paul, about her first novel, *Jonah's Gourd Vine*, "I tried to be natural and not pander to the folks who expect a clown and a villain in every Negro. Neither did I want to pander to those 'race' people among us who see nothing but perfection in all of us." In the end, this desire for a clear vision and an honest accounting led her far to the right, thereby offering up another contradiction—the celebrant of African American cultural life who became a critic of African American political tradition: "Now as to segregation, I have no viewpoint on the subject particularly, other than a fierce desire for human justice. The rest is up to the individual."

In the end, however, the greatest tribute should go to all of Zora's correspondents who recognized her genius and kept her letters, convinced that Zora's fame would one day rise to the necessity of such a volume. They have enriched our lives just as Zora enriched theirs. Perhaps Zora summed up best why we find her life in letters so interesting. As she once told Countee Cullen, "I mean to live and die by my own mind." Whatever one feels about Zora Neale Hurston, she clearly accomplished this goal.

NOTE TO THE READER

My aim in editing and annotating these letters has been to make them as accessible as possible while preserving their important idiosyncrasies. Because Hurston's letters will interest readers who have varying degrees of knowledge about her life and times, I have tried to supply background on the events, controversies, and persons she refers to while still allowing the letters to speak for themselves. To keep footnotes to a minimum, much of this background information has been supplied in the introductions to specific decades, the chronology of Hurston's life, and the glossary, which is intended as a brief reader's guide. Since most readers will be reading these letters in sequence, persons mentioned in the letters are identified in footnotes on their first occurrence only, to avoid repetition. While the general introduction to this volume offers an orientation to Hurston's life, letters, politics, and writing, the introductions to specific decades add relevant cultural history, hence the overlap of some biographical information supplied in the introduction and that supplied in later sections. Hurston's correspondents are each discussed in the glossary, as are individuals, events, and organizations referred to in her letters. Occasionally, a record was available of how Hurston's letters were answered or about the letter to which she was responding. I have supplied information about such letters in the footnotes when it was possible to do so. The index will point readers toward specific names as well as issues and events and will orient the reader toward those subjects about which further information is provided in the glossary. Those readers who wish to read Hurston's letters by correspondent, rather than chronologically, may wish to consult the Index of Recipients. Works cited in footnotes are not repeated in the selected bibliog-

St. Augustine, Fla.
March 24, 1927

Dear D,

Your letter was precious! I loved it, loved it so. Your enthusiasm is certainly warming to say the least.

Yes, Dorothy, a lot of Winters have passed over my heart that have not passed over my head— more Winters have passed over my soul than over my head. Life has not been kind to me, not always, and so perhaps the heel of life has left its print in my face.

I laughed so about the bowl for you are so juvenile about it. Never you mind, the whole set of 6 only cost a dollar so you see its not worth 1/10 the thought you have given it, I had not missed it anyway.

I am writing on a novel—don't know how it will turn out. I am worked to death.

Guess what? Yes, you are right the first time. I am buying a car— a Nash Coupe, delivery Apr. 1st. I suppose I shall pay for it O.K, if not, I just want see— I am doing general things to please you, so you

I shall marry within the next month too, so you see— I am doing general things to please you.

Give Wallace Thurman my congratulations— he deserves it, too. He has great ability.

3.

Here's hoping you run away with the Contest this year, and may more.

My love to Helene, hope she writes.

I am eager to see the Eloise B. T. wonder why she wants to see me!

I shall be so happy to be back in New York again, but am lost to Bohemia forever. No more parties—just work and work, well perhaps a little domesticity.

all my love, little one

Zora Neale Hurston

forwarding address
1663 Evergreen ave
Jacksonville, Fla

Daytona next.

Letter to writer Dorothy West.

raphy, with the exception of reference works that were consulted frequently.

Hurston often complained—and rightly so—about the liberties editors took with her writing. Consequently, I have not changed Hurston's grammar, punctuation, or spelling in these letters (misspellings are indicated with "[sic]" only when failure to do so might cause confusion), and all letters are reproduced in their entirety. Some letters were partially destroyed after Hurston's death. Burned or otherwise illegible sections are marked by "[illegible]." Other information regarding the material condition of originals is supplied in brackets. Hurston's editorial changes, made either by striking out words on the keyboard or by writing over them by hand, have been indicated whenever they are legible. Most of Hurston's letters are signed by hand. If there is no indication of a signature, either the letter was unsigned or the transcription is taken from a carbon copy. The presence of brackets around the date of a letter indicates that it has been supplied by myself or an archive (marked "library dated") or that I have added it at the head of a letter for the reader's convenience when it may originally have appeared at the end.

INTRODUCTION

Overleaf: Hurston imitating a crow. Photographs by Prentiss Taylor.

*Hurston was outrageous—it appears by nature. . . . For all
her contrariness, her "chaos," her ability to stir up
dislike . . . many of us love Zora Neale Hurston.*
—ALICE WALKER, "ON REFUSING TO BE HUMBLED"[1]

She came to delight in the chaos she sometimes left behind.
—ROBERT HEMENWAY, *ZORA NEALE HURSTON:
A LITERARY BIOGRAPHY*[2]

I first had the privilege of reading some of Zora Neale Hurston's
letters nearly twenty years ago, and their biting humor, irrever-
ence, and stylistic brilliance—some of the best writing Hurston
ever did—immediately bowled me over. Her letters showcase Hurston
as writer, anthropologist, dramatist, teacher, celebrity, folklorist, and
urbanite. They also reveal her less public personas: Hurston as wife,
lover, sister, aunt, friend, entrepreneur, recluse, sailor, pet lover, gar-
dener, and cook. Hurston was famously Janus-faced and has often been
noted for dissembling and secrecy. But her letters are often star-
tlingly—even brutally—honest. They are a marvelous compendium of
information about living as an African American woman in the middle

[1]*Alice Walker, "On Refusing to Be Humbled by Second Place in a Contest You Did Not Design: A Tradition by
Now," dedication to* I Love Myself When I Am Laughing . . . and Then Again When I Am Looking Mean
and Impressive: A Zora Neale Hurston Reader, *ed. Alice Walker (New York: Feminist Press, 1979), p. 1.*
[2]*Robert E. Hemenway,* Zora Neale Hurston: A Literary Biography *(Urbana: University of Illinois Press,
1977), p. 6.*

decades of the twentieth century: a gold mine for anyone interested in the Harlem Renaissance, folklore, the Great Depression, the rise of anthropology, publishing and patronage, early black feminism, or southern American politics. Few volumes of the letters of African American writers have been published, and even fewer of African American women's letters. Hence, the letters collected here offer one of the few existing sources of personal commentary by a black female intellectual on American life and literature of the previous century.

The letters illuminate Hurston's own life. The Hurston who emerges from these letters—written to friends, patrons, colleagues, fellow writers, editors, and also to strangers—is not someone we have seen before. One of the surprises, for Hurston scholars especially, will be the political savvy these letters reveal. The flippant conservatism of Hurston's later essays has caused critics to dismiss her as naive. Though Hurston's politics were undeniably controversial, it turns out that she thought in profoundly political terms and estimated value with a steady eye to social goods. This means that her political views (including ones we find unfortunate) will have to be taken seriously, not just conveniently bracketed. The letters make clear what a serious feminist Hurston was, even more so than her novels, stories, and essays evidence. Her self-consciousness about being a writer is also a theme of her letters, as is American racism, about which she had a great deal to say that is still relevant today.

Perhaps not since W. E. B. Du Bois's description of "double-consciousness" has there been so moving a response to the question "How does it feel to be a problem?"[3] In her published writings and in interviews, Hurston proclaimed that there *was* no problem and that *she* certainly was not one, but her letters offer the other half of a "double-consciousness" that she clearly *did* experience, and they answer Du Bois's question in complex and troubling ways. In 1943, she wrote African American journalist Claude Barnett that "the iron has entered my soul. Since my god of tolerance has forsaken me, I am ready for anything to overthrow Anglo-Saxon supremacy, however desperate. I have become what I never wished to be, a good hater. I no longer even value my life if by losing it, I can do something to destroy this Anglo-Saxon monstrosity."[4] She also accused her close friend Langston Hughes of writing

---

[3]*W. E. B. Du Bois,* The Souls of Black Folk *(New York: Library of America, 1986), p. 363.*
[4]*Hurston to Claude Barnett, [February (?) 1943].*

"what the 'white folks had exalted'" by portraying blacks in stereotypical and racist ways, precisely the charge of racial pandering that Richard Wright and others would later level at her.[5] Hurston advocated color blindness, but she painted one of the most vivid pictures we have of both the advantages and disadvantages of being "other" in this society.

She was committed to her vision of an authentic black aesthetic and her letters describe her plans for a "<u>real</u> Negro art theatre" where she could "act out the folk tales, however short, with the abrupt angularity and naivete of the primitive 'bama nigger."[6] With equal passion and candor, she discusses trying to get around the "white folks as the big wigs in the city" who prevented blacks—Hurston included—from buying Florida land.[7] She also discusses her unsuccessful attempts to gain her patron's support for graduate study—"the 'Angel' is cold towards the degrees"—and to be taken seriously as one of the first African American scholars in her field.[8] She was often desperate for money. At one point she was compelled to work for half the pay of less accomplished white counterparts at the Federal Writers' Project. At another point, the press of poverty made her contemplate a career as "New York's Chicken Specialist."[9]

Hurston's letters come from a period when writing was the way to communicate with friends and business associates. Indeed, after one brief trip to the Bahamas, Hurston described "79 pieces of mail waiting for me on my return."[10] She described suitcases *filled* with correspondence, mail that would take weeks to slog through. Fortunately, Hurston saved carbons of many of her replies, and these can be found in the University of Florida archives among other papers that narrowly survived destruction after her death. Equally fortunately, many of her correspondents recognized the literary and historical value of her letters. With great foresight, and often at the urging of Hurston's friend the writer and photographer Carl Van Vechten (who devoted many years to collecting and archiving African American materials), Hurston's letters were saved and donated to the archives where they were located for this book. Letters may soon be a lost art. Few are more artful or worth preserving than Hurston's.

[5]*Hurston to Countee Cullen, March 11, 1926.*

[6]*Hurston to Langston Hughes, April 12, 1928.*

[7]*Hurston to Langston Hughes, [May 31, 1929].*

[8]*Hurston to Franz Boas, June 8, [1930?].*

[9]*Hurston to Charlotte Osgood Mason, September 25, 1931.*

[10]*Hurston to Franz Boas, October 20, 1929.*

In 1996, when the Hurston family and I first discussed this volume, perhaps two hundred or so letters had been identified in about a dozen university archives. We hoped to add a few dozen more. In excess of all our expectations, this volume includes more than six hundred letters culled from more than three dozen locations.

While it is common for literary reputations to rise and fall, not many American writers have experienced a sea change as radical as Hurston's move from obscurity to acclaim. Hurston's every unpublished word is now treasure-hunted, and the discovery of even one short story generates news reports and a flurry of scholarly activity.[11] At this writing, all of Hurston's published works are back in print; her unpublished plays, essays, stories, and folklore are forthcoming; her plays are being performed across the country; her novels are slated for production as major feature films; and there are television documentaries, graduate courses, textbooks, seminars, and hundreds of dissertations devoted to her work.[12] Her letters cannot, of course, explain this shift in public perception. But they help us put it in context.

The last letter we have of Hurston's is uncharacteristic. Written a year before her death in 1960, it is a drab query asking if Harper's would "have any interest in the book I am laboring upon at present—a life of Herod the Great."[13] This letter is unusual because even Hurston's business letters typically show remarkable wit, humor, and charm. She commonly teased people she had never met, and she shared confidences with those she hardly knew. Her letters are usually intimate; no one is held at arm's length. Across the top of one Hurston letter, writer Annie Nathan Meyer scribbled: "a faultless interesting & excellent letter."[14] Hurston's correspondents agreed. A letter from her was something special.

If her last letter is uncharacteristically restrained, her first is characteristically audacious. In 1917, Hurston went to Morgan Academy to finish high school after a particularly trying time of circulating between different relatives and working as a wardrobe girl for a traveling

[11] *Two recent instances include the republication of Hurston's short story "Under the Bridge" and the rediscovery of unpublished plays located in the Library of Congress's Copyright Division. See Bibliography of Works by Zora Neale Hurston at the end of this volume.*

[12] *Such new works include Zora Neale Hurston,* Every Tongue Got to Confess: Negro Folk-Tales from the Gulf-States, *ed. Carla Kaplan (New York: HarperCollins, 2001).*

[13] *Hurston to Harper Brothers, January 16, 1959.*

[14] *Hurston to Annie Nathan Meyer, March 7, 1927.*

theatrical troupe. She was twenty-six years old but had not yet been able to finish school and she was sick and tired of fighting the kind of grinding poverty that made people into what she called "slave ships in shoes." She entered Morgan with almost nothing: one dress, one pair of shoes, one change of underwear. School officials helped her to finance her education with a series of domestic jobs, and she worked hard to graduate, with the hope of going on to college. These were humbling circumstances. But Hurston was anything but humbled. She wrote the dean of the college, William Pickens, "I want to <u>know</u> you and Mrs. Pickens, ever so much. . . . you are interesting to me. . . . Impertinent, isnt it? But I want to get <u>All</u> that Morgan has to give. I feel that I will have done something equal to the course at Morgan, if I have really known you and Mrs. Pickens."[15]

Her determination to get "all" that every situation offered, to drain every opportunity bone-dry, delivered her into a life where she found herself the equal and intimate of some of the most famous and influential people of her day: from Fannie Hurst and Franz Boas to Langston Hughes and Paul Robeson. That determination did not always win people over to her. Her friends remember her as one of the most high-spirited women they ever knew: ambitious, adventurous, enthusiastic, dynamic, and inviting. Those with whom she clashed—and being strong-willed, she eventually clashed with many—remember her as stubborn, unyielding, and opportunistic.

She may not have taken those clashes quite as seriously as her associates did. She battled constantly with W. E. B. Du Bois, for example, and called him Dr. "Dubious": "a propagadist" [sic] and "utterly detestable . . . [a] goateed, egotistic, wishy-washy . . . haughty aristocrat."[16] She considered him a mere dabbler in the arts, locked horns with him over the "Florida Negro" project of the Federal Writers' Project, was happy to replace his encyclopedia entry on Negroes because she felt he was "the most pleadingest of all the special pleaders . . . [a] man . . . so subjective that he cannot utter a straight sentence," and was enraged when she was misquoted as saying that "DuBois was the greatest for I do not think so."[17] Yet she seemed to think nothing of writing to him, after nearly twenty years of silence, to propose he

[15]Hurston to William Pickens, [1917/1918].

[16]Hurston to Frederick Woltman, February 22, 1951; Hurston to Annie Nathan Meyer, October 7, 1927; Hurston to Maxeda Von Hesse, April 7, 1951.

[17]Hurston to Katherine Tracy L'Engle, October 24, 1945; Hurston to Langston Hughes, [May 31, 1929].

entertain her idea of building "a cemetery for the illustrious Negro dead." Her notion was to model the cemetery on Père-Lachaise in Paris, surrounded by gardens and decorated by "Negro sculptors and painters" who would re-create "scenes from our own literature and life. Mythology and all." Hurston's concern was that "no Negro celebrity, no matter what financial condition they might be in at death, [should] lie in inconspicuous forgetfulness."[18] It was a grand idea, and Hurston's good feeling for the project carried over into her letter to Du Bois. While she was not to die for another fifteen years, Hurston may well have been anticipating her own death here. Such anticipation, however—such opportunistic thinking, if one sees it that way—lessens neither the brilliance of Hurston's idea nor its horrible irony: when she died in 1960, she was buried in an unmarked grave. Neither does any possible opportunism on her part lessen the charming audacity of her reaching out to an old antagonist in hopes of joining hands for the good of "the race." This is just the sort of thing she did.

Hurston let herself go in her letters. She wrote frankly about her feelings, sharing her despair sometimes and her hilarious sense of humor other times. Most of what we know about Hurston's gift for friendship comes from these letters. They demonstrate her generosity as well as her prickliness; she was capable of dropping dear friends for slights only she could detect. She could be warm and open, or closed to the point of paranoia. In Robert Hemenway's words, Hurston was "flamboyant and yet vulnerable, self-centered and yet kind . . . Zora Hurston was a complex woman with a high tolerance for contradiction. . . . her friends were often incapable of reconciling the polarities of her personal style. Aware of this, she came to delight in the chaos she sometimes left behind."[19]

Hurston's letters reveal her life as a writer. "I shall wrassle me up a future or die trying," she declared to her wealthy white patron, Charlotte Osgood Mason.[20] With breathtaking but not atypical self-confidence, she announced to Hughes, "I have landed here in the kingdom of Marie Laveau and expect to wear her crown someday—Conjure Queen."[21] The other side of her assuredness was paralyzing self-doubt. "I have been through one of those terrible periods when I

[18] Hurston to W. E. B. Du Bois, June 11, 1945.
[19] Hemenway, Hurston, pp. 5–6.
[20] Hurston to Charlotte Osgood Mason, November 25, 1930.
[21] Hurston to Langston Hughes, August 6, 1928.

cant make myself write," she confided to Hughes.[22] "Every now and then I get a sort of phobia for paper and all its works," she wrote her Federal Writers' Project boss, Carita Corse. "I cannot bring myself to touch it. I cannot write, read or do anything at all for a period. I accumulate letters unread, even."[23]

Her letters give free expression to her unwavering commitment to the value of black folklore. With Hughes, she shared her desire to represent "His Majesty, the man in the gutter . . . the god-maker, the creator of everything that lasts."[24] When "Negro drama" came "from the life of the people," she told President Thomas E. Jones of Fisk University, it would be "the brightest flame in America."[25] Great African American art, she insisted, would come from "some humble Negro boy or girl who has never heard of Ibsen," not from a black intellectual who "goes to Whiteland to learn his trade! Ha!"[26]

Sometimes, of course, she simply gossiped. "What, I ask with my feet turned out, are Countee [Cullen] and Eric [Walrond] going abroad to study? . . . Fat was inevitable for Countee. It will fit him nicely too. Nice, safe, middle-class[.] I am glad for Wallace [Thurman] and Bruce [Nugent]. More power to them."[27]

Although Hurston was a very private person, her letters reveal certain aspects of her life which have seemed to beg explanation. For example, they tell us how difficult she found it to combine marriage and her career. As she told her nephew in 1957, "artistic people just dont go for much tying down even for the economic safety angle."[28] Her letters contest the long-standing legend that the friendship between Hurston and Hughes, one of the richest collaborations in American literature, ended due to a struggle over the play *Mule Bone*. They won't end the long speculation on Hurston's sexuality. Instead, they remind us that love can be hard to explain, categorize, or contain. When Hurston loved, she loved both deeply and expressively. Her meaning remains ambiguous, but her letters proclaim her love at various times for her best friend, Langston Hughes; for her married, white, openly

[22]Hurston to Langston Hughes, July 10, 1928.

[23]Hurston to Carita Doggett Corse, December 3, 1938.

[24]Hurston to Langston Hughes, November 22, 1928.

[25]Hurston to Thomas E. Jones, October 12, 1934.

[26]Zora Neale Hurston, "Race Cannot Become Great Until It Recognizes Its Talent," Washington Tribune, December 29, 1934; Hurston to Langston Hughes, April 12, 1928.

[27]Hurston to Langston Hughes, April 12, 1928.

[28]Hurston to Everett Hurston, Jr., March 31, 1957.

bisexual friend, Carl Van Vechten; for elderly Charlotte Osgood Mason; and for her anthropologist friend Jane Belo, whose marriage she encouraged. About her more conventional loves—two marriages we knew of and one which she kept secret—Hurston's letters have surprisingly little to say. Hurston dedicated all of her books to white patrons and friends.[29] Yet her letters can be scathing about white patronage and condescension, including that from some of those same friends.

This is not to say that these letters answer every question. Hurston galvanizes particularly passionate and often polarized debate. Many of the questions that have troubled critics and readers are illuminated—if never fully resolved—by her letters: Why did she constantly alter her age? Did she take a job as a maid toward the end of her life out of desperation or, as she claimed, as a lark? Why did she switch from writing about blacks to writing about whites? What made her politics turn reactionary? How did she manage to placate a patron intent on "primitivism" and still play a leading role in a literary movement dedicated to antiprimitivistic aesthetic self-determination? How did she manage as a black woman in a male-identified aesthetic movement? As a black person in the white-identified academy? As a person of working-class roots among middle-class, often elitist ("talented tenth") peers?

Perhaps Hurston fascinates us so because she refused to be pigeonholed. Her letters are a case study in strategic negotiations and contradictory locations. Letters are, after all, merely *"fictions* of self-revelation"[30] addressed to readers whose particularities they take into account. We are probably more aware of our audience when we write letters than at any other time. Every letter is a performance. Because Hurston was *such* a versatile performer, her letters offer more valuable insights into the self-fashioning divergent audiences demand than they offer definitive answers to the vexing questions of her life or times.

As a trained anthropologist specializing in language, Hurston was keenly aware of how discourse conceals even while revealing. In her folklore collection *Mules and Men,* she explains that African Americans are particularly likely to avail themselves of what she calls "feather-bed resistance":

---

[29]Jonah's Gourd Vine *to Robert Wunsch;* Mules and Men *to Annie Nathan Meyer;* Their Eyes Were Watching God *to Henry Allen Moe;* Tell My Horse *to Carl Van Vechten;* Moses, Man of the Mountain *to Edwin Osgood Grover; and* Seraph on the Suwanee *to Marjorie Kinnan Rawlings and Mary Holland.*

[30]*Patricia Meyer Spacks, "Female Rhetorics," in* The Private Self: Theory and Practice of Women's Autobiographical Writings, *ed. Shari Benstock (Chapel Hill: University of North Carolina Press, 1988), p. 177, my italics.*

The Negro, in spite of his open-faced laughter, his seeming acquies-
cence, is particularly evasive. You see we are a polite people and we
do not say to our questioner, "Get out of here!" We smile and tell
him or her something that satisfies the white person because, knowing so little about us, he doesn't know what he is missing. The Indian resists curiosity by a stony silence. The Negro offers a feather-
bed resistance. That is, we let the probe enter, but it never comes
out. It gets smothered under a lot of laughter and pleasantries.

The theory behind our tactics: "The white man is always trying to know into somebody else's business. All right, I'll set something outside the door of my mind for him to play with and
handle. He can read my writing but he sho' can't read my mind.
I'll put this play toy in his hand, and he will seize it and go away.
Then I'll say my say and sing my song."[31]

"Feather-bed resistance" is not just play. It is deception necessitated by
social inequality. Hurston mastered feather-bed resistance. She performed such different selves for her various correspondents that her
letters sometimes seem written by different people.

Hurston's way of negotiating contrarieties has sometimes struck
her critics as a refusal of negotiation, even of society altogether. "The
woman, quite simply, did not play."[32] It is certainly true that Hurston
never fell into step with reigning orthodoxies, but her letters provide
many examples of the complex negotiations—some playful and some
tortured—that were necessary to her success. In this, they offer an object lesson about what it takes to be an ambitious, independent, and talented African American woman in a white man's world.

Given her situation, it should not surprise us that some of Hurston's
letters are sometimes strange, overdone, withholding, or coy. Mason,
for example, is celebrated in the most exaggerated terms: "Flowers to
you—the true conceptual Mother—not a biological accident. . . . If the
high gods in space shall find anything worthy in me, then it is of
you."[33] When she needed something, her sweet-talking and self-

[31]*Zora Neale Hurston*, Mules and Men *(Bloomington: Indiana University Press, 1978), pp. 4–5. Langston Hughes, in* The Big Sea, *includes a blues lyric that expresses the same idea: "You don't know, / You don't know my mind— / When you see me laughin', / I'm laughin' to keep from cryin'."* The Big Sea, *(New York: Hill & Wang, 1975), p. 238.*

[32]*Toni Cade Bambara, "Some Forward Remarks," in* Zora Neale Hurston, The Sanctified Church *(Berkeley, Calif.: Turtle Island for the Netzahualcoyotl Historical Society, 1983), p. 11.*

[33]*Hurston to Charlotte Osgood Mason, May 10, 1931.*

deprecation could know no bounds. Harold Spivacke, chief of the Music
Division of the Library of Congress, is flattered that he is "the greatest
ever."[34] She cheerily dubbed white patrons "Boss" or "Bossman," and
signed herself "your little pickaninny" or "your devoted pickaninny."
Some of her letters explain her need for secrecy or holding back. To
Langston Hughes, for example, Hurston reports that she has found "one
of the original Africans." "She is most delightful," Hurston writes, "but
no one will ever know about her but us."[35] Her patrons sometimes took
for granted what Hurston would like or need. Louise Thompson described how "whenever Mrs. Mason sent an exotic dress for Zora to
wear, Zora called Park Avenue to report that it looked stunning on her;
then she would hang up and turn to her companion, remarking with a
laugh that she would not think of wearing such a thing."[36]

Hurston explores secrecy and dissembling as fundamental to a tradition of double voice and masking, devices central to African American literature since its inception. Early slave narrators faced three
incompatible audiences: illiterate African Americans; racist, hostile,
white southerners; and distant, possibly sympathetic northerners ignorant of the harsh realities of slavery. Paul Laurence Dunbar's "We
Wear the Mask" speaks to this pain:

> We wear the mask that grins and lies,
> It hides our cheeks and shades our eyes,—
> This debt we pay to human guile;
> With torn and bleeding hearts we smile.[37]

The problem of restricted audience expectations—and the strategy of
pretending to meet them—resonates throughout African American
writing. In 1928, when Hurston was just launching her career, James
Weldon Johnson described the dilemma as

> a special problem which the plain American author knows nothing
> about . . . The moment a Negro writer takes up his pen or sits
> down to his typewriter he is immediately called upon to solve, con-

[34]*Hurston to Harold Spivacke, August 21, 1945.*

[35]*Hurston to Langston Hughes, July 10, 1928.*

[36]*Hemenway,* Hurston, *p. 139.*

[37]*Paul Laurence Dunbar, "We Wear the Mask,"* The Complete Poems of Paul Laurence Dunbar *(New York: Dodd, Mead, & Company, 1940).*

sciously or unconsciously, this problem of the double audience. To whom shall he address himself, to his own black group or to white America? . . . It may be asked why he doesn't just go ahead and write and not bother himself about audiences. That is easier said than done.[38]

Many groups face hostile publics which call forth strategies of masking, double voice, or selective audience address, audiences for which they don masks, bury their voices, or write, pointedly, for only a selective few. "Silences. Loopholes. Interstices. Allegory. Dissemblance. Politics of respectability. These are but a few of the terms," Farah Jasmine Griffin notes, "that black women scholars use to help make sense of the silence that surrounds black women's lives and experiences. . . . many have kept the most personal aspects of their lives as well as the full range of their thoughts secret."[39] Black and white women's literature is rich with anger over this predicament. Many solitary characters decry it: Jane Eyre on the ramparts of Thornfield; Linda Brent in a cramped and airless attic; Celie writing from Georgia to a lost sister in Africa; Beloved communing from beyond the grave, so desperate is she for contact. Lacking appropriate public outlets, women's private writings (letters especially) construct the ideal audiences the writer could not find and expose the inadequacies of those they could. Letters allow the writer to turn toward one specific person and away from everyone else, to construct an audience that may not really exist. Hurston's tendency to "hide behind masks"[40] is part of this performative tradition of ironic address and disguise.

Their Eyes Were Watching God, Hurston's best novel, creates a character for whom the "oldest human longing" is "self-revelation" but who offers her story to only one person— her best friend, Pheoby. "Mouth Almighty," as she calls the townspeople, can't possibly under-

Original dust jacket,
Their Eyes Were
Watching God.

[38]*James Weldon Johnson, "The Dilemma of the Negro Author,"* American Mercury, *15, no. 60 (1928), p. 477.*
[39]*Farah Jasmine Griffin, ed.,* Beloved Sisters and Loving Friends: Letters from Rebecca Primus of Royal Oak, Maryland, and Addie Brown of Hartford, Connecticut, 1854–1868 *(New York: Knopf, 1999), p. 3.*
[40]*Hemenway,* Hurston, *p. 24.*

stand. " 'Ah ain't puttin' it in de street, Ah'm tellin' *you*,' " she says.[41] "Even if I did know all, I am supposed to have some private business to myself," Hurston wrote in her autobiography, *Dust Tracks on a Road.* "Whatever I do know, I have no intention of putting but so much in the public ears."[42]

At one point in her career, Hurston did hope to write without having to "bother" about (white) audiences. She began a novel, *The Golden Bench of God,* about black hairdressing entrepreneur and art patron Madame C. J. Walker, one of America's first black female millionaires. "Imagine that no white audience is present to hear what is said," Hurston wrote to her agent, Jean Parker Waterbury, about this novel.[43] Hurston's publisher rejected it, and Waterbury was unable to place it elsewhere. Most of Hurston's uncensored writing is lost, except in some of these letters.

Hurston had a knack for getting in on things, and for doing so in her own idiosyncratic way. She might gain recognition only to turn around and attack its very grounds. Or she'd work her way into a group, only to blast it as pretentious. She'd insist on being in the middle of whatever her friends, colleagues, and associates were doing. Then she'd stand askew of their activities, whatever they were. Not surprisingly, this rankled even her closest friends. Bold, talented, and iconoclastic, Hurston had her own view of every facet of modern American culture, from the rise of anthropology, to modern race theory, to the black pride movement, and the beginnings of black feminism. When she set herself up as observer—her favored angle of vision—she was apt to be both critical and original.

As a Barnard anthropology student, Hurston studied with Franz Boas, the father of the discipline. Boas was a wonderful teacher for Hurston, who benefited not only from his eminence but also from his challenge to then-dominant theories of race and culture based on biological determinism. Hurston founded her own antiracist writings, however, on different premises. She promoted essential, even biological, conceptions of race to celebrate blackness. Other anthropologists worried about disrupting the cultures they observed. Hurston openly participated in the rituals she recorded, including a "Nine Night" ceremony that "ended in a naked, orgiastic dance climaxed by the sacrifice of a goat" and an apprenticeship in hoodoo that required "lying nude

[41] *Zora Neale Hurston,* Their Eyes Were Watching God *(New York: HarperCollins, 1990), p. 109.*

[42] *Zora Neale Hurston,* Dust Tracks on a Road *(New York: HarperCollins, 1991), p. 189.*

[43] *Hurston to Jean Parker Waterbury, [May 1, 1951].*

for sixty-nine hours, face downward on a couch."[44] When she wrote up her research, she placed herself right in the center. This was hardly standard academic practice, as she well knew.

Refusing everything that smacked of victimization, "I am not tragically colored,"[45] Hurston declared; "I shall never join the cry-babies."[46] Nonetheless, letters written to white friends are often obsequious and ingratiating. The idea of race loyalty, an ethic central to the Harlem Renaissance, is often denounced outright by her.

In light of white racist stereotypes of so-called black licentiousness, the black press was cautioning writers to "keep away from the erotic!"[47] but Hurston insisted upon writing about "panting," "frothing," "ecstatic," "creaming" female sexuality.[48] Most Harlem Renaissance artists represented middle-class, urban black culture, deliberately presenting a picture with which white readers could identify. Yet Hurston's subject was "the Negro farthest down"[49]: rural southern blacks at as far a remove from black northern readers as can be imagined.

Hurston worked hard to win acceptance into Harlem Renaissance society, but her letters reveal a conscious decision to live on its outskirts, choosing "the muck," the turpentine camps, and the bayou over the literary salons of D.C. or New York's "Strivers' Row." She was ambitious, careful of her relationships with editors and publishers, and self-promoting (perfectly capable, for example, of dropping a friendly note and manuscript to Carl Sandburg, whom she had never met, or writing to Winston Churchill to ask him to write a preface for *Herod the Great*, a novel that no one she knew liked very much). Yet she could also be remarkably careless: failing to show up for appointments, disappearing for weeks at a time, not following through on commitments. She was close to all the key leaders of Harlem Renaissance politics and culture—Alain Locke, W. E. B. Du Bois, Charles S. Johnson, James Weldon Johnson, Walter White, and Langston Hughes—yet she was deeply critical of black leadership, complaining of too much "pandering to [the] popular palate"[50] and remarking to Countee Cullen that

[44]*Hemenway,* Hurston, *pp. 121, 230.*

[45]*Hurston, "How It Feels to Be Colored Me,"* World Tomorrow, *May 1928.*

[46]*Hurston to Countee Cullen, March 5, 1943.*

[47]*George Schuyler, "Instructions for Contributors," cited by Henry Louis Gates, Jr.,* The Signifying Monkey: A Theory of African-American Criticism *(New York: Oxford University Press, 1988), p. 179.*

[48]*Hurston,* Their Eyes, *pp. 23–24.*

[49]*Hurston,* Dust Tracks, *p. 129.*

[50]*Hurston to Ruth Benedict, spring 1929.*

*A young Zora Neale Hurston,
probably in the early 1920s.*

"some of the stuff that has passed for courage among Negro 'leaders' is nauseating."[51]

Her writing did not always succeed in reaching—let alone pleasing—her multiple audiences. While white reviewers lauded her for opening an "authentic"[52] window on an exotic and fascinating "different world,"[53] her black contemporaries attacked her as an apolitical opportunist complicit with racist stereotypes of blacks as simple, rural, uncultured folk. Richard Wright charged *Their Eyes Were Watching God* with pandering "to a white audience" by exploiting "the phase of Negro life which is 'quaint,' the phase which evokes a piteous smile on the lips of the 'superior' race." Her writing, he declared, has "no theme, no message, no thought."[54] And Alain Locke, whose imprimatur was crucial to success in Harlem Renaissance circles, concurred that Hurston was guilty of "oversimplification" and that she failed to "come to grips" with what she should have.[55] Indeed, Hurston may be American literature's most controversial writer.

American literary tastes changed dramatically during Hurston's lifetime. And the dizzying ups and downs of her career reflect these changes. Her letters reveal—in sometimes painful detail—how hard they were for her to negotiate. Locke's one-paragraph review of *Their Eyes Were Watching God,* for example, so enraged Hurston—despite the fact that he called her "talented" and dubbed the novel "folklore fiction at its best"[56]—that she never forgave him. In an angry, unpublished response, she accused him of being a know-nothing show-off, "abstifically a fraud," and offered to "debate him on what he knows

[51] *Hurston to Countee Cullen, March 5, 1943.*

[52] *George Stevens, "Negroes by Themselves," Saturday Review of Literature, 16, no. 21 (September 18, 1937), p. 3.*

[53] *Otis Ferguson, "You Can't Hear Their Voices," New Republic, 92, no. 1193 (October 13, 1937), p. 276.*

[54] *Richard Wright, "Between Laughter and Tears," New Masses, October 5, 1937.*

[55] *Alain Locke, review of* Their Eyes Were Watching God, Opportunity, *June 1, 1938.*

[56] *Ibid.*

about Negroes and Negro life" anytime.[57] To James Weldon Johnson, she wrote: "Alain Leroy Locke is a malicious, spiteful litt[l]e snot."[58]

Nonetheless, Hurston did become a literary sensation. Although she was a latecomer to the Harlem Renaissance, arriving in New York in January 1925 (with only $1.50 to her name) and not publishing much until the thirties, her flamboyant personality made her an instant celebrity among the artists, patrons, and intellectuals helping to spark a new appreciation of African American art. "She seemed to know almost everybody in New York," Langston Hughes declared.[59]

Her essays and short stories drew almost as much attention as her charismatic personality, and her work quickly began to appear in such important venues as *Opportunity*, the *Messenger*, *World Tomorrow*, the *Journal of Negro History*, and the groundbreaking anthologies *The New Negro* and *Ebony and Topaz*. Within a few years of her arrival in New York, Hurston had been honored with prestigious grants and awards from *Opportunity*, the Association for the Study of Negro Life and History, and Barnard College, and the support of white patrons Annie Nathan Meyer, Fannie Hurst, and Charlotte Osgood Mason, who funded Hurston's writing and research for nearly five years. Some have questioned this reliance on white patronage, suggesting it compromised Hurston's work. Others view it merely as a canny ability to take advantage of what was available. "She knew how to handle white folks," Arna Bontemps judged.[60] Perhaps all the canniness in the world couldn't have erased the costs of her success.

Hurston became the most well known black woman writer in America, the author of four novels, two collections of folklore, an autobiography, dozens of short stories, articles in such magazines as the *Saturday Evening Post* and *American Mercury*, numerous reviews, journalistic essays, a number of successful theatrical shows, collections of black music for the Library of Congress, and an editor and writer with the Florida Federal Writers' Project of the Works Progress Administration. She was profiled in *Who's Who, Current Biography, Twentieth Century Authors*, and she served as a member of such distin-

[57]Hurston, "The Chick with One Hen," typescript, James Weldon Johnson Collection, Beinecke Library, Yale University.

[58]Hurston to James Weldon Johnson, February 1938.

[59]Hughes, The Big Sea, p. 239.

[60]Robert E. Hemenway, personal interview with Arna Bontemps, cited in Robert E. Hemenway, "Zora Neale Hurston and the Harlem Renaissance," unpublished manuscript.

guished national associations as the American Folklore Society, the American Anthropological Society, the Ethnological Society, the New York Academy of Sciences, and the American Association for the Advancement of Science. In addition, she left behind a wealth of unpublished writings: novels, essays, more than a dozen plays,[61] and, of course, this remarkable trove of letters, written over a forty-year span. But in spite of her fame and flamboyance, the most well known black woman writer in America was nearly forgotten by the time of her death in 1960. How did Hurston nearly sink into oblivion?

Her last years were spent mostly in Florida, in and around the all-black town of Eatonville, where she grew up and from which she often drew her inspiration. These years were not just tragic or desperate. In the fifties, Hurston lived a quiet and reclusive life, partly, at least, by choice. She gave herself over to domestic pleasures: gardening, house-keeping, and taking care of her pets. But she never stopped writing. She covered the sensational case of Ruby McCullom, a black woman accused of killing her white lover. She wrote political essays on vote-peddling, Florida beef cattle, Southeast Asian colonialism, and communism (which she abominated). She revised a number of novels and began her biography of Herod the Great, a project that overwhelmed her final years but to which she was passionately devoted—more, it now appears from the letters, than she had been to any other work, including the books that made her famous.

Although Hurston worked constantly in her last decade, interesting publishers in her work proved difficult. With a few exceptions, the fifties were as inhospitable to black writers as the twenties had been welcoming. Although Hurston's last published novel, *Seraph on the Suwanee*, received positive reviews—"The author knows her people . . . and she knows the locale,"[62]—the novel earned no money. Black writing was no longer "in vogue." Hurston knew this. In "What White Publishers Won't Print," published in 1950, she described the "Anglo-Saxon's lack of curiosity about the internal lives and emotions of the Negroes," the absence of any "demand for incisive and full-

[61]*Among them:* Herod the Great, Mrs. Doctor, The Golden Bench of God, The Lives of Barney Turk, *"Barracoon," "Black Death," "The Bone of Contention," "Book of Harlem," "The Emperor Effaces Himself," "Joe Wiley of Magazine Point," "The Migrant Worker in Florida,"* Polk County, Cold Keener, De Turkey and de Law, Forty Yards, Meet the Momma, Poker, *"Woofing,"* Bama, Mister Frog, You May Go, *"Fire and Sweat." See Bibliography of the Works of Zora Neale Hurston at the end of this volume.*

[62]Frank G. Slaughter, *review of* Seraph on the Suwanee, New York Times Book Review, *October 31, 1948.*

dress stories around Negroes above the servant class."[63] Among the manuscripts she circulated in the late forties and fifties were *Mrs. Doctor*, which she described as a tale of "the upper strata of Negro life," and *The Lives of Barney Turk*, mostly about white people. Neither project bowed to white expectations. No publisher would take them.

Economic hardship forced Hurston into a series of unglamorous jobs in her final years. Her employment as a maid on Rivo Island occurred just as one of her last short stories, "Conscience of the Court," was appearing in the *Saturday Evening Post*. Other unsatisfying jobs followed: as a librarian at the Patrick Air Force Base in Cocoa, Florida (a job that left her livid about government corruption), as a substitute teacher, and as a columnist for a local paper, the *Fort Pierce Chronicle*, for which she wrote a sometimes sensationalist column entitled "Hoodoo and Black Magic."

On October 29, very reluctantly, she entered the Saint Lucie County welfare home in Fort Pierce and went back and forth between there, her home, and the hospital. She died on January 28, 1960, of "hypertensive heart disease."

Thanks to Hurston's friends Marjorie Silver, Anne Wilder, and especially Deputy Sheriff Patrick Duvall, many of Hurston's papers were saved. According to both Duvall and a woman who was a young friend of Hurston's at the time, however, many of her personal effects, including her typewriter, were carted away and buried.[64] "I don't know who was ignorant enough to burn her papers," Sara Lee Creech remarked.[65] But at the time, few people had the slightest idea of their value.

Although everything she wrote was out of print when she died, Hurston is no longer forgotten. Hurston's rediscovery began with Alice Walker's 1973 trip to find Hurston's unmarked grave and her *Ms.* magazine article "Looking for Zora," and continued with the Modern Language Association's first session devoted to Hurston in 1975, followed by Robert Hemenway's groundbreaking biography of Hurston in 1977 and Walker's anthology of Hurston's work in 1979. Hurston is now among the most widely read and widely taught American authors. There are more than a million copies of her 1937 novel, *Their Eyes*

[63] *"What White Publishers Won't Print,"* Negro Digest, *April 1950.*

[64] *Personal interview with "J.H." Name and interview date withheld by request.*

[65] *Personal interview with Sara Lee Creech, May 6, 2000.*

Were Watching God, in print.[66] Numerous plays, documentaries, and educational videos are devoted to her life and work. Her face appears on posters, coffee mugs, bookmarks, and calendars. She is at the center of literary study through conferences, seminars, graduate and undergraduate classes, anthologies, dissertations, critical articles, books, bibliographies, biographies, reading guides, textbooks for children, Hurston societies, and an annual festival in her hometown of Eatonville on the anniversary of her death.[67] Hurston has become a model for many scholars and writers. Barbara Christian has dubbed Hurston the foremother of African American fiction, an icon of self-love and racial pride.[68] "Many of us love Zora Neale Hurston," Alice Walker writes, "for her absolute disinterest in becoming either white or bourgeois, and for her *devoted* appreciation of her own culture, which is an inspiration to us all."[69] In this context, her letters are long overdue.

Hurston's letters are as much a record of joy and success as they are testaments to disappointment. They broaden what we know about her life and times and restore much-needed complexity to a writer who has often been loved too simply.[70] They give us the Harlem Renaissance, almost for the first time, through a black woman's eyes, the eyes of a woman who helped inaugurate yet also stood outside of one of the most exciting literary flowerings of this country. The letters help us see what it meant "for a black woman to be an artist in our grandmothers' time," in Alice Walker's words.[71] By bearing witness to a complex life and history, Hurston's letters offer hope.

---

[66] *Personal communication with HarperCollins.*

[67] *By a recent count there are now 29 books about her, 378 articles or book chapters, 177 dissertations, 23 bibliographic or reference guides to her work, 16 children's books, and 184 biographical books, articles, essays, or encyclopedia entries.*

[68] Barbara Christian, "Trajectories of Self-Definition: Placing Contemporary African-American Women's Fiction," *in* Conjuring: Black Women, Fiction, and Literary Tradition, *ed. Marjorie Pryse and Hortense J. Spillers (Bloomington: Indiana University Press, 1985).*

[69] *Alice Walker, "On Refusing to Be Humbled by Second Place," pp. 1, 2.*

[70] *A number of black feminist critics, it should be noted, are highly critical of what Ann duCille calls "Hurstonism." Hurston's iconic status, they argue, raises important questions of exceptionalism as well as larger questions about the economics of critical recuperation: who profits from bringing a "lost" writer back to life, what are the grounds on which he or she is brought back, how does that recuperation serve larger class, race, and institutional agendas? See in particular Ann duCille, "The Occult of True Black Womanhood: Critical Demeanor and Black Feminist Studies," in* Female Subjects in Black and White, *ed. Elizabeth Abel, Barbara Christian, and Helene Moglen (Berkeley: University of California Press, 1997), pp. 21–56; Michelle Wallace, "Who Owns Zora Neale Hurston? Critics Carve Up the Legend,"* Invisibility Blues *(New York: Verso, 1990), pp. 172–86; and Hazel Carby, "The Politics of Fiction, Anthropology, and the Folk: Zora Neale Hurston," in* New Essays on Their Eyes Were Watching God, *ed. Michael Awkward (New York: Cambridge University Press, 1990), pp. 71–93.*

[71] *Alice Walker,* In Search of Our Mothers' Gardens *(New York: Harcourt Brace Jovanovich, 1983), p. 233.*

These letters may, however, disrupt cherished views of Hurston. As is true in any revival, the revival of Hurston has sometimes glossed over what is objectionable in her life and writing. We have probably created the Hurston that we need and want, bracketing whatever does not fit. The Hurston who has Janie kill off her self-satisfied second husband by telling him that " 'when you pull down yo' britches, you look lak de change uh life' "[72] is more appealing than the one who describes her character Arvay's rape as "a pain remorseless sweet . . . [one of the] happiest and most consecrated moments of her lifetime."[73] And the Hurston who rails against the " 'pet' negro" system of exceptionalism and stereotyping[74] is more attractive than the one who fliply declares that "slavery is the price I paid for civilization"[75] or the Hurston who was eager to name names in the anticommunist fifties. But if these letters don't square with the iconographic Hurston, they nevertheless make possible a depth of understanding—of the

A young Zora Neale Hurston, probably in the early 1920s.

complexity of both Hurston and her times—that has never before been possible. Given Hurston's own propensity for "feather-bed resistance" and for playing with (and to) her listeners, it would be naive to expect anything but complication. The more information we gather about Hurston, it seems, the less definitive she becomes. This complexity is the greatest gift these letters offer.

More letters, no doubt, remain to be found. Some are the private property of collectors or sellers. Because African American studies is a

[72]*Hurston*, Their Eyes, *p. 75.*

[73]*Zora Neale Hurston*, Seraph on the Suwanee *(New York: HarperCollins, 1991), pp. 51, 306.*

[74]*Zora Neale Hurston, "The 'Pet' Negro System," reprinted in* I Love Myself When I Am Laughing . . . and Then Again When I Am Looking Mean and Impressive: A Zora Neale Hurston Reader, *ed. Alice Walker (New York: Feminist Press, 1979). See also* Seraph on the Suwanee, *pp. 60–61.*

[75]*Hurston, "How It Feels to Be Colored Me."*

relatively young academic field and is often underfunded, the expensive, time-consuming task of cataloging and indexing its relevant collections has often been delayed. Consequently, some Hurston letters probably remain unidentified in archives. Some letters are presumably still to be found in collections in other countries (including, perhaps, more letters to her various translators). Among the people with whom Hurston claimed to correspond but to whom letters could not be found are Winston Churchill, Bertram Lippincott, Julia Peterkin, Mary McLeod Bethune, Sarah Gertrude Knott, Bessie Smith, Ethel Waters, Aaron Douglas, Edna St. Vincent Millay, Elisabeth Marbury, and Richard Nixon. Many of Hurston's friends, particularly old friends from Eatonville, Florida, may still have Hurston letters tucked away in attics, basements, or storage areas.[76] Perhaps this volume will draw such letters out.

---

[76]*The daughter of one of those friends has remarked that her family "had a lot of [Hurston's] books and papers. . . . We don't know which way those papers and books and things went." Annie Davis, daughter of Will Davis and Armetta Jones. Interview with Anna Lillios, September 29, 1989; Anna Lillios, "Excursions into Zora Neale Hurston's Eatonville," Zora in Florida, ed. Steve Glassman and Kathryn Lee Seidel (Orlando: University of Central Florida Press, 1991), p. 23.*

"DE TALKIN' GAME"

The Twenties (and Before)

Overleaf: Zora Neale Hurston and her car, "Cherry," in the 1920s.

First and foremost a storyteller, with profound appreciation for the power of a well-crafted tale, Hurston moved to New York in 1925 and used her storytelling talent to refashion her life along mythic lines, erasing everything that didn't contribute to the new person she had determined to create. That person would have known hardships and hard times, but mostly in a general way. She might have disappointments, but they would never become obstacles. She would be tough and independent and young (in her early twenties, like her friends). Above all, she would be game for everything, full of enthusiasm and ideas. Nothing would be beyond her. She would live up to her proud heritage as a daughter of Eatonville, America's first incorporated all-black town—even if that meant starting over from scratch.

Accordingly, the only full-scale biography of Zora Neale Hurston starts by describing how "in the first week of January, 1925, Zora Neale Hurston arrived in New York."[1] Hurston begins her life over again in the twenties, establishing herself as a writer, social scientist, and active member of the nation's first major upsurge of African American arts.

During this period, she developed her own aesthetic: an embroidered realism equally committed to liveliness and accuracy. Her developing style as a writer mirrored her personality: hardheaded and sentimental, constrained and effusive, objective and fanciful, all at the same time. The Harlem Renaissance—for all its own self-conscious mythmaking—afforded Hurston the necessary ground on which to build this new life. It gave her a collective enterprise in which she could play a valued role. Among its many circles she could find the

[1]Robert E. Hemenway, Zora Neale Hurston: A Literary Biography (Urbana: University of Illinois Press, 1977), p. 9.

publishers, editors, writers, artists, scientists, intellectuals, producers, directors, and patrons she needed to develop all the venues in which she sought to bring the African American vernacular to the American public. This period opened the door to a number of intimate friendships, an inner circle of confidants among whom Hurston hoped to find soulmates who could bridge their differences of race, class, gender, and upbringing. Characteristically, Hurston seemed unfazed by the dazzle of New York's Roaring Twenties. Whereas Harlem was a revelation for many African Americans who had never before been in such a teeming community of black people, Hurston had been raised in an all-black town and was well accustomed to urban life by 1925. She knew that this brief flourishing of America's interest in black culture was a golden moment—perhaps she even sensed how very fleeting that fascination would be—and she wasted no time in using it to advance her personal and artistic goals.

Fashioning a serious career in this period meant becoming a good correspondent, keeping in touch with colleagues, friends, agents, editors, and publishers. Frequently, Hurston wrote multiple letters on a given day. Occasionally, she wrote more than one letter in a day to the same person. As far as can be determined, only one letter survives from earlier than the mid-twenties, although it is almost certain that she wrote to family and friends when she was attending Morgan State Academy and later Howard Preparatory. Without such a record, however, much of her early life remains a mystery. This may be how she wanted it.

What Hurston has written of her early years is peculiar. In her autobiography, *Dust Tracks on a Road*, she offers a story of her origins that reads like pure fiction. She even marks it as "hear-say," a tall tale in the American tradition she called "lying." As she tells it, her mother found herself without benefit of midwife, friend, or the strength to "even reach down to where I was."[2] If an elderly white gentleman had not chanced on her birthing, she would surely have died. Like a "fairy godmother," he counsels Hurston on her future. Included in his advice is an admonition not to "be a nigger" because "Niggers lie and lie." Hurston's only comment on this strange advice is to insist that he was color-blind and harmless. Why did Hurston choose to repeat—or invent—that story in her autobiography? Was she positioning herself

[2]*Zora Neale Hurston*, Dust Tracks on a Road: An Autobiography *(New York: HarperCollins, 1991), pp. 19–20. All uncited quotations in this chapter are from this autobiography.*

as a daughter of two worlds, black and white? Was she suggesting that white patronage—for good or ill—had always been a feature of her life? Did she want her life to read like a racial fairy tale? Or to make a parody of American fairy tales of race?

Wherever we look for information on Hurston's early life, we find interesting fictions she has left behind. The birth dates she gave for herself throughout her life—1898, 1899, 1900, 1901, 1902, 1903, and 1910—are all inaccurate, as scholars have recently discovered.[3] Hurston was born on January 15, 1891, making her between seven and nineteen years older than she claimed.[4] Neither was she actually born in Eatonville, as she claimed.

Like her parents, Hurston was born in Notasulga, Alabama, a place she describes as "an outlying district of landless Negroes, and whites not too much better off. It was 'over the creek,' which was just like saying on the wrong side of the railroad tracks. . . . There was no rise to the thing." Hurston speculates that "the ordeal of share-cropping on a southern Alabama cotton plantation was crushing to [her father's] ambition."

If Alabama was a desolate place, with conditions one longtime resident described as "outrageous [in] every way that you can think,"[5] Eatonville, Florida, when the Hurstons arrived in 1892,[6] represented opportunity. The Hurstons prospered there. Hurston's father, John, became a Baptist minister and pastor of the Macedonia Baptist Church, then served as Eatonville's mayor from 1912 to 1916. John Hurston was known as "a vocal and knowledgeable politician . . . instrumental in the development of some of Eatonville's first municipal laws."[7]

[3]See Cheryl Wall's chronology in her two-volume Library of America edition of Hurston's work: Zora Neale Hurston: Folklore, Memoirs and Other Writings (New York: Library of America, 1995) and Hurston: Novels & Stories (New York: Library of America, 1995). See also Pamela Bordelon's essay "New Tracks on Dust Tracks: Toward a Reassessment of the Life of Zora Neale Hurston," African American Review, 31, no. 1 (1997), pp. 5–21; and Pamela Bordelon, Go Gator and Muddy the Water: Writings by Zora Neale Hurston from the Federal Writers' Project (New York: W. W. Norton, 1999). Kristy Andersen's 1995 unpublished research report, "The Tangled Southern Roots of Zora Neale Hurston," also lists 1891 as Hurston's birth year.
[4]While Wall gives her birth date as January 7 (the day of the month Hurston generally claimed) and Bordelon gives it as January 15, the latter date takes into account the Hurston family Bible as well as census records.
[5]Pamela Bordelon interview with Nate Shaw, in Bordelon, Go Gator, p. 4.
[6]Wall gives this date as 1894, but the family Bible indicates that Hurston's brother Clifford was born in Eatonville in 1893, suggesting that the family moved from Alabama between 1891, when Zora was born, and 1893, when Clifford was born. Hurston's other siblings were Hezekiah Robert (Bob), born 1882; Isaac, born 1882/3, died shortly after; John Cornelius, born 1885; Richard William, born 1887; Sarah, born 1889; Clifford Joel, born 1893; Benjamin Johnson, born 1896; and Everett Edward, born 1898.
[7]See Frank M. Otey, Eatonville, Florida: A Brief History of One of America's First Freedmen's Towns (Winter Park, Fla.: Four-G Publishers, 1989), p. 17.

Eatonville was a fascinating small town founded in 1887 (Hurston gives the date as 1886), distinguished by being the nation's first incorporated black town—and perhaps the nation's oldest continually all-black town as well.[8] Hurston's Eatonville is more distinguished yet: a utopian, imagined world where blacks lived near whites "without a single instance of enmity," people lived a "simple" life of "open kindnesses, anger, hate, love, [and] envy," "you got what your strengths would bring you," and where the Hurston family enjoyed a nice "piece of ground with two big Chinaberry trees shading the front gate," many bushes and flowers, "plenty of orange, grapefruit, tangerine, guavas and other fruits in our yard," and an eight-room house. In Hurston's Eatonville, "we had all that we wanted."

Jonah's Gourd Vine, Hurston's first novel, is largely autobiographical and one of two novels (the other never published) that Hurston set in Eatonville. It provides as much (maybe more) information about Hurston's early life as anything else she wrote, including her own autobiography. John "Buddy" Pearson, modeled on Hurston's father, John, is a larger-than-life character. He can carry his little brother "under his arm like a shock of corn." He is a "fine stud" and "splendid specimen" who grows into manhood as "a walking orgasm" and "a living exultation."[9] John's sexual energy leads to "meandering" that proves fatal. Like this character, Hurston's father was so powerful that his children called him "Big Nigger." Like John Pearson, he was without "steering gear," a man whose "share" of weaknesses derailed his life and sabotaged his daughter's. He and Hurston were estranged for years. When he died on August 10, 1918, in Memphis, Hurston was living in Baltimore and, according to her autobiography, had already left him behind. It was her mother, not her larger-than-life father, who had always encouraged her to "jump at de sun."

Little is said about this supportive and encouraging mother, just as Hurston would have little to say in print about any of her marriages. *Jonah's Gourd Vine* and *Dust Tracks on a Road* both describe the scene of her mother's death, on September 19, 1904,[10] when Hurston was thirteen (not the "nine year old" child she claims to have been in *Dust Tracks*) in almost identical terms. With her arms pinned behind her,

[8]*Ibid.*
[9]*Zora Neale Hurston,* Jonah's Gourd Vine *(New York: HarperCollins, 1990), pp. 8, 50.*
[10]*This date is variously given as September 18 and September 19. The Hurston family Bible (which may also, of course, contain errors) records it as the 19th. See Bordelon, "New Tracks," p. 9.*

Hurston watched her neighbors perform their local rituals of death: clock and looking glass shrouded in cloth, pillow taken from under the deceased's head, deathbed turned to the east (to disable the corpse's reflection, hasten dying, and protect the household), all countermanded by her mother's own dying instructions to avoid all superstition. Hurston referred often to the "years of agony" she suffered over failing to carry out her mother's deathbed directions. My mother "depended on me for a voice," she wrote, but she had let the townswomen triumph.

Of the years immediately following her mother's death, little is known, except that they were difficult. Hurston's teen years, from 1905 to 1912, consequently, are often known as "the missing decade" or the "lost years," years Hurston hid by changing her age and by revealing nothing from that time period. What is known about these years comes largely from *Dust Tracks*, a notoriously unreliable, guardedly written, heavily censored book. That story, also fictionalized, goes like this: Hurston's father remarried shortly after her mother's death, and Hurston's new stepmother was intolerable. Rather than accept being an outsider in her own home, Hurston left: living in a boarding school, with two of her brothers in Jacksonville, with friends of the family, with families for whom she worked as a domestic, with her brother Dick in Sanford, Florida, and with her brother Bob in Memphis. Finally, she moved to Baltimore, Maryland, where her sister Sarah lived and where, after working as a waitress, she enrolled at Morgan Academy to complete her high school education. Between Memphis and Baltimore, Hurston traveled with a Gilbert & Sullivan theater troupe as a maid.

Looking for these "lost" years encoded in Hurston's writing has occupied much of the scholarship on Hurston. This research is suggested by African American women's arts which hint at a secret language: quilts, gardens, music, folk art, preaching and other forms of religious expression. This coded language, Alice Walker writes, is how "our mothers and grandmothers have, more often than not . . . handed on the creative spark . . . like a sealed letter they could not plainly read."[11] In the case of Hurston's lost years, however, we must ask whether her novels truly address a special reader who knows how to read between her lines or whether Hurston chose—as I believe is the case—to keep certain information from the public and to heavily edit her own life story.

[11] *Alice Walker*, In Search of Our Mothers' Gardens *(New York: Harcourt Brace Jovanovich, 1983), p. 240.*

In the twenties, Hurston did embrace publicity. At school, her writing quickly caught the attention of her teachers, Dwight O. W. Holmes, William Pickens, Lorenzo Dow Turner, Montgomery Gregory, and finally, Alain Locke at Howard, where Hurston joined the literary society and began to publish in its magazine, *Stylus*. The rich African American literary community of Washington, D.C., welcomed Hurston. She fell in with Bruce Nugent, Jean Toomer, Marita Bonner, Alice Dunbar-Nelson, Jessie Fauset, Angelina Grimké, May Miller, and Georgia Douglas Johnson, who became a good friend. Being accepted at Howard—"to the Negro what Harvard is to the whites"—was "ecstasy," Hurston wrote.[12]

Nonetheless, Hurston felt like an outsider. A short story from this period, "John Redding Goes to Sea," reveals some of the anxieties of these years. This story's main character is immediately set off from his community and their narrow-minded view that he was "a queer child." What John Redding wants is a bigger sphere, "the wide world—at last." His devotion to his family and town, however, pulls him back, and he ultimately drowns in the very river on which he had hoped to escape. This is not one of Hurston's best stories, but it suggests her ambivalence about the costs of leaving home. How could Hurston *not* have worried? She had arrived at Morgan Academy with one dress and no change of underwear. Her classmates had secure funding and family support, but she was scrambling. "I had heard all about the swank fraternities and sororities and the clothes and everything, and I knew I could never make it."

Hurston did, of course, "make it." Her arrival in New York City in 1925 may have been a "long step for the waif of Eatonville," but it was also a celebrated event.[13] And she could take pride in having written her way up from Florida. The story "Drenched in Light" appeared in *Opportunity* in 1924 and brought her Charles S. Johnson's attention. Johnson, the magazine's founder, was one of the "midwives" of the Harlem Renaissance, "the root" of the entire movement, Hurston called him.[14] Johnson encouraged Hurston to enter *Opportunity*'s first literary contest in 1925 and to come to New York to join the "New Ne-

[12]*Hurston*, Dust Tracks, *p. 113; see also, Hurston, "The Hue and Cry About Howard University," Messenger, 7, no. 9 (September 1925), pp. 315–38.*

[13]*Hurston, Dust Tracks, p. 172.*

[14]*"It was his work, and only his hush-mouth nature has caused it to be attributed to many others," she wrote (ibid., p. 168).*

gro" Renaissance.[15] She won second place (first place went to Langston Hughes) for the short stories "Black Death" and "Spunk" and the play *Color Struck*. This was all the letter of introduction to the Harlem literati Hurston could ever need. At the awards dinner, Hurston met Langston Hughes, Countee Cullen, Carl Van Vechten, Annie Nathan Meyer, and Fannie Hurst.

The first Hurston letter from the twenties we can locate, written in 1925, thanks writer Annie Nathan Meyer for help getting into Barnard. There, Hurston caught the attention of her future mentor, Franz Boas, among others. "I suppose you want to know how this little piece of darkish meat feels at Barnard," Hurston wrote her friend Constance Sheen. "I am received quite well. In fact I am received so well that if someone would come along and try to turn me white I'd be quite peevish at them."[16] "I am tremendously encouraged now," she told Meyer. "My typewriter is clicking away till all hours of the night."[17] Hurston could not afford to antagonize Meyer, who was helping her through Barnard: "I must not let you be disappointed in me," she wrote.[18] As Hemenway notes, "the authentication that Meyer and Hurst offered should not be underestimated. Just as William Lloyd Garrison assured readers of Frederick Douglass's *Narrative* that his life deserved white notice, Meyer and Hurst spotlighted Zora at Barnard. For her sister students to know that Barnard's one black student, despite her poverty, socialized with one of the most popular novelists in America and had dined the evening before with the college's founding mother, granted instant recognition and respect."[19] But at the same time, she clearly enjoyed talking shop with a successful fellow novelist. "I wont try to pretend that I am not thrilled," Hurston wrote Sheen of her new circle in one of the rare times when she did seem dazzled by the glitter of her new life. "I love it! I just wish that you could be here, Connie. To actually talk and eat with some of the big names that you have admired at a distance, if no more than to see what sort of a person they are."[20]

In addition to Meyer, Hurston became close to Fannie Hurst during this period. "The full nature of Fannie and Zora's financial arrange-

[15]Which Hurston called the "so-called Negro Renaissance" in her typically irreverent way (ibid.).
[16]Hurston to Constance Sheen, January 5, [1926].
[17]Hurston to Annie Nathan Meyer, May 12, 1925.
[18]Ibid.
[19]Robert Hemenway, "Zora Neale Hurston and the Harlem Renaissance," unpublished manuscript.
[20]Hurston to Contance Sheen, February 2, 1926.

ment is not known," Hurst's biographer, Brooke Kroeger, explains.[21] We do know that, like her friendship with Meyer, her friendship with Hurst—at that time the most popular writer in the nation—mixed good feeling and economics. As Kroeger has demonstrated, Hurston's employment with Hurst was a matter of mere weeks between November and December 1925.[22] She was a terrible secretary, so Hurst and Hurston resolved instead to be friends. But not equal ones. Hurst never invited Hurston to address her by her first name; in their letters "it would always be Fannie's 'Dear Zora' to Zora's 'Dear Fannie Hurst.'"[23] When they took a long car trip in 1931, Hurston drove while Hurst relaxed in the backseat. In her autobiography, Hurston wrote that Fannie Hurst "picked on me to my profit" and that Hurston loved her for it. In Hurst's sketch of Hurston, written after Hurston's death, Hurst described how they "took a shine" to one another and how Hurston proved a better friend than employee.[24] But when Hurst recommended Hurston for a Guggenheim, she patronizingly called her "erratic" and "undisciplined."[25] As much as Hurston may have enjoyed hobnobbing with Hurst and her friends, she remained skeptical. "They are OFTEN insincere," she confided to Sheen. "Their show of friendship mere patronage."[26]

Finding what she regarded as real friendship was not easy for Hurston. Her closest friend in the twenties was clearly Langston Hughes. They met almost as soon as Hurston arrived in New York, and Hughes quickly became her confidant. She told him about her writing, her relationship with her patron Charlotte Osgood Mason, her marriage, her divorce—things that Hurston rarely revealed to anyone and that only come out in her letters to Hughes and other good friends. Hurston offered money and folklore material. She promoted his poetry wherever she traveled. She suggested collaborating on a number of projects of her own design, and she trusted Hughes and depended on his advice. Some speculate that Hurston was in love with Hughes, but her letters provide scant evidence of that. Nor do they mention

[21]Brooke Kroeger, Fannie: The Talent for Success of Writer Fannie Hurst (New York: Times Books, 1999), p. 123.

[22]Although in a letter to Constance Sheen in January 1926 Hurston is still claiming to be Hurst's secretary.

[23]Kroeger, p. 126.

[24]Fannie Hurst, "Zora Neale Hurston: A Personality Sketch," Yale University Library Gazette, 35 (1960).

[25]Kroeger, p. 189.

[26]Hurston to Constance Sheen, February 2, 1926.

Hughes's sexuality, about which he, in turn, was notoriously private.[27] As close friends, Hurston and Hughes shared many passions. Both were committed to representations of what Hurston called "the Negro farthest down." They also shared a disgust for blacks who pandered to white taste (of which Hurston herself was often accused). They disdained the "polite" literature promoted by prominent race leaders. In *The Big Sea*, Hughes wrote that "in anything that white people were likely to read, they wanted to put their best foot forward, their politely polished and cultural foot."[28] Black attempts to mimic white culture particularly enraged them, as did white appropriations of black

Hurston on the Columbia University campus.

culture. Yet both were fervent in defending their friend Carl Van Vechten against that very charge. In 1927, Hurston and Hughes traveled the South in Hurston's car. Along the way they planned collaborative work, collected folklore, and met with hoodoo doctors. "I knew it would be fun traveling with her. It was," Hughes wrote.[29]

This decade forged other important friendships, such as Hurston's lifelong relationship with Carl Van Vechten. Van Vechten was—and remains—controversial. Some credit him with inaugurating serious white interest in black arts. Others criticize him for appropriating black culture and promoting exoticism. In response to an ongoing symposium in the *Crisis* called "The Negro in Art: How Shall He Be Portrayed?" Van Vechten (who also wrote the questions) replied that African American writers should concentrate on the "fresh material"

---

[27]*So much so, in fact, that many Hughes scholars avoid the subject altogether. His sexuality remains a controversial question: friends remember him as gay while most biographies conclude that he was asexual.*

[28]*Langston Hughes,* The Big Sea *(New York: Hill & Wang, 1975), pp. 266–67.*

[29]*Ibid., p. 296.*

of working-class, jazz-loving, speakeasy-going black culture "while it is still fresh" or run the risk that white writers would "exploit it until not a drop of vitality remains."[30] His novel *Nigger Heaven* (a reference to segregated seating in theaters) seemed to many—Alain Locke, Countee Cullen, and W. E. B. Du Bois, for example—to do exactly that. It touched off a firestorm. In the late 1940s, Hurston thought seriously of writing a book to defend Van Vechten from ongoing criticisms. "Dear Carlo," she wrote, "nothing would give me greater pleasure than to do a book around you. You have had such a tremendous influence on the arts of the last twenty-five years, that I think it ought to be precipitated out of the mass of lies that are now growing up. People are brazenly claiming credit for the many things that you were responsible for."[31] During the worst period of her life, when Hurston resolved to kill herself, it was to Carl Van Vechten that she wrote her farewells: "All that I have ever tried to do has proved useless," she confided. "All that I believed in has failed me. I have resolved to die. It will take a few days for me to set my affairs in order, and then I will go. I thank you and Fania for your kindness."[32]

The twenties also forged Hurston's associations with older men Hurston needed but did not trust. Just as she resented W. E. B. Du Bois and yet depended on the important role he played, so she had mixed reactions to figures such as Alain Locke and Walter White. On the one hand, her praise of Locke was effusive. On one letter, she drew a figure representing Hughes, Locke, and herself as "a glorious artistic triangle . . . with LH and ZH at the base, AL at the apex."[33] But Hurston resented Locke's authority, his demanding nature, and his attitudes toward women. Locke's criticism of *Their Eyes Were Watching God* finally evoked one of the most violent tongue-lashings Hurston ever gave: she called him "dishonest" and a "fraud."[34] But Locke was not easily dismissed. He was a well-connected gatekeeper, tied not only to Hurston's patron Mason but to most of the leaders of the Harlem Renaissance as well. Her relationship with Walter White, writer, secretary, and ultimately executive director of the influential NAACP, was marked by all the same tensions. When she was working with him or

[30]*Carl Van Vechten*, Crisis, *31 (March 1926)*.

[31]*Hurston to Carl Van Vechten, July 30, 1947.*

[32]*Hurston to Carl Van Vechten, [October 30, 1948].*

[33]*Hemenway,* Hurston, *p. 115. See Hurston to Alain Locke, October 11, 1927.*

[34]*Zora Neale Hurston, "The Chick with One Hen," typescript, James Weldon Johnson Collection, Beinecke Library, Yale University.*

hoping to be, she sent him love and lent him valuable theatrical properties, warmly confiding to him her views of white folklorists. When they
fell out, however, she quickly became convinced that he was both bad-
mouthing her and stealing from her, that the NAACP itself was trying
"to cramp me" as she angrily wrote him.[35] Yet just as she had thought
nothing of asking Du Bois to follow her plan for a black cemetery, in
spite of their many personal differences, so she apparently thought
nothing of asking Walter White for a letter of recommendation—
which he wrote—or his assistance, after a seven-year silence, with
what she considered scandalous treatment of black officers in southern
schools. It was evidently her view that political solidarity should over-
ride personal animus. This was, of course, the official view of most of
the veterans of the Harlem Renaissance. But it was not universally
practiced.

Many have noticed how little Hurston's autobiography has to say
about the Harlem Renaissance. Of course a movement becomes a
movement most fully in retrospect, when its historians give it coherent
narrative shape. While it is happening, a movement is a series of activities, publications, events, personalities, and places. Hurston's letters
give us a vivid sense of this movement and Hurston's involvement in it.
They show someone often living and working in direct response to it,
even when to do so most effectively meant getting away to Eatonville,
the Bahamas, Honduras, or elsewhere.

Literature and the arts were the heart of the Harlem Renaissance.
Believing that accurate representations of blacks would turn the tide of
American racism and help create equal social and economic opportunities, black artists and intellectuals of the Harlem Renaissance "promoted poetry, prose, painting, and music as if their lives depended on
it."[36]

In 1921, a *Negro World* editorial declared that "the history and literature of any race are the credentials on which that race is admitted to
the family of civilized men and are the indications of its future possibilities."[37] In the same years, James Weldon Johnson echoed these sentiments in the preface to his *The Book of American Negro Poetry:* "The

[35]*Hurston to Walter White, July 23, 1934.*

[36]*Nathan Irvin Huggins,* Harlem Renaissance *(London: Oxford University Press, 1973), p. 9.*

[37]*William Ferris, "The Arts and Black Development,"* Negro World, *April 30, 1921, as quoted by Theodore G.
Vincent and Robert Crisman, eds.,* Voices of a Black Nation: Political Journalism in the Harlem Renaissance
(San Francisco: Ramparts Press, 1973), p. 327.

final measure of the greatness of all peoples is the amount and standard of the literature and art they have produced. The world does not know that a people is great until that people produces great literature and art. No people that has produced great literature and art has ever been looked upon by the world as distinctly inferior . . . After trying 'religion, education, politics, industrial, ethical, economic [and] sociological' approaches, 'through his artistic efforts the Negro is smashing' the race barriers 'faster than he has ever done through any other method.' "[38] When asked in 1926 what business "a fighting organization" like the NAACP had with "turn[ing] aside to talk about Art," Du Bois's answer was quite simple: everything.[39] Hurston's own take on this credo—"you can't git de best of no woman in de talkin' game[.] Her tongue is all de weapon a woman got"[40]—added a comic and gendered touch.

Hurston was as passionate about art's social role as anyone else. But, along with her closest friends, she felt that "accuracy" entailed a willingness to explore *all* aspects of African American life, not just those that whites were likely to accept. The explicit program of *Fire!!*—the short-lived literary journal Hurston founded along with Hughes, Countee Cullen, Wallace Thurman, Aaron Douglas, Richard Bruce Nugent, Gwendolyn Bennett, Helene Johnson, and others—was to round out available representations of African American life by including the sexual, political, racial, and class-oriented themes that "Younger Negro Artists" (to whom the journal was devoted) had felt too constrained to explore.

The Harlem Renaissance, in other words, did not coalesce around a simple or unified vision. There were as many points of disagreement as there were of agreement among Harlem Renaissance intellectuals, especially over art's social role and the place of experimental aesthetic techniques, such as those being introduced by the white modernists, versus folk material, dialect, and the vernacular. Theatrical representations that might play into racist stereotypes yet play successfully on Broadway proved particularly vexing.

But it was, overall, a good time for African American artists, producing many black magazines, newspapers, and literary journals, and

[38] *James Weldon Johnson, Preface,* The Book of American Negro Poetry, *Revised Edition (New York: Harcourt, Brace, Jovanovich, 1931), p. 9; and James Weldon Johnson, "Race Prejudice and the Negro Artist,"* Harper's *157 (November 1928), quoted in Lewis, p. 193.*

[39] *W. E. B. Du Bois, "Criteria of Negro Art" (published text of address to the Chicago Conference of the National Association for the Advancement of Colored People),* The Crisis, *October 1926, pp. 290–97.*

[40] Mules and Men, *p. 30.*

the beginnings of cultural institutions rich with community programs, such as the Schomburg Library in Harlem. Patrons wanted to support black arts. And foundations like the Guggenheim, the Rosenwald, the Garland, and the Viking actively sought out talented African Americans. Political organizations such as the NAACP and the Urban League offered support through contests and awards such as the *Opportunity* awards, the Spingarn Medal, the Harmon Award, the Boni & Liveright award, and others. And there were many literary salons and parties—at Georgia Douglas Johnson's, at Walter White's, at the famous "Dark Tower" salon of A'Lelia Walker, and at Carl Van Vechten's—all providing space for black and white artists, intellectuals, musicians, and political leaders to mix and share ideas. And New York—as the official epicenter of the movement—was undeniably exciting. "It is," in the words of Nathan Irvin Huggins, "a rare and intriguing moment when a people decide that they are the instruments of history-making and race-building."[41] As Adam Clayton Powell, Sr., the pastor of the Abyssinian Baptist Church, put it, Harlem in the 1920s was "the symbol of liberty and the Promised Land to Negroes everywhere."[42]

Of all the arts flourishing in New York in the twenties, Hurston was particularly excited by what was happening in black theater. The celebrated all-black production of Noble Sissle and Eubie Blake's successful *Shuffle Along* (1921) seemed to open a new sphere for African American expression. Black actors like Charles Gilpin, Rose McClendon, Paul Robeson, Florence Mills, Bill "Bojangles" Robinson, Frank Wilson, Ethel Waters, and Eubie Blake starred in plays written and produced by whites: Paul Green's *In Abraham's Bosom* (1926), DuBose and Dorothy Heyward's *Porgy* (1927), Lew Leslie's *Blackbirds* (1928), and Eugene O'Neill's *The Emperor Jones* (1920) and *All God's Chillun Got Wings* (1924).

This was the context in which Hurston acquired a patron, Charlotte Osgood Mason, a wealthy New Yorker born Charlotte van der Veer Quick, probably the most complex presence in Hurston's life. Hurston described a powerful psychic bond between them and wrote to Mason with reverence. But Mason was a very difficult woman. A dedicated primitivist, her interest in African American culture, coinciding with the Harlem Renaissance, led her to support Miguel Covarrubias, Aaron

[41] *Huggins, p. 3.*
[42] *Quoted by Jervis Anderson, This Was Harlem: A Cultural Portrait, 1900–1950 (New York: Farrar, Straus, Giroux, 1981), p. 61.*

Douglas, Louise Thompson, Richmond Barthé, Hall Johnson, Alain Locke, and Langston Hughes. Mason was powerful and imperious. She also appears to have been without either humor or irony. As Robert Hemenway reports, she liked "to sit in a throne-like chair, with her protégés on footstools at her feet,"[43] apparently oblivious to what the scene connoted. Mason could be extremely generous. She was also penurious. Hurston's financial arrangements with Mason required detailing even the smallest and most mundane of items: "I really need a pair of shoes," one letter noted.[44] Hurston had to document every penny she spent, from "string beans and canned fruit" to "colon medicine (three dollars) and sanitary napkins (sixty five cents)."[45] In another, she wrote, "my health. Godmother, to be honest, I continue to have intestinal trouble but I keep it to myself. I really need medical attention but I say as little about it as possible lest I worry you. It slows me up and when I dont keep up the agar agar [a natural remedy] I lose ground. Recently I just couldnt find the money for it, and it hasnt been so good."[46] Hurston wrote that Mason "became concerned about my condition and suggested a certain white specialist at her expense." He showed Hurston into "a closet where the soiled towels and uniforms were tossed until called for by the laundry," offering her a "chair in there wedged in between the wall and the pile of soiled linen."[47] Mason wanted to be known as "Godmother." Hurston added names such as "light" and "True one." Yet Mason was also Hurston's legal "Boss."

Hurston first met Mason in September 1927, at Mason's Park Avenue penthouse. There Hurston signed a contract (on December 1, 1927) that Mason eventually extended through the fall of 1932, which gave Hurston $200 a month, a camera, and a car. It also denied her any autonomy or control over her work. The contract specified Hurston as Mason's employee. Any material collected or written by Hurston legally belonged to Mason, who was described as hiring Hurston as her "agent" in the collection of "music, folk-lore, poetry, hoodoo, conjure, manifestations of art, and kindred matters existing among the American negroes" because Mason "is unable because of the pressure of other matters to undertake the collecting of this information in person." Hurston was not to use,

[43] Hemenway, Hurston, p. 107.

[44] Hurston to Charlotte Osgood Mason, April 27, 1932.

[45] Hemenway, Hurston, p. 176.

[46] Hurston to Charlotte Osgood Mason, April 4, 1932.

[47] Zora Neale Hurston, "My Most Humiliating Jim Crow Experience," Negro Digest, June 1944.

publish, or present any of this material (her own material). Instead, she was to "faithfully perform her task. . . . return . . . and lay before said first party [Charlotte Mason] all of said information, data, transcriptions of music, etc. which she shall have obtained."[48]

It is fair to say that Mason supported Hurston's energy and recognized her brilliance. But it also must be pointed out that she curtailed Hurston's ambitions. Mason effectively forestalled the publication of Hurston's major works until well after the twenties had ended and the publishing market had become less favorable to blacks. Yet Hurston adopted the posture of the supplicant child—the irresponsible, adorable (and adoring) "pickaninny"—in her letters to "Godmother" Mason. "I see all my terrible weakness and failures, my stark stupidity and lack of vision and I am amazed that your love and confidence has carried over."[49] Should we read such letters as ironized examples of "featherbed resistance"—especially in the light of the vexed history of white patronage in this period? Does that misread a relationship in which Hurston insisted that her love and devotion—despite whatever insults she suffered—were genuine?

During this decade, Hurston seemed particularly adept at attracting the attention of powerful white people. At Barnard, she attracted eminent anthropologist Franz Boas. The twenties were a particularly interesting time to be working as an anthropologist, especially challenging if you were African American and working on African American culture. It would not be until the 1960s that African Americans would enter the field of anthropology in significant numbers.[50] As an African American woman at Columbia, studying with Franz Boas—whom Hurston called the "king of kings" or, simply, "Papa Franz"—Hurston's position was privileged. No one was more influential in the field than Boas, with his antiracist version of cultural relativism—a direct challenge to the evolutionary perspective and the amateur, unscientific ethnography popularly practiced earlier in the decade. Almost all of the leading American anthropologists of the day—Gladys Reichard, Ruth Benedict, Margaret Mead, Jane Belo, Melville Herskovits—were either associates or students of Boas. This intellectual cohort was instrumental in debunking

[48]*Contract between Zora Neale Hurston and Charlotte Osgood Mason, Alain Locke papers, Moorland-Spingarn Research Center, Howard University.*

[49]*Hurston to Charlotte Osgood Mason, April 18, 1931.*

[50]*The first African American anthropologist, John Wesley Gilbert, was an archaeologist of ancient Greece who received his degree in the 1880s.*

the racist nativism of popular writers like Madison Grant (*The Passing of the Great Race,* 1916) and Lothrop Stoddard (*The Rising Tide of Color,* 1920). And this may have helped Hurston tie her scholarly work to debates over the politics of race in Harlem.

Indeed, Hurston was positioned to bridge these two groups in a way that probably no one else was capable of doing: introducing African American culture into the project that Margaret Mead called the "Giant Rescue operation" of recording and salvaging dying cultures, and injecting anthropological methods into Harlem Renaissance artistry. Because Hurston was one of the only academically trained African American anthropologists of her day, her situation was unique, and her links to the leading folklorists of the day, particularly the Lomaxes, with whom she traveled and recorded singers such as Leadbelly, put her on the cutting edge of her field. She pioneered efforts to document black speech in glossaries and essays such as "Characteristics of Negro Expression" in line with Boas's argument that "language is a reflection of the state of culture,"[51] just as she could line that argument up with Harlem Renaissance ideas about the social role of the arts.

Methodologically, however, Hurston's fit with her fellow anthropologists was anything but seamless. On the one hand, as a storyteller rather than an empirical scientist, Hurston risked being associated with ethnographic popularizers. "Anthropology was a hit," Phillips Bradford writes in his account of the caged exhibition of an African man at both the St. Louis world's fair and the Bronx Zoo.[52] In this context, celebrating cultural difference smacked of the 1876 Philadelphia, 1893 Chicago, 1904 St. Louis, and 1939 New York world's fairs, all of which sponsored exhibitions of "native" peoples in their "natural" habitats: Eskimos, Filipinos, Japanese, South Americans, and Zulus, Balubas, and Pygmies from Africa. Hurston was in a difficult position. Her peers wanted to make white, mainstream society seem strange so that "other," "exotic" cultures might seem more familiar.[53] But since Hurston was part of a subculture already considered "other," this didn't work. She was, on the one hand, a reporter on "exotic" cultural practices and, on the other, a living example of the exotic and primitive herself.

---

[51]*Quoted in Deborah Plant,* Every Tub Must Sit on Its Own Bottom: The Philosophy and Politics of Zora Neale Hurston *(Urbana: University of Illinois Press, 1995), p. 42.*

[52]*Phillips Verner Bradford and Harvey Blume,* Ota Benga: The Pygmy in the Zoo *(New York: St. Martin's Press, 1992), p. 5.*

[53]*Alice Gambrell,* Women Intellectuals, Modernism, and Difference: Transatlantic Culture, 1919–1945 *(Cambridge: Cambridge University Press, 1997), p. 103.*

This position may help explain why Hurston felt a need for an advanced degree even as she disdained the precepts and assumptions of the university. It may also explain the license her white teachers and colleagues apparently felt to patronize and condescend to her. Franz Boas's preface to *Mules and Men*—which Hurston solicited—praises her only for "the charm of a loveable personality" that enabled her to "penetrate through that effected demeanor by which the Negro excludes the White observer effectively from participating in his true inner life." He praises her, in other words, for breaking through the "feather-bed resistance" that, *as* an anthropologist, she has identified—in this same book—as one of the most important traits of black culture. He and Ruth Benedict, even Hurston's good friend Fannie Hurst, wrote letters for Hurston's 1934 application to the Guggenheim Foundation which must have made her blood boil.[54] Neither her attempts at her own self-fashioning nor her complicated views of race could penetrate the stolid preconceptions of many of her most supportive white friends and colleagues.

Much of Hurston's writing expresses what seem to be conflicting ideas of race. "How It Feels to Be Colored Me," for example, published in 1928, argues that she had "no separate feeling about being an American citizen and colored," none of the "double consciousness" that Du Bois articulated so famously in *The Souls of Black Folk.* "I belong to no race nor time," she declared.[55] But all of her anthropological work in the twenties and thirties and her lifelong commitment to bringing African American folklore to the public is devoted to demonstrating precisely the opposite. She gave herself over to showing what was both different and special in African American history.

Her first book-length manuscript and the only one she completed during the twenties was a concerted effort to represent African American culture with neither apology nor adjustment. During her travels from 1927 to 1929, Hurston collected vast amounts of material. It is easy to romanticize Hurston with Model T and pistol, searching out

---

[54]*There is no clear record that Hurston was aware of these lukewarm letters, but when she reapplied to the Guggenheim in 1936 (and this time received the grant), she went with very different recommenders, most of them less academically prestigious but much more effusive in their praise: Melville Herskovits; Edwin O. Grover, her friend from Rollins College; Lewis Gannett, a journalist, editor, and publisher whom Hurston knew only slightly; Carl Van Vechten (this letter goes to seven lines); and Harry Lydenberg from the New York Public Library, another person who was forced to confess in his letter that he knew the recommendee only slightly. All materials referred to above are in the John Simon Guggenheim Memorial Foundation files.*

[55]*Zora Neale Hurston, "How It Feels to Be Colored Me," World Tomorrow, 11 (May 1928). See also W. E. B. Du Bois, The Souls of Black Folk.*

"the Negro farthest down" and "woofing" in "jooks" along the way. But the truth is that she worked hard under harsh conditions: traveling in blistering heat, sleeping in her car when "colored" hotel rooms couldn't be had, defending herself against jealous women, putting up with bedbugs, lack of sanitation, and poor food in some of the turpentine camps, sawmills, and phosphate mines she visited. Evidently, she cut an unusual figure: a single, black woman, driving her own car, toting a gun, sometimes passing for a bootlegger, offering prize money for the best stories and "lies."[56] I am "getting some gorgeous material down here, verse and prose, <u>magnificent,</u>" she wrote to Langston Hughes.[57] She collected so much material that she projected seven volumes: "My Plans: 1 volume of stories. 1 children's games. 1 Drama and the Negro 1 'Mules & Men' a volume of work songs with guitar arrangement[.] 1 on Religion. 1. on words & meanings. 1 volume of love letters with an introduction on Negro love."[58] Had she published these seven volumes, she could certainly have laid claim to being *the* leading folklorist of her generation. But doing so might also have derailed a career as a major American novelist. The manuscript she did create out of this material, *Negro Folk-Tales from the Gulf States,* was meant to counter the inauthentic versions of folklore Hurston saw everywhere around her. Hurston wanted to present an authentic African American folklore, not something doctored to suit either dominant aesthetics or stereotyped notions of black culture. She wanted a volume of folklore that would stand on its own, without interference, interpretation, anthropological voice-over, or her own personal "charm." "I am leaving the story material almost untouched. I have only tampered with it where the story teller was not clear. I know it is going to read different, but that is the glory of the thing, dont you think?" she wrote Langston Hughes.[59] It took almost five years for Hurston to find a publisher for her folklore, and when she finally did, it turned out that they would only publish the story material in a very different version: glossed, doctored, and threaded with Hurston's personal charm. This is the volume we now know as *Mules and Men.*

Hemenway has used the phrase "vocational schizophrenia" to describe Hurston's position, caught between Harlem Renaissance agen-

[56]*Hemenway,* Hurston, *p. 111.*
[57]*Hurston to Langston Hughes, March 17, 1927.*
[58]*Hurston to Langston Hughes, August 6, 1928.*
[59]*Hurston to Langston Hughes, April 30, 1929.*

das and those of her academic teachers. It is certainly the case that shaping a serious career as an African American woman was a difficult task. No doubt it took a heavy toll. According to her first husband, Herbert Sheen, "the demands of her career doomed [their] marriage,"[60] and her letters suggest that they may have "doomed" other love affairs. Professionally, Hurston was often forced to take odd jobs simply to keep herself afloat. Much of her professional work had to be conducted in secret to avoid angering her patron. At one point, she even apparently felt under enough pressure to engage in plagiarism, a desperate lapse for such an original writer.[61] Hurston's letters reveal the ways she negotiated such conflicts.

Young Hurston with cigarette.

Fiction may have represented some freedom from these conflicts. But even that was always subject to attack—or misguided praise— from her critics. Perhaps she wrote so many short stories in this decade because they were easy to get past her patron Mason's ever-watchful eye. These short pieces also allowed her to experiment with dialect, folklore and oral tradition, material from her childhood, and favorite themes, such as romantic triangulation.

Her letters from this decade showcase Hurston's development by suggesting the rather extraordinary odds she was up against. The twenties were a complex time in American history, affording both obstacles and opportunities which have become legendary. Hurston was well aware of this complexity and canny about seeing how she could turn it to her own advantage. She was determined, then as later, not to miss a beat.

[60]Robert E. Hemenway interview with Herbert Sheen, in Hemenway, Hurston, p. 94.

[61]"Cudjo's Own Story of the Last African Slaver," published in the Journal of Negro History in October 1927, is mostly copied verbatim from an obscure book, Historic Sketches of the Old South, written by Emma Langdon Roche. For a fuller discussion of this plagiarism episode, see Hemenway, Hurston.

TO WILLIAM PICKENS

[1917/1918]
Morgan College
Tuesday

Dear Dean,

I want to <u>know</u> you and Mrs. Pickens, ever so much, for many reasons. The first of which is, You are interesting to others. Second you are interesting to me. Third, I want to reverse the usual process, & know the writing by the writer.[1]

Greatest of all, thirty or forty years hence, The world will look for some one that has really known you to write your biography. To see you as a husband a father, & have you as a friend and teacher. Should mean that one would get beyond obvious, the superficial. I want to do that.

I would like to know to what extent, a woman of Mrs. Pickens character & accomplishments, would, influence your life.

Impertinent, isnt it? But I want to get <u>All</u> that Morgan has to give. I feel that I will have done something equal to the course at Morgan, if I have really known you and Mrs. Pickens.

Yours Respectfully,
Zora Neale Hurston.

---

[1]*Pickens was the author of numerous works, including* Abraham Lincoln: Man and Statesman, Heir to Slaves, Frederic Douglass and the Spirit of Freedom.

TO ANNIE NATHAN MEYER

163—W. 131st St
New York City.
May 12, 1925.

My [d—x-ed out] Dear Mrs. Meyer—

I have been waiting to hear from my request for a transcript of my record. It must be attended to by now.

I am tremendously encouraged now. My typewriter is clicking away till all hours of the night. I am striving desperately for a toe-hold on the world. You see, your interest keys me up wonderfully—I must not let you be disappointed in me.

No, no the little praise I have received does not affect me unless it be to make me work furiously. Instead of a pillow to rest upon, it is a goad to prod me. I know that I can only get into the sunlight by work and only remain there by more work. But you do help me immensely. It is pleasant to have someone for whom one does things. It is mighty cold comfort to do things if nobody cares whether you succeed or not. It is terribly delightful to me to have some one fearing with me and hoping for me, let alone working to make some of my dreams come true.

Is Mr. Meyer improving? I hope so, truly. I am sending a bit of ultra-free verse for him to take his medicine by (weak ending). All of the Editors of Verse magazines are panting to know who the author of this masterpiece is—but you are my friend and must not expose me.[1] Editors are violent men.

Yes, I look forward eagerly to that brief chat with you before you go away. I say brief because you have so little time and I do not wish to tax your [time—x-ed out] kindness too much.

Hoping to have another letter from you, I am, Mrs. Meyer

Your grateful and obedient servant,
Zora Neale Hurston

---

[1] Early in her career Hurston wrote, but did not publish, poems such as "Home," "Love," "Longin'," "Thou Art Mine," and "Contentment." The first lines of "Home" read: "I know a place that is full of light, / That is full of dreams and visions bright." The first line of "Contentment" reads: "When I consider how my life is spent, I am content."

TO ALAIN LOCKE

[1925]
127 E. 23ʳᵈ St.
N.Y.C.
June 5.

My dear Dr. Locke,

I am enclosing "Black Death."[1] I am very happy that you can find use for it.

I get a tremendous kick out of my Howard friendships. I certainly dislike seeing the things published about the old "Hill" that are being broadcast at present. I wonder if anyone really feels that matters are being cleared up by laundering our soiled linen on Broadway.

But the business—our business of dream weaving that we call writing is much more interesting just at this moment and I hope the volume goes over with a bang.[2] I was over to Mr. Van Vechten's[3] last week and he showed me a letter from you about the "Introduction." I think that will be very fine.

A new (I suppose it ought to be written in capitals) New Negro play company is about to be born with your humble servant as Chief mid-wife.[4] I am receiving encouragement from exceeding 'high ups.' Behold the Jimpson weed putting out roots in the solarium of the or-chid! Any contributions in the form of advice and counsel will be well received.

You, Chas. S. & J.W./Mr. Johnson ["Chas. S. & J.W." is written above "Mr. Johnson"], Walter White[5] et al[.], have been wonderful to

[1]An early short story of Hurston's, submitted to the 1925 Opportunity contest but never published.

[2]In March 1925, Alain Locke edited a special volume of Survey Graphic which he expanded later that same year into the widely influential—and for many, the definitive—anthology The New Negro, published by Al-bert and Charles Boni. "The Black Death" was not included in The New Negro, but Hurston's story "Spunk" was published under Locke's rubric of "Negro Youth Speaks."

[3]Carl Van Vechten; see glossary.

[4]This particular theater group seems not to have gotten off the ground, but there were black theater groups founded in 1929, including the Negro Art Theater, started in the Abyssinian Baptist Church, and the Negro Experimental Theater, founded in the 135th Street branch of the New York Public Library.

[5]Charles S. Johnson, James Weldon Johnson, and Walter White were all important political and artistic lead-ers of the Harlem Renaissance. See glossary.

me. I must duly give thanks. If I can eke out an existence for five weeks more I feel that I will be on pretty firm ground. Rosamond Johnson is writing the music to a play I have just finished, that is, if the heat has not overcome him.[6] I think it will go quite well. Miller of "Shuffle Along" is interested and we are having a reading next week with him.[7]

If there is time, I am sure Mr. Reiss will illustrate "Black Death" if he is asked. He is interested in the things I do, but it seemed presumptuous for me to ask him.[8]

I shall see you soon in this fair oven we call a city. Kindest wishes to all. I am

yours sincerely
Zora Neale Hurston

TO ANNIE NATHAN MEYER

163 W. 131st ST
New York City
June 23, 1923[5].[1]

Dear Mrs Meyer,

I have two or three irons in the fire and I have waited to have news to tell you. I have cause to hope that two of the three will turn out well, but nothing definite yet.[2] I wish I could look into Miss Birtwell's head.[3]

[6]*Brother of James Weldon Johnson, John Rosamond Johnson; see glossary.*

[7]Shuffle Along *was probably the most successful all-black review to open on Broadway in the twenties. Written by Flournoy Miller and Aubrey Lyles, it starred such luminaries as Florence Mills, Josephine Baker, Mae Barnes, and, briefly, Paul Robeson. Its score, written by Noble Sissle and Eubie Blake, contained many hits, including "I'm Just Wild About Harry" and "Love Will Find a Way."*

[8]*Winold Reiss, the German painter, was particularly well known for his portraits of blacks in the* Survey Graphic *and Locke's* The New Negro *(the originals are exhibited in the Fisk University Library). Also a muralist, Reiss had his work displayed in hotels, restaurants, theaters, and other public places, usually featuring different ethnic groups. Among Reiss's best-known students is African American painter Aaron Douglas.*

[1]*Hurston's typed letter is dated 1923, but this is presumably an error since she didn't arrive in New York until 1925. The date is probably 1925.*

[2]*Hurston was working on a number of short pieces at this time, including short stories such as "Muttsy," "Possum or Pig," and "The Eatonville Anthology," which she may have hoped to place in* Vanity Fair.

[3]*Birtwell was a* Vanity Fair *editor.*

If I have moderate success I will have a great deal more than my quota. I hope that I can make it all. Then I can enjoy your interest without your doing anything other than egging me on to work.

Yes, you should write another novel. You must have a number of them bottled up in you. If I knew white psychology I would attempt one on the Stillman case.[4] You have in that case:

1. The Emperor complex

a. can do no wrong

b. high disdain of women when all pleasure is squeezed out of them—cast them aside.

2 The Saul parallel

(in his the dream or vision of David's mailed fist hurling him down from his throne.)

b. His highly paid lawyers are the witch of End-Or.

c. The conventions finally get him

3 By threats to ruin her in the eyes of her children he obtains her consent ot [sic] divorce. "Perhaps I cannot convict you of immorality in a coutr [sic] of justice, but I can put a question mark after your name in the eyes of the world" etc.

a. divorces wife.

B. marries chorus girl

c deserted by society—nothing but 'regrets' at their at home.

d. Takes her abroad for that society may become reconcild [sic]

e. Return from Japan via Pacific.

f. storm; ship off its course.

g. Volcanic island

h. "House of God" bride's comment. If ever I lose myself I'd want to come here.

i. She gets it charted on map by Capt.

4 Back in N.Y.C.

a society not to be coerced

b. he wishes to rejoin associates

---

[4]*This involved J. A. Stillman, president of the National City Bank of New York, who sued his wife for divorce on March 11, 1921, in a notorious case that received a great deal of public attention because it involved questions of paternity on both sides, a "half-breed Indian guide" being named in the case of the Stillman's two-year-old son and Stillman himself being named in the case of the two-year-old son of a Mrs. Florence Leeds. To complicate matters still further, there was suspicion that Mr. Leeds and Stillman were the same person. The case remained in the public eye for months.*

c. He builds a yacht and entertains society without her.

d. Quarrels. He asks divorce.

5 She temporizes. If he will go with her to their island and stay three months she will consent if at the end of that time he still wishes it. (hopes for reconciliation)

a. He consents, knowing hat he will not change.

b. She stocks yacht secretly for a year.

c. Supplies unloaded on Island.

d. He plans to desert after a week and has the yacht to stand out in deep water "for fear the wind might drive it on the reef."

e. very happy week, for her. At the end he writes letter and escapes in early dawn but finds that the yacht has disappeared during night. He rows round among the islands for nearly a week before he gives up and exhausted is forced to return. The island is off the regular ship lanes. Events have brought out her small town religious turn. He is a thwarted, baffled emperor who has always felt that he held the fate of the financial world in his hands.

Conclusion: 1 Does she spend the rest of her days (or until rescued) turned from life, beseeching her God in hte [sic] burning mountain, while he unable to forget his former power sit always gazing out to sea for a passing ship?

2 Do they finally see themselves as they are and aided by surroundings: a. she learns to care for him instead of his money b.he ceases to despise her humbler origin and the value that "society" placed upon her and when rescued are depending upon each other in the true domestic relation?

I could plot this out even better if I thought that it would not be too much for me. I see white people do things, but I dont know that I grasp why they do them. So I fear to attempt to portray their emotions. As it is I am getting on rapidly with my novel of Negro life.[5]

I do not feel that I was too hard on my people in my last letter. Look over your mind and see how many organizations of any size that we have. I mean those that are solely ours. GET A <u>GOOD</u> MICROSCOPE! Find one educational institution supported by us. Our churches are our strongest organizations, but even those without ex-

---

[5]Jonah's Gourd Vine.

ception have suffered more than one split. There have been more than one concerted attempts to tear up Tuskegee, and at this moment there is a movement to disrupt Howard university.[6] We do not know the value of compromise. If it it cannot be as I wish it, it shall not be at all., seems to be our idea of things. THIS IN SPITE OF THE FACT THAT WE DO NOT SUPPORT HOWARD. WE HAVE NEVER SUPPORTED TUSKEGEE AND NEVER WILL. I admit gladly that there are exceptions to this general rule, but the 'let us preserve the union at all costs' are rare. This does not mean that I am ashamed of my color nor that I despise my people. But we must learn to be honest with ourselves, and know our shortcomings. We will [learn—x-ed out] acquire cohesion but we will pay dearly for being a slow pupil.

I have taken out a library card and tomorrow I am going down to get your book. I am interested to see how a person non-religious will handle the subject. I have been avioding mention of religion because I cant get off that smugness and I dont know what else, or how else to do. So I am going to your "Poor Priest"[7] for help.

Let me say again how I appreciate your efforts to help me. I am making a valiant struggle to raise $250. I feel that I will get it. I am not ashamed of receiving help, but already there were gloatings because my record did not justify a scholarship. Hope was expressed that I could not get the money otherwise. That is why I did not want the help. It is a challenge to me and I am hustling. Too much good fortune excites envy.

With deepest veneration and gratitude, I beg to remain

Your humble and obedient servant,

Zora

---

[6]*Hurston also wrote of this in her essay "The Hue and Cry About Howard University." The disruption had to do, primarily, with anger over perceived insensitivity on the part of (white) President Stanley Durkee's requirement that students sing black spirituals in chapel. Students organized a strike in protest that began on May 7, 1925, and ended on May 14. Hurston supported Durkee.*

[7]*Meyer's Robert Annys, Poor Priest, published in 1901 by Macmillan.*

TO GEORGIA DOUGLAS JOHNSON

1014 Rivington St.
Roselle, N.J.
July 18, 1925.

Dear Mrs. Johnson,

I was mightily pleased to get a letter from you. This is my chance to say to you what a wonderful poet I think you are. No, what a soulful poet I KNOW you are.

I have tried to get in touch with Mr. Wood.[1] I called his number several times, but never caught him. I wrote him too, but we had a little tiff and I suppose he does not wish to write me. I am sending you his address so that you can write him.

Clement Wood, 1 Minetta Place, N.Y.C. His telephone is: Spring 8893, in case you come in town and wish to call him.

Pleaselet me be a friend of yours always. I need you. Tell Mrs Carson I could stand a sample of her handwriting if its all the same to her.

Give her this bit of verse, too. She knows I am not trying to be a poet so she wont think that I think it's poetry.

Lots of love to you. Do write me again.

Yours lovingly,
Zora Neale Hurston

---

[1] *White novelist Clement Wood was the author of* Nigger *(1922), about three generations of an African American family, and* Deep River *(1933), about the marriage between an African American male singer and a white woman. Among his many black friends associated with the Harlem Renaissance were Walter White and Charles Johnson. Wood was the recipient in 1928 of an* Opportunity *award intended, according to Amy Spingarn's request, to benefit black writers.*

TO ANNIE NATHAN MEYER

1014 Rivington St.
Roselle, N.J.
July 18, 1925.

Dear Mrs. Meyer,

My! Robert Annys, Poor Priest is being read![1] It took me almost three weeks to get it. I went down twice and finally put in a reserve slip and got it yesterday. It is a quarter to eleven (A.M.) and I have just read the last line.

The story is powerful and Oh, so true! The failure to reach those things we crave lies in ourselves. There is another reason for the lower class of society besides the greed of the ruling class, and it is the lack of something in the ruled. You know things. Robert Annys must compromise with life like all the rest of us. You have done well, in my humble opinion. You touch human nature from the inside all the way thru.

I particularly like your descriptions of and about the min[i]ster. I dont care for detailed descriptions as a rule and often pass over them all together, but after the first line, I <u>had</u> to read yours. You are colorful. But you have a great deal of background for that. You are a poetic race of people.[2] The Old Testament is my only reason for ever opening the Bible at all. Such powers of story telling! Such magenta speech figures! You cant beat the Psalms for word music, nor the prophets for prose-poetry. Those old boys were up and at 'em. Those first chapters of Genesis are not equalled by even our best writers. And that old heathen, David! Why, he is a hundred best sellers rolled into one! He had a way with him. He could do <u>anything</u> and make it respectable. I love the old devil more than any character in either history or literature With one hand he plays divinely upon the harp, slays his enemies with the other, keeping one eye ont the ladies and the other on his workmen building cities. He went in quite extensively on the son business too, I believe.

Mrs. Meyer, please forget that I mentioned that leak to you. It is nothing. You were perfectly right. There is no way on earth to attach

[1]Meyer's novel; see Hurston to Annie Nathan Meyer, June 23, 1923[5].
[2]Meyer was Jewish.

anything like blame to you. You were trying to help your little pickaninny[3] and ran into a racial trait that you could not have known about. Of course, all of us dont do that, I am sure that Mr. Jones would not. However, if one wishes to be sincere, one cannot deny that it is pretty prevalent among us.

Should I write to Mr. Villard[4] and thank him, or should I do that thru you?. I am most grateful for all that you have done for me. I think Mrs, Annie Pope Malone, head of the Poro college, a very successful hairdressing concern with headquarters in St. Louis Mo. will help me.[5] She has expressed herself as being interested in me. She is probably the wealthiest Negro in America, and interested in education among us.

I hope that my long letter is not too tiresome. But I like to think of myself as talking to you.

Your humble and obedient little 'pick',

Zora

TO ANNIE NATHAN MEYER

624 W. 4th St.
Plainfield, N.J.
Sept. 15, 1925

My dear Mrs. Meyer,

Your little pickaninny was considerably cheered by your letter. By now, I have completely climbed back out of the depths into which I had fallen.

---

[3] Hurston refers to herself this way in a number of letters. See especially those to Charlotte Osgood Mason. Also see Hurston's essay "The 'Pet Negro' System," which she wrote in 1943 and which would seem to argue against such usage, even if Hurston is being ironic here.

[4] Oswald Garrison Villard (1872–1949) was the editor of the New York Evening Post from 1897 to 1918 and the editor of the Nation from 1918 to 1932. The author of numerous books and articles, he campaigned on behalf of blacks, women, and other minorities. His middle name, Garrison, comes from his maternal grandfather, the abolitionist William Lloyd Garrison. Senator Carter Glass of Virginia called Villard "the rankest Negrophile in America."

[5] Annie Pope Malone was the first black female millionaire, a remarkable philanthropist, and the inventor of popular hair-straightening techniques for African American hair. See glossary.

I thought the article not so bad. Mr. Van Vechten thought it rather good. It was he who introduced me to Vanity Fair—or rather to Miss Birtwell, and asked her to try something by me.[1]

Please pardon my sending you the yellow sheets. The story is in first draft. I came upon the germ of this story quite accidently, but I am shaky about using it. You can readily see the dynamite in such a subject.

The other two have been done this summer. After you have read them, I shall re-type them and start them on their travels.[2]

I have not my Barnard Catalogue with me, but I shall be thru out here by the 20th and go in for good. I do not know how much money I shall need at present, but if I have to get more I shall let you know so you can communicate with the Dean.

Seeing my record again after four years, I was not at all dissatisfied with myself. I hope that Dean Gildersleeve will let you see it.[3] Considering the handicaps I studied under at Howard, it is not so bad. I am going after a record at Barnard, tho [sho?]. In addition I am going after a prize in playwriting. I shall not let you be sorry if I have to sit up all night and uproot every ancestral kink on my head. You are a magnificent princess to me. I kiss the earth before you. I am so happy! I am so proud!

> Most humbly and obediently yours,
> Zora.

[Nearly illegible notes are scrawled on the back of this letter in a different handwriting than Hurston's, probably Meyer's.]

---

[1]Hurston's work did not appear in Vanity Fair.

[2]"Muttsy" was published in August 1926 in Opportunity and "Possum or Pig" in September 1926 in Forum. "The Eatonville Anthology" was published in September, October, and November 1926 in Messenger. Hurston may be referring to any of these here as well as a story apparently rejected by Vanity Fair.

[3]On June 9, 1925, Dean Virginia G. Gildersleeve (Barnard College dean 1911–47) wrote to Meyer to say that they had received Hurston's record from Howard and that although it contained a number of high grades it was not what they would normally consider adequate for admission to Barnard. Gildersleeve went on, however, to note that since Hurston was such an interesting candidate—and since Meyer was evidently interested in seeing her admitted—she would be prepared to make an exception. She did not, however, believe that Hurston was qualified for scholarship support.

TO ANNIE NATHAN MEYER

260–W. 139th St–
New York City
Sept. 28, 1925

Dear Mrs. Meyer,

Not thru registration yet, but hope to be O.K. by the time this reaches you. Miss Libby's[1] letter will explain a lot. I have the duplicates now and turned them in to the Registrar's office today. So I think things will move off smoothly. But <u>I never took any records away from the office</u>. I never dreamed of even <u>asking</u> to <u>see them</u>. She probably confused my case with some other. It has made me several days late, anyway. I hated to contradict her—it looked too much like accusing her of either lying or carelessness or both—so I have said very little. I merely telegraphed for duplicate.

I have a letter from Dr. Durkee[2] with his note to sign. I want to live at International House very much. And if any money is left after tuition is paid would you be in favor of it? I wish the contacts to be had by living there. I don't know whether I can make it or not. room rent $5–$9 per week a cheaper scale than Harlem's.[3] I think I have some after school work also.

Your criticisms were just the things I needed on the stories. I am doing them over but cant do much until the worry of registration is over.

I received the MSS. O.K.

Thanking you again for your magnificent work for me, I am—

Yours most humbly & gratefully,

Zora—

[In hand below Hurston's signature are names of people, numbers, and check marks after some names.]

[1]Mary V. Libby, assistant to the dean of admissions at Barnard from 1921 to 1946.

[2]James Stanley Durkee (1866–1951), the president of Howard University while Hurston was a student there. Her essay "The Hue and Cry About Howard University" is partly a defense of Durkee.

[3]In its 1927 report on Harlem rents, the Urban League noted that almost half of black renters in Harlem spent more than twice the amount on rent that white renters were paying for comparable apartments elsewhere. Average monthly rent for a four-room apartment in Harlem was $55.70; the average family yearly income was $1,300.

TO ANNIE NATHAN MEYER

260 W. 139th St.
New York City
Oct. 12, 1925.

Dear Mrs. Meyer,

No, I am certain that the next semester will not be so expensive. You see, if I am to get a degree, there are certain subjects that I must have and so Miss Meyer[1] put them on my program as absolute necessities. I expected to be a full fledged Senior but I have lost some points in the transfer (one always does) and there is a half year's work more for me. I have thought things over pretty thoroughly and concluded that this term is about all that I can do unless some more of the people to whom I have appealed send in something substantial. You see I am in class until 5 oclock three days in the week—so the job is out of the question if I am to prepare my lessons. There is no point in going to class unprepared. All I can do is make the most of this semester and then take a job. I am gaining a more secure footing in New York all of the time and I am sure of places. There are two rather good ones open to me now. The time I spend at Barnard will enhance my reputation considerably and boost my earning power. So it will do some good at that. I would love to graduate of course, but I can keep taking two or three subjects at the time in Extension and offer them towards a degree when I have enough. I can do that in about a year and neither strain myself mentally nor financially. I am going to try to sell something after this week. My routine is beginning to work smoothly now.

I shall be <u>so</u> <u>very</u> <u>happy</u> to have you to lunch with me! Will you return soon? Miss Fannie Hurst[2] has just written to say that she will have me at her home for tea and visit—lunch with me at Barnard. Isnt she kind to me?

I had to spend so much money for necessities—books, gym outfit, shoes, stockings, maps, tennis raquet, I still must get a bathing suit, gloves and if I am here in the Spring, I will need a golf outfit. It is

---

[1] *Anna E. H. Meyer, Barnard '98, Barnard registrar from 1912 to 1942; unrelated to Annie Nathan Meyer.*
[2] *Novelist, friend, and benefactor of Hurston's; see glossary.*

cheaper to "elect" that than riding. I <u>could</u> elect canoeing tho instead, I suppose.

You have been very kind, you are being warm and staunch. I hope that I can deserve you and never let you regret.

Yours humbly and gratefully,

Zora—

TO ANNIE NATHAN MEYER

260 W. 139th St—
N.Y.C.
Oct. 17, 1925

My dear Mrs. Meyer,

Your very kind letter of three days ago came to me.

Yes, I would be glad if you would write to Miss Hurst. I am sure she would help but I felt a little 'delicate' about asking her.

I am still trying to match a job to my schedule. The one I had, I lost because they wanted me by three oclock at least and on three days of the week I could not get there until 5:30. Today I have 11 cents— all that is left of my savings, so you see there is some justification for my doubts as to whether I can remain there. I must somehow pay my room-rent and I must have food.

You see, Mrs. Meyer, I have been my own sole support since I was 13 years old. You will appreciate the tremendous struggle necessary for me to merely live to say nothing of educating myself in a community indifferent to anything except creature comfort. Being "different" has its drawbacks in such an atmosphere. You can see then, that nothing would be done to soften my circumstances. For to them that would be encouraging me in my freakishness. I've taken some tremendous losses and survived terrific shocks. I am not telling you this in search of sympathy. No melodrama. If I am losing my capacity for shock absorbing, if privation is beginning to terrify me, you will appreciate the situation and see that it isnt cowardice but that being pounded so often on the anvil of life I am growing less resilient. physical suffering unnerves me now.

I will be glad to come whenever you say that I may.

Everything is going on very well at school. French is hardest for me, but I am getting that much better every day.

Hoping to see you soon, I am

> Most humbly and obediently yours,
> Zora.

TO ANNIE NATHAN MEYER

27 West 67th St
New York City
November 10, 1925.

My dear Mrs Meyer,

I have been with Miss Hurst one week today. I am very happy with the arrangement and I think that she is satisfied, too. I answer letters for her, the telephone, go errands and anything she wants done.

I am enclosing the letter from Mrs. Malone from whom I had hoped so mch. Mr. Schomburg[1] has not even answered so it does not look so bright.[2] I love it at Barnard, but if it requires a great deal of your time and effort, please dont let me be too selfish. You have done more for me than anyone else on earth. It is a splendid demonstration of pure disinterested service. You, and thru you yours have done for me what none of mine would never consider. If the money is not easily forthcoming, Miss Hurst will keep me and let me learn to be a good secretary, she says.

How is the novel coming on?[3] Miss Hurst has a new one coming out in Jan.[4] I am reading the proof now.

My French is improving. I shall write my next letter to you in that language. Oh, Barnard is the thing. I am getting a great deal out of it. It was a little difficult at first, but by now I [am] getting my sea-legs and expect my grades to climb steadily.

[1] *Arthur A. Schomburg, librarian and bibliophile; see glossary.*
[2] *Hurston hoped one of them would help support her at Barnard.*
[3] *It is not clear which of Meyer's novels Hurston refers to here. Her play* The New Way *was performed on radio the next year.*
[4] *Hurst's novel* Mannequin *appeared in 1926.*

Will you come to see me here, please? If so, when? I should love nothing better.

I have made a number of friendships now. Two that I particularly enjoy. One is Miss Florence Friedman of Jersey City, and the other Miss Claire Barkman of Morristown N.J. Oh yes, a Miss Sorrell of this city who is coming to see me on Friday. I have been out to Morristown to see Claire, and Florence has been here to see me. Claire is coming here on Sat. And next Wed. she is having me to tea in Brooks Hall.

The Negro Art Theatre of Harlem is fairly launched now and the first program will include my "Color Struck" I am hoping that you will find time to come.[5] It will be near the end of the year, the presentation. Do come and like a good Zora rooter Yell "Author, author".!!

All, everything I owe to you. I strive so much harder now for those things that I want. You see, being at Barnard and measuring arms with others known to be strong increases my self love and stiffens my spine. They dont laugh in French when I recite, and one of those laughers ha[s] asked to quizz with me. I knew getting mad would not help any, I had to get my lessons so well that their laughter would seem silly.

Have you given up the idea of coming to lunch with me at Barnard? I hope not.

This telephone number is Trafalger: 4157.

Hoping to see you soon, I am

> Your most humble and obedient servant,
> [unsigned]

[5]Color Struck *had won a second prize in that year's* Opportunity *contest. The Negro Art Theater did not launch its first full production until 1929 when it produced* Wade in the Water, *with the participation of Adam Clayton Powell, Jr., and Laura Bowman.*

TO ANNIE NATHAN MEYER

108 West 131st St
New York City.
Dec 6, 1925.

My dear Mrs. Meyer,

The enclosed letter will explain itself. I am already installed in my new Harlem room, and think that I have a place to earn my expenses. I think I also know someone from whomI can get some money on my next semester's tuition. On the whole, I am not distressed.

Hoping that you are fully recovered by this time I beg to remain

Your humble and obedient servant,
Zora.

TO CARL VAN VECHTEN

108 W. 131st St
New York City
Dec. 6 [1925–library dated]

Dear Mr. VanVechten,

Here are the poems I spoke of to you. Miss Barkman is a very delightfulm person in addition to her capabilities.[1] What you can do for her if you will, and if you think she merits it, is to tell her to go ahead. She is that shy and retiring. Her people have an estate near Morristown, she is not pressed for money—she just writes because she says she has to. I do hope you will like her work.

---

[1] Presumably Claire Barkman, mentioned as a new friend in Hurston's November 10, 1925, letter to Meyer.

Has Nora [Holt][2] told you the good news? We have something up our sleeves.[3]

Most cordially yours,
Zora

TO ANNIE NATHAN MEYER

108 West 131st Street
December 13, 1925.

My dear Mrs. Meyer,

I shall be very happy to get the dinners for Mrs. Levy.[1] On the days suggested, I am practically free half a day. I only wish it were three days instead of two. I shall call her and make the engagement for Tuesday afternoon. Again I am indebted to you.

Oh, Mrs. Meyer, the girls at Barnard are perfectly wonderful to me. They literally drag me to the teas on Wednesdays and then behave as if I am the guest of honor—so eager are they to assure me that I am desired there. At the Senior tea on Friday to Freshmen and transfers, the President of Student Govt. asked me why I did not live in Brooks Hall,[2] and wouldnt I come in for the Next semester. They have urged me to come to the Junior prom at the Ritz-Carlton in Feb. and several girls have offered to exchange dances with me if I will bring a man as light as myself. Their frankness on that score is amusing, but not offensive in that dancing is such an intimate thing that it is not unreasonable for a girl to say who she wishes to do it with.[3]

I do not yet know how many credits I shall be given by Barnard, but I shall be pretty well off Miss Meyer assures me, which I take it, means that I shall be a Senior. They have held back on giving me a count until they could see what kind of a student I would make. I shall

[2]Nora Holt was a flamboyant music critic and well-known Harlem Renaissance performer; see glossary.
[3]In the thirties, they talked of making a trip to Asia together, which had been considered for some time.

[1]A part-time employer and friend of Meyer's.
[2]Barnard dormitory.
[3]Discouraged from going to this dance, on the grounds that it would be racially inappropriate to do so, Hurston would later feign relief to Meyer at not having had to spend the money for a dress.

know at the end of this semester. Oh, how I hope for the best! She told me that all of my instructors had given me a good report for the mid-term, so that'[s] that.

Have you begun your new novel yet? I hope so. Also I wish you a speedy recovery. Miss Hurst is going to take two articles and a story to the Editors for me this week. She says she will always do that for me. She suggested certain changes which I have made with reservations. I do not wish to become Hurstized. There would be no point in my being an imitation Fannie Hurst, however faithful the copy while the world has the real article at hand. I am very eager to make my bow to the market, and she says she will do all she can for me with her Editors. Victory, O Lord!

In one of the articles, I am mentioning you.

I have spared you the French letter, but do not begin to gloat over your escape, I am merely waiting for a little more technique.

Thanking you again for your your marvellous care of me, I am

Your humble and obedient servant,

Zora

ANNIE NATHAN MEYER

108 West 131st Street
New York City
Dec. 17. [1925]

My dear Mrs. Meyer,

I have done my first afternoon's work wity [sic] Mrs. Levy. She is very, very nice I think. Now I must look around and find another place for the rest of the week.

No doubt you are right about the Prom. But even if things were different, I could not go. Paying 12.50 plus a new frock and shoes and a wrap and all the other things necessary is not my idea of a good time. I am not that 'Ritzy' yet. If I can simply continue to exist until June, I shall award myself the Croix de Guerre with palms. I was pleased, however that the girls tried to make me feel good about it. Of course I dont want to make any false steps and I am most fortunate in having you to halt me before I sprout donkey ears.

I shall send you a copy of the article[1] as soon as Miss Hurst hands it back. If she doesnt care for it at all, I'll not send it. It will not be an article then, but just so much paper and time wasted.

Hoping that you will soon be able to start on your new novel, I am

Cordially yours,

Zora

TO ANNIE NATHAN MEYER

[1925]

I have rec'd the [illegible] I got the scholarship!!![1] — — — — —
Many Thanks, I shall choose Wed. Night the 10th. Mr. Light[2] called me about your play. Half through the reading and likes it very much.

Zora—

TO ANNIE NATHAN MEYER

[winter 1925/26]
108 W. 131st St—
Saturday

Dear Mrs. Meyer,

I have written [Mrs.—x-ed out] Mr. Shay.[1] I have been scouting around for material. For the greater part, I am trying to pick them up off of Lenox Ave. because one is likely to find a great deal of talent

---

[1]*The only published essay of Hurston's that makes sense in this context is "The Eatonville Anthology." She may refer here, however, to something that was never published.*

---

[1]*According to Robert Hemenway, this scholarship was arranged for by Annie Nathan Meyer. Hurston had also applied for assistance from Annie Pope Malone and Arthur Schomburg.*

[2]*James Light (1894–1964) staged Meyer's* Black Souls *at the Provincetown Playhouse on March 30, 1932. He also directed Eugene O'Neill's* All God's Chillun Got Wings *(1924).*

---

[1]*Frank Shay (d. 1947) was a theater manager in New York.*

that will be easily handled—that is, free from great ideas of their own great worth, and from complexes and inhibitions.

Thanks for the money. Thru Miss Weeks[2] the College is granting me 76^{00} to finish out the year. I could not have gone on otherwise. <u>They were eager for me to stay</u>! Isnt that splendid? Miss Weeks is a jewel, is she not? And the Dean was <u>splendid.</u> They would rather let me have it than have me either drop out, or endanger my record by too much work. One <u>really needs</u> ones time at Barnard.

Oh, I hope Mr. Shay can <u>see</u> me. I want to be the principal's wife so badly.

Most Cordially yours,
Zora

[on back of letter:] Went down to Hotel McAlpin to Glee Club luncheon and everything went off well. The other members insisted on my being there.[3]

TO CONSTANCE SHEEN

[at top, Hurston's hand: "This is the Fannie Monogram also."]

Barnard College
116th Street and Broadway
New York City
Jan. 5th [1926]

My dear Constance,

I have just returned from my vacation — we got out on the 18th and returned to class on the 4th—and found your card waiting for me. I assure you, it was mighty welcome.

Do you remember how we used to talk of Fannie Hurst? Well I am secretary to her now. Of course she could get a better one, but she just likes me and so I sit up and peck her letters out on the machine. All this, of course after school hours.

[2]Mabel F. Weeks was assistant to the dean of social affairs at Barnard from 1922 to 1939.
[3]In other words, they did not try to exclude her because of race.

I suppose you want to know how this little piece of darkish meat feels at Barnard. I am received quite well. In fact I am received so well that if someone would come along and try to turn me white I'd be quite peevish at them.

Here is a [letter—x-ed out] match container of Miss Hurst's. I took out the remaining matches for fear of fire in the mails. It was used on the evening of Dec. 19th by Fannie Hurst, Stefanson(the explorer)[1] Chas. Morris, and myself. Irvin S. Cobb[2] was there but he used another pack. with Jesse L. Lasky[3] and Margaret Anglin.[4] You can get one of your brothers to put in another pack of matches. I just thought you might like a souvenir of F.H. since you admire her so much. Her new novel APPASSIONATA will be out Jan. 23rd.

I am glad that you remembered me. Write me a line sometimes when you have some moments to kill.

Sincerely and cordially,
Zora Neale Hurston.

TO CARL VAN VECHTEN

[January 5, 1926—library dated]
108 West 131st Street
New York City

My dear Mr. Van Vechten,

I have found something this time which I am sure will stir you up immensely. I HAVE COME YPON THE MOST MARVELLOUS SET OF SPIRITUALS SINGERS YET! I can get three of them to come down to your place with their tambourines, guitars etc. whenever you say. Please hear them sing just one song and you will experience a rev-

---

[1]Hurst's lover, Vilhjalmur "Stef" Stefansson, Arctic explorer, Eskimo ethnographer, and author of My Life with the Eskimo and The Friendly Arctic.

[2]Local-color writer Cobb's portrayals of the South were popular and influential. The author of over five dozen books, Cobb (1876–1944) sometimes published up to half a dozen titles a year.

[3]Jesse Lasky (1880–1958) was one of Hollywood's founding fathers, the cofounder of Paramount Pictures, and an independent producer.

[4]Actress Margaret Mary Anglin (1876–1958) went from melodrama to comedy to success as a theater manager.

elation. I, Zora, vouch for it. This will be the church I spoke of brought to you. I beseech, I beg you to do this for your own pleasure. You will hear a spiritual done SPIRITUALLY!

Thanks for the very kind criticism in the Herald-Tribune.[1] Miss Hurst has three things of mine that she is showing to Ray Long.[2] Hope they take.

Much success to you and yours.

Cordially,
Zora

TO ANNIE NATHAN MEYER

[January 1926—library dated]
Saturday Morning.

My dear Mrs. Meyer,

Your rebuke is just. I have been guilty of gross forgetfulness. It is a state of mind of which I am trying to rid my self., but I dislike routine and it is hard for me to remember all of it. This is no excuse, for I am part of a machine and should play my part intelligently. I had made out my program and carried it in to the office, but held up thing trying to get that course in the drama under Miss Latham that I am very keen about.[1] She is even as I does not keep her office hours regularly— very erratic, but I did not know until I got my bill that I had overstayed the time. I did not get the course either, for it is a closed one. About the History exam, I did not show up the next day for it. I copied the exam schedule and somehow confused the hour. It was at nine. I thought it was at 1:10. I was there in the building at a quarter to nine, going over my notes etc. Sort of gloating in my preparedness, and eager for the race. Imagine my consternation when I went up at 1:10 and saw a strange class! I felt wretched about it. But I have paid my fee,

---

[1]*Possibly "Negro Work Songs" and "Street Cries and Spirituals," appearing in the December 20, 1925, edition.*
[2]*Ray Long (1878–1935), president of the International Magazine Company, which included* Cosmopolitan, Good Housekeeping, *and* Harper's Bazaar, *and editor of* Cosmopolitan *from 1918 to 1931.*

---

[1]*Minor W. Latham was a Barnard instructor in English, teaching drama and speech courses, during the 1925–26 academic year.*

and registered for the exam in good time. I am very much ashamed of myself. Very frankly, I hope you would not know of. I must be cured of my dreaming somwhow. I have written to someone for the $16.00 to make up the deficiency.

I shall try to lay my dreaming aside. Try hard. But, Oh, if you knwe my dreams! my vaulting ambition! How I constantly live in fancy in seven league boots, taking mighty strides across the world, but conscious all the time of being a mouse on a treadmill. Madness ensues. I am beside myself with chagrin half of the time, the way to the blue hills is not on tortoise back, it seems to me, but on wings. I havent the wings, and must ride the tortoise. The eagerness, the burning within, I wonder the actual sparks do not fly so that they be seen by all men. Prometheus on his rock with his liver being continually consumed as fast as he grows another, is nothing to my dreams. I dream such wonderfully complete ones, so radiant in astral beauty. I have not the power yet to make them come true. they always die. But even as they fade, I have others.

All this is [not—x-ed out] a reason, not an excuse. There is no excuse for a person who lives on Earth, trying to board in Heaven.

Most cordially yours,
Zora Neale Hurston

Thanks again for the ticket and other favors. Mr. Light was very glad that I wrote him about the play. He likes it very much so far and I am to have a talk with him about it tonight.

TO ANNIE NATHAN MEYER

108 West 131st Street
Jan. 15th [1926]

Dear Mrs. Meyer,

Things are going better with me, but I was right. The next day (Tuesday) I went in with blood in my eyes. Talk about your "Twelve Pound Look" (Barrie)![1] Mine would have weighed a ton. And it

[1]The Twelve-Pound Look, *a play in one act by James Matthew Barrie (author of* Peter Pan).

worked! I have been carried to Brooks Hall to visit and made much of
to see what I had to say. I SAID THE EXAM SURPRISED ME. We
talked on. I mentioned that I had called on you the evening before and
had enjoyed myself immensely. Everybody knows that you are a
trustee. My hot look warmed the whole class up. They are all cordial.
Mr. Collins[2] told me today in the presence of Miss Barkman that I
could take the exam on the day set for it, if I wished, but I had a grade
of C already. WHY? Why must I be offered that privilege? I have not
said a word to Mr. Collins.

Clever is not a good word for Black Souls.[3] It is immensely moving.
It is accurate, it is very, very brave without bathos. There are some
mighty fine literary passages too. Once or twice I noted a trite figure.
There is some excellent philosophy. You have not forgotten the truths
of life, however. To be brave costs something. We must all make our
compromises with life. Andrew is the real hero to me. It is so much
easier to die out of ones troubles than it is to live with them. It is
much less painful to die for a principle than to live for it; to have ones
manhood chipped away by the chisel of circumstances. Ah it is a brave
man indeed who can sentence himself to cowardice for life out of love!
To suffer with a strong heart the ignominy of submission for those
who are preopering [sic] by it, but scorning the sufferer no less.

Mrs. Robeson[4] should praise BLACK SOULS. She could hardly do
otherwise.

To close, I feel better. But if I had not made a show of resistance,
my name would have been mud. I assure you Mr. Collins was thoroly
frightened. But I have been trying and shall try harder to be a Negro
Extra. I know I must in all things. Florence Friedman and I discuss
it often.

I shall make you a cake at my own home on Sunday—three layers
this time.

Yours cordially,
Zora

[2]Robert F. Collins, assistant in geology.

[3]Meyer's play about a black poet who is involved with a white senator's daughter in Paris and who is eventually lynched. Produced in 1932 at the Provincetown Playhouse. The New York Times reviewer described the writing as "clumsy" and the characterizations as "inept."

[4]Eslanda Robeson; see glossary.

TO ANNIE NATHAN MEYER

108 West 131st Street
January 31, 1926.

My dear Mrs. Meyer,

At last I am through with my exams and I am consequently feeling much improved. I do not know my grades yet, but I found the exams less of a monster than I believed.

In this same mail I am writing Mr. Light. Anything that I can do to bring BLACK SOULS before a large group will be a pleasure to me.

I completely submerged before and during exams for I felt that I needed the time for my subjects. Because of unsettled living conditions, I had had already too much distraction, so that to be sure that I overlooked no chances, I abruptly went out of circulation, if you know what I mean.

I wanted to make you a cake last Sunday, but my landlady said that she needed the kitchen so I put it off until this week. But today, I got a chance to wait a dinner and make three dollars and I took it. I shall make it <u>very</u> soon, but since I am afraid that something might come up, I wont give the day.

I wrote the letter promptly to the committee and I have been in for the personal interview with Prof. Langford[1] also. She told me to take my bill and go on into the bursar's office with what money I had, explaining there that I was applying for scholarship. She didnt guarantee anything, but I feel quite hopeful after the interview. I forgot to add, in telling you about my bill, that there is always $5.00 for Phys. Ed. And $6.00 for registration fee.

I am eager to talk to you about a number of things.

I hope this bad weather is not treating you badly. It is trying even to a well person

Oh, yes, I had read the Barrie play "THE TWELVE POUND LOOK" but I could not resist the play on words.

If the weather permits, I hope to see you at Barnard soon.

As ever yours,
Zora

---

[1]*Grace Langford, assistant professor of physics.*

TO CONSTANCE SHEEN

February 2, 1926.

My dear Connie,

I wonder if I have hurt you by sending you those little things! I hope not, for nothing was further from my thoughts. You see, I like to have those little intimates of the people well known, and knowing that you are a Hurst fan, I thought you would feel the same way. Your letter seemed a little,—well, as if I had done something not quite pretty.

I wont try to pretend that I am not thrilled at the chance to see and do what I am. I love it! I just wish that you could be here, Connie. To actually talk and eat with some of the big names that you have admired at a distance, if no more than to see what sort of a person they are. I wish that I could say to you 'jump on the next train'. We would dive into all those places on the East Side etc. You know how interested I am in the theatre, and I am just running wild in every direction, trying to see everything at once. But you must try to come. I dont say I would make you happy, but I certainly would see that you got excitement.

And lastly, Connie, please dont think me braggish. If I seem that way, its because new experiences have me flustered. Frankly I cant appear blase' when I am pleased. I know it wont last always, so I am playing with my toy while I may. Besides, there are drawbacks and I am not happy at all <u>often</u>. I am just an ordinary person who is lucky sometimes. A kind letter from you gives me just as much or more pleasure as one from <u>any</u> celebrity. They are OFTEN insincere. Their show of friendship mere patronage.

Perhaps I should have written long ago, but you see, I had no way of knowing that I had a friend in Chicago who was thinking of me. I wish that I had. There have been times in the past year when it would have helped a lot. I hope that you will believe me when I say I really wanted your friendship, Connie, for it is true. I have remembered often with a twisted smile how you used to go to the library without saying a word and get the books I showed interest in. You impressed me as having something very, very warm and stuanch about you that you kept under cover. Yes, I wanted you to keep on liking me. I still do.. The fact that you have been strong enough to write me after so long a lapse puts you infinitely above my little friendship that feared to show itself.

I hope that you find it possible to snatch another minute or two from your business and write me another letter. Tell Prudence[1] she is A.W.O.L on my mail.

> Yours, yours, yours,
> Zora
> Barnard College
> 116th St. and Broadway.
> New York City.

I shall ask Miss Hurst, in some moment of relaxation, to write you herself and send you her autograph. She is working on a new novel now, and is consequently digging in quite furiously. But she will write you, watch and see.

TO ANNIE NATHAN MEYER

[January—x-ed out]
February 22nd [1926?]

Dear Mrs. Meyer,

I am wondering how you are getting on during this most temperamental weather.

Just finished the History exam. and feel quite all right about it. My mind is a little tired, however, from my many activities. Mr. Charles Boni[1] just called me up and said that he would be interested in a collection of folk tales by me. I want to start on it, but I have so little time what with making a living and everything.

I suppose Mr. Light has communicated with you about the play by this time.[2] I have had only a brief conversation with him, and he

---

[1] *Prudence Sheen, sister of Constance and Herbert Sheen.*

[1] *Of Boni & Liveright publishers, one of the best-known and most active publishers of Harlem Renaissance authors.*

[2] *This could refer to either the project on which Hurston and Meyer had considered collaborating or a work of Hurston's, most likely* Color Struck, *published in* Fire!! *in November 1926. Meyer's play* Black Souls *was produced in Provincetown in 1932.*

thought well of it. I think that the negroes of Harlem should raise the money for its production if it is not taken by any of the big producers.

Dr. Durkee sent the money, but I have been forced to use some of it for rent. I have the promise of $18.00 from my brother to make up the deficiency.

I am a mere hunk of mud today, and so this letter is words, just words. The turnip has no blood.

Cordially yours,
Zora

TO ANNIE NATHAN MEYER

[spring 1926?]
108 West 131 St
Thursday Night.

My dear Mrs. Meyer,

I thought that I would have been with you before this to talk about the play.[1] Mr. Holstein[2] told me at first that he was very eager to come, and that he would get in touch with you at once. I thought that he had gone, but Monday I saw him on the street and asked him how he enjoyed his visit, and he said something about business, etc., and was generally evasive. I cant explain it since he gave me none. I think he has been tampered with. You see, I have talked to every one of the literary people about the play, and he probably told some of them he was going to see you, and they got up a scare crow to keep him away and try to interest him in some plan of theirs.

I am being trained for Anthropometry[3] and Dr. Herskovitch [sic][4] is calling me at irregular intervals to do measuring.[5] Each day, I plan

---

[1]See n. 2, p. 81.

[2]*Caspar Holstein, Harlem numbers king and philanthropist who underwrote the* Opportunity *awards.*

[3]*Human body measurements used in anthropological classification and comparison; used especially by Herskovits and Boas to dispute racist phrenology and ideas of racial inferiority.*

[4]*Dr. Melville Herskovits, anthropologist; see glossary.*

[5]*According to Robert Hemenway, Hurston would "take a pair of calipers and stand on a Harlem street corner measuring people's skulls—an act that many contemporaries felt only Zora Hurston, with her relaxed insouciance, could have gotten away with."*

to come to you, and each day he works me all day in two or three hour spurts. But I have a Job for the Summer and that makes me happy. Dr. Boas[6] says if I make good, there are more jobs in store for me. Elsie Clews Parsons[7] is interested in me too, he says and so I must learn as quickly as possible, and be quite accurate. Friday is my last day of coaching, and from then on, I am on my own with a glorious career before me, if I make good.

Would you like to come to Harlem and visit me before you go away? I should love nothing better. Of course, I am coming down tomorrow as soon as Dr. H. [Herskovits] lets me free from coaching and shall help on Sunday too, if you need me.

Oh, I am so tired tonight! Dr. [Herskovits] is putting me thru under pressure, as Boas is eager to have me start.

Goodnight, Most sincerely yours,

Zora

[on left side:] I should love to take you to a Sanctified Church—that is, all of the members are Saints—they admit it. The service is <u>most</u> primitive. Sunday Evening is a good time.

TO COUNTEE CULLEN

Barnard College
In the city of New York
March 11. [1926]

My dear Countee,

I know that I am a reprobate, I'm cross eyed, and my feet aint mates. All of this I acknowledge before you say it, so save your breath and temper. Now!

---

[6]*Dr. Franz Boas, Columbia anthropologist and Hurston's teacher; see glossary.*

[7]*(1874–1941), folklorist, anthropologist, sociologist, feminist, and social activist. Worked with Boas on research on southwestern U.S. Indians, helped to found the New School for Social Research, the* New Republic *magazine, and the American Folklore Society. Author of numerous books on the family, Mexico, and Pueblo Indians and collector of folklore from the Carolina coastal islands.*

I received your letter of encouragement and it helped a lot, I can tell you. I do not intend to talk about "Color" because you commended "John Redding"[1] But it is a wonderful volume of poems. I just sit and wonder as I read poem after poem and wonder how you can keep it up so long. I can understand one hitting off a few like that, butI cannot see where it all comes from!

By the way, [Langston] Hughes ought to stop publishing all those secular folk-songs as his poetry. Now when he got off the "Weary Blues["][2] (most of it a song I and most southerners have known all our lives) I said nothing for I knew I'd never be forgiven by certain people for crying down what the 'white folks had exalted', but when he gets off another 'Me and mah honey got two mo' days tuh do de buck' I dont see how I can refrain from speaking. I am at least going to speak to [Carl] VanVechten.

Dreary days for me. The regular grind at Barnard is beginning to drive me lopsided. Dont be surprised to hear that I have suddenly takent to the woods. I hate routine.

You must tell me something about historic old Cambridge,[3] and all that it has done to and for you. I hope I shall see something of you during the Easter Holidays.

We are playing with the idea of a Little theatre now. I shall be doing the thing reall by June, I hope.

The warmest greetings to you old pal, and a reluctant good-bye. All the success in the world.

Cordially, I am

Zora

are you in any of the contests?[4]

[1]Color, Countee Cullen's first book of poetry, was published in 1925. "John Redding Goes to Sea" was Hurston's first publication. It appeared in the Howard University literary society journal Stylus in May 1921 and was reprinted in Opportunity in January 1926.

[2]Langston Hughes's first volume of poetry, The Weary Blues, was published by Knopf in 1926.

[3]Cullen attended graduate school at Harvard.

[4]Among the literary contests of the Harlem Renaissance were those sponsored by such periodicals as the Urban League's Opportunity.

TO FANNIE HURST

Barnard College
March 16th [1926]
108 W. 131ˢᵗ St.

My dear Fannie Hurst,

I am conscious of he fact that I have sinned most grievously in not coming down for that minute on Washington's Birthday, but the truth is, I got a csll to go wait a dinner shortly after, and $3.50 is not a sneezing matter. I know you did not mind so much my not coming as my not having let you know of my changed plans. But you must allow for my mental mixups. This year has been a great trial of endurance for me. I dont mind saying that more than once I have almost said that I couldnt endure. I shall hold on, but every time I see a cat slinking in an alley—fearing to walk upright lest again she is crushed back into her slink—I shall go to her and acknowledge the sisterhood in spite of the skin.

I made quite a satisfactory record for last term. And partly because you took me under your shelter, I have had no trouble in making friends. Your friendship was a tremendous help to me at a critical time. It made both faculty and students <u>see</u> me when I needed seeing. I wish some of these Spring days that you could come up to the school to Anthropology 110. It is all about thr religions of primitive peoples and is as full of things a writer could use as a dog is of fleas. Maybe you would eat lunch with me. But with all that you do in the course of the day, I almost know that it is out of the question.[1]

I have not been to see Mr. Wells because I have lost faith in myself for the present. Perhaps it will return. I dont know.

Cordially yours,
Zora Hurston

---

[1] *At top of letter, someone, probably Hurst to her secretary, has noted the following: "Dear Zora, I can lunch with you Thursday 25ᵗʰ or Friday 26ᵗʰ—sign & mail."*

TO FANNIE HURST

[March 1926]
108 W. 131st St
Sunday Night.

Dear Miss Hurst,

I shall be so proud and happy to have you come on Thursday to lunch at Barnard. I have my last class on that day from 11–12 M. and will consequently be free for the rest of the day.

That class is Greek Civilization—a most interesting course under Miss Putnam—of the well-known publishing firm and we are now studying <u>Plato's Republic</u>. If you wish, I will come to the subway to meet you or wait for you at the entrance to Student Hall (Jacob Schiff) where you spoke last time. If you can only spare the lunch hour, I shall be there at 12 oclock.

Oh, I am so very happy!

Sincerely,
Zora

[At bottom left corner, Hurston has drawn a smiley-face and the word "Captured!"]

TO W. E. B. DU BOIS

[stamped July 3, 1926]
43 West 66th Street
Friday

Dear Dr. DuBois,

I have been going through all the hells of moving into a flat. I am now in my flat and flattened out by honest but grimy toil. Will turn my attention to the revising of the play at once.[1] Could you, or would you bring it past my place soon? In that way, I shall get a visit out of you without your suspecting it.

Do you think Krigwa[2] would be interested in a play with music? I have been absent by necessity, but I am working for the project just the same.

Cordially yours,
Zora Hurston

TO MELVILLE HERSKOVITS

43 West 66th Street
New York City
July 20th [1926—library dated]

My dear Dr. Herskovits,

I am getting on but not so fast as at first. so many of the wives and children are going away that I am unable to finish the families at once. I am getting the fathers though. Dr. Boas told me to search a little harder for families of more than on child and to be very discriminating as to economic rating, since you and King[1] had gotten the others. So I am trying to be very selective.

A number of people remember you and send regards. George

---

[1] In March 1926, Hurston had sent Du Bois a play entitled The Lilac Bush with which Du Bois was not impressed. He advised her not to produce it. The play to which Hurston refers here, then, is obviously something submitted since that time. In June, regarding this newer play, Du Bois wrote enthusiastically, calling the work "beautiful" and requesting revisions so that her black biblical characters not view blackness as a curse. This suggests that Color Struck, published in Fire!! in 1926, might be the play she is speaking of here. Other possibilities include The First One: A Play, which was published in Ebony and Topaz in 1927, and a play version of her unpublished short story "The Bone of Contention."

[2] The "little Negro theatre" organized by Du Bois in 1926 and originally called the Crigwa Players (Crisis Guild of Writers and Artists). Crigwa was responsible for a number of productions, some taking place in the basement of the New York Public Library's Harlem branch (later the Schomburg Center for Research in Black Culture) at 135th Street, and for influencing black theater productions in other cities throughout the country.

[1] Hurston often called Franz Boas the "king of kings."

Schuyler[2] is back in town and eager to talk to you. I am sending copies of the papers carrying your article[3] under separate cover.

Family number: Z57
Ind.   " 　 Z149
Hoping that you are having a great vacation, I am

Sincerely yours,
Zora Neale Hurston

TO CARL VAN VECHTEN

[postcard postmarked 1926]
[Postcard front: "BIGGEST SENSATION SINCE THE
ARMISTICE. C. Wm. Morganstern PRESENTS Mae West
in 'SEX': A Comedy Drama of Life By Jane Mast,
Staged by Edward Elsner.
Dalys 63rd St. Theatre New York Now"]

Dear Carl—

You must come and see Mae West.[1] She does the most perfect Harlem bit of any person on the White stage

Zora Neale Hurston

---

[2] *African American journalist, satirist, and novelist; see glossary.*
[3] *In 1926, Herskovits published both "Age Changes in Pigmentation of American Negroes" in the* American Journal of Physical Anthropology *and "The Cattle Complex in East Africa" in* American Anthropologist.

---

[1] *Mae West wrote* Sex *under the pseudonym Jane Mast. West performed the work until the show was raided by police, and she was sent to prison for six days on obscenity charges.*

TO LANGSTON HUGHES

[December 1926]

> *[front: burning log with leaves and holly;*
> *printed inside: "With ardor and fire I wish*
> *you a Merry Oolde Christmas and a Happy New Year";*
> *signed Zora Neale Hurston][1]*
> *Thank you, thank you dear Langston.*
> *You warmed me tremendously in my dark hour.*
> *I shall never forget.*

Sincerely,
Zora

TO FANNIE HURST

[December 1926]
    To Fannie Hurst because she's worth a billion of <u>anything</u> you choose to count————(I wouldnt count nothing but diamonds and emeralds.)

Zora Neale Hurston

---

[1] *Hurston's standard (hand-painted?) Christmas card. A number of copies can be seen in her papers at the University of Florida and at the Beinecke Library. See also Hurston to Marjorie Kinnan Rawlings and Norton Baskin, [December 22, 1948].*

TO LAWRENCE JORDAN

[postmarked Savannah, Ga., February 18, 1927]
[on Barnard stationery]

Forwarding address
1663 Evergreen ave
Jacksonville, Fla.

Dear Larry,

I am answering at once, but you dont deserve such attention for you waited two full weeks before answering my note. Put this eary reply on my part down to female weakness, or something like that. My head tells me I should take at least two weeks more.

Thanks for the spiffy new word. Yes, it has taken its niche in the little red "memory." I'll probably give you a part of the royalty. See if I dont.

Well, you could do several things that would aggravate me more than coming down here. But I cannot imagine an ultra like you forsaking the creature comforts of New York for these shacks that suffice in the sub-tropics. I cannot see you forsaking the classic halls of Universities for the songs and tales of camp and road-chain gangs and what-not. I challenge you—I dare you to try it!

I am looking at cars—you see I think it best—and my brother does too, that I avoid common carriers. So I am trying out cars now. There is a marvelous Oakland Coupe 1927 model fully equipped, been driven 3500 miles. They want $870–$300 down $54.50 per month. There are others cheaper, but gee, I want that one. My brother is trying to divert me—thinks a Ford Coupe would be fine, and I'd be foolish to pay more. I think so too, but dont be surprised if I own that pretty mama by April 1ˢᵗ. Gee, I wish you could be here to see it, you'd love it too. I think you'd think foolishness was sense in this case. My brother plays so safe. He doesnt lose anything, but he doesnt get any fun either—the terrific kick that comes from taking a chance.

I'm not so sure that you are safe—that the things you named as sort of emotional disinfectants are sufficient. But any way, I suppose there's nothing to be done about it. Selah.[1]

---

[1] *A Hebrew term used in the Psalms to indicate a pause, sometimes with the sense of "so sayeth the Lord."*

Well, write me a letter next time and dont wait until you are dressing to go out to a dance to dash me off a line. Deliberately write me on purpose.

Sincerely,
Zora.

TO ANNIE NATHAN MEYER

[added—presumably by Meyer—at top of letter:]
a faultless interesting & excellent letter

Fernandina, Fla.
March 7, 1927.

Dear Friend,

Congratulations! I have been searching far and wide for some late orange blossoms for you but it seems I'm out of luck. I found one tree and was about to borrow a few sprigs when the owner came along and persuaded me I really <u>must</u> desist.

About the French, I dont feel badly since I have three more trys. No one ever passes it on the first trip. I was unfortunate in that my first was at graduation as I told you, I was frightened cold—realizing how much hung on it. Then too, Prof. L.[1] is nervous and consequently he makes others so. Third I didnt know so much French that I could afford to forget a word, but I forgot even simple adverbs and prepositions. I didnt regain my composure for three days after. But I shall be <u>well</u> prepared for the next try. I really dont know a great deal of French, but I shall study it hard. It is trying to do so now, however, when I want to be free to write.

I have written about 30 pages on your novel[2] which I shall send to you as soon as typed. I have struck my stride down here now, and have a good schedule worked out. I hope you will like what I have done on

---

[1] *Louis Auguste Loiseaux, associate professor of French.*
[2] *Intended as an expansion of Meyer's play* Black Souls, *produced in Provincetown in 1932.*

the story. I take the mornings for writing and the afternoons and evenings for anthropology, and get a great deal done for both.

I shall mail you $20 for Dr. Durkee on the 15th of this month, and $25⁰⁰ on the first. But $50⁰⁰ May 1st. I am so eager to repay his great kindness to me. How much do I owe him?

I had a lovely letter from Miss Meyer. She has been precious to me. The students in general fear her, but from the first day, I saw her smileless face was kind—It was a busy frown rather than a harsh one. I shall send her some magnolias when I send yours. They are magnificent down here, in bloom in April.

These woods are drugging. They are too powerful. I cant describe the grandeur of it all. Nature has upended her horn-of-plenty here. I really do think you'd go mad with pleasure if the ignorance and squalor that is "swaddled" all over did not depress you too much.

Going back to the French exit—I think Prof. L. wanted to help me out the worst way. I was not sufficiently prepared and in addition had a brainstorm.[3] I shall write him about books and courses.

So sorry I flunked that exit. It is the first course I have ever flunked. Of course I did not flunk the course, but I did the exam so I feel just the same about it.

The poor whites down here have the harshest and most unlovely faces on earth. The Negroes are disfigured by ignorance, but [it] is a slinking shrinkiness. The white just stares aggressive intolerance. But they are kind to me.

[Barnard seal on stationery appears here upside down.]
Whoops! seal of Barnard upside down.

lovingly,
Zora.

---

[3] *In* Their Eyes Were Watching God, *Hurston uses this word in the same way—to mean period of intense confusion, rather than bright or brilliant idea.*

TO LANGSTON HUGHES

general delivery
Fernandino [sic], Fla
March, 17, 1927.

Dear Pal,

Please send me Wallace's address.[1] I have 110 guarranteed subscribers for "Fire".[2] I shall get more in every town that number is for Jacksonville alone. Or I can have them sent thru you if I find that this letter reached you safely.

My story for the next issue was left in my apartment in N.Y. so I must do it again. (by 18th in your hands)

Say, I am stopping at the most gorgeous colored home in U.S.A. The <u>walls of every room are hand carved in wood for every inch</u>! It is the most wonderful bit of Negro art work in America. I am having it photographed, and he is making me sample blocks for the next issue of Fire.[3]

Getting some gorgeous material down here, verse and prose, <u>magnificent</u>. Shall save some juicy bits for you and me. Wish you could join me after school closes. Well, I believe we can run the other magazines ragged. I shall send the money I owe with my story. There are 9 copies in my apt. in N.Y. but I cannot get at them so I guess I'll have to pay up.[4]

So long old timer. Let me hear at once.

Lovingly, Zora

Oh, left my copy of "Fine Clothes"[5] on the mantle shelf so I am handicapped, but shall buy a copy and finish my review. I have spoken to 3 groups and I have urged them all to buy your books.

---

[1]*Wallace Thurman, Harlem Renaissance writer and personality; see glossary.*

[2]*A literary journal launched by Hurston, Langston Hughes, Wallace Thurman, Richard Bruce Nugent, Gwendolyn Bennett, and Aaron Douglas; see Fire!! in glossary.*

[3]*In "Art and Such," an unpublished essay originally intended for inclusion in* The Florida Negro, *Hurston credited the Fernandina carvings to an ex-slave named Brooks Thompson. "Without ever having known anything about African art, he has achieved something very close to African concepts," she wrote.*

[4]*The Fire!! editors all contributed money to produce the magazine, which had only one issue, most copies of which were destroyed, ironically enough, in a fire.*

[5]Fine Clothes to the Jew, *Hughes's second volume of poetry, published in 1927.*

TO LAWRENCE JORDAN

St. Augustine Fla
3-24-1927

Dear Sir:—

I was weak and run down with spots before my eyes every time I read a letter from New York City, and bearing down pains around the heart. I was so weak I couldnt help from answering letters as soon they arrived, but after taking three bottles of your medicine, I can wait an entire week. Please send me three more bottles and I'll forget how to Write altogether.

Yours truly
Seattle Slappey
Hellshepecker, Fla.

Dear Larry,

Please dont take my flippancy seriously. I just wanted a longer letter—I feel a little lonely cut off from all of my friends—when I cracked you about that dressing for a dance. I take it all back.

You have a tremendously alive sense of humor. I laughed heartily and long.

Flowers are gorgeous now, crackers not troubling me at all—hope they dont begin as I go farther down state. I'll be very glad to be back in New York City, however.

I am finding interesting people and things and love it all.

Class rooms irk me too, this time of year. I take a positive grudge against the faculty.

Shall be in Daytona next,

Yours,
Zora

Somehow, on reading this over, it seems dreadfully stupid and cold. Sorry, I meant it otherwise.

Z.

TO DOROTHY WEST

St. Augustine, Fla
March 24, 1927

Dear D.,

Your letter was precious! I loved it, <u>loved</u> it so. Your enthusiasm is certainly warming to say the least.

Yes, Dorothy, a lot of winters have passed over my heart that have not passed over my head. To put it better——more winters have passed over my soul than over my head. Life has not been kind to me, not always, and so perhaps the heel of life has left its print in my face.

I laughed so about the bowl for you are so juvenile about it. Never you mind, the whole set of 6 only cost a dollar so you see its not worth 1/10 the thought you have given it. I had not missed it anyway.

I am writing on a novel——don't know how it will turn out. I am worked to death.[1]

Guess what? Yes, you are right the first time. I am buying a car——a Nash Coupe,[2] delivery Apr. 1st. I suppose I shall pay for it O.K. if not, I just wont.

I shall marry within the next month too, so you see I am doing several things to please you.[3]

Give Wallace Thurman my congratulations——he deserves it, too. He has great ability.

Here's hoping <u>you</u> run away with the contest[4] this year, and many more.

My love to Helene, hope she writes.[5]

I am eager to see the Eloise B.T. wonder why she wants to see me![6]

---

[1] Jonah's Gourd Vine *was published in 1934.*

[2] *Franz Boas gave references for Hurston on a $200 loan application for her car.*

[3] *Hurston married Herbert Sheen on May 19, 1927. Although there is very little mention of Sheen in the letters leading up to their marriage, she speaks of Sheen much more often than she does her second and third husbands, whom her letters never mention.*

[4] *The* Opportunity *contest was held on July 27, 1927. It was suspended for financial reasons from 1927 to 1934.*

[5] *Helene Johnson (1907–95) was a Harlem Renaissance poet who frequently published in* Opportunity. *She was Dorothy West's cousin.*

[6] *Eloise Bibb Thompson (1878–1928) was a writer and journalist (*Los Angeles Times *and* Tribune*). She won the playwright's award in the 1925* Opportunity *contest.*

I shall be so happy to be back in New York again, but I am lost to Bohemia forever. No more parties—just work and <u>work,</u> well perhaps a little domesticity.

All my love, little one,
Zora Neale Hurston
forwarding address
1663 Evergreen ave
Jacksonville, Fla

Daytona next.

TO CARL VAN VECHTEN

[postcard postmarked March 28, 1927, St. Augustine, Fla.]
[postcard front: huge swimming pool at Alcazar Casino, St. Augustine, with white bathers]

In which I did not take a dip.

Zora

TO FRANZ BOAS

1663 Evergreen Ave
Jacksonville, Fla
March 29, 1927

My dear Dr. Boas,
Arrived in town today to meet Dr. Woodson[1] who is here for Negro History Week, and found your letter.
I am not borrowing any money. I suppose that came out of looking into the matter of buying a used car for $300. They asked me for whom I

---

[1] *Historian Carter G. Woodson, founder of the Association for the Study of Negro Life and History; see glossary.*

worked as a matter of routine, and I told them. I am getting the car because it is terribly hard to get about down here. The places I ought to go are usually far from transportation, and it is discouraging to walk. So I thought that I would get it, since I felt that I could keep up the monthly payments—26.80—even when the work was over. I had no idea that it would cause you any worry at all. In fact, I thought I was doing business with the Martin-Nash Motor Company, I have had no dealings, nor communication with this Investment Securities Corporation at all. But some one is telling me that that is the way cars are sold if not bought for cash.

Enclosed [on side: "under separate cover"] find all of the material that I have transcribed into ink.[2] It is fortunate that it is being collected now, for a great many people say, "I used to know some of that old stuff, but I done forgot it all." You see, the negro is not living his lore to the extent of the Indian. He is not on a reservation, being kept pure. His negroness is being rubbed off by close contact with white culture.

I have a "hand", a powerful piece of conjure for the museum, and I have bargained for two more pieces, from a still more powerful "doctor." By the way, I found in Fernandina, a man [Brooks Thompson] seventy years old, who is a most marvelous wood-carver. Born a slave, unable to read or write. The interior of his house is all carved, every inch! His doors and casements are of such wondrous beauty, that in my opinion the compare favorably with the best that has come out of Africa. He is doing a 2 ft. square piece for you to see.

I am sorry that I have kept you waiting, I have a great deal of material in pencil, and I am transcribing it in odd moments. The reason that it is not typed, is that it is hard for me to lug a machine along country roads in addition to my bag. That was one of the first things, in addition to the fatigue, that made me think of getting the used car. I knew that there was not enough—that I could not get a car furnished me, so I decided to do as Dr. Reichard[3] had done—and buy an old one cheaply. I can sell it again when I am thru.

Respectfully yours,
Zora Neale Hurston

Next towns, 1Armstrong, 2 Palatka. (general delivery)
3Sanford.

---

[2]*This material became* Negro Folk-Tales from the Gulf States, *and some was published in* Mules and Men.
[3]*Gladys Reichard, Columbia University anthropologist.*

Dr. Woodson told me to say to you that if a recording machine can be had for $100 or less that the <u>Association</u>" will pay for it if you can find one.[4] I am wondering if I can operate it. Is it very difficult? I am eager to learn.

TO LAWRENCE JORDAN

[return address on envelope: Gen. Del., Sanford]

Palatka, Fla
May 3, 1927.

Dear Larry,

Your letter has just been forwarded to me, and I am very happy to find that you have not forgotten me altogether. I was beginning to fear.

Of course I have no feeling of injury. You have been lovely. Your letters are the best things in envelopes.

These are excerpts from my note-book.

1. A man arrested for "vacancy" (vagrancy) but when the police found out that he was working, they fined him for carrying concealed cards and attempt to gamble.

2. Hot papa! dont have to warm up

3. Shut dat hash-pen! (mouth)

4. I wouldnt give a poor, consumpted, crippled crab a crutch to cross the river Jordan.

5. your head is full of apes

6. Hot as Tucker when de mule kicked his mammy

7. great grand noble (of lodge)

8. I'll bop you in de mouf so hard till you lay a egg.

9. Damn de water-works in Hellshepecker!

10 Youse a cotton-tail dispute! (lie)

11 De lyingest man dat ever hollered "titty, mama."

12 I'm walkin down de road wid de law in my mouf. (this woman was very angry, determined, and heavily armed)

---

[4]*Securing appropriate equipment was a problem throughout Hurston's career. See, for example, her October 6, 1944, letter to Benjamin Botkin.*

13. I'm so sobbing hearted

14 Looking like de devil's doll baby.

15 You eats mocking bird eggs (tell everything you know)

I am glad you are doing something that pleases you more, but I know it must be dull for you in Kimball. I am getting a certain amount of entertainment out of my work, but sometimes, I yearn to point the nose of my car due North and throw her into high. Believe or not, Larry, I want to see you tremendously.

Florida: gorgeous sunlight, fleas, flowers, frogs ferns, alligators, poincianas, flies, cypress, roses, magnolias, roaches, hyacinths by the mile, fleas, fruit, flies, cool nights, fleas, roaches, bouganvilla, gnats, pines, roaches, china berry trees, fleas, bedbugs and magnolias amid dazzling palms and stretches of waters. Wish you could see it all.

Like my proto-type (according to Larry) I am casting myself upon the ground, rending my garments and throwing ashes around sorter careless. I shall not sin again in that wise. But remember, your letters reach me by devious ways of rural post offices so dont count delays against me.

Do write me soon & let me know your summer plans, if any.

Sincerely,

Zora.

[on back of letter] The little red-kercheif is always in my handbag, but never used for anything but a memory.

TO LANGSTON HUGHES

[spring/summer 1927]

Dear Langston—

Finished work and got my check today. [Carter] Woodson cut me a week.[1] I thought I'd get pay for the month but he only paid me for two weeks. Have only 100^{00}. Rather depressed. I hate that improperly born wretch.

---

[1] *From her $1,400 fellowship.*

Shall we drive, or shall I sell car? shall see you in five days at the outside.

Zora.

TO ANNIE NATHAN MEYER

Gen. Delivery,
Sanford, Fla
May 22, 1927.

My dear Mrs. Meyer,

No, I am <u>not</u> dead nor damned, but both Dr. Boas and Dr. Woodson are rushing me like thunder along. I need at least [an—x-ed out] a whole year to do what I am doing in six months.

About the novel. Since I have been down here, I have a first hand account of a lynching—but by a million to one chance, the victim survived. Left for dead he regained consciousness the following day and crawled 4 miles and hid away in a Negro home until he could escape north.

Why not let us begin our story with the lynching and loop back to the beginning and the Senator's visit? This new structure seems to me to be much better. I shall briefly outline it.[1]

A handsome young Negro and a lovely white girl are out in the grounds of the school, but some distance from the buildings. They are in a friendly, somewhat emotionally bantering conversation. Sounds of shots in the distance, baying of hounds, a burly Negro crashes through the woods, sees them and bolts away desperately. They wonder what has happened. Dogs come on almost at once followed by posse of armed white men. No sign of fugitive and they are furious. He has quarreled with foreman over wages and the white man is dead.

---

[1]*Meyer suggested that Hurston turn her play* Black Souls *into a novel, and, according to Robert Hemenway, she assured Hurston that "if the book were published she would acknowledge Zora's work in a preface and give her half the profits." In spite of two years of effort on the project, Hurston could not make it work. (Robert E. Hemenway, "Zora Neale Hurston and the Harlem Renaissance," unpublished manuscript.) See Hurston to Annie Nathan Meyer, January 15, [1926]. It is not clear if Hurston was ever credited for her work on the play when it was produced in Provincetown in 1932.*

"Here, Nigger you seen a—I'll be damned! Got a <u>white</u> girl out here in the woods." Fugitive passed up for the time being. White girl attempts to explain that it was <u>she</u> who suggested the walk, but is hushed aside. "Uppish Nigger, got to be made an example for other biggity darkies." lynching, recovery next day and escape north. Loop back from lynching to Senator, school, etc and in the end to a meeting in the North "Race Relations Committee on which the Senator serves & to which a young man slightly lame, prematurely gray who carries his head peculiarly to the side comes & is not recognized by the young lady with the Senator.

I am so rushed that I must work it out thoroughly in July. But I have lots of lead pencil work, but so many pages to work over.

Let me know what you think of it as I have worked it out so far.

Lovingly,

Zora.

TO DOROTHY WEST AND HELENE JOHNSON

Gen. Delivery, Sanford, Fla
May 22, 1927

Dear Little Sisters D & H—

Yes, I'm married now, Mrs. Herbert Arnold Sheen, if you please.[1] He is in his last year at the U. of Chicago Med. school, but is going to stay out until we get a good start. We are all quite happy now. But write me still by my maiden name as I dont want my mail balled up.

Darlings, see can you find me a copy of Elmer Gantry.[2] I am submerged down here in this wilderness, where such books are not for sale.

Things going dull down here. Working hard, but the people are impossible—all except my husband. The scenery is gorgeous, though.

I have given up writing things until the expedition[3] is over. Then I shall try again. By the way, I hope you two ran away with the "O"

[1] Hurston and Sheen were married on May 19, 1927.
[2] Sinclair Lewis's novel of 1927 about the success of a corrupt midwestern preacher.
[3] Folklore collecting expedition; supported by Woodson's Association for the Study of Negro Life and History.

[*Opportunity*] contest. I <u>know</u> you did even though I have heard nor seen a thing down here in the swamps.

Tired and full of indigestion so I shall not write at length. My love to all the bunch.

Lovingly your sister, Zora

P.S. Do you girls want my apartment for 3 months? You can keep it cheaper than you can your present quarters besides greater comfort insured. I shall not return until Sept & by that time, I might be able to get a front apartment and let you keep it, having a hubby to look out for me, now.

Any way, let me hear from you at once as I know several people who want it, and I cannot afford to keep it vacant. The man who had it is ill in Chicago, and had to give it up.

Lovingly
Zora.

TO DOROTHY WEST

[postcard postmarked June 14, 1927]
[added at top:]

please give my husband a ring. He is at the apt, and Eatonville, Fla. I am afraid lonesome

Dear "D"—<u>Congratulations</u>! Get 1st next time.

Your letter and the book[1] overtook me. look for a letter & money from Mobile, Ala (c/o gen. Del.) Lots of love to you. Eatonville is lovely and gave me a big hand.

Lovingly,
Zora.

---

[1] *Hurston had previously requested a copy of Sinclair Lewis's 1927 novel,* Elmer Gantry.

TO CARTER WOODSON

[July/August 1927]
To the Association for the Study of Negro Life and History.[1]
Dr. Carter G. Woodson.
1538 Ninth St. N.W.
Washington, D.C.

Dear 'Sir:—

This month has been given to the searching out of beliefs and customs, and many strange things have come to light. I have recorded already 89 beliefs an numerous nuances or adaptations of customs.

I shall report on the two Negro towns in the state within ten days. The report is finished except for a disputed point—about the first mayor of Eatonville[—]as soon as that can be cleared up I shall mail it.

In Ocala I have discovered another unsung Artist—again a house interior—beautifully done with a hickory-nut motif.

Expense Account
May 28–June 30

Stamps	1.00	
(from Sanford) To Orlando (May 29	1.10	
Room	7.00	Cora Walker
Board	9.60	
	18.70	

Winter Park (June 9):	.09
(Mrs. I.W. Williams) Room	5.00
R.R. Camp Entertainment	2.35
Board	8.85
Church	.85
	17.14

[1]Hurston had a $1,400 grant from the association to conduct fieldwork, but she was also designated as an "investigator" for the association and therefore owed reports such as one that followed here, on a Florida streetcar line and one that Hurston sent, in October of 1927, on Fort Moosa, in Florida. Both reports would have been part of the obligation of Hurston's $1,400 fellowship. Both reports can be viewed in their entirety at the Library of Congress.

To Woodbridge (June 17–20)	.19
(Della Lewis) Room and board	4.00
Entertainment	.90
transportation to camps	2.40
	5.30
	+.19

To Eatonville (June 20–30)

	.12
(Mrs. Armetta Jones) Room	9.00
groceries & wood	11.01
To R.R. & turp. Camps	6.90
Watermelon cutting	2.65
Music	3.00
Church	1.25
	33.93
Total—————	75.07

Respectfully submitted
Zora Neale Hurston

The folks in Jacksonville forward my mail so slowly that I would appreciate your mailing the check to me at Maitland, Fla. I shall wait there for it. I thank you.

TO CARL VAN VECHTEN

[from Langston Hughes and Zora Neale Hurston]
[telegram]
[from Fort Valley, Georgia]

August 16, 1927

HERE WITH DOROTHY HARRIS PARENTS[1] BESSIE SMITH
IN MACON COME DOWN JOIN FUN FOR WEEK ALL RETURN
TOGETHER.

LANGSTON AND ZARA [sic]

TO CARL VAN VECHTEN

Cheran, S.C.
Aug. 26, 1927.

Dear Carl,

We rolled into this town tonight tired but happy. One or two
mishaps on our run up from Charleston.

1. The car, known as Sassy Susie had a puncture on a front tire, re-
paired at Columbia, S.C.

2. Somehow all the back of my skirt got torn away, so that my little
panties were panting right out in public. I suppose this accident will
be classed as more tire trouble.

I have about fifteen nice juicy songs to sing and I wish that Nora
Holt Ray was there to assist. So sorry I missed [yo—x-ed out] her.
Hope I see her on her return.

---

[1] *Dorothy Hunt Harris and her husband, artist Jimmy Harris, were at this time supplying* Fire!! *with office space in their Greenwich Village apartment. Five years later, when Hurston was financially strapped, in poor health, and at odds with both Mason and Locke, Jimmy Harris apparently suggested that Hurston visit Dorothy's parents again. See Hurston to Charlotte Osgood Mason, April 16, 1932.*

Langston and I are making a collection of art objects and expect to hold a joint exhibition on our return. Oh by the way, what Langston was bringing you from Cuba is no longer among the living.[1]

My love to the handsome "debutante" broker of East 30th st, and the charming T.R.S.[2] So eager to see you all. Hope Harry Block is in town.[3]

Shall try to be in Richmond Sat. night and see H. Stagg[4] and be home by Monday. Love to Fania.[5]

Yours sincerely,
Zora.

We have been having a Root doctor to conjure T.R.S. Not that we had anything against him but we had to have a victim and since he is free single, and childless we thought he was the best one to use. If he should turn up one day with his limbs all tied up in a knot dont tell that we conjured him.[6]

TO LANGSTON HUGHES

43 W. 66th St., New York City
Sept. 21, 1927.

Dear Bambino,

I went to see Mrs. Mason[1] and I think that we got on famously. God, I hope so! She likes the idea of the opera, but says that we must do it with so much power that it will halt all these spurious efforts on the part of white writers.[2] Of course we both agreed that it would take

---

[1]*Hurston refers to a gift of Chinese whiskey which she and Hughes, presumably, have now drunk.*

[2]*Tom R. Smith, editor at Horace Liveright and friend of Van Vechten's.*

[3]*Block was a senior editor at Knopf.*

[4]*Hunter Stagg, literary editor of the* Richmond Times Dispatch *and editor of the* Reviewer, *a magazine based in Richmond, from 1921 to 1924.*

[5]*Fania Marinoff, Carl Van Vechten's wife; see glossary.*

[6]*On August 15, Hughes had written Van Vechten that they had "decided to get somebody conjured while we're down here."* Remember Me to Harlem: The Letters of Langston Hughes and Carl Van Vechten, 1925–1964, *ed. Emily Bernard (New York: Knopf, 2001), p. 58.*

---

[1]*Charlotte Osgood Mason; see glossary.*

[2]*A folk opera that did not materialize; their later collaboration,* Mule Bone, *was never staged during either's lifetime.*

time as you couldnt find time to work at it now, and we must do it deliberately and with the greatest of care and art. She does not believe that any one but us could do it. At any rate, she would not give her aid in any way to any one else.

I am going to take her to our church. I only wish that you might be here to be with us. It would make it quite nice if [I—x-ed out] you could. But it is this Sunday night, for she must go away on the 28th.

I am enclosing the correspondence on "Washington". This synopsis of "SPUNK", "TUSH HAWG" (tusk hog) or "TURPENTINE" is a working synopsis, not final so that you may suggest as many changes as you like.[3] If Hall Johnson's play does not go on, or if it is a failure, which I seriously believe it will be with the present book, I need FIRE in the opera.[4]

I do hope to see you in New York soo. Oh, by the way, will you please say to the couple that had us to lunch there at Lincoln, that I think Dr. Herskovits will make a splendid lecturer for his boys. He is vivid and colorful and knows his subject.

Hoping that things are well with you I am

Most sincerely yours,
Zora

TO ANNIE NATHAN MEYER

43 W. 66th St
New York City
Oct. 7, 1927.

My dear Mrs. Meyer,

I have been back in town for three weeks now, but I have been— and still am—working on my report for Dr. Boas.

---

[3] Hurston had published a short story entitled "Spunk" in the June 1925 issue of Opportunity. She listed a play also entitled Spunk with the Copyright Office in 1935. She included an essay entitled "Turpentine" in her writings completed for the Federal Writers' Project in the thirties and intended for publication in a volume to have been called The Florida Negro. "Tush Hawg" has not been found.

[4] Johnson was a choral director and composer; see glossary. At the time of this writing, he was concentrating on presentations of black spirituals, and the play to which Hurston refers appears not to have been produced.

The novel is beside me now. The more I see of the South, the more am I convinced that it would strike a terribly false note.[1]

1. There is no opposition to schools of higher learning in the South. The southerner merely refuses to support Negro schools. His argument is that Negroes buy everything else they want why not support their own schools?

2. Negro men can take their women wherever they please, provided, she the woman, has not previously compromised herself with a white man who wants his property.

3. I am absolutely certain that the daughter of a <u>Southern Senator</u> would never follow any Negro man to the woods however handsome he might be, or brilliant. You must go South and touch the upper class whites to appreciate the taboo. A white child of 3 years old would know better than to eat with a Negro. She probably would let down in France, but Alabama, Never!

You have followed the writings of Dr. DuBois[2] too carefully and he is a propagadist with all the distorted mind of his kind. He is doing a great service perhaps for his race, but he must use propaganda methods and those methods never follow actual conditions very accurately.

4. That Negro principal would <u>never</u> have laid his hands upon that white Senator! I would love to think that he would, but I <u>know</u> he wouldn't—no matter what the Senator had done.

As soon as I can get my material all in, I would love to go over it with you page by page. I shall probably be thru by the last of next week. Will you let me see you then?

My trip was most fascinating and I'd love to tell you about that too. I am worn down to 124 pounds but it was well worth it.

Most sincerely yours,

Zora Neale Hurston

Endicott: 2744

---

[1] *Hurston refers to her attempts to turn Meyer's* Black Souls *into a novel.*

[2] *Leading black intellectual W. E. B. Du Bois; see glossary. Hurston often criticized him in her letters and offered favorable depictions of Booker T. Washington, his intellectual rival, in some of her fiction.*

TO ALAIN LOCKE

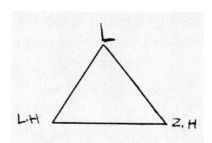

43 W. 66ᵗʰ St.
New York City
Oct. 11, 1927.

Dear Friend,

I have been practising your physiology of French sans cesse and
M. Jean Adam[1] thinks I am getting on fine. I am very grateful.

I suppose that "Fire"[2] has gone to ashes quite, but I still think the
idea is good. We needed better management thats all. Don't <u>you</u> think
there ought to be a purely literary magazine in our group? The way I
look at it, "The Crisis" is the house org. of the N.A.A.C.P and "Opportunity is the same to the Urban League.[3] They are in literature on the
side, as it were. Mr. Johnson is an excellent man and full of zeal but he
has a great deal on his hands.[4] The same is true of Dr. DuBois. Dont
you think too that it is not good that there should be only two outlets
for Negro fire? Your work in Philosophy is less confining than either of
the others, why cant our triangle—Locke—Hughes—Hurston do
something with you at the apex? Besides I am certain that you can
bind groups with more ease than any other man in America. Will you
think it over?

---

[1]*Professor.*
[2]*Literary journal started by Hurston, Hughes, and others; copies were destroyed in a house fire.*
[3]*The two most important journals of the Harlem Renaissance; see* Crisis *and* Opportunity *in glossary.*
[4]*Charles S. Johnson founded* Opportunity *in 1923 and left it in 1928 to join the faculty of Fisk.*

Prof. Adam tells me that he was with you and Maran[5] in N. Africa. I wonder if he could get a chance to teach in the Washington High School? I wanted to suggest it to him, but I thought there might be some bar to a foreigner unnaturalized. Is it feasible? I think he wants to establish himself permanently. Do you think [Remainder of this letter is missing.]

TO LANGSTON HUGHES

43 W. 66 St
New York City
Dec. 9, 1927

Dear Langston,

I am leaving for the South on Wed. 14th on the 3:40 from the Penn Station enroute to Mobile. I shall see Cudjoe Lewis[1] first as he is old and may die before I get to him otherwise. Wish that I could see you for the few minutes I will be in Phila. My car is either K-G or K-9 It is indistinct.

There is a tea at Roberta Bosley's[2] on Sunday afternoon for Rose McClendon.[3] Wish you would come up. Also there is a marvelous exhibit of pictures from Haiti at the Ainslie Galeries [sic] 677 Fifth Ave. Honest they are wonderful, Langston. So many fine Negro subjects. I had just been trying to persuade Richard Reid to stop whining for a while and go South and work some. He says he has no sympathy for them so I desisted and left him to his chase of John Barrymore etc.[4]

---

[5]*René Maran, author of the novel* Batouala, *about life in the French Congo.*

[1]*Cudjo Lewis was an eighty-year-old survivor of the* Chlotilde, *the last ship to bring African slaves to the United States in 1859 and the source for Hurston's article "Cudjo's Own Story of the Last African Slaver," published in the* Journal of Negro History, October 1927.

[2]*Associate of Carl Van Vechten's and, later, active member of the James Weldon Johnson Literary Guild.*

[3]*Actress and activist Rose McClendon (1884–1936) was known for her work in such productions as* Deep River, In Abraham's Bosom, Never No More, *and Annie Nathan Meyer's* Black Souls. *McClendon worked with the Negro Experimental Theater and the Negro People's Theater. The Rose McClendon Players were founded in 1937. She starred in Hughes's* Mulatto *just before her death.*

[4]*Born in Eaton, Georgia, in 1898, Reid received mention from the Harmon Foundation. In "Art and Such," Hurston wrote that "O. Richard Reid of Fernandino . . . at one time created a stir in New York art circles with his portraits of Fannie Hurst, John Barrymore, and H. L. Mencken. Of his recent works we hear nothing."*

You MUST promise to join me as soon as school is out. It will be different this time, Langston. By the way, I am going to send you something out of the first check. I have wanted to so much, but I just couldnt before. I know that you NEEDS. What I mean by it will be different, I will have a better car ALL PAID FOR, and a better salary. Also, you MUST promise to ask ME first when you get strapped.

Hope I see you old dear. I must write to Miss Settles when I get South. So rushed now.

Lovingly,
Zora

TO CHARLOTTE OSGOOD MASON

[December 1927]
43 W. 66th St.
New York City

Dear Darling Godmother,

You have given me the happiest Christmas season of all my life. For the first time ever, I was among friends <u>and</u> Well fed and warm. I could give and receive. It was nothing expensive that I had to give, but I could give <u>something</u> as well as receive. I had love. I felt you warm and close and urging me on to happiness. <u>Nothing</u> was lacking, even to the traditional egg-nogg.

Godmother dearest, far-seeing one, you have given me my <u>first</u> Christmas. I mean the first Yule season when reality met my dreams. The kind of Christmas that my half-starved child-hood painted.

Thank You, dear Godmother.

Zora.

TO LANGSTON HUGHES

[postcard postmarked January 31, 1928]
[postcard front: "Bird's Eye View
of an Orange Grove, Florida."]

Dear Langston

Here on the works Living in the quarters of the Everglades Cypress Lumber Co. Please Write me.

> Lots of Love
> Zora
> Box 181 LOUGHAM, FLA.

TO DOROTHY WEST AND HELENE JOHNSON

[postcard postmarked February 23, 1928]
[postcard front: "The Alligator Quartet singing 'Way
Down upon the Suwannee River' Florida"]

Dear Children,

How are you? Send me a card perhaps to Lakeland, Fla, Gen. Del. Thanks for the Xmas present, old beans. You shall hear from me.

> Zora H.

TO LANGSTON HUGHES

Eatonville Fla
March 8, 1928.

Dear Langston,

Your letter was so timely and vital. You answered a big question for me—the age of folk lore. I had collected several very good modern stories which I knew [was—x-ed out] were good, but I was wondering if anybody else would see it that way. For instance (as dictated)"

"uh white man uz (was) drivin his car by auh cotton patch when uh boll weevil flew outa his steerin' wheel.

" 'Lemme drive yo car," he says to de white man.

" 'Naw, you cant drive it" de white man says to 'im, "you cant drive no car."

"Dont tell <u>me</u> Ah cant drive no car. Ah drove in uh thousand las' year an' Ahm gwine drive in two thousand dis year."

Now about the show.[1] I have not written a line of anything since I have been down here and I left all of my MSS. in Newark[2] in storage. I have several good ideas, but nothing worked out. I am truly dedicated to the work [in is over-written] at hand and so I am not even writing, but living every moment with the people.

I believe I have almost as many stories now as I got on my entire trip last year.

I think I'll slip back to Mobile and get some more wood for Godmother and send it whole as you suggested. In fact, I think I'll try to get four to six boards so that a frieze may be carved on it telling the story of Negro slavery from capture in battle in Africa to the "Weary Blues." (figure of Jazz player at piano)

By the way, I read from "Fine Clothes"[3] to the group at Loughman[4] and <u>they got the point</u> and enjoyed it <u>immensely</u>. So you <u>are</u> really a great poet for you truly represent your people. You shall hear more of this later.

I dont mind writing <u>you</u>, in fact I like to but I have refrained to keep from obligating <u>you</u> to write. Your letter was the most helpful thing and <u>please</u> do that whenever you think of anything that might help. Remember I am new and we want to do this tremendous thing with all the fire that genius can bring. I need your hand.

If they can rumor me in Harlem at this distance, then I know that the champion "rumorist" of all time is in New York.

[1]*A collaborative folk opera.*

[2]*Probably Westfield, New Jersey, a city six miles from Newark. Hughes lived there in 1928, and Hurston had moved into a rooming house nearby. These manuscripts would have included her folklore notes for* Negro Folk-Tales from the Gulf States, *as well as other materials.*

[3]*Hughes's second volume of poems,* Fine Clothes to the Jew, *published in 1927.*

[4]*A group at the Everglades Cypress Lumber Company in Loughman, Florida. The camp proved to be a rich source of folk material.*

I am going to divorce Herbert as soon as this is over. He tries to hold me back and be generally obstructive so I have broken off relations since early Jan. and thats that.[5]

I am enclosing an intercepted love letter from Mobile. Keep it in your files as I have not copied it.[6]

Here is a page of Negro verse.[7] Note that the two first lines have no meaning other than to rhyme with the [of—x-ed out] last one which tells the story. I note this trait in all Negro verse and I wonder if you have.

I am getting inside of Negro art and lore. I am beginning to see really and when you join me I shall point things out and see if you see them as I do. You are coming as soon as school closes arent you? Langston, Langston this is going to be big. Most gorgeous possibilities are showing themselves constantly.

I have the street scene still & 2 others in my mind—if you want them you can use them for yourself and its O.K. by me. Godmother asked me not to publish and as I am making money I hope you can use them.[8]

I am sending her some orange blossoms.

Lovingly yours
Zora

I am collecting the expressions, similes, etc as you suggested but that is another instance of our thoughts clicking[9]

[5]Hurston obtained the divorce from her first husband, Herbert Sheen, on July 7, 1931.

[6]Langston Hughes had the idea of collecting love letters, and Hurston collected many of them for a volume that never materialized. None of these letters survive in her papers.

[7]Not found with the letter.

[8]Hurston seems here to be withdrawing from their folk opera and offering him the material. This is relevant in light of the later dispute they would have over their one collaborative project, the play Mule Bone; see Mule Bone in glossary.

[9]This material may have contributed to Hurston's essay "Characteristics of Negro Expression," published in Nancy Cunard's Negro: An Anthology in 1934.

TO LANGSTON HUGHES

Maitland, Fla.
April 12, 1928.

Dear Langston,
  Your helpful letter to hand and I am already collecting letters. I have a collection written to one local sheik—about 16–20 and they are rich. That was a <u>noble</u> idea of yours, Langston.
  I can <u>really</u> write a Village Anthology now, but I am wary about mentioning it to Godmother for fear she will think I am shirking but <u>boy</u> I think [I] could lay 'em something now. I told you I must not publish without her consent.[1]
  Hope that you see the Loughman report.[2] I like it a little.
  I had written to Dr. Locke[3] at H.U. [Howard University] about March 6.[4] I wonder if he ever got it. I have written again however. I sent him a wire to Fisk, but it came back undelivered.
  Are you planning to join me vacation? I hope so. I promise you one saw-mill and one phosphate mine as special added attractions.
  I am working hard & broadening some. I have come to 5 general laws, but I shall not mention them to Godmother or Locke until I have worked them out. Locke would hustle out a volume right away.
  1. The Negro's outstanding characteristic is drama. That is why he appears so imitative. Drama is mimicry. note gesture is place of words.
  2. Negro is lacking in reverence. note number of stories in which God, Church & heaven are treated lightly.
  3. <u>Angularity</u> in everything, sculpture, dancing, abrupt story telling.
  4. Redundance. Examples: low-down, Cap'n high sheriff, top-superior, the number of times—usually three—that a feature is re-peated in a story. Repetition of single simple strain in music.

[1]*Hurston had published "The Eatonville Anthology" in the* Messenger *in 1926 and may have wanted to work on a longer version of such a piece.*
[2]*Her folklore materials from the Everglades Cypress Lumber Company which went into* Negro Folk-Tales *from the Gulf States.*
[3]*Alain Locke; see glossary.*
[4]*This letter is not in Locke's papers.*

5. Restrained ferocity in everything. There is a tense ferocity beneath the casual exterior that stirs the onlooker to hysteria. note effect of negro music, dancing, gestures on the staid nordic

6. Some laws in dialect. The same form is not always used. Some {syllables/words ["syllables" is written above "words"] are long before or after certain words and short in the same positions[.] Example: You as subject gets full value but is shortened to yuh as an object. Him in certain positions and 'im in others depending on the consonant preceding. Several laws of aspirate H.[5]

I have touched on all these briefly because I know a word is enough to make you grasp it all.

What, I ask with my feet turned out, are Countee [Cullen] and Eric [Walrond] going abroad to study? In the words of H—Hannibal, "O Carthage, I see thy fate!" (when he saw the [decapitat—x-ed out] cut-off head of his brother.) A negro goes to Whiteland to learn his trade! Ha!

Fat was inevitable for Countee. It will fit him nicely too. Nice, safe, middle-class

I am glad for Wallace and Bruce. More power to them.[6]

Did I tell you before I left about the new, the _real_ Negro art theatre I plan? Well, I shall, or rather _we_ shall act out the folk tales, however short, with the abrupt angularity and naivete of the primitive 'bama nigger. Just that with naive settings. What do you think?

I think I shall try a stenographer. I use up a deal of time I might be making contacts with the setting down. I think it would be cheaper since I'd get more work done in a shorter time. _Please_ tell me what you think. And I want to collect like a new broom.

I shall give the last half of the year to conjure, or do you think 3 months is enough?

Lovingly,
Zora.

discovery 7. Negro folk-lore is _still_ in the making
a new kind is crowding out the old.

---

[5]_Much of this material went into "Characteristics of Negro Expression."_

[6]_Wallace Thurman and Bruce Nugent were close friends who lived together at "Niggerati Manor" on West 138th Street. Nugent was openly gay, and Thurman was, according to Arnold Rampersad, "both guilty about his active bisexuality and eager to satisfy it." Hurston's letter was written at the time of Thurman's separation from his wife, Louise Thompson._

TO LANGSTON HUGHES

Box 394
Mulberry, Fla
May 1, 1928.

Dear Langston,

You have a <u>noble</u> list of guests at your Prom.[1] Its top superior to all I have seen. I wish I was there.

Sorry to my heart that you are not coming South this year. Nevertheless, I know you will be with me in spirit.

Of <u>course,</u> you know I didnt dream of that theatre as a one-man stunt. I had you helping 50-50 from the start. In fact, I am perfectly willing to be 40 to your 60 since you are always so much more practical than I. But I <u>know</u> it is going to be <u>Glorious</u>! A really new departure in the drama.[2]

Please send me your mother's address. I want to write her.

Off to the phosphate mines for the day. Shall be here sometime I think.

Sincerely,
Zora.

---

[1] *The Diamond Jubilee celebration at Hughes's Lincoln University.*
[2] *This suggests that their idea for a collaborative folk opera was still under consideration, in spite of Hurston's sense that Charlotte Osgood Mason wanted them to drop it.*

TO ALAIN LOCKE

Box 394
Mulberry, Fla.
May 1, 1928.

My Dear Alain,

I believe some monstrous ole paper-eating ogre is grabbing my letters to you and swallowing them up tiddy-umpty. I hope a St. George arises to chop him into doll-rags.

Things are going Well, I think, here. I have just read "The Negro and His Songs" Odom [sic] and Johnson and it is not so stupendous as the critics make out.[1] It is inaccurate in a dozen places. He has several songs cut into bits and each bit labelled another song. Perfectly honest, no doubt, but misinformed. I get that sort of thing but I keep searching after other bits until they match up.

Are you coming down? When? Please let me hear.

Sincerely,
Zora

TO ALAIN LOCKE

Box 394, Mulberry, Fla.
May 10, 1928.

Dear Alain,

I was very happy to hear from you. I had just had a letter from both Godmother and Langston so the circuit is complete.

---

[1] *Howard W. Odum and Guy B. Johnson were faculty members at the University of North Carolina. Published in 1926,* The Negro and His Songs *included recordings and argued for folk music as the derivation of the blues. In the spring 1925 issue of* Survey, *Countee Cullen called* The Negro and His Songs *"an interesting collection. It is done with a scholarly acumen for detail and a dispassionate notation on the specimens."*

I am sending you under separate cover two vertebra of pre-historic sea animals. These were taken from the phosphate mines here about fifty feet below the surface of the ground. I believe the huge phosphate deposits in this state are the sites of sea animal graveyards before the Quartenary when Florida is believed to have emerged from the sea. Perhaps the rising land trapped great numbers of fish in deep depressions where they died as the water evaporated. You can see by comparison with present day fish that the bones are fish bones and not mammal. But what fish! You can do as you like about them—either give them to the Geological Dept. or keep them. Is Prof. Shuh still there?

The bit of wood is from the ship in Mobile Bay. (Cudjoe Lewis)

Thanks a lot for the Tulane U. contact. They sent an application blank in case I might wish to enroll in some of the social science classes. Dont laugh.

Could you come down in June immediately after school closes? I earnestly hope so. I have a great deal to show and tell you.

I know that teaching must be a little colorless to you with all the great prism that you have inside you. It must make you feel sorta like a lightning bug. Drab on the outside but fire underneath. You can only show your light by flashes.

My actual degree came from Barnard this week. I have sent it on to Godmother. I am a little bit happy too.

I shall be glad to hear from you.

Most sincerely,
Zora (pen dry)

P.S. Godmother sent me the Negro Wor[k]aday Songs of Odom and Johnson and I am not nearly depressed as I feared I would be. I was almost afraid to read it, fearful lest they had beat us to it in the matter of songs. But, boy! They have done the book just about like Nicholas Murray Butler[1] would do the black-bottom. They evidently know nothing of the how folk-songs grow. What is merely incremental (or en) [they— x-d out] repetition, they have taken for another song. He has the song "Ike and Jerry" cut up into eight or ten songs. He has the "Love, O

---

[1]President of Columbia University.

careless Love" English ballad, in a garbled form as negro work song. It should have been under the head of adaptation; he has taken several things from the phonograph records, and heavens knows there has never appeared one genuine Negro bit on there. I certainly would like to see an honest criticism of the work published, but we couldnt do it lest we be accused of jealousy. Read the book and you will see he misses the point in numerous places. I would love to read it with you.

This is a terrible bit of typing, but the heat has me. Excuse it please.

Z.

TO ALAIN LOCKE

Box 32
Magazine, Ala
June 14, 1928.

Dear Alain,

I was so glad to hear from you. It does help to get a word from an ally.

I'll break in right here with an explanation.

Do you remember when you visited me in New York I spoke of the article I had sent to "The World Tomorrow" because of the debt we owed them on "Fire?" You said that some white lady had thought of giving us some help, but you were sure that Wallace Thurman was not being ethical about the money. Well, the article went to them in Sept. or Oct. They sent to me & Langston for more or contributions. Thats how "How it Feels to be Colored Me" came to be published. I had no money. Godmother didnt understand but I have explained to her now.

The work is going splendidly. I have a real thriller to hand you within a week.[1]

---

[1] Hurston's next published essay, "Dance Songs and Tales of the Bahamas," was a serious piece of anthropological writing and not a "thriller." She probably refers here to her manuscript in process, Negro Folk-Tales from the Gulf States.

Where is Langston? I owe him a letter, and want to write.

Yes, I hope the work goes on as well as at the first. I certainly am doing my best. About a month ago I wrote a short criticism of "Negro Workaday Songs"[2] to Godmother in which I said that white people could not be trusted to collect the lore of others, and that the Indians were right.[3] I was quoting Godmother's words, but somehow she felt that I included her in that category. I hurriedly explained to her and she said she was satisfied. I was so sure we understood each other that I didnt say present company excepted. I am too sorry but I cant see how I could have avoided it—me feeling as I did about the [illegible word] between us.[4]

TO LANGSTON HUGHES

Magazine, Ala
July 10, 1928.

Dear Langston,

I have been through one of those terrible periods when I cant make myself write But you understand, since you have 'em yourself.

In every town I hold 1 or 2 story-telling contests, and at each I begin by telling them who you are and all, then I read poems from "Fine Clothes".[1] Boy! they eat it up. Two or three of them are too subtle and they dont get it. "Mulatto" for instance and "Sport"[2] but the others they just eat up. You are being quoted in R.R. camps, phosphate mines, Turpentine stills etc. I went into a house Saturday night (last) and the men were skinning—you remember my telling you about that game—and when the dealer saw his opponent was on the turn (and losing consequently) He chanted

[2] *Odum and Johnson's* The Negro and His Songs.

[3] *This predates Hurston's reference to "feather-bed resistance" in* Mules and Men *and her belief that Indians offer white society resistance as "stony silence."*

[4] *A portion of this letter is missing, including Hurston's signature.*

[1] Fine Clothes to the Jew, *Hughes's second volume of poetry, published in 1927.*

[2] *The first lines read: "Life / For him / Must be / The shivering of / A great drum."*

"When hard luck overtakes you
Nothin for you to do
Grab up yo' fine clothes
An' sell em to-ooo-de Jew Hah!!"

(slaps the card down on the table)
The other fellow was visibly cast down when the dealer picked up his money. Dealer gloating continued: "If you wuz a mule

I'd git you a waggin to haul—
But youse <u>so</u> low down-hown [?]
you aint even got uh stall."

So you see they are making it so much a part of themselves they go to improvising on it.

For some reason they call it "De Party Book." They come specially to be read to & I know you could sell them if you only had a supply. I think I'd like a dozen as an experiment. They <u>adore</u> "Saturday Night"[3] and "Evil Woman,"[4] "Bad Man"[5] "Gypsy Man"[6]

They sing the poems right off, and July 1, two men came over with guitars and sang the whole book. Everybody joined in. It was the strangest & most <u>thrilling</u> thing. They played it well too. You'd be surprised. One man was giving the words out-lining them out as the preacher does a hymn and the others would take it up and sing. It was glorious!

Work going on well. I am getting much more material in a given area/space ["area" is written above "space"] & time than before because I am learning better technique. Getting more love letters too. Am keeping close tab on expressions of double meaning too, also compiling lists of double words. They—to give emphasis—use the noun and put the [use of—x'd out] function of the noun before it as an adjective. Example, sitting-chair, suck-bottle, cook-pot, hair-comb.[7]

Without flattery, Langston, you are the brains of this argosy. All the ideas have come out of your head.

[3]*The first lines read: "Play it once. / O, play some more."*
[4]*The first lines read: "I ain't gonna mistreat ma / Good gal any more."*
[5]*The first lines read: "I'm a bad, bad man / Cause everybody tells me so."*
[6]*The first lines read: "Ma man's a gypsy / Cause he never does come home."*
[7]*This material went into "Characteristics of Negro Expression," Hurston's 1934 essay for Nancy Cunard's* Negro: An Anthology.

I have about enough for a good volume of stories but I shall miss nothing. I shall go to New Orleans from here. Oh! almost forgot. Found another one of the original Africans, older than Cudjoe about 200 miles up state on the Tombighee river. She is most delightful, but no one will ever know about her but us. She is a better talker than Cudjoe.

Had a letter from Alain. Wrote him at his Paris address.

Be here for two weeks more at least.

Lovingly,
Zora.

I wanted to let your publishers know what a hit you [wer—x-ed out] are with the people you write about, but Godmother doesnt want <u>me</u> to say anything at present. But I shall do it as soon as this is over.

TO CHARLOTTE OSGOOD MASON

Magazine Point, Ala.
July 25, 1928.

Dearest Godmother,

This is to wish you a perfect crossing. I am enclosing something for you to read, so that you can have a Zora hour at sea. The material is duplicated so that you need not worry about saving it when you are through.

Joe Wiley is one of the Magazine boys and these bits are all taken from his stuff. There are more of them with the Mobile material.[1]

Dearest, little mother of the primitive world, take good care not to overtire yourself abroad.

I am attempting a volume of work songs with music for piano and guitar. I have just thought out a method, sort of graphic way. I shall send you the first song asa soon as I get it finished to see if you like it.

All my love, Godmother.
Humbly and sincerely,
Zora

---

[1] *Joe Wiley is listed as a source in both* Mules and Men *and* Negro Folk-Tales from the Gulf States. *Hurston included a number of tales from Wiley in this letter. Some were later published.*

TO LANGSTON HUGHES

7 Bellville Court
Algiers, La.
Aug. 6, 1928.

Dear Langston—

I have landed here in the kingdom of Marie Laveau and expect to wear her crown someday—Conjure Queen as you suggested.

Loved your letter. Books almost all gone.[1] Check will be forwarded as soon as the last one is in. People like you immensely.

I have taken a 3 room house here in a splendid neighborhood from the point of view of collecting materieal. Besides it is cheaper than room rent. 10^{00} month with electric lights & running water. I have furnished it for 16^{00}. Someday I wish you could camp here to write.

My Plans: 1 volume of stories. 1 children's games. 1 Drama and the Negro 1 "Mules & Men" a volume of work songs with guitar arrangement 1 on Religion. 1. on words & meanings. 1 volume of love letters with an introduction on Negro love.[2]

Send Godmother a melon a week before sailing, a bit of intended-to-be-humorous MS.S. as you suggested, & a steamer letter.

I am putting you up for the Society of Am. Folk-lore this week.[3] Do you think Dr. Locke would like it also if I can find grounds for proposing him?

You shall hear from me soon again. Glad to hear that you are tooling some new songs. Speaking of songs Porter Grainger[4] has notified me that one of the bits of funk. I handed him will be paying a royalty this month. Something about "Jelly Roll."[5]

Most Sincerely,
Zora.

---

[1] *Hurston was selling Hughes's books of poetry* The Weary Blues *and* Fine Clothes to the Jew *as she traveled collecting folklore.*

[2] *The volume of stories was originally called* Negro Folk-Tales from the Gulf States; Mules and Men *combined stories, work songs, games, and religious material.*

[3] *The Society of American Folklore was probably the most prestigious national organization devoted to folklore at the time.*

[4] *Actor, writer, arranger; see glossary.*

[5] *Slang for sex; vagina. Hurston found a "Jelly Roll" song which she had given to Grainger.*

TO LANGSTON HUGHES

#7 Belville Court
New Orleans (Algiers) La.
Aug. 16, 1928.

Dear Langston,

I sold 7 books and gave 3. Hence the 14^{00}. Please send me 10 copies of "Weary Blues." I could do with some more "Fine Clothes" too.

The copy you autographed for me has done me lots of good. When I have to meet people in group & am asked to tell about myself— which I dont want to do for fear of saying that which I dont wish—I say I cant talk, but I'll read some verses from a Negro poet. You know these self-conscious Negroes are dynamite. Some are likely to object to my work so I can keep from explaining myself & still satisfy by talking about poets.

I am rushed today so for the present. Oh! Found a Negro artist who can <u>draw</u>. Cant paint. But <u>how</u> he can draw. You shall have a sample within ten days. I have also a sculptor, woodcarver to be exact. and he is equal to Gutzon Borglum I tell you seriously.[1] Not only is his hand sure, but he has conception. Drunkard, and I must go back to Mobile frequently to keep him at work but already I have one finished figure. It shall be a surprise for Godmother on her return.

Lovingly,

Zora.

[1] *Gutzon Borglum (1867–1941) was an American- and French-trained sculptor famous for his huge statues of noted figures, including the presidents at Mount Rushmore, the Twelve Apostles at New York City's Cathedral of St. John the Divine, and Abraham Lincoln's head at the Capitol rotunda.*

TO LANGSTON HUGHES

7 Bellville Court
Sept. 20, 1928

Dear Langston,

The books came O.K. I have had time for no exploiting yet for I have been "between the snakes." Things are beginning to go well now. I am getting on with the top of the profession. I know 18 tasks, including how to crown the spirit of death, and kill.

It makes me sick to see how these cheap white folks are grabbing our stuff and ruining it. I am almost sick—my one consolation being that they never do it right and so there is still a chance for us. I would like to know what Rosamond and Gordon[1] are singing

Under separate cover I am sending two portraits of you done by Joe Mitchell[2] from a snap I have of you. I gave him a copy of each of your books. What I want you to tell me is, do you think he ought to come to New York, and if so, this Fall? He has some extra fine work that I am sending to Godmother by the time she returns. I think he draws better than Douglas,[3] but he has just picked up things and knows nothing about modern art. Will you let me know at once what you think? I am giving him 3–5 per week so that he may work. Do you think he rates the help? He is sending the drawings in return for your books, and he is doing another which I think is going to be good. He sees the defects in the others and is working them out in the next.

Heard from Godmother at Bournemouth, I am writing her a letter today to celebrate our anniversary of meeting.

Hope that you enjoyed your vacation, and that your class work will be light.

Lovingly,
Zora

---

[1]*John Rosamond Johnson was in a vaudeville act with Emmanuel Taylor Gordon called* The Inimitable Five. *Johnson and Gordon performed in concerts in Europe and America after the Johnson brothers'* Book of American Negro Spirituals *was published in 1925.*

[2]*Like many of the rural artists Hurston was proud of discovering, Mitchell does not seem to have acquired enough fame to appear in any of the standard indexes or biographies.*

[3]*Artist Aaron Douglas; see glossary.*

TO LANGSTON HUGHES

2744 Amelia St.
New Orleans, La.
October 15, 1928.

Dear Langston,

Things are ok by me. How is it with you? The conjure business is looking up, and I expect little more than duplication from now on. I am going out to Bogaloosa [sic] tomorrow to see a supposedly great one, and hope that he is not too hard to deal with. They certainly charge steeply. I have gotten everyone I have met yet, but they tell me he is enormously rich.

I stayed a week at 834 Orleans, but the bed bugs routed me, so I moved up here. It is better anyway for I am sort of in the lap of the activities. Algiers, is as dead as Babylon. It seems that police activities is responsible for the removal. Oh, I have a marvelous dance ritual from the ceremony of death. Lots of thrilling things to make your heart glad.

Shall have a check for you in a few days. Since I have been over in N.O. I am meeting more interesting people and having a thrill reading poetry. One man who heard me reading a few in a drug-store at 3000 S. Rampart came to my house yesterday morning and asked me to let him read the books, and I did. I knew he would never be able to buy one. I am giving a copy of each to the town library at Eatonville Fla. and one to the lib. of Robert Hungerford Industrial School at the same place

You are very accurate in your observations. I found the addresses a lot of help.[1] Particularly the drugstore on Rampart. I got a splendid "experience" from the old man at 834 too. Thanks a lot.

I heard that Gwen Bennet[2] was in Florida. Is that true? It puts me on the wonder if she is. Hope you got your folk-lore journals. I got

---

[1] Hughes had spent time in New Orleans in the summer of 1927, living first in a rooming house on Rampart Street, a black area of town, and later in the French Quarter.
[2] Gwendolyn Bennett, Harlem Renaissance poet; see glossary.

mine and noted A.H. Fausett's[3] contrib. I am exultant for they are set down just as I thought they would be. I note also children's games from Cincinnati, with the Negro games all wrong, for which I give thanks.

I know that the paragraphs in this letter violate all rules, but what difference does it make. You will understand me.

Sincerely,

Zora

TO ALAIN LOCKE

2744 Amelia St.
New Orleans, La.
Oct. 15, 1928.

Dear Alain,

I lost your address and I have been waiting for your return to write you. I know that you have looked to hear.

Well, things are going well with me. I am getting a great deal of conjure material. We are just in the knick of time too, for I find its greatest era is about forty years in the past. I have gotten on to a lead that promises something good from out of the past, if it pans out.

Lots of Howardites are here. Sue Brown, and her brother Dr. Felton Brown, Dr. Cherrie, Joe Dejoie, PhC.[1] and some others I have not seen yet.[2]

Godmother has said that I may return to Florida to finish the folklore after I get thru here. That will be about the first of the year. Could you join me then for a week or two—maybe the Holidays? I am very eager that you see the things and the people.

---

[3] *Arthur Huff Fauset, folklorist, writer, teacher, and half-brother of novelist Jessie Fauset. In the October–December issue of the* Journal of American Folklore *(Vol. 41, no. 162, pp. 529–57) he published "Tales and Riddles Collected in Philadelphia." A fellow protégé of Mason, Arthur Fauset wrote* For Freedom: A Biographical Story of the American Negro *(1927) and contributed to* Fire!! *and Alain Locke's* New Negro.

---

[1] *This is apparently Hurston's designation for a degree in pharmacy.*

[2] *Susie Ione Brown Waxwood graduated in 1925 with a B.A. in liberal arts; Ernest Cherrie received an M.D. in 1927; Joseph John Dejoie received his pharmacy degree in 1925.*

I ahve [sic] found a wonderful wood-carver at Mobile who is greater by a handsome margin than the Fernandina man. He does human figures as well [as] Gutzon Borglum. Really. Wait till you see what I send Godmother. In New Orleans, I have found a fellow who can draw too. He is crude, but with you to point out his errors he could arrive. At present, he has greater skill than Douglas, but knows nothing but just what he has picked up. I am sending samples of his work also.

You are going to have plenty of editing to do after this expedition is over, I promise you. I am using the vacuum method, grabbing everything I see. Langston is responsible for that to a great extent. He writes and suggests other phases continually. I wish you would help me that way also. By the way, would you like to become a member of the Americam Folk-Lore Society? I think it would be good for you. Let me hear.

I hope to stop at Washington on my way, Godmother willing. Was your trip abroad successful and happy? I hope so.

Lovingly yours,
Zora

TO DOROTHY WEST

[envelope postmarked November 5, 1928]

Dear Dorothy,

Wally[1] should perk up. I know that it is annoying for his mother-in-law to keep on living and pestering him, but then there are gunmen down on the East Side who hire out for as low as $25.00. He should be a very happy man by Thanksgiving.

You are a love, Dot, no less, to put my parcel away so carefully. It is my fault for not wrapping better, and for not writing the letter first. It all turns out to be futile, for I must now take those duplicates I sent you and go to work from an entirely different angle than at first. Would you send me all the typed sheets, secretly, and by registered mail? I'll be eternally grateful if you will.[2]

---

[1] *Wallace Thurman.*

[2] *Hurston had told Langston Hughes she was working on a volume of stories, a book of children's games, a piece on Negroes and drama, a volume of work songs, a volume on religion, a volume on words and meanings, a volume of love songs, and* Mules and Men.

Of course you are near my heart and always will be. I trust you and Helene [Johnson] more than anyone else in this world. You are the fine gold in New York's show and shine. I have a lot in store for you.

I am O.K. in every way and hope to see you early in the year. But do not think of leaping out of 43.[3] I proabably wont have time to stop long.

PLEASE DONT LET ANYONE KNOW THAT YOU HAVE HEARD FROM ME OR SEE MY PAPERS BEFORE YOU MAIL THEM.[4]

Lovingly yours,
Zora

P.O. Box 5201
Station B
New Orleans, La.

TO LANGSTON HUGHES

[postcard front: "Cutting 'Bogalusa Brand' timber in logging operations, Great Southern Lumber Co. Bogalusa, La."]

Monday [November] 19, '28

Dear Langston,

Read "Fine Clothes" to enthusiastic bunch of lumber-jacks here Sat. Big colorful jook[1] here. You'd love it. I am full of impressions.

Love
Zora

[3]Hurston's apartment, loaned or sublet to West and Johnson.
[4]Such secrecy no doubt had to do with Hurston's contract with her patron Charlotte Osgood Mason; it specified that Hurston could show work only to those Mason had approved.

[1]A jook joint is a private bar or dance hall with live music.

TO LANGSTON HUGHES

P.O. Box 5201, Station B
New Orleans, La.
Nov. 22, 1928.

Dear Langston,

I have purposely held back the enclosure till now so that you would be in funds for Thanksgiving. I hope that you have a very good time.

I am getting on in the conjure splendidly. Tell me this, should I go to every one of them as I am doing, or merely learn what the greatest have to teach? I have been going to every one I hear of for the sake of thoroughness. This necessarily means duplication in detail, but it seems to me best as the little ones know some detail not known to the great. It costs more money to see so many, however, and keeps me pressed. I dont mind that, if its necessary. Tell me what you think.

Yes, I WILL conjure you too, but only for good luck. Oh, honey, I have the most marvellous ceremony. The dance of the nine snakes! Just you wait till you see that. You were right again in saying that it would take six months to do the conjure. I am knee deep in it with a long way to go.

I am outlining the materials for the books. I want to have the rough outlines for Godmother to see on my return. Shall send you a copy as soon as possible.

By the way, what is this I hear about a new magazine in Harlem[1] Wish that I might participate. I know that you are doing your bit to make it go.

Know what, you ought to make a loafing tour oft the South like the blind Homer, singing your songs. Not in auditoriums, but in camps, on water-fronts and the like. You are the poet of the people and your subjects are crazy about you. Why not? There never has been a poet who has been acceptable to His Majesty, the man in the gutter before, and laugh if you will, but that man in the gutter is the god-maker, the cre-

[1]*Edited by Wallace Thurman,* Harlem: A Forum of Negro Life *began publication in 1928. Contributors and editors included Dorothy West, Helene Johnson, Walter White, Langston Hughes, Richard Bruce Nugent, Aaron Douglas, Alain Locke, and George Schuyler.*

ator of evrything that lasts. That could be a long theme, but your intelligence saves me the trouble, and you the boredom. Why not think it over?

Got plenty story material for the book. This is a miscellaneous paragraph, look for anything. Saw the great "doctor" Redmond at Bogalusa. Income over 500 a day. He isa a rusty black nigger with a piece of greasy flannel around his neck. Never allows the patient to tell him one symtom. Looks at them and prescribes. Clientele mostly white. I could have married the old scalawag. Claims to cure appendicitis by making the patient pass it or bringing it out of the throat. Gettiny [sic] plenty letters for book,[2] and about enough [pl—x-ed out] children's games, and enough work songs. Of course, not letting anything slip by me willingly. Have not heard from Locke, tho I wrote him some weeks ago.

Luck and love,
Zora

TO ALAIN LOCKE

P.O. Box 5201, Station B
New Orleans, La.
Nov. 22, 1928.

My dear Dr. Locke,

How come? I want to hear from you. I want to know all about your European trip and everything. Have you seen the wooden figure I sent Godmother? I want to know what you think about it.

I dont want to seem impatient, Alain, but wrassle me out something and put it in the mail. I know that you lead a strenous life, but my tongue is all lolled out, waiting to lap up that letter from you which is so long overdue.

Luck and love,
Zora

---

[2]*Projected volume of love letters.*

TO DOROTHY WEST AND HELENE JOHNSON

Box 5201, Sta. B
New Orleans, La
Nov, 22, [1928]

Dear My Children,

Thanks for your favors. Look for a parcel for yourselves in a day or two. Dont look for coherence in this letter. I am merely trying to get it said.

Things going fine. Have a brilliant new idea towork out, hence my request for the material. Sure you will be thrilled. Bully for the new magazine,[1] shall hurry home to do what I can. Got lots of things for you to help me work out as soon as I get there.

My love to all the folks, no I guess you better not say anything.

Shall see perhaps sooner than I had anticipated.

Luck and love,
Zora

TO DOROTHY WEST

Wednesday-12-5-28

Dear Dot Child,

If I gave you the idea I was coming home soon it was during one of my trance periods. I wont be home for months & when I <u>do</u>, it will be

---

[1]Harlem: A Forum of Negro Life, *edited by Wallace Thurman. Later, West would edit her own magazine,* Challenge, *eventually retitled* New Challenge.

so sketchy that you can just stick me on the day-bed. I'll be in & out of town so I probably wont need any apartment.

Did you get the box of pecans I sent you for Thanksgiving?

Love to my Helene
Zora.

Same P.O. address
wish I could help out on "Harlem" but it is impossible at present. I'm heartbroken over being bound to silence.[1]
[in left margin:] are you tired of the place?

TO ALAIN LOCKE

256 N. Dearborn ST.
Mobile, Ala.
Dec. 16, 1928

My dear Alain Locke,

I wanted very much to stop, but I made a promise that I would not. Godmother said that you had mentioned it to her, but she was afraid. So here I am, and at work.

She was very anxious that I should say to you that the plans— rather the hazy dreams ocf the theatre that I talked to you about should never be mentioned again. She trusts her three children [Locke, Hughes, and Hurston] to never let those words pass their lips again until the gods decree that they shall materialize. Nobody knows but us anyway so it is safe.

I do hope that I shall see you in the South before many weeks have elapsed.

Very late, I thank you for the royalty checks. Did I need them?

Sincerely yours,
Zora H

---

[1]*Hurston refers here to the restrictions placed in her contract with Charlotte Osgood Mason.*

TO FRANZ BOAS

Box 5201, Station B
New Orleans, La.
Dec. 27, 1928.

My dear Dr. Boas,

I was very proud to hear from you. I have wanted to write you but a promise was exacted of me [by Mason] that I would write <u>no one.</u> Of course I have intended from the very beginning to show you what I have, but after I had returned. Thus I could keep my word and at the same time have your guidance.

I am finding lots of things which will intrigue you. I find Odom and Johnson in error constantly. A too hasty generalization. The subject of sympathetic magic is being looked into as thoroughly as I can, and folk-lore collected, religious expression noted.

This is confidential. I accepted the money on the condition that I should write no one. It is unthinkable, of course, that I go past the collecting stage without consulting you, however I came by the money. I shall probably be in New York by the Fall. I have not forgotten your interest in Creole languages, but I have had little time to note anything. I am getting on very well. The experience that I had under you was a splendid foundation, for whereas, I got little for you, now, I know where to look and how. Sometimes I have gotten in a week as much as I gathered for you through out. I regret it too, but I know that you understand, and will be pleased with me when I return

Most affectionately yours,
Zora Hurston

TO LANGSTON HUGHES

1663 Evergreen Ave.
Jacksonville, Fla.
April 3, 1929.

Dear Langston,

Say! isnt Wallie getting away? I think its just too wonderful. I am so proud and thrilled.[1]

I had a letter from Locke and he told me that Jessie Fauset was getting married and he got off one of the best wise cracks of the year.[2] If Jessie ever hears of it he will have to live abroad for a long time.

Do let me hear from you. I get worried sometimes and feel that you have gotten so intellectual that you are forgetting a low-brow like me. I want you to hurry and come out of that knowledge works and be human. But maybe the business of graduating has you very occupied. I can understand that. But at that I think Lincoln is presumptious to give YOU an exam.

Locke is utterly disgusted at Wallie.

I am sitting down to sum up and I am getting on very well at it. I feel full of my subjects, but there are going to be lots of hollering as various corns get stepped on.

My last night in New Orleans I spoke on poetry at New Orleans College and read some poems from WEARY BLUES and read FINE CLOTHES clean through.[3] My they liked it. One old maid matron of the dormitory nearly finished dying when I read "Saturday night," but the boys et it up. I read 6 poems from Helene Johnson too, and talked a little on poetic form.

I shall go down state as soon as I get all the material on the African princess who married a white man out beyond the three mile limit

---

[1]*Wallace Thurman was professionally active at this time. In 1928, he wrote* Negro Life in New York's Harlem *and launched the short-lived literary magazine* Harlem: A Forum of Negro Life; *in 1929, he published his first novel,* The Blacker the Berry, *and wrote the play* Harlem.

[2]*Editor and novelist Jessie Redmon Fauset married businessman Herbert Harris in 1929.*

[3]*Hughes's first two books of poetry, published in 1926 and 1927.*

and lived on an island off Jacksonville.[4] I am photographing that carved house at Fernandina, too.

Wait till you see my conjure material. Oh, Langston, my "crowning" ceremonies were thrilling!

Well, you must write. They will forward from here, but you shall have a card as soon as I get down state—about five days.

Love,
Zora

I have some dandy theatrical ideas for us to work out.

TO FRANZ BOAS

Box 815, Eau Gallie, Fla.
April 21, 1929.

My dear Dr. Boas,

I am through collecting and I am sitting down to write up. I have more than 95,000 words of story material, a collection of children's games, conjure material, and religious material with a great number of photographs.

As soon as I can get the typing done, I shall send you the carbons.[1]

Is it safe for me to say that baptism is an extension of water worship as a part of pantheism just as the sacrament is an extension of cannibalism? Isnt the use of candles in the Catholic church a relic of fire worship? Are not all the uses of fire upon the altars the same thing? Is not the christian ritual rather one of attenuated nature-worship, in the fire, water, and blood? Might not the frequently mentioned fire of the Holy Ghost not be an unconscious fire worship. May it not be a deification of fire?

---

[4]*The daughter of slave trader Zephaniah Kingsley, Jr. (1765–1843), and Anna Madgigene Jai, the daughter of an African king. Kingsley and Jai moved to Florida in 1803 and Jai and her four children by Kingsley relocated to Haiti in 1835 to escape Florida's harsh laws regarding free blacks. Jai and her children returned to Florida after the Civil War. Both daughters, named Martha and Anna, married white men and, hence, either could be the legendary princess to whom Hurston refers.*

[1]*Presumably the manuscript that became* Negro Folk-Tales from the Gulf States.

May I say that the decoration in clothing is an extension of tthe primitive application of paint (coloring) to the body?

May I say that all primitive music originated about the drum, and that singing was an attenuation of the drum-beat. The nearer to the primitive, the more prominent the part of the drum. Finally the music (the singers) reach that stage where they can maintain the attenuation independently of, and unconscious of the drum. Such is the European grand opera. Unrithmic attenuation. I mean by attenuation, the listener to the drum will feel the space between beats and will think up devices to fill those spaces. The between-beat becomes more and more complicated untill the music is all between-beat and the consciousness of the dependence upon the drum id lost.

Perhaps in a week or ten days, you shall have the materials. It is very difficult to get a typist down here. The few I find are maddening botches. Thus I am slowed up considerably. Oh, for a New York typist for a month. A great deal of the work is done, in a way. Thus I am hopeful of getting it to you soon.

I hope that you are in the best of health. I hope to see you by the late Summer. I hope that Mrs. Boas is quite well. My love to Drs. Reichard and Benedict.[2]

Love,
Zora Hurston

TO LANGSTON HUGHES

[April 30, 1929—dated at end of letter]

Dear Langston,

You seem to be commanding me to write you before I went to bed. I have been working very strenuously on my religious material today and I am so grateful that you suggested so many phases of it. Really I think our material is going to be grand, Langston.

I am just beginning to hit my stride. At first I tried to do too much in a day. Now I am satisfied with a few pages if they say what I want. I

[2] *Anthropology professors Gladys Reichard and Ruth Benedict; see glossary.*

have to rewrite a lot as you can understand. For I not only want to present the material with all the life and color of my people, I want to leave no loop-holes for the scientific crowd to rend and tear us. But as I work, my, I find new phases from moment to moment. I am convinced that christianity as practised is an attenuated form of nature-worship. Let me explain. The essentials are a belief in the Trinity, baptism, sacrament. Baptism is nothing more than water worship as has been done in one form or the other down thru the ages. Venus rises from the sea (All life coming up out of the water, i.e. water one great necessity of man) Neptune and the other water gods, in every mythology. The name is missing in christianity, but the tribute is paid nevertheless. "Uness ye be born of the water—" I find fire-worship in Christianity too. What was the original purpose of the altar in all churches? For sacred fire and sacrifices BY FIRE. This has been brought over from Judaism. The burnt offering is no longer made, but we keep the symbol in the candles, the alter and the term sacrifice. Symbols my opponents are going to say. But they cannot deny that both water and fire are purely material things and that they symbolize man's tendency to worship those thing which benefit him to a great extent. I believe that the holy ghost is deified fire. It is spoken of too often as fire. On the day of pentecost it was claimed that it appeared as actual tongues of fire. You know of course that the [bapti—x-ed out] sacrament is a relic of cannibalism when men ate men not so much for food as to gain certain qualities the eaten man had. Sympathetic magic pure and simple. They have a nerve to laugh at conjure. I shall ask is the Trinity, Fire, Water, and Earth? Who shall say me nay without making a purely emotional appeal?

Within the week you shall have some copy to read. Be very drastic. I think I shall ask Locke to do some editing as soon as I can get a large batch in shape.

I am leaving the story material almost untouched. I have only tampered with it where the story teller was not clear. I know it is going to read different, but that is the glory of the thing, dont you think?

Yes, I got your Easter letter and I was very happy to have it too. You are always helpful. In fact you are the expedition. I am so glad t that you are soon to graduate I dont know what to do. I know you will feel free. You must feel like Gin Mary[1] shut up in a classroom I know I did.

---

[1]Heroine of Hughes's poem "Ballad of Gin Mary"; she is forced to dry out for a year and a half behind bars.

Oh, I love my religious material. Some of it is priceless. Know what I am attempting? To set an entire Bapt. service word for word and note for note. The prayers are to be done in blank verse for thats what they are, prose poetry. I have four dandy ones. I dont like my sermon as well, but I shall prop it up on every leaning side. I shall cut the dull spots in the service to the minimum and play up the art.

I photographed the house in Fernandina and Godmother thinks its wonderful. I have the picture of two hoodoo doctors and a marvelous woman preacher. I shall illustrate freely.

I know it is a busy time with you, old timer. So if you cant find time for more than cards, I understand. But I do love to hear.

Lovingly,

Zora

Box 815, Eau Gallie, Fla
April 30, 1929.

TO RUTH BENEDICT

[spring 1929?]
c/o Gen. Delivery, Palatka, Fla
or 1663 Evergreen Ave, Jacksonville.

Dear Dr. Benedict,

You have no idea how your kindly letter touched me. Things looked pretty dark just then. My task is harder at times than I had anticipated.

You see there are Negroes with "Race Consciousness" and "Race pride" drilled into them and they resent any thing that looks like harking back to slavery. I am getting along splendidly in a group— everybody digging their heads to tell me things when some "race man" or woman shows up with something like this:

"Whuts all this fur, nohow? some white folks is trying tuh get something so they kin poke fun at us. They want us back in slavery. Why dont they write something bout our school principal—<u>Professah</u> Smith? now they wants tuh drag us down an y'all sittin here like a pack uh dunces pewking yo' guts." Reproachful glances at me. Of course I never let things rest there. That person must be won over, and I havent failed so far, but sometimes it sets the spirit back a few days and delays me.

I am sorry that I did not talk to Dr. Boas about the car first, but I thought he might feel I was trying to get him to get it for me. So I went on so I could carry things out to a satisfactory conclusion, down here and get into the out of the way places—always the most fruitful.

The meeting of the Negro Historical Society[1] was <u>terrible</u>! <u>unspeakable</u>! Such a pandering to popular palate! Dishing up the old race superiority stuff and dragging emperors, queens, statesmen, wholesale into the colored race. I was so shocked at Dr. Woodson's 45 minute flapdoodle fling that I was ashamed to admit I was working for the Association.[2] He had me to return to Jacksonville for it, and wanted me to speak at first. But at the opening "get-together dinner" (such a business for a supposedly scientific meet—sounds so Kiwanis if you get my meaning) [that—x-ed out] I told him how I felt. I simply could not betray Dr. Boas by becoming a soap-box orator to flatter the bishops and elders out of coin. I told him Dr. Boas was the most scientific Anthro. on earth and I must stick to facts so he didn't <u>want</u> <u>me</u> to say a <u>thing</u> after that.

I am enclosing cards for you, Dr. Boas and perhaps Dr. Herskovits would like one. I worked "Dr" Robert's town and he is making me some "hands" (amulets) they will cost $7.00 each. I want them for museum pieces. I wonder if the Dept could spare $14.00 for such a thing! he usually gets $10.00 each but is trying to vamp me—hence the reduction.

Really, I am working very hard. These roads are <u>some</u> rough with palmetto roots, etc. But the little old car gets me anywhere. I send all the material in by hand because I am a little weary by bed-time but I shall type it all as soon as I arrive in New York. I send it so that Dr. Boas will know that I am hustling. By the way he has not answered my letter yet—or it has not been forwarded at any rate.

These snapshots will visualize scenes for you as you read the stories. There are notes on the back of each, note.

[1]Hurston refers to the Association for the Study of Negro Life and History, formed in Chicago in 1915 by Carter Woodson. Its primary purpose was to promote self-awareness among blacks.
[2]Hurston worked for Woodson in 1927.

My right hand gets pretty tired of writing by bed-time as I must take down so much irrelevant stuff in order not to offend, but I shall write you again soon, as shall write Dr. Boas often.

Sincerely yours,
Zora.

Daytona (gen. del.) after 24th of Apr.

TO LANGSTON HUGHES

[spring/summer 1929]
Box 815, Eau Gallie, Fla.

Dear Pal,

I am glad that you saw the other material in New York for I was very eager to know what you thought about it. I am glad you like. About AL,[1] he approves anything that has already been approved.

I told him nothing but asked him about editing the material, and I only asked him tjat because G.[2] said she wanted me to be more cordial to him. I have only written him about four times since I have been down. But thanks for the tip. I shall be even more reticent from now on. I'll keep my big mouf shut.

No, never would I speak of any of the things you tell me. I know they are for me only and I am most discreet. I know that you tell me things to guard my relations with G.

I am trying to get some more children's games all the time. I dont seem to find anymore now. I do hope that I get some down around Miami.

Perhaps there are some slight Negro-Indian admixture in the state, but I doubdt it. The Seminoles are singularly pure. I think they say that there never has been but one half-breed in the Everglades. I hope to see a great deal of them when I go down. I have had them in mind ever since I came to the state

---

[1] *Alain Locke.*
[2] *"Godmother."*

I shall write her every week now, I mean Godmother. Yes, I do think that she is wonderful. Could you broach the magazine article to her? I couldnt very easily. But there is plenty of time for that.

Do you want to look over what I have on our show? Lets call it ""JOOK" that is the word for baudy house in its general sense. It is the club house on these saw-mills and terpentine stills. Then we can bring in all of the songs and gags I have. Shall we work on it at once? I am willing if you are. I know that G. would never consent for me to do so, so you will have to take it all in your name. Man, I got some jook songs! I am getting enough for a volume by itself and I am pushing it close. The folks call playing and singing those songs "jooking". For ex. "Man, he sho kin jook."

I am headed for Miami and some more conjure. Start tomorrow or Sunday. Shall write you from here. Also shall run up to New Orleans on my return and do as you suggest about the lives of some of the doctors.

Yes, I shall fix up the material at once and send it on to New York out of my way. I am eager to do that too. It is a weight upon my mind. I shall hold back the conjure untill I get the other from Miami and put it all together.

NO, I haven't told G. that I sent you the material. I wanted to get your reaction before sending it to her. I have been full of fear and trembling for what I have done. I feel that I have been honest, but the question was, how will it strike others. I started out to manufacture some conclusions and found that I didnt have to. There is too much that is true to say.

I shall get a typist as soon as possible and get it off, after I have classified it. I made no attempt to do that at first. I wrote in bits as I worked it out and felt that you would see that.

Poor Wallie [Thurman], I can sympathize with him. How are the Bontempts[3] getting on? And the Douglases? I am glad Aaron is getting on well. He deserves it. I hope Wallie does something else fine. I am eager to see them all. I hope that I can come up Thanksgiving or Xmas.

Langston, really, MULATTO is superb. I have read it about the hundredth time and it is so good. So truly negroid. Little bits of drama thrust in without notice. Pictures. I dont want to be sloppy, but the tears come every time I read "MOTHER TO SON". You are a

---

[3] *Arna Bontemps, poet, novelist, critic, and librarian, and his wife, Alberta: see glossary.*

great poet. May I dedicate one of my volumes to you?⁴ I hope they
will rate it.

Give me a picture, old thing. I'd like to gaze upon thy pan.

Let me hear when you have time.

Sincerely,

Zora

[on sides and bottom:] Dont you think you had better edit <u>with</u> me?
I need your selection. Taxes very little on that place. No, I wasnt impatient for the material I was collecting jook songs. Pornographic
The trouble with Locke is that he is intellectually dishonest. He is too
eager to be with the winner, if you get what I mean. He wants to autograph all successes, but is afraid to risk an opinion first hand.

TO LANGSTON HUGHES

[May 31, 1929]

Dear Langston,

The stuff is on the rails at last. I thought I was ready before I was
and had to make a lot of changes. Can you read things at once and get
it back to me so that I can get it typed and off to Godmother? Thanks
if you can. I am very eager for her to see what I have done.

I know that you are having a terrific time, in your last few under-
grad days. I am wondering if I should not wait till it is all over before
putting it before you.

Make plenty suggestions. You know I depend on you so much.

I read the Lit. Digest for May 11,¹ and Langston! I was so thrilled.
But it was just as I had said at both New Orleans U. and Straight. I did

---

⁴*None of her volumes was dedicated to Hughes. All were dedicated to white patrons and friends:* Jonah's
Gourd Vine *to Robert Wunsch;* Mules and Men *to Annie Nathan Meyer;* Their Eyes Were Watching God *to
Henry Allen Moe;* Tell My Horse *to Carl Van Vechten; and* Seraph on the Suwannee *to Marjorie Kinnan
Rawlings and Mary Holland.*

---

¹*The* Literary Digest *article referred to is "The Black Belt Now Circles the Globe" and was about Hughes
and other Harlem Renaissance figures who traveled and studied internationally, including Du Bois, "Jossie"
Fauset, Alain Locke, and Walter White. The article calls Hughes the "greatest living, altho still quite young,
Negro poet."*

not say that DuBoise was the greatest for I do not think so, but the
other I did.

I am very eager to see and talk with you now. I have so much to say
and so many things for us to do together. I got a dandy filling-station
skit worked out.

I am thru with the first writing of both the lore and the religion
I shall now set it aside to cool till it grows inside me.

I think what follows is exciting. I have a chance to buy a beautiful
tract of land slap on the Indian river, which as you probably know,
passes for the most beautiful river in the world.[2] It parallels the ocean
all the way with the merest strip of land between so that one has the
river and the ocean together. Now there are fifteen lots in the plat all
surveyed, cleared, and with what could be used for a dandy club house
right on the water. $4,000 is the price. $1,500 down and any terms I
want to make for the rest. Know what I thought of? A Negro art
colony. You, and Wallie, and AAron Douglas and Bruce and me and all
our crowd.[3] It is about three miles from Eau Gallie prper and so we
would be isolated. It is on the Dixie Highway, as fine a piece of road
engineering as there is in the U.S.A. Honest Langston it is a good buy.
You know that everybody down here is dead broke, dont you? They
have never allowed a Negro to buy on the Dixie or the Indian river before and they are not doing it now, except in this case. We dont need to
worry about the white folks as the big wigs in the city have held a
meeting and decided to sell to me. I can, if I choose sell to any of my
friends so long as they belong to my social caste. They want no niggers
in that neighborhood and were quite frank about it, but they said that,
they were agreeably surprised in me, and the last man of the white
business world tip their hats to me, treat me with the utmost respect.
They are all yankees anyway. They say they do not mind Negroes having the plat, but NO niggers. They do not want the property to lose its
future value. I mean the adjacent property. They said, that we can
have a R.R. station there if we ask the R.R.co and have a little town of
our own. I think that would be dandy. I introduced them to you thru
"Fine Clothes" and they had it at the Chamber of Commerce meeting, and you have been discussed at the P.O. for two weeks. The man

[2]*The Indian River runs along the central southeastern coast of Florida.*
[3]*Wallace Thurman, Aaron Douglas, Bruce Nugent.*

who wants to sell is a bootlegger and the Govt. has been hard on him and he is about to lose everything. I think I can get it cheaper than 4000 if I can raise the down payment. That is what he is eager to get. What do you think? I spoke at length of the white attitude because I know you would wonder about it at once. It looks absolutely safe to me, and we could have lots of fun and a lovely place to retire and write on occasion. I am not asking you in a snide way to help on the payment, I really want your opinion. Thats all. I think Aleilia Walker[4] might like the idea don't you? We dont need too many. No big society stuff. Just a neat little colony of kindred souls. I'm crazy to build me a house that looks something like an African king's menage. More alaborate of course.

Love and luck, honey.

[on back of envelope:] Decided at last minute to send material on to G.M. Felt she was anxious. Hope for it back by June 7th.

TO LANGSTON HUGHES

July 23 '29

Dear Langston,

I have been very ill at the Flagler Hosp. in St. Augustine, but the attack was fortunate for by rushing to the Hosp. I found that my stomach was O.K. but my liver was out of order—been pulling me down for 2 years.[1] I am getting on splendidly. Happy with the shadow of stomach operation removed. Shall go to Miami very soon now.

Love—Zora.

---

[4]*A'Lelia Walker, the daughter of millionaire Madame C. J. (Sarah Breedlove) Walker, supported black artists and intellectuals through salons held in her home and was a famous Harlem Renaissance figure.*

---

[1]*Hurston suffered from intestinal and digestive problems her entire life.*

TO LANGSTON HUGHES

Box 42
Sta. Lemon City
Miami, Fla.
Aug. 17, 1929.

Dear Langston,

I am here where it is very nice and I am getting a lot of work done. Wish you here because such good likker can be had. I know that will upset for a week but calm yourself. I shall bring you some if life lasts.

So much improved in health. Glad the doctors had made an error about my stomach. I am getting on fine now and eating plenty.

Wired G. my new address. That stenog. is so slow. I wanted her and you to see things, but you will have to wait a week perhaps. She has promised me so many times that I am afraid to say untill I get the stuff in my hands.

Got some new ideas for skits. One is "White Folks Love." Negro will first try to win the girl by making dicty[1] love, but will fail. then he gets real common and is a knockout. Another is "School" I know that has been done, but not the way I am going to do it. I have something startling in that connection. Another "Cock Robin gets killed in Nigger Town." A travesty on Who killed Cock Robin.? A R.R. track-gang skit and the Jook scenes and the coach scene from my play "Color struck."[2] Dont you think that was the best part of the play? Do you think it could be made a good skit separated from the rest? Thus I have about seven skits about ready. How many could you get together? I am now writing music, and if I do say so, I have one or two snappy airs. I am trying to get the whole together so that you can have a copy and make your additions ad lib.

> Love old thing.
> Zora

[1] *Swell; grand; high-toned.*
[2] *Published in* Fire!!, *November 1926.*

TO LANGSTON HUGHES

[envelope postmarked September 5, 1929]
[sent to Lincoln University, Pa.; forwarded to
128 W. 131st St., New York, N.Y.]

Box 24 Lemon City Sta.
Miami, Fla.

Dear Langston,

Collection going at a rapid rate, but little depressed spiritually at present. I know you must be very busy.

Love,
Zora.

TO LANGSTON HUGHES

[October 15, 1929]

Dear, dear Langston—

Your wonderful wire missed me by a few days. I went to Nassau, Bahamas on the 12th.[1] But found it on my return.

The hurricane was awful. Thought once I'd never get back. That felt like h——— to me too, for I had just collected 20 marvelous Bahamian songs and learned the two native folk dances, and gotten a Congo drum (called Gimbay, accent on last syllable) for us. That would be terrible to miss bringing back now wouldnt it. I got 3 reels of the dancing too.

I know G. told you we are going to press with the stories.[2] Can you not take them & edit them and indicate changes and generally touch

---

[1] *Hurston was there during a violent hurricane, which inspired some of the most memorable scenes in* Their Eyes Were Watching God.

[2] *They didn't. Most of this material did not appear until its 1935 publication in* Mules and Men.

up? I wish that you might be with me personally to point out. We could do it so much quicker. She says the dirty words must be toned down. Of course I knew that. but first I wanted to collect them as they are.

You can use the originals from the safety deposit box in N.Y. and [indicate—x-ed out] make notes for me down here.[5]

Now, Alain said that I was not definite enough about some of the religious cults of New Orleans so I am thinking of returning there shortly and correcting the errors and closing up the conjure volume too. He said I needed to clinch some of my statements by photostatic copies of documents, plus some more definite information, which I had seemed to take for granted the reader would understand. I shall go in November for by that time I shall be about cleaned up here.

I wanted the Nassau material for: (1) There are so many of them in America that their folk lore definitely influences ours in South Fla. (2) For contrast with ours.

The great tragedy is, I found the greatest of the Island hoodoo men the day before I left Nassau. I had only my return ticket and 24 cents so I had to come on. I didnt even have enough to cable G. and they wouldnt send it collect. Should I go back for a week? I could do him in that time as he is favorably worked up to me. Got some good fragments, however before I found him.

Well, honey, your wire did me so much good. Gee, I felt forlorn. Too tired. Been working two years without rest, & behind that all my school life with no rest, no peace of mind. But the Bahamas trip did me a world of good. I got rested while working hard. No flattery, though. You are my mainstay in all crises. No matter what may happen, I feel you can fix it.

Let me hear soon, honey

Lovingly yours,
Zora

Do you need some money?

---

[5] *Much of Hurston's material was apparently stored in Mason's safe-deposit box.*

TO FRANZ BOAS

Box 24, Lemon City Sta.
Miami, Florida
Oct. 20, 1929.

Dear Dr. Boas,

I have been trying to get to this letter for a week. But I wanted to be deliberate about it, and I had 79 pieces of mail waiting for me on my return from the Bahamas and that took some time to dispose of.

Now I find that there is a new birth of creative singing among Negroes. The old songs are not sung so much. New ones are flooding everywhere. New Orleans is the womb of cults and there I find the Protestant churches being as individual as one can imagine. Pagan. I know that you and Dr. Klineberg[1] will be delighted with what you will find. I know of other places where there is some good singing, but it is sort of hit and miss so therefore not so reliable as New Orleans. Mobile is one of those places.

About the material I have been collecting. It is decided that the stories shall be one volume.[2] With what I have here with me, it is complete. Conjure and religion a volume each.[3] Unfinished. I have not quite located all that I want. I hope that you will have time to read the naterial soon. I have tried to be as exact as possible. Keep-to the exact dialect as closely as I could, having the story teller to tell it to me word for word as I write it. This after it has been told to me off hand until I know it myself. But the writing down from the lips is to insure the correct dialect and wording so that I shall not let myself creep in unconsciously.[4]

I thought you might be interested in the Bahamas. The Negroes there are more African, actually know the tribes from which their ancestors came. Some still speak the dialects. I know that you were interested in finding out as near as possible the tribes and localities of the

---

[1] *Anthropologist Dr. Otto Klineberg; see glossary.*

[2] *Originally* Negro Folk-Tales from the Gulf States.

[3] *Combined with the stories to create* Mules and Men.

[4] Mules and Men *includes significant narration of her own experiences and perceptions.*

slaves. The idioms of their dialects appear in the English. The possessive s is dropped. The auxillary verb <u>to be</u> is missing. The plural is
lacking.

Now in the stories, I have omitted all Pat and Mike stories. It is obvious that these are not negroid, but very casual borrowings. The same
goes for the Jewish and Italian stories.

I have been following the works of Odum and Johnson closely and
find that they could hardly be less exact. They have made six or seven
songs out of one song and made one song out of six or seven. There
are instances of English ballads being mistaken for Negro songs. They
have distorted by tearing segments from a whole and bloating the bit
out of all proportion. Let them but hit upon a well turned phrase and
another volume slops off the press. Some of it would be funny if they
were not serious scientists! Or are they?

I shall be in New Orleans before the first and have my address to
you and Dr. Klineberg by then.

Hoping that you are quite well and happy, I am

Most sincerely yours,
Zora Hurston

TO OTTO KLINEBERG

[carbon copy]

Box 24
Lemon City Sta.
Miami, Fla.
Oct. 22, 1929.

My dear Dr. Klineberg,

I find that I am restrained from leaving the employ of my present
employers.[1] I shall be in New Orleans, all right, but to do something
else. Shall be leaving here tomorrow by motor for that city. I cannot
tell you how sorry I am, but I cannot say anything More.

---

[1] *In other words, restricted by the contract with her patron Charlotte Osgood Mason.*

Some good persons to cultivate are: Mr. A. Mabin, 1521 S. Rampart St., Rev. J.A. Alexander, 1205 Perdido St., Wm. Gardner, 410 Saratoga St.. Visit Pilgrim Rest Bapt. church, Howard Ave. between Clio and Erato on Sunday nights, second Sundays in the month. Israel Bapt. Church at Jackson and Clairborne, 1st Sunday nights. (Ada Myles, 2825 Philips St. a member and good singer) Ebenezer Bapt. 2415 Clairborne 4th Sunday. Wm. Gardner, 410 Saratoga, a marvellous singer, both as an improvisor and singer.[2]

My old mail box is 5201, Sta. B, New Orleans. I am writing to tell them to hold my mail there. I have friends at 1900 Jackson Ave., the Blanchets, Mr. Cleo, and his wife Mollie.

I thought I could do it. I felt very sure. I will do anything I

Sincerely and sorrowfully,
(Signed) Zora Hurston

TO FRANZ BOAS

[October 1929]

My dear Dr. Boas,

I am in a trying situation.[1] If Dr. Klineberg will come on, I will give him all the assistance possible.. Perhaps just as much as if I were entirely at liberty. But I wanted you to understand what I am up against. I thought I might drop my work and do this thing with Dr. Klineberg, but I find that I am restrained from doing anything of the sort. However I cannot bear to think of your plans miscarrying. I shall see to it that Dr. K. has the proper openings, help, contacts and whatever else you want. I am in a terrible nervous state. I have been brought up so shortly.. But you shall not be disappointed. When I gave my word I felt safe. Now that things are out of my power to change, I am letting you know, and offering to do my best. I shall be in New Orleans anyway, and so be of service. The salary is not important. In fact I am glad to

---

[2]*Unable to assist Klineberg more directly, Hurston suggests sources and research subjects.*

[1]*In other words, having promised to work with Klineberg but having to answer to Mason's demand that she not do so.*

[be] able to serve you without a cent. Really things will work out better than they sound. I pray that you trust me and send Dr. K. along.

Humbly and sincerely yours,
Zora

I am waiting here as your wire suggested for more from you. Saturday.

TO LANGSTON HUGHES

[postcard postmarked November 2, 1929]
[postcard front: "Seminole Wedding, Miami Florida"]

Dear Lang,

Off to Bahamas again.[1] Was to have gone yesterday but boat delayed. Write you from there. Hope you like your shirt. Will bring you something <u>hard</u> <u>fine</u> from Nassau.[2]

Z.

TO FRANZ BOAS

Box 5201
Sta. B
New Orleans, La.
Dec. 10, 1929.

My dear Dr. Boas,

I think that we are getting on fine here. We have succeeded in breaking down resistance and overcoming the Moens[1] handicap. You remember that unfortunate affair, I think.

---

[1] *Hurston had spent two weeks in the Bahamas the previous month.*
[2] *Liquor?*

---

[1] *Probably Lars Moen (b. 1901), writer, filmmaker, and scientist. Possibly Dutch anthropologist J. L. Moens, who taught Asian studies and art history at Cornell University.*

The collecting of conjure is going on apace. It has just occurred to me to also collect the stories about the doctors as well. That might seem far-fetched, but I think they are important because they show the attitude of the people towards the whole thing.

I am getting much more material. I have much less difficulty now in working so I am beginning to feel that, even if I had not collected much since I have been down here, I have acquired a certain technique.

I want to make this conjure work very thorough and inclusive. As soon as I have the latest material assembled in some order, I shall let you have it.

I am not seeking stories particularly now, but of course all that I can find, I grab. I am just breaking down the Creole resistance so I hope now to include some of theirs too.

Many more song-dances have been added to the material you have. Thirty-five from the Bahamas.

There is a young Negro Prof. of Psychology teaching at one of [the] colleges here who is tremendously interested in helping us, and we think he is going to be lots of use. Hawkins is his name. He is eager to go into Anthro. now and says that he is coming to see you when he comes to New York.

I suppose Dr. Klineberg has gone over the ground so that I wrote to speak of the things he doesnt know about.

> Much love and reverence,
> Sincerely,
> Zora Hurston

[on side:] Dr. Klineberg is <u>very</u> fine to work with

TO LANGSTON HUGHES

[December 10, 1929—dated at end of letter]

Dearest Langston

Your wires and your letters have all come safely. All helped but your last letter comforted my soul like dreamless sleep.

Now I am getting much more conjure material here in New Orleans, and I shall fet a great deal more in the Bahamas. I am hoping for enough material to make an entire volume of just that. The religion would not be out of place in the volume, but I do think the song would jar. I have enough of them for a separate volume anyway. About a hundred. That ought to be enough I think. But we can discuss that when I am there.

It is so good to have the counsel of both you and Alain.

So sorry about the packing, but I thought I had done a good job in each case. That gold thing had some bits falling off when I got it, I hope it was not further damaged.

Well, I tell you, Langston, I am nothing without you. Thats no flattery either. We will talk a lot when I get there.

I shall try to get back to the Bahamas for Xmas so that I can get some more pictures. That is their carnival season, and besides I have a letter saying that my man is back again, but may leave before long for Haiti. I shall sail from there for New York. That means I am running here with my tongue hanging out to get everything I see. I have come to the conclusion that the birth certificate of Marie Laveau is not so important. It is pretty well established about her birth, life and death.[1] I shall photograph her tomb. I am finding so much more on my return here than I thought. Shows that I am getting better as a collector. I may have to ask for more time, but I hope not. G. has said that I may have it if I wish.

> Love ad everything deep and fine, Honey
> Lovingly,
> Zora

Dec. 10, 1929

---

[1] *To this day, the birth and death dates of Marie Laveau, legendary hoodoo priestess of New Orleans, remain in debate; see glossary.*

TO LANGSTON HUGHES

[winter 1929/30]

Dear Langston,

New Orleans again. I was expecting to go to Nassau, but my look-
out over there warned me not to come for a few weeks. You see the
Govt. is prosecuting obear [obeah] men (hoodoo doctors) pretty stre-
nously at present and my man found he was under suspicion so he
went to one of the outer islands to lie low till things calm down.

Now I need you. I am simply wasting away with fear. You see, I
had to have a new car. Just HAD to. I had mentioned the matter to G
once and she simply elploded. You can see how I felt for the insinua-
tion was that I was extravagant or took her for a good thing. Neither
was soothing to my self-respect. So this time when I foud I must spend
about $95. to put the old bus in shape I just took in on myself to go
and dicker for one and keep my big mouth shut. The company, however wrote to see if my references were right, so she learned of it. She
wrote me a letter that hurt me thru and thru. She asked "Why couldnt
Negroes be trusted?" But she later sent the $400 to pay for the car.
Now another situation arose. You know that the auto business has succeeded the horse in more ways than one. The used-car dealer is every
bit the match of the horse trader. They will lie like cross-ties from
Montreal to Mexico. The car is delivered 'as is' so that anything wrong
is just too bad after you have traded. They know how to dope them too
so that the first 50–100 miles will go just dandy. Then the trouble
commences. This one I bought started to knocking before the hundred
miles so I decided I wasnt going to be bothered any more so I turned it
in at once and put the credit on a new car. Balance nearly $300. Now I
can pay it out of my allowance. I am just praying that she wont find
out what I have done. I dont feel that I have done wrong for nobody
knows what inconvenience I have suffered fooling with old cars. Always something to fix. Money I ought to spend on my work is spent on
the old can and keeping me strapped. I just feel that she ought not to
exert herself to supervise every little detail. It destroys my self-respect
and utterly demoralizes me for weeks. I know you can appreciate what

I mean. I do care for her deeply, dont forget that. That is why I cant endure to get at odds with her. I dont want anything but to get at my work with the least possible trouble.

No, I havent heard a word about the trip yet. But then I didnt write, waiting to see what I should do about Nassau or New Orleans. But I am writing tonight. I have been so full of apprehensions too that I am half ill. I'd love to come and talk to you more than anything I know, Langston.

I am getting some conjure stories to include in my book of conjure with the actual ceremonies I already have. Do you like the idea? It just occurred to me to put down all the miraculous tales the people tell me about conjure and witchcraft. Sort of throw them in to break the monotony.

Working on religion again too. This is a fine city for it too. I want to close out all the volumes as soon as I can. When it is all in you and I can take plenty of time to edit it. Locke will be a great help too, but I am afraid he will not see it just as we do.

Do you think I have enough conversions, experiences, etc.? I can get more. Should I get another sermon? More prayers? I am now tracing some of the variations on the Protestant theme like the Sanctified, Rollers, Jumpers, Spiritualists. I mean their influence on Negro religious experience. I find them very important. They are a revolt against the sterile rituals of the Protestant church. A reversion to paganism.

I am glad to hear you say you think of writing prose.[1] A poet should turn out marvelous prose. Kipling, Sir Walter Scott, Shakespeare, are fine examples of men who did both. Do let us see as soon as you feel right to do so. I am stuffed with things I'd like to write now and I shall get down hard at it as soon as I clear this work up.

Hope you see the Nassau dances I sent G. Three reels if they dont cut them at the laborotory. The drum is in New York now.

Poor Wallie! I wish he might get a divorce.[2] That is what I am going to do. Should I do it now, or should I wait till the job is over? Herbert is interning at the City Hosp. in St. Louis. I am just not going to let myself be annoyed. I have too much to do and too much to live for to have some one nagging me and destroying my nervous force.

---

[1] *Hughes published the novel* Not Without Laughter *in 1930.*

[2] *Although reportedly homosexual, Thurman attempted a brief but unsuccessful marriage to Louise Thompson.*

Are you thinking of taking any further degrees, or is one enough for you? I have been wondering about that since your graduation.

Had a letter from Dorothy West. She wants me to come to Paris with her. Says Eric [Walrond] and Countee [Cullen] and Agusta Savage[3] are there and so she and I ought to be there. What is the matter with Helene [Johnson]?

Well, darling, do what you can for me. I want to come up there very much for Thanksgiving. Save me in the other matter if you have the chance. I have told you all about it so you would have the facts in hand. I feel skeered to death, still I think I did the sensible thing after all, but, Oh, I fear getting caught!

> Love and so long, Langston.
> Most sincerely,
> Zora.

Your quarters sound lovely! I can play a little golf and I have been to that very club.

> Box 5201
> Sta. B
> New Orleans, La.

[on back of page two, Hughes drafted:] Don't be afraid for if one thing ends there's always something else[.] would advise telling about car although may explode again[.] she loves you too much to completely blow you out[.] best way work with her is nothing hidden then you have solid foundation to go on[.] explosions are part of the business.

---

[1]*Sculptor Augusta Savage; see glossary.*

"I LIKE WORKING HARD"

The Thirties

Overleaf:
Hurston collecting folklore from Rochelle French and Gabrielle Brown,
Eatonville, 1935.

"The depression did away with money for research," Hurston noted in her autobiography.[1] Actually, for the black artists and intellectuals of the Harlem Renaissance, the Depression did away with just about everything. The magazines, salons, foundations, public programs, awards, prizes, and travel opportunities that fed the Harlem Renaissance did not dry up overnight. But the stock market's crash was the beginning of the end for the "vogue"[2] in African American arts.

African Americans were harder hit than whites during the Depression. Black unemployment was as much as three times higher than it was for whites. Hurston noted a sense of exhaustion and disappointment replacing the energetic spirit of the Harlem Renaissance. "Some of my friends are all tired and worn out—looking like death eating crackers," she wrote Lawrence Jordan.[3]

What conditions did black, female, working-class New Yorkers face in the thirties? Did Hurston know about New York City's infamous "slave markets"? It was virtually impossible to live in New York and not know about them. African American women by the thousands, many of whom had never done domestic work before, lined the streets of Manhattan, Brooklyn, and the Bronx hoping for a day's domestic work. According to black feminist historian Jacqueline Jones, there were as many as two hundred of these "marts" in New York City alone. The sight of these women willing to work for low wages, in

[1] *Zora Neale Hurston*, Dust Tracks on a Road *(New York: HarperCollins, 1991)*, p. 153.
[2] *David Levering Lewis*, When Harlem Was in Vogue *(New York: Oxford University Press, 1979)*.
[3] *Hurston to Lawrence Jordan, May 31, 1930.*

some cases merely for carfare and food, must have been chilling. By the end of the decade, Jones reports, over 80 percent of black women in the nation would say that they had done domestic work.[4] How insulated was a writer and scholar like Hurston from such economic devastation?

Harlem was especially hard hit in the Depression, partly because blacks had seen larger economic gains there than elsewhere. Black ownership of real estate slid from 35 percent to a mere 5 percent, according to Urban League figures. Black-owned businesses suffered similar declines. The "don't buy where you can't work" movement, much discussed throughout Harlem, protested these conditions but could do little to change them. Many of Harlem's blacks—more than half by some accounts—had already experienced significant displacement in migrating from the South. The upheaval wrought by the Depression added to that sense. The unique black businesses that had produced some of the nation's first black millionaires—hair-care entrepreneurs Madame C. J. Walker and Hurston's friend Annie Pope Malone among them—were all but destroyed by the new economic conditions.

Hurston's autobiography says little about the Depression, perhaps because she was never fully a member of those circles most affected. Or perhaps it was not really new to *her*. As Jones puts it, "depression-like conditions were not new for the vast majority of black Americans."[5]

At no time in her life had Hurston been able to count on economic security. The 1930s, however, were Hurston's professional heyday, and for the first time, she *could* count on the security of a career, if not many of its financial rewards. At the start of the decade, she wrote Boas that "at present I am working furiously."[6] "Working like a slave and liking it," she reiterated to a friend in 1935.[7]

By far the largest number of Hurston's surviving letters were written in the thirties. While constantly busy and often on the road, she was careful to stay in touch with friends and benefactors, keeping them apprised of her whereabouts and plans. It was not uncommon for her to write as many as two or three letters on a given day, many of them three- or four-page, single-spaced, laboriously typed documents (in her

[4]*Jacqueline Jones,* Labor of Love, Labor of Sorrow: Black Women, Work, and the Family, from Slavery to the Present *(New York: Vintage, 1986).*

[5]*Ibid., p. 196.*

[6]*Hurston to Franz Boas, April 16, 1930.*

[7]*Hurston to Edwin Osgood Grover, May 14, 1935.*

entire life she never owned a dependable typewriter) that sometimes served as outlines or rough drafts of essays and articles to come. There were days when she traveled, drafted an essay, organized and attended an elaborate rehearsal, and still made time to type as many as a dozen pages of letters, including extensive correspondence with Langston Hughes, Melville Herskovits, Franz Boas, Charlotte Osgood Mason, Carl Van Vechten, Ruth Benedict, Dorothy West, Walter White, and James Weldon Johnson.

Amazingly enough, these voluminous letters are not the bulk of what she produced in this decade. Most of her major publications—*Jonah's Gourd Vine, Mules and Men, Their Eyes Were Watching God, Tell My Horse, Moses, Man of the Mountain, Barracoon,* and *Mule Bone*—were written in the thirties. Additionally, Hurston's fieldwork in the Bahamas, Jamaica, and Haiti was completed during these years, involving demanding travel, field notes, and reports. She worked on theater productions, including *Fast and Furious, Batouala, Mules and Men, The Great Day, From Sun to Sun,* and *Singing Steel,* hauling a troupe that numbered as many as sixty people from New York to Washington, D.C., St. Louis, Chicago, Nashville, and Florida. She taught at a number of colleges, including Rollins, Bethune-Cookman, and North Carolina College for Negroes. She collected folk music. She worked for the Federal Theater Project and the Federal Writers' Project, supervising its Florida Negro Division. She was seriously ill with a persistent and recurrent stomach ailment, various aches and pains, and a mysterious wrist problem, yet somehow she found time and energy for at least one serious love affair (Hurston was particularly secretive about her love life) and a brief marriage to a man twenty-five years her junior. No wonder Hurston didn't have much to say about the Depression. Freed from the restraints of her various patronage relationships by 1932—she never accepted patronage again—this was a professionally rich and liberating time for her, although she certainly did have to "work hard" to reap its rewards.

When she ended her contract with Mason early in 1931, Hurston could not have predicted her financial future or the risks she would be taking by pursuing her dreams for scholarship, publishing, and the theater. Just prior to ending the contract, the *Mule Bone* collaboration with Langston Hughes had broken down, a loss she described to Arna Bontemps as "the cross of my life." *Fast and Furious,* for which she had held high hopes, opened and closed in one September week. Her collaboration with Hall Johnson—meant to compensate for the *Fast and Furious* disappointment—also collapsed at the end of 1931. *Barracoon* was finished, but even with editor Harry Block's assistance, it didn't seem to be going anywhere. The intriguing possibility of working with Paul Robeson and others on an opera of René Maran's enormously popular and controversial French novel about Africa, *Batouala*, finally came to nothing.

The year 1932 did not produce more income. Although her folklore production *The Great Day* was a success with New York critics, it left her hundreds of dollars in debt to Mason. To make matters worse, Hurston had reason to believe that both Mason and Locke had written her off as a failure. In April she received a formal dressing-down from Locke. Her letter to Mason, written a few days later, rings with resignation. "I understand," she wrote, that "both you and Alain feel that I have lost my grip." She was ready to leave New York and return to Eatonville, she told Mason. "I cannot comment on that because anything I might say could be construed as a bid for my own comfort. I shall leave that to time. For after all you are the last word, no matter what I do or dont. I can neither be present when you sit in judgment, nor cry out under sentence. You cannot be wrong, for everything that I am, I am because you made me. You can smile upon me, and you can look off towards immensity and be equally right. You have been gracious, but you were following no law except your inclination."[8]

There were other disappointments as well. Hurston spent many years trying to publish, first, *Negro Folk-Tales from the Gulf States* and then its much-amended version, *Mules and Men*. Her experience with the Lippincott Company in 1933 finally turned the tide. Bertram Lippincott gave Hurston the confirmation that she could *write*. After seeing a short story of hers, he contacted her to ask if she was working on a novel. She wasn't. But in a burst of self-confidence, she answered "yes" and set about to produce one. *Jonah's Gourd Vine* was written in a mere nine weeks, while Hurston was supported by small loans from neighbors and family. Lippincott accepted it right away, paving the way to also accept *Mules and Men* a few months later, in the spring of 1934. To get one book published, Hurston had needed to write another one, but suddenly, she was a two-book author. The fruit of her frenzied two-month effort was safely placed with one of the country's most

[8]*Hurston to Charlotte Osgood Mason, April 4, 1932.*

prestigious publishers, and the folklore book to which she had given her heart finally had a home. In *Dust Tracks,* she described her feelings: "I never expect to have a greater thrill than that wire [of acceptance from Lippincott] gave me. You know the feeling when you found your first pubic hair. Greater than that."[9] There are no letters to Mason, Locke, Hughes, or any of her friends describing her good fortune. In fact, there are no surviving letters at all from the crucial months between March and December 1933. Perhaps Hurston was too busy working to keep up her usual level of correspondence.

Lippincott's interest ushered in more "working hard." At the end of 1933, Hurston was invited to start a drama school at Bethune-Cookman College, followed by the possibility of a similar project at Fisk, and then by successful national performances of her theater production *The Great Day.* Contrary to her claim that "the Depression did away with money for research," Hurston received more research funding in the thirties than at any other time. After a performance of *The Great Day* in Chicago,[10] she was invited to apply for a Rosenwald Fellowship. The Rosenwald Foundation suggested that she pursue a Ph.D., a longtime ambition which Mason had thwarted. "Oh, Dr. Boas, you dont know how I have longed for a chance to stay at Columbia and study," she wrote.[11]

Incorporated in Chicago in 1917, the Rosenwald Foundation had as its mission the advancement of "Negro welfare" and "black-white relations." Over a period of thirty-one years, it raised more than $20 million and gave grants to James Baldwin, Arna Bontemps, Sterling Brown, W. E. B. Du Bois, Aaron Douglas, William S. Braithwaite, and others. In the thirties, the Rosenwald was one of the few funding sources available to African Americans, and it was the only major funding source that made the support of African Americans its main objective. The Rosenwald sought out Hurston, not the other way around. This was a telling measure of her status.

In her Rosenwald application, Hurston adopted all the self-possession appropriate to a seasoned professional. "The major problem in my field," she wrote, is that collecting "must be done by individuals feeling the material as well as seeing it objectively. In order to feel and appreciate the nuances one must be of the group." She did more than

[9]*Hurston,* Dust Tracks, *p. 155.*
[10]*Retitled* The Singing Steel.
[11]*Hurston to Franz Boas, December 14, 1934.*

capitalize on her insider status. She also expressed her interest in furthering scholarly work and acknowledged that she needed "further training and discipline in order to better adapt methods of work to the material."[12] Her budget proposal asked for $4,407.50 to complete her Ph.D., which she anticipated could be done in a mere two and a half years, including fieldwork. The application was accepted on December 19, five days after Hurston mailed it. The foundation offered $3,000 to be spent as follows: $100 a month for up to twenty-four months of graduate study; $500 for fieldwork; and $100 to return to New York. This was solid support.

Almost immediately, however, the arrangement began to collapse. On December 20, just one day after awarding Hurston the fellowship, Rosenwald director Edwin Embree wrote a letter to Charles S. Johnson describing what he and the other Rosenwald officials saw as Hurston's "conspicuous outs." "She seems to all of us to need, very badly, further discipline both intellectually and personally. The tempering which comes from hard, even, routine study," he wrote, "may turn what in part is still crude iron into fine steel." They felt that for her to attempt a school of black drama in Nashville, as she and Fisk president Thomas Jones had discussed, would "add to her personal distress and create for herself intellectual confusion." She would be likely to "cause a great deal of trouble" at a college, he added.[13] Hurston, at the time these patronizing remarks were penned, was a mature woman of forty-three (her application gave her birth date as 1902, or thirty-two years old), the published author of many short stories and two books, and a successful producer of folklore productions. Embree, moreover, was a trained sociologist and the son of famous abolitionists. He was widely known and well regarded among African Americans for his antiracist politics. It is difficult to explain why the Rosenwald—or Embree himself—so suddenly lost faith in Hurston. The condescension, coming so quickly on the heels of strong support, must have been baffling to her.

Franz Boas tried to intervene. He backed Hurston's research plan, and she enrolled at Columbia, as planned. In January, Embree reiterated to Boas that so long as "you and your associates at Columbia are willing to assume direction of her work, we are willing to provide her with modest support for a two-year period."[14] Boas wrote back immedi-

[12]*Fellowship application to the Julius Rosenwald Fund, Fisk University, December 14, 1934.*

[13]*Edwin Embree to Charles S. Johnson, December 20, 1934, Rosenwald Papers, Fisk University.*

[14]*Edwin Embree to Franz Boaz [sic], January 2, 1935, Rosenwald Papers, Fisk University.*

ately that "we all believe in the ability of Miss Hurston and are willing to undertake a rather detailed direction of her studies."[15] There was some question, early in January, of whether Hurston would be better off at Columbia—which had no courses at all on African Americans— or with Melville Herskovits at Northwestern, where a graduate curriculum on Africa and African Americans was getting under way. By January 14, she and Boas had resolved in favor of Columbia and were keeping Embree carefully apprised of their plans.

But on January 21, the foundation reduced Hurston's promised, multiyear $3,000 grant to a one-semester fellowship totaling only $700, hardly adequate for the pursuit of the serious, rigorous, and "disciplined" graduate study they claimed she needed. Their assertion, strangely enough, was that her letters "do not indicate a permanent plan."[16] Boas wrote Embree in March to protest. Embree responded that they were "distressed" at Hurston's "over-zealousness in her own behalf" and at what they called "her lack of tendency to serious quiet scholarship." Apparently taking it for granted that all whites were as patronizing about blacks (or women?) as he was, Embree declared that "I write thus frankly because I know your interest in such matters is the same as ours."[17] Boas protested again, but Embree was unmoved. Hurston's response was to skip her spring classes. Her summary report to the foundation later stated that while a single semester's support was not sufficient to help "appreciably in Anthropology," she had made use of the semester's time to write two plays and her next novel. The Rosenwald experience, coming on the heels of the demise of her professional and personal relationships with Mason, Hughes, Hall Johnson, and Louise Thompson, could not have done much good for Hurston's opinion of outside help.

But in early 1936, Hurston was awarded and accepted a Guggenheim Fellowship. Founded in 1925 by Senator Simon Guggenheim, the Guggenheim Foundation was one of the most farsighted and beneficent foundations in the country. Built on the principle that philanthropies should find smart people, fund them, and leave them alone, the Guggenheim Foundation did not scrutinize its fellows as did the Rosenwald. The secretary-general of the foundation, Henry Allen Moe, was in many ways Embree's opposite. Hurston developed a close

[15]*Franz Boas to Edwin Embree, January 7, 1935, Rosenwald Papers, Fisk University.*

[16]*Edwin Embree to Zora Neale Hurston, January 21, 1935, Rosenwald Papers, Fisk University.*

[17]*Edwin Embree to Franz Boas, March 26, 1935, Rosenwald Papers, Fisk University.*

personal relationship with Moe, as did most of the fellows he funded. Her long, newsy letters to him are among the most crafted and interesting she ever wrote. Having internalized too many lessons from her Rosenwald experience, perhaps, Hurston was, however, uncomfortably deferential to Moe. Her attempts to ingratiate herself by constantly soliciting Moe's advice prompted a curt reply. When she persisted in calling him "Bossman," Moe replied that "I am not <u>busha</u> [boss]. The Fellows are <u>busha</u>. The Foundation exists for them. So, busha (or whatever the feminine is), don't hesitate please, to let me know what's what and what you want."[18]

With this fellowship's support, Hurston lived in Jamaica from April through September 1936, studying the culture of the Maroons (descendants of escaped slaves). In September, she went to Haiti, where she began important research on hoodoo culture and wrote her finest work, *Their Eyes Were Watching God*, a novel she completed in only seven weeks. In spite of differences in temperament, Hurston and Moe's friendship was warm and cordial, and Hurston dedicated *Their Eyes Were Watching God* to him. Hurston returned to the United States briefly in the winter, applied for a second Guggenheim, which she received, and arrived in Haiti again in March.

This was a difficult trip. While completing her work on hoodoo culture, Hurston became violently ill. She had been plagued with stomach problems for years, possibly from tension and fatigue and possibly from bacteria picked up on her travels. But this bout was severe enough that Hurston feared for her life. She believed that she had gone too far in her work on the "terrible" Petro gods and was being either punished or warned. She backed off, spent a month recuperating, then returned to the United States in September, arriving in time for the appearance of *Their Eyes Were Watching God* and a switch of professional gears. Having combined folklore and fiction during her time in Haiti, she now looked to mix folklore and drama.

Hurston's status as a folklorist has never been fully appreciated. In part, this may be because the letters that express many of her most important folklore ideas have never before been available. But folklore's place in 1930s culture is also under-studied. Often romanticized today as an esoteric or ephemeral field, folklore had solid academic standing

---

[18] *Henry Allen Moe to Zora Neale Hurston, September 28, 1936.*

in the thirties. It was a volatile site of competing interests. Academics, patriots, and leftists all sought to claim folklore as their own.

For academics, folklore was a central aspect of American culture, closely tied to sociology and anthropology. The best folklore department in the nation was Columbia University's folk-song department. Hurston's collections of blues and folk music were a natural outgrowth of her anthropological training there. Ruth Benedict, the acting head of Columbia's renowned anthropology department, also served as editor of the *Journal of American Folklore.*

Nonacademic interest in folklore was even stronger. Folk dancing had been widely promoted since the early 1900s as a "wholesome" way to educate children about the nation. Schools and colleges across the nation formed folk-dance clubs. Hurston's alma mater, Barnard, had— and continues—a tradition of extracurricular folk dance. The New School for Social Research offered classes in "Folk Songs and Dances of Many Peoples," and anthropologists who specialized in dance, such as Hurston's friends Jane Belo and Katharane Mershon and her rival, Katherine Dunham, were instrumental in founding influential folk-dance schools.

Much of the general interest in folklore was nationalistic. President Franklin D. Roosevelt wrote playwright and folklorist Paul Green: "We in the United States are amazingly rich in the elements from which to weave a culture. We have the best of man's past on which to draw, brought to us by our native folk and folk from all parts of the world." Many saw academics as the advance guard of a movement to save that rich culture of American diversity. Concerned that American folk culture could become "as uniform, as uninteresting and as impermanent as a factory-made quilt," the *Washington Post* reporter trusted that "the scholars with their notebooks and recording machines, are doing their best to salvage something from the ruins."[19] Not all folklorists were quite so sanguine about academics, however. Sarah Gertrude Knott, the director of the National Folk Festival Association, which sponsored folk festivals across the country to educate the nation about its various cultures, took the position that "academic research is of no value in prolonging the active life of a traditional song or dance."[20]

---

[19] *Jean Delaney,* Washington Post, *February 19, 1939.*
[20] Washington Post, *February 19, 1939.*

The national folklore movement was the product of collaboration between academics and nonacademics, a collaboration for which Hurston was a natural. Her letters show a particularly nuanced understanding of the gaps between academic and nonacademic appreciations of folklore. Her friend Paul Green served as president of Knott's folklore association. And its planning commission included many academics, including Hurston's associates Robert Wunsch of Rollins and Thomas E. Jones of Fisk. According to the "Draft Statement of the Program for the National Folk Festival and Cooperating Agencies," the national organization would depend heavily on university courses in folklore. Among the schools committed to this agenda were the Black Mountain College of North Carolina, Rollins College, Harvard University, the University of New Mexico (which offered a course on "Spanish Folk Lore" given by another of Hurston's correspondents, folklorist and director of the Library of Congress's folklore program, Benjamin A. Botkin), the University of Oklahoma, the University of North Carolina, Fisk University, and Vanderbilt University. These courses were designed to "recognize and appreciate the value and charm of this material to our national life," and the national organization, echoing Roosevelt, felt that it was crucial to preserve "folk materials from the disintegrating influences of the 'American melting pot.'"[21] In spite of this commitment to cultural diversity, Hurston appears to have been the only black person appointed to the national committee, and she was not given the high-level position her background called for.

The first National Folk Festival, at which Hurston and her theater troupe performed, was held in St. Louis in April 1934. It opened with a thousand-member choir singing Negro spirituals. Hurston's troupe performed along with various other shows of "authentic" music and dance presented by: lumberjacks, Indians, Spanish Americans, Appalachian fiddlers, cowboys, "mountain musicians," French Creole singers and dancers, harp players, square dancers, New England "sea chantey" singers, "Ozark legend" storytellers, singers from the Old Sailors' Home of Staten Island, Vermont balladeers, Carolina "country courtship" performers, and Mormons.[22] This festival was an enormous success, as were the subsequent local and national festivals that copied it. All American folklore may have been lumped together indiscrimi-

[21] *Draft Statement of the Program for the National Folk Festival and Cooperating Agencies, Thomas Jones Papers, Fisk University.*
[22] St. Louis Globe, *April 22, 1934.*

nately. But it was also well loved. Her letters show us that Hurston welcomed the enthusiasm while resenting its naïveté.

If the St. Louis festivals and others like it were important to building a spirit of national patriotism, the American Left had its own reasons to celebrate folklore and cultural diversity. According to Michael Denning, "the folk music revival was spearheaded by Communists."[23] Although it was jazz and not the folk music of singers like Woody Guthrie, Huddie "Leadbelly" Ledbetter, and Pete Seeger that formed "the soundtrack of the Popular Front,"[24] the kind of vernacular music Hurston collected was much sought after by leftist groups like the Industrial Workers of the World (IWW). Unions and other leftist organizations used blues and folk music to educate people about the value of denigrated cultures. Hurston expressed a consistent antagonism toward American communists in her essays and her letters,[25] but in this one instance, she and the Communist Party saw eye-to-eye. Her letters reveal a flexibility in her political thought about this matter that is evident in none of her other writing.

Given her training in folklore, Hurston was an obvious choice for the Federal Theater Project, newly organized in 1935 through the Works Progress Administration. She was hired as a drama coach at $28.36 a week and worked with such professionals as Orson Welles and John Houseman. Unfortunately, there are no letters about the six months she worked on the project, but we know that Hurston was kept in a coaching or "helping" role, a serious underutilization of her vast experience with the theater, and a rehearsal for her bad experience with the Federal Writers' Project later in the decade.

Hurston's interests throughout the thirties had already been more or less evenly divided between her academic publications—*Mules and Men, Tell My Horse,* and her essays—and her efforts to stage folklore for popular audiences. While she had more success with the former, her letters reveal that theatrical production was, in fact, much more impor-

---

[21]*Michael Denning,* The Cultural Front: The Laboring of American Culture in the Twentieth Century *(London: Verso, 1996), p. 283.*

[24]*Ibid., p. 329.*

[21]*Nowhere more forcefully than in "Why The Negro Won't Buy Communism," which Hurston published in the* American Legion Magazine *in June 1951, under a banner headline that read, "Despite the high-pressure selling of the Paul Robesons, the Benjamin Davises and the Howard Fasts, the American Negro is too smart to fall for Joe Stalin's brand of up-to-date slavery." Hurston's thesis here, one she also expresses in some of her letters, is that the "communists hope and pray to use us to do their dirty work in the way of sabotage and espionage." Deeply resenting the idea that communists cast American blacks as "pitiful," Hurston scornfully rejected any proffered "help" from the Party.*

tant to her. She saw drama as the heart of black experience. In "Characteristics of Negro Expression," Hurston wrote that there is one thing "that permeates [the Negro's] entire self. And that thing is drama."[26] Hurston was not alone in singling out black theater. As Henry Louis Gates, Jr., puts it: "among all of the black arts, greater expectations were held for none more than for black theatre."[27]

It is not surprising, then, that Hurston would be upset to see black drama appropriated by whites. As early as the twenties, Hurston had been disturbed by white folklorists staging black material. In a letter to Alain Locke in May 1928, Hurston wrote that she had just received a recent folklore collection by white folklorists Howard Odum and Guy Johnson and that although she had been "almost afraid to read it, fearful lest they had beat us to it in the matter of songs," she was relieved to see that "they evidently know nothing of the how folk-songs grow."[28] "It makes me sick," Hurston confided to Hughes, "to see how these cheap white folks are grabbing our stuff and ruining it. I am almost sick—my one consolation being that they never do it right and so there is still a chance for us."[29] The ignorance of white collectors was cold comfort, however, when they had all the resources and connections. In the forties, she was still expressing concern that whites would appropriate and exploit black materials.

Hurston felt that most of the so-called black drama available to the public was inauthentic, watered down, and washed out. She wanted true black drama brought to the American stage: "<u>real</u> Negro art theatre."[30] Drama could be profitable. Even the "inauthentic" Broadway shows Hurston detested were often a success. *Shuffle Along,* for example, the first black show of the twenties, had a run of over five hundred performances. It attracted so many people that the street where it played had to be blocked off to traffic. Other white shows about blacks, such as *Porgy and Bess* and *The Green Pastures,* were also hits. Hurston had been involved in two white-authored black dramas—*Fast and Furious* and *Jungle Scandals*—and was horrified to see how the producers "squeezed all Negro-ness out of every thing."[31] Meanwhile, black the-

[26] *Nancy Cunard, ed.,* Negro: An Anthology *(London: Wishart, 1934).*

[27] *Henry Louis Gates, Jr., ed.,* Mule Bone: A Comedy of Negro Life, *by Langston Hughes and Zora Neale Hurston (New York: HarperCollins, 1991), p. 15.*

[28] *Hurston to Alain Locke, May 10, 1928.*

[29] *Hurston to Langston Hughes, September 20, 1928.*

[30] *Hurston to Langston Hughes, April 12, 1928.*

[31] *Hurston to Charlotte Osgood Mason, September 25, 1931.*

ater companies such as the Krigwa Players, the New Negro Art Theater, the Harlem Experimental Theater, and the Gilpin Players struggled along on promises and debt. Hurston's idea of theater resonated
with Du Bois's view that black art must advance "the cause." "Her dramatic productions revealed the artistic content of the Afro-American
heritage," Hemenway writes; "they were intended to instill race
pride."[32] Pride could only come, Hurston argued, from making visible
what was real and intrinsic in the "Negro self," never from imitating
others. "Fawn as you will," Hurston wrote. "Spend an eternity standing awe struck. Roll your eyes in ecstasy and ape his [the white man's]
every move, but until we have placed something upon his street corner
that is our own, we are right back where we were when they filed our
iron collar off."[33]

Hurston's theatrical ambitions were difficult to realize. Mason was
determined that Hurston not "waste" her material on the commercial
stage. Funding was difficult to come by. The public preferred white
dramas about blacks—where holdovers from minstrelsy such as shuf-
fling, banjos, and overblown speech were still being shown—to the
kind of drama Hurston produced. She lacked the right Broadway connections and was known as a folklorist and anthropologist, not a reliable commercial producer. The Federal Theater Project could have
helped Hurston realize these ambitions. Unfortunately, its administra-
tors clung to their own agendas.

Hurston persisted. Her first attempt to bring a native, authentic,
black theater to the stage was the ill-fated *Mule Bone*. Set in Eatonville,
Mule Bone is about a quarrel between two boys—one Methodist and
one Baptist—over a girl. The story of the *Mule Bone* fiasco is a long
and complicated one.[34] Hurston's letters are virtually the only record of
her side of the story. *Mule Bone* was never produced during Hurston's
(or Hughes's) lifetime. Worse, it seemed to precipitate the breakdown
of her friendship with Hughes. An accurate picture of the rupture
helps explain her later attitudes toward theater, collaboration, friend-

[32]*Robert Hemenway, Zora Neale Hurston: A Literary Biography (Urbana: University of Illinois Press, 1977),
p. 205.*
[33]*Zora Neale Hurston, "Race Cannot Become Great Until It Recognizes Its Talent," Washington Tribune,
December 29, 1934.*
[34]*Readers with a particular interest in the Mule Bone story should consult Hemenway's biography, Langston
Hughes's The Big Sea, Arnold Rampersad's biography of Langston Hughes, or the edition of Mule Bone
edited by George Houston Bass and Henry Louis Gates, Jr. (New York: HarperCollins, 1991). In their edition,
Bass and Gates reprint material from Hemenway, Hughes, and Rampersad, as well as relevant correspondence.*

ship, and trust. Her letters about this episode are some of the most painful and heartfelt she ever wrote.

Is it possible to have an accurate picture of something that has been called "the most notorious literary quarrel in African-American cultural history"?[35] Perhaps not. Every Harlem Renaissance historian has his or her own theory of blame. In Hemenway's words, "the circumstances surrounding the play will always remain a mystery."[36] His view is that the *Mule Bone* disaster was "an honest misunderstanding exacerbated by . . . special pressures," a "tangled" story, "filled with bad behavior, shrill voices, and feigned innocence."[37] There are many things that we will never know about *Mule Bone*, gaps in the story that no amount of correspondence can fill in.

What we do know about *Mule Bone* is easy to narrate. Hurston and Hughes collaborated on the play in the spring of 1930 when they were both staying in New Jersey rooming houses, under Mason's direction. Mason hired Louise Thompson as their typist. Hurston gave a draft of *Mule Bone* to Carl Van Vechten in October of that year. Unbeknown to Hurston, he sent it to Barrett Clark of the Theater Guild. Clark, in turn, sent it to Rowena Jelliffe and the Gilpin Players in Cleveland: "the outstanding amateur black theatrical organization in the nation."[38] Meanwhile, Hurston went back south, promising Hughes she would finish the second act in Florida. When she returned to New York, she was busy and evasive, apparently not interested in the play. Hughes ran into Jelliffe in Cleveland and learned that she wanted to produce the play and that she was surprised to hear he had had anything to do with it. A series of phone calls and letters ensued. Hurston expressed her anger at Hughes for—in her view—indulging Louise Thompson's inappropriate attempts to capitalize on *Mule Bone*'s commercial value. Hurston insisted that the bulk of the play was her own. Ultimately, Hurston and Hughes resolved in favor of a Cleveland production under both names. Hurston went to Cleveland to meet with Hughes and Jelliffe and attend rehearsals. But while she was there she learned that Thompson had also been in Cleveland (on unrelated matters). Suspecting sabotage, she called off the production.

[35]*Bass and Gates, p. 5.*

[36]*Hemenway,* Hurston, *p. 147.*

[37]*Hemenway,* Hurston, *pp. 136, 146.*

[38]*Arnold Rampersad,* The Life of Langston Hughes, *vol. 1 (New York: Oxford University Press, 1986), p. 194.*

Some—probably most—scholars blame Hurston, claiming that jealousy derailed one of the great black productions of our time. Others blame Langston Hughes for doing too little work while trying to claim too much credit. Hughes's biographer, Arnold Rampersad, concludes that Hurston was "deceptive." But virtually everyone agrees that the cancellation of the production, in early February 1931, put a definitive end to their friendship. Since Hurston was the angry and injured party that day, she is generally seen as responsible for ending that friendship.

There are, however, two overlooked events in this sad tale, ones that we would not be aware of without Hurston's letters. After their final scene at his parents' home, Hughes states, "I never heard from Miss Hurston again."[39] Thus, scholars have taken it for granted that *Mule Bone* ended their communication. We now know that this is not true. On March 18, 1931, only a month after the *Mule Bone* crisis had come to a head, Hurston wrote Hughes what can only be described as a friendly letter. "DEAR LANGSTON," Hurston wrote:

> I got your clipping today. Thanks. I read it. . . . it was kind of you to want to help me. I am glad to hear that your throat is well. I have yet to undergo what you have just passed thru. I am feeling fine and well, but that throat is just waiting to spring on me again.

This letter makes it plain that the two were still in touch (as does another, written on Valentine's Day), even as the *Mule Bone* collaboration became a legal stalemate. There is not the slightest expression of malice or ill will here, or any mention of the *Mule Bone* disagreement itself. Hurston continued expressing goodwill toward Hughes as late as 1940 when she was planning to write a positive review of *The Big Sea,* the very book in which Hughes maligned her. "I have a review copy of Langston's book and I am in the midst of it now," she wrote a friend. "So far very good. I shall write a review, but I do not know where to send it. I have decided to send it to Mrs. Knopf and if she feels like using it, she can send it where she wishes."[40] A review copy of the book would presumably have come directly from Hughes's publisher and almost certainly at his own request. Neither Hughes nor Hurston, in

---

[39]*Langston Hughes,* The Big Sea *(New York: Hill & Wang, 1963), p. 334.*
[40]*Hurston to Fannie Hurst, August 4, 1940.*

other words, fully severed their emotional ties. Rampersad reports that "incredibly, when Hurston needed help during the most humiliating episode of her life, in which she faced prosecution on a sordid (but unfounded) morals charge, she would turn for a testament to her good character to—Langston Hughes,"[41] who was apparently willing to come to court in New York, if needed." This was in 1948. Whatever happened between Hurston and Hughes, we must now conclude that it was *not* all Hurston's doing and that *Mule Bone* was not its sole cause.

Not all of Hurston's theatrical forays were failures. Her most successful production, *The Great Day*, opened in New York at the John Golden Theatre on January 10, 1932. For this production, according to Hemenway, "she organized some of her best material for presentation in revue form, adding Bahamian dances to worksongs, children's games, conjure ceremonies, and jook scenes. . . . Hurston put it all together in a show . . . loosely structured around a single day in the life of a railroad work camp."[42] Although Hurston had to fund the play herself, saddling her with a huge debt to Mason (who loaned her the money), *The Great Day* received excellent reviews. One reason for its success, ironically enough, was the play's promise to lift the veil of "feather-bed resistance." Alain Locke, who wrote the program notes for the play, said that Hurston had given the public "the true elements of this Negro heart."[43]

Hurston offered many performances of this drama. In New York, it was presented at the New School for Social Research and at the Vanderbilt Hotel, under the auspices of the Folk Dance Society of America. She took the play on tour throughout the country, sometimes in association with folklore societies, sometimes under the auspices of the National Folk Festival Association, sometimes by invitation, sometimes on her own. Hurston was able to tour such a complex performance because of the institutional affiliations she developed throughout this period, beginning with Rollins College and including Bethune-Cookman College, the North Carolina College for Negroes, and Fisk University.

In April 1932, Hurston had left New York to go back to Florida, where she wanted to work on *Mules and Men* and rest. But instead she launched a whole new arena of activity. That spring she met Hamilton

---

[41] *Rampersad, pp. 199–200.*
[42] *Hemenway, Hurston, pp. 177–78.*
[43] *Alain Locke, advertising flyer.*

Holt, president of Rollins College, along with Edwin Osgood Grover and Robert Wunsch, both professors there. The importance of these latter two can hardly be overstated. In 1934, Hurston dedicated *Jonah's Gourd Vine* to Wunsch, and in 1939, she dedicated *Moses, Man of the Mountain* to Grover. These men opened up connections for her, both local and national, of exactly the sort she wanted.

Eatonville was a charming but poor and dusty town. Rollins College, just one town away, in Winter Park, Florida, was wealthy and lush, with a beautiful campus built of Spanish-style white buildings with red-tiled roofs. The expensively landscaped campus featured winding stone paths and huge oaks draped with Spanish moss. Founded in 1885, Rollins was a small, coeducational, white, liberal arts college. When Hamilton Holt took over the college in 1925, it was in poor shape financially and materially. By the time Hurston's connection began, it had undergone major physical and pedagogical revisions that were drawing national attention. Holt did away with the lecture and recitation system, replacing it with a curriculum based on small seminars, workshops, and tutorials with faculty. This was a good atmosphere for Hurston, who was eager to do hands-on work with students. Although the college was whites-only, it gave Hurston an exciting venue for her dramatic art.

The student body was, no doubt, a bit odd for a dramatist devoted to working with "the Negro farthest down." Most of the Rollins students were decidedly well off. And they were not especially gifted academically. But the college's powerful emphasis on individualism—Holt had done away for the most part with admissions requirements, entrance examinations, and standardized curricula—resonated well with Hurston's ideas of education. Also to her advantage was the fact that as a black woman she was not eligible for a regular faculty appointment. Instead, she assumed the status of celebrity visitor, the college's exciting—and no doubt exotic—outsider. The Depression had forced colleges like Rollins to downscale. Faced with declining endowments, the president cut faculty salaries by half in 1932. Many of the college's most popular experimental programs had been scaled back or dropped. The presence of a famous African American artist was a great boon to a college experiencing lean times but eager for experimentation. Holt was an unabashed celebrity hound, skilled at using famous people to focus national attention on his school. And Hurston was able to entice some of her famous friends, including Fannie Hurst, to bolster the

Rollins image. In other words, as much as Hurston got from Rollins, she probably gave them even more.

In spite of their many differences, Hurston found kindred spirits in Holt, Grover, and Wunsch. Holt was a charismatic, powerful, and strong-willed administrator who liked to try radically new ideas. Among them was an innovative program of faculty chairs, which included "a Professor of Books, Professor of Evil, Professor of Hunting and Fishing, Professor of Things in General, and a Professor of Leisure." In addition, he added a Department of Books, headed by Edwin Osgood Grover. Grover, a former editor, author, and publisher, offered courses called "Literary Personalities," the "History of the Book," and "Recreational Reading" in an effort to instill the ideal of self-education. This ideal would have appealed to Hurston, who, in spite of her time at Barnard and Columbia, was mostly self-trained. And the farcical chairs would have appealed to her disdain for academic pretentiousness. Holt shared Hurston's interest in the person "farthest down" or what he liked to call "Undistinguished Americans."[44] And Grover shared her love of animals, nature, and Florida.[45]

Hurston, Grover, and Wunsch planned a folk concert at Rollins. Wunsch helped Hurston assemble and train a troupe culled from local talent. What she wanted, she told Grover, was to produce "real Negro theatre."[46] Their first production was offered in January 1933. Titled *From Sun to Sun*, the production was based largely on *The Great Day*. When it proved popular, another production of it was given in the school's main auditorium. As we see from her letters, Hurston was pleased with these successes but distressed that she could not persuade Rollins to allow blacks to attend the performances. "I come up against solid rock," she wrote to Charlotte Osgood Mason.[47] In response to her urgings, a special performance open to blacks was scheduled in Eatonville in February.[48]

---

[44]*See Hamilton Holt, ed.,* The Life Stories of Undistinguished Americans *(1906; reprint, New York: Routledge, 1990).*

[45]*See Edwin O. Grover,* The Animal Lover's Knapsack: An Anthology of Poems for Lovers of Our Animal Friends *(New York: Thomas Y. Crowell, 1929), and* The Nature Lover's Knapsack *(New York: Thomas Y. Crowell, 1927).*

[46]*Hurston to Edwin Osgood Grover, June 15, 1932.*

[47]*Hurston to Charlotte Osgood Mason, January 6, 1933.*

[48]*The information on Rollins College comes primarily from four sources: Robert Hemenway's biography of Hurston, Warren F. Kuehl's* Hamilton Holt: Journalist, Internationalist, Educator *(Gainesville: University of Florida Press, 1960), Brooke Kroeger's* Fannie: The Talent for Success of Writer Fannie Hurst *(New York: Times Books, 1999), and a visit to Rollins College in January 1998, which included discussions with Rollins College archivist Kate Reich.*

Rollins was the most successful of Hurston's institutional affiliations in this period. While she also tried to start schools of black drama at North Carolina College for Negroes and at Bethune-Cookman College, working as a regular faculty member didn't suit her personality. Instead of being treated like a fascinating "exotic," these schools saw Hurston as one of their own and demanded that she labor accordingly. As her letters show, she found such demands decidedly unpleasant. Hemenway notes that Hurston "did not submit well to authority and was . . . very soon at odds with Mrs. Bethune."[49] It was one thing to perform black folklore to white audiences who found it new and exciting. It was altogether another thing to stage black folklore in a black context with audiences experiencing various scenarios as overly familiar, embarrassing, or belittling. I have been "plugging away in the dark," she wrote Locke of her time at Bethune-Cookman.[50]

Toward the end of the decade, Hurston tried, once again, to work with the federal government. This time, she became involved in the Federal Writers' Project of the Works Progress Administration, working on their guide to Florida and a book on "The Florida Negro." In the winter of 1938, she had gone to Maitland, Florida, to finish *Tell My Horse.* As soon as it was done, she returned to her interest in folklore, which necessitated the steady income to be had from joining the Florida program of the Federal Writers' Project. Hurston scholars believe that Hurston was ashamed of this position, because it was government relief. There is no question that she was secretive about it, guarding it from family and friends. But her letters suggest that the problem may have been not so much one of going on relief—although Hurston detested anything that smacked of a handout—as it was her mistreatment by the FWP.

Hurston was qualified for a position as an editor, even *the* editor, of the FWP's project *The Florida Negro.* "No other staff member could boast of having a full-fledged book in print," Stetson Kennedy points out, "but by this time Zora already had three."[51] Nevertheless, she was hired as a "junior interviewer," which paid $67.20 a month, $5.00 less per month than the unit's typist. Eventually, she contacted the national director of the program, Henry Alsberg, to complain. He attempted to

[49]*Hemenway, Hurston, p. 201.*

[50]*Hurston to Alain Locke, March 24, 1934.*

[51]*Stetson Kennedy, "Working with Zora," in* All About Zora, *ed. Alice Morgan Grant (Winter Park, Fla.: Four-G Publishers, 1991), p. 62.*

Hurston at an FWP exhibit in 1938.

persuade Hurston's boss, Carita Doggett Corse, to promote Hurston to an editorial position. According to Pamela Bordelon, "Alsberg's liberal recommendation that Hurston be made an editor sent shock waves through Florida's WPA organization, which controlled the state FWP's employment and finances. In the Southern scheme of things, blacks were not given supervisory positions, even if they were more capable or better suited."[52] But Corse "sidestepped the issue and suggested that Hurston be given an additional $75 in travel allowance" rather than a promotion.[53] In one letter to Corse, Hurston pointedly refers to her accomplishments and national standing and also refers to herself as Corse's "pet darkey."[54] Although she had often used such language with

[52]*Pamela Bordelon, ed.,* Go Gator and Muddy the Water: Writings by Zora Neale Hurston from the Federal Writers' Project *(New York: Norton, 1999), p. 16.*
[53]*Ibid.*
[54]*Hurston to Carita Doggett Corse, December 3, 1938.*

white patrons, here she explicitly alludes to her published essay "The 'Pet Negro' System." In that essay, she excoriates the practice of exceptionalism by which racists can enjoy "their" favorite black person without attending to questions of social injustice. Perhaps the frustrations of the decade had built up to a point where Hurston could no longer contain her anger. The bitterness of her "double-voiced" irony was becoming more apparent.

Activist and writer Stetson Kennedy, Hurston's supervisor at the Florida FWP, recalls that the project gave writers a considerable measure of freedom. "It was characteristic of many of us 'field workers,' " he writes, "to take advantage of being our own boss by submitting ma-

Hurston on a WPA fieldwork trip in the 1930s.
"Racially 'mixed' teams travelling together were virtually unheard of in those days, and there were almost no hotels or 'motor courts' for blacks, which meant that Zora frequently had to sleep in her beat-up Chevy. . . . Sometimes when the target group was black, Zora was sent ahead, as a scout. . . . She was . . . there [in Cross Creek] when we arrived, sitting on the porch of a turpentiner's shack, rocking and smoking. I couldn't resist taking a candid shot." —Stetson Kennedy

terial on a somewhat sporadic basis."[55] His recollection is that Hurston was simply too accomplished and opinionated to fit into the agenda laid out for the "Negro Unit." "There we editors were," Kennedy remembers, "doing our very best to see to it that everything that went into the *Guide* was couched not only in staid Federalese but also in the specific guidebook jargon set forth in the FWP *Style Manual;* and there was Zora, turning in these veritable prose poems of African eloquence and imagery! What to do? Inevitably, the inferior triumphed over the superior, and not much of Zora, beyond her inimitable folksongs and tales, got into the *Guide.*"[56]

If little of her material was used, Hurston nonetheless exerted a powerful influence on the outcome of the *Guide,* according to Kennedy. Sent to Washington, D.C., to adjudicate the ongoing "editorial battle" over the volume, Hurston promptly "locked horns" with both Sterling Brown, who was acting as national director for Negro affairs for the FWP, and W. E. B. Du Bois, who was consulting on the project. " 'I went in and asked them to fight with all knives and razors out,' " Hurston apparently reported to Corse. Among other topics, the three fell out over varying accounts of the terrible massacre of blacks that had taken place some years earlier (November 1920), in Ocoee, Florida. To shore up her own version of events, which was a minimalist account of the murders and destruction, Hurston claimed to have been present in Ocoee at the time—" 'I told them I was an eye-witness—gave them names, dates, everything' "—thus forcing Corse to send her to Ocoee "(18 years after the event) to cover her tracks."[57]

Following her work with the FWP, Hurston made one last attempt to work in an institutional framework. James Shepherd, president of North Carolina College for Negroes, hired her in 1939 to teach drama and organize a theater program for the school. North Carolina appears to have been even more disappointing than Bethune-Cookman. During her stay in Durham, Hurston never produced a single play and seems, in fact, to have only sporadically taught her classes. Instead, she became involved with a playwriting group of Paul Green's and with the Carolina Playmakers, a white theater group associated with the University of North Carolina. It is evident from her letters to Green that Hurston still had theatrical ambitions. "My mind is hitting on sixteen cylin-

[55]*Kennedy, p. 61.*
[56]*Ibid., p. 65.*
[57]*Ibid., p. 67.*

ders," she wrote to Green of their possible collaboration on a play based on her story "John De Conqueror."[58] Sadly, the play was never produced.

In every sense, then, the thirties seem to have offered Hurston a decade of both promise and disappointment. And the letters indicate that this was as true of her personal and romantic life as it was of her professional life. Hurston wrote some of her most romantic fiction during this decade: to "embalm all the tenderness of my passion"[59] for a young man she met and had an affair with in 1931, she said of her reasons for writing *Their Eyes Were Watching God*. *Their Eyes Were Watching God* has been described by Alice Walker as one of the "most 'healthily' rendered heterosexual love stories in our literature"[60] or, in June Jordan's words, "the most successful, convincing, and exemplary novel of Blacklove that we have. Period."[61] According to Hemenway, the relationship memorialized in this novel was "doomed from the first" for the same reasons that her marriage to Sheen and later to the young Albert Price would also prove "doomed." The men Hurston loved could not accommodate her dreams. "This man" (memorialized in *Their Eyes Were Watching God*), Hurston wrote in her autobiography, "meant to be the head . . . [and] my career balked the completeness of his ideal."[62] "No matter how soaked we were in ecstasy," she went on, "the telephone or the doorbell would ring, and there would be my career again."[63] Her letters, however, are never self-pitying. Instead, she is flip and amusing, no doubt masking whatever she really felt about the difficulty of blending intimacy into her hardworking life. It is clear that she meant it when she wrote: "I am supposed to have some private business to myself. Whatever I do know [about love], I have no intention of putting but so much in the public ears."[64] Hurston's letters throughout this decade are so guarded about her love life that even the identity of this much-lamented lover was kept out of her private correspondence, including letters written to people who must have seen them together or known of the affair.

[58]Hurston to Paul Green, January 24, 1940.

[59]Hurston, Dust Tracks, pp. 188–89.

[60]Alice Walker, "Zora Neale Hurston: A Cautionary Tale and a Partisan View," In Search of Our Mothers' Gardens (New York: Harcourt Brace Jovanovich, 1983), p. 88.

[61]June Jordan, "On Richard Wright and Zora Neale Hurston: Notes Toward a Balancing of Love and Hatred," Black World, 23, no. 10 (August 1974), p. 6.

[62]Hurston, Dust Tracks, p. 184.

[63]Ibid., p. 188.

[64]Ibid., p. 261.

Hurston in profile,
photograph by Carl Van Vechten, 1934.

How much to keep secret? What to put in "public ears"? In many ways, this was the question of the thirties for Hurston, one she had answered optimistically in the twenties. Every book she published in the thirties wrestles with the question of "public ears." *Jonah's Gourd Vine* concerns a couple who cannot communicate the crucial information each holds to his or her heart. *Mules and Men* presents many instances of "feather-bed resistance," as does her second folklore collection, *Tell My Horse. Their Eyes Were Watching God* posits that our greatest desire, "the oldest human longing," is for "self-revelation." Then it goes on to document the difficulties of revealing ourselves to others. *Moses, Man of the Mountain* takes this thesis one step further, exploring the many reasons that humankind, as a whole, cannot hear God's voice or keep in mind God's edicts. Interestingly enough, this concern with the limits of language—along with its possibilities—has often been lost on Hurston's own advocates. Franz Boas's preface to *Mules and Men*, for example, claims that Hurston "penetrated" black culture for whites. Reading Hurston's letters from the thirties reopens questions of "feather-bed resistance," of what Hurston was revealing and what she was withholding. No group of letters is as revealing as those she wrote during these years. What these letters sometimes reveal is how much Hurston would always strive to keep to herself.

TO LANGSTON HUGHES

[postcard postmarked January 2, 1930]
[postcard front: "The Water Works—Main Pumping
Station—Nassau, Bahamas"]

Trip a little disappointing but satisfactory. See you soon Love & everything.

Zora.

TO MELVILLE HERSKOVITS

Box 5201
Sta. B
New Orleans, La.
Jan. 24, 1930.

Dr. Melville Herskovits
Dept. of Anthro.
Northwestern U.
Evanston, Ill.

My Dear Dr. Herskovits,
    Dr. Otto Klineberg[1] and I are doing some work down here and he thinks we should do some color-top work and some lip and nose measurements. We need some tops (2)[2] and a sliding caliper. Could you

---

[1] *Anthropologist; see glossary.*
[2] *This was part of Hurston's work in anthropometry, which had included measuring heads on Harlem streets.*

loan us a pair of calipers and send us the tops? We are asking you because we need them at once and we are afraid that the ordinary routine method of getting them may take too long.

I hear that your work at the University is getting along fine and I am very glad. Dr. Klineberg sends best regards and hopes to see you as he goes west.

Thanking you in advance, I am

Most sincerely,
Zora Hurston

We will gladly pay postage.

TO FRANZ BOAS

Box 35
Westfield, N.J.
April 14, 1930

My dear Dr. Boas,

The letter I sent to Mrs. Margaret Smith, the Bahamian woman I had spoken of has returned to me. I am getting in touch with Mrs. Edith Illige, 250 W. 154 St. who is said to know and keep track of the Islanders. I have written her already and as soon as she consents to see me I shall arrange to get the people you wish to see.

Most sincerely yours,
Zora Hurston

TO FRANZ BOAS

Box 35
Westfield, N.J.
April 16, 1930

Dear Dr. Boas,

I have just received a word from headquarters[1] telling me to come over Friday at three and bring materials for discussion. So I shall have to drop by for that Essay. It is all right if you have not had time to look it over.[2] I suppose it is merely intended to see how I am coming on.

As soon as I can get this book[3] in shape (about ten days) I shall be able to spend some mornings in town on our project. But I am urged to do things as quickly as possible and so at present I am working furiously.

Most sincerely yours
Zora Hurston

TO CHARLOTTE OSGOOD MASON

May 18, 1930

Darling my God-Flower,

Spring means birth, but the real upspringing of life comes on May 18,[1] when you renew your promise to the world to shine and brill for another year. You are God's flower, and my flower and Miss Chapin's[2] flower and Langston's flower and the world's blossom.

---

[1] *i.e., Charlotte Osgood Mason.*
[2] *This may refer to "Hoodoo in America," published in the* Journal of American Folklore, *October–December 1931, or it could refer to a section of* Negro Folk-Tales from the Gulf States, Mules and Men, *or* Tell My Horse.
[3] Negro Folk-Tales from the Gulf States.

---

[1] *Mason was born on May 18, 1854.*
[2] *Cornelia Chapin, a sculptor, Mason's occasional secretary, and the sister of Katherine Garrison Chapin Biddle, poet.*

Hurston sketch on letter to Charlotte Osgood Mason.

May 18 is here and now comes <u>Courtesy</u> and <u>Understanding</u> to soothe the minds of men. It is like Prosephone, the daughter of Dame Ceres come back to Earth that men may have something other that [than] brute-wants in their hearts; that the behavior of love may emerge from the shell of human indifference and heal us of our grevious wounds.[3] Oh, you are born!

May I, on your emergence day sing with my broken harp the small song of love that I am able to sing? It is a small song from a big heart. Oh, my lovely just-born flower, if back there when you fluttered pink into this drab world—if they had but known how much joy and love you would/should ["would" is written above "should"] bring! How much of the white light of God you would diffuse into soft radiance for the eyes of the primitives, the wise ones would have stood awed before your cradle and brought great gifts from afar. I am not very wise but let me lay the gift of eternal devotion within your little manger. But I dont want it to lie there passively. I want it to be a green thing <u>of</u> the color of life and grow and grow till it shadows the sun at noon.

I wish that I were three Wise Men or only wise enough for one. Since I am neither I am trying to make up for it by bringing you the three Wish-Boxes shown above.

I really should not extend my congratulations to you on this day, but to all those who have been fortunate enough to touch you. It is you who gives out life and light and we who receive. I wonder, often, what is there in the world one half so precious for you to get as the thing you give so bountifully. That is merely an oratorical question—I know there isnt.

<hr />

[3]*Persephone, daughter of Demeter (Ceres in Roman mythology), was queen of the underworld and the goddess of fertility in Greek mythology.*

May I be spared for a long long time so that I may throw back a bit of the radiance you shed on me. And may the reds and blues and greens and perples of the untrammeled gods of the primitives wrap you forever and never may your light beams waver.

Life is a road with one end in heaven the other in hell. I wish I knew how many you have dragged from everlasting unseeing to heaven! I wish I knew. Here I am one of the rescued. I was laid back in eternity for your consideration.

My joy that this day brought you to us—that the inner spring comes with you; That you will bless us for another year.

My most pure and uprushing love, darling flower.

Most devotedly,
Zora.

TO LAWRENCE JORDAN

[postmarked Palatka, Fla.]

Box 35, Westfield N.J.
May 31, 1930.

Dear Larry,

I was glad, really very glad to get your letter.

Yes. Larry I still yell with joy on the slightest provocation. I have been away and kept down to business for almost three years and I am dying to spread my flannel with friends.[1]

As soon as you arrive (you see I am assuming you wouldnt be mean enough to stay away) I shall tell you all about the books. Louise Thompson, whom you know has typed them for me.[2] She did a dandy job too. No doubt, I shall be back in the old flat by the time you arrive and I shall see you sitting in the big chair where last I saw you.

---

[1] *To have a good time, to sing or enjoy music, to have sex, or to talk nonsense.*
[2] *Educator, labor organizer, activist, radical, Thompson was hired by Charlotte Osgood Mason to act as secretary to Hughes and Hurston in 1931; see Thompson in glossary.*

I was in Harlem yesterday for the first time. Some of my friends are all tired and worn out—looking like death eating crackers. All of them cried to me to come and put some life into the gang again. I dont feel any older or tired a bit. Perhaps the hectic life of Harlem wore them out faster while I was in the South getting my rest as well as getting some work done.

Please write before you come and let me know the date. I have a little car now, and I have made some plans for motor trips up the Hudson, Storm King Road,[3] Boston Post Road, etc. And I am waiting only for the equipment that is now being held at Kimball W. Va. to arrive.

Sincerely,

Zora.

TO FRANZ BOAS

June 8 [1930?]

Dear Dr. Boas,

At last I come up for air. Its been very hard to get material in any shape at all.

The "Angel"[1] is cold towards the degrees, but will put up money for further research. I have broached the subject from several angles but it got chill blains no matter how I put it.

I have at last found the woman we sought and shall make a date for us on Tuesday when I see her. I shall then let you know what she says and you can let me know when you can come.

Most sincerely,

Zora.

---

[1]*Sometimes called Storm King Highway, this road goes across the face of Storm King Mountain in Orange County, New York.*

[1]*Charlotte Osgood Mason, Hurston's patron. Hurston was not allowed to reveal her name to anyone, and, apparently, Boas never learned it.*

TO CHARLOTTE OSGOOD MASON

[draft of telegram, possibly recopied by Mason]

N.Y. Straight telegram July 7th 1930. Darling Godmother Was waiting to hear from you I about normal again at 43 West 66th Street again—love—letter following.

Zora.

TO LANGSTON HUGHES

[postcard postmarked August 11, 1930, from Westfield, N.J.]

Box 31
Magazine Point, Ala.

Dear Langston,
    Off at last. Will be back by the end of August.
    Dreamed last night that you were working on the play.[1]

Lots of love—
Zora

---

[1]Mule Bone.

TO CHARLOTTE OSGOOD MASON

[telegram]

September 24, [1930?]
MRS R OSGOOD MASON CARE L H PAUL CHAPIN[1]
    63 WALL ST

DARLING GODMOTHER SAFELY HOME WORKING WHILE
AWAITING ORDERS FROM YOU MOST DEVOTEDLY
    ZORA

TO CHARLOTTE OSGOOD MASON

[November 11, 1930]

Darling Godmother,

I can see you with the eye of faith during this fine weather building your temple out under the sky. you dont belong in a house, of
course. You belong to Space, and I am always glad when you can escape to his arms.

Harry Block's[1] address is 38 W. 57th St. Phone Circle 3745.

I am beginning to feel fagged. The weariness is beginning to break
thru my subconsciousness & call itself to my attention.

You perhaps saw how much I enjoyed your reading of Mrs.
Biddle's[2] poems. You read so well. The verse is alive. It is more than
that. It is not the chance melody of some minstrel, but songs of philosophy. Thanks again for the reading.

---

[1] *Brother of Cornelia Chapin and Katherine Garrison Chapin Biddle.*

[1] Mule Bone *Knopf editor.*

[2] *Katherine Garrison Chapin Biddle (1890–1977), poet, sister of Cornelia Chapin.*

In the last chapters of the book I shall let Kossula[3] tell his little parables. When I see you next tell me what you think of the idea.

Love and love, and love,
Zora.

Nov. 11, 1930
43 W. 66th St.

TO CARL VAN VECHTEN

43 W. 66th St.
New York City
Nov. 14, 1930

Dear Carl,

Here is the play at last.[1] Of course it is tentative. It is my first serious whack at the play business.

Langston and I started out together on the idea of the story I used to tell you about Eatonville, but being so much apart from rush of business, I started all over again while in Mobile and this is the result of my work alone.

Please read it when you have time. I know that you are very busy so I am grateful that you consent to read it at all.

I hope that you are still sticking 'em strong and that your wife [Fania Marinoff] is still lovely and fragile looking. Awkward looking sentence, but you know "nigger" enough to know what I mean.

Sincerely
Zora.

---

[3]*Cudjo Lewis, last survivor of the* Chlotilde, *the last slave ship to come to the United States. The manuscript of* Negro Folk-Tales from the Gulf States *contains a typed list of 482 "Stories Kossula Told Me," most of which were not included in the manuscript.*

---

[1]Mule Bone.

TO CHARLOTTE OSGOOD MASON

2109 Springwood Ave
Asbury Park, N.J.
Nov. 25, 1930

Darling Godmother,

Perhaps my silence has been terrible, but I have been trying to get something done while resting.[1] That is, I have been trying to find the gate to the future. I dont want to commit myself at this moment, but the quest does no seem hopeless. I held utterly silent to hold my spiritual forces together.

Now, I think I must hurry back to town to see about certain things. I am sure you dont mind my silence at this stage of the game.

I am feeling fine. I have done a few local trips. Knowing all that I do, I didnt want to get too far from base now, so that I would be too hard to reach. I wanted to be so that I could be on the scene within a few hours after I got any word, good or bad.

You see, Darling Godmother, I am trying to get some bone in my legs so that you can see me standing so that I shall cease to worry you. I dont want all your worry and generosity to go in vain. Thus I feel that I must let no grass grow under my feet. I dont need to call upon your ebbing strength for every little thing. So I shall wrassle me up a future or die trying. I have spent the last four days re-writing the first act and polishing it up a bit.[2] I am going after things. Because your behavior of love makes you you willing to give your life, is no reason why I should be willing to take it. You love me. You have proved it. It is up to me now to let you see what my behavior of love looks like. So watch your sun-burnt child do some scuffling. That is the thing that I have lacked—the urge to push hard and insist on a hearing.

I shall be back in town immediately and see what a certain person has to say to me.[3] Then I shall proceed on down in Va. That is,

[1]Hurston is probably visiting her sister, Sarah Emmeline Hurston Mack, who lived at this time in Asbury Park.
[2]Mule Bone.
[3]She was working on both "Kossula" and Mule Bone and had spoken of them, by letter, to Van Vechten and Hughes, as well as to Mason.

if I am not held on business. I shall call immediately on reaching town.[4]

You remember that we talked about selling the car. I have gotten a few appraisals. Whooeee!! They dont think so much of it. The Chevrolet company put out their new car this year two months ahead of time to help the unemployment. Then they added so many improvements and are selling it for much less than mine cost that I am afraid we are not going to get the $500.00 I had in mind. Nothing like that has been offered, except as a turn-in, and that isnt in our plans.

Until I see you in town, all, all my love.

Most devotedly yours,
Zora

TO CHARLOTTE OSGOOD MASON

[telegram]

November 27, 1930
MRS R OSGOOD MASON
399 PARK AVE

MANY HAPPY RETURNS OF THE DAY I GIVE THANKS FOR
HAVING YOU
LOVE AND DEVOTION
ZORA

---

[4]*Hurston may have been interested in teaching in West Virginia. She also mentions "equipment" being stored there for her.*

TO RUTH BENEDICT

[December 1930]
C/O United Fruit Company
Puerto Cortes
Honduras, C.A.

Dear Dr. Benedict:

I talked with Dr. Reichard[1] about the matter of coming down here, which I hope has already been discussed with you. If I had been certain of what I would find here, I would have hurried to you at the time, but I had only hear-say at that time.

After three months of observation, I call three things to your attention.

1. THE BLACK CARIBS. This group are not pure Caribs. These are interesting because in a matter of 300 years, they have, by isolation which is deliberate, established a stable ethnic unit. It is Carib, Arawak and Negro. The cannibal Caribs, eating their way north in the Antilles, ate up the Arawak men in their path, married the women, and moved on. The ancestors of our subject accepted runaway Negro slaves from the Spanish in the early days of colonization, adding a [t]hird element. On the penetration of the British into the Spanish islands, they seized a great number of these war-like and troublesome people and dumped them on them on the coast of what is now Honduras, and they have been here ever since, living in isolation from all others. They live in their own crude pueblos, having nothing to do with others. They have their own language, which one of them told me (in Spanish) is a bastard idiom. Many of the men speak some Spanish, but the women speak only the bastard language to prevent admixture. Also, no outside men are aloowed in the pueblos after sundown.

2. The Zamboes, on the Guatemalan border, who have an elaborate language of their own, and had a high culture even before the Spainiards came here. They are still intact and live thier own lives. a dictionary of their language, in addition to other studies of them seem indicated.

3. The Icaques, in a mountain near Cedros, have been in isolation

[1]Anthropologist Dr. Gladys Reichard.

up there since the coming of the Spaniards. So far, they have permitted no outside[r] to enter their pueblo. They are the one example of the absolutely uncontaminated people left. From what I can learn, they fear the diseases of the White man, especially tuberculosis, and so keep themselves apart. All objects from the outside are especially fumigated before being allowed inside.

There are several other phings which I [t]hink that you would be interested in. I hope so anyway. I wish that you or Dr. Reichard could see your way to come down. I was not sure that Dr. Gladys [Reichard] would be at Barnard during the vacation, or I would write her too. Do give her my very best. If you are interested, I could do some anthropometry before you arrive. Do please drop me a line to let me know if you have any interest whatsoever. I can send more detailed information if you wish. My very best to you and yours.

Respectfully yours,
Zora.
Zora Neale Hurston

TO CHARLOTTE OSGOOD MASON

[December 3, 1930]
43 W. 66 St.
Wednesday night.

Darling, my poor Godmother,

My heart is so torn for you and Mrs. Biddle. The news has simply tromped my sensibilities down into the mud. I just cant conceive of it.[1]

Shall I write Mrs. Biddle, or would it be better to let her forget as best she may?

What can I do to cheer you up and help to sustain your precious life?

love and utmost devotion, Darling.

Most Sincerely,
your
Zora

---

[1] *Garrison Biddle, one of Katherine Biddle's two sons, had died just before Thanksgiving.*

TO CHARLOTTE OSGOOD MASON

43 W. 66th St.
New York City
Dec. 15, 1930

Darling Godmother,
 You seem to say to me, "Yes, Zora, you may say it." So, Darling, I love you and want you to know that I amthinking of you and working hard. Things donr look so impossible for my career. Only I have been told that I am too impatient, that it takes time, and large sums are not invested without due thought.
 I hope that your children, Mrs. Biddle and Mrs. Chapin are in in better spirit and health.

Most sincerely and devotedly,
Zora.

TO CHARLOTTE OSGOOD MASON

[December 20, 1930]

Dear Godmother,
 Here is the other ham. They came from Mr. H.W. Brock, Brock Hotel, New Market, Va.

THE HURSTONS

H.R. Hurston, Physician and surgeon, Memphis, Tenn.
John Cornelius Hurston, Meat market and Florist shop, Jacksonville, Fla.
Richard William Hurston, mechanic, Newark, N.J.
Sara Emmeline Hurston Mack, housewife, Asbury Park, N.J.
Joel Clifford Hurston, Rural Education, Montgomery, Ala.
Ben Franklin Hurston, PhC., Drugstore prop., Memphis, Tenn.

Zora Neale Hurston, bum and Godmother's pickaninny, New York City
Edward Everett Hale Hurston, P.O. clerk, Brooklyn, N.Y.

> Devotedly,
> Zora

TO ALAIN LOCKE

[1930?]
Saturday night

Dear Alain—

Sorry you couldnt come up this week end, but I shall be eye-
balling every train for you next week-end. Going to spread some jenk
for you so dont fail.[1]

Now, please give Barthé my love and ask him to come up too.[2] If he
cant, then write. I like him <u>ever</u> so much. I want to hear from him. If
he could come we could have a swell party in a small way.

Now, be prepared to play a little this time. I am coming out from
under my heavy load.

> So long, old cabbage,
> Zora

TO DOROTHY WEST

[envelope postmarked January [?], 1931]

Sat. Night.

Dearest Dot,

I'll take you up on the proposition on two conditions. #1.Please
dont expect me to keep a very tidy kitchen. I aint that kind of a person. Sometimes I clean it up beautifully & often I walk out on it.

---

[1]*In* Mules and Men, *Hurston defines "to spread one's jenk" as "have a good time."*
[2]*Richmond Barthé, sculptor; see glossary.*

#2. That you just feel at home & dont expect to be company.
#2A—That you tell yo' pa to send a can of asparagus along.

Dont mind me at anytime—just spread your jenk in your own way. Dont feel anymore obligations to the dish-pan than I do. It is on an incident in life—not life itself. The Willises are gone & I expect to move into their apartment. Wish you would take the old place. I suppose I shall move on Monday or so.

Love to the whole works up there in Boston.

Devotedly,
Zora.

TO CHARLOTTE OSGOOD MASON

43 W. 66th St.
New York City
Jan. 12, 1931.

Darling Godmother,

This writing you was in the fore part of my mind always. This is the reason I did not do it. Last month I wrote you a note to cheer you up, just that and nothing more. Perhaps I was clumsy about it for I gave you the impression in some way that I was jogging your memory in money matters. That hurt. I can never tell you how much. I hope that my saying it doesnt hurt <u>you</u>. That is the last thing I'd like to do. I didnt want to repeat my blunder.

Miss Elizabeth Marbury sent for me last Saturday to call at her home.[1] I went and met those 2 German dancers, the Krentzman or Krentzburg or something like that who seem to have won American audiences last year. But that was not the reason for which I was called. She wanted to have me try out for the radio. I was asked to sing one song to get my voice range, & to see if my personality got over. She expressed satisfaction on both points. I was told to prepare a 15 minute program & come back to her. I had hoped to have seen her before now, but on Friday night before I went to her house, my throat had started to grate like it had been sand-papered and by the time I got home from my visit to her the next day, I

---

[1]Hurston hired Elisabeth Marbury as her agent in 1931.

was pretty far gone. Muscles & bones aching, eyes watering, nose, throat all involved. I got busy, of course with quinine, rhinitis and hot lemonade, nose spray, 15% Argyrol etc. and so I feel all right today. I have worked on the act even when my potato-grater voice was at its worst and it is getting smooth so that I can work to a schedule. I shall make a date with her as soon as I am sure my voice is clear, tomorrow (Tuesday) or Wed.

Second writing of Kossula[2] all done and about typed.

I am truly sorry to hear that you have been ill also. I read in the "World" that there is an epidemic of flu-grippe going on. Fannie Hurst called today to say that she was down & would I come to see her. But I had to decline. I dont want any relapse or as we say down home "git took wid de laps."

The car is still with us. Just no sale. Even a 3-day ad in "The World" brought only one answer and that from a Pontiac-Oakland dealer who wanted to trade it in on a new car. The hour is bad. I agree with you that it should have been done in the Spring. Maybe tomorrow's ad may stir up a sale. My price has dropped to $200.00 but still no takers.

Miss Chapin's voice sounded so vibrant and alive. The sun and sea have done her good. I was glad to hear it.

I have just washed up the accumulation of clothes and I shall get this to the letter-box & commence to press the thin things like kerchiefs, etc and as the heavier things dry, I shall do them to the end. Lucy Ann Hurston[3] always did both in one operation & had it over with & so do I.

Love and love, Godmother darling. I shall be so glad to see you, and fumigate accordingly. Lovingly, Zora.

TO LANGSTON HUGHES

43 W. 66th St.
New York City
January 18, 1931

DEAR LANGSTON,

I had written you a letter last week, but I have moved and in my distraction I put it in the desk drawer and found it again yesterday.

[2]*One working title for her work on Cudjo Lewis; also called* Barracoon.
[3]*Hurston's mother.*

Now Langston, let us have a heart to heart chat about this play business.[1] Please believe that what I am saying is absolutely sincere. I mean every word, so that you can bank upon it.

In the beginning, Langston, I was very eager to do the play with you. ANYthing you said would go over big with me. But scarcely had we gotten under way before you made three propositions that shook me to the foundation of myself. First: That three-way split with Louise.[2] Now Langston, nobody has in the history of the world given a typist an interest in a work for typing it. Nobody would think of it unless they were prejudiced in favor of the typist. Not that I care what you give of yourself and your things. As Kossula says, dat don't reaches me. But I do object to having my work hi-jacked. There is no other word for it. I don't see how, even if in your magnificent gallantry you had offered it, she could have accepted it. But next day she voiced the matter herself when the subject of her pay came up. I offered to pay her five dollars a day and she said to you, trying to look hurt, "Pay me, Langston! No, I don't want a thing now, but when it goes over, then you all can take care of me then." So then I saw that the thin[g] had been agreed upon between you. First I was astounded that such a suggestion should have come from you, and next I was just plain hurt.

Then your argument that if we paid her money, that it ought to be something fancy. I still don't follow your reasoning. First you give me no credit for intelligence at all. Knowing the current prices for typists, you must despise my mental processes to have broached the subject at all. You know what you said, so I don't need to go into that.

Then when these had failed you come forward with the Louise-for-business-manager plan. That struck me as merely funny. With all the experienced and capable agents on Broadway, I should put my business in the hands of some one who knows less about the subject than I.

From all these things I could not but get the idea that your efforts were bent on turning everything into a benefit for somebody else. I say again, I have nothing to do with what you do with your own things, but I choose to bestow mine where I will. Therefore, I felt that I was among strangers, and the only thing to do was to go on away from there.

Now about the play itself. It was my story from beginning to end. It is my dialogue; my situations. But I am not concerned about that.

[1]Mule Bone.

[2]*Louise Thompson, hired by Charlotte Osgood Mason to work as a secretary with Hughes and Hurston, typing* Mule Bone; *see glossary.*

Langston, with God as my judge, I don't care anything about the money it might make nor the glory. I'd be willing to give it all to you off-hand. But the idea of <u>you</u>, LANGSTON HUGHES, trying to use the tremendous influence that you knew you had with me that some one else might exploit me cut me to the quick. I am only human, you know. I'll be willing to bet that if you told Mrs. Mason what you did exactly, she would agree with me.

I told Godmother that I had done my play all by myself, and so I did, and for the reasons stated before. Perhaps you know that a firm is bound by the contracts of any of its members. Therefore, with what had been proposed in mind, I realized that I could expect you to be promising many things that wouldn't do me a bit of good. That and that only is my reason for going it alone. I haven't gone happily. Just felt obliged to. I didn't intend to be evasive. With anyone else but you I could have said a plenty. Would have done so long ago but I have been thinking of you as my best friend for so long, and as I am not in love with anyone, that naturally made you the nearest person to me on earth, and the things I had in mind seemed too awful to say to you, I just couldn't say them. I tried for a long time to bring the subject up with you, but I just couldn't. I just kept trying to make a joke of it to myself, but somehow the sentences in my mind wouldn't laugh themselves off. So now, it is all said.

I am sorry that you are having intestine trouble. That is what has harrassed me for a long time. I am glad that you are home with your mother so that you can get your stomach right. I have discovered that New York and ambition and the nervous condition that accompanies it are hard on stomachs.[3]

Now, Langston, I have not wanted to grab things for myself. I don't want to thrust you forth or anything like that. It was just self-preservation. Suppose I had proposed such an arrangement with say, Harry Block as the beneficiary. No matter who it was, you would have acted to save yourself.

I didnt quite understand the wire from the Gilpin Players.[4] I know no Mr. French[5] and so I wondered what the reference meant. I don't know what you meant by it either. I should like to see the play worked

[3]Hughes had been ill for months, according to Arnold Rampersad, in reaction to his deteriorating relationship with Mason. "I was violently and physically ill, with my stomach turning over and over," Hughes later wrote.
[4]Black theater troupe working with Rowena and Russell Jelliffe out of their Karamu House in Cleveland.
[5]Samuel French, theatrical producer, employer of Barrett Clark, who sent Mule Bone to the Jelliffes to read.

out so that the things that read well but don't act well can be elimi-
nated. I'd like to be there to offer explanations as to folk habits, etc.
But I don't know how it could be arranged just now. At any rate I wonder if the producing of it would do much good. I wish to think it over.
Let me hear from you about it.

With all good wishes, I am sincerely yours,

Zora

P.S. First act recently rewritten. Synopsis of "Papa Passes" done for
the first time. You say over the phone "my version of the play". Are
not both copies my version? I don't think that you can point out any
situations or dialogue that are yours. You made some suggestions, but
they are not incorporated in the play.

TO LANGSTON HUGHES

43 W. 66th St.
New York City
January 20, 1931.

Dear Langston,

Gee, I was glad to get your letter!

I don't feel bad about the Guild[1] refusing my offering, for I have
learned that they thought well of it, and more things besides merit
entered into the refusal. That is why Clark took it over to French's office—because he felt that it would not be hard to place, and that is
why he gave it to Mrs(?) Jeliffe. However, it may be rotten as heck.

Now, I suppose that both of us got worked up unnecessarily. I have
explained myself so that I see no need to rehash it. I know that you
are nervously constituted like me and so the less emotion the better. I
am busy smoothing out my lovely brow at present and returning to
normal. I am in fault in the end and you were in fault in the beginning. I shall freely acknowledge my share at anytime and place. Some-

[1]*The Theater Guild, which initially rejected* Mule Bone.

how I don't mind re-versing myself, especially when it moves me towards pleasanter relationship. Perhaps I am just a coward who loves to
laugh at life better than I do to cry with it. But when I <u>do</u> get to crying, boy, I can roll a mean tear.

I shall write Godmother a letter leaving you in a white light. Not
that you have been slandered, but she dotes so on our rock-bottom sincerity that she would be upset to know of a spat, however trivial it
might turn out for us.

Hope to see you in Cleveland in a few days. Until then,

Most sincerely,
Zora

P.S. How dare you use the word "nigger" to me. You know I don't use
such a nasty word. I'm a refined lady and such a word simply upsets
my conglomeration. What do you think I was doing in Washington all
that time if not getting cultured. I got my foot in society just as well as
the rest. Treat me refined.

TO ROWENA JELLIFFE

[wire; 5:32 P.M.]

January 20, 1931

Okay

Zora H.

TO ROWENA JELLIFFE

[wire; 7:04 P.M.]

January 20, 1931

Mr. Clark at French feels badly over complications thru unauthorized sending script but says you can be trusted for integrity of script material copyright not one word must be altered except by me script not to leave your hands N.Y. agent not available now but decision tomorrow.

TO CHARLOTTE OSGOOD MASON

[January 20, 1931—library dated]

Darling Godmother,

You will note that Langston makes no claim of authorship. In the letter, over the phone and thru his friends, he attempts to set up the claim that he is due something because I didnt tell him to get out. You cant talk about a work with a person and then do it alone unless you pay them.

Now I noted in his NOT WITHOUT LAUGHTER[1] that he used several bits that I had given him. Now I am not using one single solitary bit in dialogue, plot nor situation from him and yet he tries to muscle in. I am enclosing the letter I wrote him and spoke to you about. I have since sent him a practical duplicate of it.

I wish it were possible for Locke to get him before you and then call me in and let him state his claims.

But my nigger mess aside, I hope that you are well as can be expected and that your dear C.[2] is the same. My heart goes out to Mrs. Biddle in her bad hour. She is being crushed like grapes in the press,

[1]*Hughes's novel, set in Kansas, published in 1930.*
[2]*Cornelia Chapin.*

but she has been singled out by the gods to bear heavenly fire to men. So she must suffer. Like Prometheus. Perhaps the grapes cry out under the press until a voice whispers, "Hush! The gods are making wine." Blessed and cursed is the bearer of heavenly fire.

The man is still haggling over the car. He wants me to pay for having the carbon ground and I am not going to do it. The price is too low anyway. Having made that sacrificing price [$200], he concludes that I am lacking in a sense of values. But I wont give another inch.

All my love to you, Godmother. I told Langston that you knew that I had written the play. Take good care of your precious life.

Devotedly,
Zora.

TO CHARLOTTE OSGOOD MASON

43 W. 66th St.
New York City
Jan. 20, 1931.

Dearest Godmother,

Things are happening hot and fast. Now it has developed that Langston did not start the bidding for the play to Cleveland. You know that Mr. MacGowan is connected with the Guild.[1] So the play has been read there. It seems that they really want this company to try out the play. It has tried out other plays that the Guild was interested in. So it looks both to be a better proposition, and better for Langston than it did at first glance. It came to his notice after it had been mentioned to the head of the organization out there.

AND BEHOLD! It begins to look like Langston has at last gotten one eye open. He seems to have gone to Cleveland to escape certain entanglements. He is staying on there indefinitely.[2] He is a little pa-

---

[1] *The Dramatists Guild, which had a long-standing interest in producing a "real comedy" about blacks.*

[2] *Hurston intimates that he went to his mother's in Cleveland to escape Louise Thompson. Rampersad writes that he expected to visit his mother briefly, then go to Florida, but was staying on in Cleveland because of financial difficulties brought on by the deterioration of his relation to Mason.*

thetic in his wish to make up with you. He told me that in a registered
letter I have just received, but someone else called me up to say that he
is wretched and sick because he feels that he has fallen in the esteem
of many folks, including me. He is fed up on New York for the time
being. I thought he had a very hang-dog look the last time I saw him.
He is highly emotional, and I can see how realization of how he looks
to others would affect him. [added in hand: "that is why he stays ill."]
At any rate, he wrote me a pathetic letter. It is just as we know,
Langston is weak. Weak as water. When he has a vile wretch to push
him[3] he gets vile. When he is under noble influences like yours, you
know how fine he can be. Personally, I think that he has so much in
him, that it is worth my swallowing and forgetting if by extending a
friendly hand I can bring him back into the fold. I think we are in a
spot now to make a grand slam.

I hurry to end these lines to you, because I dont want to be unjust
to anyone ever. Especially Langston. I did not get my facts about the
play from him, however. I got them from the agency downtown[4] that
is connected with the Guild.

I shall write Langston at once. I am sure that if he felt that he
could get your confidence again he would worh hard to earn it. He is
ashamed of his attitude about the play and apologized to me for it. Isnt
that like the Langston of old? He says he feels so badly about going
down to certain friends of his the way he did. I know just what happened. After he had spent a night or two in town and had been fed and
flattered, he was told what a sucker he was not to fight for his rights. I
was held up to him as a double-crossing monster. Plenty sighs went up
over the fickleness of friends, etc. After all, Langston, you are so fine
and generous and the crass word robs you. I think it is just magnificent
of you to love Zora the way you do, but you poor dear, nobody ever
seems to love you. Lie down, let mama fix you some cocoa. Maybe you
ought to have a cocktail. I'll run right out and fix you one. Umph!
Umph! I for got that all the liquor was gone. Better let me run get
some. Now where is my purse? Oh, you'll get some? NO! I couldnt let
you do that. You are so good to us. Well, if you will, but remember
next time I do the buying. I wouldnt take advantage of you like others.
Etc. By the third cocktail and the tenth ton of flattery, the Galahad

[3] *i.e., Louise Thompson.*
[4] *The Samuel French Agency.*

goes forth to defend his rights, and tell that flat-foot sea buzzard of a Zora just where she get off. "And while you are about it, dear, free yourself from the strings of these people who give you a few pennies just to dominate you."

Godmother, I am so happy that Langston has taken an honorable view of the thing, that I would give him part. I shant say that to him right now, but it takes all the sting out of things. The money didnt mean anything, Godmother really. You know how I felt.

So Mr. Clarke, one of the Guild people, thinks that I ought to go to Cleveland and work the thing out. I dont know, but it looks like a build-up for New York production. He says that it, the play, is so exotic that they would like to see how it works up.

Please see me with your inner vision, waving a fan gaily.

Lovingly,
Zora.

TO CHARLOTTE OSGOOD MASON

[telegram]
[from Cleveland, Ohio]

February 3, 1931
MRS R OSGOOD MASON
399 PARK AVE

DARLING GODMOTHER ARRIVED SAFELY HAVE PUT THE PERSON ON THE RUN PLAY STOPPED LOUISE THOMPSON HAD BEEN SENT FOR TO BOLSTER AND CASE I SMASHED THEM ALL BE HOME BY WEEK END ALL MY LOVE
ZORA.

TO CHARLOTTE OSGOOD MASON

[telegram]

[February 3, 1931?]
MRS R OSGOOD MASON
399 PARK AVE

HELD BY BAD WEATHER AT HARRISBURG PENNA AT ONE
NAUGHT NAUGHT SIX NORTH SIXTH STREET HOME
TOMORROW. I HOPE SAFE ALL MY LOVE
    ZORA.

TO LANGSTON HUGHES

43 W. 66th St.
New York City
February 14, 1931.

DEAR LANGSTON,

Arrived safely back in New York. Stopped in Westfield and got two
books of mine that I needed. Asked Mrs. Peoples[1] to tell you that I had
taken them.

In case that my letter to Mrs. Jeliffe mis-carries, tell her that I just
found the check this afternoon. My nephew put part of the mail on
my desk, and put the rest in the dresser drawer so I just found it, and
am returning it to her. That is, I enclosed it in the letter I wrote her.
In view of the fact that we did no business, I don't know whether I am
due it. In addition it was incorrectly made out.

Sorry that you are having so much throat trouble.[2] You are late on
that again as you were on the intestinal trouble. I have wrassled with

<hr />

[1] *Westfield landlady?*
[2] *Hughes had his tonsils out in January 1931.*

my throat for ages. Helene Johnson is in the hospital now having her
tonsils out and I think I shall do the same before warm weather.

Lots of luck.

Sincerely,

ZORA NEALE HURSTON

TO CHARLOTTE OSGOOD MASON

43 W. 66 St.
New York City.
March 9, 1931.

Darling Godmother,

The sun is shining beautifull and golden and my heart rises to do
honor to it and to you the God and Gaurd-Mother in the Twelfth
Heaven.

Harry [Block] has the Ms.[1] and he is going to work on it at once.
He is very enthusiastic about it. So much so that he is shunting something else aside to look after it. Besides he wants to help me and in his
great kindness of heart, he is pledging all of his recreational and rest
hours until it is done.

Mrs. Grace Randolph Wood of Westfield N.J. is here with me now.
She called Sunday A.M. and said she had nothing to do today and
would love to come & finish setting the work songs. So I told her to
come on. We have set 9 songs already and I am very happy about it.
When she has all of the melodies correct she can work on the harmonies alone. She is getting a marvellous "feeling" for the songs
which she didnt have at first. She is a graduate of Howard U. Conservatory and knows her technique. All she needed was the feel of her
people and she is doing extra special in that.

Going back to Harry Block. He has been very generous in his offers to help me. He has not once mentioned pay. But I think I'd be
lacking in feeling if I did not offer him something for I know he does
not earn any princely salary at the publishing house. I'd like to take

[1]Mules and Men.

only $90 [$40?] for myself next month and give him the rest. I wont starve on that. I'll merely have to be very careful. If it calls for a little self denial on my part then I rejoice in doing something for my own future. Surely if you have sacrificed so much love and time and love and material things and love for me, I should be willing to go thru hell-fire for myself. But I can and will manage on it. Please believe me sincere and trust me to keep myself in good shape.

I feel in fine shape. Things are working out fine. I feel very bouyant and full of zeal to work. I am writing Alain an outline of my activities. I know he will be pleased.

As soon as the song collection is finished, please let Grace come and play them all to you. You can judge then whether they are true and worth offering to a publisher. I love the children's game-songs more than any for some reason or other.

Next Monday Grace is coming again and we hope to finish all by then.

Love to—all. Your love is curing my sick soul and I am feeling fine. Your gratitude.

Devotedly,
Zora.

TO CHARLOTTE OSGOOD MASON

43 W. 66th St
New York City
March 10, 1931.

Darling Godmother,

The Guard-mother who sits in the Twelfth Heaven and shapes the destinies of the primitives. This is another day and therefore another thought of you. There is no sun to warm me, so I must stand at my window and look towards the east to warm my heart.

I had an interview with Harry [Block] again last night and he said that I must rewrite the conjure material into an geographical and chronological narrative, and put in the religious material according to place and time, instead of making it something apart. It sounds very sensible to me and so I shall get back to it as soon as Kossula[1] is definitely off of hand. He says that he can do nothing until I have done my narrative, and then I must bring it to him and he will edit it. But he says he thinks the material is glorious. I am not at all cast down by his telling me that I had no book, but <u>notes</u> for a book. The point is, he has shown me what to do and this is the im[por]tant thing.[2]

Lovingly your
Zora.

TO LANGSTON HUGHES

43 W. 66th St.
New York City
March 18, 1931

DEAR LANGSTON,

I got your clipping today.[1] Thanks. I read it. I dont know whether you sent it to me so that I might know that this sort of thing happens to lots of folks, or whether some part of it appeared to you to fit the case.

At any rate, it was kind of you to want to help me. I am glad to hear that your throat is well. I have yet to undergo what you have just passed thru. I am feeling fine and well, but that throat is just waiting to spring on me again. I am calm again and went to a party and had a nice time. Hard at work on the African thing and plan to have it all done by next week.[2] Then I shall re-write the conjure book.[3] I have a good scheme for doing it now.

Sincerely,
Zora

---

[1]One of Hurston's working titles for her book-length manuscript on Cudjo Lewis; also called Barracoon.
[2]One of the main differences between the presentation of folklore in Negro Folk-Tales from the Gulf States and Mules and Men is the amount of narrative included in the latter.

---

[1]Evidently a story similar to the literary struggle between Hurston and Hughes.
[2]Book on Cudjo Lewis, variously called Kossula and Barracoon.
[3]Tell My Horse.

TO CHARLOTTE OSGOOD MASON

43 West 66 St.
New York City
March 25, 1931.

Darling Godmother,

My work is coming along well. I have taken a great deal of pains to rewrite certain passages and feel satisfied for the moment with the introduction. I have done over two entire chapters and now I am within a few paragraphs of the end of the whole thing. Then for the final typing.[1]

I found at the library an actual account of the raid as Kossula said that it happened. Also the tribe name. It was not on the maps because the entire tribe was wiped out by the Dahomey troops. The king who conquered them preserved carefully the skull of Kossula's king as a most worthy foe.[2]

Harry's not being able to help me [with *Mules and Men*] makes it unnecessary to give him anything at present. I would want to offer him part of my allowance as a gift if and when he does something for me. He says that he cannot do anything until I have done it over myself.

I find that Langston is in town and that he copied whole hunks out of my play [*Mule Bone*] in Cleveland and NOW tries to say that while he didnt write the thing in the beginning, he made all those "emendations" on the play last Fall. I cant conceive of such lying and falsehood. But then there are many things in earth and sky that I dont know about.

All my love Godmother. I am very well and I have even learned to live above Langston's vileness. So I am happy.

Love and love and love, and many prayers for your ow [sic] own good health and happiness. I am making a supreme effort at this time to make you happy and strengthen your faith in my creative ability.

Devotedly,
Zora

I'd love for Langston to face me in your presence.

[1]Kossula.
[2]*Hurston's interview with Cudjo Lewis led her, in part, to this research.*

TO ARTHUR SPINGARN

43 W. 66 St.
New York City
March, 25, 1931.

My dear Mr. Spingarn,[1]

This is to deny your assertion that you have seen the original script. You have seen what your client <u>says</u> is the original script. You evidently for get that your client had my script out in Cleveland and I see did not hesitate to copy of some "emendations." The whole matter is absolutely without honor from start to finish and this latest evidence of tying to make a case by actual theft, "emendations" as you call them, makes me lose respect for the thin[g] altogether. From the very beginning it has been an attempt to build up a case by inference and construction rather than by fact. But all the liberal construction in the world cannot stand against certain things which I have in my possession.

I think it would be lovely for your client to be a play-wright but I'm afraid that I am too tight to make him one at my expense. You have written plays, why not do him one yourself? Or perhaps a nice box of apples and a well chosen corner. But never no play of mine.

Most emphatically yours,
[unsigned carbon]

---

[1]*Hughes retained Arthur Spingarn as his attorney to handle matters regarding* Mule Bone; *see Arthur Spingarn in glossary.*

TO CHARLOTTE OSGOOD MASON

43 W. 66 St.
New York City
April 7, 1931

Darling my Godmother,

I jumped on a bus Friday night and rode down to Washington to blow the dust out of my head. It did me a lot of good. I was back home by midnight Sunday. The person I left to watch things during my absence said that you called Sat. I am so sorry I missed the call.

Yesterday I re-read the material and made several minor changes. That is why I took the trip—to give me perspective. Now I feel safer in putting it into type.[1]

I would have loved to talk to Alain. I find that he is much beloved by the students at Howard. You know of course, that Mordecai Johnson[2] is under fire. It seems that he wont be President of Howard University much longer. It is interesting to note that he is charged with the same things that Dr. Durkee was charged with—being an autocrat by the milder ones and a tyrant by the violent. The Washington papers are full of it.[3]

This dreary day depresses me, but I know that The Great Gods in Space are fathers and so I expect them to send me sunlight tomorrow.

The dress looks swell on me. I wore it to Washington. A great calm came to me out of that crazy rushing off. The sense of motion soothed me like the sea and long before Washington was reached I was in high spirits with brightest hope. Do not despair of me, Godmother, I shall come thru this time.

---

[1]Most likely Kossula.

[2]President of Howard University from 1926 to 1960 and Howard's first black president. Educated at Morehouse, Harvard, and the University of Chicago, Johnson was also active in the NAACP and was a minister of the First Baptist Church.

[3]Stanley Durkee was president of Howard from 1918 to 1926. A former Congregational minister and a white man, Durkee came under heavy fire toward the end of his presidency for what some perceived as racial insensitivity in suggesting that students and faculty sing black spirituals. His presidency was a period of growth and expansion for Howard. While some, like Hurston, strongly supported Durkee, others felt that he was out of touch with his constituency and taking Howard too far. Hurston's essay "The Hue and Cry About Howard University" details this controversy.

May your pains be borne away on the shoulders of the wind, and a big and bountiful cloud of love hang over you.

Devotedly your
Zora.

Would you come to the museum with me on Thursday? I think you might like the paintings of India.

TO CHARLOTTE OSGOOD MASON

April 18, 1931

Darling Godmother,

At last "Barracoon" is ready for your eyes.[1] I pray so earnestly that I have done something that can come somewhere near your expectations.

The pictures at the museum were magnificent. I am sending you the catalog so that you may know what the subjects are. The exhibit lasts until April 20th or thru that date.

I have been working on the conjure book this week.[2] It is getting easier now. I wrote Alain too. He is very busy I know but I hope for an answer.

Godmother darling, you dont know how the thought of you comforts me these devilish days. Sometimes what is inside me breaks out and destroys me for hours. Usually I am calm, but sometimes I need a refuge to run to. So I light a candle in your name and wait for you to send the peace.

The dress looks magnificent on me so I bought a hat to go with it. I am so grateful to you that you remember me always and try to drag me up to the light.

---

[1]Hurston had worked on this earlier, leading to publication of "Cudjo's Own Story of the Last African Slaver" in the Journal of Negro History, 12 (October 1927). As revealed in Robert Hemenway's biography, three-quarters of this essay was plagiarized from a book entitled Historic Sketches of the Old South, by Emma Langdon Roche, a fact that, fortunately for Hurston, escaped the notice of both her patrons and her critics. Unlike that earlier essay, Hemenway reports, the book manuscript Hurston refers to here was a fictionalized account intended for the general reader. It was never published.
[2]Presumably an early draft of Tell My Horse.

I saw Alta Douglas[3] last week and she asked of you. This is the first time that she has said anything about you. She says she wants to write you but she knows you [were—x-ed out] are not well.

I know that Langston says he was going to Cuba, but I suspect he is really gone to hunt up Eatonville to pretend that he knew about it all along.[4]

When I look back on the three and a half years that I have known you, Godmother, I am amazed. I see all my terrible weakness and failures, my stark stupidity and lack of vision and I am amazed that your love and confidence has carried over. That is why I am plugging away so diligently now, so that your faith will have something to live on. I know that your perfect understanding of me will read all the volumes that are compressed in this paragraph.

I fear that the tonsils will have to come out soon. They stay sore and lower my vitality too much. I am only half of me at least a third of the time.

With a prayer for greater understanding on my part, a continued love from you and some achievements from my pen to nourish you, I am

Your Own

Zora.

TO CHARLOTTE OSGOOD MASON

[May 10, 1931—dated at end of letter]
Sunday Morning

Darling my God Mother,

These flowers for the day set apart to honor those to whom God gives the care of the world in his absence.

Flowers to you—the true conceptual Mother—not a biological accident. To you of the immaculate conception where everything is conceived in beauty and every child is hovered in truth.

[3]*Aaron Douglas's wife.*
[4]*Hughes traveled to Cuba, for the third time, in April 1931, in the company of Zell Ingram, an aspiring young artist.*

If the high gods in space shall find anything worthy in me, then it is of you. Then shall I glory and sing a new song. I open my mouth and sing

"Out of the essence of my Godmother
Out of the True one
Out of the Wise One I am made
        to be
From her breath I am born
Yes, as the world is made new
        by the breath of Spring
And is strengthened by the winds of Summer
        The Sea is stirred by its Passion.
Thus, I have taken form from the
        breath of your mouth
From the vapor of your soul am
        I made to be
By the warmth of your love I am
        made to stand erect
You are the Spring and Summer
of my existence.
You, who permits me to call you
        Godmother.

                                        Devotedly,
                                        Zora.

May 10, 1931

TO CHARLOTTE OSGOOD MASON

43 W. 66th St.
New York City
June 4, 1931.

Darling Godmother,

Sitting here at work, I turned a phrase or two that pleased me and I naturally began to think that you were here with me, pulling for me and hurrying me on.

Miss Grace Mott Johnson, who is a minor sculptress, has invited me to spend a week up state with her.[1] It is very quiet there at Pleasantville she says and she also has a place at Bedford Hills. It sounds pleasant to me, for I want to do some most intensive work in the next month and they are tearing up 66th street and the noise is awful. Besides, other things make New York unpleasant to me at times, so that I am utterly disorganized for short periods.

I don't see, really, how <u>this</u> month I can make the $100.00 do. I think by July 1st I can make some arrangements that will help tide me over. I fully appreciate the present economic situation. You have been most magnificent and generous to me in <u>every</u> way. Please dont think I shall feel, now that things are such that you must curtail, that I shall forget your absolute spontaneity in giving me. Personally, I feel that it has all been to good purpose and that I shall succeed. Even if you feel that you can do nothing for me anymore in a material way, I shall know that you are behind me, and taking me on your wings when you soar with the High Gods in Space; that your love is sustaining me.

Most devotedly your
Zora.

[1] Sculptor and civil rights activist; see glossary.

TO DOROTHY WEST

[on stationery from Walper House, Kitchener, Ontario][1]

Kitchener, June 11, 1931

Darling Dot,

Just a pound or two of love from me to let you know I remember.

Devotedly,
Zora.

TO CHARLOTTE OSGOOD MASON

43 W. 66th St.
New York City
July 23, 1931

Darling, My Angel Godmother,

I know you think I am either dead, damned or delivered. But several things were in the air and I wanted [to] report something.

II *Now*, there is a revue called "Fast and Furious"[1] due to open Aug. 3, place yet undetermined. Either Brooklyn or Boston. I have the greater number of skits in it. I am so happy to be able to tell you this. It was in the air before you went away but very indefinite. It was pretty certain when I got your letter on the 9th but we were fighting over terms.

II I am now doing the book of another show at present called "Jungle Scandals" It will be ready to go into rehearsal within the month. This seems definitely settled so that I feel safe in speaking of it.

---

[1]Hurston was traveling at this time with Fannie Hurst. Ostensibly, the two had left New York to visit Elisabeth Marbury, friend and agent of both. In fact, Fannie Hurst had engineered the trip north with Hurston as a way to rendezvous with her lover, the explorer Vilhjalmur "Stef" Stefansson, who was lecturing on the Chautauqua circuit.

---

[1]A musical revue; see glossary.

Two other things seem certain but at this moment nothing definite has been done so they wait for a future letter to you. I am told that it is announced in "Variety" for this week that I am responsible for the book of "Fast and Furious." I shall secure a copy and forward it to you if it is there. Rosamond Johnson has some lovely music in the play. He and Porter Granger [sic] did the music. Porter Granger is doing the music for "Jungle Scandals."

Godmother darling, I do not consider either of the revues as great work, but they are making the public know me and come to me, and that is important. I shall do something good with "Spunk." I am working on that also and it looks like a very good play can be made from it.[2] Anyway, I like the idea of going from the light and trivial to something better, rather than coming down from a "Spunk" to "Fast and Furious." The public will see growth rather than decline, you see.

I work so hard to justify your faith in me. To tell you the truth, often I have been so discouraged that I could see no further excuse for living. But I said to myself, "Godmother sees something so it is there. Stand up, coward and look to every horizon and and fight. Thus often I have been just stumbling along with no other light for me except your faith. I had no lamp within myself.

I hear that my husband has divorced me, so that's that.[3] Dont think I am upset, for your lil Zora is playing on her harp like David. He was one of the obstacles that worried me.

> Godmother, for love, I thank you
> For kindnesses and love I thank you
> For Courtesy that passes earthy bounds
>   I thank you
> For light, I thank you
> For light whereby one walks, I thank you.
> For the giving of beauty, I thank you
> For the giving of light that I might
>   <u>see</u> beauty, I thank you

---

[2] "Spunk" was originally published as a short story in Opportunity of June 1925 and was reprinted in Locke's The New Negro. Hurston apparently took an early version of a much-revised "Spunk" to Hall Johnson, who was not encouraging about the possibility of straightforwardly presented black music. Ultimately, Hurston's work at this time resulted in the performance of The Great Day.

[3] Hurston and Herbert Sheen were divorced on July 7, 1931.

For extending your arms, for the thrusting
    forth of your hands
That roll back the uttermost horizons
    and extend the living world, I thank
      you.
The world is enlarged, that I might find
places of beauty, and roads thereto;
That there might be room for the lowly
That the seed of the humble
might be lifted up.
That their voices should sing in the wilder-
    ness
and their glory shine in the plain.
From the morning wind that sings
From the wind of the night that cries
From the stormy wind
That rages up and down
You have made wings
And from the rainbow, got them hues
You have wrought wondrous wings
and made your worms to fly
Godmother, you sit with Eternity
In one hand peace and pardon
In the other, <u>Courtesy</u> and love.

                            Devotedly, your pickaninny,
                            Zora.

another letter tomorrow or next day.

TO CHARLOTTE OSGOOD MASON

43 W. 66th St.
New York City
Aug. 14, 1931

Darling My Godmother,

You have been with me every day in the spirit and I have felt you there. My silence has neither been negligence nor illness. Things have been in such a fluid condition from day to day that there was not a statement I could safely make, except to acknowledge your gift to me. For about 15 days, the revue "Fast and Furious" looked <u>bad</u>. Financial difficulties. One day it would look hopeful, the next very black. Yesterday the producer got the money and the house all settled. Somehow my inner self tells me that even now something is not well. Perhaps he and I shall disagree about changes in my material. Godmother, they take all the life and soul out of everything and make it fit what their idea of Broadway should be like. Its sickening at times.[1]

Langston is back in town. I received an announcement that he was to lecture on the West Indies, or his travels, to be exact, under the auspices of the "Crisis."[2] He went down to my agent's[3] with a long line of most malicious lies in an effort to prejudice them against me. He took along some woman whom he introduced as his aunt to help him talk.[4] All he got for his trouble was to be called a vicious liar to his face, a sneak and a weakling. The woman was asked what she was doing there and to keep her mouth shut or get out of the office. He was made out a liar on five different counts, and told to do anything that he wished, for there was able legal backing behind me. So he finally shrunk at telling Mr. Crossett that he was collaborating on a play with Wallace Thurman and he would like for the Marbury office to handle it. Mr. Crossett told him that he handled Thurman's affairs, but that the office would positively refuse to touch anything that he had anything to do with as he had shown himself to be a person of no honor.

[1]Fast and Furious *opened on September 15 and closed one week later.*
[2]*One of the two most important journals of the Harlem Renaissance; see glossary.*
[3]*Elisabeth Marbury.*
[4]*Ethel Dudley Brown Harper, whom Hughes referred to as "Aunt Toy," was a close family friend.*

Nobody had to convict him of being a liar. He convicted himself. With his own letter of Oct. 6, before Mr. Crossett in which he asks me to send him the second act of the play, he tells Mr. Crossett that he had written the play himself in January and that I had stolen it and made a copy of his play and submitted it to the Guild. Then of course, Mr. C. showed him my copyright card of Oct. 29, 1930 and he all but fainted, for he thought he had played a sharp trick by making a copy while it was in Cleveland & getting it copyrighted.

He tried to tell the agent those things which you had told me he was saying—that it was a personal affair and that I had taken his play because I was jealous of Louise [Thompson]. The agent of course cut him short and told him that he [had] no interest in anything except the authorship of the play, and that his place was an office and not a clearing house for Harlem gossip. He wanted him to point out what he had done on the play. He said that he had taken a page and a half of my notes—all that there was of my story—and built it into seventy magnificent pages of a play. Whereupon he was again told that he was a stupid liar. He told him (I mean L. told C) that I was a person of a most violent disposition and had called him and his Cleveland friends liars and crooks, etc. Mr. C again reminded him that he was only interested in the business and commented that if his tactics were the same in Cleveland as they were in his office, I was more than justified and much too mild, really. So much for that. It no longer even annoys me. Give a calf enough rope—

Had a card from Alain. He gave me a nice bawling out. I loved it. It was the first time he had noticed me and I was so glad he had calmed down enough to speak to me at all. I shall write him c/o Cook's Place Madelaine, Paris

Now about the money, Godmother, darling. By the time for you to send me my next allowance, I shall be receiving money from the theatre.[5] I should love to keep up our original arrangement. I'd like to send you all monies and have you then give me an allowance as usual. If you say, "Now that you are earning money, go for yourself," I'll feel alone in the world again. And Godmother, that would be too awful.

What would happen if I were to jump in our car and come up to talk with you?

Thanks and thanks Godmother, darling. I love you truly.

Devotedly,
Zora.

[5]*Anticipated pay for participation in* Fast and Furious.

TO CHARLOTTE OSGOOD MASON

[on stationery from Glimpsewood,
Dublin, New Hampshire]

NY City.
Sept 15 6$^{\underline{19}}$ [1931]

Review Fast & Furious opens tonight at New Yorker Theatre Business deal unsettled until last moment—Hence my failure to communicate A letter coming full of many thanks. Good wishes for health & all my love

Devotedly   Zora—

TO CHARLOTTE OSGOOD MASON

43 W. 66th St.
New York City
Sept. 25, 1931.

Darling Godmother,

The contracts and the reviews mailed to you under separate cover tell you all about my part in the show.[1] It closed last Monday but it did not surprise me as you remember I had complained to you that the man at the head of things[2] was stupid and trite and squeezed all Negro-ness out of every thing and substituted what he thought <u>ought</u> to be Negro humor. We argued about it a good deal. Then I became well, sort of reconciled. I decided to take what ever monies came out of the thing and wait for another chance. Unfortunately, the life of the play was so short that I didnt even get the money due me. I should have gotten 175^{00} per week, all told. I actually got one 75^{00} and all the rest is still [owed—x-ed out] owing to me with small chance of getting it.

---

[1]Fast and Furious.
[2]*Forbes Randolph, composer and theater director, directed the Kentucky Jubilee Choir.*

Well, I have learned a lot about the mechanics of the stage, which will do me good in playwriting. I have received a good deal of publicity which is helpful <u>and</u> I did earn a little money. The 75⁰⁰ I sent to Dr. Durkee.[3] He had loaned me $119 while I was at Barnard and I had never had a chance to pay him anything on it. I had planned to buy some clothes and move back to New Jersey with the rest, but thats out now. I didnt expect a long run of the show [and—x-ed out] but it would have done a few months if Randolph had had enough cash to have paid salaries for the first two weeks in town. He didnt and the show had to close while playing to good houses. You see a show seldom carries itself in the first two weeks. The producer carries it, but by the third week, if it has a chance it carries itself.

No, I didnt do anything with Rosamond Johnson. He had a skit in there which he wrote with a white person. It was very good. The white person, Mr. Allie Wrukel[4] taking credit for the greater part of the creation. I think that it was fair because Mr. Johnson has an old mind. His youth has left him. Not many persons retain their mental youth. Their minds stop long ahead of their bodies. That is why <u>you</u> are so remarkable. Your mind is the granddaughter of your body. No that is not a good way to put it. Your mind has kept up with your body and projected itself out and beyond your physical limitations. It has wings. Johnson is either always in the act of imitating some one else or imitating the Rosamond Johnson of 35 years ago. He is responsible for the failure of the show to a great extent. You see Mr. Randolph trusted a good deal to Mr. Johnson's age and experience in selecting both cast and material, and he steered him too often off the high way to success. He, more than once used his influence with Randolph to palm off friends of his, as good performers. People of no ability and doomed to failure. And he discouraged anything that spoke the real Negro. Hence what the critics said was inevitable.

You see Godmother, with you, that is why I am so reluctant to recommend <u>any</u>one to you. Often we discuss people and I try to make it clear to you that I am <u>not</u> trying to interest <u>you</u> in them. I'd want to be <u>very</u> sure before I persuaded you to give of your time and energy and blessed spirit and money to worthless people just because I like them. I

[3]*President of Howard University.*
[4]*Probably Allie Wrubel (1905–73), saxophonist, contract composer for Warner Bros., popular composer. Wrubel would have been twenty-six years old at the time.*

want you to remember me as worthy of your trust, however imperfect I may prove to be otherwise.

The Viking press again asks for the Life of Kossula,[5] but in language rather than dialect. It lies here and I know your mind about that and so I do not answer them except with your tongue.

Covici Friede[6] has asked for the story book and suggested that the stories be put in a framework. They also ask for first choice of the conjure book.[7]

Miss Nancy Cunard[8] of the well know[n] steamship line has written me and also sent George Antheil, who is in this country at present, to to see me.[9] She has heard of my work and wants to publish a book of Negro-ness in Paris.[10] She seems very interested both in me and what I am doing and hinted at my joining her in Paris. I have three letters from her in rapid succession and she cabled Mr. Antheil to come to me in her behalf.

Fannie Hurst came around yesterday and suggested that since the show had closed I probably would like to make a trip with her to St. Louis Mo. and Cincinnatti to visit her folks. She has an old Reo and wanted me to drive it. I declined of course and told her I had too much to do to even look out of the window let alone make trips.

Now Godmother darling, outside of getting the story & conjure books ready for another try, I am planning a Negro concert of the most intensely black type. Early November is the time. A theatre-owner has agreed to let me have the house and the program is being worked out. I am setting the date when I find out just when you will be back. I need you there of course to be with me both as a friend and critic.

Another project. You know Godmother, I know how to cook a few things well. Among them is chicken. I have been thinking since June of making a very fine chicken boullion, chicken salad, chicken a la king, and be ready to supply hot, fried chicken at a moment's notice to the carriage trade. In other words to set up as a chicken specialist. I

[5]Also called Barracoon by Hurston; unpublished.

[6]Publishing house.

[7]The "story book" would be Negro Folk-Tales from the Gulf States, later Mules and Men, and the "conjure book" Tell My Horse.

[8]Heiress and editor of Negro: An Anthology, published in 1934; see glossary.

[9]George Antheil (1900–59), avant-garde American composer, spent much of his career in Europe as the self-proclaimed "Bad Boy of Music."

[10]Published in 1934; see Negro: An Anthology in glossary.

have been sampling the chicken soups already on the market and find not one really fine one. I'd not attempt to do this wholesale. I'd like a list of 50–100 customers and supply them without advertising or any thing of the sort. Just an exclusive mouth to mouth service. I aim to make the soup so well that it can be served as cold consommé or hot as clear soup or used as stock by the client in her own kitchen. The breasts of chicken I would cut off before the chicken was put in the soup-pot. I'd steam these breasts almost without water and when thoroughly done, they'd be my salad material. The other part of the chicken would emerge as a la king. Then I'd have a certain amount of fresh chicken livers to dispose of also.

Why do I think of this? I firmly believe that I shall succeed as a writer, but the time element is important. I know that you worry about my future. Therefore if I had a paying business—which after all could not take up a great deal of my time,—I'd cease to be a problem. Besides I like to cook. I dont need any real capital to do it. A few glass jars made to my order for the soup. Perhaps a half dozen gallon thermos jugs in which to deliver hot fried chicken. Oiled paper-lined cartons for salad & a la king. I can manage it by denying myself a few things for a short while. I'd like you for my first client, and if I please you then I'll write personal letters to some of the finer hostesses and try to establish myself as New York's Chicken Specialist.

I am in good health and most hopeful. I am beginning to find my self. It has been a most intense summer. Not a moment of relaxation but I like working hard.

As soon as the story book[11] can be typed (I am doing it myself) you shall see what I have done with it. Then back to polish off the conjure.[12] Then to the play "Spunk,"[13] then to the novel.[14] That is my program.

<u>But</u> Godmother darling, after I have tried some of these things and if the world will have none of me, then I want to remain in your love, but I shall take nothing further from you in a material way. I shall feel that perhaps some one with a greater gift deserves your help more than I. You are most magnificent and I feel justified in accepting from you only if you are fostering ability. If I am convinced that I have

[11]Negro Folk-Tales from the Gulf States, *later* Mules and Men.
[12]Tell My Horse.
[13]*Based on her earlier short story by the same title; never produced; filed for copyright in 1935.*
[14]*Probably* Jonah's Gourd Vine.

nothing the world wants then you are too high for my mediocrity to weigh down. But <u>please</u> let me stay in your love no matter what happens.

I had expected to have money to send you but we stayed in rehearsal three weeks longer than is usual and so if you had not sent the 100^{00} I would have been minus. But every day and day by day I thought I'd have my royalties to send you. I should have had 525^{00} in those three weeks, but I only got 75^{00}. Mr. Randolph says he will pay it all when he can, but when oh when? Thats show business.

With your great soul always in my consciousness, with your love and courtesy before me like a pillar of fire I am struggling forward Godmother. I say a fervent prayer for your health, and well being. Thanks for all that you are and all that you do.

Most devotedly,
Zora.

The August-Sept expense accounts follows shortly[15]

TO CHARLOTTE OSGOOD MASON

43 W. 66th St.
New York City
Oct. 10, 1931.

Dear Godmother,

I feel very sad because you are ill. I want to know if you are able to eat anything at all. May I cook you a chicken as I did once before? Please let me do <u>some</u>thing.

Promptly at twelve oclock last night I set the altar for you and asked the powers invisible for your health in fire. I know that you will improve. The end candle fell at the moment when I uttered the words.

Thanks Godmother for what you sent me thru Miss Chapin. She was <u>very</u> nice to me, but I was disappointed in not seeing you, you must know.

Please, little flower of the world, lift up your petals again. As I said

---

[15]*Hurston submitted detailed accounts of all expenses for food, medicine, clothes, and incidentals, even sanitary supplies.*

in an earlier paragraph, I know that you are gaining. It is three A.M. and I have been working here since ten. You come to me so fragrantly and strong that I left off to write you. At six A.M. and again at twelve I shall set the altar for you and you shall be lifted up.

I know that you will know that I have felt your radiating spiritual self before this letter arrives. I am writing it as a confirmation. I am here, Godmother, receiving from you and sending to you.

With that peculiar understanding of me that you have, I know that you understand this letter in a way that no one else can. It is a message that only Zora could send to Godmother alone of all the millions upon this earth and be understood. I am meeting you at the altar-places and I am acquiescent. Yes, Godmother, I dont get all the words that you are sending, but I do know that you are stretching out to me, and if I have not been strong enough to send my answer thru the ether, this stumbling letter will have to do until I can gain more strength.

Please know that you are utterly beloved. Please be assured that your every gesture is appreciated for what it really means—your courtesy, your behavior of love.

Most devotedly
Your
Zora.

TO CHARLOTTE OSGOOD MASON

43 W. 66th St.
New York City
Oct. 15, 1931

Darling, My Mother-God,

I am so very delighted to hear that you are better. I know of course that you are far from well still and yet.

I am bogged up to the waist in rehearsals for the concert in the raw.[1] Monday I go down to Steinway[2] for a brief audition with or for

---

[1] *Presumably an early version of* The Great Day; *see September 25, 1931.*
[2] *The new Steinway Hall on West 57 Street opened in 1925 as a replacement for the Steinway Hall on 14th Street, which closed earlier that year.*

Mr. Colledge.[3] I had planned to have this part over by now, but I had a little trouble with my first baritone. He is the wonderful voice I told you about from New Orleans. No fooling, he has both more volume and more quality than Paul Robeson.[4] A bit gawky at present and quite naive.

Everything was going along well until his landlady, who is a graduate of Howard Conservatory of music began to cultivate him. She is a close friend and devout admirer of Melville Charlton, a Negro organist who plays at Union Theological Seminary (Columbia U.)[5]

They want to exploit him and so they began to show him this deep point where I wasnt doing his voice justice. The songs should be "treated" by a _real_ musician before he could sing them. Dr. Charlton should be allowed to supervise everything. Mrs. Upshun _must_ be his accompanist etc., etc. All this from an ex-lumberjack whom I have befriended in more ways than one. This Dr. Charlton is an intimate of Harry T. Burleigh who has less understanding of and sympathy for Negroes than any person I can imagine.[6] You know very well what he wanted to do to the work-songs. Make them in to Bach Chorals. And he and Mrs. Upshun wanted to make something like themselves out of Aleck Moody. So I merely shrugged my shoulders & dismissed him. Now, where do you think this lady intellectual took the boy to sing? At the doings of the Imperial Monarch Elks in 129th St. where they collected $6[25] for them.[7] Then he saw the light—that she merely wanted to hold onto him as a source of income for herself. She has been out of college for nine years and has not caused the faintest irritation to the skin of the world, let alone dent it. So dragging his great voice around would give her a small place in the sun and some small change. She couldnt get into any place where they could be heard, really.

[3]George Leydon Colledge (d. 1964) was concert manager for the Arthur Judson Company and opened his own concert bureau in New York in 1932.

[4]Actor, singer, activist; see glossary.

[5]Dr. Melville Charlton (1880–1973) was organist for many New York churches and synagogues; he was the first black member of the American Guild of Organists.

[6]It is unclear whether Hurston refers here to Charlton or Burleigh, who was black. Burleigh was a composer known for his work with Negro spirituals in the teens and twenties. He was awarded a Spingarn Medal for these arrangements in 1917, was awarded honorary degrees from Atlanta and Howard Universities, composed ninety pieces, and arranged more than four dozen spirituals. The Harry T. Burleigh Association for the study of Negro music was founded in his name.

[7]According to Elks historian Mike Kelly, the organization did not end its policy of race-restricted membership (whites only) until 1975.

So he came back most humbly and made his peace with me. I have done a great deal for him in many ways, for his gift rates it. I have gotten him a job and looked after him generally. He is twenty-one but quite naive and young mentally. I know what you would advise under the circumstances and I am going ahead and doing it. I dont want him spoiled by getting conceited.

Enclosed is the program as submitted to Mr. Colledge.

The Guild Theatre is the place in mind and Dec. 13, the tentative date.

I have a fine black girl as contralto soloist, and a lovely black girl as soprano. This baritone is a dark brown also. No mulattoes at all.

Godmother, may I show Mr. Colledge the fire-dance films from the Bahamas? I'd see to it that no one saw them outside the Judson offices,[8] and I'd see that they were handled carefully and returned immediately. It would save time if I could. He wants to see first a sample of all the materials and while I am training the group it takes so long for the preliminary showing and thats holds back definite arrangements. Then too, seeing the films would refresh my memory on details. Please, may I?

I type all morning and rehearse in the afternoon. It keeps me a little tired but I dont mind it so long as I feel it is getting me somewhere.

Mr. John Golden sent for me to be Negro adviser on a play he is to produce soon.[9] It was written by white people and they want to be sure of the atmosphere. I shall insist on program credit along with salary. If the play he is producing at present clicks, it will be about January before he does the Negro play. If it flops he will do the Negro play at once.

Godmother,—as I see it, unless some of the young Negroes return to their gods, we are lost. My short theatrical experience has shown me that the old bunch have neither gift nor honor. They stand around tin-pan alley and imitate the Jews.[10] If a Negro comes along with an idea they attempt first to steal it & then crush the idea-bearing individual. Crush him so that he wont be around accusing them. Rosamond Johnson is one of the rottenest of the lot too. I was startled

---

[8]Theatrical agents.

[9]John Golden (1874–1955), successful theater producer and lyricist, established the John Golden Theatre in 1926, which closed during the Depression but was reestablished later.

[10]Tin Pan Alley was the center of the popular music business in New York City. Coined by composer Monroe H. Rosenfeld, the term at one time referred to two blocks of 28th Street between Fifth and Sixth Avenues. "Tin Pan Alley" composers concentrated on vaudeville, while "Broadway" composers concentrated on musicals.

when I saw some of the things he does to make a dollar or two. And the trajedy is that he is not by himself. They all attempt to clean themselves with their tongues like a cat by saying "other people do it." And the worst of it is they choose to take their ethics from the tin-pan alley Jew, who in turn despises them for being not only petty crooks, but lacking in originality in even that. George Antheil, the French composer paid me the compliment of saying I would be the most stolen-from Negro in the world for the next ten years at least. He said that this sort of theivery is unavoidable. Unpleasant of course but at the bottom a tribute to one's originality. But of course it is due to you in my case, because you sent me to look and see.

I know that this is distressing to you, the mother of the primitives, but it is the unlovely fact. Our so-called leaders are a degenerate and self-seeking lot. The poor Negro, the real one in the furrows and cane brakes are the least of his thoughts. A few paltry dollars and some white person's tea table is his goal. Alain is different but all the others are awful. He is not popular with them either and I can see why. You must hang with the gang or be shot in the back. <u>Please</u>, if you want their backing, dont disturb the existing order of things. Get on the band wagon, that is the backs of the poor Negro and ride his misery to glory. Complain in lyric verse about the fate of the black man, but kick him in the face if you meet him. He is supposed to be a figment of the printed page at so much per line. He must not walk in daylight and disturb the cogitations of our intellectuals. They have done enough for the poor brute when they plead for a seat for him in a pull-man—where he'll never have enough money to go anyway—and when they let him furnish them a gang plank to board the publicity ship. In other words, the things our "leaders" are fighting for are privileges for the intellectuals and not benefits for the humble. we have had black, inky battles for Pullman reservations, hotel privileges, white neighborhood residences, white wives for Negro doctors, appointment of indigient Negro lawyers to Federal jobs etc. But oh so little to improve the lot of the man in the street. And nobody is going to waste time and golden syllables telling the bottom black what to do to help himself. Unctous syllables are reserved for tea-table conferences where the leaders secretly boast "no other Negro was present besides me." But it is not the Negro leader's fault if the Negro didnt hear his burning periods. The white people were there and heard him—some of them not only shook hands with him, they pulled him down on a seat beside them—his absence just goes to prove that the Negro is backward. He doesnt take advantage of his opportunities. He should have been in the gold-room of the Biltmore at Mrs. Van Whoosis' tea. Is a race champion supposed to go hunt these wretches down? When he announces that he is champing for them at so much per champ (paid by white people) they ought to be happy. He is not supposed to know the hardships the poor intellectual has to endure for his sake. Struggling along on 5000–7000 a year & scalding his throat with hot tea and cock-tails as he is dragged from hotel to drawing-room singing of the woes of his people. The man farthest down shouldnt expect the man of brains to know or care about his humble problems either. He is a Harvard-Yale-Columbia man. And if any white person insinuates that he ought to know anything of the kind, it is a subtle thrust that he is not just as good as a white man. For surely no <u>white</u> man on his intellectual level would know anything about plowing. Plows are literary devices to be beaten into sword shares or vice versa on a type writer. Not to be waved—in all their earthiness under the noses of intellectuals. Certainly barn yards are out of his experiences. He is as good as a white man. He has his Kappa Key to prove it.

I suppose you will get the idea from what I have said that I am thoroughly disillusioned about my leaders. That is correct.

But that is not serious. I am on fire about my people. I need not concern myself with the few individuals who have quit the race via the tea table.

All my love, Godmother. I have you next my heart always. If I could only give you health! How happy I would be.

Most devotedly,
Zora.

TO CHARLOTTE OSGOOD MASON

43 W. 66th St
New York City
Oct. 26, 1931

Darling Godmother,

I want to tell you the result of my conference with Hall Johnson.[1]
He was <u>very</u> glad to get a message from you. He is happy to do anything that pleases you. He is very eager to help on the concert. In fact
he feels that it is a privilege. He thinks it is a great idea. He is going to
do the casting. Also we are in perfect agreement about Aleck Moody. I
want him to do the sermon, and I think he will have him do it. But of
course everything waits a bit on Alain.

Rehearsal is going on at this moment[2] and I wish that you could
hear these five huskies yelling "Mule on de Mount". It would do
you good.

Mr. Colledge says that he realizes that we are not letter perfect
yet on the material btu he would rather hear the real people and see
the dancers than the pictures. So thats that. I will return them to the
vault, [Mason's safe-deposit box] as soon as I look at them myself and
refresh my memory as to the details of the dances.

Hold tight to your little hoard of strength, dear Godmother and let
me add to it where I can.

Most devotedly your black spasm,
Zora.

---

[1] *Choral director, composer; see glossary.*
[2] *For the play* The Great Day, *a collection of spirituals and folk music built into the plot of a day at a railroad camp.*

TO CHARLOTTE OSGOOD MASON

43 W. 66 Street
New York City
Dec. 16, 1931.

Darling Godmother,

I know that you have seen our Alain, but I have even later news
than that which he brought.

First I have had the date set back as you suggested. It is now fixed
for the tenth [of January] instead of the third.

Alain probably told you about the audition so I shall not go into
that except to say that I felt very good that afternoon.[1]

Now I must get right down to the business side of it and the advertising comes first of course. I think Miss Dalrymple[2] has written to
you about it. She waits at all times for your approval in the publicity
matters./

She told me that she must have $200.00 right away for the printing
of the announcements and for the papers, and there must be some
photographing done. Not a great deal, but certainly a little. Now I feel
that it is highly probable that I shall be able to borrow enough cash on
prospects to do the thing, but the publicity simply cannot wait. It must
begin immediately. And the photography cannot be done until the
dancers have their costumes, and the publicity, that is, the folders wait
on the pictures. So I need to provide costumes at once. It costs three to
five dollars to costume each of the sixteen dancers. So that you can see
that I need 250.00 at once. I disposed of my car and put up the deposit
on the theatre, and my radio brought in 16.00 which I have used to
pay carfares for my group. 52 persons are a great responsibility I have
found. But now I have nothing more to sell. I am on the brink [of]
putting the thing over and it will break my heart to fall down now. Especially since no question of merit is involved, merely getting my advertising done on time. That is in time to do the concert any good.

[1] *Auditions for* The Great Day.
[2] *Jean Dalrymple (1910–?), theater publicist, manager, writer, and producer. Began her career writing vaudeville sketches; worked for a time with John Golden.*

Will you be generous yet some more and loan me that amount? I will turn over the entire box receipts to you to guarrantee the loan. I have worked harder on this than I have anything else except collecting it, and now that you have denied yourself that it might be collected, now that I have gone thru the rigors of it, and worked so hard to get it into shape, I am willing to make <u>any</u> sacrifice, meet any terms to give it a chance of success. The easiest part of it all is now before us. Most any producer down town would take it over.

The singers are only looking forward to one night's pay and so my hold on the[m] would be lost at once if there are indefinite delays. I say this because I am almost certain that I shall be able to borrow money to finish the thing, but it wont be available tomorrow., If it were a regular show and they could look forward to steady employment they would be more patient, but to rehearse for weeks and weeks for one night's pay is a great deal to ask, especially, when they see nothing happening. The Negro singers and actors have been deceived and exploited so often that they are always on the defensive. I have whole hearted co-operation now and I want to keep them at white heat, and pull off the thing while everybody has heart in it. A week is a long time to them and now that I have set back the date, if I dont begin the publicity, they will conclude that they are being trifled with. I say all this to explain and in a manner, excuse my seeming rashness in asking the loan. If ever I needed you Godmother, I need you now. You and you only understand all that I have wrapped up in that sentence.

I do hope that you can come to a rehearsal.

> Most faithfully and devotedly,
> Zora [in pencil]
> (broke pen)

TO CHARLOTTE OSGOOD MASON

43 West 66 Street
New York City
December 21, 1931

Dearest Godmother,

Rehearsals are getting on well. The business side is coming on too. That is a point that I want to take up with you now. How many announcements do you want sent to you for your own private mailing list? I know that it would be out of place for any one else to see your list.

I shall send Alain the program material as soon as I get it definitely lined up. I dont want to send it until it has some shape that he can depend upon as rather permanent. I have changed it about a great deal in the last few days. But by the end of the week hw shall have it all. He is going to make all the notes and explanations.

I am afraid that I shall have to cut down some of the scenery that I wanted on account of the Stage-Hands Union. They make all kinds of trouble about scenery for Sunday night's shows and insist on double pay for the men. More over they make you put on a stage hand for every little thing. So learning all this, I am contriving to use as little as possible. In addition, the Scenery Movers' Union demand double pay for cartage on Sundays. Their terms are positively criminal. $60.00 each way for three back-drops and one interior. So I must watch my step.

Music going magnificently, but I dont want you to come to rehearsals until afeter Christmas as a number of people are busy with holiday activities and come late. A few are absent. But after the Christmas, I know it will be different.

With high hopes for our venture and glory bulging from my pores, I am

Most lovingly and devotedly,
Zora

P.S. Not just an after thought. This is deliberate. I want it to stand out. Thanks again and again for your magnificence.

TO ALAIN LOCKE

[telegram]

January 5, 1932
DR ALAIN L. LOCKE
HOWARD UNIVERSITY 1326 R ST NORTHWEST

PLEASE WIRE FOREWORD TO DALRYMPH AT MY EXPENSE
PROGRAM SET COME SOON
    ZORA.

TO CARL VAN VECHTEN

[January 10, 1932—library dated]

> *[written on program for "Great Day," January 10, 1932,*
> *at John Golden Theatre, "A Program of Original Negro*
> *Folklore, Compiled by Miss Zora Hurston, Presented by a*
> *Choral and Dramatic Cast of Eighty Negro Players."*
> *Orchestra $2.50; balcony $2.00, $1.50, and $1.00. "Best*
> *locations for seats are being held for those to whom this*
> *announcement is addressed, and as there is a large*
> *demand, an early reply is advisable. Applications will be*
> *filled in the order of their receipt."]*

Dear Carl,
    Please let me see you in a close-up seat.

                                Love,
                                Zora

TO CHARLOTTE OSGOOD MASON

43 W. 66th St.
New York City
Jan. 14, 1932

Darling Godmother,

Conscious as I am that I failed you in certain respects, I still am filled with the vibrant hope that you got <u>some</u> pleasure out of your concert.[1]

Alain has shown you the financial statement and so you know what is what in that respect. I was almost able to [re-pay—x-ed out] pay off all of the people, but not quite. Now, I wish to know your pleasure as to the future of the material in the concert. It is yours in every way, and while I know it has great commercial value, I have no right to make a move except as you direct. I want to do something in order that I might repay your loan of 530[00].

I am showered with letters and phone calls and my nerves are twanging. In fact I have been waiting for some sort of calm to write you. I have no feeling of glory, however, I am too keenly conscious of how far short I fell of the mark at which I aimed.[2]

Most lovingly, gratefully & devotedly,
Your Zora.

[1] The Great Day.
[2] *According to Robert Hemenway,* The Great Day *was "an unqualified success" and received good reviews. The* Herald Tribune *praised it (January 17, 1932) and* Theatre Arts Monthly *noted that "a responsive New York audience" enjoyed its "artistic values." Financially, the concert was unsuccessful.*

TO CHARLOTTE OSGOOD MASON

43 West 66th St.
Hew York City
January 21, 1932.

Darling Godmother,

Forgot to tell you yesterday that I had had a letter from Langston from Jacksonville, Fla. saying that my brother and his wife had entertained him magnificently and helped out his affair a lot.[1] He was very grateful and wanted me to thank them for him.

About the concert. Godmother, I am so sorry that my thickness has distressed you so. You see, you and Alain to a lesser degree are garden flowers, while I am a jimpson weed flourishing on a fertilizer heap in the barn-yard. See the difference that makes! I didnt even remember to ask about paper quality in the program and nearly kill you sensitive souls by my crassness. I am afraid that I am hopelessly crude, Godmother darling. Please dont let my clumsiness distress you too keenly. My wish is not to shorten your years and make miserable your days. Just the opposite. Dont pay me no mind. In your magnificence, shut your eyes and ears to my crudities, and focus your glasses on my tiny goodnesses. That is the inner courtesy, of which you are the high priestess. I mean to give you pleasure always.

Here is the clipping that you did not see. I thought that perhaps Alain had shown it to you as we looked at both THE POST and THE SUN together. I am sending it to you so that you wont feel quite so badly about it all.[2] My great wish was for you to be proud of me for once.

Most lovingly yours,
Zora.

---

[1] Her brother John Cornelius Hurston ran a meat market and flower shop in Jacksonville. Langston Hughes, accompanied by fellow Lincoln graduate Radcliffe Lucas, was on an extended book tour throughout the South.

[2] The Great Day received good reviews in these papers.

TO ALAIN LOCKE

43 West 66 St.
February 28, 1932

Dear Alain,

I am too sorry to hear that you are sick with an infected tooth. It must be awful to be ill and alone in the house. Now if you need me at all, I can come down and keep house and keep your gums sterilized and see that you get your meals on time and decently. Wire me if you need me. I'd be too glad to do something to show my huge appreciation.

By the way, when you asked me about that pamphlet of poems, I thought you were asking me if I had one. Today I cleaned off my chest of drawers and found what you were talking about—your copy and notes. I shall send them to you on Monday.

Saw G. not so well. Worried about you. I am getting on well as usual. Book coming on but not too swiftly as I have been in a slump. Doing things but tearing them up, but nevertheless finishing the book at last.[1] Have a copy of Wallace Thurman's "INFANTS OF THE SPRING" You and I are in it in a small way.[2] Not a bad book at all. Havent seen Countee's book yet.[3]

Let me hear and give ME a chance to show my appreciation.

Love,
Zora

---

[1] *Presumably a reference to either of her two folklore books,* Mules and Men *or* Tell My Horse.

[2] *Hurston's character in this roman à clef, Sweetie May Carr, is described as a "short story writer" with a "ribald wit and personal effervescence" who was "a great favorite among . . . whites" and whose written work was "turgid and unpolished."*

[3] *In 1932, Countee Cullen published a roman à clef entitled* One Way to Heaven *about the Harlem Renaissance, a love story about a con artist and a domestic worker.*

TO CORNELIA CHAPIN

43 West 66th St.
New York City
February 29, 1932

Dear Miss Chapin,

I want to thank you for the dresses. They are first very pretty, and second a good fit and third something that I could not have bought for myself. But greatest of all I am joyful because your generosity has made me bloom like the desert after a rain. I am not forgetting for a single second the part my Godmother played in my good fortune, but I do not wish to fall short in my appreciation of your kindness either.

I look very beautiful in the dresses and you will perhaps feel a tiny twinge of jealousy when you gaze upon me, but the artist in you will be so delighted at the sight of such a perfect union of clothes and woman that you will stifle your jealousy at once and rejoice with me.

Thanks and thanks and thanks.

Most sincerely,
Zora.

TO CHARLOTTE OSGOOD MASON

43 West 66th Street
New York City
February 29, 1932.

Dearest Mother of the Primitives,

It is raining great smaddles of wet snow outside, but there is sunshine a'plenty inside me. You smiled at me and I am very, very happy to be alive.

The dresses fitted me perfectly and I shall wear one the next time that you let me see you so that you can admire my blond beauty.

I wrote Alain at once and murmured a word for him to the proper forces. He is too valuable a man for the world to lose and particularly for the Negro world to lose. Besides he has so many social qualities that give light in dim places.

This is not a news letter. Just a throb from inside of me that I want to make sure that it arrives at its destination. Dear dear Godmother it is blessed to be loved by you.

Most devotedly your
Zora

TO CHARLOTTE OSGOOD MASON

43 W. 66th St.
New York City
March 19, 1932.

Darling, My Godmother,

Your black gal has been stepping right along. Now I am bogged up in the concert details[1] and I'm rushing, writing notes, phoning, and scratching my nappy head. Rehearsal everyday at 4:00

Please let me know if you want any announcements this time. I am working furiously to bring on a crowd. I want to make good in your eyes.

This time I have a preacher that you will like. I am taking no chances. He <u>must</u> rehearse every day with me.

Miss Lewisohn is going to use us after all.[2] Very early in April. I shall know the exact date Monday night.[3]

---

[1] The Great Day *was about to be performed at the New School for Social Research.*
[2] *Alice or Irene Lewisohn. Alice was a theater director and writer; Irene was a playwright, director, choreographer, and founder of the Neighborhood Playhouse.*
[3] *On April 22, under the auspices of the Folk Dance Society,* The Great Day *was produced at the Vanderbilt Hotel.*

I went to Paul Robeson's concert and your predictions are coming true. He still has his voice, but he had to exert himself visibly more than once to get his effects. Also he is getting too white in his singing. But on two or three of his extra numbers he let himself go and was his old time self.

My meeting with Alain on Sunday was very, <u>very</u> happy. I have been singing ever since. I shall ask him to make the announcement about one or two minor changes in the program. I hope he wont refuse. Also I want him to say a few words about the type of material in the concert.

The cast is cut down slightly, but it is good. The dancing is 100% better. Oh yes, we are in the April issue of Theatre Arts Monthly.[4] I havent seen it yet, but several people have called me and spoken of it.

Several more things are being talked of, but nothing more that is settled at this moment. We have been approached (dancers) about a London engagement this summer. Someone else has suggested a continental tour for the whole group.

With love, Godmother, with <u>great</u> <u>great</u> love.

I am
Your own,
Zora

P.S. I saw to the paper the programs are printed on. It is even different from that used for Hall Johnson when he was there in October.

---

[4]*The issue includes a photograph of Hurston and the company entitled "Bahaman Dance." The caption reads: "The artistic values to be found in racial backgrounds and in communally created materials were recognized in Zorah [sic] Hurston's program of folk song and dance, Great Day, the result of her research in the field of negro lore. A responsive New York audience particularly favored this grotesquely costumed number."*

TO CHARLOTTE OSGOOD MASON

43 W. 66th St.
New York City
March 27, 1932.

Darling Godmother,

The holiday is about over and here I am writing you on the tail end of it instead of before. But Godmother, dear, Good Friday found me absolutely penniless. I had not the first stamp. But my brother came over to call on by tonight and gave me six stamps. So before I close my eyes I am greeting you in celebration of the rebirth of the flowers. Surely I shall live again and spread my wings for the sun shall shine again and the trees will flutter forth in trembling green and blooming color shall drive away the winter drab.

Darling, My Godmother, Easter Greetings and love and life!

Langston is here at the Grampion Hotel. Miss Kay [Kaj] Gynt got me to call him up.[1] He had spoken to her very harshly over the phone and she was upset about it. I talked to him and he was polite and rather cordial. He leaves on Monday. Wished me to give you his regards but said he was too busy to write, and besides you perhaps were too ill to read it anyway.

Have not heard from Alain since I sent the announcement. Hope he is not angry about anything.

Again, all my love. Fondest Easter greetings. May it bring you more strength and health.

Most Devotedly,
Zora.

---

[1] *Hughes had worked with Kaj Gynt, a Swedish playwright who wrote the 1927 black musical* Rang Tang *or* Cock o' the Walk, *intended for Paul Robeson. When Robeson declined to participate, Hughes may have felt betrayed by the high expectations Gynt had encouraged, and this rift between Gynt and Hughes appears to have prompted Hurston to intervene. Although this project was revived as a film ten years later with music written by Duke Ellington and, again, hopes of Robeson's participation, the play was never produced.*

TO RUTH BENEDICT

[winter/spring 1932]

My dear Dr. Benedict,

I have tried to get in touch with Mr. Workus [sic],[1] the man I spoke of in connection with Hayti[2] & La Gonave. He does not seem to be around much or the people where he lives are uncommunicative. They spoke shortly I know. Perhaps you can succeed where I have failed.

Mr. Sanftus [sic] Workus [sic]

240 Washington Ave

Prospect 9-8866

He told me I could always get information about him thru Walter White[3]—409 Edgecombe Ave. Ed. 4-9311.

He is a valuable man and eager to do something. He has equipment & everything.

Thanks and thanks for fixing up the MS[4] so well. You <u>must</u> say you edited & otherwise fixed it up. I shall have the 15^{00} For the extra copies May 1st-3rd.

Love

Zora

[written on back:] I wonder if there is any chance of getting anything from the Rosenwald fund? Dr. Boas suggested it to me once. <u>I want to go to Cat Island</u>,[5] I have a chance to go South for the summer & shall do so if nothing else turns up. Do you think I might get something from the Rosenwald for the Fall? Then I could go to Cat Islands.

---

[1] *Faustin Wirkus, author of* The White King of La Gonave; *see Hurston to Ruth Benedict, April 17, 1932.*

[2] *A once-common spelling.*

[3] *NAACP leader; see glossary.*

[4] *Mules and Men, revised now to include some of the "story" material from* Negro Folk-Tales from the Gulf States *and the conjure material from the South (her Haitian and Jamaican hoodoo materials went into* Tell My Horse*) and threaded together with the narrative sections Harry Block and the Covici Friede editors had suggested.*

[5] *Cat Island, in the Bahamas, named either for a British sea captain or for the wild cats found all over the island. A particularly lush island, it contains a medieval monastery and the ruins of numerous cotton plantations and slave villages. Cat Island is home to inventive vernacular music played on such instruments as combs, saws, and handmade goatskin drums, and Hurston may have been interested in the folk music of the Bahamas which originated there.*

TO CHARLOTTE OSGOOD MASON

43 W. 66th St.
New York City
April 4, 1932.

Darling Godmother,

Alain and I had a long and intimate session on Sunday. He has told you all about it by this time, I am sure, but I want to tell you also.

I we took up the matter of my living quarters. I [am] assuming that he came from you, otherwise I know he is too busy to worry about my petty household details. After carefully mulling over matters, we both came to the conclusion that my present income is insufficient to maintain the establishment. I found it out before, but said nothing about it for fear you might think me ungrateful for what was being done for me. I know you are not in the same circumstances you were and perhaps you were denying yourself of things to give me anything at all.

A. I can move to some less expensive place. I can find one where I do not have to furnish my own heat and hot water as I do here. I could scarcely find a cheaper rent. Even a room would cost as much as I am paying here.

B. I can go south.

Both of these plans call for funds that I do not possess.

II my finding employment. I am writing to two schools and hope for a favorable answer. Either will do so long as I am able to earn my living and my self-respect and find time to do some writing. Alain has said that he will help me in this.

III my work. I understand that both you and Alain feel that I have lost my grip on things. I cannot comment on that because anything I might say could be construed as a bid for my own comfort. I shall leave that to time. For after all you are the last word, no matter what I do or dont. I can [not—x-ed out] neither be present when you sit in judgment, nor cry out under sentence. You cannot be wrong, for [any—x-ed out] everything that I am, I am because you made me. You can smile upon me, and you can look off towards immensity and be equally right. You have been gracious, but you were following no law except your inclination.

Alain somehow has the idea that one story follows upon the heel of the other in the new arrangement of my story-book. I am wondering if he is not re-reading one of the first writings for the second. This thought is strengthened by the statement from him that the two books are just alike. They are in reality far apart.[1] The concert[2] follows the pattern of the last writing of the book, while you remember the first writing was just the stories themselves.

IV my health. Godmother, to be honest, I continue to have intestinal trouble but I keep it to myself. I really need medical attention but I say as little about it as possible lest I worry you. It slows me up and when I dont keep up the agar agar[3] I lose ground. Recently I just couldnt find the money for it, and it hasnt been so good. But as I said I would [not] be saying anything now except that I begin to realize that while my silence might keep you from worrying about my health, it sets you to feeling that I have lost interest in my work.

I made no money on the last concert,[4] but I lost none, so I am happy. I made lots of new connections. A Miss Burchenal sought me out. I told Alain all about it and he will speak of it to you I know.

I'd love to go South if I could. There are several good reasons. 1. atmosphere to work. 2. Escape New York. 3. Health 4. Chance of self-support.

> Most lovingly and with all the behavior of love,
> Zora.

I addressed the Barnard alumnae last night at the Barbizan Court 140 E. 63rd. Well-received.

---

[1] *Negro Folk-Tales* from the Gulf States *does not contain any of the narrative sections Hurston added to* Mules and Men.

[2] The Great Day.

[3] *Laxative derived from red algae.*

[4] *Performed at the New School for Social Research.*

TO CHARLOTTE OSGOOD MASON

43 West 66th St.
New York City
April 16, 1932

Dear Godmother,

The sun, your and my exclusive property, is out today and so I am writing you in all cheerfulness. I hope that you are in better health than you have been for the past few months. I hope that from somewhere you have found strength.

Mr. Hunt's son-in-law called me today and said that he thought that it would be O.K. at Fort Valley, Ga. in the fall. He had a letter from his father-inlaw and he asked of me and said that he would be glad to hear from me. Evidently when he wrote he had not received my letter.[1]

There is no great news. The concert (Miss Dehn) of last Sunday night went well. I think that Mura Dehn has more talent than most dancers and for that very reason she will not be so easily understood.[2] Her African primitive number was exceedingly fine.

I hope that you will come to the Vanderbilt to see the dancing.[3] There will be a great deal to see.

I met Max Eastman[4] on Wednesday and he was very nice to me. I think that he is a brilliant thinker. Not because he talked to me, but I have read his writings.

With all good wishes, and love and gratitude, I am

Most devotedly,
Zora

Somebody sent me a pound of agar agar and I know it was you.

---

[1] Black artist Jimmy Harris. Dorothy Hunt had married Jimmy Harris, and the couple had provided office space for Fire!! in their Greenwich Village apartment. In August 1927, Hurston and Hughes had stayed with the Hunts, Dorothy's parents, in Fort Valley, Georgia.

[2] Mura Ziperovich Dehn (1902–37), dancer, choreographer, authority on minstrel shows and African American social dances.

[3] The Folk Dance Society sponsored an exhibition of The Great Day at the Hotel Vanderbilt on April 22.

[4] Publisher, writer, and activist; see glossary.

TO RUTH BENEDICT

43 West 66th Street
New York City
April 17, 1932

Dear Dr. Benedict,

Recently I have met Mr. Workus [sic], this ex-marine who was the
"king" of La Gonave, one of the Haitien Islands, and he has some
motion-picture films of dances and two conjure ceremonies that I
know you want to see. He is also most eager to talk to you before his
return. He wants to do more of that kind of thing and needs directions as he has no formal preparation for the work. But he is an excellent photographer and an intelligent man. We talked about the
Bahamas and Hayti and found that we had traces of the same thing
and decided that we should do a comparative work on the West Indies
and the U.S. on conjure. I wonder if the Dept. or any private individual could be induced to put up a little money for me to go to the Bahamas for a few months. Remember I scarcely scratched the surface
there. I could do it very cheaply as living conditions there are easy if
one goes native as I certainly would do. $500 or less would be enough
for transportation and six months work.

Please let me know what you think about it and also when you can
see Mr. Workus. My phone is temporarily disconnected. I can receive
calls but can make none, hence the letter.

Most eagerly and faithfully,
Zora

[added by hand:] I am applying for a Guggenheim. If I can get it, I
shall do my "foreign" work in the West Indies, Bahamas, St. Martinique & perhaps a month or two of Hayti.[1]

---

[1]*Hurston first applied to the Guggenheim Foundation on July 25, 1933. She listed Benedict as one of her references. Benedict's Confidential Report claimed that Hurston lacked the discipline and order necessary for fieldwork and that a more appropriate source of funds would be an individual patron.*

TO CHARLOTTE OSGOOD MASON

43 W. 66th St.
New York City
April 27, 1932.

Dear Godmother,

This is to let you know that I am ready to go except clearing out the place.

I am enclosing the bills I owe, which I must settle before I can leave. I can get the things moved to Brooklyn and the place cleaned out for $23.00. The man will begin the moment I notify him. One other item of expense, Godmother. I really need a pair of shoes. You remember that we discussed the matter in the fall and agreed that I should own only one pair at a time. I bought a pair in mid-December and they have held up until now. My big toe is about to burst out of my right shoe and so I must do something about it. Otherwise I have clothes enough.

I know that my bills are huge, but there they are.[1] I paid my light bill of $8.56 out of the money I got from Miss Lewisohn.

I am saving my books, pictures, desk, cabinet, piano and lamps. The rugs are very worn and the chairs are wrecks. I hate to give up my heavy iron skillets but my brother's place is small.

I am doing my washing tonight so that I can iron tomorrow. My books are packed in a box but I am wondering if I ought not to pack all books and papers in the trunk that is down at the Manhattan storage warehouse. I had thought of taking them with me but it costs a lot to ship books, and I can do without them.

I am going to Eatonville, Fla. and keep in touch with schools from there.[2]

Somehow a great weight seems lifted from me. I have been trying to analyze myself and see why I feel so happy. But I do.

---

[1] *The next day Mason wrote back directing Zora to store her trunk but to be sure and pay her bills, not let them sit and then send them to Mason. Her phone bill of $34.40, Mason angrily pointed out, was higher than her own. In the same letter, Mason asked Hurston how much living in Eatonville would cost her and reminded Hurston that she had once told Mason she could live there for free.*
[2] *Schools in which she hoped to teach.*

In all happiness, Godmother, in all love in all earnestness I beg to remain,

> Lovingly and devotedly,
> Zora

P.S. Sunday is May 1, and I want to get out by then or I shall owe more rent.

TO CHARLOTTE OSGOOD MASON

Maitland, Florida
May 8, 1932.

Darling My Godmother,

I am happy here, happier than I have been for years. The air is sweet, yes literally sweet. Summer is in full swing. The days are hot but the nights are cool. The mocking birds sing off and on all night long and the honey suckle and magnolia are in bloom.

I have finished one short story that I had had in mind to write for the last four years[1] and tomorrow I shall resume work on the story book.[2] That does not seem to me to be hard work at this stage of its construction. Mostly polishing and trimming. Then to the novel that I have wanted to write since 1928.[3]

Godmother I am so grateful to you for letting me be here in Eatonville. I am renewed like the eagle. The clang and clamor of New York drops away like a last years dream. I am so glad to be here. I awake with the sun and go to bed early. No special plans to do so, it just comes about naturally.

On my way down I met a man who has fairly thin lips and a nose not too negroid. He butted in with me and was quite pushing and sure of himself. Finally he sensed that he wasnt getting on with me as well as he thought that he should so he said, "Look at me! I aint no every-

---

[1] *"The Gilded Six-Bits" was published in* Story *in August 1933.*
[2] Mules and Men.
[3] Jonah's Gourd Vine.

day man. I'm featured! I aint got ne [sic] big flat nose and no liver-lips. I'm featured like a white man. You aint foolin wid no trash, girlie, you done run up on somethin' swell and you're dumb to de fact." After giving me one more chance to mend my ways he left me in a huff and went back to his own seat.

Hoping that you will be able to write me a line sometimes

I am devotedly your
Zora.

"Dis ole track dont line by steam, it lines by de motion of lima beans."

TO CHARLOTTE OSGOOD MASON

Eatonville Fla. Via Maitland.
May 17, 1932.

Darling My Godmother,

My work is coming on most satisfactorily and I feel fine. I get up before sunrise and work on a tiny garden I am raising to keep in physical trim. I have peas (black-eye) watermelons, pole beans, lima beans, okra and tomatoes all up in spite of the terrible drought we are suffering in South-Central Florida.

I have a most ungracious letter from Langston in which he renounces his claim upon the play.[1] It is one of the most unworthy things he ever did. His manner of doing so. What moved him to do so, I dont know, but it is certain he hopes to gain something from me or from some one connected with me. The woman, Kay [Kaj] Gynt whose dialect he is correcting on her play[2] has tremendous faith in me, I know. I have been wondering if you had brought pressure to bear upon him. I know that Carl Van Vechten is no longer behind him in the matter for he put himself out of the way in April to send me word thru some one else that he knew Langston had lied atrociously in the matter. I can see by [his—x-ed out] Langston's letter that he thinks it

[1] Mule Bone.
[2] Cock o' the Walk.

expedient to placate me. On the back of the envelope he wrote a conciliatory phrase, but in the letter he "regrets that I dont choose to tell the truth about the matter." Honest Godmother it requires all my self-restraint to keep from tearing the gin-hound to pieces. If I followed my emotions I'd take a weapon and go around the ham-bone looking for meat. He <u>knows</u> full well he hasnt one word in all that script. He knows that the plot is mine, the dialogue mine. He has nothing, <u>nothing</u> there except the suggestion "Zora, lets write a play." If that is the way to become co-author I shall write to Shaw, O'Neil and Barry[3] at once and horn in on all that they do.

Eatonville now has a paved street. Do you know that in more than fifty years of this town's existence that never has a white man's child been born here? My father was a mulatto but he was born in Alabama and moved here while young, following his employer and father who settled in the white community. There is no known case of white-negro affair around here. No white-Negro prostitution even.

At a church supper the other night a man offered to buy me some baked chicken. He was informed that there was no more chicken. He was embarrassed and said to me "There <u>was</u> some chicken, there a little while ago." The serving woman said "Oh so you tryin to offer her some chicken-<u>was.</u>

Hoping that you are improving in health, I am

Devotedly and faithfully,
Your Zora.

TO CHARLOTTE OSGOOD MASON

Maitland, Fla.
May 26, 1932.

Darling My Godmother,

<u>Please</u> be especially careful. I had a most remarkably clear vision of a group planning to rob you with violence. A young woman was at the head of the group with six to eight men to do the actual work. She

<hr>

[3]*George Bernard Shaw, Eugene O'Neill, and James Matthew Barrie, author of* The Twelve-Pound Look *and* Peter Pan.

was not even present when the deed was done, however I saw her with
3,400^{00} which were obtained. I saw her as she fled, as she contacted
three of the men and gave them 10^{00} each to get away & meet her
somewhere. But she was caught by a tall detective and jailed. It was
<u>awful</u>.

I have written to Claudia Thornton to check up on Kossula[1] and all
about things. I have also asked the Post Office at Plateau to check any
letters coming to Cudjoe Lewis from New York. You are quite right in
not trusting his daughter-in-law and grand daughter. They are probably hard up and are now taking Kussola's money from him.

Work coming on fine. I havent typed the short story yet.[2] I shall
wait until I am stable on the book,[3] then I shall go back and re-read
the story, make corrections and type it. I think I shall try one of the
larger, better-paying magazines as I feel it is a very good story and
should sell.

Thanks <u>so</u> <u>much</u> for the letter. It did me a lot of good.

You have passed another milestone in safety and I pray that many,
many more will stand along your trail, marking the line where passed
understanding, love, generosity and courtesy such as no one except
Mahatma Ghandi, and possibly a few others can understand and properly evaluate.

> Most lovingly, most humbly, most devotedly,
> Your Zora.

1. "Bucks above suspicion" = a lot of money
2. "And what makes it so cool" = furthermore.
3. "Beat it to the red" = Beat your head until it bleeds.
4. "Apeing on down de road" = running
5. "You got plenty meat on yo' head" = you have sense

---

[1] *Cudjo Lewis.*
[2] *"The Gilded Six-Bits," published in* Story *in August 1933.*
[3] *Mules and Men.*

TO WALTER WHITE

[telegram June 6, 1932]

Received at Maitland, Fla.
WALTER WHITE
409 EDGECOMBE AVE. NYK

YOUR LETTER REACHED ME TODAY SORRY HOPE YOU CAN
STILL ARRANGE TO INCLUDE ME[1] CAN GUARANTEE ALL
DANCERS AND DRUMMERS THANKS FOR REMEMBERING
CAN RETURN AS SOON AS NEEDED LOVE TO GLADYS[2]

ZORA.

TO EDWIN OSGOOD GROVER

*[written at top: "my first letter from Zora,"
followed by Grover's initials, EOG]*

Eatonville, Fla.
June 8, 1932.

Dear Prof. Grover,
    The spirit of the H-A-U-N-T-E-D B-O-O-K-S-H-o-P, whose name
I cant quite make out on the receipt, advised me to see you about a
folk-lore concert that I plan to give in the Fall.[1]

---

[1]*In* Batouala. Batouala *was based on René Maran's novel of the same name, published in 1922 in French and
translated into English by Adele Szold Seltzer. The highly controversial novel's graphic depictions of sex and
primitivism caused a sensation. It was backed by Leopold Stokowski of the Philadelphia Orchestra and cast
Paul Robeson in the lead. The opera was never produced.*
[2]*Gladys White, Walter White's wife.*

---

[1]*Bought by Myrtle and Henry Thompson in 1926, this local bookstore, also known as the Bookery, was managed by Mrs. Hack Thompson, a friend of both Hurston's and Edwin Osgood Grover's.*

I hope that you will see me and let me tell you my plans. You see, I am a Negro, born here in Eatonville but educated in New York City. I majored in Anthro. under Dr. Boas at Columbia with folk-lore as my particular field. Under Dr. B. I have done three years research among my people and possibly I know as much about the matter as anyone else.

Seeing the stuff that is being put forth by overwrought members of my own race, and well-meaning but uninformed white people, I conceived the idea of giving a series of concerts of untampered-with Negro folk material so that people may see what we are really like. I gave two of these this past winter in New York and they met with instant success.[2] All of the first string critics came out and gave me excellent notices.

Now the material used in these concerts was gathered for the most part in Orange county. All of it came from Florida and so I thought that it would be fine to give a series, or one at least in the native habitat of the songs and tales. And I wondered if Rollins College would be interested thru its Dept. of Anthro., its Music dept., and since I am setting down the tales in a book, if the Chair of Books [Grover] would not like to assist in putting the world right on Negro expression.

Sincerely,
Zora Neale Hurston

TO EDWIN OSGOOD GROVER

Eatonville, Fla.
June 15, 1932.

Dear Dr. Grover,

I shall be glad to tell you all that I have in mind. You see, I feel that the real Negro theatre is yet to be born and I dont see why it should not first see the light of day in Eatonville, the first colored town in the U.S.A. I have lots of material prepared to this end and would love to work it out with the help of some one who knows a lot that I dont know.

---

[2]*There were three performances of* The Great Day *in New York: one at the John Golden Theatre, one at the New School for Social Research, and one at the Vanderbilt Hotel.*

My plan was not particularly to make money for Hungerford[1]—not that it is not deserving, but I think Eatonville is in a much worse fix. I think that a community centre and some outdoor sports would help this, I wont say immoral just unmoral, town a lot. I would love more than anything else to build a playhouse for our use here. The whole town is excited about the project. You know we are a dramatic people. I mean that literally. We dramatize every waking moment of our lives.[2] And while this town is luke warm to schools, civic improvement, etc. everybody except the preachers are keen to take part in the concerts and the dramas.

There is not enough room at Hungerford for a good concert. You see, the men go thru all the gestures of the work songs. They lay the tracks and spike them down. We act out the jook, church, folk-tales, and make a setting for the Bahaman dances. It would be lovely to have it right here in the Negro setting, but I think Orlando would be the only thing.

I wonder too, if you would consent to read even a part of the ms. of my book.[3] This is my first for the general public and I am not at all sure of myself. I know what is true, but I dont know how much truth the public wants. Of course I am not interested in Sociology and see no need for a mention of problems of the kind and I am wondering if the publishers will think I ought to appear slightly wrought up. I am leaving everything out but folk-tales and brief accounts of how I collected them—background material—but I am wondering if I am right somf far as public and publishers are concerned.

I shall be glad to see you either here or at your home in Winter Park. But you must name the time and the place. You see, I know that you are more bound than I am for time and I'd hate to break in upon you and spoil things. But I can meet your convenience both as to time and place.

Thanking you for your kindnesses, I am

Sincerely,

Zora

Hurston [different hand]

---

[1]*Robert Hungerford Industrial School, founded in 1889 by Russell C. Calhoun and his wife on the model of Booker T. Washington's Tuskegee Institute. Hungerford was the first and only school for African Americans in central Florida for many years. Its land was donated by white patrons Edward C. and Anna Hungerford of Connecticut and Maitland, and the school was named for their son, who died treating black children for malaria in Louisiana.*

[2]*Hurston also made this argument in "Characteristics of Negro Expression," published in* Negro *in 1934.*

[3]Mules and Men.

P.S. I live with Mrs. Lulu Moseley, second lane to the left and up the hill as you come into Eatonville. We can hold a plain singing concert at Hungerford. Capt. Hall is an excellent person and the school is certainly needed.[4]

TO GLADYS AND WALTER WHITE

Eatonville, Fla.
(Maitland P.O.)
June 15, 1932

Dear Gladys and Walter,

I was rushed off here to finish my book[1] and I shall be here until the fall. I am about thru with the book on folk-tales and I am starting another.[2]

You dont know how much I appreciate your mentioning me in connection with Batoula. I want to help with that more than anything I can think of. I want to be the witch doctor but that is a man, so I shall be glad to do anything that I can if only to offer suggestions on conjure. I hope that the dancers can fit in. In fact I know of no other group in America who could. In addition, I am bringing up another drummer. The one I have is good, but he gets drunk too often.

The air here is marvellous and there is plenty of fruit and vegetables. Chickens for forty cents. Melons a dime.

I am getting some backing from Rollins College at Winter Park for Negro music and drama. I will let you know the details later. It may turn out to be something very big. In that case I shall need some help in construction.

Lots of love to all. I am really working very hard and seeing my way clear.

Most sincerely yours,
Zora.

[4]Captain L. E. Hall, principal of Hungerford School from 1931 to 1940.

[1]Mules and Men.
[2]Jonah's Gourd Vine.

TO CHARLOTTE OSGOOD MASON

Maitland, Fla.
July 6, 1932

Darling My Godmother,

Some sort of a vicious insect bit me on the right wrist and it has been pretty bad, but it is getting better.

My garden is in full swing. I got a full hamper of peas today and there is another hamper on the vines. I shall get somebody to take them to town and sell them for me since it is obvious that I cannot eat them all. I wonder if you would care to try some. Nothing would give me more pleasure than to send you something I raised. But if your cook does not know how to cook them it would be no use. Still, I can send a recipe.

Mr. Josten,[1] wrote me in behalf of Mr. Stokowsky of the Phila. Phil.[2] and asks that I take a part in the musical setting of Maran's "Batoula."

Thank you Godmother for your extra kindness in sending the August allowance so soon. I am still wondering if I should not go see about Kossula, but you didnt say.

On account of my wrist, my book is not quite finished, but I have the drive and stamina, the lack of which has been my hold-back in the past year. So another week ought to see it done.[3]

Mrs. Mary McLeod Bethune,[4] a real Negro woman whose school at Daytona Beach is quite well known, is having her 57th birthday on July 10, and has asked me over to the celebration. I shall go because I consider her very worth while. You perhaps have heard of Bethune-Cookman School at Daytona Beach. She has some very powerful friends among conservative white people.

Well, Langston, Louise [Thompson] and a crowd of white Negroes

---

[1]*Werner Josten, theatrical producer.*
[2]*Leopold Stokowski of the Philadelphia Orchestra.*
[3]Mules and Men.
[4]*Educator and leader; see glossary.*

have sailed to Russia to make a Negro movie.[5] Only two in the crowd look anything like Negroes. In this connection I remember your comment on Miguel's monkeys.[6] So I'm still wondering where they will get the Negro movie out of that. Who will they use for actors? The world certainly will not know that the ones they have are colored, except by foot-notes. I learned that Langston wanted some material from me before he sailed. Hence, what he considered the overture.

I am founding an adult school here.[7] The need is so great. Somebody ought to consider the great body of Negroes and leave the special cases alone for awhile. I mean by that, that nothing is done to point out to the lowly a better way of conquering his clods. So I shall teach the cooking of stews, beans, breads, vegetables, simple pastries & sewing & indoor painting & furniture making etc. The village is responding beautifully. One wholesale grocer is giving us groceries as soon as we can fix up our model kitchen and an Orlando store is giving the dress goods. The people are pitifully eager to learn.

I shall write often, now that my wrist is improving.

All my love and gratitude and Devotion.

Most earnestly & lovingly,
Your Zora.

1- I wouldnt give you Abraham = I wouldnt even give you a cent. (i.e. Lincoln pennies)

2- A brick lick = a blow with a thrown brick

3- Give 'im a road-map = make him run

4- Hip-slinger = a woman who walks seriously, also hip-wringer.

5- De big road = a main highway.

6- Shut up dollars while de nickel speak

7- A soap-wrapper = a cheap dress

8- Put bad mouth on you = to actually speak a curse.

9- As hot as July jam, or jelly.

---

[5] *The movie was entitled* Black and White, *and the trip was sponsored by James W. Ford, the first black man to run for national office as vice president on the Communist Party ticket. Thompson published an article about the trip, entitled "With Langston Hughes in the USSR," in* Freedomways *in the spring of 1968. Among the group of twenty-two travelers were journalists Henry Lee Moon and Ted Poston, writer Dorothy West, actors Sylvia Garner and Wayland Rudd, singer Juanita Lewis, and social workers Constance White and Leonard Hill. The film was never produced.*

[6] *Miguel Covarrubias, Mexican painter and illustrator of* Mules and Men; *see glossary.*

[7] *This did not take place.*

10- Now, you done stepped on my Zillerator (accellerator) = Now you've got me started

11- I'm goin' in drownin' = going swimmin

12- coon-dick = raw liquor.

13 Commisary license—common law marriage

14 Corn worm got you = You are poor, thin or generally in bad luck.

15- I wouldnt give a stomach-ache a grunt.= I wouldnt give anything.

TO CHARLOTTE OSGOOD MASON

Eatonville, Fla.
July 20, 1932.

Dear, dear, Godmother,

The hot dry spell has killed my garden but I do not consider it a major tragedy because I did it mostly for the exercise. Still I hate to see poor little plants burnt to death in the ground.

I have finished the writing of the book and now I am going thru correcting phrases etc. I am very, very happy at the thought.[1]

Perhaps I told you last time that I went into the lending library in Winter Park & the keeper of the place recognized my name and was very kind. Also he introduced me to his wife who in turn introduced me to three members of the Rollins College faculty and they have asked me to visit the creative art department in the fall.[2]

They have a most original idea in the enclosed magazine, dont you think? I know that you must know the president of the school, Hamilton Holt. The faculty is almost entirely Northern. I tried to get a copy of all of the numbers of the magazine so that you could see the great array of talent, but they simply cannot be had. Only a few are printed & they are usually kept as souvenirs.

---

[1] Mules and Men.
[2] *Probably Professors Robert Wunsch, Edwin Osgood Grover, and John A. Rice; see Rollins College and Edwin Osgood Grover in glossary.*

Dr. Edwin Grover is the originator of the animated magazine idea[3] & he is the one who had me invited to appear at the college.

I shall be typing my book[4] by the time that this reaches you. I shall prepare for publication all that I have done so far & send them on their journey then I shall turn to the polishing of the play. I think that there is now a <u>very</u> definite arrangement for it.[5]

The other evening a man was saying that the women were always waiting for the men to draw their pay so that they could read Sears, Roebuck's bible (catalog) and holler gimme. Shug Milton[6] retorted that if the womens seen anything in Sears and Roebuck dat dey wanted, dey sho better gwan to de white folks' kitchen and make de money & git it, cause de mens didnt give 'em nothin. Talkin' bout waitin till de mens draw dey pay! Dese here mens dont do nothin but stand round & draw lightnin.'

Dialogue of Quarrel between man & woman

Eugene Brazzle: Gold, you always 'feudin & provin'! Every full-size
    lie dats gits out in dis country, you starts it. I jus' come cross
    Steele's place & you round here strowin it I stole his melons.

Gold: Youse a liar, a big black liar. You <u>did</u> steal Sam Steele's knots
    (small, second-growth water-melons) I seen you layin on you
    belly in de grass eatin melon wid yo' hands. You had melon
    seeds sticking all over yo' chin. Stop cryin' & tell de truth.

Eugene: Who cryin? I know I aint. See <u>me</u> cryin its sign of a funeral.

Gold: Aw, you aint bad, Gene. I seen badder mens dan you down at
    de mourner's bench.

Eugene: Somebody's gointer <u>bleed!</u>

Gold: Look out it aint you. I'll whip you wid dis switch-blade
    (knife) to de very red. (bleed excessively)

Eugene: I dont say I'm detrimental, but if Gold keep on botherin
    me, I'm gointer get her to go. (run)

(Here friend intervened & carried Gene off)

---

[3]*The* Animated Magazine, *edited by Holt (president of Rollins College; see Hamilton Holt in glossary) and published by Grover, began as a series of twelve five-minute oral presentations by national celebrities each February during the school's founder's week. These presentations attracted great attention to the college. In 1934, Hurston helped ensure that Fannie Hurst delivered one of these addresses at Rollins during a trip that included Helen Worden Erskine as well.*

[4]Mules and Men.

[5]*Her Rollins College production of the play was retitled* From Sun to Sun.

[6]*Local storyteller.*

"Seaboard" Hamilton said that Richard Jones was wrong. Joe Stone (a white man in Maitland) had not been made a policeman. He was a fireman.

Richard (after a long dispute) Well, he's got his badge & his billy and hes wearin a gun. I dont believe he's gointer whip no house for catchin on fire and he aint gointer shoot it for burnin. (He must be a cop)

Godmother darling, I love you so. I'm really working <u>hard</u>. I'm willing to stay here forever. In fact, I think I'll buy me a home since I can buy one on the lake front for less than a year's rent in New York. Since you are giving me all that I have I am gointer wait until I have sold something before I try it, however. But Godmother, I can buy 3 acres on a beautiful lake for $300 and pay for it in dribbles. So I have made up my mind that the first thing I sell, I shall buy me a home & feel a little less like a tramp.[7]

With infinite gratitude and a cloak-wrapping love to warm you and clothe you, I am

Most lovingly,
Your Zora.

TO CHARLOTTE OSGOOD MASON

Eatonville, Fla.
July 29, 1932.

Darling My Godmother,

I certainly wish that you would change your rule and visit Florida this Winter. Three miles from Eatonville is a small town called Winter Park. It is quiet and beautiful. Not full of the pushing tourists. Twenty-seven millionaires live there in Winter. I do not mention the rich because I think that you would be impressed by mere wealth. I mention it because it shows what kind of people those millionaires are, that there could be so many of them and still keep the place so quiet and reserved. No one outside of the circle knows of those charm-

---

[7]*Hurston never realized this dream.*

ing estates smothered down in their sub-tropical settings. One family is Van der Pool.[1] The Packards[2] of copper interests, Irving Bacheller,[3] and so on. In fact this part of the state is full of that kind of people. Those who come for the winter and not the spot-light. Oh darling Godmother, <u>please</u> come. You'd get so many delightful surprises.

Weather has been so dry for a while that even the weeds are parched, but the nights are cool enough for comfort.

I am still in the drudgery of typing. I have done a short story, an article and the story-book.[4] It has been completely re-done. Now to finish typing.

You said that I might do the concert down here if I chose. Do you still feel that way? It is possible that the residents of Winter Park may see me thru. I have told Mrs. Martin,[5] Mrs. Little[6] and Drs. Grover, Rice [either Cale Young or John A.] and [Hamilton] Holt that you must be consulted so they know. There is no hurry, nothing being contemplated before early winter.

I have now learned the chicken-dance from a local child.

Youse in de majority = you are the strongest.

Godmother, I have changed my mind about the place. If I make some money when my manuscripts go in I shall put it in the Post Office.[7] Places are all right. I'd love one but this locality has so many draw-backs. They steal everything here, even greens out of a garden.

As ugly as Cinderella's sisters = Negro synonim.

Godmother, you'd love a Florida rain-storm. Raindrops huge and pelting. The sky ripped open by lightning, the heavens rocked by

---

[1] *Isaac Vanderpool helped found Eatonville "for the Negroes of Maitland" and built the first Maitland Library in 1907. Two of the Vanderpool sons—Harry and Charles—attended Rollins. Vanderpool's daughter worked as Mrs. Thompson's assistant at the Bookery.*

[2] *Edward Packard bought Rollins College President (1902–15) Dr. Blackman's Winter Park home in 1915. His first wife, Elizabeth Blydenbery, died in 1906 and he was remarried to Helen P. Oakes.*

[3] *Novelist Irving Bacheller (1859–1950) was a trustee of Rollins College and lived in Winter Park, Florida. It was at Bacheller's request that President Hamilton Holt came to Rollins in 1925. In 1928, Bacheller was appointed a "master teacher" in Holt's "Winter School" program. A journalist, author, and editor of* New York World, *he founded the first American newspaper syndicate. See Hurston to Carl Van Vechten, July 20, 1934.*

[4] *"The Gilded Six-Bits"; "Characteristics of Negro Expression";* Mules and Men.

[5] *Prestonia Mann Martin, journalist and author of* Prohibiting Poverty: Being Suggestions for a Method of Obtaining Economic Security.

[6] *Edith Todd Little (1882–1960) was a cousin of a Rollins trustee and worked in the Rollins administration from 1951 to 1960.*

[7] *By an act of Congress in 1910 a postal savings system was established to encourage immigrants accustomed to such savings programs. In the 1930s more than $1 billion was saved in this system. The program ended in 1967.*

thunder. Then a sky so blue that there is no word to name its color, and birds bursting open with song.

I do hope that the family is happy, and that Alain and Miguel [Covarrubias] are doing fine.

Most devotedly, I am
Your own Zora.

TO WALTER AND GLADYS WHITE

[July/August 1932]

Hello Folks,

Hot and lazy out of this world. Work griping me nearly to death.

How is it that you did not go to Russia with the great migration?[1] But seriously if the list of people that I have that went, I am wondering who they are going to use for actors.

The folk theatre business here is coming along great. I seriously fear that it is going to happen.

Mrs. Mary McLeod Bethune is having her birthday party on Sunday at Daytona and I hope that you all will send her a greeting of some kind. She would love it.

If you want to borrow my drums until I return, go to 442 St. Nicholas Ave and see the Supt. John Dawson and tell him that I say to let you have them until my return. But I am getting you one made down here from the genuine goat-hide and properly and authentically decorated. Get the two snake-skin costumes also. One consists of three pieces. A cape for the shoulders, a breech piece, a head-peice. The other is merely a moccasin hide breech piece. Ther is another all over paper costume that might intrigue you. If you want to keep them until my return, I'd like it very much and feel safe about them. Tell John that it is very temporary so that he will not think that I dont trust him, for I do.

---

[1] *Langston Hughes, Louise Thompson, Dorothy West, and others.*

Much love to all. I dont know what publisher I shall try to way-lay, but I know T.R. Smith, Mrs. Knopf, Harry Block at Covici Friede.[2] Would you read the book[3] when it is finished and suggest somewhere? I think you will like it. It is folk tales with background so that theyn are in atmosphere and not just stuck out into cold space. I want the reader to see why Negroes tell such glorious tales. He has more images within his skull than any other human in circulation. That is why it makes me furious when some ham like Cohen or Roark Bradford[4] gets off a nothing else but and calls it a high spot of Negro humor and imagery.

I do hope that Stokowsy gets that money for Batoula. I want to be in that. If I can be Paul's[5] 42nd wife in the play for one night, think of the people who would be glad to be that. Put me on the staff, you all, if you can.

Love to your two lovely kids and to Carl, et al.

Most sincerely,

Zora

TO EDWIN OSGOOD GROVER

Maitland, Fla.
Aug. 7, 1932

Dear Dr. Grover,

I have read the Mss. you left with me very carefully. I find it consists of tiny fragments of negro folk lore which is to the whole of Folk-custom as toe-nail clipping to the body. It is background material, [not plot—x-ed out] torn from context, not plot. To put it in its proper

[2]*Tom R. Smith was an editor with Horace Liveright; Mrs. Knopf was Blanche Knopf, wife of Alfred Knopf; Harry Block was an editor and friend; Covici-Friede was a publishing house.*
[3]*Mules and Men.*
[4]*Octavius Roy Cohen (1891–1959) was a white writer whose detective novels featured racist depictions of black characters. Roark Bradford (1896–1948) was a white humorist, folklorist, and novelist whose 1928 novel, Ol'-Man Adam an' His Chillun, was adapted by Marc Connelly into the Pulitzer Prize–winning play* Green Pastures, *noted by many black literati as patronizing and stereotypical in its portrayal of blacks.*
[5]*Robeson.*

relation to Negro life I must take a plot and add what she has as color. But the matters are nothing new to me. It has all been collected and I wouldnt be indebted to her for a thing, in all honesty.

Mrs. Thompson has been very, very kind to me. So has Mrs. Martin and Mrs. Green. I think that Mrs. Martin is very keen mentally and so is Mrs. Little.

I am looking forward very eagerly to the theatricals we discussed. I have met Prof. Rice[1] and he is enthusiastic; but Mrs. T[hompson]. says that—well, I mustnt expect too much from him. He assured me however, that he had written Dr. Wunsch,[2] but I knew you had done that before. I have found a lovely Negro girl who would be <u>grand</u> as an actress.

Now, in spite of the first paragraph I can write a story using one of the episodes in Mrs. Ward's[3] collection, if you desire it. I'll do it immediately as I am about finishing my book.[4] Then with the two before you, you can see my point.

Oh, by the way! Mrs. Martin's book [*Prohibiting Poverty*] is out. Came out Aug. 6th

This has been a <u>busy</u> summer for me but I am glad of it all. Hope that yours has been as profitable.

The Orlando-Sentinel of Aug. 10, says that Ruth Bryan Owen will move to Orlando to live and join the Rollins faculty.[5]

Mrs. Thompson's daughter is home. Very lovely. Poor Mrs. T. must go to a hospital for a small operation.

Dr. Blackman died Aug 9.[6] I was out there last Monday, no it was Sat. I'm as bad as Graham McNamee.[7]

I have so much to thank you for. If there is any reason [why—x-ed out] for you to, I mean if for any reason you wish to see Mrs. Ward's

---

[1]*John A. Rice, professor of classical studies at Rollins College. Caustic and unconventional in his teaching style, Rice was described by Rollins president Hamilton Holt as having "the most intelligence and the least wisdom of anyone on the faculty."*

[2]*William Robert Wunsch was a graduate student at Rollins from 1931 to 1932 and served on the faculty, in English, from 1932 to 1933. In 1933, he left to teach high school in Louisville, Kentucky. He and Hurston became close friends.*

[3]*Clara Benedict Ward (Layton) (1874–1958) attended Rollins from 1891 to 1896 where she also taught religion from 1929 to 1933. In 1939 she published a history of Winter Park.*

[4]*Mules and Men.*

[5]*Daughter of William Jennings Bryan, Ruth Bryan Owen (1885–1964) worked as a war nurse, a Chautauqua circuit lecturer, and a professor at the University of Miami, where she settled. She served as a congresswoman from Florida from 1929 to 1932, as an ambassador to Denmark, and as a U.N. delegate.*

[6]*William Fremont Blackman (1855–1932) was a professor of social sciences at Rollins, served as president of the college from 1902 to 1915, and was professor emeritus from 1927 to 1932.*

[7]*Sports broadcaster for radio, known for long-winded and colorful descriptions.*

material worked into something I'll be glad to do it, because you have
been so wondrous kind to me.

Cordially,
Zora Neale Hurston

TO CHARLOTTE OSGOOD MASON

Aug 11, 1932.

Darling My Godmother,

No need for me to come North. I wired Hall Johnson's manager
and he hedged and backed water. Pretended to be so indignant at the
very thought. But I have word from three or four quarters that he was
messing with our stuff.[1]

Nerves burnt out but calm. I am glad that I made the frontal attack and forced his hand.

Love and love and love. Please forgive me for disturbing you.

Yours most lovingly,
Zora.

TO CHARLOTTE OSGOOD MASON

53 E. 132nd St.
New York City
Sept. 16, 1932.

Dear, dear Godmother,

A thousand thanks for the money you sent me. I am very grateful.

I think my concert plans in the South are pretty definite for the
fall and winter. I shall not be teaching at all. First of all, Mrs. Bethune
was most lovely to me when I went to call on her, but she is having to

---

[1]*This was a constant concern of Hurston's. She suspected Johnson of stealing material for his folk opera* Run,
Little Chillun.

reduce her faculty instead of adding to it. She said, however, that she would be glad to have me if she can raise a certain amount of money by the time school opens, late in September.[1]

Now, I know that you are wondering what I am doing in New York. Well, the Athenaeum Concert agency in Steinway Hall wired me a ticket to come at once. They saw the concerts last year and want to book 8 of them this fall. I dont know whether to undertake them or not because I have a very good proposition in the South and feel rather secure there.

Therefore, Godmother darling, it seems that I am about to make a living at last. I know that these last months have been an awful drain on your reduced income and I have appreciated keenly your kindness in continuing it. By the 15th of October I shall be in actual work in Florida and so shall be making money on my own. More than that, I shall have a chance to make a name for myself without the Broadway drawbacks. If you will, therefore, give me the allowance for October, to allow me to function until my salary begins, I shall be off of your financial hands forever. Of course, I hope that you will still be interested in me and want to know how I am getting on, and will let me see you from time to time.

I met Sterling Brown,[2] Alain's good friend. Will Marion Cook[3] introduced me to him. He is also in New York on call as I am. (Countee Cullen's play)[4]

I hope that Bendiner (concert manager) will soon have done with me and hand me my return fare. New York is painful to me now. I feel so out of place.

With adoration, with love, with reverence, with gratitude and loving [ly—x-ed out] humility, I am

> Your devoted,
> Zora.

Hope to be on my way by Monday 19th.

---

[1] *Hurston taught there in the winter of 1933.*

[2] *Writer and professor; see glossary.*

[3] *Cook was a composer, conductor, and violinist who turned to popular music after racism blocked his career as a concert violinist. His musicals, as well as his Southern Syncopated Orchestra, were popular from the turn of the century through the twenties, in both the United States and Europe.*

[4] *Probably a stage version (not produced) of his 1932 novel,* One Way to Heaven, *or an early version of* St. Louis Woman, *Cullen's adaptation of Arna Bontemps's 1931 novel,* God Sends Sunday. *Produced, finally, in 1945,* St. Louis Woman *was a Broadway success.*

TO CHARLOTTE OSGOOD MASON

53 East 132nd St.
New York, N.Y.
Sept. 28, 1932.

Dearest Godmother,

I am leaving for the South tomorrow. Many, many things have happened since I have been here in New York.

Believe me, Godmother, [as——x-ed out] I am truly sorry that you had to prod my memory as to what I was going to do. But I had been scuffling mighty hard to make a place for myself never the less. I can see my way out now. You shall have details in printed matter soon.

Again let me say how grateful I am for all that you have done for me. Thru your kindness all the opportunities that I have to make a place for myself have come.

Whether you feel that you wish to help me thru October or not, will you please let me hear from you in the South? I have had no letter from you in such a long time, that I am starved for a [rep——x-ed out] word from you.

I have a violent tooth ache at present, but outside of that I am feeling very good. I do hope and pray that the mother of the primitives is feeling the best possible.

Do you know Godmother darling, that it is a long, long time since you have held me in your inner temple. But I have been waiting outside the gate until you should pull back the curtain again. Please consider that I am always, forever, outside your temple door, waiting. I believe that the material side has befogged the clearness of the vision and I pray that when I no longer am a drain upon you financially that you can see me, the Zora of the Eatonville gatepost, again.[1] You have been so much to the world thru the primitive man, to art, to letters, to science, I do not consider my own self as important, but you have meant soul and spirit to me. I purposely do not mention the physical

[1] *While Hurston's tone is sincere, this sentence has an ironic undertone. In short stories and in her autobiography (published after this letter) Hurston describes herself as a young girl perched on top of the gatepost in Eatonville, watching the world go by on the road in front of her house and performing for the white passersby to charm them into various small favors.*

side, important as it is, because I do not wish you to feel that the flesh-pots have been all in all to me.

So darling, I depart for the South to chisel out a figure in art. I want it to have all the rhythm, harmony, asymmetry of an African sculptured figure. But you shall hear and judge for yourself. You will hear something about Hall Johnson that will surprise you, but I leave you to find out all those things for yourself.

With all devotion, with all love, with all gratitude and reverence, I commit you to the high gods in space. I know that I cannot fail for you have brought me too close to eternal truth for me to miss my road again. Knowing you is like Sir Percival's [vision—x-ed out] glimpse of the holy grail. Next to Mahatma Gandhi, you are the most spiritual person on earth.

Hoping to find a word from you on my arrival in Maitland, I am

With All love,
Your Zora.

P.S. I have not forgotten that you were only to help me until the beginning of the school year. But if you will see me thru October I shall be in position to look out for myself henceforth.

TO FANNIE HURST

Maitland, Fla.
Nov. 5, 1932.

Dear Miss Hurst,

Your picture "Back Streets" is exciting most favorable criticism here.[1]

Rollins College is all worked up over the possibility of having you down this winter. Dr. Holt is a broad, high minded forward looking person and so Rollins College is not a typical southern college. To begin with, it has money and was founded for the sons & daughters of the wealthy who come down for the winter. It is situated in Winter

[1]Based on Hurst's novel of the same name, this film was very popular.

Park, a village of 26 millionaires and a quiet culture. But I know that Ruth Bryan Owen has told you about it. Her son attended Rollins last year.

John Erskine was the guest of honor last year[2] and I do hope that you will find it possible to come when it is formally put up to you. They will <u>love</u> <u>you</u> and I and I think you'll like the experience.

I am doing Negro concert here under Prof. Wunsch, Dept. of Creative lit. because the College like the U. of N. Car. wishes to make use of the Negro folk-lore in its state.

Most sincerely,
Zora

TO CHARLOTTE OSGOOD MASON

Eatonville, Fla.
Jan. 6, 193[2—x-ed out]3.

Dear My Godmother,

I had written you a letter on Dec. 30, but some thing I cannot explain, prevented my mailing it to you. You can understand such impulses.

First you will want to know how I have spent my time. Well, I, in cooperation with the Creative Literature Dept. of Rollins College at Winter Park, have been working out concert programs. Our first program will come off on Jan. 20 at Fern Park. Profs. Wunsch and Rice have secured a small theatre there as a drama laboratory for the Dept. and my group is to open that as our first bow to the local public. All by special invitation. Only 150 to be asked. But on the 27th we sing at Recreation Hall, the campus which seats 1800. Tickets to the general public—except Negroes. I tried to have a space set aside, but find that there I come up against solid rock. So early in Feb. we sing at Hungerford, the Negro school so that our own people may hear us. The interest here is tremendous, among whites & blacks.

---

[2]*Writer and husband of Hurston's friend Helen Worden Erskine.*

But the concert work is only the opening wedge. The Dept. is going in for Creative Negro art as it never has been done. We[1] shall surpass by <u>far</u> (thanks to <u>you</u>) what has been done by Paul Green[2] et al at the University of North Carolina. Special stress on music and drama, but painting carving, sculpture—all forms of art to be encouraged. The very thing that you and I have dreamed of doing for so long, but realized the handicap of Harlem and all that it means. The art dept. is doing the scenery and the posters, etc but we shall have national publicity. All is arranged for. We are scheduled for the Un. of N. Car. at Chapel Hill March 31. In addition to the singing the group will do a one act play by me. We are offered a Town Hall recital in March also by Mr. Bendiner of Steinway Hall and Profs. Wunsch and Rice are debating the pro and con of it now. Mr. Bendiner is the one who sent for me to discuss "Mule Bone." He is still interested but <u>I</u> want to try it out here in our laboratory and work out mistakes. <u>Then</u> New York. You probably know Mrs. Aldis, the playwright.[3] She is here and interested in the work. <u>Nothing</u> would please me more than for you to come down now. Wish Miguel[4] could be here to design scenery. My group is infinitely finer than the New York crowd.

Now I know you want to know how I have been living. I want to know too. But here I am. I have made two addresses before women's clubs for which I was paid. $10.[00] & $15.[00]. I have asked none of them for any favors because I realized that to do so would injure my prestige. They have been very nice in sending their cars to take me to and from rehearsals. The hall is in Winter Park, 3 miles away so you can see that walking isnt pleasant. I can have all the fruit I want and frequently I am offered vegetables from gardens, which I always accept. So you see, Godmother Darling, your Christmas present was the finest thing that could have happened to me. I needed shoes badly and I hadnt a <u>pair</u> of stockings. I hadnt tooth paste and I was washing my face with laundry soap. You ask me then, why would I do this instead of something that would bring me an immediate return? Well, Godmother, you know we have talked and dreamed of this for so long. I

---

[1]*Hurston's new performance troupe, for which she drew mostly on local talent, including friends from Eatonville.*

[2]*White playwright and professor at University of North Carolina; see glossary.*

[3]*Could be Zoë Akins (1886–1958), Pulitzer Prize–winning playwright. Hurston was notorious for inventing her own spellings, even of the names of close friends.*

[4]*Mexican painter Miguel Covarrubias.*

know how you wept when the African Art Museum went up in smoke because you saw the need for it. You said so often that you had planned an auditorium in connection with it so that <u>real</u> Negro folk music could be heard in the midst of it all. I saw a chance here to make our dreams come true if only I could forget the flesh pots of my own personal comfort long enough to get a foothold. I have that now, Godmother. The small amount of personal comfort I have given up is so little to pay for what will come back to me. Perhaps I shall never roll in wealth. That is not the point. If we can give <u>real</u> creative urge a push forward here, the world will see a New Negro[5] and justify our efforts. That is pay. The only real discomfort is that I am ill. I conducted rehearsal last night on an automobile cushion. Wanted to stay home in bed but the 20th is too near and I am too eager for complete success, such as I had no chance to win in New York with the material I had to work on. But I am worried about my colon again. I have been very ill for the last eight days. At any rate in doing what I have done, I have merely followed your example in going into the Indian Country.[6] So <u>you</u> can understand it. I dont expect everybody to do so.

Thanks Godmother for your loving kindness to me. Your courtesy, your behavior of love.

No, I dont know what is happening in New York I hear from no one now, because now I know how expensive an extensive correspondence can be. So one by one I have dropped off from people. I did want to write you though, but I hated to be vague, and I hated to speak of projects before they were accomplished. It was hard <u>not</u> telling you. Like holding my breath.

I pray that your frail body is comfortable at this writing. I hope for a letter from you and that I shall come to New York before you leave for the summer.

Most lovingly and devotedly,
Zora.

P.S. Could you use some more grape fruit rind? Its no trouble to make.

---

[5]*While the term "New Negro" was much in use among Harlem literati, including Hurston's fellow editors of* Fire!!, *this is one of the very few instances of Hurston's own use of it.*
[6]*According to Robert Hemenway, as a young woman Mason had "spent long months covered with prairie dust, living among the Plains Indians"—her interest before encountering black culture.*

TO EDWIN OSGOOD GROVER

Ishpeming
Feb. 1, 1933.

My dear Dr. Grover,

Do you still contemplate having Fannie Hurst for your "Animated"?[1] I hope so because she wrote me some time ago and said she was delighted at the prospect.

Then another matter. I'd like to take my group to a few places in the state to further polish them before New York.[2] I thought that the Uni. of Miami might have us. The Pres.[3] seemed enthusiastic when you brought him to our rehearsal. Should I write him myself or would it be best if you wrote him for me? If we are to approach him at all, we ought to do so while enthusiasm runs high here, both with the audience and the performers.

Is this too much to ask on top of all the other things that you have done for me? I feel that I lack the proper prestige to approach him directly.

Sincerely,
Zora Hurston

---

[1]*The* Animated Magazine, *a Rollins College innovation for live radio shows with celebrities which began as public lectures.*

[2]*Hurston's* From Sun to Sun *troupe. They had given a performance in January and would perform at Rollins College, at Eatonville, and at other Florida locations.*

[3]*Bowman F. Ashe was the first president of the University of Miami. He held the office from 1926 to 1952.*

TO RUTH BENEDICT

[stationery stamped:]
Estate of William H. Johnston [sic][1]
Maitland, Florida

Feb. 23, 1933

Dear Dr. Benedict,

As soon as I can get into town and get some strong wrapping paper, I shall mail the story material.[2]

I shall send for the reprints within a week I know.[3] You see I am down here on very small income. Nothing from Mrs. Mason anymore because I gave the conjure material to the Folk-lore Society. I dont care. I am getting on anyway. But it was touch [sic] for the first month or two after her sudden cutting me off. So friends here are subscribing one dollar each to make up the ten dollars I need to send you for the reprints. Already I have six dollars and I have three others pledged. I have made some powerful friends here and if times were not so tight, I could easily get the funds necessary for my doctorate. 26 millionaires (in normal times) and most of them more than friendly to me. They turned out beautifull[y] to my concert and I made enough to pay off my most pressing debts.[4]

Mr. Irving Bacheller suggested to the others that they pay for my reprints and I admitted that I'd be very happy to have it done.

Rollins College here is getting so interested in Anthro that I think they'd put in a dept. and push it with a little urge.[5] Dr. Hamilton Holt

---

[1] *William H. Johnson (1847–1927) had been the director of the bank in Winter Park and purchased his estate in 1915 from the Hungerford family.*

[2] *Negro Folk-Tales from the Gulf States. In a letter dated February 11, 1933, Benedict asks if Zora will send her "the manuscript of Tokula" for publication in the* Journal of American Folklore, *which Benedict edited. In this same letter, Benedict asks for "the unedited manuscript that was the result of your first field trip." Evidently, Hurston had decided to publish the narrative version,* Mules *and* Men, *as a trade book and the original version,* Negro Folk-Tales from the Gulf States, *as an academic work. "Tokula" appears to have been unpublished and is not among the unpublished writings that Hurston registered for copyright with the Library of Congress.*

[3] *Hurston refers here to reprints of her article "Hoodoo in America," published in the* Journal of American Folklore, *44 (October–December 1931).*

[4] *Hurston refers here to the presentation of* From Sun to Sun, *in Recreation Hall at Rollins College in February.*

[5] *Rollins College did not establish an anthropology program until 1972.*

is <u>very</u> modern and open to suggestion. He is prexy here. Profs. W.R. Wunsch and Rice[6] and <u>tremendously</u> interested in the folk-lore of the state. So perhaps a graduate of your Dept. could find a place here. I'll get Wunsch or Rice to write you about something and off hand they can be asked why not have a dept. here and collect all the Couch (obscure white element in South Florida analogous to backward mountaineers in Va-Tenn) Negro and Indian lore? Your dept. at Columbia could get a lot of new stuff and extends [sic] its influence here and at the same time make another opening.

If I am flush with funds (10[00] or over) I shall send you some fruit next week. No, I <u>dont want</u> you to pay express. I want to do it myself.

Lovingly,

Zora

TO RUTH BENEDICT

March 6, 1933

Dear Dr. Benedict,

I have just finished looking thru the pages and comparing the stories with my original notes as to story-tellers. Believe that I have them all corrected at last.[1]

It has just struck me that your name is latin and means "good saying." That is correct too. Maybe its "The good word."

Is there enough story-material for a publication? I hope so.[2]

---

[6]Hurston probably refers here to Cale Young Rice, who began teaching at Rollins in 1928 under President Holt's "Winter School" program. John A. Rice, a classics professor, was involved in a dispute with Holt over fraternities, resulting, this same month, in Rice's dismissal. The dismissal involved Rollins in a lengthy and bitter conflict, and the college was consequently removed from the American Association of University Professors' list of approved colleges. With others, Rice then founded the experimental Black Mountain College. Given the timing of this letter and the extent of that controversy, it is unlikely that Hurston refers to Holt and John Rice in the same paragraph.

[1]The manuscript of Negro Folk-Tales from the Gulf States.

[2]On April 12, Benedict wrote Hurston to say that her material could not appear in the next issue of the Journal of American Folklore because sufficient funds for a special Negro issue had not been collected and that the next issue would therefore be devoted to Indians. Although Benedict promised that Negro Folk-Tales from the Gulf States would be published the next year; and, again, that it would be published in 1934, Hurston's last publication in the Journal of American Folklore seems to have been in late 1931. Negro Folk-Tales from the Gulf States remained unpublished.

Fruit just going to waste here. Wish so much that I was flush so I could deluge you and Dr. Boas. I shall be in New York before long and then I shall see you and talk over many things.

Mrs. Mason fell and broke her hip and wrote me by air-mail. I think she is very sorry now for what she did to me.[5]

So sorry for the terrible task you have ahead of you on these stories.

Lovingly
Zora.

TO ALAIN LOCKE

Box 14, Maitland, Fla.
March 20, 1933.
[in left margin:] I did not mention G. in the program because I didnt know how she'd feel about it. Why they left out about Howard U. I dont know.

Dear Alain,

Miss Chapin wrote me of Godmother's fall. I am tremendously grieved. I am writing you because thru G. we are akin. I know you feel as I do. Only you have been closer than I in the past year and feel no remorse. I feel it. I know you are too big in this hour to rub my face in the dirt because I kneel before you.

Personally, I am growing. Now I am <u>doing</u> some of the things that we used to dream of. For one thing I have the chance to build a Negro theatre. Not just the building but the heart, the reason for the building to be. Rollins College, the most powerful white college in the state is with me. The two professors of Creative Writing are both North Carolinians and tied with Chapel Hill. They planned to take my group with theirs up there March 31st for the play tournament, but now it looks as if none of us can go on account of money. Rollins was to furnish all expenses but the school feels now that they cant spare the $385^{00}. So

---

[5] *i.e., not extending payments beyond the termination of their contract in September.*

it looks as if whites and blacks will all stay home and plan for next Fall. But we have gotten on. It has been decided to send our plays up to be read anyway. Of course the students are disappointed but————

I have two plays to go. Would you like to see them? "Lord of the Rainbow"[1] I think is good myself even if I shouldnt say so.

Would you like to come down next fall at our presentation? We are to be a feature at Rollins every year from now on. It is a wonderful chance for Negro playwrights and young actors to grow. We have even found a Negro scenic artist here who is attracting a great deal of attention. He is a handsome Greek God in brown. The College gave him the award (see program) last year over all the whites. Of course he is not a student. [He is—x-ed out] This is a strictly white college but it shows its breadth.

At my suggestion the Creative English group has read your "New Negro."[2] Honest, Alain a lot can be done here. With your help we can build here a theatre that will be talked of around the world. Paul Green and the entire U.C.[3] crowd is with us. If we had Bruce Nugent and one or two others, Lawd, Lawd! We are planning an outdoor theatre for the fall. Ruth St. Denis was here and saw us and wishes to appear with us as soloist-dancer.[4] I know its novelty-publicity seeking but it will help us never-the-less.

My sister [Sarah] died very recently in New Jersey and I am so unhappy about it. I havent spoken of it to a soul. I dont see why I should make others sad, but honest Alain, I am hard hit. Then Godmother falls! Its as if the sun had lain down in the cradle of eternity. I am doing more and better work than ever, somehow.

Please answer my letter

Most sincerely,

Zora.

Just had a letter from Clarence C. White,[5] inviting our group to Hampton. Pres. of Hampton was here in [illegible word] at Rollins.

---

[1]This play does not appear among her papers; nor is it among the unpublished materials she registered with the Copyright Office.

[2]The New Negro; see glossary.

[3]University of North Carolina.

[4]Ruth St. Denis (1879–1968), dancer and founder (with Ted Shawn) of the Denishawn dance troupe and school.

[5]Director of the Hampton School of Music, White had been an early student of Will Marion Cook and also of Samuel Coleridge-Taylor. He taught at West Virginia State College from 1924 to 1931, collected folklore and music in Haiti in 1928, and received Rosenwald support for his opera Ounga. White received a Harmon Gold Medal Award in 1927 and honorary degrees from Atlanta University and Wilberforce.

TO CARL VAN VECHTEN

[postcard]

1105 E. 9th St.
Sanford, Fla.
Dec. 4, 1933

Dear Carl,

Have a novel "Jonah's Gourd Vine" accepted enthusiastically by Lippincotts. Would love to have you mess with it in any way that you see fit—Advance review would be just fine.

Hope to see you before Christmas.

Most sincerely,
Zora.

TO RUTH BENEDICT

1105 E. 9th St.
Sanford, Fla
Dec. 4, 1933

Dear Dr. Benedict,

I have just placed my first novel with J.B. Lippincott of Philadelphia.[1] It is intended at present for Spring publication. Will you write me an advance review?[2] I'd love one from Dr. Boas also if he could be approached without massacre to my person.

I wonder if the Museum of Nat. Hist. would loan me a sliding caliper, [of—x-ed out] and a pair of spreading calipers too. I am working on my Negro ear placement and getting on fine. Now that I am

---

[1]Jonah's Gourd Vine *had been accepted by Lippincott on October 16.*
[2]*Benedict wrote a paragraph in which she praised the book for letting "us" backstage to see black life "off guard." Bertram Lippincott promised to use the paragraph in advance publicity for the book.*

going to get some cash from my book as well as some from another source you will see me in New York soon. I have applied for a Guggenheim Fellowship and I am told by someone in the know that I cannot fail. West Coast of Africa my objective.

If I can have the use of the head-measuring instruments, I can turn in something that Papa Franz will like I am sure.

I have kicked loose from the Park Avenue dragon and still I am alive![3] It cost me a lot for the first few months but I have found my way again.

Hope to see you soon. But I shall certainly see that you have some fruit when it gets thoroughly tree-ripened.

Lovingly
Zora.

Shall pay up all the society dues <u>very</u> shortly—as soon as I receive the first advance royalty check.[4]

TO FANNIE HURST

1105 E. 9th St
Sanford, Florida
Dec. 4, 1933

Dear Miss Hurst,

I have just placed my book—a novel I began in July and finished in September with the J.B. Lippincott Co. The title is "Jonah's Gourd Vine"

I have been wishing for you to write an introduction to the book. Would you?[1] They plan a Spring publication

---

[3] This reference to Mason is one of the most pointed and bitter in Hurston's correspondence.

[4] Hurston refers to the Folklore Society dues. Benedict was serving as president.

---

[1] In February 1934, Hurst sent Hurston the following carbon copy, published by Lippincott's virtually without emendation and rarely reprinted since:

Here in this work of Zora Hurston there springs, with validity and vitality a fresh note which, to this commentator, is unique.

Here is negro folk lore interpreted at its authentic best in fiction form of a high order.

A brilliantly facile spade has turned over rich new earth. Worms lift up, the hottish smells of soil rise, negro toes dredge into that soil, smells of racial fecundity are about.

Have you finished your new book yet?[2]
I hope to be in New York before Christmas now.

Most Sincerely
Zora.

TO FANNIE HURST

1105 E. 9th St.
Sanford, Fla.
[December 1933]

Dear Miss Hurst,

Thanks for even considering writing the introduction and the fine letter to the Guggenheim Foundation. I loved it.[1]

As a matter of fact, not even excepting Langston Hughes, it is doubtful if there is any literary precedent for the particular type of accomplishment that characterizes "JONAH'S GOURD VINE."

Miss Hurston has penetrated into the complicated lore and mythology of her people with an authority and an unselfconsciousness that has not its equal in similar annals. Even through what might easily be dialectic mists, her negroes emerge on the authenticity of her story-telling.

John, fretted with desires, Lucy, "pretty as a speckled pup" are as real and unspecial as their problems are special to them. Lucy with her bed pulled out from under her while practically in the pangs of childbirth; Lucy clouded in dialect, brown every one of her ninety-eight pounds, never for a moment fails to reveal that just a scratch under her skin lurks her universality.

Simultaneously, these characters are negroes and people.

The author's treatment of whites is as natural and without change of key as it would need to be if she is to succeed in keeping universality the dominant tone of her book.

Humor, heartache, ambition, frustration, superstition, fear, cussedness, fidelity and infidelity flow naturally behind white and black pores.

Point of departure between races leaps from the spring-board of the teeth rather than from the deeper recesses of the heart, and whatever racial issues are raised, are borne out of the grandly natural sources of the power of the author's story-telling.

Jean and Pearson, Lucy and every inhabitant of the narrative move against a background embroidered in folklore and symbolism, yet themselves so real and so human and so true, that rising above the complicated machinery of color differentiations, they bring the reader to fresh realization that races, regardless of pigmentation, behave like human beings.

[2]Anitra's Dance, *published in 1934.*

---

[1]*In November of 1933, Hurst wrote a somewhat qualified letter to the Guggenheim Foundation in support of Hurston's application. The letter praises Hurston's talents, abilities, and experience as well as what Hurst considered Hurston's lack of racial self-consciousness. In her view, one of Hurston's greatest strengths was that she retained the "natural" and "humble" characteristics that too many "sophisticated" Negroes had lost. She also cautioned the Foundation that Hurston could be "erratic" and "undisciplined."*

I guess its just routine, but five publishers have asked me for book-length work since the appearance of my short-story "The Gilded Six-Bits" in the August issue of "Story." I have another book all but finished now.[2]

I am most delighted with my publishers. Mr. Lippincott is very nice.

Mr. B. Lippincott says he will send you the manuscript. He is almost as delighted as I am to have you consider doing the introduction. It may not be literature, but it certainly is sincere work, Miss Hurst. It is from the middle of the Negro out—not the reverse. I hold no brief for anyone. I do not attempt to solve any problems. I know I cannot straighten out with a few pen-strokes what God and men took centuries to mess up. So I tried to deal with life as we actually live it—not as the Sociologists imagine it.

But I go on and on.

Most sincerely,
Zora.

TO HAROLD JACKMAN

1105 E. 9th St.
Sanford, Fla.
Dec. 15, 1933

Dear Harold,

Thanks for the big compliment. That is of asking for my play. I have been doing a book[1] and concert work and only a few days ago decided to rewrite "Mule-Bone." Maybe three weeks or more before I am thru. Then you shall have it if you still want it.

Sincerely—
Zora.

I agree with <u>all</u> that you say.

---

[2] Mules and Men.

[1] Jonah's Gourd Vine.

TO JAMES WELDON JOHNSON

1105 E. 9th St.
Sanford, Florida
Jan. 22, 1934

Dear Mr. Johnson,

The J.B. Lippincott Company is bringing out my "Jonah's Gourd Vine" a novel, in May. They have made out a [long—x-ed out] list of people to whom they plan to send advance copies, but no Negro names were on there because they are not familiar with Negroes and did not know to whom they should send.

May I place your name on the list? I <u>want</u> to do it very much. It is a story of Florida life. You <u>ought</u> to have something to say. <u>Please</u>.

Hope Mrs. Johnson is O.K. My love to her

Most sincerely
Zora Hurston

TO CARL VAN VECHTEN

[January 22, 1934]
School of Dramatic Arts
Bethune-Cookman College
Daytona Beach, Fla.

Dear Carl,

You are still and yet the same prince as before.[1] Thanks for the good word to Miss Hull.[2] I have touched up "Mule-Bone" a lot and

---

[1] *According to Bruce Kellner in* Carl Van Vechten and the Irreverent Decades, *Hurston told Fannie Hurst that "if Carl was a people instead of a person, I could then say, These are my people."*
[2] *Probably Elizabeth Hull, Van Vechten's niece and the daughter of Emma Van Vechten Shaffer.*

feel that it is much improved. Be thru typing in a week I know. Maybe sooner. So scared I will be too late and she will tell me so.

Mr. Lippincott likes my book a lot.[3] He is making some move about a movie and he wants to get in touch with Paul [Robeson?] about it. It seems that if Paul likes it, it will be bought.[4] I dont know where he is at present, but I know you do. Will you please see that he gets the enclosure? Thanks.

Mrs. Bethune has invited me to establish a school of dramatic arts based on pure Negro expression at her school in Daytona Beach. I have accepted. I wish to work out some good nigger themes and show what can be done with our magnificent imagery instead of fooling around with bastard drama that cant be white and is too lacking in self respect to be gorgeously Negro. She and I hope that we can induce you to visit us. She is after my own heart. But immediately, we want a picture of you to adorn our walls as one of the first real Negroes in literature. You get my meaning I am sure. No reflection on your mother at all.

Think I have placed my second book. "Mules and Men" The folktales done over and put back into their natural juices. Two more books planned for the near future.[5]

How is Fania?[6] Love to T.R.[7] and all the gang. Expect to be up there in the spring.

Most cordially,
Zora.

Either of the addresses will do. Even here at Maitland (Eatonville) will reach me.

Z.

[3]Jonah's Gourd Vine.

[4]Jonah *was submitted to the Warner Bros. Studios story department in October 1934. It was not purchased by the studio.*

[5]*Possibly* Negro Folk-Tales from the Gulf States *and* Tell My Horse.

[6]*Fania Marinoff, wife of Carl Van Vechten.*

[7]*Tom R. Smith, editor at Horace Liveright and friend of Van Vechten's.*

TO CARL VAN VECHTEN

Bethune-Cookman College
Feb. 6, 1934

Dear Carl,

Your picture came O.K. and it is <u>grand</u>! But immediately a problem arises out of it. Mrs. Bethune thinks it is meant for her office and <u>I</u> think it is meant for the walls of the Dramatic School. Show us and tell us so that we can know. At any rate, I have it in my possession and shall not let go unless you say so. And I'll hate like the devil to do so then.

So you are responsible for the Mills brothers also![1] Considering all of the other colored talent that you have fathered it looks like a case of "Ol' Man Hagar and his Chillun"

I think Lippincott is going to have me up in March. I'll be so glad to see you. I am beginning a new work and full of it right now.[2]

Love,

Zora.

[1]*David, John, Harry, Herbert, and Donald Mills began singing together in 1922 and were the first black singing group to have a nationally broadcast radio show. Their hits included "Tiger Rag," "Paper Doll," and "You Always Hurt the One You Love."*
[2]*Probably* Tell My Horse.

TO CARL VAN VECHTEN

[telegram]

February 17, 1934
DAYTONABEACH FLO 17
CARL VAN VECHTEN
150 WEST 55 ST NYK

THANKS YOUR COMPLIMENTS PLACE ME OUT ON ETHERS
BLUE BOSOM WITH THE SIX WINGDED ANGELS PHOTO
ARRIVED OK THANKS LETTER FOLLOWS

LOVE
ZORA.

TO CARL VAN VECHTEN

[February 28, 1934]

Dear Carl,

   Thanks awful. Fannie Hurst was down here for THE ANIMATED
MAGA ZINE at Rollins College and we ahd a fine lot of talk. She told
me that you would have written the introduction if she had not done
so.[1] When Mr. Lippincott found that I knew Fannie Hurst he proposed
at once that I ask her to write the introduction. I told him that you
were more up on the subject, but he had sent a letter off to her the
same time he wrote me and so when he came down here to talk to me,
I told him about your being king of the Niggerati[2] and he laughed a
lot and said he wished he knew how he could get out of having her

---

[1]For Jonah's Gourd Vine, *published in May 1934.*
[2]*Hurston's phrase.*

write it without making her mad.[3] You sounded better. She wrote a swell piece. Short but pointed. It was grand. Now they have taken my second book the folk-tales which I call MULES AND MEN. It is for fall publication. I'm hoping that you will consent to write the introduction for that.[4] They have sent me a contract to sign that calls for three more books. I have a novel planned that I like, and if it sells like I hope it will, I'd love more than anything for you to be midwife to it. Miss Worden or Worthing,[5] who came down with Miss Hurst, went out to Eatonville from Winter Park (3 miles) and took pictures. She plans an article in the WORLD-TELEGRAM about our town. If you could be induced to come down in the fall, I'd strow it around that you are to run for mayor. That would be NEWS! I could write a funny article about that. Last time (Aug. 18) Hiram [sic] Lester won by 11 to 6.[6] Dont worry, you wont have to kiss all the babies. Candidates are not allowed any such privilege here. Sleeping with the wives is enough to do to folks without kissing the babies too.

Oh yes, the title you didnt understand.(Jonah 4:6-10)[7] You see the prophet of God sat up under a gourd vine that had grown up in one night. But a cut worm came along and cut it down. Great and sudden growth. One act of malice and it is withered and gone. The book of a thousand million leaves was closed.

I plan to be in New York in May.[8] Hope that you will not be gone by then.

Most sincerely,
Zora

---

[3]The same explanations would be offered to Ruth Benedict later—by Bertram Lippincott but perhaps at Hurston's request—to account for asking Boas and not Benedict to write the introduction for Mules and Men.
[4]Boas wrote the preface.
[5]Writer Helen Worden Erskine; see glossary.
[6]Hirum Lester was mayor of Eatonville from 1922 to 1924; he operated the small store and post office originally started by Joe Clark on whom Hurston based Jody (or Joe) Starks in Their Eyes Were Watching God.
[7]For Jonah's Gourd Vine.
[8]Hurston was probably in New York City during most of May that year.

TO FANNIE HURST

Bethune-Cookman College
Daytona Beach, Florida
March 8, 1934

Miss Fannie Hurst
27 W. 67th St.
New York City

Dear Miss Hurst,

This is to try to turn you some humble thanks for all the lovely things that you have done for me. Words seem so useless, so I pledge that which I know you value most. I promise to work, and to turn out the best literature that I can; to keep my perspective wholesome and not to descend to deceit in literature no more than I would in friendship. In other words, not to blind myself nor attempt to create the artificial concerning my people for outside consumption, however much I am tempted. Somebody has already suggested that I could have put a little humor into that sermon. I could have done so, but it certainly would have not been true. I'd be no better than Roark Bradford.

I am writing to thank Miss Worden also. Both of you have been very fine. But I know that you were back of her interest in me.

Gratefully and sincerely,
Zora

TO WALTER WHITE

Bethune-Cookman College
Daytona Beach, Florida
March 8, 1934

Mr. Walter F. White
409 Edgecombe Ave.
New York? N.Y.

Mr. dear Mr. White:

It is extremely difficult for me under stand your recent attitude to-wards me. The one question that stands out above the others in my mind is, why you feel that I am not due any answer about my cos-tumes? I have thought about it intensely for months and still I am too dense to see why I should not have my things. I could understand the cupidity of Hall Johnson and those miserable wretches that he cor-rupted for his own ends, but I cannot see why any of it should touch <u>you</u>. I am determined to know.

Sincerely,
Zora Neale Hurston

TO ALAIN LOCKE

[on Bethune-Cookman College stationery]

March 24, 1934
Alain L. Locke
1326 N.W. Rst.
Washington, D.C.

Dear Alain:

It has been a long time between drinks, but I've kept you in mind all along. The strain of hard work has kept me silent to everyone. But you know the circumstances under which I have been working—plugging away in the dark.

Bravo! I saw your article on Sterling Brown in THE NEGRO AN-THOLOGY by Nancy Cunard. It was so true and fine I felt that I had to take a moment and tell you how I felt about it. I met him in New York last fall and was mightily impressed with him. I agree with you that even Negroes ought to know something about Negroes before they write things.[1]

Now I have found something down here that will interest you a great deal. I have found an artist of the first water. Honest, his portraiture is swell and he has never had a lesson in his life. He runs the elevator in a hospital in Orlando and is about 23. Tall and well built, Rich brown. The white people are already paying him to do their portraits. His name is Iven Tate, Orange General Hospital. He is simple, intelligent and TALENTED. He did the scenery for my concert last year. Won the prize for original art over all the whites in the state.

There is a young man here from Chicago, of very good family who plans to come to Howard next fall. I have told him that he must look you up. He has a really fine mind and under the proper influences will turn out to be a good writer. He can coin some grand phrases but has that awkwardness of youth. He is quite light in color, his mother being white I understand, and almost as big as Paul Robeson. He has lots of kinds of talent and I sincerely expect big things of him. I have taken the liberty of advising him to write you him self. Please dont squelch him. He is really something in the making. You have a chance in him to guide talent. He is motherless and almost fatherless in that he is somewhat neglected. And being a sensitive soul he erects barriers between himself and his father's indifference. Name, Frederick Wall, of Chicago and this school.

Hope that Godmother is well. I wrote her several months ago but she never answered so I assumed that she did not want to hear from me anymore.

Most sincerely yours,
Zora Hurston

---

[1] *In this article, Locke hails Brown for "meeting the objective of Negro poetry": "the poetic portrayal of Negro folk-life true in both letter and spirit to the idiom of the folk's own way of feeling and thinking." Brown's "racial touch," Locke wrote, "gives the genuine earthy folk-touch" that had been missing from the soul of Negro poetry.*

TO CARL VAN VECHTEN

Bethune-Cookman College
Daytona Beach, Florida
March 24, 1934

Dear Carl,

I am very glad that you liked "The Gilded Six-Bits."[1] I had been wallowing it around in my head for three years before I put it on paper. It brought letters from four publishing houses, Lippincott's being among the number. It will not be in the book "Mules and Men." That is the folk-tales done in a style that I think you will like.[2] I think Mr. Lippincott likes it better than "Jonah's Gourd Vine." He thinks it too short, however. He wants 180 pages more than the 65,000 words I turned in. He wants a $3.50 book.[3] Shall send on the first part in a few days so that you can offer suggestions if you like.

"Jonah's Gourd Vine" is reccommended by the Book-of-the-Month Club for May.

Seen Nancy Cunard's "Negro Anthology" yet? I got my copy yesterday. It is well done on good paper.

I am invited to come to St. Louis to the National Folk Festival of which Paul Green is the head. Walter Prichard Eaton,[4] Gertrude Knott[5] and lots of other <u>grand</u> folks behind the thing. It will bring me no money to take my dancers there, but it will give my books a push—especially "Mules and Men," in that it will increase my standing as a Negro folk-lorist outside of calling attention to me generally. The

---

[1] *Published in* Story, *August 1933.*

[2] *i.e., connected by narrative rather than standing alone.*

[3] *In fact, it was Lippincott's request that Hurston's hoodoo material (the second half of the published book) be added to the manuscript. On July 3, 1934, Bertram Lippincott wrote Franz Boas to tell him that they were requesting permission to reprint two of Hurston's* Journal of American Folklore *articles ("Dance Songs and Tales from the Bahamas" and "Hoodoo in America"), as an additional section of* Mules and Men. *As this letter from Lippincott to Boas also makes clear, Boas's preface was heavily edited by the publisher.*

[4] *Walter Pichard Eaton (1878–1957), associate professor of playwriting at Yale, was an author, playwright, teacher, lecturer, drama critic, and theater expert. He was the drama critic for the* New York Tribune *(1902–7), the* New York Sun *(1907–8), and* American Magazine *(1909–19).*

[5] *Gertrude Knott (1895–1984), founder and program director of the National Folk Festival; staged the first festival in St. Louis in 1934.*

dates are April 29, 30, May 1, 2. I am giving a concert[6] in the big Auditorium on the Beach to earn the transportation fare. Everything looks
favorable for it. Wish you could find time to come out to St. Louis for
the thing. I know you'd love it. Ozark Mountaineers, lumberjacks,
Indians, and Aunt Hagar's low visibility chillun. Even Pres. Roosevelt
is steamed up about it. Enclosed letter will show who is behind it all.

Love to Fania, Harold Jackman and all who may ask of me.

Yours indeed,
Zora.

TO DOROTHY WEST

Bethune-Cookman College
Daytona Beach, Fla.
March 24, 1934

Dearest Dot,

Yes, to all questions. I'm too delighted at your nerve in running a
magazine not to help all I can.[1] I <u>love</u> your audacity. You have learned
at last the glorious lesson of living dangerously. Thats the stuff! Let
the sun go down on you like King Harold at the battle of Hastings—
fighting gloriously. Maybe a loser, but what a loser! Greater in defeat
than the Conqueror. Certainly not a coward that rusted out lurking in
his tent—too afraid to cross your steel with fate.[2]

If you do not like this un-Negro story, why not go to "Story" Magazine 20 East 57th St. and get permission to re-publish "The Gilded
Six-Bits"? The story brought me a lot of recognition and I havent time
to write anything good in so short a time. Anything hurried and
shoddy would hurt you as a publisher and me as a writer.

---

[6] *A production of* From Sun to Sun.

---

[1] Challenge; *see glossary.*

[2] *In the battle of Hastings (October 14, 1066), William (the Conqueror), duke of Normandy, defeated Harold,
king of England, for the English throne. Although Harold put up a strong resistance against William, his
armies were exhausted from an earlier victory over the Vikings in the north.*

I'd love to be in the issue with R. Fisher. He is greater than the Negroes rate him generally. That is because he is too honest to pander to our inferiority complex and write "race" propaganda.[3]

In a big hurry darling

Yours indeed,

Zora.

My novel "Jonah's Gourd Vine" is a May publication (Lippincotts.) It is recommended by the Book-of-the-Month Club for May.

My next book "Mules and Men" is for fall publication. Same publishers.

Did you like Nancy Cunard's "Anthology"? I think it is great.

Perhaps it would be better to use the enclosed story than to reprint, but you are the editor.

Hurston seated,
photograph by Prentiss Taylor.

[3]*Rudolph Fisher (1897–1934) was a physician and writer. His books include* The Walls of Jericho *(1928),* The Conjure-Man Dies: A Mystery Tale of Dark Harlem *(1932), and numerous short stories. He won the Spingarn Medal in 1925 for "High Yaller."*

TO JAMES WELDON JOHNSON

Box 74, Longwood, Florida
April 16, 1934

My dear Dr. Johnson,

I referred the lady to you. I think that there is enough misinformation out about the Negroes without my adding a thing. I know that you know what she needs.

Just a word about my novel[1] before you read it. I have tried to present a Negro, preacher who is neither funny nor an imitation Puritan ram-rod in pants. Just the human being and poet that he must be to succeed in a Negro pulpit. I do not speak of those among us who have been tampered with and consequently have gone Presbyterian or Episcopal. I mean the common run of us who love magnificence, beauty, poetry and color so much that there can never be too much of it. Who do not feel that the ridiculous has been achieved when some one decorates a decoration. That is my viewpoint. I see a preacher as a man outside of the pulpit and so far as I am concerned he should be free to follow his bent as other men. He becomes the voice of the spirit when he ascends the rostrum.

I am reading ALONG THIS WAY[2] now. It is <u>grand</u>! My sister and I used to go around the house claiming things like that—what you and your brother did at the what-not. By the way, Prof. France[3] of Rollins College is having it read in his class. Prof. Sproul[4] in English (His sister married Dorothy Peters brother) is using it in his class-room also.

If the sponsors get the rest of the money I will see you in St. Louis.[5]

Sincerely yours,

Zora Hurston

Some white folks have given me the use of this cottage so that I may write in peace and quiet.

---

[1] Jonah's Gourd Vine.

[2] *Johnson's autobiography* Along This Way, *was published in 1933.*

[3] *Royal Wilbur France (1883–1962), professor of economics and human relations at Rollins from 1928 to 1952.*

[4] *Kathleen Sproul was an instructor in English at Rollins in the early 1930s and the author of* The Birthday Murder *and* Death and the Professors.

[5] *For the folk festival. The St. Louis Folk Festival was the first National Folk Festival and is the oldest consecutively held folk festival in the United States.*

TO ESLANDA ROBESON

Box 74
Longwood, Fla.
April 18, 1934

Dear Essie,

Your letter was altogether satisfactory. I had not written you because I feared that I might be seeming to lay an obligation upon you—to be trading on sentiment. I could have had a book on the press three years ago if I had wanted to do that. Carl [Van Vechten] told me to get one all ready and take it to Knopf because he had spoken for me. I appreciated his good will but I wanted to just naturally win my way by worth. I know that sounds like conceit, but it isnt. For the opposite of that statement is that if I could not sell a book on merit, I'd just never be heard from. I think that I got heard from too early as it was. So I just sat back and waited until I had heard from you. I know that if every anyone bought the movie rights to the book and if ever anyone wrote a satisfactory scenario and if it suited you all, I mean if you liked it, Paul will act in it anyway so I feel fine. I am glad that you liked the book.[1] I tried to be natural and not pander to the folks who expect a clown and a villian in every Negro. Neither did I want to pander to those "Race" people among us who see nothing but perfection in all of us.

What you tell me about your studies is thrilling. I feel so keenly that you have at last set your feet on the right road.[2] You know that we dont know anything about ourselves. You are realizing every day how silly our "leaders" sound—talknig what they dont know. I am laughing now at a recent article by Harry T. Burliegh [sic].[3] Because of his

---

[1]Jonah's Gourd Vine *did not appear until the following month. Hurston had probably sent the Robesons an advance copy of the book; perhaps she had even shared a draft or partial draft with them. She may have had Paul Robeson in mind for the part of the preacher, modeled on her father.*

[2]*Eslanda Robeson had begun a course of study in anthropology at the London School of Economics and University College. Along with her husband, Paul, who was studying African linguistics, philology, phonetics, and folklore, Eslanda Robeson was specializing in the anthropology of African cultures. She and Paul were considering a permanent move to Africa.*

[3]*Harry Thacker Burleigh (1866–1949) was a black singer and composer who worked with Antonín Dvořák on his symphony* From the New World, *singing African American songs and helping Dvořák with spirituals. As an editor and arranger, Burleigh was responsible for many of the spirituals that became famous in the early 1900s, including "Deep River." The Harry T. Burleigh Association, in Indiana, was named in his honor.*

posotion Roland Hayes[4] has let himself be led into talking some of the same rot. I am truly happy that you and Paul are going to sources. Of course, your learning the West African languages can mean nothing else but that you are going to Africa to study at first hand. That is glorious. Just what I have wanted to do for the past four years, but no funds. I also know Malinowski very well indeed.[5] Give both him and Fortune my best. I shall assist some one from the Uni. of Texas in recording Negro songs this summer under the Library of Congress.[6] There is a huge National Folk Festival being held in St. Louis Mo. April 29, 30 May 1, 2 to which I am urgently invited but it takes too much money to go with a group $600 and I cant see that, you know. But anyway, America is acknowledging my past efforts. One night, Alan Locke, Langston Hughes and Louise Thompson wrassled with me nearly all night long that folk sources were no[t] important, nobody was interested, waste of time, it wasnt art nor even necessary thereto, ought to be suppressed, etc. etc., but I stuck to my guns and the world is certainly coming my way in regards to the Negro. I have staedily maintained that the real us was infinitly superior to the synthetic minstrel version, and once they have had a glimpse, the imitation is rapidly losing ground. MORE POWER TO YOU. I know that it is your idea because I heard you say that you wanted to do this when I saw you in America last. I can see a marvelous future for both you and Paul. No limitations, really. Arent your subjects thrilling and your daily advances like travelling in new lands? I'd study a great deal more if I could afford it. Wish that I could go with you and Paul. Wish that I had a chance to learn the languages.

My second book "MULES AND MEN" is sold now and I have a contract for three more.[7] Luck to you and yours.

Yours indeed,
Zora Neale Hurston

---

[4]*Roland Hayes (1887–1976), the son of former slaves, was one of the most highly regarded African American singers of the century. Performing originally with Harry Burleigh, Hayes toured North America and Europe, offering as many as 125 concerts a year. Hayes was the first African American solo singer to regularly add spirituals to his repertoire and was a member of the Fisk Jubilee Singers.*

[5]*Anthropologist Bronislaw Malinowski (1884–1942) was particularly influential in creating cultural authority for the professional ethnographer acting, as Hurston did, as a participant-observer. Malinowski stressed objectivity in his ethnographic accounts and aimed to give the reader a sense of actually being there and witnessing a different culture—getting "inside" the culture. Malinowski married Elsie Masson, who died of multiple sclerosis in 1935.*

[6]*"Some one" is the folklorist Alan Lomax; see glossary.*

[7]*In addition to* Mules and Men, *the following Hurston books were published by Lippincott:* Jonah's Gourd Vine *(1934),* Their Eyes Were Watching God *(1937),* Tell My Horse *(1938),* Moses, Man of the Mountain *(1939), and* Dust Tracks on a Road *(1942). Hurston also contracted a second volume of her autobiography, but this was never published.*

TO CARL VAN VECHTEN

[April 26, 1934—library dated]
Box 74
Longwood, Fla.

Dear Carl,

I havent seen one either.[1] Maybe the publisher is treating us like home folks. I'm sure I dont know how come. As soon as I get a copy you shall have one. Maybe he is only sending it to folks he expects advance criticism from.

Love and 10,000 little squaddly toad frogs.[2]

Yours,
Zora.

P.S. I'd rather send <u>you</u> one myself anyway. Scared to <u>death</u> of reviews.

TO RUTH BENEDICT

[spring 1934]
Longwood, FLA
Box 74

Dear Friend,

<u>So</u> glad to have a line from you. Here I am in Longwood very pleasantly located and finishing my second book—a popupar version of the folk tales.[1] Off the press in October. Mr. Lippincott

---

[1]*Copy of* Jonah's Gourd Vine.

[2]*Hurston is here imitating a typical Carl Van Vechten closing for a letter.*

---

[1]Mules and Men—*a popular version, as opposed to* Negro Folk-Tales from the Gulf States, *sent to Benedict for the* Journal of American Folklore.

want Dr. Boas or you to write introduction. May I have him
write you?

Glad to straighten out those names & places. Send it along.

Sincerely, Zora.

TO JAMES WELDON JOHNSON

Longwood, Florida
May 8, 1934

Dear Friend,

I am just back from St. Louis. I did not stop thru Nashville because
I had four people in my car and nowhere to put them and it was about
11:20 P.M. when we got in. Shall be up soon at my leisure.

I suppose that you have seen the criticism of my book in The New
York Times. He means well, I guess, but I never saw such a lack of information about us. It just seems that he is unwilling to believe that a
Negro preacher could have so much poetry in him.[1] When you and I
(who seem to be the only ones even among Negroes who recognize the
barbaric poetry in their sermons) know that there are hundreds of
preachers who are equalling that sermon weekly.[2] He does not know
that merely being a good man is not enough to hold a Negro preacher
in an important charge. He must also be an artist. He must be both a
poet and an actor of a very high order, and then he must have the
voice and figure. He does not realize or is unwilling to admit that the
light that shone from GOD'S TROMBONES[3] was handed to you, as
was the sermon to me in Jonah's Gourd Vine.

Folk Festival was interesting and I met lots of people whom I
should know, but the long drive left me very tired.

I wish that yiu would write an article about Negro preachers that
would explain their hold upon their people truthfully. That is, because

[1] *In his May 3, 1934, review of* Jonah's Gourd Vine, *John Chamberlain argues that "Miss Hurston is writing
poetry and giving us anthropology; her sermon is too good, too brilliantly splashed with poetic imagery, to be
the product of any one Negro preacher."*

[2] *Hurston based this sermon on one she had collected by the Reverend C.C. Lovelace of Eau Gallie, Florida,
and which she published portions of as "The Sermon" in Nancy Cunard's* Negro.

[3] *Johnson published* God's Trombones: Seven Negro Sermons in Verse *in 1927.*

they are the first artists, the ones intelligible to the masses. Like Adam
Bede,[4] a voice has told them to sing of the beginning of things.

My best to Mrs. Johnson and all who may ask of me.

Most sincerely,

Zora

TO LEWIS GANNETT

Box 74
Longwood, Florida
May 12, 1934

Mr. Lewis Gannett
New York Herald-Tribune
New York City

My dear Mr. Gannett,

Mr. Lippincott sent me the clipping of your criticism of "Jonah's
Gourd Vine" and I received it yesterday. At the same time I found
your letter in my mail-box.

Your criticism is so full of understanding kindness that by the time
I got half-way thru, my feelings were running all over me. Maybe authors are not supposed to write to critics. I dont know because nobody
didnt tell me. I'm just following my feelings.

Your opening paragraph is literature of a very high order because
it sings and says things on the music strings that were put inside us
from the foundation of the world. Way back there before they hauled
the rocks to build the rocky mountains. I tried it on my box (guitar)
and it just fit some chords as I frammed[?] [word illegible] them out.

I am glad you recognize that intimacy between us and the heavenly inhabitants. You see I note that most people consider us over-
religious and fearful, when nothing is further from the truth. We are
ceremonial—lovers of color and magnificence. While white people
strive to achieve restraint, we strive to pile beauty on beauty, and mag-

[4]Title character of 1859 novel by George Eliot.

304   ZORA NEALE HURSTON

nificence on glory. Our preachers are talented men even though <u>many</u> of them are barely literate. The masses do not read literature, do not visit theatres nor museums of fine arts. The preacher must satisfy their beauty-hunger himself. He <u>must</u> be a poet and an actor and posess a body and voice. It is good if at the same time he is of high moral character. <u>But</u> like all the rest of the world, we forgive a great artist much that would never be forgiven the mediocre. <u>Many</u> great poems are breathed out every Sunday in our numerous churches and the acting out of the epic is magnificent. It is not admitted as such by our "classes." Only James Weldon Johnson and I give it praise. It is utterly scorned by the "Niggerati" (Negro literati, a word I coined in my 1927 undergraduate days) But the truth is, the greatest poets among us are in our pulpits and the greatest poetry has come out of them. It is merely not set down. It passes from mouth to mouth as in the days of Homer.

My six books would be

1. The Return of the Hero (Irish author, name slipped me) [above this line, Gannett wrote: Darrell Figgis (Boni Gooles)]
2. Penguin Island Anatole France Dodd Mead
3. Back Streets—Fannie Hurst—Hayer
4. Along This Way—James Weldon Johnson [Viking—Gannett's note]
5. The Good Earth—Pearl Buck [Day—Gannett's note]
6. My Antonia—Willa Cather [H.M.—Gannett's note]

[Jonah—Robt Nathan—McBride—Gannett's notes]

The order here means nothing. I want very much to set down a book about the life of Jonah by a man named Nathan but I am not certain of his first name, nor of the exact title of the book. But I think it is marvellous. It has been some months since I read it.

I am much more than mouth-glad at your kindness to me, and then too and again, I thank you. You encourage me to work and try to improve up the next time I say to a volume "go gator and muddy the water."

Yours indeed,
Zora Neale Hurston.
[Jonah's Gourd Vine—Gannett's note]

TO ALAIN LOCKE

[postcard postmarked May 16, 1934]

Box 74
Longwood, Fla.

Dear Alain,

Thanks for your letter and suggestions. I had yearned to do just that,[1] but fear of the consequences had me. It shall be mailed tomorrow.[2] Wish I could see her just once before it is too late.[3]

Sincerely,
Zora.

TO ALAIN LOCKE

Box 74
Longwood, Fla.
May 21, 1934

Dear Alain,

The books did not arrive from the publishers until Saturday—too late for even the northbound mail on that date because the office closes at noon on Saturdays. Too bad. But I got it[1] off today bright and early.

My mail is terrible now. I have so many letters to answer that I cant get down to work.

No, I shant be with Mrs. Bethune next year. She is a swell person, but the affair is too full of distraction for thought. There is more social life than at Howard and you are sort of compelled to appear. Then

---

[1]*Send Mason a copy of her novel or, possibly, dedicate the novel to her.*
[2]*A copy of* Jonah's Gourd Vine.
[3]*Hurston refers here to the ill health and imminent death of Charlotte Osgood Mason.*

---

[1]*A copy of* Jonah's Gourd Vine *for Mason.*

there is no money. Mr. Lippincott is dead set against it. I may be at Wilberforce in the fall.

Thanks again for the chance to show Godmother my inner thoughts. Sincerely, Zora.

TO CARL VAN VECHTEN

[June 12, 1934—library dated]

Dear Carl,

I am here [in New York] at the Dewey Square Hotel and I have been trying to find your telephone number for a long time. So I am writing you to ask you to please see me before I have to leave town the end of the week. It has all been so hectic since I have been here.

Lots of love. I want to talk to you so bad.

Yours indeed,
Zora

TO CARL VAN VECHTEN

[postcard postmarked July 20, 1934]
[postcard front: "Home of Irving Batcheller [sic], (Widely Known Writer), Winter Park, Fla."]

Darling Carl

Home and found your lovely card. So glad to hear you are home. I told Spencer Tocus[1] to see you. He is a most colorful musician out of St. Louis. See you in August for that photo.

Love, Zora

---

[1]*Clarence Spencer Tocus, who later wrote "The Negro Idiom in American Musical Composition" (master's thesis, University of Southern California, 1941).*

TO WALTER WHITE

Box 74
Longwood, Florida
July 23, 1934

Dear Walter White,

Two questions have been ploughing about in my consciousness for weeks. I had planned to wait until I returned to New York in September to find out the answers, but my curiosity got the better of me this morning and so I am asking it now.

I noticed at Kings Mountain, N.C. that you kept up some sort of a joke that I was liable to use bad language or do something lacking in respectability. That has been puzzling me for I'd like to know the name of the man—or woman—in New York with whom my name has been connected in that way. And I'd certainly like to know when anyone has ever heard me us[e] vile language. It has always puzzled me just why you wanted to make that joke, if you meant it to be one.

Now, the next thing that is puzzling me, is why you said—even tho you laughed as if that also were a joke—that Langston Hughes wrote a play with me. Of course you might have been joking when you uttered the slander but I have been wondering why you never corrected it. I'd like to know your reason for making that joke also. Maybe you think you ought to say that. Alright. Let us have your facts. A statement like that is a vile accusation and surely a man like you wouldnt do that unless he had some good substantial reason for doing so. I think this slander of me never would have gone so far had I not been so complacent. So I have taken advice and decided not to let this thing be so one-sided. From one thing and another, I've noted a tendency on the part of your organization[1] to try to cramp me. Why, I dont know. But I have the incidents before me, and moreover, others have noted it.[2]

Cordially
Zora Neale Hurston

[1]The NAACP.
[2]White's reply was shocked but cordial; he denied all of Hurston's charges and told her he thought she was more thick-skinned.

TO FRANZ BOAS

Longwood, Fla.
Aug. 20, 1934

Dear Dr. Boas,

I am full of tremors, lest you decide that you do not want to write the introduction to my "Mules and Men." I want you to do it so very much. Also I want Dr. Benedict to read the Ms. and offer suggestions. Sort of edit it you know.

Mr. Lippincott likes the book very much and will push it. His firm, as you know probably publishes more text-books than any other in America and he is conservative. He wants a very readable book that the average reader can understand, at the same time one that will have value as a reference book. I have inserted the between-story conversation and business because when I offered it without it,[1] every publisher said it was too monotonous. Now three houses want to publish it. So I hope that the unscientific matter that must be there for the sake of the average reader will not keep you from writing the introduction. It so happens that the conversations and incidents are true. But of course I never would have set them down for scientists to read. I know that the learned societies are interested in the story in many ways that would never interest the average mind. He needs no stimulation. But the man in the street is different.

So <u>please</u> consider all this and do not refuse Mr. Lippincott's request to write the introduction to <u>Mules</u> <u>and</u> <u>Men</u>. And then in addition, I feel that the persons who have the most information on a subject should teach the public. Who knows more about folk-lore than you and Dr. Benedict? Therefore the stuff published in America should pass under your eye. <u>You</u> see some of the preposterous stuff put out by various persons on various folk-subjects. This is not said merely

---

[1] *The version titled* Negro Folk-Tales from the Gulf States.

to get you to write the introduction to my book. No. But an enormous amount of loose writing is being done.[2]

My best to Drs. Klineberg and Reichard.

Most sincerely,
Zora Hurston

TO JAMES WELDON JOHNSON

[on Chicago YWCA stationery]

October 7, 1934
Dr. James Weldon Johnson
Fisk University
Nashville, Tenn.

Dear Dr. Johnson,

I stopped by Fisk on my way up here to give a concert and to make three speeches to see you, but alas, I find that New York University has borrowed you and so you are not to be seen, more's the pity for me. I saw your pretty shiny house with its green shutters and paid a little visit to all my old friends and came on up here.

But while I was there I made some interesting contacts. John Work[1] and others. Everyone seemed glad that I had come along at that time with my interest in Negro folk-lore concerts. So a great deal was said about Fisk doing something about Negro drama. The Carles S. Johnsons said that you had been talking about it for some time and felt keenly the need. Prof. Turner, Lorenzo Dow,[2] surprised me by being tremendously interested too. So I had a long talk with President Jones and he also is enthusiastic. He has tentetively proposed that I write him a letter telling him things about myself.[3] He wants to talk with you, Dr.

---

[2]*Boas did write a preface which praises Hurston's ability "to penetrate through that affected demeanor by which the Negro excludes the white observer." He also applauded "the charm of a loveable personality" in Hurston's style.*

---

[1]*John Wesley Work, Jr., was an associate professor of music theory, director of the Fisk Jubilee Singers, head of Fisk's music department, and conductor of the men's glee club at Fisk.*
[2]*From 1929 to 1946, Lorenzo Dow Turner was a professor and head of the English department at Fisk.*
[3]*See Hurston to Thomas E. Jones, October 12, 1934.*

Charles S. Johnson, Dr. Turner and Work. If it seems the thing to do after consulting you (he has the opinion of the others) he proposes to send me to Yale for a year of study in directing and the allied dramatic arts and bring me back to establish the experimental theatre at Fisk. He feels that he has the perfect set-up for it if he adds me to you, the material Charles S. and Turner has collected tp say nothing of what I have on hand. The idea being to create Negro drama out of the Negro himself. At the same time he wishes me to have additional training so that we can present all types of drama. He wants Fisk to lead the world in this matter and he wants to do it before some of the other schools do it. Frankly I am asking you to use your prestige, well, not against me. I have worked very hard in this particular direction and that I can do it better than most people or I wouldnt want to assume the responsibility for such an important thing only to see it fail.

I am writing to Dr. Jones today stating the things he suggested that I tell him. One point that he wants to be sure on is that after Fisk has spent her money on me that I will stick. I certainly will. You know that I have spent nearly five years now in reserach where it was certainly less attractive than the Fisk campus.

My love to your stately Grace Nail.[4] My next book is out in December, I think. Delayed by the illustrator.[5]

Most sincerely yours,

Zora

Zora Neale Hurston

P.S. Dr. Jones feels that actual creative drama belongs in your department[6] and is the logical development of things that you are working out.

---

[4] *Johnson's wife.*

[5] *This was initially Cyrus Leroy Baldridge (1889–1975), who had also done illustrations for Arna Bontemps and Langston Hughes, but was later changed to Miguel Covarrubias.*

[6] *Johnson's department was Creative Literature/English.*

TO CHARLES S. JOHNSON

[on Chicago YWCA stationery]

October 8, 1934.
Dr. Charles S. Johnson,
Fisk University,
Nashville, Tenn.

Dear Charles S. and Mrs:

Arrived safely. Drove the stretch from Nashville to Chicago in one day, but I suppose you do that as a rule.

I have written to Dr. James W. Johnson about the matter of the Dramatics at Fisk. I am writing to Dr. Jones today. I do hope and pray that it all goes through successfully. I am very eager to do the thing.

My best love to Mrs. Johnson and the children. A whole heap to Dorothy Steel, she is just O.K.

Everything going grand here. I muzzled Grimes and got here safely. Drop me a line when you have time.

Most sincerely yours,
Zora Neale Hurston

ZNH:mp[1]

---

[1] *YWCA secretary/typist. Hurston complained about typists' errors, but also used typists whenever they were available, as they were when she was staying at the YWCA.*

TO ALAIN LOCKE

[on Chicago YWCA stationery]

October 8, 1934.
Dr. Alain Leroy Locke,
Howard University,
Washington, D. C.

Dear Dr. Locke:

Glad you are back in America, so I can talk with you. I want to dedicate my forthcoming book to Godmother. To me it is unthinkable to dedicate it to anyone else.[1] I have no way of knowing how she feels about it, as she can no longer write letters to anyone. May I have your opinion in the matter?

I am here in Chicago to direct a Folk Concert the same as the one in New York, with splendid backing. The Concert will come off before Thanksgiving. A big Loop affair.[2]

Miss Baber send[s] regards to you. I am to speak before her Womans' Club October 17th. I am to speak in the Civic Opera Building at the Deltas'[3] Formal dinner, October 11th. Very shortly I am to address the Womens' Civic Glee of Chicago, so you see I am very busy earning a living. But I am earning it, not chiseling as our friend Langston is doing. They tell a lurid tale of his brazen antics at Fisk.[4]

---

[1]*Hurston's first two books,* Jonah's Gourd Vine *(1934) and* Mules and Men *(1935), are dedicated to Bob Wunsch and Annie Nathan Meyer, respectively.*

[2]*The concert, modeled after* The Great Day *and* From Sun to Sun *and entitled* Singing Steel, *became the basis for the Rosenwald's suggestion that Hurston apply for a fellowship for doctoral study in anthropology.* Singing Steel *was performed on November 23 and 24, was well received, and reportedly earned Hurston $500. Chicago's downtown is referred to as the "Loop" because it is encircled by the raised tracks of the "el'" train.*

[3]*Black sorority Delta Sigma Theta, founded in 1913 at Howard University.*

[4]*Hurston may be referring to incidents in Hughes's 1931 book tour—at Hampton, not Fisk—in which Hughes fell out with the administration over his desire to join in student protests over racism. She could also be referring to Hughes's political protests in 1932 while on a book tour of the South with Radcliffe Lucas. Hughes caused a particular stir at the University of North Carolina at Chapel Hill, where his poem "Christ in Alabama"—"Christ Is a Nigger"—enraged southern whites. According to his biographers, Hughes was not at Fisk in 1934.*

Hope to see you very soon, maybe I will be at the football game. I do hope you are in Chicago before that time.

Sincerely,
Zora Hurston.

ZH:mp

TO HAMILTON HOLT

[on Chicago YWCA Stationery]

October 8, 1934
Dr. Hamilton Holt
Rollins College
Winter Park, Fla.

Dear Dr. Holt,

I am offered five hundred dollars to direct a concert here which will probably be given at the Chicago Civic Opera house. The only reason that it might not be held there is the fact that the building seats so many that even 2000 people would look scarce in it.

On the way up I stopped by Fisk University in Nashville, Tenn. and the president Dr. Jones, asked me to apply for the job as head of the Drama dept. Fisk is the second most important Negro college in America, and under its white president, much more progressive than Howard in Washington, which is the ranking college. He thinks well of my approach to the matter and asked if I had ever had any sort of training outside of just experience, and I told him about Mr. Wunsch and the Rollins Experimental Theatre coming to my rehearsals and showing me what to do. That is true. They began almost as soon as my rehearsals began and helped down to the last. He is most favorably disposed towards me, and likes my work and speaks of giving me the rest of this school year at Yale to study drama and directing, and bringing me to Fisk next year as a full professor. He read the Rollins program and notices and was much impressed. He fully understands that Rollins is a white college and that the interest was in advancing Negro drama. I hope that you will not be offended at my mentioning your school. I have gained a lot from the contact. I had planned to ask the group here for 150.00 for my services when he asked me if 500 would do, so I said yes.

So now I find myself with comfortable quarters, maid service and a secretary. The hard work that I did around Winter Park is bearing fruit.

Thanking you for your past kindnesses, which have been many—in fact Rollins has been back of everything that I have done for the past two years—and for your present interest, I am

Sincerely,
Zora Neale Hurston

P.S. James Weldon Johnson will be working on the same project if I get the job at Fisk.

TO THOMAS E. JONES

[October 12, 1934—dated at end of letter]
THE YOUNG WOMENS CHRISTIAN ASSOCIATION
of Chicago
4559 South Parkway
Chicago, Illinois

Dr Thomas E Jones, President
Fisk University
Nashville, Tennessee

Dear Dr Jones:

Following the suggestions you made during our very pleasant conversation, I am writing you certain information about myself.

I suppose it is easiest to begin at the beginning. Born, January 7, 1902 at Eatonville, Florida.

Grammar School—Eatonville

High School—Morgan College, Baltimore, Maryland

Barnard College—Bachelors Degree—Columbia

University in the City of New York.

Began college life as an English Major, and satisfied the requirements practically during my Freshman-Sophomore years, which

were spent at Howard University, Washington, D C. My interest was
by accident switched to Anthropology by writing a term paper at
Barnard in a course under Dr Gladys Reichard. Dr Franz Boas,
world's most noted Anthropologist, who heads that department at
Columbia University sent for me. Began active participation. Field
work in Physical measurements with Herskovits and election to Ethnological Society before graduation. On graduation found a fellowship awaiting me.

Went to Florida and worked six months,[1] back to New York for
four months, weighed down by the thought that practically nothing
had been done in Negro folklore when the greatest cultural wealth on
the continent was disappearing without the world ever realizing that it
had ever been. Money was found[2] and I returned to the south and
spent three years 1928–1931 studying and collecting

  (a) Negro folk tales
  (b) Negro secular songs
  (c) Religious expressions
  (d) Hoodoo practises

Returned to New York and began to re-write and arrange the material for Scientific publications, and while doing so, began to see the
pity of all the flaming glory of being buried in scientific Journals.
Took the music to Hall Johnson, thinking that he would see what I saw
and be glad to use it. I had heard all of the Negro concert Artists, both
soloists and groups and was depressed by the fact that while they were
often great artists in the white manner, they fell so far below the folk-
art level of Negroes. I thought that it was because the material was
lacking. But later I found that to be true, but in addition it was
thought that no negro vocalist was an artist unless he or she could take
good negro music and turn it into mediocre white sounds.

Hall Johnson held the music six months and returned it to me with
the statement that the world was not ready for Negro music unless it
were highly arranged. The barbaric melodies and harmonies were
simply unfit for musical ears. I knew better. So in October, 1931 I decided to present Negro music, with emphasis on the secular, since that
was practically unknown. I decided to include folk-dancing. Hall Johnson agreed to help me, but after a date had been set for a concert early

---

[1]*Hurston collected folklore during this time (1927) with the help of a research fellowship from the Association for the Study of Negro Life and History.*

[2]*Mason's money: Hurston met Mason about this time.*

in December, he kept my singers standing around his studio for three weeks without one rehearsal, so I finally realized that I must do it alone. We gave our Concert January 1, 1933 at the John Golden Theatre (see appended copies of press notices for results). We were invited to do it again at the New School of Social Research in March, which we did. I had proved my point. Even Deems Taylor[3] sat until the last note was sung and came back stage to congratulate me. Louise Homer[4] also wrote me. Otto Kahn[5] was most enthusiastic. The world wanted to hear the glorious voice of my people.

I had also decided that the world ought to know about the folktales of Negroes. The Uncle Remus tales were true in spirit and wonderfully done, but hardly scratched the surface. There should be a chance for the world to know more. I decided to arrange the large collection and offer it for publication. So I returned to my native village for quiet, atmosphere and economical existence in addition to my love of the place. But Winter Park, home of Rollins College is three miles away and somebody there had read of the concert at the John Golden Theatre, so I was invited to do it at Rollins.

For (a) Rollins College interests itself in the folklore of the entire state.

(b) Prof W R Wunsch, Dr Hamilton Holt, and Dr Edwin Dagood [sic] Grover and Mrs Prestonia Man Martin with others are of the opinion that Negro drama if and when it arrives will be the brightest flame in America. So they wanted to have a helpful hand in stimulating it, and believed with me, that if it ever is to exist, that it must come out of the life of the people. So under Prof Wunsch's tutelage we trained a group at Winter Park, and opened the Museum, the experimental Theatre at Rollins three weeks later we gave a second performance (January 11, 1933) at Recreation Hall, Rollins Campus, to a very full house. We were invited to give performances at Lake Wales, Florida, Mountain Lake Club (Bok Tower) under Mrs Paula Dohme, Sanford, Florida. Twice

[3]*Writer and friend of Carl Van Vechten's, composer, music critic, editor, and radio commentator, Joseph Deems Taylor (1885–1966), along with Burton Rascoe, was a habitué of the Round Table at the Algonquin Hotel.*

[4]*Louise Dilworth Beatty Homer (1871–1947) was a dramatic contralto who performed from about 1900 to 1929, beginning with a world debut in France in 1898 and a U.S. debut in Verdi's Aïda with the Metropolitan Opera Company in 1900, and including performances with Enrico Caruso, Giovanni Martinelli, and Beniamino Gigli. She taught voice at Rollins College after retiring to Winter Park, Florida, in 1941. She was married to composer Sidney Homer (1864–1953).*

[5]*Banker Otto Kahn (1867–1934) chaired the Metropolitan Opera Company from 1908 to 1931 and was probably the most powerful and influential patron of the arts in New York at this time.*

Orland Municipal Auditorium, Daytona Beach Auditorium. I was invited to do the concert at Daytona Beach while I was attached to Bethune-Cookman College in that city, to develop the drama at the school. I found it impossible to do anything worthwhile for (A) student body of only 226 and the same students were needed for all the Choral groups, Major athletics, social groups, <u>various</u> dramatic groups at the same time. An instance of the sort of thing that happened, a Pageant was planned for the 30th Anniversary of the school. I was told to work from the script that a member of the faculty had written who had no more idea of drama than I have about relativity. I was urged to make it a grand performance. Then the entire faculty was summoned to help me direct. No one besides myself had had any experience in the field. One day eight people were trying to direct one scene at the same time. I went to the President and pointed out the impossibility and was told that the President wanted to be fair to all the members of the faculty and give each a chance to fame and glory. She couldn't be partial to <u>me</u>. I have not been able to rationalize the statement yet. Anyway the performance was just some students stumbling around on the stage.

I was given the old hospital building without a cent of money and told to turn it into a theatre. I even had difficulty getting a light bulb for my office.

The President had tried for four years to secure the Auditorium on the beach for a performance, and in spite of the fact that the head of the concern was a trustee of the school, it was refused each time. It was offered to me however on the strength of my record, with the hope that I'd do something akin to the things I had done at Rollins College. The President was jubilant when she learned that the Auditorium had been secured, but stated that no new program was needed. The people always wanted to hear the same songs and recitations that were done at Community Meeting. That was exactly what Dr Holmes said the people didn't want to hear. I must pledge myself to something different. So I had to say to the President that, I couldn't accept her program. So I went into preparation, but was given no authority to call rehearsals, only my personal popularity with the student body carried me over at all. Once when I complained to the President that the director of the chorus who was a student was giving me no co-operation she retorted that if the present arrangement didn't suit me, I could get my cast the best way I could. I finally made the cast see the importance of the thing, and in the last two days left of the rehearsal they responded like heroes and put the thing over. 2100 people were in the audience, and most enthusiastic. The President was proud, but I was a wreck from the exertions. I could never go through that again. My novel "Jonah's Gourd Vine" had been sold and I was contracted to my publisher for four more books, the second one for immediate delivery. So I decided to abandon the farce of Bethune-Cookman's Dramatic department and get on with my work.

I tell you this so that you will understand that I am not a quitter. There was nothing that I could do there that was constructive. In fact I felt it was hurting me. For all the dramatic presentation of the various groups would naturally be supposed to be my work by the general public. In fact Mrs Davidson, Editor of the Daytona Beach News-Journal, knowing the situation, advised me of the hopelessness of it. I was invited to bring my group from Winter Park to participate in the National Folk Festival that was held at the opening of the new $6,000,000 Municipal Auditorium in St Louis, which I did. On my return, I went on with my writing exclusively.

I would love to work out some of my visions at Fisk University because there, more than anywhere else in America, is the perfect machinery. There is James Weldon Johnson with his vision and breadth, heading Creative literature. Dr Charles S Johnson with his infinite horizon in spite of his silence. His tremendous love of Negro creative instincts. He has backed it in a manner that all the world knows about. He has further shown that he is not just a Sociologist by the fact that his data is high above statistics. It pulsates with the life of his people. He is happy to give his talents and material to building the project at Fisk. Mrs Johnson is eager to do her utmost. It has always been her desire.

You have Dr Lorenzo Dow Turner with his preparation, his talents and collection to contribute to the success. And his is an unbounded enthusiasm.

I believe that I can add something to your already rich endowment and in the belief, I submit myself for your consideration.

Sincerely yours,
Zora Neale Hurston

ZNH:mp
October
Twelfth
1 9 3 4

TO FRANZ BOAS

[on Chicago YWCA stationery]

[October 23, 1934—dated at end of letter]
Dr. Franz Boaz [sic],
Columbia University,
New York, N. Y.

Dear Dr. Boaz [sic]:

The reason that the publishers did not send the last half of my book on to you, was they were getting me to revise certain parts. They felt that it was too technical for the average reader. I was required to do something more acceptable for public reading.[1]

It is in their hands now, and as they are very, very eager for you to do the introduction, you will no doubt receive the completed copy immediately.

I myself am very enthusiastic about having you say a word in the book.

I say nothing at present of my tremendous esteem for you, for fear that it may sound like bribery to get you to do the introduction.

Dr. Herskovits called me since I have been here in Chicago, and had me out to his home last Sunday afternoon for tea. There was a great crowd, and reminded me of the parties at your home when Mrs. Boaz [sic] used to serve her delicous oatmeal cookies.

Hope you like the manuscript.

My love to Dr. Reichard, Dr. Benedict, Dr. Klynberg [sic] and the rest.

Most sincerely,
Zora Neale Hurston

October
Twenty-Third
1 9 3 4
ZNH/mp

[1]*They had specifically requested that Hurston's hoodoo material, already published in the* Journal of American Folklore, *be added to* Mules and Men.

TO ALAIN LOCKE

[on Chicago YWCA stationery]

[October 29, 1934—dated at end of letter]
Dr. Alain Leroy Locke,
1326 R. Street,
Washington, D. C.

Dear Alain:

I have written godmother for the permission to dedicate the new book.[1]

Did I tell you in the last letter that it is being illustrated by Baldridge?[2] It would have been off the press in November but for that. It will be out in January now.

Instead of feeling less need of godmother and more independent as success approaches me, I need her more and feel her great goodness to me more deeply. If I am acclaimed by the world, and make a million in money, I would feel still that she was responsible for it. I have not written often because I did not get answers and thought she did not want to hear from me. Just did not understand. She shall have a weekly letter from me—from now on.

I do hope that you come to Chicago, within the next few days. I wish that you could be here for my concert on the 23rd of November. I would like very much to have you tell the audience what godmother has meant to Negro literature and art. She is where she can do no more, but before she passes I think there ought to be some acknowledgment to the world, from at least one of the people that she has saved or tried to save, and what she has meant to America.

There will be three performances, two evening performances on the 23rd and 24th of November and a matinee on the 24th.

I am beginning my third book as soon as the concert is over.[3]

---

[1]Mules and Men *was dedicated to Annie Nathan Meyer.*
[2]Mules and Men *was instead illustrated by Mexican artist Miguel Covarrubias.*
[3]*Probably* Tell My Horse.

My play "Mule Bone" has been asked for by the Little Theatre in New York. Same director as for "Run Little Chillun."[4] I am wondering whether to send it there or to produce it myself here. I have a very good opening. Since all funds for the play and everything else can be had right here, I am wondering if I could not do a better job of interpreting Negro material than any white director ever could.

Most sincerely,

Zora

Zora Neale Hurston

October
Twenty-ninth
1 9 3 4
ZNH/mp

TO CARL VAN VECHTEN

[on Chicago YWCA stationery]

[November 3, 1934—dated at end of letter]
Mr. Carl VanVechter [sic]
150-W—55th, Street
New York City;

My Dear Carl:—

A flock of purple rabbits to you.

I just read in the newspaper that you are flying to Chicago on Wednesday, with Gertrude Stein,[1] so you know I want to

---

[4] *Hall Johnson's play, 1933; staged by Clarence Muse and Frank Merlin.*

[1] *Gertrude Stein (1874–1946), one of the most important modernist writers, was praised by many African Americans for her experiments in black voice and point of view, especially in "Melanctha," a long section of her trilogy* Three Lives. *She was accompanied by Van Vechten to Chicago for an opera performance on which she collaborated with Virgil Thomson and which featured an all-black cast.*

see you. The fact is, I am determine to do that little brown
thing.
>   Adoringly
>   Zora

4559 So. Parkway
C/O Y.W.C.A
Chicago, Ill
Call, Atl.1434
NOVEMBER
THIRD
1 9 3 4
ZNH/vs

TO MELVILLE HERSKOVITS

[on Chicago YWCA stationery]

[November 7, 1934—dated at end of letter]

Dr. Melville J. Herskovits,
Northwestern University,
Evanston, Illinois.

Dear Dr. Herskovits:

So glad to receive the letter from you this morning.

The cold is a thing of the past now. I feel fit as a fiddle this morning, and am ready to lick the whole world if necessary.

It was very thoughtful of you to enclose the clipping. Thank you.

This coming Sunday (November 11th) will be alright. Besure and
come early, because the best of the service will be early in the evening.
Meet me here at the Y, no later than seven-o'-clock.

It warms my heart everytime I think of what good friends you and
Mrs. Herskovits have proven to be.

>   Sincerely,
>   Zora
>   Zora Neale Hurston

11/7/34
ZNH/mp

TO CARL VAN VECHTEN

[November 29, 1934]
4559 So. Parkway [YWCA]
Chicago, Ill.
Thanksgiving Day

Carl Darling,

Send the pictures here. I am so excited about them I can hardly wait. Frankly I feel flattered that you wanted to photograph me. I am conscious of the honor you do me.[1]

I saw Nora Holt twice and we are talking seriously of the trip to the orient. If we can get some dates in California, as we think we can, the project is assured. I hope and think that I can sell Ethel Waters[2] a song. If she takes it for $200.00 I will be copasetti[3] for China.

If I dont get to gom to China and Russia I shall be in the East before Christmas. Publicity has been grand here.[4]

Little Margaret has an awful crush on you. Because she wanted it so much I let her take the card you sent me with your picture on it for the time being. But I wouldnt give it away for good.

Thanking you in the humblest way that I know how, I am

Zora
Z.N.H.

---

[1]*Carl Van Vechten did a series of photos of Hurston, most of which can be seen at the Beinecke Library, Yale University.*

[2]*Singer and actress; see glossary. Hurston and Waters were friends, but there is no evidence that a song was sold.*

[3]*Version of "kopasetee," defined by Van Vechten in his 1926* Nigger Heaven *as "an approbatory epithet somewhat stronger than all right." "Copesettic" or "copacetic" in more recent usage.*

[4]*Hurston's* Singing Steel, *a version of* The Great Day, *was performed in Chicago in late November; as a result of this performance Hurston was invited to apply for a Rosenwald Foundation Fellowship to attend Columbia.*

TO CARL VAN VECHTEN

[December 10, 1934—dated at end of letter]
Y. W. C. A.,
4559 South Parkway,
Chicago, Illinois.

Mr. Carl Van Vechten,
150 West 55th. Street,
New York, N. Y.

Dear Carl:

The pictures are swell! I love myself when I am laughing. And then again when I am looking mean and impressive. You are a long tall angel with that "Balsm of Gilead" in your hips. I am wearing out my loud singing symbol talking about you.

Did you have things like you wanted them for Thanksgiving? I had plenty dinners here, just couldn't get around to all of them, but I went the limit. I buried many turkey bosoms that day, to say nothing of turkey hammers.

Thanks for the new picture, you look like a red-hot spider man in the center of your web, looking for a sizzling fly. I like that.

Expect to see you before Christmas.

Lovingly,
Zora
Zora Neale Hurston

December
Tenth,
1 9 3 4
ZNH/mp

TO EDWIN OSGOOD GROVER

4559 South Parkway [YWCA]
Chicago, Illinous
Dec. 13, 1934

Dear, dear Friend,

I know that I have been awful to the people who love and to the ones I love most. But life has picked me up bodaciously and throwed me over the fence. Letter-writing has gotten to be an ordeal by reason of quanttity and insisstence.

I have sent the most of the clippings to Mr. Lippincott, but here are some of the duplicates. I am speechless from public appearances and speech-making.

The Rosenwald Fund, the organization that had previously proposed me for a chair at Fisk Univ. now feels that they want to do something bigger. I am asked to fill out an application blank for a fellowship so that I may take my doctor's degree. Perhaps that is best after all for I can do first the one then the other. I will be eligble for a full professorship, for more extensive field work which has already been suggested, while at the same time my interest in the theatre need not die.

Hope that I can be in Florida before Mr. Lippincott gets there. I will if this matter does [not] hold me up. Love to the Thompsons, Dr. Holt, Prof. and Mrs. France and all who may ask of me.

Most sincerely,
Zora

I'd love to know all your friends here.

TO FRANZ BOAS

4559 So. Parkway [YWCA]
Chicago, Ill.
Dec. 14, 1934

Dr. Franz Boas
Columbia U.
New York City

Dear Dr. Boas,

Great news! I think that I have secured a Rosenwald scholarship to return to Columbia and work for my doctorate. If all goes well I shall be entering immediately after the holidays. I have wanted the training very keenly and tried very hard to get Mrs. Mason to do it for me. She would give money for everything else but that. I have been so concerned to get more training so that I might work out two projects that I have in mind. Is it all right for me to enter at this time of year?

Now I realize that this is going to call for rigorous routine and discipline, which every body seems to feel that I need. So be it. I want to do it. I have always wanted to do it and nobody will have any trouble about my applying myself. I wonder if it ought not to be taken into consideration that I have been on my own since fourteen years old and went to high school, college and everything progressive that I have done because I wanted to, and not because I was being pushed? All of these things have been done under most trying circumstances and I stuck. I have had two or three people say to me, why dont you go and take a master's or a doctor's degree in Anthropology since you love it so much? They never seem to realize that it takes money to do that. I had such a hard time getting the money to take my bachelor's that I could appreciate what it meant to attempt to attend a college on nothing. Another thing, it is hard to apply ones self to study when there is no money to pay for food and lodging. I almost never explain these things when folks are asking me why dont I do this and that. I have to make a living, and consequently I have to do the jobs that will support me.

But oh, Dr. Boas, you dont know how I have longed for a chance to stay at Columbia and study. Otherwise there would be no point to my using evry thing possible to get this scholarship.

Hoping that all goes well with you and yours, I am

Most sincerely,
[unsigned carbon]

P.S. Do you remember Miguel Covarrubias, the Mexican artist that you met one Sunday night with me when we went to the Sanctified church? He has just returned from four years study in Bali and is to do the illustrations for MULES AND MEN.

TO EDWIN EMBREE

442 Manhattan Avenue
New York City
December 29, 1934

Mr. Edwin Embree
4900 Ellis Ave.
Chicago, Ill.

Dear Mr. Embree,

Dr. Boas has been ill for the past month, but I have seen him through Miss Bryant, his secretary. He has agreed to take me and said that he would write you to that effect.[1] I need not say how pleased I am, for you would already sense it.

As soon as this holiday mob gets out of the city I shall find some permanent living quarters. Maybe dormitory for graduate students or International house. The only thing about that is that it seems a fraud for me to go there since I am a plain American. Not unless they need some Americans to mingle with the foreigners for flavor.

---

[1]Boas wrote to Embree on December 27 and again on January 7, stating his support for Hurston and his willingness to supervise her doctoral work.

I shall write you again as soon as Papa Franz gets over to the office. He thinks that will be only a few days now.

Hoping that you had a pleasing Christmas and that the New Year will be equally satisfactory, I am,

Sincerely yours,

Zora Neale Hurston

TO THOMAS E. JONES

442 Manhattan Ave.
c/o Jackman
New York City
December 29, 1934.

Dr. Thomas Elsa Jones
Fisk University
Nashville, Tenn.

My dear Dr. Jones:

Your letter was forwarded to me here and I was glad to hear from you after a long silence.

If you happen to come to New York during the next two years I shall be very glad to see you. I have a fellowship at Columbia University for that length of time under the Rosenwald. I shall be in residence during the school terms, but provisions have been made for foreign travel during the summer months.

So you see, there would be no point in holding that application blank for me as the Board would hardly wait as long as it would have to before I could think of accepting anything there. Happily for all of us that need not alter any plans. I think that it would be nice to give it to Mr. John Work[1] in acknowledgment of his strenuous ef-

---

[1] *Informing Jones that she could do better through the Rosenwald than through Fisk, Hurston is reacting to Jones's lack of sustained interest in the proposal that she join the drama faculty there. Ironically enough, Work attended Juilliard for two years on a Rosenwald Fellowship prior to joining Fisk.*

forts in that direction.[2] He is a bright young man and deserves some recognition of his talents. It must be genius. Nothing short of that would enable him to know so much about me in one short conversation and one glimpse. The short conversation taking place in Dr. Charles S. Johnson's backyard when I did Mr. Work the favor of giving him two songs that he had heard me do over the radio. The glimpse when he was in New York some years ago and Miss Lydia Mason brought him to my studio for the briefest introduction. Give him the job by all means and if he runs out of ideas he can always come to me under the guise of friendship and get some more, maybe.

Hoping that your holidays have been most pleasant and wishing you all good things for the future, I am

Sincerely,
ZORA NEALE HURSTON
[unsigned carbon]

TO RUTH BENEDICT

[1934?]
[in upper right:] An Indian book of tales & ceremonies from the view point of a spectator or participant with plenty of *color* would be a big success.

Dear Dr. Benedict,

Yes, Lippincott is publishing the folk-tales and making an elaborate edition of it.[1] Only as I said, they want it done, not for scientists, but for the average reader. Hence the lack of documentation and the inter-story dialogue. The last half of the book is hoodoo material and they are insisting now that I make it more suitable for the general reading public. Why dont you do an Indian book in the same manner? It would be worth money. Lippincott would be interested. Zora.

---

[2]*In other words, Hurston suggests here that Jones give Work the job slated for her.*

[1]Mules and Men.

TO EDWIN OSGOOD GROVER

[winter 1934/35]
442 Manhattan Ave.
c/o Jackman
New York City

Dear Dr. Grover,

The fellowship with provisions for foreign travel has been granted.[1] School in winter, travel in summer. I had to come on to New York at once and so I cannot come to Florida this winter. Too sorry about it too.

Tried to get east in time to catch Mr. Lippincott, but couldnt. Shall run down to talk to him as soon as I find hat he has returned. I shall be envying you all your pleasures. I shall wish that I were you talking with him, and I shall wish I were he(?) talking with you. I feel wofully cheated. I still think that he is wonderful.

I have been snatched about so much in the last ten days that I have had no holiday pleasures at all. I havent the faintest idea of a present or a card. When my mail is forwarded from Chicago, perhaps I shall find some. I didnt try to write until I had a temporary adress, at least. Please give my love to all that you know I am fond of.

Most sincerely,
Zora

[1] A Rosenwald, initially for $3,000.

TO FRANZ BOAS

c/o Jackman
442 Manhattan Avenue
New York, N.Y.
January 4, 1935

Myn dear Dr. Boas,

I would rather stay here and work towards a degree than g go to Chicago unless it would amount to the same thing in the long run. That is, if the work I do at Northwestern would count with what I do next year here under you. I really do feel the need of discipline in research and I want to use this grant of money to that end. I might want to teach some day and I want the degree as well as the discipline for thoroughness.[1]

Of course I realize that Dr. Herskovits has been to Haiti and otherwise worked with Negroes and that he could be a great deal of help to me.[2] I am writing because I do not know whether I gave the impression that I was indifferent to a degree or not. I want the routine work and Dr. Embree wants me to have it and to work for a degree.

Most sincerely,

Zora

Zora Neale Hurston

P.S. I dont know whether I have expressed myself clearly or not. W What I really want to say is that I want to work towards a degree and while I like to be in New York, I'll cheerfully go to Evanston if you think that is the best for me. Perhaps Dr. Herskovits can with my feeble contribution work out something that would help others who wish to study the American Negro as well as me.

---

[1] Hurston had actually expressed a long-standing disinterest in teaching and taught in short spells only at Bethune-Cookman, North Carolina College for Negroes, and Lincoln Academy.
[2] Melville Herskovits was primarily an Africanist.

TO CARL VAN VECHTEN

[January 5, 1935—dated at end of letter]
442 Manhattan Avenue,
c/o Harold Jackmann [sic],
New York, N. Y.

Mr. Carl Van Vechten,
150 West 55th. Street,
New York, N. Y.

Dear Carl:

This is all I have been able to find about that Historic presentation
at the Mecca. I also heard some scattering talk here and there. Hope I
see you soon. Did you see this other clipping about this heavy belly
guy.[1] We ought to try to hear them. I have already written to Lomax,[2]
who knows me, and asked me to work with him. I have written for a
date asking him at the same time to hear brother Lead Belly. If the
date comes through I will let you know.

Regards to Fania.

Ten thousand little guinea pigs,

Zora

P.S. Met the "King," his name is Adams. Glad to be photographed.

January
Fifth,
1 9 3 5
ZNH/mp

[1]Huddie "Leadbelly" Ledbetter (1888–1949), folk and blues singer, born to Louisiana sharecroppers. For most
of his life, Ledbetter was in and out of prison, where he learned and performed songs. Texas governor Pat Neff
pardoned Ledbetter for murder after hearing him sing. Ledbetter was released, but soon returned to prison after allegedly knifing a white citizen. There he met folklore collector John Lomax, who helped to make Leadbelly known to the world.

[2]Alan Lomax, folklorist and son of folklorist John Lomax, went on a folklore collecting expedition with
Hurston and Mary Barnicle in 1935. He called Hurston "probably the best informed person today on Western
Negro Folklore." See glossary.

TO JOHN LOMAX

442 Manhattan Ave.
New York, New York
January 5, 1935

Mr. John A. Lomax
181 Sulliven St.
New York City

Dear Mr. Lomax,

I am very glad to find that you are in New York at the same time that I am. "Little Boss" Lomax[1] wrote to me while I was in Florida about collecting Negro work songs, but it seems that you were down with the fever and nothing came of it.

I am writing now because I admire your work, and knowing what I am talking about, feel that it is something fine and necessary to American culture and art. May I have the pleasure of talking with both of the Lomaxes as well as listening to Leadbelly? This is the sort of thing I have been advocating all along.

Sincerely yours,
Zora Neale Hurston

Tel. Monument 8718
    Mo. 2-8718

P.S. I followed you at Mandel Hall at Chicago U.[2]

[At the bottom, Lomax has written: "A negro author See her excellent book."]

---

[1] *Alan Lomax.*
[2] *Mandel Hall at the University of Chicago was known for folk music and folk dancing.*

TO EDWIN EMBREE

442 Manhattan Avenue
C/o Jackman
New York, New York
January 6, 1935

Dr. Edwin R. Embree
4900 Ellis Avenue
Chicago, Ill

Dear Dr. Embree,

Dr. Boas said that he would write you but I thought that I ought to write also.

It seems that there is very little here to be taken that would lead directly to my special field. Most of the Anthropologists in America have specialized on Indians.[1] The more reason I should be trained to do this work, seeing that there are so few courses in any American college on the Negro, but at the same time for the present it hampers me in getting my own self trained. Of course I can take the phonetics, linguistics, etc, but the language of the Pawnees is not likely to help me much in say, Alabama. Nor Hayti. In fact, school room French, which I know reasonably well is not going to be made much use in Hayti. Right now, I need to rub up against some average Haitiens.

Dr. Boas is considering shipping me back to Evanston to study under Dr. Herskovits for the semester approaching so that he can prepare me for Hayti. There is nothing at Columbia that would help me practically for that. Dr. Boas says the following year beginning September he will then put me thru some rigorous courses but they will not have any very direct bearing on my field. It will be the sort of thing that will be general background and methods like (1) Diffusion (2) phonetics (3) Linguistics, graphs and the like. Filed [sic] work one has to learn in the field, and that I know.

---

[1] *An anthropological focus on African Americans did not emerge until well into the 1900s, with the exception of such collections as* Slave Songs of the United States *(1867) and* Uncle Remus: His Songs and His Sayings *(1880), a popularized collection.*

He will talk to me again in a day or two but I wanted to keep you informed of developments. Dr. Herskovits has done more than any American anthropologists on Negro subjects. That is why Dr. Boas thinks of sending me to him for the present/.

Most sincerely,
Zora Neale Hurston

TO MELVILLE HERSKOVITS

442 Manhattan Avenue
New York, New York
January 6, 1935

Dear Dr. Herskovits,

I got the grant from the Rosenwald and they rushed me off to talk with Dr. Boas and arrange things. But lo and behold when I get here it turns out that there is nothing here to prepare me for my special field. You see, what you have done and what I have collected is all that there is to this Negro phase. Of course Dr. Benedict suggested that I go into linguistics, but Dr. Boas couldnt see [why—x-ed out] the language of the Pawnees would help me any in Hayti. Nor the language of the Plains Indians in Alabama. So he thinks that the only way I can be prepared for my trip to Hayti this summer is for me to return to you and work with you this semester. (Approaching)

Now an idea has just struck me. With what you have and what I have and what both of us can get in the next two years, (I have a two year fellowship) we can furnish the texts that are so needed in America. You of course , being better trained, at the top and me second to you. You said that we could work up something if you could get the money and now I have it. The Rosenwald was set on either Harvard or Columbia, but you see, Dr. Boas himself is sending me back there where didnt want me to stop so the responsibility is not on me and I have my way after all. I would like for the work I do to count towards my distant goal, a doctorate. The Rosenwald says that if the work is done well in the first two years I can have a third year and with intensive work and study I ought to be near my degree by then.

I am granted two years with summer trips. (1) Hayti (2) Martinique. Maybe we can go together and with Mrs. Herskovits we can make a clean sweep. I am joyful. Please let me hear from you right away. Love to Mrs. Melville J.

Most sincerely,
Zora

TO RICHMOND BARTHÉ

[January 7, 1935—dated at end of letter]

My brother in heart and fable
My brother in pot and at table
My brother in like and kind
My brother in soul and mind
My brother in dreams and heart
My brother who molds black souls
    with art

Zora Neale Hurston
Jan. 7, 1935

TO EDWIN EMBREE

[January 8, 1935—dated at end of letter]
c/o Harold Jackman
New York, N.Y.

Dr. Edwin Embry [sic],
4900 Ellis Avenue,
Chicago, Illinois.

My dear Dr. Embry:

Dr. Boas has decided to keep me here and give me systematic training under his own hand. I shall get a permanent address as soon as possible.

As Dr. Boas has probably told you, I shall need $160.00 (one hundred and sixty dollars) for my tuition before February 1st.[1]

Thanking you again and again for your consideration.

I am

Sincerely,
Zora Neale Hurston

January
Eighth
1 9 3 5
ZNH/p

---

[1]*In the left corner, Embree has penned, "Send check & note saying we will subtract this at rate of $25 per month from her monthly check." His note is followed by one signed with the initials "DE" (his secretary, Miss Dorothy Elvidge), which reads, "ck [check] sent prior to receiving this note."*

TO MELVILLE HERSKOVITS

[January 17, 1935—dated at end of letter]
1925 - 7th. Avenue,
House 3,
Apartment 2-J.
New York, N. Y.

Dr. Melville J. Herskovits,
Northwestern University,
Evanston, Illinois.

Dear Dr. Herskovits:

Dr. Boas had decided it best for me to stay in New York, and study at Columbia University. I expect to plunge into a very interesting whirl of study soon.

I hope everything is going along fine for you and Mrs. Herskovits. Please drop me a line now and then.

With best wishes,

Sincerely,
Zora Neale Hurston.

January
Seventeenth,
1 9 3 5
ZNH/mp

P.S. Am referring Mr. Richardson to you.[1]

---

[1] *On December 18, 1934, R. C. Richardson wrote to Hurston in Hungerford, Florida, requesting information on the Ethnological Society of which Hurston was an "officer." This letter was apparently forwarded to Herskovits, who occasionally handled such inquiries for Hurston.*

TO DOROTHY ELVIDGE

Apt. 2-J, 1925 Seventh Avenue
New York, New York
January 18, 1935.

Dear Miss Elvidge,

My intentions when I asked for the $160.00 was to pay my tuition for the semester beginning February 1, all in a lump as is the custom. But I neglected to say that I needed that much in addition to the amount needed for my maintenance for one month. I understand of course that the larger sums necessary this first month will be deducted from later months.

You see, I had to get a permanent place to live as I am so consti-tuted that I must be alone.[1] So now I am all settled and ready to begin study. I have conferred with Dr. Boas and his staff and my program has been tentatively filled. It calls for 160.00 for the semester. 15 points at 10.00 each plus 10.00 registration. Since I had to use part of it for maintenance, Dr. Boas says that he will arrange for me to pay something every month of the four (Feb. thru May) forty dollars every month and that will be the same thing. [Then—x-ed out] So on the first of every month if I could have $120.00 I could make things come out. Dr. Boas says that I can make out on less in the field during the summer months, to balance it.

My program is most interesting. I am to have Mythology[,] Primi-tive Art, French phonetics, General Methods, Evolution. In addition I am to work up something in comparative myths with Dr. Benedict. I am very happy over it all.

I think that I am about to get a theatre connection as Dr. Embree suggested. A chance to study with a director who knows his business. Until I have the final word, I shall say no more.

The weather here is ever so much milder than that I left behind me in Chicago. But all the same I have not frogotten the youthful

---

[1]*Indeed, except for short periods of living with one of her nieces, Hurston rarely lived with anyone else, includ-ing her husbands. One exception to this would prove to be time spent on houseboats later in her life.*

vigor and challenge of Chicago. New York seems sort of tired and old beside it.

My deep regards to Mr. Arthur[2] and Dr. Embree. I shall certainly work hard to justify their faith.

Most sincerely,
Zora Neale Hurston

The theatre connection would mean that I could hang around and observe while important things were being done. Not any really formal class-work.

TO CARL VAN VECHTEN

[postcard]

January 18, 1935.

Mr. Carl Van Vechten;
    Just wished to notify you of change of address: 1925-7th. Avenue, House 3, Apartment 2-J. Haven't a phone yet.

As B.4.
ZORA
Zora Neale Hurston

ZNH/mp

---

[2]*George Arthur of the Rosenwald Foundation.*

Zora Neale Hurston, striking a bold pose in the 1920s. *Photographer unknown.*
Courtesy of Yale Collection of American Literature, Beinecke Rare Book and Manuscript Library.

Jessie Fauset,
Langston Hughes,
and Zora Neale Hurston,
Tuskegee Institute.
Photographer unknown.
Courtesy of Yale Collection of
American Literature, Beinecke
Rare Book and Manuscript Library.

Marjorie Kinnan Rawlings, Cross
Creek, 1933–34, Rawlings Collection,
University of Florida. *Photographer*
unknown. Courtesy of Zora Neale Hurston
Collection, George A. Smathers Libraries,
University of Florida, Department of
Special Collections.

Alain Leroy Locke.
Photographer unknown. Courtesy of Yale
Collection of American Literature, Beinecke
Rare Book and Manuscript Library.

Charlotte Osgood Mason (aka
"Godmother"). *Photographer unknown.
Courtesy of Yale Collection of American Literature,
Beinecke Rare Book and Manuscript Library.*

Carl Van Vechten. *Nickolas Muray
photographer. Courtesy of Yale Collection of
American Literature, Beinecke Rare Book
and Manuscript Library.*

Young Zora Neale Hurston (center) with
friends. *Photographer unknown. Courtesy of
Zora Neale Hurston Collection, George A. Smathers
Libraries, University of Florida, Department
of Special Collections.*

Cousins Helene Johnson
and Dorothy West. *Photographer unknown.
Courtesy of The Schlesinger Library, Radcliffe
Institute, Harvard University.*

Amelia Street, New Orleans home where Hurston lived in 1928. *Carla Kaplan photographer.*

The Roof Garden Hotel Belle Glade, Florida, where Hurston lived in 1950. *Carla Kaplan photographer.*

Hurston's final home, 1734 School Court, Fort Pierce, Florida. Now designated a landmark, this building was moved when the Lincoln Park Academy expanded into the home's original location. *Carla Kaplan photographer.*

Hurston on a folklore trip
in South Carolina.

Photographer unknown.

Courtesy of Library of Congress.

Zora Neale Hurston with drum.

Photographer unknown.

Courtesy of Library of Congress,

Prints and Photographs.

Zora Neale Hurston (far right) at a rehearsal of *The Great Day*, 1932.

Photographer unknown. Courtesy of Zora Neale Hurston Collection,

George A. Smathers Libraries, University of Florida, Department of Special Collections.

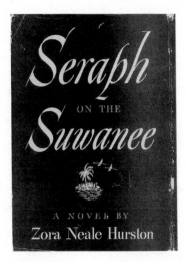

Original book jacket, *Seraph on the Suwanee.* Courtesy of Sara Lee Creech.

Book jacket, *Mules and Men,* British edition. *Courtesy of the Florida Authors Collection, Miami-Dade Public Library* and *the Historical Museum of Southern Florida.*

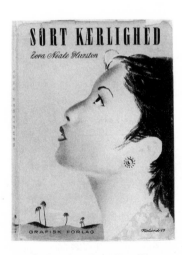

Book jacket, *Their Eyes Were Watching God,* Danish edition. *Courtesy of the Florida Authors Collection, Miami-Dade Public Library* and *the Historical Museum of Southern Florida.*

Book jacket, *Caribbean Melodies,* Zora Neale Hurston and William Grant Still. *Courtesy of the Florida Authors Collection, Miami-Dade Public Library* and *the Historical Museum of Southern Florida.*

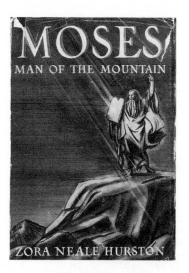

Original book jacket,
Moses, Man of the Mountain.
Courtesy of Sara Lee Creech.

Original book jacket, *Tell My
Horse.* *Courtesy of the Florida Authors
Collection, Miami-Dade Public Library and
the Historical Museum of Southern Florida.*

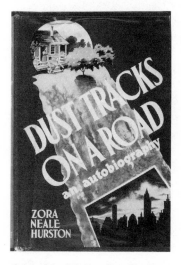

Original book jacket, *Dust Tracks on
a Road.* *Courtesy of the Florida Authors
Collection, Miami-Dade Public Library and
the Historical Museum of Southern Florida.*

Book jacket, *Dust Tracks
on a Road,* Japanese edition.
Courtesy of Stetson Kennedy.

Zora Neale Hurston.

Carl Van Vechten photographer.
Courtesy of Yale Collection of American Literature,
Beinecke Rare Book and Manuscript Library.

TO DOROTHY ELVIDGE

1925 Seventh Avenue
Apt. 2-J
New York City
Jan. 26, 1935

Dear Miss Elvidge,

I shall get along all right on the financial arrangement. Tho classes have not started as yet, I have begun my home work in French. I have a splendid new dictionary, and I am translating some modern French plays. I have the good fortune to know Mrs. Joseph Shrank who was attached to the American Embassy in London as translator for six years.[1] We see each other every day and talk. She is contacting some one at the Haitian Consulate for my benefit, so that phase is moving along nicely.

Lots and lots of snow here, but the weather is warming up, thanks to the high gods in space.

Most sincerely,
Zora Neale Hurston

[1] *Wife of playwright Joseph Schrank, author of* Page Miss Glory.

TO EDWIN EMBREE

1925 Seventh Avenue
Apt. 2-J
New York, N.Y.
January 26, 1935

Dr. Edwin R. Embree
4901 Ellis Avenue
Chicago, Illinois

Dear Dr. Embree,

This is not to over-persuade you in the matter of the two-year plan,[1] but by way of being very fair to Dr. Boas. Since my first letter to you he has mapped out a scheme of study which seems very satisfactory to him. I was to learn routines and methods with him for two semesters. Then the third term (Spring 1936) to go to Herskovits at Northwestern and work under him as he has done more in the Negro field than any one else. The trouble is, that nearly every Anthropologist in America has specialized in some aspect of the American Indian.

Then tahat brings me to Dr. Boas' other conclusion. I am not being trained to do a routine job. I am being trained to do what has not been done and that which cries out to be done. My ground is practically untouched. But so was the Indian field when Dr. Boas came to it. There would be no need for me to spend good time and money to do something that has already been done so well that there was nothing but minor detail for me to do. He is very eager for the American Negro field to be done (that includes the Islands) as thoroughly as the Indians. When I should return from Northwestern he had advanced study schemes thought out for me which he thinks excellent.[2]

[1]On January 21, 1935, Embree wrote Hurston a letter that essentially rescinded the Rosenwald's offer of a two-year fellowship on the grounds that she had not shown a sufficiently exacting plan of work, as required in their December 19, 1934, letter of award. That letter offered Hurston $100 a month for two years provided that she work closely with advisers in her field. The award also specified travel funds for research and her return to New York.
[2]On March 20, 1935, Boas wrote Embree that he was upset to learn that Hurston's fellowship had been cut back, and expressed his confusion over what the foundation had found unsatisfactory in her plan for work or in his statement of support for that work. His letter was answered by one of Embree's, also in March 1935, which said that the foundation found Hurston's approach chaotic and uncertain, but that if she showed careful work, they might consider renewing the grant after June. Boas's response of April 1, 1935, reiterated his support of

Just saying this so that you would know that things are not as sketchy as they seemed at first.

I am perfectly willing to accept your terms and make a later application for I feel that it will work out to the satisfaction of all.[3]

My budget does not allow me to do much theatre going, but I have had the good fortune to meet some of the people who count. I am keeping in mind that you told me to observe the theatre as closely as possible while here in New York. Walter Prichard Eaton has invited me up to Yale to visit his classes. I met him in Florida and when a friend told him that I was here he sent me all good wishes thru her and hoped that I came up. He might come down to literary tea in February and says that he will be sure to see me if he does.

Most sincerely yours,
Zora Neale Hurston

TO MIGUEL COVARRUBIAS

1925 Seventh Ave.
Apt. 2-J
New York City.
Jan.31, 1935

Dear Miguel,

Mr. Lippincott was up to see me yesterday and he is about to lay an egg because he has not heard from you. I told him what a lousy letter writer you wree and not to concern himself about the drawings because I knew that you wree going to do them. He felt a whole lot better then. But, boy, he was worried before he talked to me. Mrs [sic] He told me that he had made you a better proposition than the first one

---

Hurston and his unhappiness with the changed conditions of her grant, and reminded Embree that their letter of December 19, 1934, constituted a definite promise of two-year support.
[3]This later application does not appear to have been made.

because I reminded him that you were a world famous artist and so rated good money. So I feel better. Harry Block laid me out for going to Lippincott's but you see, I had a bid from them before Jonah's Gourd Vine was even written and you know a bird in the hand is worth a whole covey up a tree.

I have an apartment now nad I want you and Rose[1] to park your most agreeable selves there the first free morning, afternoon or evening that you have after arriving in New York.

Went to a big party given for Charles Studin[2] and everybody was there. Had a grand time. There is some talk abiut a Negro show and I suggested that they get you to do the scenery and I'll hear more about it within a week and let you know. A big theatrical firm is handling it so that it will mean money if it goes through.

Do let he have a card or something from you and Rose. Here are some suggestions for illustrations as you asked me to make. But please dont feel bound by them. You will probably feel what you want to do as you go thru the script.

With lots of love to you and Rose,

Zora

TO DOROTHY ELVIDGE

[February 4, 1935]
1925 Seventh Avenue
Apt. 2-J
New York, N.Y.

Miss Dorothy A. Elvidge
4901 Ellis Avenue
Chicago, Illinois

Dear Miss Elvidge,

Sorry if I seem troublesome, but I can not complete my registration until I hear from you. Class work work begins on Thursday of this week.

---

[1] *Rose Rolanda Covarrubias, Miguel Covarrubias's wife.*
[2] *Charles H. Studin was an attorney who specialized in music and theater. He died in New York in 1950.*

I know that this is the fourth and that I am slow in calling attention to the fact that the Feb. check has not come, but I felt that it would reach me by Monday (today) certainly. But since it didnt, I began to wonder if it might not be lost in the mails. Please forgive me if I seem to be troublesome, but I am eager to keep my class-room record clear of cuts.

The Writer's Tea, an annual affair, which will come off this Wednesday, will have me for the Guest of honor. On Sunday Feb. 10, Mrs. Annie Nathan Meyer, 1225 Park Ave. is giving a tea for me. Pearl Buck,[1] Fannie Hurst, Robert Nathan,[2] the British Ambassador[3] and 35 other notables are coming, I am told. Really, I am cold all over. What does one say to an ambassador? Darned if I know. The Barnard Club in E. 63rd is pouring tea for me on the [8th—x-ed out] 18th.

Hoping that all goes well with Dr. Embree, Mr. Arthur and all, I am

Sincerely yours,

Zora Neale Hurston

TO GEORGE ARTHUR

1925 Seventh Avenue
New York City
Apt. 2-J
Feb.5, 1935

Dear Mr. Arthur,

Of course you must be right about this new arrangement being good for me. You have always been right so far so I am willing to believe that the ame thing holds true in this instance. At any rate, I feel puzzled and helpless to a certain extent.

Now I face a new difficulty. You see when I told you that I needed $160.00 to register in school, that meant in addition to my living ex-

---

[1] *Writer Pearl Buck (1892–1973) published stories and essays in the* Nation, Atlantic Monthly, Asia, *and the* Chinese Recorder. The Good Earth *(1931) won a Pulitzer Prize and the Howells Medal. In 1938, Buck was the first American woman to win a Nobel Prize in literature.*

[2] *Writer Robert Gruntal Nathan (1894–1985) was the nephew of Annie Nathan Meyer. He was the author of numerous novels and books of poetry. During World War II, he was a screenwriter for MGM.*

[3] *The British ambassador to the United States from 1930 to 1939 was Sir Ronald Charles Lindsay, a career diplomat who had served previously as ambassador to Constantinople (1924–26) and Berlin (1926–28).*

penses for the month. The money was sent but I explained to the comptroller that I was obliged to spend some of it to pay living expenses which never stop. I explained that I was taking an apartment, which is a one-room affair and when all is taken into consideration just as cheap as a furnished room and in addition I have that privacy which is so precious to me. So I received a letter from Dr. Embree about the new arrangement,[1] and one from Miss Elvidge also in which she said that I would receive 108 dollars on the first of every month beginning Feb.1 and ending June 1. So I went to the Bursar at Columbia and made arrangements to that effect. Now the new semester has started and I have my program all made out and not enough money to carry it out. The Feb. check has not come. And I must keep on living and the class work will go on and I'll be starting out with cuts unless I have completed my registration by Thursday. This is the 5th. I hope I am not too troublesome. But I am like Will Rogers. All I know is what I read in the papers. So I made my arrangements according to what I was told. Frankly I am half ill with worry, not knowing what to do. How to explain my tardiness to the Dr. Boas and the University authorities and what to expect. Will you please, exert yourself in my behalf just once more and let me have some understanding from either Dr. Embree or Miss Elvidge whether the money will be paid according to agreement or not.[2]

Perhaps this is not a good letter. But considering my mental state you will please excuse akward phrasing. But please let me know why the money has not been sent and what to expect in the future. I think I ought to know that at least.[3]

The literary world is taking due notice of me. The annual Writer's Tea at Barnard College has me for the guest of honor. I am being given another tea on Park Ave. Sunday and the British Ambassador, Pearl Buck, Fannie Hurst, Robert Nathan, Judge Cardoza[4] and 35 other celebrities will be present. Walter Prichard Eaton, head of the

---

[1]The "new arrangement" reduced Hurston's Rosenwald Fellowship from two years to seven months, contingent upon her satisfying the conditions that had been set forth upon giving her the award.

[2]Arthur followed this letter with one of his own to Embree on February 7 stating that he did not understand what was going on with Hurston's money and asking that Embree and his secretary (Dorothy Elvidge) try to clear things up.

[3]Dorothy Elvidge wrote on January 21, 1935, that Hurston would receive five monthly payments of $108 and one single payment of $160 for a total of $700.

[4]Benjamin Nathan Cardozo (1870–1938) was appointed associate justice of the United States Supreme Court on February 15, 1932.

Dramatic dept. at Yale is coming down also. Two or three big wigs from Philadelphia also. Wish that you were here to go.

Most sincerely,
Zora Neale Hurston

P.S. How is your book[5] coming along? Just had a conference with Mr. Lippincott about the new book which is to be out in the fall.[6] Did I tell you that Miguel Covarrubias is illustrating it? Saw him just before he sailed for Mexico and he is very enthusiastic about it. I read the galley proof back in January.

TO DOROTHY ELVIDGE

1925 Seventh Avenue
Apt. 2-J
New York, New York
Feb.11, 1935

Dear Miss Elvidge,

If my letter full of anxiety about not getting registered on the first gave the impression that I do not appreciate my very good fortune then I have bungled my words exceedingly. I didnt mean it that way. I just wanted to be sure that I would be paying my pledge to the University each month on a certain date. (the first) and Mr. Arthur told me to always ask him advice. You see I have no wish to appear troublesome for fear that you will regret me, so I wrote Mr. Arthur. And now I see that I have been clumsily bothersome to everyone. I am most sorry. Please forgive me and charge it up to my anxiety to make good, plus my native clumsiness. Again I'm sorry.

Most sincerely,
Zora Neale Hurston
Zoranealehurston

---

[5]*George Robert Arthur's* Life on the Negro Frontier: A Study of the Objectives and the Success of the Activities Promoted in the Young Men's Christian Associations Operating in "Rosenwald" Buildings *was published in 1934.*
[6]Mules and Men.

TO RUTH BENEDICT

[on monogrammed stationery: ZHN]

1925 Seventh Avenue
Apartment 2-J
New York City
March 6, 1935

Dear Dr. Benedict,

I am ill. It started on me early last week, but I tried to fight it off. I all but fainted sitting at your desk Thursday. And then to add to it all, this Rosenwald Fund business has me worried.

They rush at me and <u>ask</u> me to send in an application for a fellowship. They gladly give me two years and tell me that I can select the college, suggesting that Harvard would be very nice. I agree, but state a that I wish to come to Columbia. They agree, but still insissting that Warner at Harvard is the last word in the field.[1] I told Dr. Herskovits about it all and he warned me not to take a thing for granted as he had had some experience with them and said to get a <u>written</u> agreement before I refused a job that the state of Florida was offering me. So I did. You have seen it. I also showed it to Dr. Boas.

Now a little more than a month ago I had a letter from Dr Embree saying that he had had two letters from Dr. Boas and the arrangement here at Columbia did not seem permanent enough to warrant the two year grant. That I must make a new application in June. Of course that puzzled me a lot because I was wondering how he would be able to correct Dr. Boas, but I said nothing, thinking the[y] merely wanted to watch me thru a probationary period. I did write and say that it was very hard for both me and Dr. Boas to plan anything unless we knew more than a few months ahead whether there would be any money. No answer to that. Then money that was promised on the first of each month did not get here until Feb. 6. A day after registration closed

---

[1] *W. Lloyd Warner (1898–1970) was known for his application of anthropology to the study of American society and industry. He became an assistant professor at Harvard in 1929.*

making me subject to a late fee, beside forcing cuts in courses. I wrote and asked that some effort be made to get the money here on the first and I get a letter from the comptroller practically chiding me for impertinence. Yes, really! Now it is the 6th of March and the money for this month has not arrived as yet. What to do? They seem to have <u>no</u> appreciation of the fact that scholarship calls for peace of mind. Their word doesnt seem to mean a thing.

Most sincerely,

Zora

TO ANNIE NATHAN MEYER

[on monogrammed stationery: ZHN]

[April 25, 1935—dated at end of letter]

Dear, my Annie Nathan Meyer,

I am working very hard just now which is what folks were born for I reckon. You are the hardest worker I know.

Do you know who Annot is? Just in case, she is a great artist who was chased out of Germany by the Hitler. She had a large art school there and was told to exclude Jewish students from her classes. She did not obey this command and just got out in time to escape a concentration camp. It has been hinted that her husband, Jacobi, is Jewish. Anyway, she is a grand person and a great artist. She has come to America and has now taken out citizenship papers. She has a studio at 980 RKO Building and I hope that you get to know her.[1]

Will you please ask Miss Mary Eliz. Barnicle[2] to come to the tea? She is teaching the ballad at N.Y.U. Oh, she is grand!! And her friend, Miss Margaret Conklin,[3] both at 30 Gansvoort St. New York City. And

---

[1] *Annot Krigar-Menzel Jacobi (b. 1894) was a painter, illustrator, lecturer, and teacher. She was a member of the New York Society of Women Artists and, like Hurston and Fannie Hurst, gave talks on the radio.*
[2] *Anthropologist, traveled with Hurston and Alan Lomax; see glossary.*
[3] *Margaret Swancott Conklin, author of guidebooks to Tarrytown and North Tarrytown and friend of writer Sara Teasdale.*

Annot, and Dr. Ruth Landes,[4] 1940 Andrews Ave, Bronx, and Drs
Ruth Benedict and Gladys Reichard of Columbia U. Dept. of Anthro.
Ruth Aley, 510 E. 89th St.[5]

I had luncheon with Julia Peterkin[6] last Wednesday and we got on
well. We have promised to write constantly.[7]

These last few months have seen me working harded than at any
time in my life, but I have gotten to the place that I like it. So no com-
plaint. I stay tired, but that is not bad. I only feel badly when I feel
that I have wasted a day

Did I make that address 30 Gansvoort Street clear?

I hope that You and Dr. Meyer are feeling fine these Spring days.
My very best to you.

Most sincerely as always,

Zora

P.S. I see the spelling is Gansevoort St.

1925 Seventh Ave
New York City
April 25, 1935

---

[4]*Ruth Landes (1908–91) was an author and anthropologist (Ph.D. Columbia, 1935) who studied black Jews,
Marcus Garvey's back-to-Africa movement, black Brazilians, Indians, and Hispanic Americans. The author of
many books, perhaps her best known was* The City of Women, *published in 1947, which documented women's
roles in a society of descendants of African slaves.*

[5]*Literary agent (died 1987).*

[6]*White writer Julia Peterkin (1880–1961) was well known (and admired) by many black intellectuals for*
Roll, Jordan, Roll, Green Thursday, *and* Black April, *all based on her experiences on her plantation, Lang
Syne, which employed four hundred to five hundred blacks. She was interested in the lives of the descendants of
escaped slaves on the Gulla-speaking sea islands off South Carolina.*

[7]*If they did, Hurston's letters to Peterkin are yet to surface.*

TO EDWIN OSGOOD GROVER

[on monogrammed stationery: ZHN]

1925 Seventh Avenue
New York City
May 14, 1935

Dear Friend,

I posted the cards[1] but I wish that you had sent me more. I can place some at Barnard, City College, Hunter College, and New York U.

Working like a slave and liking it. But I have lost all my zest for a doctorate. I have definitely decided that I never want to teach, so what is the use of the degree? It seems that I am wasting two good years out of my life when I should be working. Then too, I love my Florida. I am sick of these dull gray skies and what not. I want to be back home!

I have now had lunch with Julia Peterkin and we got on swell. She is back on her plantation agai. Univ. Women gave me a big tea on Friday. Celebs too numerous to mention were there. I like Pearl Buck. She is so simple. Robt. Nathan and I get on together.

My yearnful regards to all my friends. I know that Mrs. Thompson thinks that I have forgotten her, but its just this awful hectic life I'm living. If I told you all the things that I have gotten done since Jan. you would open your eyes.

Send me some more announcements so that I can post them around. Especially with summer school for teachers coming on. You know what that means at Columbia.

My love to the family.

Most sincerely,
Zora
Zora Neale Hurston

How is Robert Hungerford[2] [added in hand: "(School)"] making out? Can it keep going?

[1]*Probably announcements for the college's "Animated Magazine" of short celebrity addresses, created and edited by Grover.*
[2]*Eatonville's Normal and Industrial School, founded in 1889 on the model of Booker T. Washington's Tuskegee Institute.*

TO MIGUEL AND ROSE COVARRUBIAS

[on monogrammed stationery: ZHN]

1925 Seventh Avenue
New York City
May 21, 1935

Dear Miguel and Rose,

Mr. Lippincott came up to see me worried about the illustrations for the book. I hinted that you might not be satisfied with the financial arrangement. He said that he had made you a better proposition. I thought that still it was not satisfactory to you and so you were waiting for something better. Is that the trouble? Of course you know that I will do all that I can to make it better if I can. If that is why will you let me know the quickest way possible so that I can take it up with him? I shall be so unhappy if you do not do the book. And I hope, that it can be a fall publication as advertised. Please let me know if there is ANYTHING that I can do to help the matter along.

I may get a chance to come down your way soon. Fannie Hurst and I are planning a trip to the Southwest, and I am strongly suggesting that we keep on to Mexico City. It may work out. She seems enthused over the idea. Then of course I hope to see you.[1]

Life must be good to you two with all that you have to bring to life. I wish you everything. And when I say evrything, I mean EVERY-THING that is good. I still feel the golden glow of those days when we were all here in New York playing around so carefree.

Most sincerely,
Zora

P.S. Plesae forgive me, but I am more worried than Mr. L. [Lippincott] is. And he is very concerned. But you can understand that it is a difference in the angles from which he and I are looking at the thing. It is business with him. I cant conceive of you letting me down without an explanation. I'd go all thru life wondering what happened.

---

[1] *Hurston traveled with Hurst to Canada in 1931 and in Florida in 1934. The trip she mentions here did not take place.*

TO RUTH BENEDICT

[on monogrammed stationery: ZHN]

(P.O. address, Gen. Del. West Palm Beach, Fla.)
Belle Glade, Fla.
June 28, 1935
    [written sideways in top right:] The Everglades is a most rich, and
gorgeous field. We have been on the Ga. islands also.

Dear Dr. Benedict
    I am down here in the Everglades collecting material in a fine way.
I am working with Alan Lomax and we are getting some grand material. He has a new, sensitive recording machine from the library of
Congress and he is a good operator. I know the material & where to
get it. So I am counteracting his tendencies to hasty generalization.
We are collecting more than songs. Trying to get as many kinds of folk
expression as exist.

   1. Songs
      a. Unknown spirituals
      b. Social songs
      c. work songs
      d. chants
   2. Sermons
      a. prayers
      b. How I got religion
      c. Calls to preach, etc.
   3. Children's games
      a. songs
      b. chants

[written along left side:] Look on the map of Florida & see Lake Okechobee, in the Everglades, our locale.
[written sideways in bottom right:] latest address: Gen. Del. Lemon
City Sta. Miami, Fla.

[written sideways in top right:] a good job can be done on Negro
    instrumentalization as you can see from the records.

    3. "Woofing" (characteristic talks)
      (Varied kinds)
    4. Instrumentation
      a. Guitar
      b. mouth organ
      c. Home made instruments
      d. Drums.

I have no money to work with, but all my expenses are being paid
by Lomax. All that I need is enough to pay for a copy of the records. I
thought that the department might want a copy of each of these.
They will probably be 150-200 by August 1.

I mean to say that I do not need the cash at all. If the dept. would
see that the records are copied, it would give Dr. Boas a great deal that
he has been wanting. I am doing a careful and thorough job and I
<u>would</u> love for Columbia to have the collection.[1] The originals are al-
ways a little better than the copies and I am sorry now that I did not
come to see you & see couldnt I have had 100 blanks of our own. 100
would cost about $32.00 they are aluminum. These are turning out
swell.

                           Most sincerely,
                           Zora Neale Hurston

[1] *Hurston's known recordings are housed primarily at the Library of Congress Folklore Division.*

TO EDWIN EMBREE

[on monogrammed stationery: ZHN]

Gen. Del
[West Palm Beach, Florida—x-ed out]
[June 28—x-ed out], 1935
Miami, Fla. July 1.
Lemon City Station.

My dear Dr. Embree,

I am a little tardy with this letter but life has been rushing.

I want to express my appreciation for all that I was able to do under your grant.

You would understand that I would not be able to do anything important toward a doctorate with a single semester of work.[1] So I did what could amount to some thing. I wrote two plays, both of which have a more than even chance of being produced in the fall. I wrote the first draft of my next novel which has already been accepted by my publishers.[2] It was six months of most intensive labor, because I considered it <u>simply</u> <u>must</u> count constructive

Now, since the first week in the month I have been south doing research with Alan Lomax, whom you know and we are doing some excellent recordings Both of us feel that we belong together as workers. It is the chance I have wanted so long.

Please accept my profound thanks for all that you have done thru the Foundation for me. It was short but important in my career.

---

[1] *In March 1936, Hurston filled out a Rosenwald form asking her to evaluate her grant. In it, she reiterated the negative effects of its changed conditions: "since the grant was first made to me for two years, but somehow in a way I do not understand, ended in six months, I do not feel it helped appreciably in Anthropology. But I was able to do some very good creative work during the period. I finished a play that has a very good chance of getting somewhere. I plotted out two new books and submitted the general plan of one of them to my publishers and had it accepted. As it turned out, I feel I gained a great deal from the grant because I am very happy when I can find the leisure to work creatively. And since my work is being favorably received, I feel justified. I would have loved to have studied more, however in Anthro and achieved my doctorate. But full of gratitude for what I received."*

[2] *An early draft of* Moses, Man of the Mountain.

Perhaps Dr. Jones <u>did</u> feel badly over my letter [regarding working at Fisk], but so did I over his and all that it implied.

Most sincerely

Zora Neale Hurston

Belle Glade, Florida

lastest address:

(Gen. Del. Lemon City Station, Miami Florida.

If the Rosenwald would like copies of the records we are making as the beginning of a library of Negro folk expression, I'd be glad to arrange with Mr. John Lomax for copies to be made. I think it would be a wonderful collection if carried <u>far</u> enough, and could be the source for all the scientists who wish to work on such material <u>and</u> the Rosenwald is the organization to do it. Impertinent eh? Perhaps, but stating fact.[3]

TO JOHN LOMAX

[on monogrammed stationery: ZHN]

[August 30, 1935—dated at end of letter]

1925 7th Avenue

Apt. 2-J

New York City

[in pen in different handwriting:] send back at once

My dear Mr. Lomax,

Your very kind letter has just reached me here. I see that I should have had it two weeks ago, so it was somehow not forwarded promptly.

---

[3]*On July 9, Embree answered that he was glad the foundation's support had assisted Hurston in getting something done and that he was delighted she was working with Alan Lomax, whose work Embree admired. He felt the Rosenwald was not the right place for the recordings and advised Hurston to place them elsewhere.*

I deserve no thanks if I have been helpful to Allan [Lomax] in any way. He is such a lovely person that anybody would want to do all that they could to please him. He will go a long way.

Because he told me that he plans to take his degree at U. of T. [University of Texas] this year and then continue in folk-lore, I carefully insisted that he see further than the surface of things. There has been too much loose talk and conclusions arrived at without sufficient proof. So I tried to make him do and see clearly so that no one can come after him and refute him.

He has such an admiration for you that I'm certain that your love for him is not greater than his for you. He says that he is just seeing you as you are and appreciating your bigness and your tenderness. Dont be cross with him, but he told me how you used to take him in your arms when he was a small boy & restless and walk the sidewalks with him and sing to him and tell him tales. I saw him myself turn his back on all urgings to come to New York this fall. "My father has plans for me and he is right, too. I am just seeing that he knows best." On another occasion he repudiated the Communist Party for the same reason. "It is as my father says. I couldnt, wouldnt hurt him ever again by refusing to accept his judgment in such matters." He kept me up until four oclock one night talking John Lomax. So I have a tremendous, shall I say curiousity? about you as a man, and a huge interest in you as a folk-lorist.

Thanks for any notice you might take of me in the work. I regret that the time was so short. Hope to mend the lick next time if there ever is a next time. I have resolved to bring Allan to the notice of Dr. Boas. He told me that Boas was very cold to him when he went to see him. But I shall introduce him in a way to catch the eye of Boas.

Thanks again for your kindness. If ever you are in New York City please look me up. I should like to discuss certain phase of the work with you.

Sincerely,
Zora Neale Hurston

Aug. 30, 1935
[in different handwriting:] this is the Negro woman
novelist who was with Miss B [Barnicle] and Alan a part
of the summer. The two females "fell out."

TO CARL VAN VECHTEN

[on monogrammed stationery: ZHN]

[September 6, 1935—library dated]
1925—7ᵗʰ Ave.
Friday.

Dear Carl,

Every day I have been running from place to place thinking that I'd be placed in a job before night. Then I could come home and write you a letter and say "thanks for the kind favor, I shall return it on such a date." But I kept getting put off and my feet got more tired and my spirits lower. But it looks like I really am going to have a job now.[1] I shall hear definitely—this evening. So I am saying "thank you" with an upturn in my voice.

I have lived thru a horrible period of grim stagnation but I see my way out of the woods at last. My mental state was such that I could neither think nor plan.

Thanks for befriending me in such a noble manner, in the hour of my my dumb agony. A love affair was going wrong too at the time. I think it is O.K. now. You know about it already.[2]

I was up in the country last week-end and it was nice. Guest of the James Huberts'[3] of the Urban League. That restored my sanity I believe. Honest, Carlo, I had got to the place I was talking to myself.

Most lovingly,
Zora.

---

[1] *Hurston was hired by the WPA Federal Theater Project in Harlem as a drama coach.*

[2] *This is the love affair memorialized in* Their Eyes Were Watching God, *an affair with a man referred to by Robert Hemenway with the deliberately misleading initials "AWP" (he asked not to be identified). A fellow student, "AWP" (Percival Punter) was a handsome West Indian who had been a member of the cast of Hurston's* The Great Day. *According to Hemenway, AWP was "studying to be a minister." AWP could not tolerate Hurston's career and she would not give it up, a pattern in her relationships. As was also true in other relationships, there was a significant age difference between the two. AWP was twenty-three at the time; Hurston was in her mid-forties.*

[3] *James Hubert was the executive secretary and founder of the New York Urban League.*

TO JOHN LOMAX

[on monogrammed stationery: ZHN]

1925 Seventh Avenue
New York City
Sept. 16, 1935

My dear Mr. Lomax,

I thought once that this letter would not be necessary, but what I heard two nights ago make me feel that it is.

Miss Barnicle[1] is not the generous disinterested friend of yours that <u>you</u> think. If she has her wish, Allan [sic] will not be back with you for years to come, if ever. She is trying to get him something to do so that he will not return to college this year, but will stay here in New York. For one thing she has a certain attachment for the boy and the next, she is trying to build herself a reputation as a folklorist thru the name of Lomax.

When she proposed that I go on this trip with them one of the things she earnestly urged upon me was that I must help her to get this lovely young man [in—x-ed out] out of his stifling atmosphere. He had a backward father who was smothering Allan with fogy ideas both of mind and body. I heard how you took that gentle poet and artist Leadbelly and dogged him around and only her sympathetic attitude and talks with him (when you were not present, of course) kept the poor fellow alive and believing in himself. Leadbelly got no ideas of persecution from the Negroes in the village as you supposed. He got them right there in the house in Wilton. Why? She was attracted to him as a man by her own admission. And next, she like allo other Communists are making a play of being the friend of the Negro at present and stopping at nothing, <u>absolutely nothing</u> to accomplish their ends. They feel that the party needs numbers and the Negro seems to them the best bet at present. They just dont know us is the reason they feel that way. One of the things that she is working hardest for is that Allan shall not return to Texas this fall. She says he does not need the schoolin and he needs New York and freedom.

---

[1]*Anthropologist Mary Elizabeth Barnicle, who traveled with Hurston and Alan Lomax.*

I promised that I would help all I could to persuade him to that end. But Mr. Lomax when I met Allan and he told me his plans and talked about you in the way he did, I just could not find it in my heart to help destroy the boy. That is just what it will amount to in the end. I know whereof I speak and I would much rather confront her in front of you than write this letter. She even gloated that she meant to take your daughter, whom she describes as a beautiful intelligent creature who is also being ruined by your cruel control, and let her "grow." Your name came up in a restaurant Friday night where I sat at a table. Twom men present were Reds and they spoke of how at Miss Barnicle's house they heard of your holding poor Allan down.

When I left Allan in early August he was in the notion of doing what you wished. Saturday night he came here and told me that did not intend to return to Texas unless he couldnt find anything to do here. That you had written urging him to come home as soon as possible but that he wasnt going if he could help it. So you see, what she said was her objective on this trip south seems accomplished. I have not mentioned details and incidents because that would be too tiresome but I do know what I'm talking about. And none of it would add to your happiness. She knows that I see thru her and do not approve. She has used a great deal of sophistry on Allan to cover up and I have merely let him know that I do not think that she is clean. He is so terribly young and men are dumb for the most part before the tricks of women anyway. He merely sees himself hugely approved of and urged to free himself of all inhibitions. The very things he had been told at home were indecent and to be avoided like the plague.

You know very well that I would not take the liberty of saying these things if I had not plenty proof to back it. Out in the Bahamas <u>MANY</u> folks felt that both the white race and Americans had been shamed.[2] Further, the works of John and Allan Lomax are being deviously diverted to the works of Elizabeth Barnicle. Allan is being told that he must build himself up independently of you. Ostensibly a build-up for him. But all these activities will center around the English dept. at N.Y.U.

Dont take my word fot it. Investigate. Wish that you could happen up here unexpectedly. Allan has promise. I was outraged that she opposed every effort on my part to make him a serious worker. Selling him the idea that the way to collect folk-lore was to stay half drunk.

[2] *Presumably by Barnicle's work.*

Horrible to me from the view point of a worker who feels that one needs all ones faculties plus every machanical help to do the job. And then again from my small town Florida background to see a fifty year old woman plying a twenty year old kid with likker.[5]

I am not asking you not to say I told you for I am so sure of my facts that I dont care. But it would be nice if you just watched developments on your own. She knows that I know, Oh God, just too much, but I am certain that she feels sure of you to the extent that you would never believe a word against her. Further you are a white southerner and I am a Negro and so I am certain that she feels that she could be daring and you would never believe me. GFor that reason I wish that you could wait awhile and see what happens and interpret events in the light of what I have told you.

Most sincerely,
Zora Neale Hurston

What I, meant to say is that at present she is making him feel that he has arrived at the place where he can stand alone and is a folk-lorist independent of your reputation and consequently does not need you nor any further education. You know that both those conclusions are very pathetic and will be disastrous for him.

TO WALTER WHITE

[on monogrammed stationery: ZHN]

1925—7th Ave.,
Apt. 2 J,
New York, N. Y.,
Oct. 24, 1935.

Dear Walter;
I was very pleased to recieve your letter of commendation and appreciated your interest in Mules and Men.

---

[5]*The age difference between Barnicle and Lomax was roughly the same as that between Hurston and her second husband.*

I am terribly conscious of the time that has expired since the receipt of your letter and I am hoping that you will pardon the delay.

Let me know whether you will or will not be busy either Thursday or Saturday evening and if not I would like very much to come over and play a game of bridge.[1]

Appreciatively,

Zora

ZH/JS

TO FANNIE HURST

[postcard]
1925 7th Ave. Apt. 2-J
Nov. 5, 1935

[hand-drawn picture of Fannie Hurst]

Dear Fannie Hurst,

Say when and I'll be there. Just settled a hard piece of work.[1]

Sincerely,

ZNH [hand-drawn picture of herself]

---

[1]*White's reply was cordial and made no mention of their previous conflict. He wrote that they were busy both nights, did not play bridge, would be happy to see her, but were just leaving town.*

[1]*Hurston may be referring either to her fieldwork with Lomax and Barnicle or to her work with the Federal Theater Project of the WPA.*

TO EDWIN OSGOOD GROVER

1925 Seventh Avenue
New York City
December 29, 1935

EDear Dr. Grover,

Holiday greetings and salutations to you and to all the delightful
Grovers! Dont mind my long silences. It is not that I am not feeling
and thinking. But I am doing the most intensive stretch of labor ever.
A whole suit-case full of unanswered mail. I am answering the seven
that I feel most urgent tonight. I am on this Federal Negro Theatre
project and I have been called upon to write a play within a week and
believe it or not, I did it and got it accepted. Must keep working on
"MOSES" for my publishers and another book besides.[1] I am requested at public places and make some of them besides getting some
reading done and some work on another play which I think is all set so
far as acceptance is concerned.

Thanks for the help with the Guggenheim Foundation. I want to
come south and write my two books, or finish them off in peace. New
York is not a good place to think in. I can do hack work here, but I
need quiet to really work.

My regards to all of the delightful folks that are still in Winter
Park. Oh, to be down there in Florida beauty once more! I love the
place.

Most sincerely,
Zora

[1]Moses, Man of the Mountain *and* Tell My Horse.

TO FANNIE HURST

1925—7th Avenue
January 10, 1936

Dear Fannie Hurst,

Just taking time out to turn you some humble thanks for all that you have done for me past, present, and future. You are magnanimous. You are understanding and kind and wonderfully generous with the most precious of your possessions—your self and your time. I am sitting here trying to find words for feelings, and sensing all the time that I am not doing a good job of revealing myself to you. But you know me. Go inside and look around. If you find anything worth the having in my heart, please take it and even if you only set it among your lesser treasures, I'll be covered with honor and glad.

I am very happy. I have been saving up and the phone company says that my phone will be in by noon on Friday. I want to as you if I may come to see you sometime soon, but I am waiting for the phone to be in so that I can call you the first one and ask. (Now, you'll hope I dont get it.)

Most sincerely,
Zora

TO HERSCHEL BRICKELL

1925 Seventh Avenue
New York City
Jan.27, 1936

Dear Herschel Brickell,

I've been sitting here nearlt two weeks with my mouth wide open and cant shut it. I never would have written so smart alecky if I had thought it was you. I just thought it was one of those ham-fats that got their gizzard all crammed full of notions and aint a one of them so. I dont know what to say because I have always, even before I became an author myself, had the most tremendous admiration for you as an artist, and now what I have written makes it look like I'm getting brash with you, when I am not. Please see it with <u>my</u> feelings and not with <u>your</u> head.[1]

So I'm grating some sweet potatoes right now to make you a nice potato pudding (tater pone, to you) because now I realize at last that you were just trying to give me some publicity. You are just too nice and I'm going to bury something in the road for you to walk over that will bring you evrything you want. I want God to point Hid good luck finger at you and dont never vary it a fraction.

Most sincerely yours,
Zora Neale Hurston

TO FANNIE HURST

[marked by Hurst: answered March 2/36]
[February 29, [1936]—dated at end of letter]

Dear Fannie Hurst

I am having a party on Thursday, March fifth, at nine o'clock, for H.P. Davis,[1] who has spent twenty years in Haiti and has written a marvelous book about it. Do come.[2]

Sincerely,
Zora Neale Hurston

1925 Seventh Avenue
February twenty ninth

---

[1]*Brickell had reviewed* Jonah's Gourd Vine *twice in 1934, once for the* New York Post *on May 5 and again for* North American Review *in July. He called the book "authentic" and the sermon "magnificent" but felt that its folklore was better than its "framework."*

---

[1]*Harold Palmer Davis (b. 1878), author of* Black Democracy: The Story of Haiti, *originally published in 1928 and revised in 1936. Davis had worked with Hurston on* Fire!!

[2]*On March 6, Hurst wrote to Hurston that she had been too tired to go to the party the previous night and regretted not being able to attend.*

TO CARL VAN VECHTEN

[library misdated as March 3, 1936]
[February 29, [1936]—dated at end of letter]

Dear Carl,

I am having a party on Thursday, March fifth, at nine o'clock, for H.P. Davis, who has spent twenty years in Haiti and has written a marvelous book about it. Do come.

Sincerely,
Zora Neale Hurston

1925 Seventh Avenue
February twenty ninth

TO WILLIAM STANLEY HOOLE

1925 Seventh Avenue
New York, New York
March 7, 1936

Mr. William Stanley Hoole
Birmingham-Southern College
Birmingham, Alabama

Dear Mr. Hoole,

I think I must be God's left-hand mule, because I have to work so hard. Thats very funny too, because no lazier mortal ever cried for breath. But the press of new things, plus the press of old things yet unfinished keep me on the treadmill all the time. Thats how come I havent answered your most kind and flattering letter before now.

My next book is to be a novel about a woman who was from childhood hungry for life and the earth, but because she had beautiful hair, was always being skotched upon a flag-pole by the men who loved her and forced to sit there. At forty she got her chance at mud. Mud, lush and fecund with a buck Negro called Teacake. He took her down into the Everglades where people worked and sweated and loved and died violently, where no such thing as flag-poles for women existed. Since I narrate mostly in dialogue, I can give you no feeling in these few lines of the life of this brown woman with her plentiful hair. But this is the barest statement of the story.[1]

I am glad in a way to see my beloved southland coming into so much prominence in literature. I wish some of it was more considered. I observe that some writers are playing to the gallery. That is, certain notions have gotten in circulation about conditions in the south and so these writers take this formula and work out so-called true stories. For instance, one Russian lady got hot under the collar and walked out of a party because I wouldnt say that I had suffered terribly down home. It seems that she had helped arrange the party for me to expose my sufferings and the <u>real</u> conditions in the south and when I said I lived pretty much the same in New York and Florida, she used that back-house word and walked out. Being poor myself I am heartily in favor of poor people getting hold of money but I fail to see the difference between an under-paid cotton-picker and an under paid factory hand. So why stress Alabama? The under dog catches heck everywhere. Nobody would love to see ideal living conditions for everyone more than I, but I sense insincerity when only one section of the country is held up for example. But I do feel that the south is taking a new high place in American literature. Caldwell,[2] [Julia] Peterkin, and that new-comer David C. Cohen [sic] (God Shakes Creation)[3] and Bliss Carmen? (Stars Fell on Alabama)[4] are definite contributers to life. Not to mention Sherwood Anderson,[5] whom I

---

[1]*This is a summary of* Their Eyes Were Watching God, *indicating that Hurston had planned out the novel carefully in advance.*

[2]*Erskine Caldwell (1903–87), southern novelist, author of* Tobacco Road *(1932), an unflinching portrayal of white poverty in the South,* God's Little Acre *(1933), and more than fifty other works.*

[3]God Shakes Creation *(1935) was written by David Lewis Cohn (1896–1960), who would go on to write* The Good Old Days *(1940),* New Orleans and Its Living Past *(1941), and other works. Hurston wrote a review of* God Shakes Creation *which appeared in* New York Herald Tribune Books *on November 3, 1934.*

[4]Stars Fell on Alabama *(1934), a prose study of southern life, was written by northern essayist, poet, and folklorist Carl Lamson Carmer (1896–1960). Bliss Carman was a Canadian poet.*

[5]*Sherwood Anderson (1876–1941), short-story writer and novelist, associated with the Chicago Renaissance along with Theodore Dreiser and Carl Sandburg. Although known primarily for portrayals of the Midwest such as* Winesburg, Ohio *(1919), Anderson drew on his own journeys in Alabama and Louisiana for his novel* Dark Laughter *(1925).*

think is almost equal to Caldwell, if not equal. T.S. STribling[6] is a monnyark, thats something like a king you know, only bigger and better. I love him.

You asked for a paragraph and this is a pretty long one that I have on this page. But I was trying to give you a peep into my mind. I thought hard and tried to make a ststement about the literature in a sentence, but I couldnt make it.

Sincerely,

Zora Neale Hurston

P.S. I come of an Alabama family. Macon County.

TO HENRY ALLEN MOE

1925 Seventh Avenue
New York City
March 11, 1936

Mr. Henry Allen Moe
Guggenheim Mem. Foundation
551 Fifth Avenue
New York City

My dear Mr. Moe,

If I were asked how cheaply an American writer could live in the British West Indies, and collect new material I would say:

A. That decent sleeping quarters could be obtained for about twenty shillings per week. This is high for services available, but rentable quarters are scarce.

---

[6]*Novelist and short-story writer T. S. Stribling (1881–1965), pioneer of the Southern Literary Renaissance. Stribling's* Birthright *(1922) was acclaimed by William Stanley Braithwaite as "the most significant novel on the Negro written by a white American."* Teeftallow *(1926) and its sequel,* Bright Metal *(1928), examined rural Tennessee hill culture. The trilogy* The Forge *(1931),* The Store *(1932), and* Unfinished Cathedral *(1934) depicts three generations of the Varden family in Florence, Alabama, from the eve of the Civil War through the 1920s.*

B. That one could buy wholesome food at about twenty to thirty shillings per week. The staples of the islands are, bolied fish, boiled yams, boiled plantain, pigeon peas and rice. This as a regular diet has been found to be rather hard on systems unaccustomed to the excessively starchy diet. These things are cheap and easy to get, but hard on elimination organs. Hence the added expense to buy leaf vegetables and the like.

C. Incidentals. That is, stationary, stamps, laundry, toiletries tips, stockings, entertainment (rum makes good friends) and the like. One pound per week.

D. Medical care. Perhaps not necessary, but sometimes is. :Perhaps ten shillings perhaps nothing at all.

E. Transportation: The most important and most uncertain of all expenses. Two to five shillings per day is the best estimate that I can make with the information at hand.

All of these estimates are made on the premise that the dollar is at par. I have heard something from travellers about exchange rates. I do not know whether it is in the favor of the American writer or not at present.

After thinking hard over the matter, this is the best estimate that I can make for the hypothetical American writer. If I had more recent and more exact information I could speak with more authority. Please consider the above as guesses based on past experiences, not on recent investigation.

Most sincerely yours,
Zora Neale Hurston

[in left-hand margin, the following numbers are written (probably by Moe):]

260
500
250
100
300
300

1710

TO HENRY ALLEN MOE

1925 Seventh Avenue
New York, New York
March 18, 1936

Mr. Henry Allen Moe
Guggenheim Foundation
551 Fifth Avenue
New York, N.Y.

My dear Mr. Moe,

    I humbly and gratefully accept the fellowship granted me by the John Simon Guggenheim Memorial Foundation through you. It is my earnest hope, and my firm determonation to add something to human understanding and to art through my great good fortune in securing this grant.

Most sincerely and respectfully yours,
Zora Neale Hurston

TO HENRY ALLEN MOE

1925 Seventh Avenue
New York City
March 30, 1936

Mr. Henry Allen Moe
Guggenheim Foundation
551 Fifth Avenue
New York City

My dear Mr. Moe:

    I shall be ready to leave any day after Wednesday, April 1st. I thought that I would have a great deal of trouble with passports, but I am advised that they will not be necessary. It was suggested that I ask you for an open letter, which you understand more about than I.

I received the official announcement a few minutes ago and saw my name thru a mist. I go to perform my vows unto God.

Most sincerely,
Zora Neale Hurston

TO CARL VAN VECHTEN AND FANIA MARINOFF

[postcard of ship]

[April 1936?]

Dear Carl and Fania,

On my way. Shall write you at length from Jamaica. Weather fine, men plentiful.

Love, Zora

TO FANNIE HURST

[postcard postmarked Port-au-Prince, Haiti]

April 13, 1936

Dear Fannie Hurst,

On my way. Weather fine. Shall write you at length from Jamaica. Deeply sincere,

Zora

TO MELVILLE HERSKOVITS

2 W. Ivy Green Crescent
Kingston Jamaica, B.W.I.
April 15, 1936

Dear M.J. and the Mrs.,

I fully intended writing you before I sailed. In fact I seriously considered a trip to Evanston to confer with you on this work of mine to the West Indies. You see I want to do what you and I talked about when I saw you last, that is, work together. You fully appreciate how much there is to be done when you realize that there is no real curricula for those Anthropologists who wish to study the Am. Negro. I was struck with it whn I went back to Columbia last year. Papa Franz knows the Indian, etc. but there was nothing to help me in my study of the Negro. I could bring more to the Dept. tha that it could give me in the matter. You are the only one with anything to offer. Suppose we set out to create the same thing for the Negro at Northwestern as Boas has done for the Indian at Columbia? I'll work like a dog to gather material and join with your superior training and knowledge to do something immortal in the matter. Maybe I can save a little money from this to come there after this is over and work under you to the great end.

I shall go to Haiti soon for a long stay and study. I stopped off there Monday and made some fine contacts to study anything I want. I went to the villa of Jules Faine and talked with him about his book of which I enclose a brief plan. I read portions of it. I hope that you will grab it, M.J. It will be a feather in your cap if it is published under your University press.[1] H.P. Davis is trying to get him a publisher, but I am asking him to do nothing about it for a few weeks. The plan that I enclose does not do the book justice. It is most carefully and scientifically worked out. He lives quietly up there at Petionville in the hills and has worked slowly for years. You are going to be enthusiastic about it.

---

[1] Merchant and scholar Jules Faine was working on a French/Creole dictionary. Faine's illegitimate daughter, Simone Ovide, married Haitian dictator François "Papa Doc" Duvalier.

Shall be here for a few days, maybe weeks if I find very much. I plan to go out in the country where I contact ther real people. With a knowledge of Jamaican obeah I will move on Haiti.[2]

Most sincerely,
Zora

TO HENRY ALLEN MOE

[stamped: received at Guggenheim, April 20, 1936]

2, West Ivy Green Crescent.,
Cross Rds. P.O.
St. Andrew.
Jamaica, B.W.I.

Henry Allen Moe, Secr.,
John Simon Guggenheim Memorial Foundation,
551 5th Ave.,
New York.

My dear Mr. Moe,

I arrived safely on Tuesday, I spent most of Monday at Port-au-Prince, and was warmly received by highly placed persons. I have been urged to return at the earliest possible moment so that my stay in Jamaica will not be as long as I had planned on leaving New York. I'm going to the country and look around a bit for material and by the end of the week I will have left Kingston.

I am very happy about every thing and I shall work very very hard. It hardly seems possible that my chance has come. I have looked and yearned so long for the chance of work as hard as I could at what I wanted to do, I've never really extended because I could'nt before.

---

[2]*Herskovits discouraged Hurston's work in Jamaica and Haiti, urging her instead to go to the Bahamas, for which, he felt, she had much more adequate background and preparation, both culturally and linguistically.*

I shall write you again immediately, as I am located in the country.

I went to Barclays Bank and everything is correct.

> Most sincerely and devotedly,
> [unsigned]

Stenographer terrible! Serves me right. I always do my own typing, but she begged so hard & offered to do it so cheaply that I weakened. Thought I'd get a lot of work done quickly. Ha!

TO W. E. B. DU BOIS

[April 1936]
2, West Ivy Green Cres.,
Cross Rds. P.O
St. Andrew.
Jamaica.

Dr. W.E.B.DuBois
Atlanta University,
Atlanta Ga.

Dear Dr. DuBois,

I quite approve of your plans for the Encyclopedia.[1] Yes, I will contribute something if you will tell me what you wanted.

By the way, I wrote George/Joel ["Joel" is written above "George"] Spengarn [sic] a letter.[2] He seems to feel that you have (being in Atlanta) is lost to him and he is unhappy about it. Pretty fresh, hey, me advising you, well, strange things do happen.

> Sincerely,
> Zora Neale Hurston

I dictated this letter to a local stenographer & this is what her notes turned out.

---

[1]*The* Encyclopedia Africana *was in some ways the biggest project of Du Bois's career. It was intended to express the Pan-Africanism he developed over his lifetime. He began working on this project after his move to Ghana in 1961 but did not complete it before his death in 1963. Henry Louis Gates, Jr., Anthony Kwame Appiah, and others recently completed the* Encyclopedia Africana *and made it available on-line and in print.*
[2]*Writer and professor Joel Spingarn; see glossary.*

TO JAMES WELDON AND
GRACE NAIL JOHNSON

[postcard]
[postcard front: "Greetings from Jamaica: The Creek
Dome—Pure Water Spring—Montego Bay."]

[April 1936?]

Dear Friends,
I am out here in this beautiful country and down at work. Wish I had
the address of the Joel Spingarns. I love them very much.

Zora Neale Hurston
Zora

Charcoal sketch of Hurston by Amy Spingarn.

TO HENRY ALLEN MOE

[stamped: received at Guggenheim, May 5, 1936]

Dear Mr. Moe,

Just this minute, as I was about to post your letter comes one from Dr. Herskovits, urging me strongly to leave Jamaica and proceed at once to the Bahamas. His arguments are:

1. That the time is past to diffuse efforts over large areas, and since I have made a start in the Bahamas I should stick there and do an intensive piece of work there.

2. I should lose no time in Haiti because he feels that my knowledge of Creole, while adequate to converse, is not good enough to permit me to grasp all the nuances that he feels made Mules and Men live. (Please, I am quoting)

3. That the accounts that I have given him previously of the Bahamas convinces him that [is—x-ed out] they are much more primitive than any of the other islands, and so I should lose no time in doing the finest thing possible there. He feels that I alone can do it best. He will be glad to help me work up the material that I gather.

Now, both you and Dr. Lydenberg[1] have advised me to gather material with the eye to a good book, not necessarily a scientific one. I was going to the Bahamas anyway in the end, but I was planning to go on to Haiti in a few days. Now I wonder whether to proceed to Haiti as planned, or to go on to the Bahamas. I'm asking.

I am beginning to gather material wholesale here. Just squat down awhile and after that things begin to happen. The people here are just as sensitive as in Haiti, I mean the upper class, these "coloured peo-

---

[1] *Harry Miller Lydenberg (1874–1960) was one of the most respected librarians of the century. As chief of the research collections of the New York Public Library from 1934 to 1941, Lydenberg fashioned New York's library system as a virtual scholarly academy, drawing together scholars, writers, artists, publishers, and editors.*

ple" who have white blood in them and feel like suing you if you call them Negroes. I hear that the late John Hope created consternation here by calling himself a Negro.[2] You see he was whiter than those who deny that they are Negroes and so they looked foolish. I have corrected several who called me a <u>coloured</u> person. They wonder why we insist on being Negroes. I shall write an article about this island where roosters lay eggs.[3] I mean by that that a mulatto b born out of wedlock, as always, never mentions his mother. Only the white father. So you finally conclude that women are not necessary to births out here. The rooster lays eggs.

Please tell me what to do in this matter of Haiti and I will promise not to worry you too much after. I am also letting Mr. Lydenberg know of my dilemma.

Most sincerely,
Zora

TO HENRY ALLEN MOE

[telegram]

May 21, 1936
LC HENRY MOE GUGGENHEIM=
FOUNDATION 551 FIFTH AVE NEW YORK=

CREDIT LETTER LOST PENNILESS BANKS WARNED=
    HURSTON.

---

[2]*Educator John Hope (1868–1936) served as president of Atlanta Baptist College (later Morehouse College), Atlanta University, and finally, Spelman. Hope was awarded the Spingarn Medal posthumously in 1936.*
[3]*The first chapter of Part I of* Tell My Horse: Voodoo and Life in Haiti and Jamaica *is titled "The Rooster's Nest."*

TO HENRY ALLEN MOE

[telegram]

May 22, 1936
LC HENRY MOE=
GUGGENHEIM FOUNDATION 551 FIFTH AVE NYK=

TRUST CORRESPONDENTS PROMPTLY WARNED
IDENTIFICATION GONE OCCURRED LEAVING BANK=
    HURSTON.

TO HENRY ALLEN MOE

Kingston, Jamaica
May 22, 1936

Dear Mr. Moe,

I wish I could make you know how sorry I am about this loss because I realize what a lot of trouble and worry I am to others.

This is the way it was. Since May 4th I have been moving about the country seeing what I could see. I found a gracious plenty. If there was nothing more than what I had already seen I meant to clear out from Jamaica. But I meant to get what was here before I left so as not to feel that I missed something later on. I found three separate cults that surprised and interested me. 1. Pukamania 2. Horsehead 3. a queer African-sounding name that is performed by the Marroons. These Marroons are worth a year's study in themselves. They are the dwscendants of men who fought their way to freedom from slavery and successfully fought off all attempts to re-enslave them. They still govern themselves and pay no taxes [or?] any other tribute to England. I have made friends there and secured permission to live among the Marrons of the West for as long as I like. I hurried back to Kingston with my last cash shilling on Monday night and prepared to get away next day to Maroontown where

so many wierd and wonderful things still happen. Took my letter of
credit to the bank on Tuesday morning and drew $100. This was the
first time I had drawn so much but I wanted to stay a long time. Up to
that day I had drawn fifty dollars on two occasions, so that altogether I
have drawn 200 on my credit since I left New York. Went from the bank
with the money, letter of credit, and my identification in a large wallet
to a beauty parlor for a hair cut. Clutching this wallet all the time. Refused to even rest it at the request of the attendant. Very hungry by that
time. Walked <u>half a block</u> to Meyers restaurant for a bowl of soup. Went
to pay and found that the wallet was gone. I had rested my things (a
book and a small package) on the end of the table where I sat alone.
The waiter was summoned and the manager and everybody. No one acknowledged seeing it. I went immediately to the police and then to the
banks and gave warning and information. Waited and hoped all next
day for some word, hating like the devil to admit the loss. Then on
Thursday felt I ought to inform you. Borrowed a pound from a friend
and cabled you. But the first day I went in the bank I tried to leave
the letter of credit and Barclays refused to accept the responsibility.
Wouldnt allow me to leave it there. I have witnesses that I tried to carry
out your instructions. I placed all the valuables in the wallet until I
could reach my room where I would separate them again as usual and
had the bad luck to have it happen in the one vulnerable moment.

I am the most unhappy person in the world because I fear your organization may feel that I am too much trouble to bother with, and just
at the time when I have come upon the most exciting material I have
even experienced. Jamaica is a seething Africa under its British exterior. The law here is most stringent. It does not stop things as it so
smugly imagines it does. It merely sends it under ground. You'd be
most astonished to find out what happens <u>right here in Kingston.</u>

I have told the detectives all that I can, notified the banks fully,
and advertised in the Gleaner, offering a reward for the return of the
wallet.[1] So now all I can do is sit here with that heavy sickening sink-
ing sensation in my stomach and wait dumbly to see what life will do
with me.

[1]*In the Guggenheim files, there is a copy of an article about this loss either published in the local paper,* Daily
Gleaner, *or intended for publication there. Its version of events is slightly different than Hurston's, describing
her discovery of the loss as having occurred not in the restaurant, but in a taxicab she hailed after she left the
restaurant. A letter to Moe from the Kingston detective inspector presents a third scenario in which the wallet
was dropped onto the street by Hurston.*

Found your letter on my return to town with my mind all made up to stay here for a while.

Most sincerely and gratefully,
Zora Hurston

TO HENRY ALLEN MOE

Poste Restante
Kingston, Jamaica
May 28, 1936

Dear Mr. Moe,

I received notice of the money you so kindly sent me on Tuesday.[1] The bank sent the notice on Saturday but Monday was Queen Victoria's birthday so I didnt go to the P.O. that day. So it was paid me on Tuesday and i needed it too. Thanks. Thank you very much.

I feel that I have not talents whatsoever in money and business matters. So maybe I ought not to have to do with it at all. I get too thoroughly immersed in my dreams. But somehow life is so organized that I find myself tied to money matters like a grazing horse to a stake.

I think a sneak theif got the bill fold. I hardly think any one could have known about the letter of credit. I feel that that has been thrown away or destroyed to avoid detection. The police still hope to recover it but as the days go by I myself am losing hope. I went to the American Consul here, a Mr. Armstrong, and he askd the officials at Barclay's to cable you all the details since I had no funds. They would consent to do it only if I paid for the cable myself. I told t them that of course I had a reasonable command of English and could send a wire myself. But since I had done business with them I and Mr. Armstrong thought that they would have extended me that courtesy. I'll never set foot in <u>that</u> bank again. The Royal bank of Canada has been more active in urging on the police than any other. If you have my other letter by the last air mail it contains all the details.

---

[1] *Moe arranged for Hurston to receive first $25 and then $100. He also reassured her that they would see to arrangements that would let her continue her fellowship work.*

Any money sent me thru the Royal Bank of Canada will reach me promptly. I am having all my mail General Delivery to avoid careless handling in residences.

I am finding some gorgeous and shining legends now. <u>Plenty</u> of material here. The Rolling Calf for instance.

The people here are beginning to like me a lot. They now seek me out to tell me things. A cabinet maker has made me a set of wooden salad plates out of the beautiful hard woods that they have here. 12 plates out of different woods. I expressed my pleasure at the compliment and now a potter is making me a set of native dishes. They are quite attractive too. I am panting to get back into the mountains with the Marroons so that I can witness that marvelous conk-shell ceremony that begins with an echo in a far-off mountain and lasts for three days. The sound and echo begin at midnight and gradually the "god" is brought in to the village from the mountain. No white person has ever witnessed it and less than five persons outside of the tribe have done so, and they were either married into the tribe or very closely connected.

On my knees I say how sorry I am that I have caused so much trouble. I'm too sorry. I've been in a black and melancholy hole of a mood and condition ever since. All the suns in the universe not enough to light it up. This morning I feel better, somehow.

Most sincerely,
Zora Hurston

TO HENRY ALLEN MOE

Poste Restante, Kingston, Jamaica
June 10, 1936.

Dear Mr. Moe,

Came down from Morant Bay yesterday and found your most kind and understanding letter. Thanks.[1]

I went straight from the Post Office to the Royal Bank of Canada to see about keeping my important paper[s] there. I was told that they

[1]Moe had written that he, too, had lost a letter of credit once and that things could be rearranged with a mere forfeit of $100 on Hurston's part, to help cover the costs of international notification to the banks.

would keep it for me for a dollar a month if I used it often. Free of charge if I didnt use it oftener than twice a month, which I wont. So its agreed that I am to bring it there.

The check for 100 dollars came to me the day I went up to St. Thomas-in-the-east of which Morant Bay is the big town. I am getting on very well there. It has occurred to me to make a collection of all the subtle poisons that Negroes know how to locate among the bush and the use of which they are so expert. No one outside of the hoodoo or bush doctors know these things. But as I am learning day by day more and more I think that I will be doing medical science a great service to identify these weeds so that antidotes can be prepared. The greatest power of voodoo rests upon this knowledge. Some of these "bushes" are quite marvelous. One of them I <u>know</u> will kill by being placed so that the wind will blow from it to the victim. Another can be rubbed on the clothing and enters thru the pores as soon as the victim sweats.

Thanks for the check. Of course I do not feel badly at paying $100. to have the letter circularized. I consider myself favored in not paying the whole amount. Thanks for your intervention.

Sincerely and happily,
Zora HURSTON ["Hurston" written in a different hand]

TO EDWIN OSGOOD GROVER

Port Maria,
Jamaica B.W.I.,
3rd July, 1936.

Dr. Edwin Osgood Grover,
Winter Park,
Florida.

Dear Dr. Grover:

Here by this gorgeous sea, I took out all of your poems and read them over again. They fit in as beautifully as if you had actually seen the sea and mountains of Jamaica.

I appreciate you—Nature's poet.

I am gathering splendid material for a book.

You know, I thank you for what you have done for me though I cant say it myself with enough feeling.

My regards to Mrs. Thompson and all my friends who have stood by me so beautifully through the years.

> With appreciation and good wishes
> Most sincerely
> Zora

TO FANNIE HURST

Port Maria,
Jamaica, B.W.I.,
3rd July, 1936.

Miss Fanny [sic] Hurst
23 West 67th Street,
New York City.

Dear Fanny Hurst:

Thanks to you, I am out here working very hard.[1] It's quite gorgeous.

I am hoping that you will join me as you said you would. There is plenty here for your note book.

Do you know that they banned the showing of your IMITATION OF LIFE here?[2] The shoe pinched too much.

> Love and appreciation.
> Zora

[1] In late 1935, at the Guggenheim's request, Hurst wrote the foundation in support of Hurston's application for funding for research in Haiti and Jamaica.

[2] The controversial film based on Hurst's novel by the same title.

TO MELVILLE HERSKOVITS

Accompongtown
Maggoty P.O.
July 30, 1936

Dear Dr. Herskovits,

I found your name up here in the visitors book and Col. Rowe told me that you had spent the night here two years ago. Also found that Catherine [sic] Dunham had been here last year carrying out the program that I had mapped out for the Rosenwald gang.[1] I can afford to laugh at them, of course, but their littleness is astounding.

Jamaica has yeilded some surprising things. There is a strong primitive survival deeply buried from the sight of prying official eyes, but very much here. I have found the answer to three phases of magic that had always puzzled me. 1. Why the frequent use of the earth from graves to injure? 2. Why the universal fear of poisoning in unlettered Negroes 3. Why the stubbornly maintained charge of poisoning when the M.D. found no justification?[2]

I go to Haiti after the big ceremony here of Aug.1. That is the big, big thing and you have not seen Maroon ceremony unless you see that. The affair begins with a purification withdrawal of the men to the mountain adjoining and they signal their return with the ceremonial horn at dawn and then things begin. It is a wonder that Miss Dunham did not stay for it.

My regards to Mrs. Herskovits. Where are you off to next time? I met Miss Edith Clarke[3] here and find her very nice.

Sincerely yours,
Zora

---

[1] Dancer, anthropologist, artist, choreographer, writer, and teacher, Katherine Dunham (b. 1910) became a specialist in Afro-Caribbean and Afro-Brazilian culture. She formed her first dance troupe in 1931, danced on Broadway, opened an influential New York school of dance in 1945, served as a U.S. State Department adviser and campaigned internationally against racism. As an anthropologist, Dunham studied with Melville Herskovits. Hurston considered her a particular rival.

[2] Hurston builds on this fear in Their Eyes Were Watching God when she makes Janie's second husband, Jody Starks, so suspicious of Janie's poisoning him that he will take no food or drink from her.

[3] Jamaican anthropologist Edith Clark (1896–1979) was particularly well known for her work on families, her social advocacy for illegitimate children, and, later, her book My Mother Who Fathered Me (1957).

TO HENRY ALLEN MOE

Hotel Bellevue
Port au-Prince
Haiti
Sept. 24, 1936

Dear Dr. Moe,

I must do that thing that I dislike to do, that is, write you a longish letter. I know that you are a very busy man. But at the same time I feel that you must know the ins and outs of everything as far as I can tell you.

You remember that shortly after I arrived in Jamaica I had a letter from Dr. Herskovits telling me that if he had laid out the plans I would not have gone to Jamaica at all because there was nothing there to see; and that my French was not good enough to come to Haiti. Of course at the time I wondered how Dr. Herskovits could pass judgment on my french seeing he knew nothing about it. I wrote you because I did not know what was behind it all and thought you might know. By your silence, I discovered that you knew no more that I did Well, late in July I got the answer to the puzzle. I went up to Accompong, the biggest Maroon settlement in the island and found that he had been there for a night and had later sent a Miss Catherine [sic] Dunham, a petty dancer of Chicago there to collect. She had been there for a monthbut had done nothing that anyone could take account of. That is [only the—x-ed out] the only place she visited in Jamaica because Herskovits didnt stay there long enough (8 days) to find out about what was really going on. Then [he had—x-ed out] she had proceeded to Haiti where he had stayed a month. She stayed here six months with <u>infinitely</u> less preparation than I have for the work. So it all comes out. From someone in Chicago I hear that after I had given the concert at the Chicago Civic Opera with the West Indian dancers that cause very favorable comment all over she thought all she needed to do was to come. But she doesnt seem to realize that I spent months over details that she doesnt even <u>see.</u> But Charles S. Johnson and Herskovits have persuaded her that they can make a great woman of her by suppressing me.

I am having no trouble at all in making myself understood. I arrived yesterday on the S.S. Haiti and already I have found the community I wish to tackle first. In Jamaica, I lived in every [one of] the parishes and studied every group. Bossman, there is plenty in Jamaicaa to see!! In the parishes of the St. Thomas, Portland and St. Elizabeth, I hardly see how Haiti can surpass them for primitive lore. I have seen things!

Here I shall take a house up in the hills so that I can write in the periods when I am not finding things. Busha, (Jamaican for boss)[1] I feel that I can justify your giving me this. chance. I think I have two books already. While I have the facts at hand, I shall go light on the strictly scientific, and bear down heavy on the matter of story-telling.

Please sir, I thank you for the new letter of credit. It had been there for some time before I came out of the bush and found it.

Nothing in Jamaica! Scarcely a week passes in Kingston someone is not prosecuted for witchcraft. I have a collection of clippings from the GLEANER on it but they are pasted up.

Busha, I cant tell you how much this chance means to me. I am straining every nerve to the goal.

                    Most sincerely,
                    Zora Hurston ["Hurston" is written in a different hand]

TO HENRY ALLEN MOE

Port-au-Prince, Haiti
October 14, 1936

Dear Dr. Moe,
    I certainly was glad to get your letter. I was wondering if [you] could understand the petty conniving and intriguing that goes on among us so-called "big niggers". I am ashamed to admit that there is more effort spent to keep somebody else from getting somewhere than there is to get somewhere ones self. For instance, I ran into Arthur

---

[1] In his reply to this letter, Moe refuses to be called "bossman"—in any language—insisting that the fellows are the "bosses" of their own research.

Schomberg [sic] one day and he insisted that I go to lunch with him as he had something to tell me that was important. It turned out that he had just returned from Fisk University. And what was he doing there? He was there secretly urging students <u>not</u> to take any subjects under James Weldon Johnson! Make him so unpopular that he must leave Fisk. When he is gone then Charles S. Johnson will take steps to see that Fisk has a Negro president. You can just imagine whom he thinks ought to be it. Schomberg will be librarian for his labors. Why get rid of James W.? Well, it would seem the natural thing to make him president if he were around. Thomas Elsa Jones must be kept there at all hazards until Jim Johnson can be eased out. He was full of glee as he told me how many students he had persuaded. I was terribly distressed because Jim Johnson is the most all-around fine fellow in the Negro race. I didnt tell him about it because he is clever and it might seem like meddling, too. But that sort of thing is plentiful. J.W.J. [James Weldon Johnson] has not injured C.S.J. [Charles S. Johnson] and is certainly worthy of any honor in the world, but there you are.

I almost forgot to ask for an application blank. November 1 will soon be here. I know that thousands of other people want a chance, but I want another one too. There is so much to write about in these waters. If I cease gathering material now and write, I will miss a great deal that I came for. If I continue to collect until March, I shall have no time to write. I have considered this dilemma a great deal recently. Nobody realizes more than I what a wonderful thing has happened to me. I have grown in every direction in these six months. May I have a form by an early mail so that I can get it in by the dead line?

There is no female word for busha in these parts. Women have not that prestige. I look forward to the day when I shall be back in U.S.A. and have my way about something. Thanks for the compliment just the same.

Most sincerely,

Zora

P.O. Box 128-B. I shall keep this permanently, no matter where I go in Haiti, so as to avoid confusion.

TO HENRY ALLEN MOE

Box 128-B
Port-au-Prince
Haiti
January 6, 1937

Dear Dr. Moe,

A detailed letter is coming on the boat. It is so much slower than the air, but I felt safer, so I sent it that way. However I did not forget that you had avised me tom have my application in by January 1. I did not forget and tried hard to do so, but I wanted to have certain accomplishments realities instead of dreams before I wrote you.

I do hope that you had a very pleasant holiday season. Mine was spent far from the joys of the city in the hinterland of La Gonave[1] but I enjoyed it just the same.

Sincerely as always,
Zora Neale Hurston

TO HENRY ALLEN MOE

Box 128-B
Port-au-Prince, Haiti
January 6, 1937

Dr. Henry Allen Moe, Sec.
John Simon Guggenheim Memorial Foundation
551 Fifth Avenue
New York, N.Y.

Dear Dr. Moe,

This is the third letter that I have sweated out of my system to you in the matter of a renewal of the fellowship. But each time I

[1]*Île de la Gonâve, an island off the coast of Haiti.*

seem not to be adequate in my explanations. It is hard to give a true picture. Perhaps I have chosen too big a canvas for my work. No, that is not right either. The picture is infinitely too huge for the canvas.

From April to September I spent in Jamaica gathering material for a book on the tropics which I had decided to call "BUSH". It was to be half and half Jamaica-Haiti. Not a strictly scientific work, but burning spots from the ensemble. I found enough material for a whole book on Jamaica, but I wish to hold to my original plan with the exception of lessening the Jamaica material in favor of haitian which is more exciting by far. Now I have a new title, "TELL MY HORSE" which is the third personal introduction of the "Gude" (pronounced geeday) spirit speaking throught the person possessed. The plan so far is:

TELL MY HORSE[1]

A. Jamaica
  1. Nine Night (spectacular ceremony to dismiss the spirit of the dead person on the ninth night after death. Truly gripping.
  2. The preparation of a young girl for love. The methods used to bring a girl utterly innocent of love matters to the bed of her husband or lover in afrenzy of pleasurable anticipation, plus the knowledge of what to do to give the man the most pleasure and at the same time, feel no pain herself. How to achieve preg-- nancy quickly and surely.
  3. Pocomania. A primitive religious sect that is many things in one. a. Obeah b. Koomunah. c. Myalism
  4. The Maroons. A few of their customs and a Hog-hunt. One of the most exciting things in the western world.
B. Haiti
  1. Zombies. Proof of their existence. Why. How. Eight authentic cases.
  2. Haitian gods and demi-gods with their signs, animals, colors and ceremonies, and meanings.
      a. Damballah, "Li qui rete n'en ciel" (he who lives in the sky) The most powerful of all the gods but whose name is sel- dom heard, it being too sacred to be spoken. He is ap- proached through other gods. His symbol is the snake.

[1]Published by Lippincott in 1938.

    b. Legba, ndxt to Damballah in power

    c. Loco, the Tree god (in Dahomey, Loki)

    d. Peidro, most terrible

    e. Agoue' god of all waters

    f. Zandour, or Canga-Zandor

    g. Balinjou, perhaps a phase of Damballah

    h. Maitresse Ezilee, the woman of Damballah

    i. Agoun Badagree

    j. Boine, La Croix, Baron Cimiterre, Baron Sambdi, all names of the Lord of the Dead who is worshipped Nov. 2 with elaborate ceremony, and whose color is brown.

    k. Cimbi, worshipped with the snake through December-Jan.

    l. Aida, female consort of Damballah

    m. Cilla, likewise.

    n. There are numerous demi-gods and phases of the known gods to be mastered by me, [but—x-ed out]

    o. There is a whole lore of sacred places and stones in connection with the worship of the gods. Also the drapeaux (flags) animals and the like that is associated with each.

    p. Houngans.

        1. Who are houngans and why

        2. The passing of power from the dead houngan to his or her successor three days after death. I have seen this wierd ceremony in which the dead sits up, opens his eyes and nods his head.

        3. The various degrees of priesthood as in masonry. I see it but do not know as yet how and why except that I know a baptism preceeds each upward step.[2]

Summary on Haiti:

I am not starved with a paucity of material as is usual, but flooded with so much that I realize the task is huge, so huge and complicated that it flings out into space more fragments than would form the whole of any other area except Africa. It is more than the sympathetic magic that is practised by the hoodoo doctors in the United States. It is as formal as the Catholic church anywhere. An ordinary volume of 100,000 words could only cover the subject by being very selective and

---

[2] *The published text of* Tell My Horse *roughly follows this outline.*

brief. So you can see why a letter is difficult for me. It is like explain-ining the planetary theory on a postage stamp. Haiti's pagan gods have captured many white people who have not gotten so far as I have in the mysteries, and who perhaps will never get any further than they are, but who are held so firmly that they cannot bear the thought of leaving Haiti. Husbands and wives, families and friends are forsaken by these whites who quietly merge themselves in the rites and are happy beyond belief. In this connection I have often wished that you could pay a visit and see and hear for yourself. I let myself be per-suaded to order a set of ceremonial drums baptised and named for you. Then I got a little afraid that you might not get the point and de-spise both the drums and my intelligence. No I have not been con-verted locally, tho I am not a christian either.

Since the middle of December I have been at La Gonave, the sup-posed island kingdom of Workus [sic], and find thatSeabrook made his royalty out of the whole cloth.[3] But I like Workus and so I shall say nothing about it on my return. Communication with the outside world is difficult from there so I came over to see this letter off. On La Go-nave, one might be in the heart of Africa for all outward signs. I loved it. Wish that I might go to West Africa some day to check up on cer-tain religious manifestations that I find here and in Jamaica. This let-ter in the mails, I shall be off to the far places again, that is to La Gonave first and then other places.

I have been trying for weeks to think out a crisp, clean-cut letter of application to you, but the subject wont let it come out like that. So I simply say, I have worked seriously during the months you have fi-nanced me and gathered a mass of material. And gathering the mate-rial so far as Haiti is concerned, makes me realize what a taks really is here. I have now a working knowledge of creole, and the pattern of the job to be done which is a hundred times bigger than it seemed the day I talked with you in your office. It has never been done, and is cry-ing to me to do it. So I come to you in the only way that I know how

---

[3]*Faustin E. Wirkus was a Marine Corps sergeant crowned king by the residents of the Île de la Gonâve, according to stories written by William B. Seabrook. Seabrook wrote the introduction to Wirkus's account of his adventures,* The White King of La Gonave *(New York: Doubleday, 1931). Wirkus's book became a cause célèbre, fascinating what Seabrook claims was an audience of "ten million" whose "dream-wish" to "be God" was fulfilled by Wirkus's tale. Seabrook also wrote* The Magic Island *(also titled* The Voodoo Island*) in 1929.*

and ask for another chance. I beg the opportunity to finish what I have
begun.

Sincerely and gratefully,

Zora Neale Hurston

P.S. If I seem to be ungrateful and to take things for granted it is because the seriousness of the occasion makes me fluster somewhat. Also
I have not mentioned all the things that I have done because I tried
that in the first version of the letter and it only succeeded in looking
like I was too mouthy.

TO FANNIE HURST

Box 128-B, Port-au-Prince, Haiti
Jan. 22, 1937

Dear Fannie Hurst,

Congratulations on your new book!![1] I have ordered it but it has
not come as yet.

There is another matter of grave importance that I must speak to
you about. Miss Hurst, drop everything and take a plane or something
and be here by the 5th of February. The Royal Dutch Line will put
you here on the 3rd. I not only promise you material for a book, but
there is something you can do for your friends, Franklin and Eleanor
Roosevelt.[2] You know that I know I am asking something big and
crazy-sounding. But the situation warrants this emergency measure
and I would not urge you to dash off on a wild goose chase at a moment's notice (I have a proper appreciation of your importance) unless

---

[1] *Fannie Hurst published* Great Laughter *in 1936.*

[2] *Hurst's friendship with the Roosevelts began in 1931, well before Franklin D. Roosevelt's presidency, and continued throughout their time in the White House, to which Hurst was a frequent visitor. In Hurst's Founder's
Day address at Rollins College in 1934 (accompanied by Hurston and Helen Worden Erskine), Hurst spoke at
some length, and warmly, about the Roosevelts.*

it were justified. Anyway a few days later than the 5th will help, but it would be better if you got here by that date.[3]

I must rush and bathe and get this off in the air mail. Hence the abrupt closing.

As ever,

Zora

TO CARL VAN VECHTEN

[postcard]
[spring, 1937]
1925—7th Ave Apt. 2-J.

Dear Pink-toe,

Back from the Caribbean and very glad to be back. Hope to see you soon. Let me hear from you. I got my tail all curled, & red in the comb.

Sincerely,

Zora.

TO ANNIE NATHAN MEYER

[postcard]
[spring, 1937]

Dear, dear Friend,

I am back after twelve strenous months and would love to see you.[1] Today I finish a piece of business with my publisher and then I shall begin reading that long list of your published works. There was no

---

[3]*I have been unable to determine what event Hurston hoped Hurst would witness in Haiti on that date. It is possible that there were already stirrings of the labor revolt that led to what is known as the Caribbean Holocaust—the massacre of ten thousand to twenty thousand day laborers in October 1937. The annual Marroon Ceremony in which she was interested was on January 6.*

[1]*In 1935, Hurston had traveled throughout the South. In 1936, she spent six months in Jamaica, then another six in Haiti in 1936 and 1937.*

possibility of my getting hold of them while in Haiti. I have really been in the wilds! Brought back some lovely material too.

My phone not connected yet so please drop me a card and say when I can come and talk with you. I hope that the Dr. is quite well and happy.

I see by the papers that Robert Nathan's great story has been dramatized.[2] I shall go to see it no later than tomorrow night if I can get tickets. He is still my favorite of all living authors.

Lovingly,

Zora

1925—7th Ave. Apt. 2-J.

TO HENRY ALLEN MOE

1925 Seventh Avenue
New York, New York
March 20, 1937

Dr. Henry Allen Moe,
John Simon Guggenheim Mem. Foundation
551 Fifth Avenue
New York, New York

Dear Dr. Moe,

I have been sitting and thinking since yesterday noontime how to write this letter so that you could understand and know my feelings.

Perhaps unfortunate for me, I have a ideal of achievement fleeing before me. Always there is the hope that I shall confine it in the written word. So far my fingers have not touched its garments. But when one has a burning bush inside one keeps on trying, whether or not. One bleeds internally when balked of effort.

So I am thanking you for the understanding soul you have to let me escape again from what destroys me here. Further, I see more clearly what is to be done. Haiti is so thrillingly real and unreal that

---

[2]*Probably* Road of Ages *or* One More Spring. *In the 1930s, Nathan was writing novels, poetry, plays, and screenplays. Many of his works were successfully adapted for the stage and the cinema.*

I have wished that the whole twelve months had been spent there. But still I would not have missed what I saw in Jamacia for anything. I am trying to show you the background for my gratitude so that when I say it is monstropolous and high, you know that I am fully aware of your great generosity. I see all forms of generosity, spiritual and material wrapped up in the same bundle, and all shining under the glow and light of your understanding. I come in the humblest way I know how to say thank you in a most particular manner. I shall strain to justify it in work.

Yours sincerely,
Zora Neale Hurston

TO DOROTHY WEST

[postcard postmarked March 22, 1937]

1925 Seventh Avenue, Apt. 2-J

Dear Dot,

I would just love to see you. Phone not connected yet. But most anytime I will be in. Come a running, honey.

Zora

TO JAMES WELDON JOHNSON

1925 Seventh Avenue
New York City
March 23, 1937

Dear James Weldon Johnson,

Thanks for your assisstance in the matter of the Book-of-the-Month Club contest. You have a fine, big heart in your bosom.

Were you mad with me that you didnt answer the letter I wrote you from Jamaica?

My very best to the regal Mrs. Jim. Let me know when you visit New York.

Most sincerely,
Zora
Zora Neale Hurston

TO BURTON RASCOE[1]

1925 Seventh Avenue
New York City
March 24, 1937

Mr. Burton Rascoe,
Literary Guild
New York City

Dear Mr. Rascoe,

I want to thank you all for remembering my name in the recent Book-Of-The-Month contest. It put my silver singing-trumpet to playing in my hand. Thank you over and again.

Sincerely and gratefully
Zora Neale Hurston

[1]*Arthur Burton Rascoe, drama critic, journalist, editor, and author; see glossary.*

TO KATHERINE TRACY L'ENGLE

1925 Seventh Avenue
New York City
April 1, 1937

Katherine Tracy L'Engle
Columbia University
New York City

Dear Miss L'Engle,

You do me a great honor in using material from MULES AND MEN. I am very happy over the matter. If Mr. Lippincott has given his consent then it [is] more than alright with me. He is the swellest publisher that ever was.[1]

It is also fine of you to invite me to your recital. You can count on me for a good customer. I wont come alone either. I wont miss.

I am delighted to see that you are another Floridian. They grow such nice people in that state. (Cheers!) Please let me see you and talk with you sometime.

With a much-felt wish for your continued success, I am

Sincerely yours,
Zora Neale Hurston

---

[1] *L'Engle wanted to use portions of* Mules and Men *in her reading series, Studies of the Negro in American Literature, at Columbia University.*

TO KATHERINE TRACY L'ENGLE

[April 1937—library dated]
1925 Seventh Avenue
Apartment 2-G
Manhattan, New York

Miss Katherine Tracy L'Engle
Whittier Hall
Columbia University
New York City

Dear Miss L'Engle:

    Please forgive what must seem ungraciousness but I have only today finished the corrections on the final proof of my book,[1] and between preparing for my lecture tour which begins on the 19th and my return to Haiti, I find an almost inhuman rush of work pressing on me.

    It makes me very happy that you want to read from "Mules & Men". Thank you for your good wishes. I am very eager to meet you and shall certainly attend your recital Wednesday.

Very Sincerely Yours,
Zora Neale Hurston

ZNH:J

---

[1] *Hurston wrote* Their Eyes Were Watching God *in November and December 1936. It appeared in the fall of 1937.*

TO MELVILLE HERSKOVITS

1925 Seventh Avenue
New York City
April 6, 1937

Dear M.J.,

CONGRATULATIONS!! It is grand to see you get additional recognition for your work, for you do work hard.[1]

I am astonished at the criticism of Williams. First of all I am astonished that he would attempt it; and then again I am stunned that he knows so little. Of course you are right and I had intended writing you a long letter about Jamaica when I got around to it. There is a wonderful amount of duplication in thefolk tales there of the American Negro tales. Truly amazing. I was not collecting the tales but I encouraged the telling of them and it was truly astonishing. Many, many of the well known tales are identical except for the change of character names. SAME THING IN HAITI.

You seemed cross with me and so I did not tell you how I felt about that Dunham business. Now, please understand in the very beginning that I have nothing against her and could in no way be jealous of her work. But you remember that the Rosenwald offered me a fellowship without my asking for it. Well, Pres. Jones of Fisk who is an intimate friend of Dr. Embree did something to me which I still think was patronizing and contemptible. I told him immediately that I resented it and thought he ran his school like a Georgia plantation, with him as "Mr. Charlie" and members of his faculty being "good niggers" by carrying tales on the others, and he ought to be above it. He evidently told Embree about it for he froze up on me at once, proving to me that down in his heart he felt that niggers should stay in their places and not talk biggity to white folks no matter how justified the provocation. By the grape vine from Fisk I heard that Charles S. Johnson, who has not been friendly to me for years was boasting that it wouldnt be long with me and that he was grooming Catherine [sic] Dunham for the place. Embree wrote me a querelous letter without saying anything definite, but objecting to Dr.

[1]Herskovits was awarded a Guggenheim Fellowship for 1937–38.

Boas. He advocated Harvard. I have a certain loyalty and felt to make the change would be to repudiate Dr. Boas and you know I think with good reason that he is tops and in addition, whatever little foothold I might have is due to him and I could not in honor turn around and tell him that I preferred to study at Harvard. So I said, no that if I was to take my doctorate it was going to be with Boas. Then he wrote me and said for me to make another application to the Rosenwald in June. Mind you, they had already provided for two years. I never made the application for two reasons. First because they would not let Dr. Boas plan the course, but Dr. Embree insisted on laying out the work and I have no faith in his equipment as an anthropologist. Next I suspected his sincerity. I half believed that he was making difficulties because he no longer wished to give the money because I had sassed out his friend. Then I heard that the organization while the money had been appropriated by a jew was anti-jewish and that was the basis for the objection to Boas. I have been told that they give the cold shoulder to all jews. I dont know. But anyway, that was my experience with the Rosenwald. Nad when I reached Jamaica and found that she [Dunham] was following the identical itenerary that I had submitted to the Rosenwald, having heard what I heard about it, I jumped to conclusions in my mind.

Now about that dance of the Maroons. They hold the real one Jan. 6. That is when they go out to the mountains 24 hours ahead and make their own costumes and come in at a ceremonial hour to the blowing of the abeng. What was put on for money was tourist stuff. They tried to get me to put up some money for one. I told the Col. that I would be back for the regular one. His son-in-law was very friendly with me and had whispered in my ear about that and some other things. The Col. was very disappointed when I refused to have a dance put on. He tried to shame me by telling me how much Miss Dunham spent. I didnt tell him I had had more experience in the field than she. I merely told him that I wanted to come again around Christmas time. The August festival is big, but political. At one time it was tremendously important but all their dances have declined. Only the old ones cling to it. The young ones want something else. Then too, there is little faith in Col. Rowe. You know that the Col. is appointed by the Gov. and so they have no real choice of their leader and from the Maroon point of view, Col Rowe was not a good choice. And only once a year do they do anything relly ceremonial and that is Jan. 6. In the first place the Maroons are highly over rated. They are the show piece of Jamaica like a Harlem night club.[2] In fact they are not nearly so interesting as some groups in St. Thomas, out from Morant Bay. I saw some marvelous stuff there. There are some groups right in Kingston who do more than the Maroons. But the government is eager to give the impression that all primitive expression has disappeared from the island except what is done by the Maroons. The most important thing that the Maroons have that is separate is their primitive medicine. THAT IS IMPORTANT. It would be worth a separate study. I only had five months to do the whole island and that was not enough to study that phase intensely with the other things that I was doing.

Dr. Simpson told me about your new book[3] which I shall buy as soon as I catch up with my letters and go outside the house. I always use you[r] wife's African translations of poetry in my lectures. I am doing that quite seriously now under the Colston Leigh Lecture Bureau.[4] Spoke at the U. of Minn. on March 11. Three more to do this month in the south. Then I sail for Haiti again. Love to Mrs. H.

Sincerely yours,
Zora

TO HENRY ALLEN MOE

1925 Seventh Avenue
New York City
April 6, 1937

Dr. Henry Allen Moe
John Simon Guggenheim Memorial Foundation
581 Fifth Avenue
New York City

Dear Dr. Moe,

This is a turn-thanks letter to you for all that I have received. I know that you know my feelings and the ranges of my mind. I shall

[2]Hurston refers here to the fact that during the Harlem Renaissance the most famous black nightclubs—such as the Cotton Club—catered to whites and did not welcome black patrons.
[2]Probably Life in a Haitian Valley, published by Knopf in 1937.
[4]Founded in 1929, the Colston Leigh Lecture Bureau represented a wide range of speakers.

work like anything to save you that feeling of futility about me. I have a great big plan in my mind which I have hesitated to speak about because I do not know whether I have the ability to carry it out. When I make the first break I'll lay it before you.

With another bow and a thank you, I am

Most sincerely,
Zora Neale Hurston

TO HENRY ALLEN MOE

Port-au-Prince, Haiti
May 23rd, 1937

Dear Dr. Moe,

I landed safely today and found the rains in progress. What looked like the dry bed of a stream when I left has become a river that has swept houses away and crumbled the walls of the hospital. A few deaths here and there, but nothing serious. I plan to leave for the south as soon as the driver is satisfied that the roads are safe. Perhaps in two or three days.

The voyage down was pleasant. People ought to begin to consider the Panama R.R. Steamship line. It is Government owned. The vessels are stabilized, food good, great big square cabins and cheaper! Wis I had known about it last time!

You shall hear from me each move I make.

Most sincerely and gratefully,
Zora Neale Hurston

TO HENRY ALLEN MOE

C/o American Consulate
Port-au-Prince, Haiti
July 6, 1937

Dear Dr. Moe,

I am writing you after a long silence. Not that I had nothing to say to you before, but it did not seem the time to say it.

The book that I wrote, that it was possible for me to write because I had a Guggenheim fellowship, will be published September 16, I am told. Title: THEIR EYES WERE WATCHING GOD.

The points that I specified in my application for a renewal of the fellowship have been met. I have succeeded beyond my own expectations. With this exception, the inflow has been so exciting and so full that there has been no opportunity for putting anything into final form. But there have been repercussions. It seems that some of my destinations and some of my accessions have been whispered into ears that heard.[1] In consequence, just as mysteriously as the information travelled, I HAVE HAD A VIOLENT GASTRIC DISTURBANCE. That happened two weeks ago and today I leave my bed for the first time under my own power. I had myself brought into Port-au-Prince a week ago and carried to the bank and drew enough money to see me back to the U.S.A. if the worst came to the worst and left it with the Consul. I am sleeping and eating at his house now. Boss, for a whole day and a night, I thought I'd never make it. But I gain strength again now, and soon I go off again. You will hear from me in Port de Paix or La Gonave, according to which way the wind blows, inside of a week. I am <u>extremely pleased</u> with the progress of the work so far.[2] But I know that I could not survive a repetition of alimentary infection and so if conditions warrant it, with your permission, I shall do my polishing on American soil. This is purely an "if" statement. I just want you to understand in case. During this last week I have been propped up in

---

[1] *i.e., Dunham's.*
[2] Their Eyes Were Watching God *was completed in seven weeks while the material for* Tell My Horse *was being collected.*

bed doing another piece of work that you will hear about later.[5] No moss is growing on my back.

My very best to you and yours. The weather at this time of year is not as bad as I was led to expect.

Most sincerely,
Zora N. Hurston

TO HENRY ALLEN MOE

Hinche, Haiti
August 26, 1937

Dear Bossman,

I am here in the central plain of Haiti and in a hot-bed of what I want. My days are taken up now with tying up all loose ends and reviewing for the sake of verification. But let me assure you, boss, the book is in the bag.[1] I mean! So I am skipping about wherever I think I need a re-check. Planning to sail Sept. 22. Wish that I could be there for the coming out of my new book Sept. 16,[2] but that is not possible because something big is coming off here on the 18th that I would not miss for anything.

As soon as I land in New York and talk to you and Lippincott I shall head for Florida to polish off this volume. It is swelling up in me like a jeenie in a bottle, or like southern Negroes would put it, like a barrel of molasses in the summertime. I cant do so well here because now the material is engulfing me. I am embarrassed with too much. It confuses plans. And since if I spent 20 years I'd never get it all, I might as well stop with two books—one for anthro. and one for the way I want to write it.[3]

<hr />

[1]*Probably the manuscript of* Tell My Horse.

[5]Tell My Horse.

[2]Their Eyes Were Watching God.

[3]*Quite possibly Hurston had dual volumes in mind on the order of* Negro Folk-Tales from the Gulf States *and* Mules and Men, *but in that case the book she described as being the way she wanted it was the former, intended* for *the anthropologists.*

Boss, you told me to mention some Negroes that I think might be worthy of help. I nominate for number one, Iven Tate, painter and elevator boy, Orange General Hospital, Orlando, Florida. He does some very original conceptions with a sure and certain hand. He won the award for most original piece of work for the state of Florida for 1932 over all the whites and, bossman, between us two, you know that he <u>had</u> to be good to do that in Florida. He is intelligent and honest and content with his wife and baby. Strange as it seems, she understands and tries to help. But in order to eat, he cannot leave that elevator. Many of the white people hire him to do portraits and pay him two or three dollars. I begged Mrs. Bethune to help him in 1934. She could have spoken a good word to some of the wealthy p people who visit her school. But she wouldnt do it. I paid his way up to Daytona one Sunday when I was teaching at her school and he brought that marvelous portrait of his sister and another composition and he got the attention of the visitors as soon as the [w]ork was displayed. She snubbed him terribly and almost quit speaking to me. Afraid attention would be directed away from herself. The heifer! The crusher of talent!

Number two, 2929[?] McCull[a]h St. Baltimore. He wrote a good article in the COMMENTATOR for August I think. (The name is Ollie A. Stewart[.])[4] He has a fine direct style and courage! Not just to complain, but to take positive trends. He will bear watching.

Number three, a school of music and dancing for all the Negroes. To formalize and make respectable Negro musical methods. A college whose professors would be the people who make the songs and dances. It could be something more dynamic than most people would realize at first glance. It could support itself by concerts and tuition fees by the second year. [written in margin:] Imagine, Duke Ellington, Fats Waller, Louis Armstrong as guest professors! Ethel Waters, Bill Robinson, etc. Cant you see the white[s] who have ambition in that direction running there, to say nothing of Negroes.

I am now in robust health again. But, boss, I was one sick 'oman for awhile. I shall always remember that you understood and sympathized.

Most sincerely,

Zora Neale Hurston

---

[4] *Correspondent Ollie Stewart wrote for the* Afro-American *as well as other publications.*

TO FANNIE HURST

[postcard postmarked October 15, 1937 (New York)]

Dear Fannie Hurstt,

Thanks for all the lovely things you do me. Sorry I had to begin by mis-spelling your name, but it seems that this machine got too smart on me.

I was interviewed by Miss Worden[1] yesterday and photographed. She is as grand as ever.

Does it mean that you are considering going to Boston?[2] I hope so. THAT would be just asterperious! Had dinner with Carl [Van Vechten] Monday night. He is as you say very wonderful and magnificent. Edna St. Vincent Millay[3] sent me a lovely telegram. Was not that generous of her? God <u>does</u> love black people, doesnt He? Or am <u>I</u> just out on parole? Whatever it is, I dont intend to worry my gut into no fiddle string over how come. I mean to get my right amount of laughing. Love,

Zora

TO EDWIN OSGOOD GROVER

104-63 165th Street
Jamaica, Long Island
October 23, 1937

Dear Dr. Grover,

Thanks for your letter that was forwarded to me through Mr. Lippincott. I save all of your letters, for each one contains some vital help for me. I owe so much to you.

---

[1]*Helen Worden Erskine, see glossary.*

[2]*For the November Boston Book Fair, which Hurston planned to attend.*

[3]*American poet (1892–1950). Pulitzer Prize–winning writer Edna St. Vincent Millay was known for both conventional sonnets and political poetry. She published numerous books of poetry, a play, an opera with Deems Taylor, and satires under the pen name Nancy Boyd. Sadly, no letters from Hurston turn up in Millay's papers.*

Yes, indeed, I am coming home for the winter. In fact I did not intend to stop when I landed. I planned to send everything I had on by freight and follow on immediately. But I am to speak at the BOOK FAIR in Boston on Nov. 8, and at Radio City BOOK FAIR Nov. 15. So Mr. Lippincott asked me to stay north for that. I am bringing all my furniture with me this time. I want peace and quiet to sit down and try to learn how to write in truth. I have always been too hurried before.

My very best to the rest of the Grover family. You must have had extraordinary parents tp produce so muvh talent in one family.

I have just received a card this morning from Carl VanVechten saying that he saw my name in the new edition of WHO'S WHO. I must look to see as soon as I have time to get around to it.

My regards to Mrs. Thompson. I brought both of you something from Haiti.

I am under the impression that one can get only two fellowships from the Guggenheim.[1] But I have so much material now, that I can do about three books without stopping to search for more.

Looking forward to seeing you soon, I am

Yours sincerely,
Zora Hurston

TO CARL VAN VECHTEN

[October 23, 1937—library dated]
104-63 165th Street
Jamaica, Long Island

Dear Carl,

Perhaps you do not know it, but you are the person that I love best of everybody. But you know, Carl, you are a rich man, and you know my background. Lots of times when I want to make over you, I am so afraid you will think I want something from you. But from the bottom

---

[1] *According to G. Thomas Tanselle, vice president of the John Simon Guggenheim Memorial Foundation, "It was possible at that time for an individual to be awarded more than two Fellowships, but it was a rare occurrence."*

of my heart, I have several of the finest emotions in the worl wrapped around your image.

Nothing in the world would give me greater pleasure than to write about you. But they asked me to write about Fannie Hurst because her new book was just out, I reckon.[1] I hope they ask me again and let me choose my subject. A per[s]on could really say something if they write about you. I think I shall write to some asterperious magazine like Scribners or Vanity Fair [of—x-ed out] or Harpers and ask them to let me do a portrait of you with trimmings. Maybe they might let me, you never can tell. Anyway I shall ask. They cant kill me for that. I'll ask all and perhaps one of them will pay me some mind.

I know Elizabeth Hull[2] thinks that I am trashy, [b]ut that is not too true. I am trying to find Helen Johnson who put a box of papers in storage for me. She has something that Elizabeth wants to see. I find that she has lost her job, broken up her home and some say that she is in Boston. Anyway some one says that they will locate her by Monday if she is in town and if in Boston she will get me her address. I have the resume written as requested, but I wanted to take both things at the same time.

Saw Grace and James Weldon Johnson last night. They are still swell.

Most lovingly,
Zora

Satirday Morning.

---

[1]*"They"* is Saturday Review, *in which Hurston published a profile of Hurst, "Fannie Hurst by Her Ex-Amanuensis," October 9, 1937.*
[2]*Elizabeth Hull, Van Vechten's niece and the daughter of Emma Van Vechten Shaffer.*

TO FANNIE HURST

[on New York Urban League stationery]

November
5th
1937

Dear Fannie Hurst:

I have decided to do a Negro Folk concert at the Ambassador Theatre[1] Sunday evening, December 12th. It wouldn't be done right unless you were there with your best dress on and your mouth all primped up like a Christmas present.

I hope you do decide to go to Boston. I think I am leaving Sunday night or Monday morning. At any rate I am bound to see you at the New York Book Fair.

Lovingly yours,
Zora

Miss Fannie Hurst
1 West 67th Street
New York, N. Y.

ZNH/p

---

[1] *Broadway theater, still operating.*

TO JAMES WELDON AND
GRACE NAIL JOHNSON

[on New York Urban League stationery]

November
5th
1937

TO THEIR ROYAL HIGHNESSES
KING JAMES AND QUEEN GRACE

If it please your Majesties, your humble servant plans to give a program of Negro folk music at the Ambassador Theatre Sunday evening, December 12th. Now, you know I wouldn't start nothing like that without consulting you, because it wouldn't be done right, you knowing all that you do about folk things.

In spite of your royal proclivities, everybody knows you are one person who has not forgotten, or maybe it's because you are royal that you do not forget. But anyhow, I want to consult with you before I go too far. Would you drop me a line and give me a date?

I plan to set aside a portion of the proceeds as a fund to encourage Negro artists.[1]

Lovingly yours,
Zora

Dr. James Weldon Johnson
413 West 148th Street, c/o Nash
New York City

---

[1]*This did not come to fruition.*

TO CARL VAN VECHTEN

[on New York Urban League stationery]

November
5th
1937

Dear Carlo:

I hope you got back safely from your stepmother's funeral. I have been looking for you to call me up and been kind of wishful about the thing.

Look, Carl, I am doing a folk concert at the Ambassador Theatre on December 12th. It is a Sunday night, and I hope you keep it open. It's going to be good singing and plenty hip-wringing.

I am going to call you up, now.

Lovingly yours,
Zora

Mr. Carl Van Vechten
158 West 55th Street
New York, N. Y.

TO CARL VAN VECHTEN

[on New York Urban League stationery]

December
1st
1937

Dear Carlo:

My publishers insist that I finish my book on Haiti immediately.[1] Consequently, I do not find the time to work on the concert at the moment. So, there will be no concert on December 12th. In fact, I do not know when I can do it. But at some future date it is going to be done, and then I want to see you there.

Sincerely yours,
Zora Neale Hurston

Mr. Carl Van Vechten
158 West 55th Street
New York, New York

ZNH/p

TO CARL VAN VECHTEN

Box 173, Maitland, Fla.
Feb. 21,1938

Carl, The Incomparable,

I ducked off down here for two reasons. One reason was that I just had to come, and the other was that I wanted to. I had to come because I could not stay in New York until I had made some more money. And I knew that I could get some as soon as I hand in the script for the

[1] Tell My Horse.

book on Haiti.[1] Then too, I wanted to come and get it out of the way so that I could get back to work on FAN THE LADY.[2] Having the tail end of the book hanging over my head was ruining my entire life. I could not work very fast in New York so I ran down here to finish it quick. The contract calls for 80,000 words and I have 62,000 on paper and corrected for the typist. I expect to finish it this week and then I head for New York again. I do sincerely hope that I am not too late for your dinner. Nothing would give me greater pleasure. Before I leave Florida I have an errand for Fania Marinoff. Once she said in my presence that she wanted a certain thing to be found only in Florida. It is near Miami, and I shall get it for her and bring it with me.

The orange trees are full of blossoms and I see you in every one of them. The bees are humming in the trees all day and the mocking birds sing all night in the moonlight.

A wreath of flame vine for your crown,
Zora

TO JAMES WELDON JOHNSON

[February 1938]

Dear Lord Jim,

I get tired of the envious picking on me. And if you will admit the truth you know that Alain Leroy Locke is a malicious, spiteful litt[l]e snot that thinks he ought to be the leading Negro because of his degrees.[1] Foiled in that, he spends his time trying to cut the ground from under everybody else. So far as the young writers are concerned, he runs a mental pawnshop. He lends out his patronage and takes in ideas which he soon passes off as his own. And God help you if you get on without letting him "represent" you! His interest in Sterling Brown

---

[1]Tell My Horse.

[2]*This work does not appear among Hurston's papers or the works she registered for copyright. This may be a title for the concert she hoped to produce.*

---

[1]*Hurston is reacting to Locke's comments (Opportunity, January 1938) on* Their Eyes Were Watching God. *Locke wrote that Hurston was "talented" and had a "gift for poetic phrase, for rare dialect, and folk humor" but that her characters were "pseudo-primitives" and her writing an "oversimplification."*

makes him see Claude McKay as a rival to Sterling. Hence his snide remarks about Claude. I sent the original of this to OPPORTUNITY. I hope that they print it.[2]

Is it sweet to be back at Fisk again? Love to the lovely Grace. I am down here at Eatonville to finish my book[3] quickly. There is a race-relations meeting at Rollins College at Winter Park (3 miles away) on Monday. The president of some Atlanta college is the main speaker. I did not get the name last night when the[y] invited me to attend. Hope that you come down to Rollis some time.

> Faithfully,
> Zora
> (Neale Hurston) [written in a different hand]

Eatonville, Florida
(Maitland, P.O.)

TO CARL VAN VECHTEN

[spring 1938]
Box 173, Maitland, Florida

Hooray, Carl!!

The book is finished and in the hands of the typist![1] Soon I will have a publisher's check and be on my way to New York and to work with Mrs. Elizabeth Hull. Three more hoorays!!!

> Sincerely,
> Zora

---

[2]Opportunity *chose not to publish Hurston's response to Locke's criticism, titled "The Chick with One Hen." Here Hurston wrote that Locke "knows nothing about Negroes" and that his review was "rank dishonesty . . . a conscious fraud." "The one who lives by quotations trying to criticize people who live by life," she angrily retorted.*
[3]Tell My Horse.

---

[1]Tell My Horse.

TO CARITA DOGGETT CORSE

[carbon copy]
[on FLORIDA WORKS PROGRESS ADMINISTRATION
stationery (Jacksonville)]

Maitland, Florida
June 16, 1938

Dr. Carita Doggett Corse, Director
Florida Writers' Project
Jacksonville, Florida

Dear Dr. Corse:

I find many folk songs of the type that you discussed with me in the office, but the difficulty in collecting them is that it is hard to set them down correctly at one sitting, and the informant usually grows self conscious if asked to sing them over and over again so that they may be set down so that one does not secure the same thing as when they are sung naturally. The answer is a recording machine. If you could secure one of these for my use I could knock about the state a bit and secure some very good samples for the project.[1] Florida is very fortunate in having so many types of songs and music. It is perhaps the richest state in the Union that way if we except New York City. In the same connection, would it be possible for you to get enough expense money for me to visit the phosphate country around Bartow and Lakeland, and a short trip to the Everglades? It would be to the great advantage of the project if this could be done. You know that I have had a great deal of experience collecting under Dr. Boas, and also I made it possible for Mr. Lomax to get the records that he did in Florida and Georgia in 1935.

Most sincerely,
(Signed) Zora Neale Hurston

---

[1]On June 22, Corse forwarded Hurston's letter to Henry Alsberg, director of the Federal Writers' Project, and asked if he could loan the Florida project the recording machine he had in his office.

TO JANE BELO

Box 173, Maitland, Florida
December 3, 1938.

Darling Jane,

Why did I not show up to meet Dr. Masrow?[1] Well, I had not the funds available to keep me in New York another minute. So I just had to head south. I was on a spot. You see, if I had said that to you, you might have thought that I was trying to work you for something. I wanted to meet the Dr. the worst way, and I wanted to talk with you again. I thought it all over and decided not to risk it. Your inner confidence is worth a lot to me, so I paid for it with a bit of heart-meat.

But this letter is not to talk about me. My feelings are not so valuable after all. This is about little Jane Belo—a tiny ivory casket housing infinite beauty and worth. This valuable container of priceless things has been in the hands of careless handlers, who not only had not the intelligence to look inside, they lacked the appreciation for the marvelous handiwork of the casket itself. Now this precious thing must be retrieved from the hands of the blind and the dumb and placed where its worth can be appreciated. I put this priceless thing with all it holds into the hands of Jane Belo. She must care for it and protect it from the bruising contact of the puling insensitive. If you, Jane Belo, fail in this your stewardship, then you have failed, not yourself alone, you have failed humanity. Your care of the precious thing I entrust to you may seem to others to be egocentric and the like. But there must be singleness of purpose in any great endeavor and so you must risk the accusation of self-interest in the interest of what is inside the cosmic box. For once let out a glimmer of the inner light,, and you shall be that other Jane Belo which was from the beginning, but which has been mutilated in attempts to follow the pattern of the common herd. Your first great work will be THE TRANCE.[2] But that is only a beginning. Like Hercules, scramble on

[1]*Probably humanistic psychologist Abraham H. Maslow (1908–70). Maslow taught at Columbia University and Brooklyn College.*
[2]*Columbia University Press published this work in 1960 as* The Trance in Bali. *Its preface was written by Margaret Mead.*

up your narrow and rugged path with the light of the blue hills of fame and glory for your light. You have genius within your jewel box. Use it. You are fortunate enough to have financial means. Cease to apologize for it and begin to use it as a weapon to clear your path to your destiny. It was meant to be.

Bon Voyage! Go, my little Jane with the light of the future in your eyes. You cannot fail. You have not been successful in your other experiments because the butterfly was attempting to return to the caterpillar stage. Spread your wings and soar!! You have no place in your life for the puling weaklings who would sap your vital fluid. Be true to your destiny and Jane Belo.

My love, my love, my love, my love, my love, my love!

Faithfully,
Zora

TO CARITA DOGGETT CORSE

Maitland, Florida
December 3, 1938

Dear Dr. Corse,

I have just returned from the Book Fair in Boston and had to stop in New York, too.

I am sitting down this time to write you a much-felt letter, Boss. I am risking it because you are an author yourself and I feel that you can understand my form of insanity perhaps. Dr., every now and then I get a sort of phobia for paper and all its works. I cannot bring myself to touch it. I cannot [read—x-ed out] write, read or do anything at all for a period. I accumulate letters unread, even. I have just been through one of those periods that lasted about nine days. It is stronger than I am, boss. But when I do come out of it I am as if I had just been born again. So at last I am back at work. What I had to do when I bogged down was so little that I might have finished it in 48 hours with ease, but I just couldn't. My dumb and silent period had me. When I was a child I used to go hide under the house away from the rest of the family and mood away. The only thing that could drive me bact to human associaition was darkness. I was and still am afraid of the dark. So now you know. You have been too decent for me to lie to you andpretend that I was ill or something. Just something grabs hold of me and holds me mute, miserable and helpless until it lets me go. I feel as if I have been marooned on a planet by myself. But I find that it is the prelude to creative effort.

It would have been lovely if you had been in Boston with me.[1] Everything was so restrained and polished that you would have been right in your element. Somehow they (the town) showed [me—x-ed out] a great enthusiasm for me, which I cannot make out. Back Bay and Beacon Street turned out for me. You might have been a little proud of your pet darkey. Yes, I know that I belong to you and that Sterling Brown belongs to Allsberg [sic].[2] I laugh at the little phenagling he does to give Sterling the edge over me. BUT, he cannot make him no new head with inside trimmings and thats where he falls down. You ought to see Sterling exhibiting hisjealousy as I top him time after time.

I shall positively be in your office no later than Tuesday morning, with the book ready for the typist.[3] My broadcast was set back at my request until Dec. 9. I hope that it can be postponed until spring. Gee! I hate that cold weather!

Most sincerely,
Zora
Zora Neale Hurston

[1]For the book fair.
[2]Henry G. Alsberg, director of the Federal Writers' Project.
[3]Probably the manuscript of The Florida Negro.

TO FANNIE HURST

[postcard postmarked February 10, 1939]

Manse Hotel
1004 Chapel St.
Cincinnati, Ohio

I am here in the setting of "Back Street."[1] Feel your spirit all over the place. Here on a business trip.[2] Wish I were in New York.

Love,
Zora.

TO CARL VAN VECHTEN

The Manse Hotel
1004 Chapel Street
Cincinnati, Ohio
February 19, 1939

Dear, dear Carl,

Thanks so much for the lovely pictures of Ethel Waters that you sent me. Thanks, and thanks and thanks!! You are always doing something fine for people.

Carl, I want to do something public to show how much I admire Ethel and her work. What you and other artists did was very wonderful and I wish my name could have been on there too.[1] But if I do that

---

[1] *Hurst's novel.*

[2] *Doing radio broadcasts for WCW studios.*

---

[1] *In response to a negative review of Ethel Waters's performance in* Mamba's Daughters *which he felt was unjustified, Van Vechten wrote an open letter to the* New York Times *in September 1938. He solicited signatures for the letter and contributions to pay for the advertisement space. It read in part, "The undersigned feel that Ethel Waters's superb performance in* Mamba's Daughters *at the Empire Theatre is a profound emotional experience which any playgoer would be the poorer for missing." He also wrote a glowing review for the February 1939 edition of* Opportunity.

now, it would look too copy-cat, or would it? I am out here to do a series of broadcasts on a local station and cannot come to New York for a
while yet, (unless I bolt the program as I feel like doing) and I want to
do it now. That is I want to make some public expression now. I want
to take some space and do as you did, or something like that. It might
be all right if I said something as a Negro. Tell me if you think I
ought not to do that now on account of following you all too closely.

Thanks also for the clipping from P. Taylor.[2] It was very kind. My
back aches this morning, so I say goodbye for the moment.

Faithfully yours,

Zora

TO CLAUDE BARNETT

Manse Hotel, 1004 Chapel Street
Cincinnati, Ohio
February 25, 1939

[at upper left and top:]
Dear Claude, This is the letter I wrote you, but sent it
down in Florida to a white friend of mine down there Z.

Dear Claude Barnett,

I am here in Cincinnati for a series of commercial broadcasts,
signed up for 13 weeks. I have never been here before and I do not
know anyone here as yet and do not know whether I even like the
town. But I am close to Chicago, and wish that I could see you and
Etta. This is wretched driving weather or I would shove the wheels of
my Chevvie on to Chicago. But never mind, this snow and ice cannot
keep up forever and then--------

How is Your Royal Highness? And how is the scrumptious Etta
Moton [sic] Barnett?[1] You must let me know.

---

[2]*Prentiss Taylor (1907–91), lithographer and photographer. Along with Langston Hughes, Taylor founded a
short-lived publishing house called Golden Stair Press. Some of his photographs are reprinted here.*

---

[1]*Etta Moten Barnett, Claude's wife; see glossary.*

It is curious that I am so much better known among the whites than among my own people. Nobody in brownskin seems to have heard of me in this hotel. (I have not been out to meet anyone else) But down at WLW [studious—x-ed out] studios several knew of me. There seems to be some law that I must be interviewed on the air everywhere I stop. I was on the American School of the Air CBS on the "FAMOUS AUTHORS SERIES" from New York Dec. 9. On next Wednesday they interview me on the "MEET THE AUTHOR" hour here over WLW NBC network at 10:30 A.M. I have been interviewed at Orlando Florida, and Chicago also. So I dont get a thrill anymore.

My latest book which was published last Oct. as TELL MY HORSE by Lippincott has been bought by a swank English firm and is being published over there under the title of VOODOO GODS. I am getting very keen about the English. My publisher (J.M. Dent, London) came over to talk with me and we got along swell. His wife had such faultless social manners. My last book, THEIR EYES WERE WATCHING GOD was published by them and it went very well indeed in England, so I am asked over there for a speaking tour in the Spring. If my present enthusiasm for the English keeps up, I will stay a long time if and when I go. I like them!! From England THEIR EYES [ATTRACTED ATT—x-ed out] WERE WATCHING GOD attracted attention on the continent and was translated by Ada Prospero and published in Rome last summer. I get such lovely letters from all over England and the Dominions and several from continental Europe. I think it would be fun if Etta and I made a tour of Europe. Let her sing and me speak. Dont you think it might be interesteing?

Anyhow, wont you write me in this lonesome town? This is the first time that I have even been anywhere and didnt know a soul.

Sincerely yours,
Zora Neale Hurston

TO EDWIN OSGOOD GROVER

Box 407
Durhan [sic], North Carolina
October, 12, 1939

Dear Dr. Grover,

I am here at the N. C. College, heading the Drama department, and I believe I shall have a successful year. I have the good fortune to be inculded in the play writing class of Paul Green at the University of North Carolina at Chapel Hill and I am proud of that. I think that is one of the most pleasant things that has ever happened to me, and I think I'll benefit by it. My last book on MOSES will be off the press November 2.[1] It is dedicated to you and I hope that you will not be disappointed at the work. I have the feeling of disappointment about it. I don't think that I achieved all that I set out to do. I thought that in this book I would achieve my ideal, but it seems that I have not reached it yet but I shall keep trying as I know you want me to.

Perhaps you would be interested to know that TELL MY HORSE which came out in England as VOODOO GODS, [It—x-ed out] was a <u>book</u> <u>of</u> <u>the</u> <u>month</u> [and there was a—x-ed out] and it sold the $500.00 advance[ment—x-ed out] on it in the first week. Since then, I have received a second check for $263.00. You remember it came out in London on May 4. They are asking for the manuscript of MOSES before it is published in America. My American publishers are very enthusiastic about the manuscript. I wish I shared their enthusiasm.

Carl Van Vechten says it is the best thing that I have done. Perhaps he is right but it still doesn't say all that I want it to say.

Morgan College, Baltimore, Maryland, conferred the degree of [Dr.—x-ed out] Litt. D., last June. I thought you would be interested to know. I think most of my friends in Winter Park will be happy for me.

I am going to make a speech before an exclusive womens' club in Milwaukee on October 24, then I am going on to Boston to speak at the Book Fair on October 26.

[1]Moses, Man of the Mountain.

I think my work here will be interesting. I am very happy to have a chance to work with the crowd at Chapel Hill. I think it is the door to a new phase of my career.

My best to the whole Grover family and to all who may ask of me.

Most sincerely,

Zora

P.S. I have a very dumb stenographer to whom I dictated this letter, hence the confusion..

TO CARL VAN VECHTEN

[in hand at top of letter:] Do you think that Ethel Waters would accept an invitation to speak here? I would be delighted to arrange it if she would consider it. It would be a grand experience for the college.

Box 407
Durham, North Carolina
October 12, 1939

Darling Carlo,

Your letter reached me after a long delay. Somehow or other, it was delayed in the College Post Office. You can never know how happy it made me. In the first place it is always a Christmas present to get a letter from you, it's just like Christmas and Easter coming at the same time. That is how I feel about you, and in the next place you made me feel very much happier about the book because I feel that I fell far short of my ideal in the writing.[1]

I am going to speak in Milwaukee and Boston on the 24 and 26, respectively. I hope that you will let me see you as I go through New York on my way to Boston or on my return from Boston. I must see you and run my big mouth awhile. You know that is the best thing us darkies got—that is our mouths.

[1] Moses, Man of the Mountain.

Carl darling, I know you don't like to make speeches, but I to wish
you would visit the school here and let them see you. You're a great
figure in Literature as well as a great man, and the rest of the Negroes
neet to know more about you. I feel that I would be doing the college a
great favor if I could get you to come down.

My best to everyone who may ask of me. Ten thousand lilies and
orang blossoms for you and your swell blurb on my book. You are always the magnificient Carl.

Most affectionately,

Zora

TO JAMES E. SHEPHERD

[December 14, 1939—library dated]
Box 606
North Carolina College
Durham, North Carolina

Dr. James E. Shepard [sic], President
North Carolina College
Durham, North Carolina

My dear Dr. Shepard:

I am writing to you about my work here at the institution. I am
very concerned about it for several reasons. The first is, because I set
out to make a success of anything that I do. The second is, because the
frama [sic] department of the University of North Carolina is very eager that this project here should succeed.

On the several occasions in which I have discussed with you my
small opportunities to do anything very strenuous in the matter that
would lead to any important consequence, there has been no conclusion
reached for expansion. On one occasion, you did say to me that the
school had not organized my work as yet—that it had not been planned
out. I have talked to Dean Elder about my difficulties and also to Dean
Rush. Dean Elder assured me that he would try to plan something

more comprehensive for the approaching quarter, but it is already upon us and I have received no notification of any plan whatsoever.

Since no one as yet seems to have made any plans for the work, I assume that it is not indifferent to the program, but that no member of the administration knows what to do about it.

You remember the registrar's office scheduled one course for me, English 261, from 2:30 to 3:30 which, as you know, was at an hour when none of the students interested in drama, could attend and the listing of the course was not understood so that no one registered for it—that this was not a lack of interest on the students was proven—that since they understood that was for the drama course, more that a hundred people registered for it. It can be seen from this that there is no lack of interest on the part of the students, and I assure you that there is none on my part, if a proper frame is provided for me to work.

May I, at long last, offer some suggestions for the work? I suggest a course in playwriting, a course in play direction, a course in play production which would include, lighting, scenic designing, construction, costume designing, etc. These courses are not only basic and necessary, they are irreducible minimum if anything at all is to be accomplished, and I assume that you do want something accomplished or you would not have invited me to join the faculty in the first place.

I find with the little time that we have had to prepare a presentation that it will not be what I wish to have represented as my work, so I beg you leave, not to present a play on the 18th of this month here on the campus. Dr. Koch[1] and Mr. Paul Green suggested that I carry it over until sometime in January and make my first presentation at the Play-Makers Theater at the University of North Carolina at Chapel Hill.

May I have a letter from you stating your position in all the matters that I have brought up to you in this communication?

With all good wishes, I am

> Very truly yours,
> Zora Neale Hurston
> [unsigned carbon]

ZNH:RJH

---

[1]*Frederick Koch (1877–1944) was the director of the Carolina Playmakers, at the University of North Carolina, where he also taught dramatic literature.*

"IT IS TOO HARD TO REVEAL ONE'S INNER SELF"

The Forties

Overleaf: Hurston in a hat.

Hurston's 1940s were bracketed by terrible disappointment and heartbreaking betrayal. Her letters from this period total less than half of those from the thirties. Yet they are some of the most important letters she ever wrote. They detail many successes, and her joy in friendships and work, but also unfulfilled desires. Relationships went sour. There were professional disappointments, including struggles with her publishers and major shifts in her writing. While in the twenties, Hurston wrote mostly short fiction, and in the thirties, she devoted herself to novels, folklore, and plays, in the forties, she wrote little drama and no folklore at all, concentrating instead on novels, journalism, and political essays. "Her mission to celebrate black folkways lost its public intensity."[1] Her letters from this period help us understand why. They also tell us that the problem of "public ears" returned with a vengeance in this decade. More than anything else, this determined what Hurston wrote and did not write.

Approaching her fiftieth birthday (while passing for her late thirties), Hurston had lost none of her ambition. Her autobiography and her final published novel were written in this decade, as were many short stories and a range of other publications, from Caribbean music to essays on normal schools and cattle ranching. From her letters, we learn of the many projects she planned but never completed: an essay on Florida's Indian River; material on language for *Reader's Digest*; a book-length study of folklore figures; a book on Carl Van Vechten's

---

[1]Robert E. Hemenway, Zora Neale Hurston: A Literary Biography *(Urbana: University of Illinois Press, 1977), p. 288.*

contributions to African American culture; new plays; pieces on the 1943 Detroit riot and youth gangs; and a cookbook. Also significant was her growing interest in film. Hurston introduced film into her field-work, oversaw an aggressive effort by her publisher and agent to interest Hollywood studios in adapting her work, and even spent a brief period in Hollywood, working for Paramount Pictures.

Hurston's politics have often baffled her admirers, and this decade inaugurates the paradoxical blend of militancy and conservatism that characterizes the rest of her life. During the war, Hurston became involved in a number of political projects, from congressional campaigns to a proposed Florida cemetery for "illustrious Negro dead,"[2] to struggles over segregation in the military. She wrote optimistically of racial progress and lambasted all who disagreed with her increasingly idiosyncratic views.

During the forties, Hurston had two—possibly more—love affairs and a short-lived, secret, third marriage. She described herself as "in love" with friend and fellow anthropologist Jane Belo and began important new friendships with blues singer Ethel Waters, fellow Florida writer Marjorie Kinnan Rawlings (famous for *The Yearling*), schooner captain Fred Irvine, and New York writer and journalist Helen Worden Erskine. She attempted to arrange speaking tours for Fannie Hurst in North Carolina and Ethel Waters at Rollins College. She contacted powerful people she believed could help her, including Winston Churchill and Edna St. Vincent Millay.

For Hurston, however, the difficulty of making meaningful personal, artistic, or political connections was sharpening in the forties. One of Hurston's most telling letters from this period concludes that "it is too hard to reveal one's inner self."[3] Language was proving inadequate and understanding rare. And this may have been devastating for an artist committed to communication and an anthropologist enthralled with community. In the twenties and thirties, she had been more concerned with resisting *pressure* to reveal her inner self, a pressure that came from whites eager to make her an exotic sensation as well as from blacks anxious to make her defend her iconoclastic views. But in the forties, Hurston seemed to fear misunderstanding more than anything else. In fact, she increasingly seemed to take misunderstanding and failure as a given.

[2]*Hurston to W. E. B. Du Bois, June 11, 1945.*
[3]*Hurston to Hamilton Holt, February 11, 1943.*

One source of misunderstanding was evidently her second divorce. Neither Hurston's letters nor her autobiography make any mention of Albert Price, III, her twenty-three-year-old second husband (Hurston was forty-eight). The two presumably met while both were with the WPA in Jacksonville, Hurston as a writer and Price as a recreation worker. They married on June 27, 1939, in Fernandina, Florida, and lived together there, very briefly, in the home of Price's mother. Even Hurston's family was unaware that this marriage had taken place.[4] Perhaps Hurston felt vulnerable to criticism about their age difference. Perhaps she was uncomfortable with Price's well-heeled background. Perhaps she recognized that the union would be short-lived. Court records claim that Hurston and Price had a "mutual understanding" to keep the marriage secret. And when Hurston went to North Carolina in the fall of 1939, Price remained at home. Hurston's divorce suit, filed in February 1940, claimed that she "had hoped for support and protection from the defendant as her husband but he . . . refuses to work." Hurston represented herself as "meek and humble . . . easy to be imposed upon," a woman who neither "use[s] obscene language" nor visits places of "ill repute." She accused Price of "habitual drunkenness" (a charge she later withdrew), "sprees," and having "threatened to beat the hell out of her if she should carry out her desire to divorce him." Price's countersuit was filed in April. It claimed that Hurston had made false promises of financial support and had shown "disregard [for] the youth of the defendant." Price contended that she had "a mean, uncontrollable temper" and put him "in fear of his life" from her " 'BLACK MAGIC' " and " 'VOODOOISM'." Hurston withdrew some of her complaints, and the couple apparently reconciled briefly. When Hurston went to South Carolina in the spring of 1940, Price accompanied her. But the reunion did not last. They shared a house for no more than a few days at a time and did not stay together during that summer or in the months that followed. Divorce papers were finalized in 1943, at which time the court found in Hurston's favor.[5]

Certainly their twenty-five-year age difference "divided Albert and

[4]See Pamela Bordelon, "New Tracks on Dust Tracks: Toward a Reassessment of the Life of Zora Neale Hurston," African-American Review, 31, no. 1 (1997), p. 17.

[5]Zora Neale Hurston v. Albert Price, Divorce Bill, February 9, 1940, Duval County, Florida; Zora Neale Hurston v. Albert Price, Answer and Counter Claim, Circuit Court of Duval County, Florida, April 1, 1940; Zora Neale Hurston Price v. Albert Price, Special Master's Report, Duval County, Florida, November 9, 1943.

Zora."[6] Class differences also loomed large. Price was a member of one of Jacksonville's best black families, the grandson of one of the co-founders of the Afro-American Life Insurance Company and a founder of American Beach, one of the nation's first African American resort towns.[7]

A letter from Hurston to Jane Belo suggests a third, if much more speculative, possibility for the failure of this marriage. This letter, written between Hurston filing for divorce and Price's legal response, discloses Hurston's interest in another man. "To tell you the truth," she wrote Belo, "I am a little 'tetched' with love myself, though it has not gone beyond the palpitating stage. No committments [sic] as yet. He has a magnificent bass voice. I am trying to find out if that is what I am stuck on or if it is the man himself. I do like strong, big wrassly men and he seems to fit the bill in many ways. I wish he had some money, but then I have never been wealthy, so————."[8] The letter makes no mention of Price. The man with the magnificent voice is not mentioned again.

It is possible that this is the man Hurston secretly married in the 1940s, a marriage that Hurston's biography surmised "never took place."[9] One reason that Hurston's marriage to James Howell Pitts has been so hard to learn about is that an account of the engagement, reported in the *New York Amsterdam News*, February 5, 1944, is misleading, suggesting that the marriage was to take place in Cleveland when it had already taken place one month prior in Florida. Pitts had been living in Cleveland—at East 79th Street—at the time of his 1943 divorce. Hurston and Pitts married on January 18, 1944, in Volusia County, Florida, near Daytona Beach, where Hurston was living on the houseboat *Wanago*. Presumably, Pitts accompanied Hurston back to the *Wanago*, and they lived there together for some time prior to their divorce ten months later, on October 31, 1944, also in Volusia County. On their application for a marriage license, Pitts gave his address as 1606 Albany Street in Brunswick, Georgia, his age as forty-five, his race as "colored," and his occupation as "merchant." He listed his birthplace as Aiken, South Carolina. Hurston listed her address simply as Daytona

[6]*Hemenway*, Hurston, p. 273.
[7]*See Russ Rymer*, American Beach: How "Progress" Robbed a Black Town—and Nation—of History, Wealth, and Power *(New York: HarperPerennial, 2000).*
[8]*Hurston to Jane Belo, March 20, 1940.*
[9]*Hemenway*, Hurston, p. 318 n. 35.

Beach. She listed her age as forty, although in 1944 she would have been fifty-three, thirteen years older than she claimed and eight years older than her husband. She gave Eatonville as her birthplace and "writer" as her occupation.

Eight letters written by Hurston during this period survive, but she does not mention her marriage—or Pitts—in any of them. In fact, she creates the deliberate impression that she is living alone on the *Wanago*. Perhaps she was alone most of the time. In writing to her friend Harold Jackman in March, she describes herself as having "an interesting amphibious existence" on her houseboat, and reports being "lonesome," although she has just had friend Katharane Mershon as her guest for a month (the month that would have been the second month of her marriage). Again, there is no mention of Pitts.[10] In a letter to Henry Allen Moe, written in September, she described her houseboat as providing her "the solitude that I love."[11] Other letters discuss Chinese politics, race politics, literary criticism, and various plans for work and travel, including to Honduras—again with no mention of her husband. In the fall, she wrote a series of letters to her good friend Jane Belo, pleading with her to "join me on an expedition."[12] "I want to stay in the field for two years," she told Benjamin Botkin, again with no mention that to do so would mean leaving somebody behind.[13]

Hurston's closest confidante at the time was evidently Jane Belo, with whom Hurston had shared an intimate correspondence about Belo's own marriage to Frank Tannenbaum. Some readers, upon discovering Hurston's letters to Belo, may wonder if it was Hurston's feelings for Belo that jeopardized her marriage to Pitts. The Belo letters are unlike any of the more than six hundred in this book—"Darling Jane," one letter concludes: "My love, my love, my love, my love, my love, my love!"[14] "Darling, darling, darling, darling, darling, darling. Dear, dear, dear, dear, dear, dear, dear, dear. Love, love, love, love, love, love, love. . . . Most devotedly your own," another ends.[15] Belo's marriage to fellow anthropologist Frank Tannenbaum marks the end of

[10] *Hurston to Harold Jackman, March 29, 1944.*
[11] *Hurston to Henry Allen Moe, September 8, 1944.*
[12] *Hurston to Jane Belo, October 1, 1944.*
[13] *Hurston to Benjamin Botkin, October 6, 1944.*
[14] *Hurston to Jane Belo, December 3, 1938.*
[15] *Hurston to Jane Belo, May 2, 1940.*

such language, although Hurston and Belo remained friends and correspondents for years. In her autobiography, Hurston states matter-of-factly that she "fell in love with Jane Belo."[16] What should we conclude? Both Harlem and Columbia University were known for sexual experimentation at the time, but Hurston's exuberant language may be merely the language of passionate female friendship found for centuries in women's letters to one another. Hurston was often exuberant. There is no reason to doubt that Hurston was "in love" with Belo, as she said. At the same time, we do not know exactly what she meant by that.

Hurston quit her teaching job at North Carolina College in March 1940. She and Belo had plans to collect material on unusual religious practices in South Carolina that they hoped would match those in Bali and Haiti. Hurston was eager to explore the possibilities of film and anxious to master the medium. "I found that the pictures didnt com[e] out and I was in the depths of despair," she wrote Belo in early May of work they had done filming religious trances and "sanctified" churches. "<u>Please</u> send the men with the equipment and let me go on finding out things."[17]

But all was not completely well with their collaboration. Hurston's letters to her playwright friend Paul Green express considerable anxiety about the very cameramen she begged Jane Belo to send. Hurston feared that, once again, important African American cultural materials would be appropriated by exploitive whites. "I am in a panic," she wrote Green one day later. "She [Belo] has secured a movie outfit . . . with two very enthusiastic Jews who want to take the spirituals for <u>commercial</u> <u>purposes.</u>! Now, dont sit there, Paul Green, just thinking. DO SOMETHING! We cant let all that swell music get away from us like that."[18] She suggested that she and Green make their own recordings before Belo's cameramen arrived.

Belo's crew arrived early. Instead of "two Jews," there were three: Louis Brandt, Bob Lawrence, and Norman Chalfin. They, along with Hurston, wrote a collective, enthusiastic letter to Belo on May 20 to let her know that "we've been shooting, shooting and shooting—We been begging and wheedling . . . But we've got records.—that much we

[16]Zora Neale Hurston, Dust Tracks on a Road, *from "The Inside Light—Being a Salute to Friendship," un-published in the original 1942 edition (New York: HarperCollins, 1996), p. 228.*
[17]*Hurston to Jane Belo, May 2, 1940.*
[18]*Hurston to Paul Green, May 3, 1940.*

know."[19] Chalfin, the project's sound engineer, insists that the "commercial" uses of this material were minimal: a musicologist used some of it as background for the Broadway plays *Battle of Angels* and *Holy Roller*, and some of the tapes were aired on the radio. Hurston, he remembered, may have been upset about that.[20]

In the spring of 1941, Hurston finished her work with Belo and accepted friend Katharane Mershon's invitation to visit California. Almost nothing is known about Hurston's time in Hollywood. But recent research into film studio archives, combined with statements in Hurston's letters, tells us a great deal about the context in which Hurston tried to break into film and how difficult it would have been for an African American woman to get very far.

Hurston's interest in Hollywood had been building from the midthirties on, when she had been regularly submitting her work to the studios. Some of her closest friends, such as writers Marjorie Kinnan Rawlings and Fannie Hurst, saw their writing adapted for very popular movies, and Hurston may have hoped to follow their example.[21] As Elizabeth Binggeli shows, Hollywood had a voracious appetite for cinematic material of all kinds.[22] So, in spite of manifest racial prejudice in Hollywood, Hurston's efforts to break into film may not have been entirely quixotic. None of Hurston's work for film was produced in her lifetime. But it *was* taken seriously by the studios. *Their Eyes Were Watching God* was reviewed by Warner Bros. two months before its publication. Multiple studios reviewed *Dust Tracks on a Road* immediately upon publication. *Seraph on the Suwanee* was reviewed in galleys by both MGM and Warner Bros., and the latter considered producing a film. They saw *Seraph* as a story with "tried and true" elements that wouldn't be "too expensive to film" and that might serve as a good vehicle for Jane Wyman.[23] Kenneth Mackenna of MGM told Whitney Darrow that they found the novel fresh and "delightful."[24]

[19]Chalfin, Brandt, Lawrence, and Hurston to Jane Belo, May 20, 1940.

[20]Personal interview with Dr. Norman Chalfin, August 15, 1999.

[21]The film version of Rawlings's novel The Yearling, starring Gregory Peck and Jane Wyman, was released in 1945 and made Rawlings a celebrity. Well over two dozen movies were made from novels, stories, and scenarios written by Fannie Hurst, including Humoresque, Mannequin, The Younger Generation, Back Pay, Back Street, Imitation of Life, and Young at Heart.

[22]Elizabeth Binggeli, " 'Obviously Not for the Screen': Studio Reading and the Revenge of Unfilmable Narrative," (Ph.D. diss.). My reconstruction of Hurston's experience with Hollywood draws primarily from Binggeli's research.

[23]Ibid.

[24]Kenneth Mackenna to Whitney Darrow, December 9, 1948, Scribner's Archive, Princeton University.

Hurston's Paramount employment preceded Warner Bros.' interest by a few years. She was hired in October 1941 as a Paramount "story consultant," a position roughly equivalent to assistant editor or "first reader" for a publisher. "When producer Arthur Hornblow took me to lunch at Lucey's and hired me at Paramount, it was nice—very nice. I was most elated. But I had had five books accepted then, been a Guggenheim fellow twice, spoken at three book fairs with all the literary greats of America and some from abroad, and so I was a little more used to things."[25] She left in January 1942.

The bulk of Hurston's time in California was spent not in Hollywood studios but hard at work on her autobiography, a project she had accepted only reluctantly. "I did not want to do it now," she wrote to Grover, "but my publishers wanted it very much."[26] "I did not want to write it at all . . . it is too hard to reveal one's inner self."[27] *Dust Tracks* bears out that claim by being one of the most un-self-revealing autobiographies ever written. "Apparently written self-consciously with a white audience in mind . . . it is an autobiography at war with itself."[28] *Dust Tracks* has damaged Hurston's reputation. Alice Walker views it as "the most unfortunate thing Zora ever wrote." "It rings false," she writes.[29] The book particularly disappointed Hurston's black contemporaries. Arna Bontemps wrote that "Miss Hurston deals very simply with the more serious aspects of Negro life in America—she ignores them."[30]

Pearl Harbor was bombed as Hurston was revising her manuscript, and the United States' entry into the war created a climate in which publishers were unwilling to risk an African American woman's criticism of U.S. foreign policy. Lippincott made drastic demands for revision. "Suggest eliminating international opinions as irrelevant to autobiography," her editor wrote across the manuscript.[31] Hurston took out the offending materials, but she made a public record of the changes. Across the type-

[25]*Hurston*, Dust Tracks, *p. 155.*

[26]*Hurston to Edwin Osgood Grover, December 30, 1941.*

[27]*Hurston to Hamilton Holt, February 11, 1943.*

[28]*Hemenway*, Hurston, *pp. 277–78.*

[29]*Alice Walker, "Zora Neale Hurston—a Cautionary Tale and a Partisan View," foreword to* Zora Neale Hurston: A Literary Biography, *by Robert E. Hemenway (Urbana: University of Illinois Press, 1980), p. xvii.*

[30]*Arna Bontemps, "From Eatonville, Florida, to Harlem,"* New York Herald Tribune, *November 22, 1942, p. 3, quoted in Kathleen Hassall, "Text and Personality in Disguise and in the Open: Zora Neale Hurston's Dust Tracks on a Road," in* Zora in Florida, *ed. Steve Glassman and Kathryn Lee Feidel (Orlando: University of Central Florida Press, 1991), p. 159.*

[31]*Typescript manuscript of* Dust Tracks on a Road, *James Weldon Johnson Collection, Beinecke Library, Yale University.*

script of the unrevised version of *Dust Tracks*, donated to Carl Van Vechten's growing James Weldon Johnson Memorial Collection of Negro Arts and Letters at Yale University, she wrote: "Parts of this manuscript were not used in the final composition of the book for publisher's reasons."[32] "Rather than get across all the things which you want to say," Hurston told an interviewer in the 1940s, "you must compromise and work within the limitations [of those people] who have the final authority in deciding whether or not a book shall be printed."[33]

The excised chapters are some of the most radical political statements Hurston ever made. She attacked missionary work and organized religion for "screaming for blood in Jesus' name." She assailed the practice of imperialism by France, Germany, England, and the United States. "We, too, have our marines in China," she reminded readers, painting a vivid portrait of the injustices of American arrogance and world domination. America, she argued, was an international hypocrite. "We, too, consider machine gun bullets good laxatives for heathens who get constipated with toxic ideas about a country of their own. If the patient dies from the treatment, it was not because the medicine was not good."[34]

Addressed primarily to white audiences, *Dust Tracks* was fairly successful exactly as it appeared.[35] It sold well (five thousand copies at first publication) and brought Hurston to the attention of a wider public than her other published books had done. In some white circles, she was promoted to the dubious status of instant spokeswoman for the race. Oblivious to the caginess that bothered black readers, the *New York Times* reviewer called *Dust Tracks* "a thumping story," "forthright and without frills." "There is no 'hush-mouth modesty' about the book," the reviewer wrongly declared.[36] The *Saturday Review of Literature* praised the autobiography for being "full of humor, color, and good sense" rather than the "race consciousness that spoils so much

---

[32] *Ibid.*

[33] *"Zora Neale Hurston Reveals Key to Her Literary Success,"* New York Amsterdam News, *November 18, 1944, quoted in Hemenway,* Hurston, *pp. 286–87.*

[34] *Zora Neale Hurston, "Seeing the World as It Is," typescript, James Weldon Johnson Collection, Beinecke Library, Yale University. Some of Hurston's excised chapters have been published in the HarperCollins reprint of* Dust Tracks. *All of the excised chapters are in Cheryl Wall's edition of* Dust Tracks *for the Library of America.*

[35] *Radical white writer Harold Preece, however, wrote that Hurston had completely sold out to white racist expectations. "[It is] the tragedy of a gifted, sensitive mind, eaten up by an egocentrism fed on the patronizing admiration of the dominant white world." Clipping, "Dust Tracks on a Road," Tomorrow, February 1943, Schomburg Center for Research in Black Culture.*

[36] *Beatrice Sherman, review of* Dust Tracks on a Road, New York Times Book Review, *November 29, 1942.*

Negro literature" and praised its author for not taking "an arrogant, self-made Negro attitude, or the conventional bitter and downtrodden one." *Dust Tracks on a Road,* this reviewer declared, "is told in exactly the right manner, simply and with candor, with a seasoning—not over-done—of the marvelous locutions of the imaginative field nigger."[37] *Dust Tracks on a Road* was awarded *Saturday Review*'s Anisfield-Wolf Award in Racial Relations for "the best book of the year concerned with racial problems in the field of creative literature." One wonders, reading such reviews, about the politics of this "race-relations" prize.

The excision of Hurston's political writing from her autobiography has helped support a misunderstanding of her as apolitical, a misper-ception that she sometimes helped create. Hurston was involved in one political controversy after another in the forties. The war had been a particular catalyst for her. She was outraged over U.S. foreign policy and disappointed that the African American community failed to protest atrocities committed against other people of color:

> Thruman [sic] is a monster. I can think of him as nothing else but the BUTCHER OF ASIA. Of his grin of triumph on giving the or-der to drop the Atom bombs on Japan. Of his maintaining troops in China who are shooting the starving Chinese for stealing a handful of food. . . . Is it that we are so devoted to a "good Massa" that we feel that we ought not to even protest such crimes?[38]

Domestically, she was incensed over segregation in the military. She experienced some of the War Department's policies firsthand when she went to the North Carolina College for Negroes to teach drama. "Well, the Negroes have been bitched again!" she wrote Alain Locke of the training school she found there.

> I mean this Signal Corps sxhool [sic] which the Govt. has set up here. . . . You must remember that these men in the Signal Corp are college men for the most part, and represent the best Negro families in America. And here they are stuck off in this out of the way hole, and being insulted. . . . I feel that the whole body of Negroes are being insulted and mocked.[39]

[37] *Phil Strong, review of* Dust Tracks on a Road, Saturday Review, *November 28, 1942.*

[38] *Hurston to Claude Barnett, [July 21–26, 1946].*

[39] *Hurston to Walter White, November 24, 1942.*

According to historian Gordon Patterson, Hurston may have been making a mountain out of a molehill. "In less than a month," he writes, "she managed to turn a local dispute which revolved around the quality of cafeteria food and dormitory overcrowding into an indictment that reached the highest levels in the War Department."[40] There were, however, large issues at stake. The Signal Corps had resisted training African American pilots. Florida Normal was an inappropriate school for a Signal Corps, and its choice signaled the "leadership's continued effort to limit the number of blacks admitted to the Corps."[41] Walter White dispatched the NAACP's special counsel, Prentice Thomas, to investigate Hurston's charges; he confirmed them without qualification, and William Gray, college president, was put on notice by the War Department.

Events such as the Detroit race riot of 1943, in which thirty-four people were killed, convinced Hurston that there was a need for greater black militancy in response to entrenched racism. She wrote Alain Locke that "we are being foolish, we Negroes, if we let it rest as we have done other riots." She urged him to help her dispel myths about northern racial equity: "the false premise that northerners love Negroes, and that all the intolerance is in the South," as she put it. "The truth of the matter," she wrote, "is that the Anglo-Saxon is the most intolereant [sic] of human beings in the matter of <u>any</u> other group darker than themselves."[42]

While Hurston railed against segregation in the military, she was quoted by journalist Douglas Gilbert as saying that "the Jim Crow system works."[43] The comment touched off a firestorm in the black press. "Now is not the time for Negro writers like Zora Hurston to come out with publicity wisecracks about the South being better for the Negro than the North. . . . The race is fighting a battle that may determine its status for fifty years. Those who are not for us, are against us," Roy Wilkins, NAACP secretary and coeditor of the *Crisis,* shot back.[44] Hurston was devastated. "Nothing has ever upset me so much as this

<hr>

[40]Gordon Patterson, *"Hurston Goes to War: The Army Signal Corps in Saint Augustine,"* Florida Historical Quarterly, *fall 1995, p. 166. I am grateful to Professor Patterson for sharing his essay and his knowledge of the Signal Corps controversy with me.*

[41]*Ibid., p. 170.*

[42]*Hurston to Alain Locke, July 23, 1943.*

[43]*Douglas Gilbert, "When Negro Succeeds, South Is Proud, Zora Hurston Says," New York World-Telegram, February 1, 1943.*

[44]*Roy Wilkins, "The Watchtower," New York Amsterdam News, February 27, 1943.*

printed thing with Douglas Gilbert," she wrote Claude Barnett. "It is so untrue, so twisted! . . . I deny categorically that I ever said that Negroes were better off in the South. Perhaps that is his own sentiments. Neither did I approve of segregation in the South or anywhere else. . . . I am positively ill over it. I know how impossible it is to get a retraction from a newspaper. I merely feel like dying, since I can get no chance to kill him. At any rate, the iron has entered my soul. I am now a bitter person."[45]

Hurston came away from this episode convinced that "editors and the powers that be will have their way" and sure that she would not be "permitted to depart from a standard pattern" without attack. It was one thing to be unable to share one's "inside feelings" with an abstract public or with narrow-minded whites. It was another thing altogether to find herself misrepresented and thoroughly misunderstood by blacks.[46]

In December 1944, Hurston wrote to Carl Van Vechten that she was losing hope of being understood. The failure of her third marriage must have contributed to her sense of despair over being able to share her "inside feelings" publicly or privately, personally or politically.[47] "I have learned to know that the thing we call misunderstanding—that blind bumping of one vessel against the other as they grope for nearness," she wrote, probably in reference to her failed marriage, "is the greates[t] tragedy of humanity. Of all animate life. This cosmic blindness that prevents even the very near from being clearly seen. That is when it hurts most. One feels the futility of life when even those closest to one cannot be clearly seen."[48] She confided to Barnett: "I am often so disillusioned that it hardly seems worthwhile to even be interested in a general way."[49]

Hurston became involved in one of the most contentious black political battles of the decade, a contest famous for tearing apart the cohesion of Harlem politics. In 1946, Harlem's native son Adam Clayton Powell, Jr., descendant of the founder of Harlem's Abyssinian Baptist

---

[45] Hurston to Claude Barnett, [February 4?, 1943].

[46] Hurston to Douglas Gilbert, February 4, 1943.

[47] As was true in the case of the love affair that became the basis for Their Eyes Were Watching God and to which Hurston devoted a chapter in Dust Tracks (cautiously giving him the misleading initials "A.W.P.") as well as the case of her second marriage, to Albert Price, Hurston's letters do not mention her third husband, James Howell Pitts.

[48] Hurston to Carl Van Vechten, December 10, 1944.

[49] Hurston to Claude Barnett, [July 21–26, 1946].

Church, ran for Congress against Republican candidate Grant Reynolds, a black state corrections commissioner and relatively unseasoned politician whom Powell called "Uncle Tom."[50] Urged into the race by liberal New York governor Thomas Dewey, Reynolds was an adamant integrationist. Friends such as Thurgood Marshall, Joe Louis, and Walter White respected his militant protests against segregation in the military. But Powell's record, which included important work on the People's Committee, the Equal Employment Coordinating Committee, and publication of the widely read black paper *People's Voice*, was widely seen as even more impressive.[51]

Hurston supported Reynolds and campaigned hard for him among her friends. The Harlem vote was two to one in favor of Adam Clayton Powell, and Powell won the election easily, becoming the first black member of the U.S. House of Representatives. There are many reasons that Hurston may have chosen to go against the grain. While Powell was politically well regarded, he was also seen as too arrogant to work well with other black leaders and as a maverick whose support could damage progressive legislation. He was a known playboy, behavior of which Hurston disapproved. And Powell had the support of the Communist Party and its sympathizers. Hurston was already well on her way to the rabid anti-communism she would be known for in the fifties. So Powell's perceived communist support alone might have pushed her into Reynolds's camp. She would not have been the only African American to defect from the Democratic Party in the mid-1940s. Many African Americans were fed up with the Democrats' southern alliances, their foot-dragging on integration, and their support of the poll tax. But perhaps Hurston also liked being different, enjoyed demonstrating her individuality and lack of concern for what others might think. Perhaps she relished the scandal of campaigning against Harlem's homegrown hero. Perhaps supporting Reynolds over Powell was a way to thumb her nose at her political detractors, to be politically provocative, yet remain, as she put it, in "the good fight."[52]

In the middle of the decade, Hurston took on an assignment for an encyclopedia entry. She was so enthusiastic that she described the sort of work most writers find routine as "the greatest honor that has come

[50]*Edwin R. Lewinson*, Black Politics in New York City *(New York: Twayne, 1974), p. 118.*

[51]*Wil Haygood*, King of the Cats: The Life and Times of Adam Clayton Powell, Jr. *(Boston: Houghton Mifflin, 1993).*

[52]*Hurston to Claude Barnett, [July 1–16, 1946].*

my way so far."[53] Much of the excitement stemmed from the fact that Hurston's entry would replace the "Negro in America" essay written by W. E. B. Du Bois which had run in the *Encyclopedia Americana* with updates, revisions, and sometimes a different title since 1904. Hurston was not shy about using the occasion to celebrate Booker T. Washington for making a place for "Negro 'untouchables' " and for never uttering "a public word or [writing] a line concerning what came to be known as the controversy between himself and Dr. Du Bois," whereas Du Bois, she insinuated, did nothing for " 'the man farthest down' " and used his writings to attack Washington unfairly. Hurston's entry differed from Du Bois's in a number of particulars. Whereas Du Bois's essay begins with a reminder that the slave trade "cost Negro Africa millions of souls" and focuses mostly on the social conditions of blacks in America, Hurston's essay repeats a mostly southern claim that some free Negroes under slavery "even held slaves" and is as critical of northern carpetbaggers as it is of slaveholders, taking up the often-articulated southern view that during Reconstruction "what should have come to the Negro after a period of preparation, was thrust upon him while he was still in a state of unreadiness, leaving him not only maladjusted to his surroundings, but retarded in progress for generations." Both Du Bois and Hurston cover segregation, lynching, voting, and disfranchisement in their essays. Hurston's essay devotes considerably more space to black arts.[54] This assignment was quickly followed by another assignment for an encyclopedia entry, this time for *The New International Year Book*. Hurston's essay placed particular emphasis on the "considerable progress toward interracial understanding" made by blacks and provided synopses of accomplishments in education, religion, politics, sports, journalism, the arts, and the military.[55] Both encyclopedia entries offered Hurston the opportunity to write from a position of cultural authority, a position she was pleased to use provocatively.

---

[53]*Hurston to Katherine Tracy L'Engle, October 24, 1945.*

[54]*Zora Neale Hurston, "The Negro in the United States," Encyclopedia Americana, 1947; W. E. B. Du Bois, "The Negro in America," Encyclopedia Americana, 1904–46. Quotations in this paragraph are taken from the 1954 edition of Hurston's essay (pp. 47–52) and the 1940 edition of Du Bois's (pp. 47–52). I am especially grateful to Frank Orser, archivist of the Zora Neale Hurston Collection at the University of Florida, Gainesville, for his help in locating these entries.*

[55]*Zora Neale Hurston, "Negroes," in Charles Earle Funk and Henry Wysham Lanier, eds., The New International Year Book (New York: Funk & Wagnalls, 1946), pp. 418–19.*

If Hurston had resigned herself to being provocative in place of being understood, *Seraph on the Suwanee*, the one novel published in this decade, would have been a sure bet. The novel's theme is misunderstanding and failed communication. It is the story of a largely failed marriage between Arvay and her husband, Jim Meserve, or Me-Serve, as he is appropriately named. Their marriage founders because both are unable to reveal their "inner selves" to the other. This theme is clearly grounded in Hurston's own experiences of disappointment and misunderstanding. Yet *Seraph on the Suwanee* proves confusing and hard to understand. Rather, it is hard to understand *why* Hurston would have written it. Why, for example, would she go from depicting the black community she knew so well, portrayed so lovingly, and criticized so handily to a story about southern crackers and their difficult rise to financial success? Why would she go from using rape as a central metaphor for exploitation in *Their Eyes Were Watching God* to a story in which rape is merely misunderstanding: a "pain remorseless sweet" and a "memory inexpressibly sweet"?[56] Why does she paint a positive and comic image of the very "pet negro system"—"every Southern white man has his pet Negro"[57]—which she decried elsewhere as "a residue of feudalism"?[58]

Was Hurston demonstrating that she could write about whites as perceptively and interestingly as she had about blacks? As early as 1942 she had declared her intent to break "that old silly rule about Negroes not writing about white people."[59] Was she attempting to please Scribner's, her new publisher? She had left Lippincott's after it rejected two novels about black life and interfered with her political views in her autobiography. Was she worried that editor Maxwell Perkins would prove another "timid soul," as she had called Lippincott?[60] Her letters to Burroughs Mitchell, who succeeded Perkins as her Scribner's editor, display Hurston's willingness to compromise and take direction. At one point, Mitchell even expressed some surprise at how easygoing and cooperative Hurston was about suggested changes to her work.[61] "Please remember that I am neither Moses nor any of the writing apostles,"

[56]Zora Neale Hurston, Seraph on the Suwanne (New York: Scribner's, 1948; reprint, New York: Harper-Collins, 1991), pp. 51, 134.

[57]Ibid., p. 61.

[58]Zora Neale Hurston, "The 'Pet Negro' System," American Mercury, May 1943.

[59]Hurston to Carl Van Vechten, November 2, 1942.

[60]Hurston to Carl Van Vechten, September 12, 1945.

[61]Burroughs Mitchell to Zora Neale Hurston, November 24, 1947.

she told Mitchell. "Nothing that I set down is sacred. Any word or sentence can be changed or even cut out. What we want is success."[62] What kind of success? Success in whose estimation?

Regardless of whom it might have been trying to please, *Seraph* was not as successful as Hurston must have wished. It sold 4,638 copies. The *New York Times* praised her, declaring that "the author knows her people, the Florida cracker of the swamps and turpentine camps." But it also criticized the novel's lack of depth, concluding that it amounted to an "excellent background drawing against which move a group of half-human puppets."[63] Another reviewer summed up the novel for the *New York Herald Tribune Weekly Book Review* by declaring that "one could go on indefinitely reiterating this novel's contradictions."[64] Whether or not Hurston knew "her people"—i.e., Florida crackers— the novel never quite brings them off. It remains too caught between contrary audiences to satisfy any one of them.

Hurston evidently wanted *Seraph* to convey a racial message. Unfortunately, Hurston's view of race is notoriously complex. It does not translate easily into fiction. Nor is it very accessible to the mainstream audiences she wanted the novel to reach. In *Dust Tracks*, she had declared herself an individualist firmly opposed to any unified concept of "The Negro." "There is no *The Negro* here," she wrote. "Maybe, after all the Negro doesn't really exist." "Race Pride" is not only nonsensical, "it is a sapping vice," detracting attention from *individual* achievement to "the solace of easy generalization."[65] "I freely admit that we can match the white race scoundrel-beast for scoundrel-beast, and skunk for skunk. But as <u>individuals,</u> not as a whole," she wrote in one letter.[66] "I want nothing done as a favor to me [as a Negro]," Hurston wrote in another letter.[67]

Her paradoxical treatment of "race consciousness" is more complex than mere individualism. Accepting neither the position that race is "essential" biology nor the position that it is myth and "social construction," Hurston also eschewed the third alternative or compromise position that was then current. This compromise argued that race was

[62]*Hurston to Burroughs Mitchell, October "Something Late," 1947.*

[63]*Frank G. Slaughter, review of* Seraph on the Suwanee, New York Times Book Review, *October 31, 1948.*

[64]*Worth Tuttle Hedden, review of* Seraph on the Suwanee, New York Herald Tribune Weekly Book Review, *October 10, 1948.*

[65]*Hurston,* Dust Tracks, *pp. 172, 222, 239, 238.*

[66]*Hurston to Burton Rascoe, September 8, 1944.*

[67]*Hurston to Claude Barnett, [July 1–16, 1946].*

an *ethics,* that one had an *ethical* obligation to one's own race, *however* the "true meaning" of race might be philosophically understood. Writing *Seraph* may have been a way to demonstrate her belief that being a black writer did not oblige her to black subjects and themes. At the same time, she did not reject "The Negro" outright. In "Negroes Without Self-Pity," she argued for defending "The Negro" and being accountable to one's people: "the upper-class Negro . . . must take responsibility" for what was done by "The Negro" outside of his or her sphere, she argued.[68] In "Crazy for This Democracy," published squarely in the middle of the decade, Hurston unabashedly took up the voice of "The Negro" in her attack on the " 'arse-and-all' " of a democracy that touted its virtues around the globe while "subjugating the dark world completely."[69] Passionate individualism and passionate racial pride are both consistent hallmarks of Hurston's writing and her politics, however contradictory the mix may seem.

In the forties, however, Hurston's individualism appears to respond to personal disappointment. Her politics of individualism seems increasingly inflected by personal bitterness, a sense that there were not trustworthy "others" with whom to ally herself.

Throughout much of the decade, Hurston was hell-bent on a trip to Honduras with her friend Fred Irvine. They hoped to find a lost Mayan village described to Hurston by Reginald Brett, an English gold miner who insisted he had located and seen phenomenal ruins. "Jane, darling, I want you to join me on an expedition," Hurston wrote to Belo. "I want it very much. I am going to Honduras to gather some material that I am told is exceedingly rich, varied and so far, untouched. I know that you would fairly wallow in it like a cat in catnip if it is even half as rich as I am lead to believe. Some truly wonderful and history-making things which we may work on. PLEASE, do come and go with me, darling."[70] She seems to have invited nearly everyone she knew to join her in Honduras, perhaps wanting to revive some of the sense of collective and collaborative work she had enjoyed in the thirties. At one point, in a letter to Ruth Benedict, Hurston went so far as to suggest that "instead of attempting the whole thing myself, [I should] turn over the direction to you, and work on some detail that you may assign to me."[71]

[68]Zora Neale Hurston, *"Negroes Without Self-Pity,"* American Mercury, *November 1943.*

[69]Zora Neale Hurston, *"Crazy for This Democracy,"* Negro Digest, *December 1945.*

[70]Hurston to Jane Belo, October 1, 1944.

[71]Hurston to Ruth Benedict, June 19, 1945.

Might Hurston have been desperate to go to Honduras for other than purely research reasons? Could it have represented a much-desired escape for her? From Honduras, she told Van Vechten that she had been finding New York abysmal, "everybody busy hating and speaking in . . . brazen lies."[72] In an earlier letter to Belo and Tannenbaum, she had also spoken of her desire to leave the country. "These howling war years so filled with hate and lack of faith and illusion, plus the years of hate-urge that preceeded [sic] them have caused me to fear that all youth and enthusiasm had gone out of America."[73] Whether she went to Honduras to escape these conditions, being there did Hurston a world of good. "I shall always be grateful to Honduras," she wrote to her editor Maxwell Perkins; "it has given me back myself. I am my old brash self again."[74]

But if escape from controversy and misunderstanding was what Hurston wanted, it turned out that even Honduras wasn't far enough away. Shortly after her arrival back in New York, a final misunderstanding imposed itself on Hurston. This one nearly killed her.

On September 14, 1948, Hurston was arrested for committing immoral acts with a ten-year-old boy. The sodomy charges for which Hurston was indicted on October 1 were false, resulting from a neighbor's anger over Hurston's advice regarding her troubled son.[75] "The thing is too fantastic, too evil, too far from reality for me to conceive of it. I am charged with meeting this boy at 4:30 every Saturday afternoon in the basement of a house where I have never been and in company with two other adults whom I have never seen. This was said to be going on for more than a year, the very time when I was in Honduras," Hurston wrote to Van Vechten and Fania Marinoff.[76] The charges were outrageous and unsubstantiated. Nevertheless, they took months for Hurston to clear up. Much worse was the fact that the press caught wind of the scandal, and Hurston was publicly vilified. On October 23, 1948, the *Baltimore Afro-American* carried a front-page story under the banner headline "Boys, 10, Accuse Zora." This attack by the black press, which paused neither to gather facts nor to allow Hurston to speak, was an unthinkable betrayal, as was the fact that the story was

[72]Hurston to Carl Van Vechten, July 30, 1947.

[73]Hurston to Jane Belo and Frank Tannenbaum, October 14, 1944.

[74]Hurston to Maxwell Perkins, May 20, 1947.

[75]The People of the State of New York v. Zora Hurston, October 1, 1948.

[76]Hurston to Carl Van Vechten and Fania Marinoff, [October 30, 1948].

leaked by a black court employee. "You should know," she told Van Vechten and Marinoff, "that a Negro who works down in the courts secured the matter and went around peddling it to papers. That is the blow that knocked me loose from all that I have ever looked to and cherished." The race disloyalty took her to the brink of suicide. "I have resolved to die," she told Van Vechten and Marinoff. "It will take a few days for me to set my affairs in order, and then I will go."[77]

Luckily, Hurston's closest friends stuck by her. Burroughs Mitchell arranged her release on the night of her arrest, brought her back to his home that night, paid her $1,500 bail, hired her lawyer, Louis Waldman, and loaned her the initial legal fees.[78] Van Vechten and Marinoff sent love and support. Marjorie Kinnan Rawlings lent money. Helen Worden Erskine supported Hurston, as did Fannie Hurst, who helped Hurston through the trial and then to get back on her feet afterward. "Please help me," Hurston was forced to write Hurst after the case was finally dropped. "What I must have now is enough to keep me alive for two weeks. After that I can go to work. I owe room rent now and other things. I have used up every available resource before appealing to you—even to pawning my typewriter."[79] Even Langston Hughes was prepared to come to court and testify on her behalf.

It was impossible to fully clear her name with the public, but Hurston was determined to get to the bottom of this episode for her own sake. In February, she wrote to Fannie Hurst that she had "ferreted out the source of the matter and know my enemy and whom and how to fight."[80] The "enemy" was a man named Richard Rochester. His place in Hurston's life was extremely complicated, as we can see from Hurston's detailed letters about him to Erskine and Hurst. Rochester, described erroneously and anonymously in the *Afro-American* as a "Harlem Republican leader," had filed two small-claims suits against Hurston for money he claimed she owed him for damages to his car. Apparently, he also filed a vote-fraud claim against Hurston regarding a supposed double registration in 1946.[81] Hurston won the small-claims cases and reported to Hurst that "the Judge was right in

[77]*Ibid.*

[78]*Correspondence between Hurston and Mitchell, September and October 1948.* The People and Alexander Miller v. Zora Neale Hurston, *City Magistrate's Files, September 14, 1948.*

[79]*Hurston to Fannie Hurst, February 10, 1949.*

[80]*Ibid.*

[81]Afro-American, *February 5 and February 19, 1949, as cited by Kristy Anderson, unpublished research report,* "The Tangled Southern Roots of Zora Neale Hurston," *pp. 9–10.*

there defeating the unholy purpose of Richard D. Rochester at every move."[82] Rochester, Hurston was sure, was "the source and foundation of the whole business" of the unfounded sodomy charge.[83]

The origin of the war between Rochester and Hurston is not clear. One witness at the small-claims trial, according to newspaper reports, suggested "that Rochester was Miss Hurston's lover."[84] This seems highly unlikely. There may have been a connection to the 1946 Reynolds/Powell campaign. It is possible that some of the controversy engendered by Hurston's participation in that campaign came back to haunt her in the form of this antagonist, a man who dogged her even to her publisher's offices, harassing first the secretary to Scribner's publicity director, then the publicity director, then Whitney Darrow's secretary, then Whitney Darrow, with his version of events.[85]

Whatever Rochester's role in the morals charge, the trial cost Hurston both her peace of mind and the book she was working on at the end of the decade, a novel entitled *The Lives of Barney Turk*, the story of a young white man on a Florida produce farm who goes through a series of "lives," in Central America and Hollywood, that lead him to greater self-awareness. By October 1949, Hurston had completed a first installment of the novel, based on an earlier précis. Mitchell liked the plot, the Hollywood angle, and the main character. A few months later he was even happier with the new book and noted that, through her work, Hurston seemed to be putting her recent ordeal behind her. Only two months after that, in March 1950, he was writing that neither he nor Hurston's agent thought the novel was working out. The gist of his letter was that the novel was unfocused and unbelievable and that Hurston was not working on it efficiently. In October, he rejected the book outright. Hurston's publishing career suffered from this point on. She never regained the kind of surefootedness—almost a sixth sense—that had once given her insight into what her readers would like.

In her last dated letter of the decade, written in December 1949, Hurston told Van Vechten and Marinoff, "I have regained my peace of mind and cheerfulness."[86] Whether she held on to this "peace" or not,

[82] Hurston to Fannie Hurst, February 10, 1949.
[83] Ibid.
[84] Anderson, "Tangled Southern Roots," pp. 9–10.
[85] Burroughs Mitchell to Louis Waldman, January 24, 1949.
[86] Hurston to Carl Van Vechten and Fania Marinoff, December 22, 1949.

Hurston on a folklore trip.

there is considerable evidence that her trust in other people and her desire to reveal anything of her "inner self" were irreparably damaged.
In *Their Eyes Were Watching God*, Hurston developed the metaphor of
"kissing friends" to describe mutual revelation and understanding so
perfect and complete that it was as if "mah tongue is in mah friend's
mouf." She came back to this metaphor at the end of her autobiography. "Let us all be kissing-friends," she wrote on the final page.[87] In
light of the misunderstandings and conflicts Hurston endured in the
forties and the loneliness she would experience in the fifties as well,
this invitation has a tragic and ironic ring.

[87]*Hurston,* Dust Tracks, *p. 209.*

TO PAUL GREEN

Box 407
Durham, North Carolina
January 24, 1940

Mr. Paul Green
Drama Department
University of North Carolina
Chapel Hill, North Carolina

Dear Paul Green:

If you have decided to work on JOHN DE CONQUEROR,[1] you do not need to concern yourself with the situation here at the school. I won't care what happens here or if nothing happens here so long as I do the bigger thing with you. My mind is hitting [overwritten on heating] on sixteen cylinders on the play now. I am so stimulated by you, so I am utterly unconcerned if I can work with you on that. Your last remark to me last night was that you wanted to write a very funny play, and I think we have the material for it by blending John De Conqueror with John Henry, Marcus Garvey,[2] Father Devine [sic],[3] etc. There is also the element of a touch of grandeur in the thing.

I can continually [feature—x-ed out] feed you with grist for the framework. All the critics have said that I can write good dialogue and I notice both, from reading your work and listening to you, that, that is one of your strong points. So I believe that we can hit the ball for a

[1] A Hurston story which she and Green wanted to produce as a play.

[2] One of the most charismatic and extraordinary black political leaders of the period, Jamaican orator Marcus Aurelius Garvey (1887–1940) arrived in Harlem in 1916. He formed the weekly paper Negro World (1918–33, reaching a circulation of 200,000 at its peak) and the Universal Negro Improvement Association, "to work for the general uplift of the Negro peoples of the world." Advocating "Africa for the Africans," Garvey founded an all-black shipping company (the Black Star Line) and worked to colonize Africa with American blacks. Garvey was deported in 1927 after serving more than two years in the Atlanta Federal Penitentiary for mail fraud, but many continued in his efforts.

[3] Father Divine (George Baker) (1880–1965) was one of the country's most successful religious leaders. Known as God to many followers, Divine's "Peace Mission" established itself in Harlem in 1933 after Divine finished serving a prison sentence on "public nuisance" charges. Like Garvey, Divine had a highly flamboyant style that drew both followers and criticism. Divine was famous for his personal excesses, especially his extravagance in homes, cars, and female followers. He was also famous for powerful personal charisma.

long run. If JOHN DE CONQUEROR succeeds, there is the play about the mayor of my village, which I think is very funny.[4] Carl Van Vechten thinks it's the funniest play that he has ever read, and is continually urging me to finish it. He has even told producers about it, for me, and assures me that he will stand by to push it.

I have intended to say something about this each time that I see you, but I get so excited in your presence that I forget it. Hence, the letter, in fact, I see no reason why the firm of Green and Hurston should not take charge of the Negro playwriting business in America, and I can see many reasons why we should. I was tremendously interested in the radio group last night. This coming Sunday night, I must make a speech in Greensboro at the College Womens' Club, but on the other meeting nights I'll be there. Let me turn you some humble thanks for giving me the chance.

Very sincerely yours,
Zora Neale Hurston

ZNH:RJH

TO FANNIE HURST

North Carolina College
Durham, North Carolina
January 30, 1940

Dear Genius Fannie Hurst:

I am here in North Carolina teaching drama. I find it rather interesting work. The school is a State school, and just beginning to do graduate work.

Thank you so much for the Christmas greetings. It was good to be remembered by you at Christmas.

I find that there are a large number of admirers of "Imitation of Life" in this section, especially in Raleigh and Durham. You have been discussed often when people found out that I knew you.

---

[4]Hurston had worked the Eatonville materials into many different forms, including a number of plays and short stories centered on the mayor of the town. Van Vechten had forwarded Mule Bone to producers.

It would be a great treat to have you come here to speak. I am a member of an organization that sponsors a Finer Womanhood program every year during the month of February. It is their purpose to bring before the public, an outstanding woman exemplifying such qualities as you possess, as an inspiration to the women of this section. I know what your presence here would mean to "Womanhood". Please do not refuse me. I want to see you and let others see you, so that they may realize more fully that you are not only a genius, but a broad, dynamic person who has an intelligent interest in my group.

Many of us read with interest your syndicated column, and think it good.

I know that you do not like to speak, but please do me this favor. Many heard your radio talk and were enthusiastic about it.

If you will come we would like to have you during the week of February 19th or February 26th, any evening during that time, but if these dates are not convenient we shall be glad to have you whenever you find it convenient.

I feel that both Duke University and the University of North Carolina would be too glad to have you also.

May I hear from you as early as you find it convenient.

Your devoted disciple,
Zora Neale Hurston.

TO FANNIE HURST

Box Box [sic]
Durham, N.C
February 6, 1940

Dear Fanny [sic] Hurst,[1]

I call it a treat to get a letter from the fountain head. Yes, I got a letter from that fat-head down in Florida and she sent me eight typewritten pages of questions to be answered, going back to my grandparents

---

[1] *This letter was included with other Hurston letters in the Hurst Collection at the University of Texas. The content is clearly Hurston's, but the letter appears to be a handwritten transcription prepared by someone else (perhaps Hurst).*

and what they meant to the community.[2] I'm not going to answer it, naturally. Why should a person, who doesn't even read be doing a thesis on a subject like that—on any subject at all? I'm often struck with the fact, how many Negroes are more impressed with the fact that I was your secretary [and—x-ed out] than all the other things that I've done.

You have a grand set of admirers in this part of the world because of "Imitation of Life". So it seems that Sterling Brown[3] is not in the majority. He picks on me all the time now. He tells people that he wants to riddle me, and otherwise deflate me because he says that I stand convicted of having furnished you with the material of "IMITATION." I let it stand without contradiction because I feel [it—x-ed out] he does me honor. In so saying, he pays you an unconscious tribute because he is admitting the truth of the work. What he and his kind resent is just that. It is too accurate to be comfortable, but I see through him very clearly. He is jealous to pieces because I have out-stripped him so far. So he adds the two things up and hates me like poison. Not that I care a tinker's.

Hope to be in New York soon and will surely see you. If you have time. Then I will tell you all about this mess around here that they call education. You can get another good book out of it.

Merrily and cheerily,

Zora

TO JANE BELO

Box 407, Durham, N.C.
March 20, 1940

Dear Miss Jane,

Resigned my job March 1,[1] and sat down out at my log cabin to await your majesty, and here it is March 20th and so I have come to the conclusion that the great thing of your life has arrived—love.

Now, you must not feel badly if life has changed your plans. You

---

[2] *On January 27, Hurst had written Hurston in regard to a letter from Lottie Clark, who was writing a thesis on Negro women leaders of Florida and who, much to Hurst's upset, seems to have been unaware of Hurston.*
[3] *Writer and critic; see glossary.*

[1] *Hurston had been teaching drama at the North Carolina College for Negroes in Durham.*

must not consider for a moment that I shall feel badly. Rather I am happy that it has come to you. I have wanted it to happen. You are a gentle little thing that needs love and protection and I am most happy that it has come. So if it is your inclination to abandon the trip altogether, dont hesitate to tell me. Your welfare and happiness concern me a great deal, and I am sure that I would do the same thing under the same circumstances. All I hope is that you will not forget me and that I shall hear from time to time what is happening. But let me know the final word so that I can make some plans for the Spring.

I should like to see what you have done in Bali very much. I was eager for you to come here because I know that both Duke University and University of North Carolina would have loved to know about your work.

Well, to tell you the truth, I am a little "tetched" with love myself, though it has not gone beyond the palpitating stage. No committments as yet. He has a magnificent bass voice. I am trying to find out if that is what I am stuck on or if it is the man himself. I do like strong, big wrassly men and he seems to fit the bill in many ways. I wish he had some money, but then I have never been wealthy, so————[2]

I have no telephone out at the shack, which is out on Highway #15, Hope Valley Road about two mile[s] on the town side of the Country Club. But if you will send me a wire to my mail box, (which I am watching these days like a cat watches a mouse hole,) I will know what is what. Also in case you decide to come tell me where to meet you. The Washington Duke is considered the best hotel in Durham. My log house is in a yard with two little log cabins in back. It used to be a tourist camp, complete with filling station. None of it is in use now. I just live in the house which is on the left side of the road as you drive out towards the golf club.

I know that I shall love the man who loves you and brings you so much happiness. I want to be the first person to congratulate him on his great good fortune. Hurry up and let me see him.

Most sincerely,
Z.N.H.
Zora Neale Hurston

[2]Hurston had filed for divorce from her second husband, Albert Price, in February 1940. While it has usually been assumed that their substantial "age differential" (he was twenty-three and she was forty-eight when they married) doomed their marriage, this letter suggests that Hurston's interest in another man—possibly the man who was to become her third husband—may have had more to do with her on-again, off-again relationship with Price; their 1940 divorce suit was withdrawn and not fully realized until 1943, just before Hurston remarried.

I had arranged with a storage warehouse to take care of my furniture, and he is standing around waiting on me. So drop me a word right quick so I can know what to tell him.

TO PAUL GREEN

Box 407, Chapel Hill, N.C.
March 21, 1940

Dear Paul Green,

Sure enough, your letter was in the P.O. when I got back from Chapel Hill, and it was kind of you to write me. Frankly, I had made some sort of arrangements inside of myself to stuff up the hole that was gaping after the staff of the CAROLINA PLAYMAKERS went out of me. You see, I heard of a rumored boast that you all had been talked to and that my name was being spit at in Chapel Hill. So I was sad and sort of gutted. I pondered "With so much truth in evidence, how can a pack of lies be so popular?" So I said, "Well, it just goes to show how much disillusionment a person can harbor and still not quit breathing." For I was around and making the motions of life as usual. I didnt know that any of you had tried to get in touch with me.

Reading your letter over for the third time, I have the uncomfortable feeling that I have pestered you too much about this HIGH JOHN DE CONQUER. You have tried to feel it and you cant. So I will take High John out of your lap and go off an[d] sit up with him awhile. As I said, I will write through the thing and let you see what I have done. If you then feel like bothering with the thing again I will be very happy. If not, well then, you just dont feel that way. Maybe I shall never find a way out with the story, but I feel it very strong, and somehow I think I shall.

My, it was nice seeing the Green family the other night! It put me right back on my feet. Such things prove to me that there is no such thing as an absolute big or little. Its size depends upon time and circumstance. [N]obody can know what is big or little until Time has passed upon it. So a casual conversation of an evening may have some tremendous effects. The evening might have seemed trivial, even boring a trifle to you all, but it did something to me which it will take a long time to see the end results. It unbuttoned my horizon from around my waist and shoved it out towards the rim-bones of nothing.

> Most sincerely, gratefully anf humbly yours,
> Z.N.H.
> Zora Neale Hurston

TO JANE BELO

[in upper left corner:] Madame Veronica of Beaufort is Daisy Middleton

Box 174
Beaufort, S.C.
May 2, 1940

Jane, the Incomparable, greetings,

Dear Beloved, this is to thank you for easing my terrible disappointment Just the day before your letter reached me I found that the pictures didnt com out and I was in the depths of despair I am sending on the reel that shows a little. Please send the men with the equipment and let me go on finding out things. I am having great luck at that, and leave the instruments alone.[1] I have in notes

A. a swell story of the splitting of the two churches complete with intrigue love interest, etc. Alma (she of the good voice, Carrie's youngest daughter) and the Bishop!

B. Family ramifications & personal tangles and angles of both churches.

C. The relations between those who "come under deep-teaching" and the others of [illegible line]

D. Exact description of the trance by those who have experienced it, with suh conscious wishes and fears laid bare through the visions.

E. The meaning of the "Prophet" in the church.

---

[1] *Hurston had been experimenting with film to record the "sanctified" church practices she was studying with Belo.*

Now I went to work right away to lay the foundation for the white men to come in to take the sound pictures.[2] I think we had better make them (Geo Washington & his main supporters, I mean) a present because they a not taking to it any too kindly. I have the matter of the time when they shall come to work to you. If you prefer to see the work before you sail for Mexico, then send them along now. If you prefer to have them work in June, let me know. I will do whatever pleases you. I am glad that you can get the two young fellows to send along and I have a nice tourist camp picked out for them, right close to the churches. It is right on the highway, and inside of Beaufort.

I will be sure to keep my $150[00] from getting mixed up with yours. I dont see why you could not state that it was 5 x 300 on your income tax statement. Would anybody be the wiser? It would not hurt anybody that I could see.

So far as your family ganging up on you on the Jewish question, you can point with pride to Secretary of State Cordell Hull.[3] His wife is a Jew from an old Virginia family. If that isnt precedent for the daughter of an old southern family, I dont know what is and remember that Sec. Hull is from Tenn. That ought to settle the family hash, that side of it that needs settling, anyway. However, I opened a window in my soul and sent out my spirit to help you safely into Frank's[4] arms. It cant be otherwise, darling. You will see. I shall put a Ounga on your mama that shall keep her silent until all is over. I am sending a mouth-gag in a spiritual way. I love you and I want you to be free to meet "the day" bravely.

Darling, darling, darling, darling, darling, darling. Dear, dear, dear, dear, dear, dear, dear, dear. Love, love, love, love, love, love, love, I want you to know that I am working down here to make a study that you can use to your eternal power and glory.

So, I await the two boys when you see fit to send them, now or later. Let me know at once which you prefer to do.

Most devotedly your own
Zora.

---

[2]*Norman Chalfin and his associates, Louis Brandt and Bob Lawrence.*
[3]*Cordell Hull (1871–1955) was appointed Judge of the Fifth Tennessee Circuit in 1903, was elected to Congress in 1907, and became secretary of state in 1933. In 1913, Hull authored the first federal income tax bill. He married Rose Frances Whitney of Staunton, Virginia, in 1917.*
[4]*Frank Tannenbaum.*

TO PAUL GREEN

Box 174, Beaufort, S.C.
May 3, 1940

Dear Paul Green,

I am in a panic. I am down here in South Carolina doing some research in religious experience, and the trance in religion in particular for Miss Jane Belo. She has gone back to New York to marry Frank Tannenbaum and I am carrying on. Now here is the rub: As we have gone about from church to church we have run across some GRAND music and I confided to her that I was going to ask you for a machine to record some of it for our plays. [Yesterday I—x-ed out] As she was leaving three weeks ago she remembered my statement about the music and asked me not to get in touch with you until she saw whether she could get a machine from Columbia U. or not. Both of us have friends there and then Frank Tannenbaum is a professor there too. So what happens? Today I get a long letter from her saying that she has secured a movie outfit with sound effects, that is for taking the movies and the sound at the same time to send down to me after June 1, with two very enthusiastic Jews who want to take the spirituals for <u>commercial purposes</u>.![1]

Now, dont sit there, Paul Green, just thinking. DO SOMETHING! We cant let all that swell music get away from us like that. You said yourself that there ought to be lots of music in the play and music that had not become hackneyed and worn out. Cant you get one of the machines from the University and run a man down here for a week? Of course I am not going to lead them [written in left margin: "I mean those two from N.Y."] to the fattest and juiciest places nohow. I feel justified because Miss Belo and I had an understanding from the start that if any recordings were done, that I was to have the use of them first. I thought that this was a swell chance for us [handwritten insertion: "you & me"] to get hold of a great deal of raw music that we could work up from time to time as

---

[1] The "two Jews" are presumably Louis Brandt and Bob Lawrence, film editors for the project. But since Norman Chalfin, sound engineer for the trip, is also Jewish, she may be referring to any of the three of them. According to Chalfin, the "commercial purposes" were small-scale: a musicologist who heard of their recording asked to use it as background to the popular Broadway plays Battle of Angels and Holy Roller. Some of the tapes were also aired on the radio. (Personal interview with Norman Chalfin.)

we needed it. But her sending of these two sharks down looks like she has forgotten, or been out-talked one. No matter which, I think that we will have to do something, and that quick. If [we] could even make fifty records we would have a great deal. I hope that we can exhaust all the fat juicy places before them two get here and then I will show them some nice places. There will be plenty still, but I dont want them to get a hold of certain tunes which I have earmarked for BIG JOHN DE CONQUER. She really does need the pictures of the services for her study in the trance,[2] [but—x-ed out] and I will do all that is in my power to get the best for her. But the songs————that is killing my dreams, AND they are unnecessary to her. It is just that she has raved about them to persons who saw what they could do with them. You see where I am at?

Please let me hear from you right away. I have such high hopes for BIG JOHN. Please do what you can about it.

Most sincerely,
Zora
Zora Neale Hurston

TO JANE BELO

[from Chalfin, Brandt, Lawrence, and Hurston]

[May 20, 1940—library dated]
Monday.

Dear Jane:

We've been shooting, shooting and shooting—We been begging and wheedling—and bluffing to get current—But we've got records.—that much we know. It's a good thing records can be played back immediately.

If the gods of anthropological investigators are with us we have some swell fotos and films.

Not all that we planned worked out—We don't have any synchronization because our motor lay down on us before we started—so we were hand cranking all the four hundred foot rolls and using the spring on the 100 foots. We have a [illegible] service, and an outdoor service and also a Sunday nite service.

[2] *Belo's book*, The Trance in Bali *(New York: Columbia University Press, 1960).*

Had we attempted to synchronize the sound the flexibility of jumping from place to place would have been impaired—

We really did shoot some wonderful reactions I hope that they prove satisfactory for study purposes.

We find that after having gone through it once that there are a number of things we'd have liked to do that our equipment did not permit.

The excellence of what we did get we'll leave up to you to judge.

Without Zora most of it would have been impossible.

Give all our records to Frank, and accept our congratulations—best wishes and all that and let us make the old standby remark about all your troubles being little ones.

> Regards, etc.
> Norman Chalfin
> and Lou[is Brandt] and Bob [Lawrence]
> and Zora

TO FANNIE HURST

P.O. Box 174
Beaufort, S.C.
Aug. 4, 1940

Dear, dear Friend,

I cannot tell you how shocked I am to hear that you have been ill at all, let alone being in a hospital![1] I have never conceived of you as either ill nor ailing. I see you always swirling the waving veils of space like a spear of flame.

Now, what can I do about it? Do you need me in any way? I am at your feet and at your service. There is nothing that I would not do for my benefactor and friend. You know that I can type now. I can cook as always, I can do many more things than I could when you scraped me up out of the street. If there is anything that you feel I could do to please you, you must let me know. I should pay back for all that I have received somehow.

---

[1] Hurst underwent a hysterectomy earlier that summer.

I have a review copy of Langston's book and I am in the midst of it now.[2] So far very good. I shall write a review, but I do not know where to send it. I have decided to send it to Mrs. Knopf and if she feels like using it, she can send it where she wishes.

I hope to be in New York before Labor Day. I want to see and to feel. This is a nice quiet place to work, but insufferably dull.

I kiss your hand, lady and salute you back to health.

Most devotedly,

Zora

Zora N. Hurston

TO ANNIE NATHAN MEYER

[postmarked January 15, 1941]

52 West 130th Street
New York City

Dear Friend,

This morning at 4:20 I put the last word down on my book.[1] Happiness unbounded. It has been so confining. Thanks for the invitation to lunch. I shall be too glad to come AND ON TIME. Ha!

Lovingly,

Zora

---

[2]*His autobiography,* The Big Sea, *published in 1940. His discussion of the* Mule Bone *episode, in which he gives his side of the story and claims (incorrectly) that he "never heard from Miss Hurston again," appears at the very end of the book; Hurston clearly had not read that section yet.*

[1]*Presumably* Dust Tracks, *which she continued revising throughout 1941.*

TO RUTH BENEDICT

2666 Cimarron Street
Los Angeles, Cal.
Sept. 16, 1941.

Dear Ruth Benedict:

Here I am out here enjoying the sunlight. I hope that all the things are going well with you. I hope that Dr. Boas is in good health.

I have been trying to recall an old Bahama song and I cannot make it exactly. I enclose a dollar for which I pray that you send me a copy of "FOLK TALES FROM THE BAHAMAS". That little pamphlet which I did around 1929 if it is still on hand.

My best to Dr. Klineberg and all the other swell people in the Department.

Most sincerely yours,
Zora
Zora Neale Hurston

Hurston's home, 2666 Cimarron (in 2001).

TO EDWIN OSGOOD GROVER

PARAMOUNT PICTURES, INC.
5451 Marathon Street
Los Angeles, Cal.
December 30, 1941.

Dear Dr. Grover,

It did me a lot of good to get a letter from you. You put me right back to work again. You always make me feel that I have to live up to something, and that is the kind of thing that keeps a creative person alive.

This job here at the studio is not the end of things for me. It is a means. My autobiography is due out in the spring.[1] I did not want to do it now, but my publishers wanted it very much. They said to my objections, that I could do another volume of it years later. I am doing an article for THE SATURDAY REVIEW OF LITERATURE at once,[2] with Theodore Pratt[3] and his new book as a springboard. After all details of my new book, DUST TRACKS ON A ROAD, are cleared up, I shall start to work on a play in dead earnest.

Until two weeks ago, I thought that I had an interesting situation to put up tp you. Mr. and Mrs. John Mershon,[4] of Saginaw Michigan, who have been living in Bali, Netherlands Indies for nine years came back home to avoid the impending trouble. She was second to Ruth St. Denis for years at her school. She was also a well-known solo dancer in her own right, besides teaching at the Denis-Shawn school. Now, she has married money and thinks that perhaps they will never be able to return to Bali. She has had two years of college work and wants a degree. He is interested in agriculture and wants to work at it. He is really marvelous with plants. So I urged them to move to Winter Park,

---

[1] Dust Tracks on a Road.

[2] *This does not appear to have materialized.*

[3] *Florida writer and journalist Theodore Pratt (1901–69) was the author of thirty-five novels and numerous essays. Pratt and Hurston became friends. Pratt lent Hurston small amounts of money and spoke at her funeral. He published a profile of Hurston in the* Florida Historical Quarterly *in July 1961.*

[4] *Dancer and anthropologist Katharane Edson Mershon (1892–1986); see glossary.*

take up their studies at Rollins where they could give something as well. She has a great collection of Balinese art. She knows their customs well. I thought that she could lecture around there on it, loan her collection to the college, teach dancing if necessary and enjoy herself while giving pleasure to others. They would not need to do it for money, for their income never comes below $500.00 per month, and sometimes it is much more. Now that we are in the war actively, they seem to be afraid to come to Florida on account of the numerous military objectives in the state, plus the excessive coast line. They plan to return to California, but to stay away from the coast. He was most excited about the ½lant possibility of Florida, since he has lived so much in the tropics, and knows Osborne Fairchild, or Fairchild Osborne at Homewood.[5] He helped him with his colleftion of tropical plants when Fairchild visited Bali. I am so disappointed that they are not coming to you. They are well-placed socially, financially, and have brains. I gave them letters to you and Mrs. Thompson when they left here for Saginaw to spend the holidays with his father, who not only made a fortune in Michigan timber, but is one of the founders of Phellps-[sic] Dodge Copper. Naturally it occurred to me that they could help out financially on new buildings, etc. I knew too, that they would love the intellectual atmosphere of Rollins, which is to say Winter Park. They were mightily impressed with Dr. Hamilton Holt, you, and the whole set-up when I told them about it. It would help her in a psychological way if she got that degree. It would give him something to [do] besides just spend money aimlessly if he could work into the tropical plant culture of the state. He has a fine mind, just never had to use it much. The home address is 1501 N. Michigan Ave., Saginaw. They plan to leave there after the holidays. Do wish for many reasons that you could get them down there. I have been their house guest out here for five months and know that they need some stimulation to make them happy. I saw how my being in the house was a godsend to them. I love them very much and want them to be happy. Work is the only answer. They just sit around and bore each other to screams. Yes, actual hysteria.

My best to you and yours, which means your immediate family,

[5]Probably Henry Fairfield Osborn, conservationist, trustee, and then president of the New York Zoological Society. Osborn also taught biology and paleontology at Columbia University.

Rollins, and all Winter Park. I might get down there late in March. I had planned to join them there. [in hand: "(the Mershons)"]

Etta Moten is here now, and we had a good talk about Rollins. She was entranced. Ethel Waters is here too, and we are good friends. With her huge following, she ought to be a sell-out at Rollins in concert. I suggested concert to her Sunday night. It had never occurred to her to give a whole evening of her varied types of song. She is a priceless personality! Wait until you meet her! Etta Moten told me that she gave a benefit out at Hungerford, and found all the students simply worshipping me. They quoted me in song and story, but she found Hall [Johnson] still trying to kill me off. He talked me down until her accompanist sprung to my defense. The girls and boys know his attitude and the more he knocks me the more they love me. I do not mind at all. All I want is that the school and the town shall go ahead. I know that he cannot block everything forever. God is in His Heaven, so things have to come right with the world.

> Most sincerely your humble and obedient servant,
> Zora
> Zora Neale Hurston, Lit.D.

TO EDWIN OSGOOD GROVER

[April 15, 1942]
C/o General Delivery
St. Augustine, Fla.

Dear Dr. Grover,

I shall be driving down towards the week end. I arrived in Florida with my whole respiratory tract congested. As sick as I have ever been in my life. So I did not try to contact anyone. I did not write Mrs. Mershon because she has enough to worry about without knowing that I had pneumonia, tonsilitis and sinus. I Think the alkaline dust of the deserts I crossed did me up. But the old vim and vigor is back again. I shall be seeing you before the week is up. My very best to the family until I get there.

> Zora

TO HENRY ALLEN MOE

[stamped: received June 25, 1942]

Howdy do, Dr. Moe!

I am down here trying to polish up my book, write three plays and keep on eating.[1] I do hope that you are strutting the Avenue in your zoot suit with the drape shape, and otherwise cooking with gas.

Faithfully yours,

[unsigned]

Box 977
St. Augustine, Fla.

TO CARL VAN VECHTEN

Box 977
St. Augustine, Fla.
November 2, 1942.

Darling Carlo:

Just got back to St. Augustine yesterday after five weeks absence,[1] and found my mailbox overflowing. I would rather be shot with tacks than to have missed that dinner to you on the 20th.[2] But the truth is, I was down with malaria over on the Gulf side of the state and could not even find the strength to drive back across, so that I could not get

---

[1]*Hurston was revising* Dust Tracks on a Road *and working on a number of plays, including some on which she hoped to collaborate with playwright Paul Green. At least one of these was centered on Eatonville life and intended as a comedy.*

---

[1]*In September and October, Hurston had been traveling throughout Florida collecting folklore.*

[2]*The James Weldon Johnson Literary Guild dinner tribute to Van Vechten, organized by Roberta Bosley, was actually November 20, not October 20.*

to the BOOK FAIR, and I did not even know that your letter, and Roberta Bosley's[3] letters were here until yesterday.

I plan to be there to your exhibition.[4] The only thing that could prevent it would be that I am forced to return to Hollywood to complete the work under contract to PARAMOUNT.[5] But I have written to say that I would start back by December 1, so I feel sure that I can have my long-desired trip to New York.

I have recently sold two articles to Saturday Evening Post,[6] and am asked for one, to be delivered in January, to Readers Digest. I want to take a crack at THE NEW YORKER. Do you think it can come off? Having been on the writing staff at PARAMOUNT for several months, I have a tiny wedge in Hollywood, and I have hopes of breaking that old silly rule about Negroes not writing about white people. In fact, I have a sort of commitment from a producer at RKO that he will help me to do it. I am working on the story now.[7]

I will send along the mss that you suggested. Just as soon as I can wear down some of the correspondence that has accumulated in these five weeks. I am most grateful to you for the kind thought in asking for them. You are so generous in your soul! Your book DUST TRACKS ON THE ROAD, will be mailed as soon as I get my six copies. My publisher has written that they have been mailed to me.

My best to you, darling Carl. I owe you so much. I wrote a chapter in my new book dedicated to friendship, but the publishers deleted it.[8] In it, I tried to show my inside feelings for certain people, because I am not

[3]Roberta Bosley was a member of the James Weldon Johnson Literary Guild and subject of a sculpture by Richmond Barthé.

[4]A new show of Van Vechten's photographs was opening in November at the Museum of the City of New York titled "The Theatre Through the Camera of Carl Van Vechten."

[5]Hurston's Paramount contract indicates that her work with the studio was as a writer and technical adviser, and lasted scarcely two months, ending in December 1941.

[6]"Lawrence of the River" appeared in the September 5, 1942, edition of the Saturday Evening Post. "Miss Catherine of Turpentine" was purchased by the Post, but never appeared.

[7]Seraph on the Suwanee, probably.

[8]In that chapter, titled "The Inside Light—Being a Salute to Friendship," Hurston acknowledges the "juice of friendship" received from Charlotte Osgood Mason, Carl Van Vechten, Fannie Hurst, the Huberts, the Beers, Amy Spingarn, Harry Burleigh, Bob Wunsch, Henry Allen Moe, Charles S. Johnson, Jane Belo, Miguel and Rose Covarrubias, Harry Block, H. P. Davis, Edna St. Vincent Millay, Herbert Childs, Katharane Mershon, and many others. Of Van Vechten, she wrote: "He has not been one of the 'white friends of the Negro' who seeks to earn it cheaply by being eternally complimentary. If he is your friend, he will point out your failings as well as your good points in the most direct manner. Take it or leave it. If you can't stand him that way, you need not bother. If he is not interested in you one way or another, he will tell you that, too, in the most off-hand manner, but he is as true as the equator if he is for you."

sure that I have ever made it clear how I feel, and as you have noted, I am such a poor letter-answerer. But I feel deeply, just the same. I regretted the loss of that chapter. My love to your beautiful Fania. I must come to New York to get a look at something pretty when she dresses up.

With faithful feelings,
Zora

TO CLAUDE AND ETTA MOTEN BARNETT

Box 977
St. Augustine, Fla.
November 24, 1942.

Dear Claude and Etta:

Congratulations first to that luscious piece of gal-meat known as Etta Moton [sic] on her success. You see, I have been saying for years that she was a great actress, and I take satisfaction in seeing my predictions proven.

Claude, there is a rotten situation down here in the matter of the Negro Signal Corps School[1] that has been established here. Look, Claude, the Govt. was forced by pressure to grant this ONE AND ONLY S.C. for Negroes, and it is a mockery to all of us in the U.S.A. Not that the teachers are not good. They are. But the living conditions surrounding them, I mean this little jerk of a school without adequate living quarters, and the food and all is a scandal. I think it is worth your sending a man from the Press to give a look-see. There was a reporter here from the PITTSBURGH COURIER, but Gray (President of the little school) grabbed him by the arm and carried him through the buildings and never gave him a chance to speak to either students or instructors. THERE IS PLENTY WRONG!!![2]

[1]The Signal Corps of the U.S. Army was created by Congress on June 21, 1860. Albert James Myer, the first Signal officer, was the founder of the corps. The Signal Corps was responsible for army signal communications and provided the United States with the first weather service. Later the corps became a training ground for pilots.
[2]William Gray (1911–72) was president of the Florida Normal and Industrial College in St. Augustine, Florida, from 1941 to 1944, when he became president of Florida A&M College in Tallahassee (1944–49). Gray also edited the Philadelphia Afro-American.

I feel that something should be done because this thing concerns all of us. It is not the affair of that little grafter Gray. This is for all of the Negroes in the U.S.A. We are being highly insulted and mocked here.

Met Etta's cousin Effie Moton [sic] Goode of Mobile on the train as I was returning from making a speech at Frankfort, Ky. She got off at Birmingham. Said she had just left you and Etta in Chicago. We had a most pleasant visit together on the train.

More success to you and Etta. My best love to you both. Etta knows that she is one of my enthusiasms. She is two great artists, and the world will see it, too.

Most sincerely,

Zora

Zora Neale Hurston

TO WALTER WHITE

Box 977

St. Augustine, Fla.

November 24, 1942.

Dear Walter White:

Well, the Negroes have been bitched again! I mean this Signal Corps sxhool which the Govt. has set up here. It would be more than worth your while to look into the matter. Through pressure from you it w was grudgingly granted. Fisk, Hampton and Tuskegee asked for it. But it is stuck down here at the Florida Normal, a most insignificant school to begin with, and then there are inadequate living quarters for the men. There was a walkout last week from the dining-room on account of the continued poor quality and quantity of the food. The President of Florida Normal is named William Gray. His wife[1] has charge of the dining room. When the men complain, she resents it, I quote, "I dont like your attitude, and your tone of voice is not respectful enough to Mrs. Dr. Gray." Then Gray tries to make the men

---

[1] *Hazel Yates Gray.*

apologize to his wife. Four men who refused to do so, feeling that they were being swindled out of their $30 for board and getting baloney sandwiches and tea, he asked these men to leave the campus in sarcastic letters. I can get them for you. The dissatisfaction is <u>tremendous.</u> There was a walkout from the dining room last week. You must remember that these men in the Signal Corp are college men for the most part, and represent the best Negro families in America. And here they are stuck off in this out of the way hole, and being insulted by this insignificant squirt because he is president of o one of the most insignificant schools in the world. He is worse than Sheppard [sic][2] of North Carolina if that is possible.

Personally, I have nothing to do with it. I am only here in this city because it is a quiet place to sit down and write. But these men from all over the U.S. hearing that I was here, sought me out to meet me as an author. Then, soon, they were telling me thier troubles. It is awful, Walter. The Government, having been forced by you to grant this Signal Corp to Negroes, dumped it in this little hole, and felt that your mouth was stopped. Remember that this is the ONLY one for Negroes in the U.S., though the whites have several. I feel that the whole body of Negroes are being insulted and mocked. Please send someone to look into things. I tell you what is going to happen before you get here. Gray is going to grab you, or whoever you send, and try to keep you from talking to either the students or the teachers. THE PITTS-BURGH COURIER sent a reporter down, and he carried him through the buildings, and never let him out of his sight until he was off the grounds. Of course all he heard was what a great man Gray was, when in fact, he has nothing whatever to do with the Govt. project. There are Negro men here, approaching genius in the field of radio, whom the mass of Negroes know nothing about, but would be proud to hear of, but he not only did not allow the reporter to speak to them, he never even mentioned them. I am only giving you a <u>hint</u>. There is plenty here to find out. It concerns us all, and I really think something ought to be done. I would rather you come and look, or send a man, than for me to try to tell you.

Love to Gladys and the family. My best to you. I want to come up there, but transportation is in such a muddle I dont know when it will

[2] *James Edward Shepherd (1875–1947) established North Carolina Central University in 1923 and served as president until his death. Hurston attacks Shepherd in her essay "The Rise of the Begging Joints," a scathing critique of a certain type of black educational institution.*

be. I regretted so much missing Carl's [Van Vechten] dinner, but I had to speak at Kentucky State College at Frankfort the night before, and I could not get transportation to New York in time.

Most sincerely,

Zora.

Zora Neale Hurston

P.S. Gray further insults the men when they complain by telling them they had nothing as good as this at home. He sarcastically asks them where they got three meals a day before they came here. He assumes that these men, Mind you educated and all that, have come from hovels. They are most outraged and insulted.

TO CLAUDE BARNETT

413 N. Spruce St.
Daytona Beach, Fla.
December 5, 1942.

Dear Claude:

I had packed up my things, that is my papers to go down the Coast for some story material, and so the notebook with your address was not at hand, so I just tried the Defender office. Sorry for the delay. Your letter reached me yesterday, (Friday 4th) because I had come on down here to talk with Mrs. Bethune and do an interview with someone else, so your letter was late reaching me too. Will next Friday do as well? I will shoot back to St. Augustine and get all the material I can and have it in the mail by Tuesday.

Goodbye, Claude, best wishes! I am so sick with a cold for the present, that I feel like falling on my face and croaking.

Most sincerely,

Zora

TO EDWIN OSGOOD GROVER

413 N. Spruce St.
Daytona Beach, Fla.
[December 10, 1942]

Dear Dr. Grover:

Thank you for your beautiful letter! It always does me so much good to hear from you. You might not know it, but you are my good angel inside. I say to myself when I contemplate something "Now, what will Dr. Grover think about that when he hears it?"

I have assignments for several short subjects for magazines, and I am trying to get them all off of hand by Christmas. I have been in St. Augustine until recently, getting material for a piece of work at the suggestion of someone in Hollywood. Now, with the war and all, it might not go through. Here in Daytona Beach, I am getting the stuff for a big story on the days when the Indian river traffic was in its hey-day. It is monumental! I had no idea that it had ever been so important to the growth of South Florida, nor so colorful.

I sent your criticism on to Lippincott. Thanks <u>so</u> much for it. There is something I want to ask of you, though it might seem a bit immodest. Something like intriguing for publicity. But publicity is part of the success of writing, and so, on that basis, I ask you to go through my works, and send to THE READER'S DIGEST expressions that might go under the head of TO A MORE PICTURESQUE LANGUAGE. I would love to appear in that department which they conduct. They pay both the sender and the author for what they use. It is not the money that I want, it is the prestige.[1] I think that there might be something in THEIR EYES WERE WATCHING GOD, TELL MY HORSE, MOSES, and even DUST TRACKS. Maybe JONAH'S GOURD VINE. But since MULES AND MEN is folk, there might not be an original of mine there worth offering.

My very best to all the Grovers. I am working harder, and more consistently now than ever in my life. I wonder if Miss Eulalie[2] would

---

[1] *Senders received five dollars in 1943, ten dollars in 1944, and twenty-five dollars in 1945.*
[2] *Eulalie Osgood Grover (1873–1958) was the sister of Edwin Osgood Grover and the author of two children's books:* Sunbonnet Baby *and* Overall Boy.

consider working over a legend with me for a child's story. As soon as I can get some urgent work off, I want to come down there and talk it over with her.

Most sincerely,
Zora Neale Hurston

TO ALAIN LOCKE

Box 1502
Daytona Beach, Fla.
January 10, 1943.

Dear Alain:

You will never know how happy your letter made me. Really, I want your approval. I am extremely happy if Godmother is pleased. She is so sure and right in her judgments.

I can see your points about the ship. It just could not be done until the war is over. But I am determined that it shall be done then. I do think it could be a significant thing for all the world.[1]

I shall speak in Washington for the Zeta Phi Betas on Feb. 23rd.[2] Do let us see each other and run around town a bit, gas permitting. Of course I shall not try to drive up, but MAYBE we can get a taxi now and then. Really, Alain, I am through being a smart-aleck. You must forget that I ever was one and let us have some fun while I am there.

Some new things have happened to me recently, that I think you will be proud of. I am working hard now. I have tried not to go north this winter because I came back from California with sinus trouble, and raw weather gets my head to going. But I must go to New York almost at once for some interviews, newspaper and radio both, plus some talks with editors. I shall be back here as soon as I can to coddle my left sinus.

I want to meet the new writers you speak of. I think that it is a very good thing. I did not get to Carl's dinner because I had to speak at

[1]Hurston was interested in raising the former slave ship the Chlotilde. See Hurston to Carita Doggett Corse, May 29, 1946.
[2]Black sorority founded at Howard University in 1920.

the State College in Frankfort, Ky. the night before, and just could not get transportation that would get me there earlier than 8:30 the next morning.[3] I ached in my heart over missing that dinner. I saw your picture in the papers. Very dignified and impressive, old thing. Read your article in THE SURVEY-GRAPHIC and have it in my scrapbook.[4] It was very thorough, I think.

My best to all who may ask of me.

Most sincerely,

Zora

TO CLAUDE BARNETT

[February 4?, 1943]

Dear Claude:

Nothing has ever upset me so much as this printed thing with Douglas Gilbert.[1] It is so untrue, so twisted! My letter to him, immediately that I had the copies, tells you how it struck me. [This letter follows.]

Now, immediately that we sat down to talk, he asked me what I thought about the Negroes in Harlem who had been convicted as Nazi sympathizers. I said that I did not know about the Nazis, but as for Japan, what those men had said out loud, millions were thinking, and he might as well know the truth. He wanted to show me where Negroes up north had nothing to worry about, but I contended that it was everywhere the Anglo-Saxon set his foot. I mean race prejudice.

You will please note how disjointed and incoherent the article reads. You can see him cutting out, and substituting. He hints at some of the things that I really did say, but twists them into something else. I deny categorically that I ever said that Negroes were better off in the South.

---

[3] *In November Hurston had told Van Vechten that malaria prevented her from receiving the invitation on time. See Hurston to Carl Van Vechten, November 2, 1942.*
[4] *Locke wrote "Harlem: Dark Weather Vane" for* Survey Graphic *in 1936.*

---

[1] *Journalist for the* New York World-Telegram. *Gilbert had quoted Hurston—misquoted her, she insisted—as saying that "the Jim Crow system works." She denied the statement, but it touched off a firestorm of criticism in the black press.*

Perhaps that is his own sentiments. Neither did I approve of segregation in the South or anywhere else. I said that it was frankly established.

He did do me a favor, which I hate not to acknowledge. He made me a fine contact with Guthrie McClintic.[2] Having done that, he probably felt that he would make me pay for it by putting all he wanted to say in my mouth. I am positively ill over it. I know how impossible it is to get a retraction from a newspaper. I merely feel like dying, since I can get no chance to kill him. At any rate, the iron has entered my soul. I am now a bitter person where once I had tolerance. So I send along to you a copy of my letter to him, so that you can know what really went on.

Sincerely yours,
Zora.
Zora Neale Hurston

But one thing is definite. The iron has entered my soul. Since my god of tolerance has forsaken me, I am ready for anything to overthrow Anglo-Saxon supremacy, however desoerate. I have become what I never wished to be, a good hater. I no longer even value my life if by losing it, I can do something to destroy this Anglo-Saxon monstrosity.

TO DOUGLAS GILBERT

P.O. Box 1502
Daytona Beach, Fla.
February 4, 1943.

Dear Douglas Gilbert:
Yes, things went off very well with Mr. Guthrie McClintic, but I cannot tell you the details until it gets a little further. Then I shall tell you all the details the very first moment that I know. It looks good, D.G. It looks good!

---

[2]*Theater producer and director McClintic (1893–1961) was particularly well known in the forties for* The Barretts of Wimpole Street, *on which he collaborated with his wife, Katharine Cornell, as well as for productions of such plays as* The Three Sisters, Antigone, The Playboy of the Western World, Antony and Cleopatra, *and* Medea.

Now, I have the three copies of the interview with you at the Algonquin Hotel.[1] I know that there is a scarcity of space in your justly distinguished daily,[2] and I am sure that you had to exert yourself to get me in at all. Perhaps that is why you had to foreshorten it so much. But what appears does not give what I was really trying to say.

For instance, you remember that I said that I did not see the business of race prejudice as a sectional one; that there was plenty of race prejudice both north and south, but that the South by opportunity of long practise, had worked out a system, while the North, caught between its declarations of no prejudice, and its actual feelings when the situation was up to northern communities was groping around for the same thing, but with fine phrases. I told you how I laughed to myself watching northerners, after saying to Negro individuals how distressed they were about the awful conditions down South, trying to keep Negroes from too close a contact with themselves. The South, having been perfectly frank all along, was unembarrassed.

In the matter of segregation, I said that the Negroes had their own theaters, and places of amusement, sometimes owned by Negroes, but often owned by whites and managed by Negroes; that Negroes were happy in their social gatherings and had no more desire to associate with the whites than the whites had to associate with them. I made this point deliberately, because this "social equality" has been the red herring that white people like Talmadge,[3] who do not want Negroes to have equal opportunity drag across the issue to becloud it. Their claim is, that Negroes are eager to marry into white families, and so they have to exert themselves to prevent it. They know that this is not true, but it has been a useful cliche for a long time. Neither did I say that Negroes are better off in the South than in the North. What I did say was, that there is a large body of Negroes in the South who never get mentioned. They are wealthy, well-educated, and generally doing good for themselves. I said that the propagandists always talk about the share-croppers and the like, but never mention these people. I said

---

[1] *The Algonquin Hotel, at 59 West 44th Street in New York, was home to the legendary Algonquin Round Table, a 1920s literary group that included Dorothy Parker, Robert Benchley, and Alexander Woollcott.*
[2] *The* New York World-Telegram.
[3] *Eugene Talmadge, Georgia governor, had been a member in the 1930s of the Black Shirt Association, which carried banners proclaiming "Niggers back to the cotton fields—city jobs are for white folks." His 1942 gubernatorial campaign has been characterized as organized "racial terror."*

that they do not move north, because they are making good where they are. That they are respected by the whites of their communities, even highly favored, and treated quite differently from the uneducated and shiftless Negroes. They hold a sort of prestige in their communities, which they would lose in the North.

Then as I told you, I hate talking about the race problem. I am a writer, and leave sociological problems to sociologists, who know more about it than I do. Therefore, I was hoping that the phases of my work that we talked about would be the spirit of the article, instead of the race problem. I am frankly distressed that the race angle has been stressed. Perhaps that is not your fault, since I know that you feel my interest, and you know how I feel about such discussions, but editors and the powers that be will have their way. It looks as if a Negro shall not not be permitted to depart from a standard pattern. As I said, the nation is too sentimental about us to know us. It has a cut-and-dried formula for us which must not be violated. Either there is no interest in knowing us, or a determination not to destroy the pattern made and provided. We are even supposed to use certain sentences at all times, and if we are too stubborn to do so, we must be made to conform to type.

Perhaps my saying that the North was prejudiced too, was too far off from the norm, and too distressing after all the fine phrases that have been poured over us up there. But I look behind the phrases and see that Harlem is a segregated neighborhood just like any in the South. I have listened to the northern abstractions about justice, and seen the cold hardness to the black individual. Therefore I stick to my point that this thing is a national problem instead of a sectional one. As I said, in some instances, the South is kinder than the North. Then the North adds the insult of insincerity to its coldness.

What I say, in no way applies to you. I feel deeply grateful for your interest and your kindness. I shall always be deeply grateful, and yearn for some way to show you my inside feelings. But I do regret the abbreviated article that leaves out the real meanings of my words. It is only one of your thousands of writings, and perhaps means little to you one way or another. But it is highly important to me. It denies all that I think and feel. My stand is that the South is wrong, but the North is not guiltless. It is only a matter of opportunity and degree. I know that you must have fought for the space you gave me, and that I need not hope for another chance, so that I am in a deep blue mood. Death would seem so restful and kind. But I suppose that unity, or the appearance of it must be kept up in the nation. So I sing my goat song and be roasted.

As soon as I have more in Guthrie McClintic's hand, I shall let you know first thing. I shall keep you posted step by step. But I shall tell no one else. Being a writer your ownself, you know the superstition among us about keeping secret until a contract is signed.

With faithful feelings,
Zora Neale Hurston

TO HAMILTON HOLT

[Across the top is added (probably by Holt): "Grover, any thing for me to do."]

Box 1502, Daytona Beach, Fla.
February 11, 1943.

Dear Dr. Holt:

I thank you so much for your kind letter. Truly I am glad that you liked DUST TRACKS. I did not want to write it at all, because it is too hard to reveal one's inner self, and still there is no use in writing that kind of book unless you do.

You know, I had a lot more about Rollins College and Winter Park in the original script,[1] but my publishers did not like it. I wanted to show more awareness of what had happened to me at Winter Park, and my gratitude twrds several people there, as well as some in New York. But it was cut out.[2] Now, I look like a hog under an acorn tree guzzling without ever looking up to see where the acorns came from.

If things break right for me, I shall be down in Winter Park not later than Monday of next week. I have been planning to come for some time, but a trip to New York, and work has kept me plugging hard. I have much to tell you and Dr. Grover about new developments, and beg his advice in some things. This looks like the break I have been waiting

---

[1] *Hurston often uses "script" as shorthand for "manuscript."*

[2] *The excised draft—"The Inside Light—Being a Salute to Friendship" (Beinecke Library)—only mentions Holt in passing and does not discuss Rollins, although both Rollins and Holt are mentioned in the published version.*

for. The minute that I have real money, I plan to own me a home out in the woods somewhere around there. I love Orange County!!

Oh, yes! I met Mrs. Mary Montagu Burghley in New York.[3] She talked of coming to Florida. She is interested in writing. I suggested Winter Park, of course. With her British drawl, she asked, "Aw, er, that is the village where Rollins College is located, isnt it?" "Thats right!" I was glad that she already knew. "Impossible place!" the Montagu Burghley went on. "That is where that Hamilton Holt sort of throws his weight around. He is fearfully lacking in the proper respect, you know." So I take it, that you have not been properly impressed with a descendant of Lord Burghley, advisor to good Queen Elizabeth. I'll tell you what went on between us when I see you. I let her Montagu-Burghley me around for a bit, then I just turned right niggerish and let her figger that out the best way she could.

Most sincerely,
Zora Neale Hurston

TO CARL VAN VECHTEN

Box 1502
Daytona Beach, Florida
Feb. 15, 1943.

Darling Carlo:

Howard University is honoring me as its alumni who has done the most distinguished post graduate work. March 2. is the date.

The award comes off at 10:30 A.M. The banquet at 8:30 P.M.

You know I have no closer friend than you. I would love for you to come down and lend me the joy of your presence for that great occasion. It would do me <u>so</u> much good to have you with me then.

On Feb. 23, I am the speaker for the National Zeta Phi Beta Sorority in Washington, D.C. on their National Finer Womanhood Week program. I do wish that I could have Edna St. Vincent Millay with me then. I admire her immensely as a poet and a woman. She has sent me

[3]*Lady Mary Montagu Douglas Scott Burghley; someone—presumably Holt—has circled her name and written "Who Is the Lady" at the bottom of the letter.*

telegrams of encouragement, though I have never met her personally.
How could I reach her quickly? It would be a very fine thing for the
fine Negro women who will be present to know the genius Millay. She
fits right into my idea of a finer woman. If you know her address,
would you wire it to me collect?

Most affectionately,
Zora

TO COUNTEE CULLEN

Box 1502
Daytona Beach, Florida
March 5, 1943

Dear Countee:

Thanks a million for your kind letter. I am always proud to have a
word of praise from you because your friendship means a great deal to
me. It means so much to me because I have never known you to make
an insincere move, neither for personal gain, nor for malice growing
out of jealousy of anyone else. Then too, you are my favorite poet now
as always since you began to write. I have always shared your approach
to art. That is, you have written from within rather than to catch the
eye of those who were making the loudest noise for the moment. I
know that hitch-hiking on band-wagons has become the rage among
Negro artists for the last ten years at least, but I have never thumbed a
ride and can feel no admiration for those who travel that way. I have
pointed you out on numerous occasions as one whose integrity I respected, and whose example I wished to follow.

Now, as to segregation, I have no viewpoint on the subject particularly, other than a fierce desire for human justice.[1] The rest of it is up

---

[1] *Twelve years later, in August 1955, Hurston published a notorious letter in the* Orlando Sentinel, *entitled
"Court Order Can't Make Races Mix." Here, in response to the ruling in* Brown v. Board of Education, *she
wrote that "the whole matter resolves around the self-respect of my people" and that there was no "satisfaction" to be had "from a court order for somebody to associate with me who does not wish me near them." She
regarded the Supreme Court's ruling as "insulting" on the grounds that "if there are adequate Negro schools
and prepared instructors and instructions, then there is nothing different except the presence of white people."
See Hurston to* Orlando Sentinel, *August 11, 1955.*

to the individual. Personally, I have no desire for white association except where I am sought and the pleasure is mutual. That feeling grows out of my own self-respect. However blue the eye or yellow the hair, I see no glory to myself in the contact unless there is something more than the accident of race. Any other viewpoint would be giving too much value to a mere white hide. I have offended several "liberals" among the whites by saying this bluntly. I have been infuriated by having them ask me outright, or by strong implication if I am not happy over the white left-wing associating with Negroes. I always say no. Then I invariably ask why the association should give a Negro so much pleasure? Why any more pleasure than association with a black "liberal"? They never fail to flare up at that which proves that they are paying for the devout worship that many Negroes give them in the cheap coin of patronage, which proves that they feel the same superiority of race that they claim to deny. Otherwise, why assume that they have done a noble deed by having contact with Negroes? Countee, I have actually had some of them to get real confidential and point out that I can be provided with a white husband by seeing things right! White wives and husbands have been provided for others, etc I invariably point out that getting hold of white men has always been easy. I dont need any help to do that. I only wish that I could get everything else as easily as I can get white men. I am utterly indifferent to the joy of other Negroes who feel that a marriage across the line is compensation for all things, even conscience. The South must laugh and gloat at the spectacle and say "I told you so! That is a black person's highest dream." If a white man or woman marries a Negro for love that is all right with me, but a Negro who considers himself or herself paid off and honored by it is a bit too much for me to take. So I shall probably <u>never</u> become a "liberal." Neither shall I ever let myself be persuaded to have my mind made up for me by a political job. I mean to live and die by my own mind. If that is cowardly, then I am a coward. When you come to analyze it, Countee, some of the stuff that has passed for courage among Negro "leaders" is nauseating. Oh yes, they are right there with the stock phrases, which the white people are used to and expect, and pay no attention to anymore. They are rather disappointed if you do not use them. <u>But</u> if you suggest something <u>real</u>, just watch them back off from it. I <u>know</u> that the Anglo-Saxon mentality is one of violence. Violence is his religion. He has gained everything he has by it, and respects nothing else. When I suggest to our "leaders" that the white man is not going to surrender for mere words what he has fought and died for and that if we want anything substantial we must speak with the <u>same</u> weapons, immediately they object that I am not practical. No, no indeed. The time is not ripe, etc, etc. Just point out that we are suffering injustices and denied our rights, as if the white people did not know that already! Why dont I put something about lynchings in my books? As if all the world did not know about Negroes being lynched! My stand is this: either we must <u>do</u> something about it that the white man will understand and respect, or shut up. No whiner ever got any respect or relief. If some of us must die for human justice, then <u>let us die</u>. For my own part, this poor body of mine is not so precious that I would not be willing to give it up for a good cause. But my own self-respect refuses to let me go to the mourners bench. Our position is like a man sitting on a tack and crying that it hurts, when all he needs to do is to get up off it. A hundred Negroes killed in the streets of Washington right now could wipe out Jim Crow in the nation so far as the law is concerned, and abate it at least 60% in actuality. If any of our leaders start something like <u>that</u> then I will be in it body and soul. But I shall never join the cry-babies.

You are right in assuming that I am indifferent to the pattern of things. I am. I have never liked stale phrases and bodyless courage. I have the nerve to walk my own way, however hard, in my search for reality, rather than clink upon the rattling wagon of wishful illusions.

I suppose you have seen my denial of the statements of Douglas Gilbert of the World-Telegram. I know I made him sore. He is one of the type of "liberals" I spoke of. They are all Russian and want our help to put them in power in the U.S. But I know that we would be liquidated soon after they were in. They will have to get there the best way they can for all I care.

Cheerio, good luck, and a happy encounter (with me) in the near future.

Sincerely,
Zora

TO CARL VAN VECHTEN

[on stationery from Lucy Diggs Slowe Hall, Washington,
D.C., "The Capitol's Most Distinctive Hotel for Women"]

[March 10, 1943]

Darling Carlo!
Everything went off well except that you were not here.[1]
Writing you from Florida.

All my love,
Zora.

TO CLAUDE BARNETT

Box 150 2
Daytona Beach, Fla.
May 16, 1943.

Dear Claude,
Thanks a million for all that you have done for me. I shall pay back in anyway that I can. Here is something on installment.
It looks as if Hell is popping at Bethune-Cookman School. Mrs. Bethune came down for commencement (May 9, 10) and Dean Bonds, and a slue of others were mysteriously ousted. Both she and Pres. Colston dodge the responsibility for the act. Naturally Bond and the others require explanation of why, [finally—x-ed out] but none was forthcoming. I hear that finally a white lawyer was retained to get at the reasons for the dismissals, and summoned Mrs. B. to his office. She answered by hurriedly jumping the next train for Washington. I was told that Pres. Colston was not in town either.

---

[1]*Hurston had traveled to Washington, D.C., to accept the Howard University Distinguished Alumnae Award.*

Now, for the background of the business: It seems that the trustees have been "urging" Madam Bethune to resign since 1934. They said that she had done a good job in starting the school, etc. but that now, the school needed a man, and a man up on the latest in modern education. The school was "growing" too slowly. 30 years old and only 126 students. They were kept under a strain to raise money to maintain it, but not enough growth was shown for the school. One of them said to me "there is too much <u>Bethune</u> and not enough school." Mrs. Bethune refused to resign. Now it is 40 years old & no bigger.

With her job in Washington and repeated illness, she consented to resign if the board would give her $3000 a year for life and let her name her successor. This was finally agreed upon, so in Dec. 1942 Colston (who is a young man, born at Winter Park, Florida, 3 miles from my home at Eatonville and who was a former student at Bethune-Cookman, and whose wife is a foster-daughter of Mrs. Bethune) was made president.

There has been bad blood between Mrs. B and Dean Bond since 1934. He is a highly trained man, has made good in his job, and the trustees spoke highly of him. Mrs. B. feared that they planned to make him prexy. She tried to fire him then, but his salary was paid by the Gen. Ed. Board, or the Slater Fund[1] or something like that and she could not touch him. I think it was a day or so before baccaleurate Sunday that he got his dismissal along with several others. Daytona Beach is <u>seething</u>, Mrs. B's popularity here is at an all-time low. Student[s] swear that they will not return, and will prevent anyone else coming that they can. They say here that she fires any teacher who buys a home, and cited several cases to me. I cannot write everything, so I think the Ass. Press should have a man on the grounds if you want to get a hot story.

Now, Claude, I own a houseboat, the WANAGO, and it is open to you and Etta at anytime that you want to take a vacation and fish. It is a 32 ft. cabin cruiser with a good motor, sleeping bunks, galley (kitchen, to you) and everything in a modest way. Do come and visit when you feel a lazy spell creeping on you.

Note Well: About Bethune-Cookman. I am not giving you my personal opinion. I am reporting. I listen to Daytona Beach and give you

---

[1]*The John F. Slater Fund, established in 1882 by John Fox Slater (1815–84), a textile manufacturer and philanthropist, to further Negro education and uplift "the lately emancipated population of the Southern States."*

what is going on. Some of it I know myself, but I am keeping mum. But <u>there is plenty to see and know.</u>

Most sincerely,
Zora

Thanks for the clippings.

TO KATHERINE TRACY L'ENGLE

Box 1502
Daytona Beach, Fla.
May 16, 1943.

Dear, dear, Friend:

Thanks for your kind letter! I was as blue as the inside of a stovepipe when it came.

The boat is bought and paid for. Still needs paint on the inside and a little carpentry work, but it is livable. Plan to take it around to Sanford before next week is over. It is <u>your</u> second home, you know.

I do hope your Palm Beach engagement was a success.

Do be home Monday or Tuesday as I will be in St. Augustine one of those days. I must talk with you to get back my soul.

Most devotedly,
Zora

Box 1502, Daytona Beach.

TO MARJORIE KINNAN RAWLINGS

Box 1502
Daytona Beach, Florida
May 16, 1943.

Dear Miss Rawlings:

Twenty-one guns! I have just read "Cross Creek"[1] carefully and prayerfully. It is a most remarkable piece of work. You turned your inside light on there community life, and it broke like day.

Whether it pleases you or not, you are my sister. You look at plants and animals and people in the way I do. You are conscious of the three layers of life, instead of the obvious thing before your nose. You see and feel the immense past, what is now, and feel inside you something of what is to come. Therefore you are not pacing the cell of the current hour. You are free because you have made your peace with the universe and its laws. You are deep and fine.

You did a thing I like in dealing with you Negro characters. You looked at them and saw them as they are, instead of slobbering over them as all of the other authors do. They talk real too, and act as I know them. You have done a remarkably able thing with the Negro idiom. It is so accurate. I am so sick and tired of that black-face minstrel patter that is put out as Negro dialect. I am not objecting to the bad grammar but the lack of imagination. You catch the thing as it is. You note the "picture-talk" that is something of a linguistic heirogliphics. I am tickled to death with you, Sugar. I love [the—x-ed out] your description of the women's behinds. "Box" and "Shingle" and they fit the thing so beautifully. You were thinking in heirogliphics your ownself.

I do wish that I had read it in time for a book review. How I would have loved to have done one on "Cross Creek"! You have written the best thing on Negroes of any white writer who has ever lived. Maybe

---

[1]Cross Creek, *a best-seller, was published in February 1943. In January, Zelma Cason entered a $100,000 libel suit against Rawlings for passages from* Cross Creek *that Cason, an old friend, considered slanderous. In 1944, the Supreme Court ruled that if the charge was changed to "invasion of privacy," the case had merit. In 1946, Rawlings won a decision that Cason appealed. Cason won the 1947 appeal.*

you have bettered me, but I hope not, for my own salvation, so I wont compare too closely to keep up my self love.

You have cut the ground from under my feet in your description of the orange-picking. I was just about to do a scene, but you have done it too well to be repeated. If I had known that you were going to do it, I could and would have given you some dialogue from the groves, as you were up at the house and therefore, couldnt get it. By the way, there is an orange picker at my home, Eatonville who goes for who tied the bear in an orange tree. It is said that he is the fastest in the state. His name is John C. Hamilton. They call him "Seaboard" because he walks so slow.[2] (The Seaboard Railroad is supposed to be much slower than the Atlantic Coast Line.) He is about 35 and one of the most colorful characters I have ever known. I know he will die with his boots on, for he dares anything. I would not say he is quarrelsome, but if it does come to a fight, he wont take tea for the fever. His favorite saying is "If you pay your way on me, I'll pay it off." and he does just that. I would say that he is a human rattlesnake. He does not seek the fight, but he certainly wont run if it starts. No gun nor knife will back him off. "I dont b'lieve it will kill me" he says, and keeps right on coming. He really knows fruit, from seed to packing house, and he "cuts" (picks) fruit so fast that he can make one orange catch another one falling into the bag. All of the packing houses like him to work for them. He not only is an expert but he works regularly and is dependable. His brashness extends to other activities. He will try work and other plans that most Negroes would not try. He has initiative, so help me! He suggested, and helped me get hold of a great deal of the material in <u>Mules and Men.</u> He is a born bossman. Somehow, the others fall in and do what he says. His only hold back is that he is bound to pitch a Saturday night drunk about every month or so—not that he wont be on the truck Monday morning, but if you cross him, or he imagines you cross him when he is drunk, well, big moose done come down from the mountain. He doesnt use weapons, but oh, that fist! Some of these days, he is bound to come up head-pecked shorty. Before that happens, I wish you could know him.

Now, I have bought a houseboat.[3] It is 32 ft. long and has a reliable motor in it (44 hp Gray motor) and sufficient sleeping space. How I wish that we could explore both the Indian and St. John's river to-

[2]*Hurston lists Seaboard Hamilton as one of her folklore sources in* Mules and Men.
[3]*The* Wanago.

gether. I am not a bad cook myself, though I know that I am not in a class with you.[4] I go for hush-puppies too and soft-shell turtle, etc, etc. though I cant make good Hollondais sauce as yet. I never even knew there was such a thing till I went north to school.

Well, thats the crop. I do hope to see you soon. I am at your feet in admiration. I hope that you have a loaf of bread under each arm and standing on a ham.

Literary secret: I am getting fat just where a cow does under the tail.

Most sincerely,
Zora Neale Hurston

TO ALAIN LOCKE

On Board Houseboat WANAGO
Howard's Boat Works
Daytona Beach, Fla.
July 23, 1943.

Dear Alain:

Twenty-one guns for your magnificent job on the seventy-fifth anniversary of our Emancipation! Grand! Scronchous!

I am so happy about your part in it. It has the essence of TAO, which, as I understand it, is the stripping away of all externals, and reaching the eternal essence or primeval. I know that Godmother is a proud and happy person over you.

There is another job for you to do. There should be a comprehensive work on HIGH JOHN DE CONQUER. As I have said, there is a great confusion of John Henry and High John. The Negroes naturally, do not tell the white people all they know and feel.[1] But High John is

---

[4] *Rawlings's popular cookbook,* Cross Creek Cookery, *was published in 1942.*

[1] *An allusion to her theory of "feather-bed resistance."*

the real hero.[2] John Henry[3] is the story of an incident like the death of
Casey Jones.[4] But High John De Conquer runs all through our folk-lore.
He is really Brer Rabbit, the hero who wins by a ruse. Now, there are
numerous stories, which if you look at the bug under the chip, proves
him to be our wish-fulfillment hero. But I would go further, and corre-
late him with the world-wide [idea—x-ed out] John concept. Have you
thought about the fact that in every country there is a great John? John,
Jack, Jaques [sic], Johannes, Juan, Giovanne? There must be some spiritual value assigned to the name John. Note that even the fore-runner of
the Messiah was John the Baptist. The well-beloved was also John. No
John appears in Hebrew lit. until the Advent. Could not the name be
some secret symbol that has escaped our modern knowledge? It is
something to speculate upon. I think that with the definite magic attached to the name HIGH JOHN DE CONQUER, and all that is attributed to him, there is the symbolic naming of a _force_ universal that has
more to it than appears on the surface. With the stories (which have
been collected only fragmentarily) and everything else including implications, something really scholarly could be done. Hundreds of thousands, perhaps millions of Negroes in America are carrying about on
their persons a bit of root known as HIGH JOHN DE CONQUER at
this moment, and it is their most valued possession. What is more, I am
always running into white people who are doing the same thing. They
have gotten the faith from association with us, of course. The point is,
IT MEANS SOMETHING TO THEM. I mean the people who carry it,
are acknowledging some sort of divinity. I have done a brief thing on it
for AMERICAN MERCURY. But it is a mere scratch on the [service—
x-ed out] surface.[5] If you are interested, I will work with you on it. You
can do some reading on the European John business, and I will con-

[2]_In the glossary that Hurston attached to_ Mules and Men, _she provided this explanation of "High John":
"Jack or John (not John Henry) is the great human culture hero in Negro folk-lore. He is like Daniel in Jewish folk-lore, the wish-fulfillment hero of the race. The one who, nevertheless, or in spite of laughter, usually
defeats Ole Massa, God and the Devil. Even when Massa seems to have him in a hopeless dilemma he wins out
by a trick. Brer Rabbit, Jack (or John) and the Devil are continuations of the same thing."_
[3]_John Henry was a legendary freed slave who worked as a steel-driver on the Big Bend Tunnel of the C&O
Railroad, started in 1870 in Talcott, West Virginia. In the glossary to_ Mules and Men, _Hurston provided the
following explanation for John Henry and printed the folk song in the appendix, under "Negro Songs with
Music": "The story told in the ballad is of John Henry, who is a great steel-driver, growing jealous when the
company installs a steam drill. He boasts that he can beat the steam drill hammering home spikes."_
[4]_John Luther Jones (1863–1900) earned the nickname "Casey" from his birthplace, Cayce, Kentucky. An engineer for the Illinois Central Railroad, Jones sacrificed his life to save others by remaining at his train's con-
trols during a collision with another train._
[5]_Entitled "High John de Conquer," this essay was published in_ American Mercury, _57 (October 1943)._

tinue to set down what is in the mouths of people. All that mass of stuff which is yet unwritten. I think that we can do something enduring for the world, when it is all worked out and correlated. What I did for the MERCURY has no scholarship of necessity. Besides, the editor had to have it sugared up to flatter the war effort. That certainly was not my idea, but sometimes you have to give something to get something. So I wrote in an opening paragraph and closing paragraph as requested. You will see what I mean when you read it.[6]

Here is an idea for your SURVEY GRAPHIC. An article, taking off from the Detroit riot,[7] showing that the basic trouble of that incident and others of its kind in the north arises out of the false premise that northerners love Negroes, and that all the intolerance is in the South. I have been touching on it in everything I have done for some time because I have seen the tragedy coming out of millions of simple, (and not so simple) Negroes rushing north with the firm belief that all is permitted there, and finding it otherwise. On the part of the northern whites, they have carried over the phraseology of the Abolition struggle. Then, all Negroes were sweet, pure noble people. They knew nothing about them, many of them never having seen a Negro at all. The tales of the Underground Railway were thrilling and made the white conductors heroes. The doctrine of the "noble savage" was everywhere. Then came UNCLE TOM'S CABIN and typed the Negro for the North. Not knowing Negroes, they [sic] characters were real. So, they have the fixed idea that we should all be sweet, long-suffering Uncle Toms, or funny Topsys. When the real us shows up, there is disillusionment. Then the northerner finds that he is no more willing to live in close communion with a number of Negroes than the southerner. One or two in a community have the benefit of novelty. As soon as Negroes become plentiful, the whites clamor for a separation of activities. He has not even the tolerance of the

---

[6] *The first paragraph of her article reads: "Maybe now, we used-to-be black African folks can be of some help to our brothers and sisters who have always been white. You will take another look at us and say that we are still black and, ethnologically speaking, you will be right. But nationally and culturally, we are as white as the next one. We have put our labor and our blood into the common causes for a long time. We have given the rest of the nation song and laughter. Maybe now, in this terrible struggle, we can give something else—the source and soul of our laughter and song. We offer you our hope-bringer, High John de Conquer." The last paragraph of her article reads: "White America, take a laugh out of your mouths, and win! We give you High John de Conquer."*
[7] *This took place in 1943 and was one of the worst northern race riots in American history. It was sparked on June 20 by a fight over the city's segregated beach and fueled by outrage over the Sojourner Truth Homes, a housing project built for blacks but turned over to white autoworkers. Twenty-five whites and nine blacks were killed over many days of violence.*

South which has already, from long association, discounted our weaknesses, which are no more than any other human failings. He has never had any illusions about us to lose. So, the northerner feels trapped. He is caught between the folk-lore he has been raised on about Negroes, and his actual feelings. But so much has happened, including the Civil War, that he hates to admit it. So he takes refuge in saying that southerners moving north did it. This is ridiculous on the face of it. The Negroes who have gloried in the nort[h] are also caught, so they join in the chorus, "Them southerners snuk up here and done it." The truth of the matter is that the Anglo-Saxon is the most intolereant of human beings in the matter of <u>any</u> other group darker than themselves. Did the southerners colonize Africa and India, and put over the outrages based on race there? Were these slaveholders southerners in the beginning? No, they were merely some more English people. Slavery did not take on in the north because they were more virtious, but because it was not practical. It did not pay. Once a thing becomes profitable to a man, he can find excuses for it and justification in his soul. Even God tells him that He made that man to make him some money. The North is now suffering from the illusions of UNCLE TOM'S CABIN. It did a magnificent job, but the characterization certainly was not realistic. The North accepted it too literally. The reaction has set in since the first rush of Negroes to the north during the last World War. I think that the SURVEY GRAPHIC could with profit, check on the number of southerners arrested in Detroit (white) also how many southerners are on the Detroit police force. I am certain that they would find the number neglible. We are being foolish, we Negroes, if we let it rest as we have done other riots. We must comeout of our rosy dream that it is only a sectional thing. It is national, and we ought to recognize it as such and attack it from that angle. It is making it too easy for the government. All they need to say when they wish to exclude us from hotels and neighborhoods is to say, "I dont care myself, but some southerners will come along and object." In England, where they Jim Crow us in hotels, it is "Some American will object" when they are doing it on their own. How is it that these southereners can get so much influence in a northern community out of all proportion to their numbers? How can a few Americans dominate England? No, we are being played for simple fools while they laugh at the ease with which they can put it over. This cliche can be done away with just as the South finally killed off white men blacking up their faces and committing rape. Once, they never looked to see. Now they do, and it has gone with the wind. If a publication like SURVEY GRAPHIC would take the count, it would go a long way in fixing responsibility, and preventing like occurences. Once the hoodlum element in the north realized the "THEM SOUTHERNERS DONE IT" was not going to be accepted, it would give them pause. They use the Negro vote up there there to get into power, and then bar us from jobs and decent living quarters, and if there is any protests, riot, and terrify Negro workers away from town and jobs, and then laugh up their sleeves while they brush it off with folk-lore about the south. The Sout[h] is certainly doing its bit toward discrimination down here, but they are not pulling off that up there. That is a monstrous insult to our intelligence, or is it?

My very best to you and to Godmother, Miss Chapin and Mrs. Biddle.

With sincere admiration,
Zora

I said what I had to say to Eugene Lyons[8] about the responsibility of the North, and he did not like it a bit. I am beginning to see that there is a great body of northerners who sympathize with the South and want no corrections made. They have so long thought of themselves as holy angels as regards the Negro, that they object to being shown up as no better than the people whom they have denounced so long.

I am living on my houseboat now, and you are invited for a visit. I can offer you a short cruise on the river, but gas is so short that we cannot do much.

Z

---

[8]Former journalist, U.S. correspondent to the Soviet news agency Tass (1923–27), Lyons (1898–1985) authored a number of books reflecting his disillusionment with the Soviet Union. From 1939 to 1944, Lyons served as editor of American Mercury. In addition to books on the Soviet Union, he wrote on Sacco and Vanzetti, Herbert Hoover, and David Sarnoff.

TO BENJAMIN BOTKIN

Box 1502
Daytona Beach, Fla.
July 25, 1943.

Dear Dr. Botkin:

I sure do want those records I ordered. But since leaving Washington, I have bought a houseboat, and the darned thing has kept me as broke as a he-hant in torment. Having the hull scraped and painted, just painting, a few things done to the motor and bilge pump and what not. Now, I have done all the hard part, and I can keep some money in my pocket again. Soon one morning before long, you are going to wake up anf find a money order from me on your desk.

A.B. Hicks went to New York, as did most of the boys who sang in my group, around 1935. He married about the time I was going to Haiti. He is from Sanford, and I know that his mother died there about two years ago. The best I can do is to run down there and see his aunt and find out where he is now. I am sure that he must be in the army. I know that his signature woulf [sic] fly back at you if he only knew. He would bust his britches with pride. I will certainly get his address for you in short order. I was don south of here picking up some material when your letter came, or it would have been answered sooner.

NOW! That which I felt to say first I am saying last. I have the copy of the Seventy-Fifth Anniversary of Negro Freedom publication and it is <u>grand</u>.[1] Not only is the work well done, the idea behind it is worthy. Then too, coming at this time, it amounts to positive genius. Not that I am not conscious of many things still to be worked out for Negroes in America, but I take the practical view that we are here, and most of us have no intention of going anywhere else. So, we must find some way of working together in peace. I am one of those people who put up or shut up. The number of Negroes in the U.S., plus other factors make it foolish to contemplate taking up arms. Wholesale emigration is impossible. There is no other road but intelligent adjust-

---

[1] *There is no record of this publication at the Library of Congress.*

ment of conditions. Why go around putting out crap that you cant
back up? That is the surest way in the world to lose respect and become ridiculous. I have plenty of personal courage, so far as that goes,
and I certainly do not mind dying if it means anything. But talk, talk,
talk to me is about as useful as a paper boat on the Atlantic, and a lot
of hate without any activation just ruins your liver. I do as much as I
can by coming down here and making adjustments through personal
contact at the seat of difficulty. I know that there are some of my own
people who would not cross the Mason-Dixon line for all the tea in
China, sit up where it is safe and say that I am a coward for not staying up north and helping them talk. Sometimes I wonder if they really care about improvement or just like to use the so-called Race
Problem as a chance for publicity.

   With all good wishes to you and yours, I am

Most sincerely,

Zora Neale Hurston

TO MARJORIE KINNAN RAWLINGS

Box 1502
Daytona Beach, Fla.
August 21, 1943.

Dear Miss Rawlings:

   How I wish that I were not doing a book too at this time![1] I would be
so glad to come and take everything off your hands until you are through
with yours. I know just what you need. You are certainly a genius and
need a buffer while you are in labor. Idella is much less intelligent than I
took her to be. What a privilege she had![2] Well, it is inevitable that people like you will waste a lot of jewelry by chunking it into hog pens.
Even though I am busy, if it gets too awful, give a whoop and a holler

---

[1] *This may have been her novel about Eatonville, rejected in 1945. No known copies exist.*
[2] *Idella Parker, a former schoolteacher and Rawlings's maid from 1940 to 1950, published her own story, enti-*
tled Idella: Marjorie Rawlings' "Perfect Maid" in 1992. Parker remembered Hurston's first visit in 1940:
"Imagine this now!" Parker writes. "Here was a black author who had come to visit Mrs. Rawlings and had
been treated like an equal all day long, talking, laughing, and drinking together on the porch for all the world

and I will do what I can for you. I really mean that. I am already looking around for somebody who would really do for you permanently.

The WANAGO is berthed at the Howard Boatworks at Daytona Beach now, and I am living on it. It is very pleasant, but a little cramped for all the books and papers that I have. But I have that solitude that I love. All the other boat-owners are very nice to me. Not a word about race.

Really, now, Miss Rawlings, if you find yourself losing your stride, let me help you out. I know so tragically what it means to be trying to concentrate and being nagged by the necessity of living. Of course yours is not financial as mine was at one time, but still with the scarcity of help in these war days, it might call for all sorts of annoyance to just get fed and bedded.[5]

Most faithfully yours,
Zora Neale Hurston

TO EDWIN OSGOOD GROVER

Box 1502
Daytona Beach, Fla.
Nov. 7, 1943.

Dear Dr. Grover:

No, you did not leave me abruptly. What happened was that I had been offered pork chops for lunch in Sanford and I could not refuse to eat them and thus offend my hostess. But pork makes me sick. My insides were roiling all the time I was at Rollins. I ran over to Eatonville to take something to quiet my stomach and change my clothes. I laid down at Armetta Jones',[1] and when I woke up it was 9 P.M. Excuse it please.

---

to see. But when it came to spending the night, Zora would be sent out to sleep with the servants. This was not for lack of bedrooms, mind you. Mrs. Rawlings had two empty bedrooms in the house, and no one else staying in either one." A second volume of Parker's memoir, From Reddick to Cross Creek, *was published by the University Press of Florida in 1999.*

[5]*According to Rawlings's biographer, Elizabeth Silverthorne, Rawlings took Hurston up on this offer and Hurston took care of her for over a week.*

---

[1]*Armetta Jones, "Domestic," is listed as one of Hurston's folklore sources in* Negro Folk-Tales from the Gulf States.

I will be only too glad to write the review.[2] The honor will be
mine. I have wondered if I did right by not boosting Bucklin Moon.[3]
But the thing was so sordid it sort of went against the grain. Then too,
it gives a falsely morbid picture of Negro life. If his picture is true,
how does he account for the thousands on thousands of wealthy, educated Negroes? He solves that by just not mentioning their existence,
but they are here, none the less. I see no good in distorting a picture to
suit your own argument. His book is a non sequiter. I wish him well,
though. But that awful picture does Negroes in general more harm
than good. One might reason "if the body of Negrodom is that weak
and shiftless and criminal, no need to bother one's head about them."

Something happened in Eatonville that night that you would be
interested in. (you remember that I have been so interested in a Civic
Center or something to give the young folks something to do besides
hang around the shop (and fornicate.) Well, a group there, thinking
that there was something in what I have been preaching so long, have
set to work. They have bought a lot next door to the Baptist Church,
and paid for it. Now they are trying to raise money to build a club
house of some kind. As soon as they knew I was in town, they came to
me to do what I could to help.) "We want you to come home and
help[.]" "We're trying to do like you told us, and now since Captain
Hall[4] aint here to break up everything we start, we can get somewhere
if you will help us." "You can talk to them white folks in Winter Park
and get 'em to help us build. You got a talent for that." That is the way
they talked to me, and I was glad to see some feeling of making
Eatonville a better place for young folks to be—especially for girls.
Can you think of anyone in Winter Park who would do something for
Eatonville in that way? (Dr. Grover if you only knew how much it is
needed!) The illegitimacy rate is awful. When I was a child, the
Hungerford School was the social center. What went on at the School
concerned Eatonville and vice versa.

But after the death of Calhoun,[5] the growth of Hungerford
stopped abruptly. Its history has been sad since then. Truthfully now it

---

[2]*Hurston did not publish any reviews under her name in 1943.*

[3]*In 1943, writer Bucklin Moon (b. 1911) published* Darker Brother.

[4]*Captain L. E. Hall, principal of Hungerford Normal and Industrial School from 1931 to 1940.*

[5]*Russell C. Calhoun, founder of Hungerford School, in 1889, died in 1909.*

is considered a sort of reformatory by the Negroes of the state. They send the unmanageable children there. Some are the children of working mothers. Seldom one for real instruction. The reason for this is that money was not available to hire a really able man for President. The little men who have been there, have sought to give themselves importance by scorning the village. It is both my school and my town so I feel things deeply. The town, deprived of any <u>uplifting</u> influence has sort of drifted, but the School is in no moral position to call names. This is just to <u>you</u> and not for general knowledge. I merely tell you so you will see the necessity of a play place for the town, as we had to get a public school of our own because of the antagonistic attitude of the School to the town. You have to have the picture. The time seems to be past for getting together again as Rollins is with Winter Park. I wish it could be different. I wish that the two could work out things together. It would be fine for both. But I shall never again try to bring it about. I'll do what I can for the town, and no longer seek any cooperation from Hungerford. Under the War Recreation plan, could Eatonville secure a Center which it could use later for a permanent thing? It is in order, because the men from the camps around flock to Eatonville and have no place to go but the shop.

Armetta Jones (at the big camphor tree) is one of the most, if not the most energetic workers for the plan. She works for Miss Treat in winter and for Mr. J.C. Chase in summer. I know that you have no money of your own to spare, but are you interested at all in the matter?

When Mr. Chase talked to me the other day about Hungerford and the new trustees, I had two or three suggestions for cooperation at the tip of my tongue, but decided not. Because I am better educated & better known, I am bound to stir up jealousy on the part of the incumbent who would say I wanted the job. I did want to go back to him, Mr. Chase, after I talked to the folks in Eatonville and ask him to help us on the Recreation Center, but I feared even that. But I would be so happy for it to happen, and I promised to come and help get the work done. The matter is very near my heart. I want to see the town spruced up and made pretty to continue the Scenic Drive on through town. They will work for me, but it seems, nobody else can get the town to do it.

Most sincerely
Zora.

TO HAROLD JACKMAN

On Board Houseboat WANAGO
Daytona Beach, Fla.
March 29, 1944.

Dear Harold:

How nice to get a line from you! I was just being lonesome for New York and old friends.

I would have loved to have seen the Covarrubiases. A friend of theirs, Mrs. Katharane Edson Mershon, whom they met out in Bali was a house (no, boat guest) of mine for a month. She just left for California on Friday last.

Thanks so much for getting the name and the address for me. That was real kind of you. Send it along. I would really love to go to South America right now. Nothing would suit me better. I want to find out something down there.[1]

Well, I am having an interesting amphibious existence right now. A houseboat-cruiser keeps you well supplied with excitement. Now dont get any picture in your mind of the Astor yacht. Nothing like that. Nothing but a 32 foot boat with a 44 h.p. engine that will sleep two. Small galley (kitchen to you, you landlubber) and toilet that you can squeeze into and close the door if your behind does not stick out too far.

How is Countee? Do give him my best. I wish that you and he could come down for a few weeks this summer and rough it some. I could use two men to pull on ropes when coming into a dock.

> Most sincerely your friend,
> Zora
> Zora Neale Hurston
> Box 1502
> Daytona Beach, Fla.

---

[1] She may have already heard about a lost Mayan city in Honduras in which she would soon become deeply interested.

TO CLAUDE BARNETT

Box 1502
Daytona Beach, Fla.
June 3, 1944.

Dear Claude:

You just will keep on being a prince, wont you, in spite of the world being like it is?

I would like the chance at that radio program more than most things in the world. I have had two or three chances before, but they were not what I wanted, and I turned them down. On one, I was asked to write the same kind of Amos and Andy thing. They wanted my name to give the air of authentic Negro to it. I have always refused to take a part in things like that. If they want to do it, okay. But I am not going to go on record as saying that it is real. I may even think that it is funny at times, but not Negro humor. If we keep on sanctioning that kind of thing, there will be no place for either Negro actors nor writers, for the whites can do that well enough themselves.

Right now, I have been asked to do a play.[1] I am bogged down in it and wonder if I know what I am doing. New York seems to like it so far. I have my fingers crossed until it sees the footlights. If I can get somewhere with this, then next time, I mean to let myself go and do what I want to do in the Negro theatre. I have always wanted to wrap something stunning around Etta Moten. She is good in PORGY AND BESS. No doubt about it. But the story is not too true to our lives and I want to do something more penetrating.

Hope to see you both in Chicago before long. Until then, my most important regards and thanks for mentioning my name. When the play gets to the casting stage, I do hope that Mr. Stephen Kelen-d'Oxylion[2] sees Etta Moten for the lead.

Yours sincerely,
Zora
Zora Neale Hurston

[1] Polk County.

[2] Broadway producer and husband of writer Dorothy Waring, with whom Hurston collaborated on the original Polk County script. According to Robert Hemenway, "When Waring urged Zora to keep a 'sort of Gershwinesque feeling' about their Polk County musical, Zora's reply was 'You don't know what the hell you're talking about.'"

TO HENRY ALLEN MOE

Box 268
Daytona Beach, Fla.
September 8, 1944.

Dr. Henry Allen Moe
The John Simon Guggenheim Memorial Foundation
551 Fifth Avenue
New York

Dear Dr. Moe:

I have achieved one of my life's pleasures by owning at last a houseboat. Nothing to delay the sun in its course. Just a 32 foot houseboat cruiser that is nearly thewnty years old, but it is very comfortable for a workshop and I can have the solitude that I love.[1] The Halifax river is very beautiful and the various natural expressions of the day on the river keep me happier than I have ever been before in my life. I do wish that you could come and stay awhile. Here, I can actually forget for short periods the greed and the brutality of man to man. I have back my faith in the ultimate good that I was losing for awhile. Oh, how I want to believe!!

Another great and tearing desire is upon me. I am hoping that you can hit a straight lick with maybe a crooked stick and do something about it.

This is it: Mr. Reginald Brett, who has been doing gold mining down in Honduras for several years, is back in the United States for the duration. He and his wife made a long trip just to meet me, and urge me to come down to Honduras and do some research and write about the country. He says that nothing of importance has been written about it at all, and that having read our TELL MY HORSE, that he feels certain that I can do it better than anyone else, and that I would be more acceptable to the Honduranians than any writer in America. He tells me that he has seen an ancient Mayan city (ruins of)

---

[1]*Hurston purchased the* Wanago *in 1943, the first of her two houseboats over the next four years. Her second, purchased in 1945, was the* Sun Tan.

that no other white person has ever looked upon. The folk lore is plentiful and virgin, so far as the outside is concerned.[2]

Dr. Moe, you know me well enough to know that that information has got me just like a mule in a tin stable. I am pitching and rearing and kicking at the walls. I just have to go, Dr. Moe, even if I have to toe-nail it all the way down there, and take my chances on eating and sleeping, someway and somehow after I get there. But go I will and must. Can you, will the Guggenheim Foundation consider an application from me? I want a recording machine this time, and a good camera to take along. And while I am set on going, I would much rather ride than walk, and I would much rather know that I am going to eat than guess about the matter. Could you? Would you? My heart is beneath my knees, and my knees are bent in some lonesome valley crying that this thing be not denied me. I have applied for a renewal of my passport already, so as to be in position to take out at the earliest possible minute.[3]

My new novel is two-thirds through, and I am marching along on it night and day so that it will be out of my hands as soon as possible, so that it need not hold me back.[4] I plan to stop by Mexico City and hail Miguel Covarrubias on the way, and maybe intrigue him into helping me photograph. Outside of Rose Rolando [sic], his wife always haggling me to go Communist, and me being stubbornly unconverted, we are very fond of each other. I keep telling her and others that if I ever meet a Communist with a sense of humor, and a sentence he or she thought up him or herself, I will take the matter under serious consideration. Pooling material things is not so bad, but if I have to quote [a]nd repeat the same identical phrases, down to the last stress on a syllable as everybody else, they can count me out of the Party. I dont see what Old Maker went to the trouble of making me a head for if He didnt expect me to use it once in a while the way I want to use it.

Well, I see that the Chungking government is either walking out, or being abandoned by the Allies as unprofitable. It is all very sad to me, and will produce tremendous cynicism all over Asia, whichever

[2]*Reginald Brett was an English gold miner who worked in British Honduras. Hurston put great stock in what Brett told her and was determined, for many years, to investigate his claims.*
[3]*Moe wrote back that, at best, Hurston might be eligible for a six-month fellowship (fellows only being allowed two years of support), and suggested that she write up her program of research.*
[4]*Her unnamed and unpublished novel on Eatonville, some of which was based on material from* Mule Bone.

way it is. It is not out in the open yet, but you will see it come to pass in the next few weeks. I made certain predictions four years ago, and even told important government people what I knew. But they could not believe I knew what I knew. But I did. If we were going to fight Japan, we should have done it in 1937 instead of hiring Chiang Kai Check to do it. He was much more eager to expel the white man from Asia than he ever was to fight Japan. But somehow, the folk-lore persists that all darker people are ever eager to serve the Anglo-Saxon. Have you ever noticed how full our literature is of Latins, Asiatics, Jews, Indians and Negroes dying for love of the Nordics? Have you ever noted the stress on <u>faithfullness</u> of others to nordics? I often wonder if they realized what the "lesser breeds outside the law" would do if they only had the guns. I have noted the maneuvering in Palestine in the last two years and thought a lot.

My very brand new best to you and yours. I hope that you have a loaf of bread under each arm, and standing on a roasted turkep bosom.

Yours faithfully,

Zora Neale Hurston

Yes, I can speak Spanish.

TO BURTON RASCOE

Box 268
Daytona Beach, Fla.
September 8, 1944.

Dear Burton Rascoe:

I glory in your spunk! In your criticism of ANNA LUCASTA[1] you say some true things. You can see way into things. I have made that same point that you make on Dr. Overstreet[2], and infuriated at least

---

[1] *Philip Yordan's 1944 play,* Anna Lucasta, *was a Broadway hit.*

[2] *Harry Allen Overstreet (1875–1970), teacher, philosopher, social psychologist. Overstreet's progressive commitments to the working poor and labor issues led him to develop innovative programs of adult education. He published numerous books on psychology and, with his wife, Bonaro W. Overstreet, on communism, the Soviet Union, and the FBI.*

two editors who are "friends" of The Negro. I told them that their condescension in fixing us in a type and place is a sort of intellectual Jim Crow and is just as insulting as the physical aspects. In fact, it helps to bolster the physical aspects when our "friends" defend us so disastrously.

Now, I will pick up my points, so you can know what I mean. In their "Liberal" championship of American negroes, they seek out and praise [written in left margin: "every"] characters of the lowest type and most sordid circumstances and portray the thing as the common state of all negroes, and end up with a conclusion that the whites, and particularly the Capitalist whites are responsible for this condition. How sad is the state of Aunt Hagar's children!

Now, I freely admit that we can match the white race scoundrel-beast for scoundrel-beast, and skunk for skunk. But as <u>individuals,</u> not as a whole. They claim to be more "liberal" than I, and better friends of negroes than I, because they blame everything on white discrimination. They charge me with never blaming the whites for laziness and skul-duggery among us. I freely admit the handicaps of race in America. but I contend that we are just like evrybody else. Black skunks are just as natural as white ones. Them thats born skunks will be skunks regardless. But I also point out that we have just as high and as fine and industrious individuals among us as any other group, and that our "friends" do us a terrible injury to put us all in a lump. If our friends portray us as sub-human varmints, the indifferent majority can only conclude that we are hopeless. They have laid down the proposition that we have no ability to survive in this civilization. I know different, and you do too. We are every kind of people from high to low. In other words, we are just people. Let us take the responsibility for our share of ill-living as well as the praise for well-doing. Just let us be people. The Overstreets insist on seeing us as both moral and mental incompetents and then defending us from our "enemies." And they get mad if I dont let them defend me. As you infer, they condescend, and then are infuriated if I dont like it, which is just another way of telling me that I am incompetent, and ought to be proud to let them stand watch-and-ward over me, and pity me. It feels <u>so</u> good to them. I say, to hell with it! My back is broad. Let me, personaly and privately, be responsible for my survival or failure to survive in this man's world. If I can stand the pace, let me get all that my ability will bring. If I cant, then let me go down in jeopardy like the moon before day. For myself, I want no double standard of measurements.

In other words, if I am a skunk, I meant to stink up the place. I am no poor, dumb something blundering around with an odor tagged onto me by the all-conquering whites. If I am a walking rosebud, I did that too. I am a conscious being, all the plaints and pleas of the pressure groups inside and outside of the race, to the contrary.

I turn you some humble thanks for your understanding. Several multitudes of intelligent negroes are going to agree with you, even if they do not write you as I did.

Most sincerely,
Zora Neale Hurston.

TO HENRY ALLEN MOE

Box 268
Daytona Beach, Fla.
September 18, 1944.

Dr. Henry Allen Moe, Secretary General
THE JOHN SIMON GUGGENHEIM MEM. FOUNDATION
New York, New York.

Dear Dr. Moe:

I wish to undertake an inportant project, which is beyond my small personal means, so I am asking the Guggenheim Foundation to assist me, if it is practical and possible. Further, I would like to do it under the auspices of the Foundation to solve many problems of prestige that are bound to arise during and after the completion of the work.

From information which I have received, and which I have every reason to believe is reliable,[1] I wish to go to Honduras to do research in folklore, and to do some explorations.

1. FOLK LORE

A. Collect materail among the PAYA Indians, the most primitive in Honduras, and thought by some to be the most primitive in all Central

---

[1]This is the information received from Reginald Brett.

America. It [will] be valuable material not only as to the customs and culture of the PAYA, but as comparative materail on other tribes as to vanished customs among the more highly developed groups. Perhaps also, lost ethnic connections.

B. Collect material among the Caribs and the Mayans now living on Roi Tan Island on the coast of Honduras. Since both the Caribs and the Mayans have disappeared everywhere else that they were known to exist, some very valuable historical and cultural material may be collected that will shed light on problems that have puzzled scientists in their investigations. Since this small residue of Mayans speak Mayan, some words may be found that could be used as keys to decipher the monuments of the ancient Mayan ruins.

C. Work extensively among the Zambu Indians of southeastern Honduras. They have a very highly developed culture of their own. They have developed a language with a very large and flexible vocabulary. They have a highly developed system of Astronomy that is comparable to our own. They know, and have named all the principal stars and constellations that we know, and worked our an accurte calender, as had the Ancient Mayans. Their knowledge should be put in writing, and a dictionary of their language, and their lore recorded.

2. EXPLORATIONS

A. List and describe the large number of medicinal plants of Honduras. Some are said to be very remarkable and may lead to some advance knowledge in the practise of medicine.

B. Learn as much as possible about the mystery city. No one knows how long this group of people have lived in this place, nor what their history is. But this town in the mountains has been there for centuries. No outsiders have ever been allowed to enter this place, for any reason whatsoever. They even expel their own sick. I do not hope to enter, but if I can talk to some of the expelled ones, I plan to get a history of the people, and perhaps penetrate the mystery of their rigid isolation. They are a healthy, well-formed people.

C. Visit and explore the Lost City up the Patuca River.[2] My informant [Reginald Brett] has discovered an Ancient Mayan city never seen and therefore looted by gold-hunting Spaniards as they did in Yucatan and elsewhere. This town escaped all sight, and the ruins are undisturbed.

---

[2] *The Patuca River in northeast Honduras empties into the Caribbean at Patuca Point. It is interrupted at numerous points by rapids, most famously the Portal del Infierno, or "Gate of Hell."*

Only one white man has ever seen it, and very few Indians. It is hidden in the deep jungles of the Mosquito District of southern Honduras.

D. Visit the vast ancient and as yet undisturbed cemetery of the Ancient Mayans. It is a vast area of burial mounds laid out in perfect geometrical order radiating out from a central point. This sope also has escaped detection up to now, and most probably holds valuable artifacts that may increase our knowledge of the past. One of the great tragedies has been that the Spaniards in their looting destroyed artifacts, stones and inscriptions ruthlessly in their search for gold and broke up many valuable works of art in order to cart off the precious metal or stones attached. It would be indeed strange if no ornaments were found in the mounds. The discovery may prove as important intellectually as the finding of the tomb of Tut-Ankarkam. At the most disappointing, they cannot fail to shed some light. It something for an intact cemetery to be found. That in itself is a contribution to science.[3]

Most respectfully submitted,
Zora Neal Hurston

TO JANE BELO

P.O. Box 268
On Board Houseboat WANAGO
Daytona Beach, Fla.
October 1, 1944.

Darling Jane:

Just had a letter from Katharane Mershon telling me that you were back in New York again and had a new apartment. I was very glxx glad to hear that. I had wanted to get in touch with you so much, but was told that it was impossible while you were at The Four Winds.

Jane, darling, I want you to join me on an expedition. I want it very much. I am going to Honduras to gather some material that I am told is exceedingly rich, varied and so far, untouched. I know that you

[3]On March 29, 1945, Moe wrote that the Guggenheim was not able to grant Hurston an additional fellowship.

would fairly wallow in it like a cat in catnip if it is even half as rich as I am lead to believe. Some truly wonderful and history-making things which we may work on. PLEASE, do come and go with me, darling.

The bearer of this letter is Reginald Frederick Irvine, born in England. He is a perfectly balanced and grand person to work with. He is not one of us, in that he is not particularly interested in anthropology, but he is an adventurer, and interested in everything. That is, he has intellectual curiosity. He has a ship, the MARIDOME (Latin for SEA HOME) and he has consented to let me charter the boat for unlimited research in the tropics. He will be the captain of his own craft, and he is a wonderful seaman, and has sailed the seven seas. All I must do is see the ship through a paint job, some new sails, and things like that. Naturally, I must "find" the ship. That is, stock her with provisions. But it is a marvelously comfortable and stout craft. He can tell you about it better than I. We plan at least two years in Central America, which your Frank loves so well.

I have never wanted to do ANYTHING so much as this piece of research. I do not wish to put on paper some of the things we will have to work on. Some one else may beat us to it. That is why I do not put it up to the Dept. of Anthro at Columbia. I have sold my car and everything else I can spare to finance the thing. So you know how I feel. A Foundation is giving me some aid.[1] I am going no matter how I get there because I know that it is going to be epoch-making. I think that it will do you good to be off there with me working on something that interests you so much. PLEASE COME!

My deepest respects to your lady-mother, and to your Frank. Is he working on another book on Latin-America?[2] There will be plenty for him to write on down there in the next few years. I see things brewing.

Have you a motion picture camera now? We will need it badly.[3] I am trying to get a recording machine for records. Mr. Irvine is a good photographer and a good technician generally, and lucky for us to have along. You can be a lot of help to the expedition, as you know methods. Together we can do something that will make Dr. Margaret Meade's [sic] "SAMOA" look like the report of the W.C.T.U.[4] I have a

[1]*Perhaps she was counting on support from the Guggenheim.*
[2]*In 1935, Tannenbaum had published* Whither Latin America? An Introduction to Its Economic and Social Problems. *His next book on Latin America,* Mexico: The Struggle for Peace and Bread, *did not appear until 1955.*
[3]*Moe had already written Hurston to suggest that she try to secure equipment on her own, since it was unlikely that the Guggenheim would pay for equipment and, in any case, he could give her no answer until March.*
[4]*Women's Christian Temperance Union.*

line on some <u>truly</u> sensational material. Come and bring all the equipment that you can rake and scrape. You know that I know what I am talking about. All I need is time and equipment, and a good, congenial worker like you. Preferably you.

Most sincerely and devotedly,
Zora
Your Zora.

TO BENJAMIN BOTKIN

Box 268
Daytona Beach, Fla.
October 6, 1944.

Dear Dr. Botkin:

The old bloodhound is on a redhot trail. I have some information about some material to be found in Honduras that is amazing! Nothing short of it. 1. The Zambu Indians who have a high culture, which they had before the landing of the Spaniards. A language of their own with a large vocabulary, many arts ans [sic] sciences, including a system of astronomy which compares most favorably with our own. 2. A lost Mayan city which has never been gazed upon, either by the Spanish looters, nor the Archeologists who have been in Yucatan and other areas. Away back in the jungla and utterly untouched. 3. A vast cemetery of burial mounds, as yet unfound, except by an Indian and definitely B.C. in date.

So I have rushed to Dr. Moe of the Guggenheim with my information and my enthusiasm, and he is bending an ear. He advised me to do something which I was going to do anyway—beg you for the loan of a recording machine to take with me. Maybe I could even pay for one if you were to point out a good used one. But I want to stay in the field for two years, and naturally, I must hoard every penny I can rake and scrape, beg and borrow. From what I have been told, it is worth it. I may even murder up a couple of old guys suspected of having research money in their pants and not donating.[1]

---

[1] *Botkin wrote back that, because of the war, he had no recording machines to loan.*

I do wish that you could dash out of your office, combing files and records out of your hair, and picking data out of your teeth as you flee away down the corridor, and come with me. Even if what my informant [Brett] tells me is only half true, it is going to be worth that year or two out of your life. Dont be so sensible all the time. Go on out of your head and come along to Honduras with the project. I know that you would get excited with me at every new find. A man here [Fred Irvine] has a 27 ton schooner lying idle, and has offered it to me for transportation, a camp and a working base that is movable with all equipment always handy. Isnt that nice? Very little money necessary because it has sails, and the engines would only be needed when the wind failed. I am applying for my passport today, or rather a renewal of it.[2] I hope and pray that they will let me go. Somebody might beat me to it if I have to wait. Maybe some German down in that neck of the woods.

I do hope that all is well with you and yours. These do be times that take all you have to scrape up a decent laugh or so. I do not refer to the battlefields, but to this enormous pest of hate that is rotting mens souls. When will people learn that you cannot quarantine hate? Once it gets loose in the world, it rides over all barriers and seeps under the doors and in the cracks of every house. I see it all around me every day. I am not talking of race hatred. Just hate. Everybody is at it. Kill, rend and tear! Women who are supposed to be the softening influence in life screaming for the kill. Once it was just Germany and Japan and Italy. Now, it is our allies as well. The people in the next county or state. The other political party. The world smells like an abattoir. It makes me very unhappy. I am all wrong in this vengeful world. I will to love.

Most sincerely yours,
Zora Neale Hurston

[2] *On September 8, Hurston told Moe she had already made the application.*

TO JANE BELO AND FRANK TANNENBAUM

Box 268
Daytona Beach, Florida
October 14, 1944.

Dear, dear Jane and Frank:

Your enthusiasm does me more good than you can ever, ever imagine. These howling war years so filled with hate and lack of faith and illusion, plus the years of hate-urge that preceeded them have caused me to fear that all youth and enthusiasm had gone out of America. It seemed like a bitter old character sitting in a chimney corner. Finding another pair of live coals under the graying ashes has sent my spirits up.

But yes, any time that you can make it convenient to join up will be glorious. I thought of you immediately when the thing came to my notice, and I only waited until it took more definite shape. By the time you get there, I will have a camp established in the field, and some definite contacts so that you can plunge right into things on your arrival. I know that I can break the ground as well as the best in the business.

The date of departure is soon, but not definite. You see, the MARIDOME[1] needs a new coat of paint, some canvas for the decking, and some more for awning purposes so that it will be a nice sitting-spot. That will be important in the tropics, you know. You see, we plan to use the boat a lot as a permanent home. I plan to establish a land base up the Belize river, but the boat is home base. So Fred suggested that we take the MARIDOME down the Indian River about 200 miles to just above Palm Beach to a little boat works where it is not so expensive to get the painting done. Here in the Daytona Beach yacht basin where both of our boats[2] are berthed now, they do what is known as "push a hard pencil" that is, lay on all that the traffic will bear. We plan to lighten costs by helping on the paint job ourselves. I have learned to do a good job of boat-painting in these two years of ownership. I can use a blow-torch with the best on removing the old paint. Then sand down

---

[1] *Fred Irvine's ship.*
[2] *The* Maridome *and the* Wanago.

good, and put on the new coat with worship. It is much more crafty than house-painting. It is almost ceremonial. I know that Frank would love to be up to the eyebrows in the doing of it. It is really craftsmanship. So our going depends upon when the boat is ready, and when we get it "found". In case you do not know, that means stocked with supplies. Not later than six weeks at the outside, we hope. The panelling in the salon is warped and cracked, but we will have to pay a ships carpenter to do that. It is of mahogany plywood of the era before they made moisture-proof plywood. So it has to be replaced. Last but not least, I must have a white tropical wool skirt and Fred some pants of the same when we go ashore in places like Havana, etc. He says that the trip will be a failure if some beautiful Senorita does not smile on him. He <u>must</u> have the fancy pants. Maybe he is getting them in New York right now. So we plan to spend about $800 on the boat and supplies before we stand out to open sea. I already have commitments with publishers for stuff after I get there, so I know that I shall not starve. The hard pull is to get the craft renovated to go. It is utterly seaworthy. The bottom is as dry as your living room floor. Oh, if you two could only be along when we weigh anchor! Just the right company. There is a woman here with money who is so eager to go with us, but Fred says no for one reason and I say no for another. He says no because she i[s] sentimental about him, and he wants no committments. He wants to be free in his mind. Impersonal relationships. I dont want her to go because I know that she is not interested in the things that you and I would be, and that she would become a problem on our hands. She would be scared of the "natives" and want to hang around the capitol and the foreign colony. That would be all right if she would cut loose altogether, but she wouldnt. She would make us feel "guilty" of neglect and things like that. Moreover, she is a damned imperialist and would flap her big mouth and turn the Indians and perhaps all the Honduranians against us. I have had that terrible thing to happen to me in the field right here in the United States. The wrong person along. One bray, and months of build-up torn down. I know that Latin America is not too fond of Americans. It is going to call for months of careful behavior. A Honduranian tells me that being a mixed-blood will be in my favor. The President himself is part Negro.[5] But even so, I am taking no chances on makeing mess-up.

[5]*Tiburcio Carías Andino was president of Honduras in the thirties and forties.*

Yes, I do plan to come to New York, perhaps in the next two weeks. I want to see and talk to Dr. Moe at the Guggenheim, and Mr. Paul Fejos at the Viking Fund.[4] Then, I want to see you very, very much. We will have to talk and TALK!

How on earth could you, Jane, lose confidence in yourself? It is <u>amazing!</u> With looks, brains, talents, place and money, I cant see how it could happen. I have nothing but some talent, and I feel mighty fine. Let the world look out for itself. On guard! I am attacking and attacking! You have the world in a jug with the stopper in your hand. All of the things I mentioned, and then love of a good, brilliant, attractive man besides. What more in this world is there to have? Three weeks shame on you! Go bag your head!

Oh, yes, you will have a kindred spirit in the arts. Fred Irvine does water colors. He is very eager to get on with it. He has no formal training, and you could help him out. What I have seen of his work looks very promising.

All tired between the shoulder blades from all night typing,

with faithful feelings,
Your Zora

TO JANE BELO AND FRANK TANNENBAUM

Box 268
Daytona Beach, Fla.
October 18, 1944.

Dear, dear Jane and Frank:

A brief note to let you know that my informant about Honduras is in New York. I just had a note from him there. I do not know where he is staying, but New York being so crowded, he is probably staying in a tree in the park, and giving the address where he can be reached C/o N.L. Bowen, 20 Pine Street.

[4] *The Wenner-Gren Foundation for Anthropological Research, Inc., is a private foundation supporting research in all branches of anthropology. Created and endowed in 1941 as the Viking Fund, Inc., by Axel Leonard Wenner-Gren, the foundation aims to encourage innovative research and foster the development of an international community of anthropologists.*

If you can talk with him, he will tell you much more than I could in a letter. He has spent most of his life in Central and South America, and I know that Frank will have many questions to ask him, as Brett is persona grata down there and knows a great deal more than most Americans who have been down. He is a mining engineer, and took his degree in Chile, I believe. He has a very keen mind, and though his principal interest is mining, he is interested in the customs, politics and the like of the countries. He is the only man, so far as he knows, who has seen this lost city of the Mayas up the Petuca [sic] River, which was probably built before Christ, and has been deserted for more than a thousand years at least. But he will tell you a hundred things, many very, very interesting to us anthropologists. If we can just get a chance to be the first to work on it, we will have the world by the ears. You, Jane, will never have cause again to lose confidence in yourself. Irvine has the boat we want, but knows nothing except what Brett has told him off-hand about the place. But Brett knows and knows and knows! Irvine is handdy to have along, too, and interesting.

A tropical hurricane is raging, and this boat is rearing and pitching like a mule in a tin stable. But I am not distressed. The boat is sound. I like violent aspects of nature, (if I am safe.)

I have some legal business that will take a few days, then I hope to take off for New York.

My best love to you and a pretty bunch of grapes besides.

Most warmly,

Zora

[on Brett's business card, attached to this letter:]
Reginald A. Brett, E.M.
Tegucigalpa, Honduras

[crossed out:]
194 Rivo Alto Canal
Zone 3
Long Beach, California

c/o N. L. Bowen
20 Pine Street.
New York City.
October 14-1944.

TO HENRY ALLEN MOE

Box 268
Daytona Beach, Fla.
October 18, 1944.

[written across the top:] Tropical hurricane is raging, and this boat is pitching rearing like a mule in a tin stable. Z

Dear Dr. Moe:

I fully intended writing you a personal letter before now, but what with getting my tonsils out, getting over the operation, and work and every day living, I am away behind my intentions.

Thank you so much for your interest. I thank you in a most particular manner. If I had a pretty, pretty bunch of grapes, I would send them to you to eat all by yourself.

My informant about Honduras, is Mr. Reginald Brett, E.M. I had a letter from him today, and find that he is in New York now. I do not know where he is staying (probably in a tree in the park if New York is half as crowded as I hear it is) but he can be reached C/o N. L. Bowen, 20 Pine Street, New York. I think that he will be there for two or three weeks more, seeing something about his mines. I think that it would be very interesting to you to talk with him.

He tells me something else that is interesting. It seems that Guggenheim-Rosario is the power that be in Honduras. I know that the Guggenheim Mining interests have nothing to do with your end of the Guggenheim, but it is interesting. I shall certainly go to see that firm as soon as I get there. Mr. Brett tells me that Guggenheim is the government down there. If they approve, you are all right. If not, you had better find out where the national border is located.

Now, if the State Department okays my passport, nothing would please me more than for you to rush out of 551 Fifth Avenue, combing applications out of your hair, and picking data out of your teeth, and jump on the boat with me, and be off to the tropics. Maybe go barefooted, and not care whether any artists or scientists got to Paris or not.

If you looked down and got too self-conscious about your bare toes, you could tie a bow of red ribbon on a toe or so and call your self in ceremonial dress. Dont be surprised if I do a trick like that. Bananas can get so they taste real good if you get good and empty. I know what I am talking about. It is bad when you have too much to eat. It gets so nothing tastes exciting anymore. Once in Haiti, I was very hungry and came upon a crowd of folks in a little town sitting around a pot of yellow corn meal mush seasoned with a little brown sugar. Not really refined brown sugar. It is raw sugar. I put down five cents Haitian and got into the scramble. My, my! It tasted good! My appetite put the rest of the flavor in. I have an awful fear that maybe something might keep me from going. Oh, Lord, I hope not.

Anyway, it is not right for you to be always fixing it so others can go off and work out their dreams, and you never go. I propose a fund to provide fund-secretaries-generals to go and see some of the places they make possible for artists and scientists to go. Maybe the artists themselves should make up a fund like that. Then I will pass on your application to go off somewhere and dream.

Most sincerely,
Zora

[written on left side:] I am doing my best to come to New York before Nov. 15

TO CARL VAN VECHTEN

Jungle Trail Farm
Holly Hill, Fla.
December 10, 1944.

Dear Carl:

What can I say to put form to my feelings? I have thought and thought. I love you very dearly. If in my struggle with life and the press of the moment, I seemed to be indifferent to you, it was less than a mist upon the surface of things.

I have learned to know that the thing we call misunderstanding—that blind bumping of one vessel against the other as they grope for nearness, is the greates tragedy of humanity. Of all animate life. This cosmic blindness that prevents even the very near from being clearly seen. That is when it hurts most. One feels the futility of life when even those closest to one cannot be clearly seen.

With sincere feelings,
Zora

TO J.A. [JACK ANDERSON?]

[1943/1944]

Dear J.A.:

Do come to see me. The boat[1] is at Daytona Beach now. It is at the Howard Boat Works. You come in on Ridgewood Avenue. When you get to Fairview Ave. Turn left and come down to Beach. At Beach, turn left at Dutcher's filling Station. If you kept straight ahead, you would cross the Main Street Bridge, so turn left of the filling station and come about ½ mile and you will see the sign, just as you cross a small bridge over the Canal. The Wanago is lying in the Canal. Park inside the Boat Works grounds, and either ask at the office, or come on through that door that says KEEP OUT EXCEPT BOAT OWNERS AND CREWS. Come on down to the last stringpiece and out the door and you will be standing right by the WANAGO. I will be home every week end except this present one.

The divorce ought to come through in a week or so now. I am working on it hard.[2] It is going to come through, too. His being in the army held me up some.

Be looking for you and the others you mentioned. Dont worry about the race angle. It will be all right.

Most sincerely,
Zora

[1] *The* Wanago.
[2] *Her divorce from Albert Price was finalized on November 9, 1943. Her divorce from James Pitts was finalized on October 31, 1944.*

TO CLAUDE BARNETT

644 S. Segrave St.
Daytona Beach, Fla.
April 28, 1945.

Dear Claude:

Will you please [give the enclosed letter to the—x-ed out] distribute the enclosed letter through your ASSOCIATED NEGRO PRESS, It explains my attitude and motives sufficiently, I think to anyone who is reasonable. I feel this way sincerely, and I do not see how any intelligent Negro can feel otherwise.

Do me another pleasure. Please send me all the data on Etta Moten. Send me also any information you have on Negro women in the United States too, or tell me where I can get hold of any. I am asked by one of the Latin countries south of the border for a factual work on Negro women in the United States, and I want to make it as comprehensive as possible. I was suggested to them by Dr. Patterson of Tuskegee. Do, please help me all you can. I particularly want to be thorough on Etta Moten, because, first she is a first class singer and actress. Our best living one at present. I mean all around. Then too, I know that Latin America is interested in Etta Moten, and I want it full and complete.

I am plugging away on a major piece of work, with my finger naiils broken back from pounding on thi typewriter.[1] But I am happiest when I am at work, so no complaints.

My very best to you and the seductive Etta. By the way, some day I want you to write for me your emotions when you first saw Etta Moten. What part of you responded first? Your eye, ear, or, shall we say your libido? Or did they all hit you in a lump? It would make a good article for THE NEGRO DIGEST. Let me know how you feel about writing it. Of course, you will not stop at that. It would only make a paragraph or two. Let us know how you fared during courtship, and how you finally got the rope on the gal. The public would be interested to know. You might want to keep the secret to yourself, but plenty men would like to know the secret of your charms. You are intellectual, of course, have a

---

[1]Hurston was working on Mrs. Doctor, *a novel about wealthy African Americans. It was rejected in the fall. No known copies survive.*

charming personality, and physical attractions. But some others feel
that they have that too, but you got the inside track. How? That will
call for an article by The Etta herself. The two things bracketted under
A FAMOUS LOVE AFFAIR.

> Most sincerely yours, with thanks,
> Zora
> Zora Neale Hurston

TO W. E. B. DU BOIS

On Board the Houseboat-Cruiser SUN TAN
(P.O. Box 268)
Daytona Beach, Fla.
June 11, 1945.

Dr. W.E.B. DuBois
Atlanta University
Atlanta, Ga.

My dear Dr. DuBois:

As Dean of American Negro Artists, I think that it is about time
that you take steps towards an important project which you have ne-
glectaed up to this time.

Why do you not propose a cemetery for the illustrious Negro dead?
Something like Pere la Chaise in Paris.[1] If you like the idea, may I
make a few suggestions to you?

1. That you secure about one hundred acres for the site in Florida. I
am not saying this because it is my birth-state, but because it lends itself
to decoration easier than any other part of the United States. I think
that was why Edward S. Bok chose Florida for the world famous Bok
Tower. I hope that you have seen it, for it is a thing of wondrous beauty.[2]
And the thing I want you to note is that two-thirds of the beauty is not

---

[1]*Père-Lachaise is the historic Paris cemetery where such notables as Proust, Wilde, and Molière, among others, are interred. The cemetery is located on Folie-Regnault, was originally used as a seventeenth-century Je-
suit nursing home, and was built by Louis XIV's confessor, Father LaChaise. In 1804, the city of Paris
purchased the property and commissioned the cemetery.*

[2]*Located near Lake Wales, Florida, Bok Tower and its 128 acres of surrounding gardens are designated a National Historic Landmark. The stone and marble tower stands over two hundred feet tall and houses a carillon
with fifty-seven bronze bells.*

in the Tower itself, but in the surroundings. You see, Dr. DuBois, the very woods of Florida afford trees and shrubs free that would cost a fortune north of here, even provided they could be made to grow. Magnolias, bay, oaks, palms, pines, all free for the taking. Beautiful shrubs while not wild, so plentiful that you could get thousands of cuttings of hibiscus, crotons, oleanders and the like for the mere asking. And dont forget the beautiful, disease and insect repelling camphor tree which grows here so free and quickly. By the time that each wellknown Negro contr[i]buted a tree or two, you would have a place of ravishing beauty. Ceremonies of tree-setting, of course. You would, like Bok, select a site in the lake country of Florida, where thousands of acres are available and as cheap as five to ten dollars an acre on lakes.

2. That there be no regular chapel, unless a tremendous amount of money be secured. Let there be a hall of meeting, and let the Negro sculptors and painters decorate it with scenes from our own literature and life. Mythology and all. Funerals can be held from there as well.

Addition to first suggestion: In Florida, the vegetation would be green the year round, so that visitors during the winter months would not see a desolate looking place. For you must know that the place would attract visitors from all over the world.

3. As far as this is possible, remove the bones of our dead celebrities to this spot.

4. Let no Negro celebrity, no matter what financial condition they might be in at death, lie in inconspicious forgetfulness. We must assume the responsibility of their graves being known and honored. You must see what a rallying spot that would be for all that we want to accomplish and do. There one ought also to see the tomb of Nat Turner.[3] Naturally, his bones have long since gone to dust, but that should not prevent his tomb being among us. Fred Douglas and all the rest.[4]

You will naturally ask me why I do not approach Mary McLeod

---

[3]*Nat Turner (1800–31) led the most significant slave rebellion in the history of the United States. Some believe that Turner's Rebellion, which preceded the Civil War by thirty years, was the first battle to end slavery. Turner felt called to the mission of freeing the slaves through spiritual visions that foretold his role as leader of the revolt. By the end of the three-day battle in August 1831, Turner and his band of about seventy slaves killed fifty-seven whites. The counterattack in Southampton County, Virginia, left one hundred blacks massacred.*

[4]*Frederick Douglass (1818–95) was an abolitionist, reformer, revolutionary, and probably the most famous orator of his day. His transition from slavery to celebrated speaker, writer, and editor drew attention to the cause of slavery across the country. Some of his publications are* Narrative of the Life of Frederick Douglass *(1845),* An American Slave, Written by Himself *(1845),* My Bondage and My Freedom *(1855), and* Life and Times of Frederick Douglass *(1881). Douglass was editor of* North Star *(1847–51),* Douglass's Monthly *(1859–63), and the* New National Era *(1870–74).*

Bethune, since she is right here in town with me. But my objection is that she has never uttered nor written a quotable line, never created any art form, nor even originated an educational idea. She has not even improved on any that have been originated. So I think that she should come into the thing later on. In fact, having made the suggestion to you, I shall do nothing more if you like the idea and take it up. I mean, nothing that is not asked of me. I am no organizer, and I know it. That is why I have never accepted any political appointment, though three have been offered to me since the War began. I like to sit and meditate and go my own way without strings, so that I can say what I want to. That is precious little at present, because the publishers seem frightened, and cut every thing out that seems strong.[5] I have come to the conclusion that for the most part, there is aan agreement among them to clamp on the lid. But I promise you, that if you like the idea and go ahead, I will fall in behind you and do all that I can.

I feel strongly that the thing should be done. I think that the lack of such a tangible thing allows our people to forget, and their spirits evaporate. But I shall not mention the matter to any one else until you accept or refuse. If you accept, there is no need for me to say anything more, as that will be your province. If you refuse, then maybe Walter White and the N.A.A.C.P. might take it up.

Oh yes, the reason that I suggested so much as 100 acres was because it would prevent white encroachment, and besides, it would afford space for an artist colony if ever the need arose. You can call on me for the first contribution. If you came down to look over sites, I could save you a lot of trouble by driving you around to look, since I know the State pretty well. I think that I know where to get some mahogany from Central America for the inside woodwork of the building.

Your own mind can furnish you plenty of details, so there is nothing more for me to say except congratulations on your stand at San Francisco,[6] and many good wishes for the future.[7]

Sincerely,
Zora Neale Hurston

[5]This may be a reference to the critique of American imperialism that Hurston had to delete from the published version of her autobiography, Dust Tracks on a Road.

[6]In 1945, W. E. B. Du Bois attended the founding conference of the United Nations in San Francisco as representative of the NAACP.

[7]Du Bois replied that he was not as enthusiastic about Florida as Hurston was and did not see her idea as practical for him. He suggested that she contact Walter White. Hurston and Du Bois had been out of touch for nearly twenty years.

TO RUTH BENEDICT

On Board the Houseboat-cruiser SUN TAN
(P.O. Box 268)
Daytona Beach, Fla.
June 19, 1945.

Dr. Ruth Benedict
Dept. of Anthro.
Columbia University
New York, N.Y.

Dear Dr. Benedict:

Nearly a year ago, I came upon some most interesting information about material in Honduras, Central America, and I have wanted so much to go. At last, I have secured the money for a year of work,[1] and nothing happening to prevent me, I shall be going down soon.

What I want to say to you is, that from the information that I have, it looks like something tremendous, and to get out of it what should be gotten, perhaps you or you might delegate Dr. Klineberg to come down and take over. I want to look the thing over first, and if it is as I am told, it will be a monumental job that will require years to work out. I will let you know as soon as I make a general survey of the area, and instead of attempting the whole thing myself, turn over the direction to you, and work on some detail that you may assign to me.

1. The Zambu Indians, who sound very interesting. They have a comprehensive language of their own, and had worked out a whole cosmogeny long before the first Spaniard landed in America. They knew all the constellations that civilization has discovered, and had names for them. Many more details. And they have never been worked on. Their dictionary is still to be written. I understand that some missionary has set down a few words, but only those that pertain to teaching them about christianity.

2. What is left of the Caribs, and their culture.

[1]From the Guggenheim Foundation.

3. An ancient cemetery that extends for miles, and is not known about by more than three people even down there. It is in an area that is uninhabited, and for some reason, held in awe by the natives, who never go to that vicinity. It probably antedates the christian era, and it is not known whether it is Mayan or whom, nor why the area was abandoned. The Spaniards did not find this place and thus ravish it as other burial sites have suffered. The burial mounds radiate out from a central point and suggests a Mayan calender. This undisturbed burial site may tell us much that is not yet known.

I have looked up the publications on Central America, and I was startled to note that while there has been much done in Archeology in Central America, practically nothing has been done in Anthropology.

Where can I get hold of some instruments for anthropometry? I want to have all those necessary for measurements and see what we find.

If we do no more than establish their norm in that direction, something has been gained. And there are several groups to measure.

In the matter of artifacts, I am told that there is a great deal of material to examine. Further, there are jades found occasionally and there is none there naturally. There is a legend that the Chinese visited the coast regularly centuries before Columbus. I saw a jade axe, made for a left-handed person that was old, old. It was dug up while beginning a mining excavation.

My informant is a person who has no interest in anthropology. He is a prospector, and got to telling me of his work down there, and then I began to question him about things that I saw bored him to death, as he is only interested in finding gold and antimony, but he answered me as fully as he could, and he is a very intelligent person, and trained as a mining-engineer. Then I sought out some Honduranians around Tampa, and got to questioning them, and they confirmed all that he said independently, and without knowing where I got the information. All but about the burial site. They said that no one ever went but so far up the Patuca river as it was cursed country. It was not well to go there. My informant, not caring about superstitions, and eager for gold, ahd penetrated where none had gone for centuries. Perhaps the awe of the natives is some forgotten reason why the area was abandoned so many centuries ago by the people who left the cemetery.

I read with interest your publication that upset the brass-hats[2] so, and smiled. Facts go down mighty hard with some folks, confirming my conviction that there is nothing so precious that men know as what they <u>want</u> to believe.

My best to you and all who may ask of me.

There are several more things that have been told to me, but I will check on things and report more fully when I am on the ground.

Most sincerely,

Zora

Zora Neale Hurston

TO CARL VAN VECHTEN

[July 15, 1945—library dated]
On Board the Houseboat Sun Tan
(P.O. Box 268)
Daytona Beach, Fla.
July Sunday Morning, 1945.

Dear Carlo, Carlo:

At last I can write you a letter. I have been sick with my colon and general guts for a long, long time. And really for a while, I thought that I would kick the bucket. So I wrote to no one to trouble them with my miseries. I would take my leave in silence. But now, I am feeling fine again. The sun is shining in my door. So I take opportunity to send you my very love.

How adventurous do you feel these days? I hope that you are full of spunk, for I have a job for you to do. For nearly a year I have wanted and desired to go to Central America to get new material for a book. But first the money needed was not in hand. Then around Christmas

---

[2]*A high-ranking officer or official, a manager or boss. Hurston probably refers to Benedict's 1943 book,* The Races of Mankind.

my guts started to raising cain. Now I see the money, I am feeling fine, and my next book is nearly finished.[1] When that is done, I want to set out for the Caribbean. I have some wonderful information about things to find down there. I wish that you would come along with me with your cameras, and document the trip in pictures. Neither do I forget that you are a writer. There is a lavish of untouched material you may be induced to get up off your stool of do-nothing (as my mama used to call it) and write a magnificent book. But if you dont feel like writing still and yet, I would love for you to illustrate with your camera, the book I mean to do.

Maybe Fania would love to come along. It would be lovely and just all right. There is a boat that belongs to an Englishman friend of mine that has plenty of cabin room. He is an adventurous soul like me, and wants to go along for the pure hell of the thing. I believe that you and I could do something remarkable together. Fred's boat is good and safe, and he is a grand navigator and full of humor. Neither is he hard-up for spending change. I think that you and he would get along swell, as he has your own trait of sincerity in things. Straight and frank, even at the risk of being unpleasant for the moment, but a staunch and loyal friend.

I do so hope that you will feel like coming with me. Please understand that I do not ask you for financial reasons. That has been arranged for me, or I would not be planning to go at all. Anyway, the way I am going (on Fred's "Maridome") guarantees me always living quarters down there. If Fred (31 years old) can just find plenty of romance down there, he will feel that it is worth the trip. He is handsome, virile and as daring as hell. He will never be short of female company anywhere, so I took him up on that. But I have money for the trip independent of Fred.

With all my love to you and Fania, I am with

Faith and feelings,
Your Zora Neale.

---

[1]*Either* Mrs. Doctor *or the unnamed Eatonville novel she had begun to write based, in part, on material from* Mule Bone.

TO CARL VAN VECHTEN

[July 24, 1945—library dated]
On Board the Sun Tan
Box 268
Daytona Beach.

Dear Carlo, Carlo:

While I regret that you and Fania cant run wild with me, I do understand, especially after my own sickness. I am peculiarly acid too. That is why I have never drank. I found out that the tiniest bit made me ill. Finally the doctors discovered that I have a very acid body. Probably that way at birth. Alcohol makes acid, you know and I could not handle it.[1]

However, if I find the ancient site down there that I expect, I hope that you will fly down for a few days. It will be history-making and you must be there with one roll of film at least.

Captain Fred Irvine was born in England. Came to the United States when he was ten. His widowed mother left him and his brother in a school in England, came here, found work and remarried. Then she brought her two sons over. His father left some money. His brother died, and he inherited it all. He has been on the go since he was 18. Raised in New York. He has no formal college training, but is most widely read. He is not a pretty sort of a man, but handsome in a dark manly way.

No, I have not tried any of it, but it must be good, because he has mobs of girls running after him all the time. And I know Fred well enough to know that he loses no time with women unless he is getting some. I have not bothered to try it, because I am going off with him, and it could cause a lot of trouble in the end. There will be lots of girls down there, and he will be sure to try them out, and that would make me jealous. There will be lots of men down there too, and I am liable to run up on something that suits and that would make him fu-

---

[1] *In the twenties, she not only drank, but reported at one point to Van Vechten that she and Hughes drank up the gift of Chinese whiskey that Hughes had intended for Van Vechten. See her letter to Van Vechten of August 26, 1927.*

rious. He got rid of a man who was going down with us because I got very friendly with him. He claimed that Ludy was too stupid, but he had been praising his intelligence for six months before that. Ludy was very gay and witty and all I did was agree with Fred. But Ludy had to go! The very next day Fred told him he could not go with us. Fred is very resourceful and capable in many ways. He is a faithful friend, and could be counted on to stand back to back with you even if it came to fighting for your life. I have talked about you and your character to him often, and said how you would be good company, besides being a great photographer, and he said "He sounds like a man I would love to know. Yes, you can ask him to go with us. I hate bastards who beat around the bush about things, and grin with people they know they dont like. If he is direct in both his likes and dislikes as you say, he is the kind of man for me. What is wrong with calling a bastard by his right name?" Fred is so like you in so many ways that it is startling. By the way, he has great talent as an artist, though he has not done much about it. Carl, he can really draw, and without any formal training. He has promised to get to work down there and see if he has enough talent to turn that way for life. I know that he has it, and that is why I have taken so much time and pains to influence him. If he gets down to work as he has promised, the world is going to hear from Fred Irvine. It is good for him to be away from the night clubs and such for a year, and really find himself.

One man who envies Fred in several ways, came on board my boat and whispered to me that Fred is part English Jew. You can imagine the laugh I got out of that. In the first place, he knows nothing about Fred's antecedents. In the next place, what could anybody make out of that if he were? I knew that the bastard had race prejudice that must include Negroes as well as Jews, so I booted his hips right off my boat. I am colored, and so can not be a regular member of the Halifax River Yacht Club, but I have lots of friends in there and am invited to the Club House, so I got that guy black-balled when he tried to join.

> With love and kisses,
> Zora, Rex.

TO HAROLD SPIVACKE

Box 268
Daytona Beach, Fla.
August 21, 1945.

Dr. Harold Spivacke, Chief
Music Division
Library of Congress
Washington, D.C.

Dear Harold Spivacke:

No, I have not got a recording machine, and that is one of my main worries. I tried to get hold of one months ago, but was told[1] that owning to the War, none were available either by purchase nor borrowing. That is very serious, because I have information of a tremendously rich field in music. (a) Zambu Indian. (b) Other Indian groups; (c) Carib (D) Carib-Negro; (e) Negro (f) Old Spanish background music.

In other ways, tales, customs, cosmology, ethnology, etc. Honduras, if my information is only half true, is the richest field that I have ever heard of. And it has not been worked. I looked up the field when I was in New York last fall, and it has hardly been touched. So I am doing all I can to get enough funds to work on. I am no longer eligible for a Guggenheim, so I am having to save up my own personal funds. It promises well for me, because the family of the President of Honduras is in my corner, and want me to come and work there. Frankly, they say that they would prefer me to a "Gringo" who would come down, patronize them and act superior in other ways. So I am burning down with eagerness to be off. I am just as sure that I am going to make history as I am that I am black. (Well, if not really black, of that denomination, so to speak.) And I am going to build you up a collection for your Department that you are going to be proud of. I dearly love research. I have no idea that I am ever going to be rich, and to tell you the truth, I am not at all concerned aout it. Just let me collect and

[1]*By Benjamin Botkin.*

set down some greaat work in my field, and I will die laughing happily. To supplement my funds, I have arrangements with two magazines for articles.[2]

My best to you, and thanks for your encouragement. I hope to hear of you, not only as a great administrator in your work, the greatest ever, but that you have a whole ham in your frigidaire, and a big turkey with a full bosom in your oven. It could happen you know, now that the War is over somewhat.

Most sincerely, and respectfully,
Zora Neale Hurston

TO CARL VAN VECHTEN

The Sun Tan
Box 268
Daytona Beach, Fla
September 12, 1945.

Dear, dear Carlo:

Oh, how I do wish that you would go to Honduras with me! Your company would be such a pleasure to me. But there is another important consideration. You have made important contributions to American literature, and I see no reason why you should stop writing as you have done. I can see that you might not be interested in doing the same kinds of books that you have done, and want a fresh turn. Except the people who write for the delight of stenographers, and who do the same sort of thing all the time with just a change of title, talent requires new food. Hence the roving and the wide scope of Somerset Maugham. So I planned to lure you down there in pastures new, and intrigue you to write again. I wish that with all my heart. You ought to write some more.[1]

---

[2] *These may have been travel articles; they may have been more articles for* Negro Digest *or* American Mercury, *where Hurston had been successfully placing essays. "Crazy for this Democracy" was published by* Negro Digest *in December 1945.*

[1] *Much of Van Vechten's time was now devoted to building up the James Weldon Johnson Collection at the Beinecke Library at Yale and to his work in photography, which had largely supplanted his writing.*

I have not gotten off myself because I have done a book for Lippincott, and I have not had as yet the editorial suggestions for possible changes and I would like that to be off my hands before I go.[2] I am waiting to hear from Tay Hohoff in the New York office [of Lippincott's]. I wanted to do a serious one on the upper strata of Negro life, and had it two-thirds done, when I think Lippincott, (timid soul) decided that the American public was not ready for it yet.[3] So I have done a book on my native village, starting with the material of Mule Bone and weaving a story about a village youth expelled from town by village politics going places, including Heaven and Hell and having adventures, and returning after seven years to achieve his childhood ambition of being a fireman on the railroad, and the town hero.[4]

But the story I am burning to write is one that will be highly controversial. I want to write the story of the 3000 years struggle of the Jewish <u>people</u> for democracy and the rights of man.[5] You know, Carl, the Christian world reads the Bible with their prejudices, and not with their eyes. The story is right there. Beginning with Sinai, and on to the final destruction of Jerusalem by the Roman emperor Titus (only he was not emperor until later) there was one long and continuous struggle of the people against the arbitrary rule of the priesthood. And from Exodus on to the fall of the Capitol City, the priests have nothing but denunciation for the people. They are "stiff-necked" "generation of evil people" "generation of vipers" all sorts of curses and maledictions are hurled at them for not adhering to the Laws. But nobody seems to consider that the Hebrews did not value those laws, nor did they ask for that new religion that Moses forced on them by terror and death. Moses was responsible for the actual death of at least a half million of the people in his efforts to force his laws upon them. 3,000 were slaughtered right at Sinai in the very beginning. It went on and on. It is all too evident that Moses did not care a fig for those Hebrew people. Moses had worked out an idea for a theocratic government, and the Hebrews were just so the available laboratory material. I am convinced that he thoroughly hated them after Sinai, if not before. At no time in the five books attributed to him, does he link him-

---

[2] *Her unnamed novel on Eatonville. No manuscript survives.*
[3] *Mrs. Doctor, never published. No manuscript survives.*
[4] *Either an early version of* The Lives of Barney Turk *or her unnamed Eatonville novel, the manuscript of which was eventually rejected. According to Robert Hemenway, Lippincott found it both sloppy and strained.*
[5] *Her plan for a history of* Herod the Great. *This book would be the focus of much of Hurston's energy for the rest of her life.*

self with them in any way except as dictator. He says "these people" and to God "thy people." <u>Never</u> "my people." He ordered them not to marry outside of the Hebrews, and slaughtered many of them for doing so. Yet he himself was married to a Mideanite Princess when he led the people out of Egypt, and later married an Ethopian woman. In every move, he shows himself as feeling superior to the people, and his scorn of them. There is not one word of love anywhere. Even in his last address to them he spends most of his time heaping curses upon them and making dire predictions. Arbitrarily, he places his stooge, Aaron, his family and tribe over the people <u>forever</u>. It is interesting to note in all the long history of the nation how few Levites ever distinguished themselves. King Saul was of Benjamin. David of Judah. Joshua of Ephraim. Herod the Great was an Idumean (descendant of Esau, and not strictly a Jew) No one but the Levites were allowed to learn to read and write. No one was allowed to write a book except the Levites. So that in 3000 years you have only 22 books! Think of that! And in all of them the Levites are reviling the people for not being obedient to them. We have no written side of the people other than the direct testimony of their behavior recorded by their oppressors. And as one artist to another, you and I cannot but weep over the countless thousands of Jewish geniuses who must have lived and died unheard. Writers, painters, sculptors, philosophers, etc. If we consider the great amount of genius displayed among the remnant of the race that is left to the world, how much more must have perished when the race and nation were numerous? It is indeed a great loss to the world. It is comparable to the loss to the world in the Middle Ages when the Christian Church had gotten a strangle hold on Europe. In the book I plan to set the struggle in Judea against like things in Greece, the Roman Empire, England, Europe and show that instead of the Jewish people being a peculiarly evil and hard-headed race of people, doomed by God to suffer and be hated, that they were just people, fighting for all those things which other people hold sacred and conducing to the rights and dignity of man. We gloat over our own Reformation and freedom from the domination of the Catholic Church when it had and exercised temporal power, yet our Sunday School lessons teach us to regard the same instincts in the Jews as evil, thus justifying any evil & suffering that they have had and further that any imposed upon them at present or in the future as being what they have coming to them for "disobedience to God." When in reality it was a revolt, or series of revolts, against the priesthood.

It can be a tremendously dramatic and magnificent work. In all those thousands of years, we have only a few sentences actually spoken, setting forth the sufferings of the muted people. "Behold, we die! We perish. Shall we be consumed with dying?["] (Numbers 17:12) Was there ever a more helpless or pathetic picture of terror and death before Hitler? They are cut down by the sword of thousands; infested by plague, burnt to death by thousands, decapitated & their heads exposed in the sun; killed by the thousands by poisonous snakes. It is a terrible picture and equal to what has gone on in our Christian lands under the Popes & Preachers. A commentary on too much power in any hand, religious or not. But I do not intend to present it as a lecture. I intend to lay my proposition, and then show a series of dramatic incidents set over against the same sort of things, in other lands. The long struggle in England from the time that the nobles stopped King John at Runnymede and wrung the Magna Carta from him, to the first Labor government in England. Same in France, Germany, Russia, etc, and the Emancipation of the slaves in the Americas.

Do the Jews have tragic eyes as some say they do? And why not? They have fought the good fight longer than anyone else in the world. 3,000 years from Sinai to Christ. No one can deny that they flocked to Christ because he brought to a head the social revolution that had been gathering so long. They bled and died for the faith and through it the social reforms that we now enjoy, from Judea through Rome, Greece and all the Near East. Nero lit his Coliseum with the bodies of burning Jews who were Christians. But now, we do not even give them credit for it. We speak of "Christian martyrs" as Gentiles, when in fact, the first century of Christianity was dominated by Jews. We have scourged them for their will and courage. In the terrible siege of Jerusalem, the people fought against (and were butchered by) their oppressors inside the walls and yet turned a brave and daring face to Titus without. They fought on in desperation, though knowing that they must lose. So when starvation had driven them to eat the last dog and cat, when many had eaten their children, and the walls were finally overthrown by Titus, the few survivors of the nation, with cosmic tragedy in their eyes, never having been loved either by their rulers, nor the strangers without, picked up their weary feet, and became The Wanderers of the earth.

Why did I go into all this detail to you? Because I want your reaction. I want you and Fania to tell me if you think it should be written. I have no doubts about the story possibilities. The stuff is there! It is the biggest story in the world. I have traced the thread through the entire Bible, through Flavius Josephus, the greatest historian of the Jews, the Maccabees, Spinoza, and contemporary Roman and Egyptian histories. I know that I am right. The Jewish people have suffered and still suffer from the slander of their own Priests. I do not mean that the present Rabbis do it. I mean that Gentiles have formed their opinion of the Jews through what is taught in Sunday Schools, and the slanders of their oppressors is taken for granted, and justifies our present-day prejudices. I like all other little Christian(?) ignoramuses was taught of the evil ways of the Jews. So evil that God just had to do away with them. They are meant to be kicked around. You see what I mean? If you think it should be done, (and I trust your judgment) I am going ahead. I know that it will make thousands mad, but "Let there be light!"

I have more manuscripts to send along to you, but I have to go through a whole box of papers & I <u>dread</u> it. I did my last book on the typewriter, but if I do the book "Under Fire and Cloud"[6] on the Jewish people, I plan to do it all in long-hand, for frankly I feel that it is going to be a really great book.

Fred is in Miami, and rearing to go, but I cant go until my affairs are in order. Do wish that your health permitted you to go. I send you my very love. I send you the world of love, with the sun and the moon thrown in.

Devotedly,
Zora, Regina

6 *Early name for* Herod the Great.

TO KATHERINE TRACY L'ENGLE

On Board the Houseboat SUN TAN
Box 268
Daytona Beach, Fla.
October 24, 1945.

Dear Tracy L'Engle:

What happened to my typewriter to make it cut a caper like that above, I really do not know.[1] Maybe its gone crazy too like the rest of the world.

Do I want to do that article![2] Oh, Miss Tracy! I want to do the very thing that you suggest—an objective piece of work. My natural honesty and self-respect is revolted at all this special pleading, and DuBois, is the most pleadingest of all the special pleaders. The man is so subjective that he cannot utter a straight sentence. For example. After reading four biographies of Alexander Hamilton, and finding nothing there about his being a Negro, I asked DuBois what were his grounds for making such a statement? He replied with a smug smile, "He was born in the West Indies, and he was illegitimate. There were few white women in the colonies, and so his mother must have been a Negro." I pointed out that his parentage was right there for all to see. True, his mother ran off from her husband and lived the rest of her life with her soldier-lover, but he was an Englishman, with his name and birth-place given. He answered that that <u>could</u> have been manufactured, and walked off from me clutching his falsehoods to his bosom. He has snatched numerous perfectly white people into the Negro race in the same way. I have decided that it comes of a monumental inferiority complex. That sort of thing is practised by the Jews too. Those who do that, wish that they were white. Failing at that, they just borrow all the distinguished white people and get into the race with them by proxy, as it were. I resent his putting that Greek slut, Cleopatra, into the same race with me. Anyway, his pretense that the

---

[1] *In the original typescript, L'Engle's name is raised up a half line in the salutation.*
[2] *To replace Du Bois's entry "Negro, American" for the* Encyclopedia Americana. *Hurston's entry, "The Negro in the United States," ran from 1947 through 1954.*

ancient Egyptians were Negroes is just as arbitrary and false. But certainly! I want to do the article. I will consider it the greatest honor that has come my way so far. You are an angel, (No, nothing inane like that) You are First Trombone in God's best band!

About this summer, now. I was down the State, and your letter had been here a week when I got to it. I was so broke, and so utterly depressed at that period, that I was mute and soundless. Like a prairie under winter snows. So deep in the darkest bottom of Hell, that it seemed that all the suns of the universe could never light it up again. Now, I am back at work. I thought once of asking you to loan me $100, then I realized that you have little money, and my asking would merely have depressed you, seeing that you could not help me. Things are much better with me now, and this great honor that you are trying to steer my way is the biggest thing that you could ever have done for me. I shall certainly mention your name to God next time that He drops in for a visit.

Now, I am only depressed and distressed by the state of the world. But you and I never expected any different from the way things were being steered, did we? That dear, departed, crippled-up so-and-so was the Anti-Christ long spoken of. I never dreamed that so much hate and negative forces could be un-leashed on the world until I wintered and summered under his dictatorship.[3] But God remembered America at last!

Maybe I can come to New York to do research on the article! Oh, that will be wonderful to be there while you are there! I can do the last part of my current book at the same time.[4]

Good night. In leaving you, I fold you warmly in all your most inside dreams.

With faith and feelings,
Zora Neale Hurston

I was down at Tampa yesterday, and did not get your letter until today.

Z

---

[3]*Franklin Roosevelt.*
[4]*Probably the Eatonville novel.*

TO KATHERINE TRACY L'ENGLE

Box 268
Daytona Beach, Fla.
November 4, 1945.

Dear Miss Tracy:

Before your last letter arrived, I had already lost my taste for coming to New York. Not that I could find no place to stay, because my brother owns three houses in Brooklyn, and there is always room at his home for me. But he tells me of the unlovely social conditions there. Robbing and cut-throating and such awful carryings on that he has resolved to move back to Florida so that his 15 year old son will have a chance to grow up decent. Then a white friend of mine went up for a month and only stayed one week. He too was distressed by what he saw there. I hate to look at things like that. That is what your blessed New Deal did for us. Crime in Harlem is rampant, and the police are helpless because the New Deal-promoted Negro politicians immediately let out a scream that Negroes are being persecuted the minute a Negro thug is arrested. I was there, and know that that is what happened about that Race riot in 1936.[1] Mayor LaGuardia and the New Deal gang passed it off as something that happened because the "poor Negroes were so hungry and down-trodden." But I happened to <u>know</u> that it was promoted by the Communists, and nothing was said about it because they had all pledged to vote for Roosevelt in the 1936 election. The blame was hurled at the door of the capitalists who did <u>not</u> vote for Roosevelt. Oh, poor America is in an awful spiritual state! I am thankful that a solid kind of a man like Truman is in. But I also see that the New Dealers are sniping at him already. His repudiation of their dizzy theories is driving dear Eleanor and her cohorts <u>wild</u>. Take good care of your self, and get rid of that cold.

Most sincerely,
Zora.

[1] *The race riot to which Hurston probably refers actually took place on March 19, 1935, incited by the beating of a sixteen-year-old Puerto Rican, Lino Rivera, accused of shoplifting a pocketknife. The Young Communist League encouraged protesters to resist the police. Three people were killed, dozens injured, and over one hundred jailed.*

TO KATHERINE TRACY L'ENGLE

Box 268
Daytona Beach, Fla.
November 27, 1945.

Dear, dear Miss Tracy:

You owe me a letter you know, and I would appreciate one too from you.

I have Mrs. Dudley's letter at last and I am just too happy about it.[1] Tongue cannot tell and words cannot express my feelings about the thing. I thank you and I thank you!!!

I still wish that I might be in New York while you are there, but the cards are really stacked against it. The cold weather, the housing and the crime situation are too much to handle all at one time. As I said, my brother will always take me in, but he is paying for his houses, and I would have to crowd in out there in Brooklyn with the family, and then too, I never did like Brooklyn anyway.

You do not know how much I appreciated your offer of help. I was so full that I did not find the words to say my feelings at once. I am getting along very well now, and as I expect to finish my new book in a few weeks, I will be getting advance royalties on that.[2] I thank you for your great spirit anyway.

When you have finished your job on the Encyclopedia, why not consider joining me in Central America? As soon as I finish my work for Mrs. Dudley, I am going down there for two years of research. You could be so much help and company and everything. Why not think about coming along?

Most sincerely,
Zora

[on back:] Miss Tracy L'Engle c/o Mrs. Dudley

---

[1] *Apparently an editor for* Encyclopedia Americana. *L'Engle helped arrange for Hurston to publish "The Negro in the United States." Her article replaced the "Negro, American" entry written by W. E. B. Du Bois, which had run in the* Americana *since 1904.*

[2] *The Eatonville novel.*

TO KATHERINE TRACY L'ENGLE

Daytona Beach, Fla
December 11, 1945.

Dear Miss Tracy:

Our letters crossed each other, but that is just all right. So long as I heard from you.

Was it you who suggested me to Mr. Henry W. Lanier of Funk & Wagnalls NEW INTERNATIONAL YEAR BOOK to do the article for them on the Negro?[1] I have a strong suspicion that it came through you. Thanks mighty much if you did. If you did not, I thank you just the same, for I know that you would have done so if you had had the chance.

Yes, I think that I would love to do the cook book with your Sarah.[2] A great deal of human interest could be worked in between the recipes. As soon as I get the book off of hand that I am doing now—which will be very soon,[3] and the work for AMERICANA, I will be ready to tackle it.

Your idea about a psychic storm stands to reason. The world could not go so crazy in a total way otherwise. That is one reason why I feel to go to Central America for awhile, where there is not so much "social consciousness" to deal with and be distressed over.

My publisher was down here to see me only yesterday. He likes what I have done on the book very much, which makes me happy no end.[4]

Do you mean that a play that does not deal with race and social strife would not be acceptable at present? I know the spirit of the current plays from the reviews, and they are all sharp angles.

The trouble with that is, they are neither true to the facts of Negro life, nor to the psychology. I have said to several people that these violent reformers ignore the present state of affairs, and go way back to present a picture that no longer exists as current. Take for instance

---

[1]Hurston's article, "Negroes," appeared in the 1945 edition, published in 1946.
[2]L'Engle's cook.
[3]The Eatonville novel.
[4]Lippincott—probably a reference to the Eatonville novel.

STRANGE FRUIT.[5] Negro girls no longer have children by white men. I challenge her to find an instance, even in her own Georgia. It is simply not being done. They heyday of the mulatto was during slavery. It kept up to a lesser degree up to 1900. From then on, it slacked off till in this generation, it practically does not exist. I have come across only two cases in the last twenty years. One was a servant girl in New York, and the other was a prostitute in Jacksonville by a policeman. The New York case with an insurance agent happened in 1926. The Jacksonville case no less than 16 years ago. As to that other play about the returning Negro soldier living in the backyard of the southern Senator, and teaching school, you know that it is false to the core. There is very little living on premises at present except in rooms, because it is too expensive for the employer, to say the least. Then he must be as trashy as all get-out to still be living there after he had got a good education. It is a reflection on him, and not on the Senator. It just would not happen. You can see what I mean by these zealots going back forty or fifty years to "correct" a situation that no longer exists. What they are really doing is working for the Communist revolution, plus the Jewish gripe against the non-marriage of Jews by gentiles as a rule. The money i[s] put up by Jews for the Negro to carry the ball for them. I could say a whole lot and tell a lot of truths that would not look pretty, and I have considered writing something about it right out loud, but I doubt if I could get it published in the present state of things. Notice how very popular it is for a Negro to kill a white man in all these things?

You know by now that I have heard from Mrs. Dudley on AMERI-CANA. By the way, does she need my work immediately? I have taken it for granted that the volume with N [Negro] would be later. But if she wants it in, I will stop everything and get it ready now.

Perhaps you can get TELL MY HORSE at the Frederick Douglass Book Center, 141 W. 125th Street, phone University 4-9312. I do hope that they have some copies, because I want six copies myself. I want 6 copies also of MULES AND MEN, and 3 of JONAH'S GOURD VINE. I have just been short of money in the last few months. But soon now, I will do it.

---

[5]*Lillian Smith (1897–1966) published* Strange Fruit *in 1944. Smith's novel, which takes place in the Deep South, is a tragic story of miscegenation between an educated black girl and a white man.*

Must get off a wire to Mr. Lanier[6] and get this letter in the Post Office by noon, so that it can get on the streamliner. I send you my very love.

Most sincerely,
Zora
Zora Neale Hurston

TO KATHERINE TRACY L'ENGLE

Houseboat SUN TAN
Box 268
Daytona Beach, Fla.
February 19, 1946.

Dear Miss Tracy:

Your life-saving letter and check came to me last Monday. Within the hour, I got a chance to go to sea on a shrimping boat I had sought the chance for some material for the book, and the two things came at once.[1] I only had a chance to get off the money to the finance corporation before jumping aboard. I got back in on Saturday night.

It was a wonderful experience! It was tough and rough, but highly informative. The men, white and black who put shrimp on the table of the nation are made of the stuff of pioneers.

Thanks to you, now I can finish my book.[2] I have been snatched back from the brink of insanity, and that is no figure of speech. Before this week is over, I shall be finished with my work, and then set out to make some quick money at once. Do some articles. I shall never forget your generosity of soul in my terrible hour. I have typed out the sentence you sent me, and posted it up on the bulkhead by my bed so that I may look at it and contemplate it at all hours of the day and night.

Do consider Central America. I think that off together, you and I might take time and do a wonderful play. Your own knowledge of the

---

[6]International Year Book *editor.*

[1]*The main character of* Seraph on the Suwanee *runs a shrimping business.*
[2]*Probably* Seraph on the Suwanee.

show business, and some ideas that I harbor might come to something practical.

With thanks, with love, I am

Your Zora

TO TRACY KATHERINE L'ENGLE

[February 1946]

Dear Miss Tracy:

Yes, I would love to do the article for the TIMES Sunday Magazine.[1] I would like the connection for just the reason that you say. There would be so many things that I could work in with them. In the long run, it would be more profitable. I have not the pictures as yet, but I can get them very easily.

Yes, I shall do the play for Ethel Waters as soon as I can get the leisure,[2] which is as soon as I get this typing[3] off my hand. I have it well laid out, and I can do it even outside of the U.S. and send it back.

I have an idea that I think is good. I think that my new book has both play and movie possibilities.[4] I would love to see these Negro parts played by good white actors. 1. I understand that Walter White, the head of the N.A.A.C.P. is now out in Hollywood for the purpose of forbidding and Negro actor from accepting a servant role in the movies. In fact, to set up a pressure group to dictate the roles that Negroes play. That, I am afraid is going to kill off the Negro in the movies, because you must realize that plays would have to be written specially to furnish roles that would meet his approval. The average movie story has no such roles because they are about white people. Since white actors have played Negro parts in the past, and now do most of that on the air, I see no reason why it cannot be done in a big way. Modern make-up would take care of the situation perfectly. 2. Negroes are acting white roles now on Broadway, and so I can see no

[1] *This seems not to have materialized.*

[2] *This seems not to have happened.*

[3] *Hurston was working on numerous pieces at once: her encyclopedia articles, the Eatonville novel, early versions of* Seraph on the Suwanee.

[4] *Probably the Eatonville material.*

reason why it should not work the other way as well. I am afraid that
the Negro politicians are about to out-smart themselves.[5]

I do hope that you can come along with me, because I feel that it
will be the beginning of a new life for you, and that you will realize
your ambitions in more than one direction. You can not only study
Latin characterization at first hand as an actor, you can also establish
yourself as a writer. Think it over.

> Most lovingly but hurriedly,
> Zora

My idea of Hell is that I would all through eternity be typing a book.

TO CARITA DOGGETT CORSE

On Board the Houseboat SUN TAN
Daytona Beach, Fla.
May 29, 1946.

Dear Dr. Corse:

How glad I was to get a line from you on any subject what so ever!
Strange, Miss Tracy L'Engle was down here to see me just last week
and we were talking about you, and I said that I was going up to Jacksonville and try to see you.

About Kingsley, now.[1] He got around Africa quite a bit, and this
dancer might be a descendant of his and not know it. I have always
been most interested in that case, and you can be sure that I will miss
no chance to pick up information on it when I find any. I thank you
for giving me the lead.

Being a historian, and interested in Negro history, I think that it
would be fine if you would set things in motion to have the ship that
brought over the last load of slaves (1859) raised from the bottom of

---

[5]*White had called for an NAACP review of Hollywood on January 28, 1946.*

[1]*Zephaniah Kingsley, Jr. (1765–1843). Kingsley, a Scotch slave trader, married Anna Madgignie Jai, the
daughter of an African king. The pair had four children and lived in East Florida from 1803 until Jai moved
to Haiti in 1835 to escape Florida's harsh laws regarding free blacks. Their marriage was a celebrated local
legend and was reported in various newspapers. Hurston discusses the marriage of their daughter and a white
man in her letter to Langston Hughes, April 3, 1929.*

the Alabama river and towed to Jacksonville. I think that it would be a great drawing card, and a feather in your cap. It is in very shallow water just above Mobile. It would be a long tow, it is true, but it could be exhibited all the way down the gulf coast from Mobile to Fort Myers, cross the state through Lake Okechobee, and into the Indian river at Stuart, then up the river to Jacksonville, taking several months, and be exhibited, while you lecture on it all the way. The boat is named the Chlotilde, built and owned by the Mayer Brothers and a Canadian named Foster. It could become a permanent exhibit at Jacksonville and arouse a lot of interest. Make a lot of money for the society.[2]

I hope to see you most any day now, though I will notify you before I get to town so that perhaps you can find a minute to see me. I want to see you so very much.

> All my love.
> With faithful feelings,
> Zora

TO WHIT BURNETT

On Board the SUN TAN
June 15, 1946.

Dear Whit:

Naturally I feel honored to be in your collection, and too happy to sign for any possible further editions.[1]

Thanks for the check. The car gets two new tires this morning. My best to you and yours.

> Most sincerely,
> Zora
> Zora Neale Hurston

---

[2]*Hurston published an article entitled "The Last Slave Ship" in* American Mercury *in March 1944. In that article, Hurston talked about the* Chlotilde, *Cudjo Lewis (the last survivor of the ship), Lewis's original village in Dahomey, how his village was raided by slavers, the shipowners (spelled "Meaher" in the article), the clandestine arrival of the ship in Alabama, the unloading of the slaves, the years of slavery that fell to those taken on that ship, and their eventual emancipation. This article and letter counter writings in which Hurston refers to slavery as a "bully adventure" and "the price I paid for civilization."*

[1]*Hurston had first published in Burnett's* Story *magazine in 1933, when he accepted "The Gilded Six-Bits," sent to him by Robert Wunsch.*

TO CLAUDE BARNETT

[July [1–16], 1946]
On Boatd the Houseboat-Cruiser SUN TAN
Box 268
Daytona Beach, Fal.

Dear Claude Barnett:

Thanks for your offer to give me a spread on my expedition to Central America. I would much prefer to feed you something after I am on the ground. I think that you will be much more satisfied with it that way.

But there is something else very important that I was just going to write you about. It may or may not interest you, but it is important.

Mr. John S. Knight[1] is the owner of 1. THE CHICAGO DAILY NEWS; 2 THE DETROIT FREE PRESS 3 THE MIAMI (Fla) HERALD 4. THE AKRON, (Ohio) shucks! I forget the name right now. Anyhow, his vigorous anti–race prejudice editorials are attracting nation-wide attention. He has made a determined fight against the KKK in his MIAMI HERALD so that he has the outfit definitely on the run here in Florida. He has put up the good fight for better Negro housing in Miami, and for justice in the courts. He fights race hatred in a way that I like. He is different from some the so-called "friends of the Negro" in that he does not approach the matter in the spirit that we are inferior wards of the nation, but citizens being denied their rights. I do not join in the hysteria of some leading Negroes over our "friends." It is an acceptance of patronage that is insulting to me. I want nothing done as a favor to me. I want it done as my RIGHT AS A CITIZEN! Why those Negroes do not see that anything that is done under favoritism can be withdrawn? That was what wrong with FEPC.[2] It should have been a law, duly passed by Congress and not a vote-getting gesture from Roosevelt. Poor Ran-

---

[1]*Journalist and publisher John S. Knight (1894–1981) established a highly successful chain of newspapers which included Akron's* Times-Press, *Miami's* Herald, *the* Detroit Free Press, *and Chicago's* Daily News. *Starting in 1936, he wrote a commentary for every Sunday edition.*
[2]*The Fair Employment Practices Committee, established by President Roosevelt in 1941.*

dolph was tricked and trapped by that committee that FDR sent into
a backroom at the White House to come back with some device that
would save the face of the Administration, and that was all that happened. Knight has a different approach. He is certainly courageous
in that he attacks the thing right in the heart of the deepest area of
prejudice. He is a Republican, extremely rich, and has four big papers in strategic localities as an outlet for publicity. Why not begin to
build him up in the Negro press? Why not suggest him for President?
Maybe he will not get the nomination, but it will let the others know
what we expect. Besides, you are in the newspaper game, and hsi
friendship will never do you and Etta any harm. I am sorry that I
have not kept all of his editorials on the Negro, but I enclose on from
yesterday's MIAMI HERALD, which incidentally he has built up so
rapidly, that now it leads the nation in advertising. Even the New
York Times. He has recently put out a Latin-American edition, and
so will exert influence down in there. The tie-in with him will do
you no harm. And if he should get the nomination, or even make a
good showing, he will feel indebted to you. I understand that he has
established citizenship in all four states, and with his publicity,
wealth and courage, I do not see how he can fail to make a good
showing in a race. The others will certainly know that they have
been in a race when they get through with Knight. He and I have
exchanged several letters, and he is open to suggestion about situations. But you know that I am not particularly interested in politics
in an active way. You are in a peculiar and powerful position if you
care to use the power in your hands. You could do some exciting
things through John S. Knight if you are interested. And his chain
could be helpful to Etta Moton in her career. He lives most of the
time in Akron, Ohio, but he is frequently in Chicago, Miami and Detroit. I know all his staff in Miami, and they are all well-disposed towards me. I rush along any angles on race-discrimination that I see,
and without mentioning me, they frequently get worked up into editorials. But please do not think that I want to get the credit for anything. I just want to see conditions improved. I am content to remain
unmentioned so long as things move ahead. I seek no office whatsoever. But I do hope that you will give some recognition to a man who
is fighting our fight for us.

My best to you and Etta and family. I plan to push off as soon as I
can get passage. The passenger lines were discontinued during the

War, and have not been re-instated as yet, so I am having one heck of a time getting off. Tomi Tinsley is ver impatient, I know, btu she does not realize the difficulties of the situation. I can make no definite plans, because I must just grab a berth at any time and at any port where I can find one. It might be at an hour's notice.

With all good wishes,

Zora

Zora Neale Hurston

I have already commented on your character to John D. Pennekamp, Associate Editor on the Herald, and told him who you were. Knight fought against the zoning in Miami and the attempt to jail those Negroes who bought in a white section, and gave the fight good publicity.

TO CLAUDE BARNETT

[July [21–26], 1946]
Wednesday A.M.

Dear Claude:

I hasten to answer you, because I want you to be sure that I seek no personal advantage in my suggestion. In all likelihood, I will be out of the country for years,[1] and since I have never been interested in politics (seeing that it is such a sorry game) I am only interested in things improving in a general way. Like you, noting the attitude of most Negroes big and little, I am often so disillusioned that it hardly seems worthwhile to even be interested in a general way. But, I thought if a man with the potentials of John S. Knight could be egged on to do something, we ought to be interested enough to egg him on.

So far as his political aspirations are concerned, he naturally denies them. He has been mentioned from Tampa, Florida, Akron, Ohio and Orlando, Florida in the last few days as presidential timber, citing his civic clean-up records. John D. Pennekamp, Miami Herald Editor

---

[1] *She hoped to be in Honduras.*

pooh-poohs it all, and says that Knight is only interested as a behind-the-scenes power for better things. That may or may not be sincere.

I too had a great admiration for Henry Wallace once, but when he did not stick with Ickes[2] (1) in his denunciation of the venial appointments of Truman; and (2) when he announced that he would not only not oppose Truman in the next campaign but support him, I felt him a hopeless bureaucrat, eager to keep his job no matter what, and he lost his charm for me. I dont care who kicks him around.

In that same connection (Truman), I am amazed at the complacency of Negro press and public. Thruman [sic] is a monster. I can think of him as nothing else but the BUTCHER OF ASIA. Of his grin of triumph on giving the order to drop the Atom bombs on Japan. Of his maintaining troops in China who are shooting the starving Chinese for stealing a handful of food. Of his slighting the Inauguration of the new nation of the Philipines by not bothering to be present. Of his lynching all the able Japanese under the guise of "War Criminals." War is war, but these men are criminals for daring to shoot at white men, and are being lynched for it without a murmur of protest from the Negro population of the U.S. Ickes has attacked him for it, and Jack Kofoed in the MIAMI HERALD, but not one word from us.[3] Do we not see that we any any too prominent Negro being morally lynched with everyone of those able Japanese. WE are being taught a lesson and given a horrible example through that. Is it that we are so devoted to a "good Massa" that we feel that we ought not to even protest such crimes? Have we no men among us? If we cannot stop it, we can at least let it be known that we are not deceived. We can make any party who condones it, let alone orders it, tremble for election time. What are we, anyhow?

My best to Etta and family. Tell her that I shall make some song records in Latin America, and any that seem to have possibilities, I shall send them along to her for study.

Most sincerely,
Zora Neale Hurston

---

[2] *Harold Ickes (1874–1952), secretary of the interior (1933–46) and head of the Public Works Administration under FDR; he resigned from Truman's cabinet in 1946.*
[3] *Magazine writer Jack Kofoed (b. 1894) began his career in Philadelphia and wrote for the* New York Post *(1924–33) before becoming a feature columnist for the* Miami Herald.

TO HELEN WORDEN ERSKINE

70 W. 55th St.
October 28, 1946.

Received from Mrs. Helen Worden Erskine, $30.00 for the campaign of Grant Reynolds, to be turned over to Grant Reynolds.[1]

Zora Neale Hurston

TO HELEN WORDEN ERSKINE

425 West 124th St.
New York 27.
February 16, 1947.

Dear Mrs. Erskine:

No, I have not been idle. I contacted the Dominican Consulate immediately, but so far I have had small success in getting anything definite outside of the regular figure which they give out. There was a sort of tension there, and one of the girls to whom I made myself agreeable whispered that the Consul was going home and another was coming to replace him.

My contact on house-rent parties is no good anymore. Under threat of arrest for being so noisy nothing has happened next door for two Saturdays, though I was invited to be present when I broached the subject. It has just quit happening, that is all.[1]

---

[1] Hurston supported Republican Reynolds in his unsuccessful congressional campaign against Harlem's native son, Adam Clayton Powell, Jr.

[1] Rent parties were fund-raising events where open-house gatherings were held to cover rent costs. Guests paid a cover charge as well as a small fee for food and drink. As Harlem Renaissance historian Bruce Kellner explains, "If rent parties were a necessary evil, they were nevertheless social events as well, as essential to Low Harlem as literary receptions were to High Harlem." They also provided a space free of white audiences, who found the Harlem nightclubs of the twenties a particularly fashionable way to go "slumming."

But I have gotten onto something else which I think is more exciting, meaning the inside workings of juvenile gangs both in Harlem and Brooklyn. A few more days, and I think that I shall have the whole thing sewed up tight, as to the number of gangs, names and territiries, which gangs are at war with which, where they get guns and everything. I have most of the material already. Also, I am getting leads on dope. It seems that the use of marijuana is declining except among the teen-agers, but cocaine, heroin, and opium have gained tremendously among the former marijuana addicts. It seems to be brought in by members of the Merchant Marine. I am making more contacts all the time and getting in deeper.

Went to the meeting of the Directors of the AWA[2] at the Beekman Tower yesterday, and enclose the agenda and notes that I took. The Kuhns were there this time and as usual objected to everything and had a grand fight with John T. Flynn.[3]

I expect to see you in a day or two on the matter of the loan you made me. I have gotten in something else since I saw you. I have a tentative agreement with a Honduranian biggie, and if things turn out as I hope, we will get material for an article from there.

My best to you and Dr. Erskine with old-time punch. I hope that READERS DIGEST will be interested in the gang stuff.[4]

Most sincerely,

Zora

Zora Neale Hurston

I am going to the tea for Mrs. Mason and do all I can to serve her. If I can "case" the gangs it will be in the name of the committee.

[2] *The American Writers' Association (AWA) was organized to protect the freedom of noncommunist authors.*
[3] *John Thomas Flynn (1882–1964) was an author, journalist, and editor* (New Haven Register, New York Globe, Collier's).
[4] *Apparently they were not.*

TO MAXWELL PERKINS

Hotel Cosenza
Puerto Cortes
Honduras, C.A.
May 20, 1947.

Mr. Max Perkins, Editor
Charles Scribners Sons
597 Fifth Ave.
New York City.

Dear Mr. Perkins:

Except for the waters of the Gulf being a most godly blue, the voyage was uneventful. I was flung safe and sounding off on the coast of Honduras.

After moving around some, visiting Tegucigalpa, the capitol and other spots, I find it best to be on the North Coast because it has the most interesting people. Any communication will reach me at the above address, even though I might be in the interior.

It is very interesting here from a writer's point of view. I am not disappointed in the venture. I confess to being frightened over inflation here. It is little different from our U.S.A. in that respect. I feel half stranded already.

I shall always be grateful to Honduras, though for it has given me back myself. I am my old brash self again. To misquote Tennyson,[1] ". . . My rusty pen strikes true. My brass is as the brass of ten because my heart is new."

My most best to our M.K. Rawlings and [Rowena] Jeliffe [sic]. She was ever so wrong in not coming on off with me. She told me that she told you she did not have enough experience in le amour to write an exciting book for you. Tell her the stuff is here! Plenty good looking men who are plenty willing. Some of these days I might even look into things myself.

---

[1] *Victorian poet Alfred, Lord Tennyson. The lines are from "Sir Galahad": "My good blade carves the casques of men, / My good lance twisteth sure, / My strength is as the strength of ten, / Because my heart is pure."*

I do hope that your health is fully recovered by now, and I wish all other good things for you.

The country is not rich like the United States, but here there are no crippling strikes, NO COMMUNISTS, and other sea-buzzards to puke all over and spoil the land.

With all good wishes,
Zora Neale Hurston

TO CARL VAN VECHTEN AND FANIA MARINOFF

Hotel Cosenza
Puerto Cortes
Honduras, C.A.
June 21, 1947.

Dear Carl and Fania:

A line to let you know that you are still very close to my heart as of old. I have been here nearly two months now, but there were so many things that I had to do that I am just finding a minute to to a few things that I want to do, and the first one was to drop you a word.

Honduras is a very interesting country. With the widely contrasting scenery you would be delighted as a photographer. And the physical types of the people would make you swear that you had reached the heaven of photographers. I do hope that you decide to fly down for a visit. You will find the people here kindly, warm and gay.

To have a chance to photograph Copan de Santa Rosa[1] will pay you for your visit alone. Do give it a serious thought.

I have gone over to Scribners now, and feel lucky to be under Max Perkins.

All the best to you both. I send you my very love.

With that old-time affection,
Zora

---

[1]*Santa Rosa de Copán was a ruined, ancient Mayan city in the extreme western part of Honduras (near the Guatemalan border). It was an important center of Mayan art and astronomy.*

TO CARL VAN VECHTEN

Hotel Cosenza
Puerto Cortes
Honduras, C.A.
July 30, 1947.

Dear, dear Carlo:

How odd you are about the death of Maxwell Perkins![1] If you will
look back just a little, you will see that he was buried June 19, 1947. I
was in his office twice during April, and had a letter from him the last
week in May. I am unhappy over his passing for more than one reason.
First I am denied the benefit of his editorial genius, then he was a
very nice man to know, and third, the literary world has lost it's
brightest editorial light. But it is easily established that he was very
much alive when I sailed May 4th.

No, Carlo, I did not go around in New Yrok [sic] last winter. The
place was too much of a basement to Hell to suit me. Everybody busy
hating and speaking in either brazen lies or using just enough truth to
season a lie up to make their viewpoint sound valid. Not hating anyone, I felt entirely out of place. I am afraid that I got a little unbal-
anced. I got so that it was tortu[r]e for me to go to meet people, fearing
the impact of all the national, class and race hate that I would have to
listen to. I am praying that my country will have returned to sanity
before I get home again.

Dear Carlo, nothing would give me greater pleasure than to do a
book around you. You have had such a tremendous influence on the
arts of the last twenty-five years, that I think it ought to be precipitated out of the mass of lies that are now growing up. People are
brazenly claiming credit for the many things that you were responsible for. I declare to my rest! It is a caution how people get so hungry
for what they didnt do, and so brazen in twisting theings to seem to
deserve the credit that they claim! I had the feeling though, that you
would resist any attempts on my part to get the information from you.

[1]Maxwell Perkins died on June 17, 1947.

I still want to do the book on you. Illustrated by Covarrubias, it would be swell.

Very seriously, Carlo, I am working out something which I hope will be classified as a play.[2] I am using the material around the fall of Jerusalem to Titus in 70 A.D. It is a whale of a story, and it's greatness lies in the fact that it is a universal matter. The struggle of the handful of Jews against the mightest army on earth, that they might be free to live their own lives in their own way, is the struggle of democracy all over the world and in all ages. With what is going on now, I think that it would be a good time for it. The Romans won the war and destroyed Jerusalem, but the Jews won in the end, because the seed of the struggle was scattered, and came at last to conquer Rome. The symbolic Gate of Justice moved westward across the world. Do take time to let me know if you think it is a good idea.

Most sincerely,
Zora

TO BURROUGHS MITCHELL

Hotel Cosenza
Puerto Cortes
Honduras, C.A.
July 31, 1947.

Dear Mr. Mitchell:

Yes, I had been informed about the death of Mr. Maxwell Perkins. It saddened me profoundly. It touched me personally as well as feeling the tremendous loss to contemporary letters. You see, I had been revering him for years, and then when I found that I was actually going to have the chance to work under him, I felt a tremendous exaltation.[1] You must know how I felt when the news came to me here. It was too late to send a message of condolence to the family. It is useless to repeat that Maxwell Perkins was easily the greatest force in the literature of our times.

[2]*A dramatic version of the Herod project.*

[1]*Perkins edited F. Scott Fitzgerald, Ernest Hemingway, and Ring Lardner, among many others. He was one of the most celebrated editors of the century.*

Now please let me congratulate you younger men who step into his
shoes. You have a great tradition to live up to, but I am sure that you
take it like the horse in the valley of Jehosaphat accept the challenge
and shout, "Aha! There never was a horse like me!" (That is what the
Book of Job <u>says</u> the horse exulted anyway.)[2]

You can see by the enclosed correspondence the stage of the book
at present. The second half of the book has been set down, but I am
re-writing it for your early inspection. Then I will go back and go over
the entire work again.[3]

Yes, <u>PLEASE</u> I do need some money for necessities. Either you are
a fortune-teller, or Ann Watkins[4] told you. A drab terror has settled
upon me by reason of my situation, though possibly you can never
know the feeling, never having been in a foriegn country and finding
yourself without. After the last few weeks, I do not think that a head-
less horror [come—x-ed out; written above it: "could"] add anything
new to what I know about terror and fear. And this is not a thing in
contemplation, but real and practical. It came about because something went wrong somewhere. By arrangement with Mike Watkins, I
was to do some articles for HOLIDAY[5] as pot-boilers. I sent in the first
with photographs, which cost me plenty down here, but the weeks go
by and I have not heard a line from the Watkins office. Maybe Mike[6]
is on his vacation, but that is no remedy for my situation.

This country has many interesting things to write about, and the
beauty of it is, that Honduras is one country that has so little written
about it. John Gunther has written about the political aspects, which
incidentally, he could know nothing about since he only spent twenty-
four hours here.[7] I have no interest in that angle at all. Artistically, it is
too trite to be taking a poke at the politics of Latin America, and patronizing to an insulting degree. I ever love to be original. What I will
do as soon as money is available, is to organize an expedition into a
part of Honduras which is practically unknown. I have already been
part of the way, and made a most sensational discovery which I am

---

[2] *Job 39: 19–25: "Hast thou given the horse strength? . . . He paweth in the valley, and rejoiceth in his strength. . . . He mocketh at fear. . . . He saith among the trumpets, Ha, ha."*

[3] The Lives of Barney Turk, *about a white youth from a Florida truck farm and his adventures in Central America and Hollywood.*

[4] *Hurston's agent. The Watkins agency was one of the most important literary agencies of the 1940s.*

[5] Holiday *was primarily a travel magazine. Both John Gunther and Miguel Covarrubias were contributors.*

[6] *Mike Watkins, Ann Watkins's husband.*

[7] *John Gunther (1901–70) was a journalist well known for his profiles of major world leaders.*

keeping under my hat until I get hold of a few hundred dollars. I have had all that the Guggenheim gives to one person, and I am stuck for means to work with on it, but I assure you that it will be worth it when I disclose my findings. Therefore, this present book must be GOOD so that I can make the money for the project that is burning my soul to attack.[8]

But enough about my hopes and fears. I assure you that I am in a creative mood and enjoy working on the book.

With all good wishes for your success in your new endeavor, I am,

Respectfully yours,
Zora Neale Hurston

TO BURROUGHS MITCHELL

Hotel Cosenza
Puerto Cortes
Honduras, C.A.
September 3, 1947.

Dear Mr. Burroughs:

Thanks a million times for your compassion. I am human again and with confidence.

I am posting the second part of the book today, which I had the mind to send to you directly, but considered that Ann Watkins might feel that I had behaved improperly, so I am sending it on to her.[1] Only, I am an impatient person, and she seems to me to move so infernally slow. For instance; now that the second part has been re-written, I would love to have her editorial comments, as she promised on the first part, so that I could go to work on that, but so far it has not arrived. If you have made any notes, it would be a great favor to me if you would let me have them to work from. No use in having SCRIBNER'S for a publisher and not be helped by that justly celebrated editorial brains. I do want to grow along as a writer.

---

[8] *i.e., finding the lost city.*

[1] Seraph on the Suwanee.

How about, SANG THE SUWANEE IN THE SPRING for a title?
Titles are always a hard thing to arrive at. I have considered several,
including 1. THE QUEEN OF THE GOLDEN HAND, 2. ANGEL
IN THE BED 3. THE SERAPH'S MAN 4. BUT THE DEVIL
WOULDNT LEAVE HER/ I have naturally tried to avoid anything
that would tempt critics to get witty. I have often noted tha a title of
that kind excites some souls to ignore the quality of a book to show off
their wit on the title.

I am conscious that the use of 'nigger' in the text will offend some
Negro readers.[2] However, I am objective in my observations, and I
know, as they know honestly, that the heroine would have certainly
used that word. However, as a publisher, the discretion is yours.

My planned expedition is to the find a lost city in the mountains of
the Department of the Mosquitia, Honduras, which travellers have
heard about for two hundred years, but has not as yet been seen. That is
not because they searched and did not find. It is a forbidding area and
for various reasons they did not try it. I have been told by the Indians,
the only ones who really know anything about that vast area, that it is
<u>there</u>. The average honduranian knows nothing about it. They take no
interest in such things. Even Copan was discovered by outsiders. The
interior of the Mosquitia is avoided with a dread that almost amounts
to awe and terror. I have been repeatedly warned not to venture there.
They point out the dangers form tigres (jaguars), leones, (pumas) and
the deadly barbes amarillos (yellow-throats, fer-de-lances) snakes and
the cascabelles (rattlesnakes) and viboras palmas (palm tree vipers)
mosquitoes and fevers, to say nothing of hostile Indians. None of these
things impress me. Possibly all of these things do exist. I discount their
quantity considerably. The are[a] is even marked 'unexplored' on the
maps. A very sparsely populated region But as an anthropologist, these
reports tell me certain things. The civilization that had vanished from
that area even before the coming of the Spaniards disappeared for
some reason. I rule out conquest by more powerful Indian nations, because those people then would have settled there. I consider either crop
failure over several seasons, or some epidemic which naturally they had
no way of controlling in those days. I am strengthened in this theory by
hearing about the Icaques, a pueblo of Indians in the mountains near

[2]Carl Van Vechten's 1926 novel, Nigger Heaven, caused a large and long-running scandal; Hurston defended
Van Vechten, but many black friends and intellectuals never forgave him.

Cedros who fear infection so much that they permit no outsiders to enter, and avoid contact with others as much as possible. On the rare occasions when they buy cloth for garments, it is sterilized by being passed over flames before being taken into the pueblo. The seriously ill among them are expelled. They might easily be the remnants of some once great nation who fled the old location because of an epidemic. They might once have peopled the now avoided area. I am further strengthened by the universal legend here that some curse hangs over the area, and it is to be avoided. Very few of the Indians will go but so far. Certainly they do not fear the snakes and animals, for they deal with them all the times and effectually. I sense that it is some handed down legend of awae.

In the face of this, I am led to wonder. Catholicism was forced on the Indians by the Spaniards, and their old temples wrecked as far as the Spaniards knew about them. It is frankly admitted that they remained pagan in spite of that, and the conquerors frequently found them holding pagan rites even as late as the middle of the last century. They still do. You follow me, I know. There might be something back in there that is not meant for the Blanco's eyes. Being what they call here a Mestizo, (mixed blood) I am getting hold of some signs and symbols through the advantage of blood. Dorothy Stone, daughter of Samuel Zamurry [sic], Pres. of United Fruit,[3] is interested in archeology in an ameteurish way, tried to go in there and her guides messed her up so that she spent a great deal of money but go nowhere. They persuaded her that there was nothing to see. She assured me that there was not <u>because they had told her so</u>. Ha!

So th[a]t is what I have in mind. That and to explore two great underground caves constructed by the pre-columbian Indians under their cities. It is curious, that three different seekers knew about these underground places, but none bothered to explore them.

My mood is thanks, and thanks, and thanks! I wish good turkey-bosom and hot biscuits on your table. I go back to work.

Most sincerely yours,
Zora Neale Hurston

---

[3]*Samuel Zemurray was a Russian immigrant whose success began in Louisiana, where he was known as "Sam the Banana Man." He moved his business to Honduras in the early 1910s, where he organized a coup against the Honduran government to create conditions more favorable to his business.*

TO BURROUGHS MITCHELL

[September 1947]
ZORA NEALE HURSTON

Second part of novel hereby submitted.[1]

TITLES SUGGESTED:

1. LADY ANGEL WITH HER MAN

2. SERAPH WITH A MAN ON HAND

3. SERAPH ON THE SUWANEE RIVER

4. SUNG THE SUWANEE IN THE SPRING

Respectfully submitted,
Zora Neale Hurston

TO BURROUGHS MITCHELL

Hotel Cosenza
Puerto Cortes
Honduras, C.A.
October 2, 1947.

Dear Mr. Burroughs Mitchell:
    Your kind and helpful letter arrived yesterday, and last night I be-
gan to do something about it. Only the night before I had finished the
re-write of part one, so now I put in to cut down and sharpen up the
second half.[1] Earl ends with the funeral. I shall bring Arvay along her
road to find herself a great deal faster. I get sick of her at times myself.

---

[1] Seraph on the Suwanee.

[1] Seraph on the Suwanee.

Have you ever been tied in close contact with a person who had a strong sense of inferiority? I have, and it is hell. They carry it like a raw sore on the end of the index finger. You go along thinking well of them and doing what you can to make them happy and suddenly you are brought up short with an accusation of looking down on them, taking them for a fool, etc., but they mean to let you know and so on and so forth. It colors <u>everything</u>. For example, I took this man that I cared for down to Carl Van Vechten's one night so that he could meet some of my literary friends, since he had complained that I was always off with them, and ignoring him. I hoped to make him feel at home with the group and included so that he would go where I went. What happened? He sat off in a corner and gloomed and uglied away, and we were hardly out on the street before he was accusing me of having dragged him down there to show off what a big shot I was and how far I was above him. He had a good mind, many excellent qualities, and I am certain that he loved me. But his feeling of inferiority would crop up and hurt me at the most unexpected moments. Right in the middle of what I considered some sweet gesture on my part, I would get my spiritual pants kicked up around my neck like a horse-collar. I asked him to bring me all the clippings on TELL MY HORSE, and he brought several and literally flung them at me. "You had read them" he accused, "and knew that they were flattering. You just asked me to get them to see how great you were." You know how many marriages in the literary and art world have broken up up such rocks, to say nothing of other paths of life. A business man is out scuffling for dear life to get things for the woman he loves, and she is off pouting and accusing him of neglecting her. She feels that way because she does not feel herself able to keep up with the pace that he is setting, and just be confident that she is wanted no matter how far he goes. Millions of women do not want their husbands to succeed for fear of losing him. It is a very common ailment. That is why I decided to write about it. The sufferers do not seem to realize that all that is needed is a change of point of view from fear into self-confidence and then there is no problem. I had not seen these reviews, and thought that it would be a gesture to make him feel included to get them for me and look what happened. Though brash enough otherwise, I got an overwhelming complex about my looks before I was grown, and it was very hard for a long time for me to believe that any man really cared for me. I set out to win my fight against this feeling, and I did. I dont care how homely I am now. I know that it doesnt really matter, and so my relations with others are easier. Perhaps I am even cocky like Tallulah Bankhead,[2] whom I admire enormously.

I am all set up because you are pleased with the idioms of the text. Right here, I think that it should be pointed out that what is known as Negro dialect in the South is no such thing. Bear in mind that the South is the purest Eng[l]ish section of the United States. You know the historical and economic background that has kept immigration low there. You realize how the existence of slavery retarded the public school system in the South nearly two centuries behind, let us say, New England. What is actually the truth is, that the South, up until the 1930's was a relic of England, and England in the days of the Tudors and the Stuarts. Certainly England before the Industrial Revolution. Leaving out the Negroes, they conceived, as they do in England, of a upper-class specially manufactured by God. Every King's birthday in England, they knight some manufaturer for outstanding success, but you so well know that the "Blood" does not accept them. They are known as "Pickle Barons".

Add to this ancestor-worship the lack of communication in the South away from the main centers, and you find the retention of old English beliefs and customs, songs and ballads and Elizabethan figures of speech. They go for the simile and especially the metaphor. As in the bloom of Elizabethan literature, they love speech for the sake of speech. This is common to white and black. The invective is practiced as a folk art from earliest childhood. You have observed that when a southern Senator or representative gets the floor, no Yankee can stand up to him so far as compelling language goes. His logic may be all wrong, but he can certainly say what he has to say in a colorful manner. He can call every Senator there something belittling and colorful and still have some names left over for rebuttal. As we say down South, they "handle the dictionary" and sling language. They did not get it from the Negroes. The Africans coming to America got it from them. If it were African, then why is it not in evidence among all Negroes in the western world? No, the agrarian system stabilized in the South by slavery slowed down change and lack of communication aided this retardation, and so the tendency towards colorful language that characterized Shakespeare and his contemporaries and made possible the beautiful and poetic language of the King James Bible got left over to an extent in the rural South. The double descriptive and all of that.

[2]*Actress.*

And behind the story is the consciousness on my part that there is more than a geographical difference between the North and the South. The New Englander came here in protest against both religious and civil abuses, and with the inclination to change. The vanguard of the new philosophy of the importance of the individual. For the most part, the people who came to the southern colonies were affiliated with the ruling class, were satisfied with it, and came for economic reasons only. To extend and build it up in this new land. The causes leading up to the Civil War have been tremendously over-simplified. Negro slavery was not the predisposing cause, but merely the exciting cause. There was not an intelligent man North nor South who did not know that human slavery had to go. In fact, Abolition arose in the South. Many prominent southerners had been prophesying against it ever since the Revolution. There was nothing that could not have been adjusted if the contending parties had been willing to concede anything to the other. They failed to make these concessions because the struggle was more fundamental than that. It was a continuation of the class struggle between Cavlier and Roundhead. The poor whites in the South fell in behind the big landowners because they were still English-minded, and that he should follow the lead of his "betters." The "Blood" in the South wanted to secede because the idea of being dominated by the "mongrel North" was intolerable to them, just as Wally Simpson is to England right now. You saw how monarchial England hurried to the aid of the Cavalier South. The South has always been English, insular, assured that what they have always believed is bound to be right, and suspicious of outsiders and new ideas. Richard P. Daniels, a prominent lawyer of Jacksonville, and a scion of one of the South's oldest families told me that he is certain that the South was hurried into the Civil War at the instigation of England. That Jeff Davis and some of his associates were bent on joining Engla[n]d as soon as the South had succeeded in making the break, but were forced to conceal this purpose by Robert E. Lee, who did not want the war at all, and was only persuaded to cast in his lot with the South on the assurance that if it won, it would remain an independent American nation. His opposition was so well known, and he was wavering so, that Fort Sumter was hurriedly fired upon to force the issue and to force him and some few other able men to go along with their section of the country. Without him and some few others, it was felt that the South had no chance of winning. Daniels states that before Jeff Davis tried to flee in women's clothes that many papers were destroyed, which had they come to public notice would have broken Lee's heart, and disillusioned many more ardent southerners, and exposed the plot directed from England of cutting off such a huge part of the U.S. an re-annex it to England. He says that several southern scholars of history have held this suspicion, but no actual papers have ever been found, [word illegible] it will remain forever a southern secret. He says that the Virginia Historical Society has documents that prove the reluctance of Lee because he feared that the South cut off from the North could not withstand England, and that both sections, taken separately, could in a short time be whipped back into the Empire.

I am attempting to give a true picture of the South by showing Jim Meserve[3] as a member of that liberal class which has always existed in the South in a minority, who believed in the benefits of the Union and advancement. As you know, many like that fled the South on the approach of the Civil War and joined the North and fought in the Union army. Eastern Tennessee sent several regiments to the Union armies. As you know, all those southerners who held such sentiments right after the War were known as Scalawags. Nor is that trite picture of the noble and freedom-loving Negro true. There were thousands and thousands of free Negroes in the South before the War, and many of them held slaves, and fought like tigers in the Confederate armies to maintain slavery. Some didnt own any, but fought for the South anyway. I am not one of those sentimentalist who love to take sides whether my stand is valid or not. In truth, the South presents a very confusing picture. Virginius Dabney and Bilbo side by side.[4] High-mindedness and savagery side by side. In my native state, look at the ignorant Governor Cone followed by the brilliant and advanced Spessard Holland (now Senator). I want the book to look like the people it is written about. In regards to Bilbo, I have never accepted the premise that he was all that ignorant and vicious. He was a man who wanted to get along, and played on the backwardsness of his constituents, that is the majority of them. He knew only too well that many intelligent men in his state were disgusted with him. In order to prosper, he had to holler them down.

[3]*The male protagonist in* Seraph on the Suwanee.

[4]*Liberal University of Virginia historian and journalist Virginius Dabney was accused by blacks during this period of being too conciliatory with southern whites over segregation. Mississippi senator Theodore Bilbo was a states' rights, anti–New Deal, antilabor racist who openly supported the Ku Klux Klan in 1946.*

I do not know how much you know about the South, and I have risked boring you to show you the matrix out of which the story arises. How and why the characters are like they are. I shall cut out hunks of Arvay and put in more incidents as you suggest to show her stumbling advance to discover herself. You know yourself that a woman is most powerful when she is weak. Men were willing to do a thousand times more for Mary, Queen of Scots than for Elizabeth, and Lizzie so well knew it. All a woman needs to have is sufficient allure, and able men will move the world for her. I am convinced the male gland produces something that puts him out ahead of the most brilliant woman in constructive ways. I mean of course an intelligent man. In the arts it is different. But no woman has ever topped the best man in any of the professions like Medicine, Law, Architecture, Engineering, etc. Nor have any "strong" women inspired that kind of love to make him get out and do it. He fights like a tiger to protect some alluring, weakly thing. Even the men whom Elizabeth advanced were ready to desert her for Mary.

I thank you.

Zora Neale Hurston

TO BURROUGHS MITCHELL

Puerto Cortes, Honduras, C.A.
October Something Late, 1947

Dear Mr. Mitchell:

I have the revision all done, and planned to get it off on the boat-mail tomorrow morning, but this afternoon came a letter from the Watkins office making some suggestions, so I will read and work tonight and tomorrow and get it off by the end of the week.[1] The Watkins letter was very kind and makes me feel better. I was afraid that she had forgotten me.

The book is about fifty pages longer than I want it to be and I hope that you can see where you can chop it down some more. I have telescoped material in the latter part of the book, and even just left out some.

[1] Seraph on the Suwanee.

But I felt that I had to add a chapter on Kenny in New York to explain his success.[2] Though no one to my knowledge has come right out and said it as yet, we have had a revolution in national expression in music that is equivalent to Chaucer's use of the native idiom in England. Gershwin's PORGY AND BESS brought to a head that which had been in the making for at least a decade. There is no more Negro music in the U.S. It has been fused and merged and become the national expression, and displaced the worship of European expression. In fact, it is now denied, (and with some truth) that it never was pure Negro music, but an adaptation of white music. That is as over-simplified as the former claim that it was something purely negroid. But the fact remains that what has evolved here is something american, and has come to be the national expression, and is as such influencing the music of the world. Kenny is only one of the thousands of white artists who in one way another work through the accepted medium, and is explained. On your suggestion, I have adopted direct presentation in several places in place og omniscience.

You are so kind. You have helped me in so many ways, and I hope that you will continue where you see the script needs some attention. I am striving to make it as easy for you as possible. Please remember that I am neither Moses nor any of the writing apostles. Nothing that I set down is sacred. Any word or sentence can be changed or even cut out. What we want is success, not my deification.

If you find a mule tied to a tree, wring his tail and think of me.

(That is, if you are able to do any thinking after you cut a caper like that.)

Zora Neale Hurston

TO BURROUGHS MITCHELL

Dec. 5, 1947

Dear Editor Burroughs Mitchell:

I have a letter from the Watkins office of Nov. 21, saying that the script has arrived.[1] I hope that it is in your hands by now.

---

[2] *The son of the two main characters in* Seraph on the Suwanee, *a musician.*

[1] Seraph on the Suwanee; *Hurston often uses "script" as shorthand for "manuscript."*

When I am certain that I am right, I can be very seadfast, as Ann Watkins very well knows by now. Having a mind full of curiosity, however, I always listen for fear that I miss something that I ought to know, but I use my own judgment after that. I did conceed to her that Arvay[2] on the toilet stool might be considered coarse reading, so I put her in the tub. I try to avoid aggravating her for fear tha[t] she will not try to sell it to the movies, nor offer it to some Book Club, and I have given a lot of work, thought and time to the book, and I pray so hard for it to succeed, for the sake of Scribners as well as for myself. I feel so deeply about Maxwell Perkins taking me, and I want to justify his and your faith in me. I have hardly slept since the book left my hands, going over paragraphs, sentences, etc. in my mind seeing where I might have failed to get the best out of a situation and the like. But I know that you can understand how wretched this period is for an author.

Thought that you might like to see this letter. MULES AND MEN has been mightily quoted from in books and on the air many times. The Library of Congress says that it is the most important book on American folk-lore, and no studies on Am. folk-lore fails to mention it. It is one of the sorrows of my life that I could not do it over in the light of greater experience.

The rainy season is on here now, and no fooling! Already I smell fishy, and another month or so of this weather, and I will be waving you a greeting with a fin.

THE ROAD TO THE SUN has just come out of my muddle to invent a title that suits me. Can you think of something more suitable? SUWANEE TO THE SEA? [HOME TO HEAVEN—x-ed out] THE GODDESS OF THE CHIMNEY CORNER? You see the muddle I am in.

Most sincerely yours,
Zora Neale Hurston

[at bottom and along left side:]

There is a recent collection out "The Best in American Humor" I believe is the title, in which I am also included.[3] It is $6.00 I hope that you see a copy. The most famous names in the U.S. from Cotton Mather on are in there.

If you want to hear a really good guitarist in the Negro manner, contact Gabriel Brown, 1254½ Washington St. Asbury Park, N.J. Also ask him about picking up rattlesnakes.

[2]*The main character of* Seraph on the Suwanee.
[3]*Probably* Best in a Hundred Years, American Humor, *published in 1945.*

I particularly want you to know about the rattlesnake, because Watkins jumped me about it. She has an idea that once you get him off the ground, he has no resource but to just dangle. All I hope is that she never tries it. He is a powerful brute.

TO BURROUGHS MITCHELL

Hotel Cosenza
Puerto Cortes, Honduras, C.A.
January 14, 1948.

Dear Burroughs Mitchell:

The suspense is awful![1] I do hope that the terrible cold spell did not do away with the town of New York.

After a long time of stirring up the fat in my head, it seems to me that GOOD MORNING, SUN is a good title.

In this same mail I am writing to the Watkins of ice to see if they have finished with the script and turned it over to you.

I hope that you had a fine Christmas with lots of eggnog, and choice cuts of turkey bosom. I was fairly happy here in spite of the endless rains of the season. We had 18 inches here in three days. It is still at it with a vengeance. There is no opportunity for me to get back into the interior and do any kind of research with this kind of weather. It is bad enough in a city, with the lack of paving, and you must know what it would be like in the woods and mountains without definite roads. And the mud here is very affectionate. Nothing for me to do much but gnaw finger-nails and do some articles from the inside of me, and listen to a group of norteamericanos who are here building a big storage tank for TEXACO bulldoze the natives, watch and listen to three of the "sheltered and protected" Senoras make promiscuous love all over the place and their neglected children run up and down the corridor screaming and yelling. And running flatfooted at that.

> Sincerely yours,
> Zora Neale Hurston

[1] *Hurston was waiting to see if* Seraph on the Suwanee *would be accepted by Mitchell; the Watkins Agency had not yet sent over her manuscript.*

TO EGON MATHIESON

Puerto Cortes, Honduras, C.A.
C/O United Fruit Company
January 220 [22], 1948.

Dear Egon Mathieson:

I am down here in the Tropics doing some research, and your book has not yet come into my hands.[1] It was received by my former publisher, Lippincott, and sent on to the address of a friend of mine, Dr. John Erskine and his wife, Helen Worden, both of whom you probably know by reputation. He is head of the Dwpt. of English at Columbia University, and has also written many distinguished books.[2] They wrote me, telling me of the arrival of two books in which I am included, yours, and another one of the United States. So I have not had the pleasure as yet of seeing the book. I did not order it sent on here because I am undecided as to how much longer I shall be here and it might get lost in transit.

MULES AND MEN is now, by the shabby negligence of my former publisher, out of print. It is hard to get, and I find that it brings $12 a copy. Nevertheless, I shall send you one as soon as I get back to the U.S., which will be in two months perhaps. If I do not find certain things here which I am looking for, it may be sooner than that. Naturally, I shall be ever so delighted to receive your books. I am not so erudite as you, and so do not know Danish, but perhaps it is time that I learned it anyway. Then I can read your books with pleasure. It will be a lovely meeting of your mind.

My present publisher is CHARLES SCRIBNERS SONS, 597 Fifth Avenue, New York, 1Y [sic], N.Y. (17)

If you ever plan visiting the U.S. you must please be kind enough to let me know. Why not make application for membership to the

[1]Aben Osvald *was published in 1947.*

[2]*John Erskine's books include* Actaeon, and Other Poems *(1907),* Adam and Eve *(1927),* American Character and Other Essays *(1927),* The Complete Life *(1943),* The Delight of Great Books *(1928),* The Private Life of Helen of Troy *(1947), and* Prohibition and Christianity, and Other Paradoxes of the American Spirit *(1927).*

American Folklore Society?[3] Submit something to Dr. Wayland D. Hand,[4] Editor, University of California, Los Angeles 24, California, U.S.A. And our Ethnological Society too.

Need I say how grateful I am to you for your notice in your work? Please be assured of it. I shall order additional copies as soon as I get back to the States. In the meanwhile, if you feel to be generous, send me a card or a letter here at your pleasure.

Sincerely yours,
Zora Neale Hurston

TO BURROUGHS MITCHELL

Puerto Cortes
Honduras, C.A.
February 3, 1948.

Dear Mr. Mitchell:

Received your letter, and two from [Ann] Watkins. In the last one, as of January 29, I was asked to cable my answer as to whether I would come or not, and that I would have a reply from you in twenty-four hours. I cabled Friday A.M. that I would make the trip, but here it is Tuesday and no word from New York as yet. And I had booked passage for tomorrow's sailing that would put me into Baltimore. From the irregularity of things here, I am not sure that the cable went on time as it would have in the U.S. Anyway, I dont know what to do.

I take it very kindly that you are willing to do so much in an editorial way for the book. I am only too glad to do what is needful. Anyway, I suppose that I am like most authors, that is, never get through writing a book. I have been longing to do some polishing myself.

I assume tha you have been noticing trends and by now you have noted the absorption of Negro art expressions into the national expres-

---

[3]*The American Folklore Society was founded in 1888 by Franz Boas et al. Its principal emphasis was publishing a scientific journal and convening an annual meeting.*
[4]*Wayland D. Hand (1907–86) was a faculty member of German languages at UCLA. He developed an interdepartmental teaching program and research institute in folklore. In 1941, he founded the California Folklore Society.*

sion and the disappearance of it into the whole. That is of course natural, but few seem to notice it. The same thing has happened in Cuba and other Latin American countries. The dances and the music like the Rumba, Samba, Conga, etc. have been taken over from the former African slaves and made national, and are no longer associated with their origins. So far as idiom is concerned in the U.S., a brief s[t]udy will show that there is no such thing as a N[e]gro dialect in the U.S. It is southern, and from the influence of the black-face minstrels, anything quaint and humorous has been attributed to the darkies. It is a comvention like the making the Scots the source of all jokes about penny-pinching, or Jews. This evaluation naturally lessens the stature of the Negro as a contributor to American expression, but it is nevertheless true. It is going to be discovered by others sooner or later anyway. I have been reading and reading in the last three months and I am astonished how pervasive the idiom is in southern literature and that of the early West. So I know that I am right on that score.

Here's to my return to cold New York and the return to the revision of the book! I wait to hear from you.

Most gratefully and warmly,
Zora Neale Hurston

TO BURROUGHS MITCHELL

Puerto Cortes
February 14th. [1948]

Dear Burroughs Mitchell:
I received the money on the 9th, for which I wish to thank you very much. That much gratitude will have to do until I can tell you in person.

I had planned to sail on Feb. 4th, but found that I had to get a Permiso de Salida to leave the country, and Brother, I have been on the strut ever since I got your first letter telling me to come. First to the local commandancia, where I thought that the matter would be all settled in half and hour. (Ooh, la, la! as I said when I used to be French.) No, I must lay my case before the Gobernador Politico at San Pedro de Sula, which is the capitol of the Department of Cortes. Four trips back

and forth, and two wires to the Minister of the Exterior at Tegucigalpa. I have done so much running that I am due four new names,
Shorty, Stumpy, Peg-leg and Nubby from the way I have worn my
gams down. I would still be at it but for the help of the American Consul at San Pedro. He was very, very firm yesterday, and I have the
promise that I will get the papers on Monday, the 16th. On the
strength of that, I have booked passage for Feb. 20, the first boat for
New York. I understand that it is a five day run.

Having been down here in the bush so many months, you might
have to run me down and catch me and sort of tie me up in the shed
until I get house-broke again. No telling what all I might do when I
see all them houses. When I get tame, I might have some interesting
things to tell you.

So far as I'm concerned, you are playing first trombone in God's
best band. Therefore I was very sorry to hear that you had been ill.

Hasta la vista

> Sincerely,
> Zora
> Zora Neale Hurston

TO WHITNEY DARROW

[postcard postmarked July 30, 1948, Rhinebeck, N.Y.]

The task is done.[1] I plan to head back to New York by Sunday.
Deeply grateful.

> Zora Neale Hurston
> c/o Mrs. William Seabrook[2]

---

[1]*Hurston had completed her revisions of* Seraph on the Suwanee *and was doing research for an article.*
[2]*Wife of William Seabrook, author of the introduction to Faustin Wirkus's* The White King of La Gonave.

TO BURROUGHS MITCHELL

[telegram]
[from Rhinebeck, N.Y.]

August 5, 1948

EDITOR BURROUGHS MITCHELL

CHARLES SCRIBNER AND SONS 597 FIFTH AVE NYK

GRATITUDE AND BEST REGARDS TO YOURSELF
DEDICATION TO MARJERIE [sic] KINNAN RAWLINGS AND MRS
SPESSARD L HOLLAND WITH LOVING ADMIRATION[1]
                                ZORA NEALE HURSTON.

TO CARL VAN VECHTEN AND FANIA MARINOFF

[October 30, 1948—library dated]
974 Ca[u]ldwell Ave
New York City.

Dear Carl and Fania:

No, you by no means invaded my privacy. A dozen times since this horror[1] struck me, I have crept to the phone to talk about it with you, but the horror and the loathing of the filth that had been spewed upon me was so great and so unbelievable, that I could not bring myself to take it in my mouth.

The thing is too fantastic, too evil, too far from reality for me to conceive of it. I am charged with meeting this boy at 4:30 every Satur-

---

[1]*This is the dedication that the published version carried.*

[1]*Of being charged with the sexual molestation of a child.*

day afternoon in the basement of a house where I have never been and in company with two other adults whom I have never seen.[2] This was said to be going on for more than a year, the very time when I was in Honduras. In spite of the fact that the woman who is doing this lying knows that I was not in the U.S. because I went from her apartment to Honduras. I laughed when Alexander Miller, [of] the SPCC (Children's Society) told me that. Then he said, with a look of disappointment on his face, "Oh, but I understood differently." I urged him to make an investigation of the matter, even give me a lie-detector test, but he brushed it aside. Then he went out into the room where the boy was, and came back to me and said, "but the boys say that it has been going on since then. You say tha you returned in the Spring. William says that you have been meeting him early in August." I laughed at that too, and said that I was not in New York City early in August. I was upstate,[3] and could not have returned earlier than the middle of the month. "Oh, maybe he could be off a week in his dates," Miller countered. When [t]he hearing came, I found that he had fixed the date, the ONLY positive one as August 15th of this year. Then the horror took me, for I saw that he was not seeking truth, but to make his charges stick. Horror of disbelief took me. I could not believe that a thing like that could be happening in the United States and least of all to me. It just could not be true! I must be having a nightmare.

One inconceivable horror after another swept over me. I went out of myself, I am sure, though no one seemed to notice. It seemed that every hour some other terror assailed me, the last being the AFRO-AMERICAN sluice of filth.[4] You should know that a Negro who works down in the courts secured the matter and went around peddling it to papers. That is the blow that knocked me loose from all that I have ever looked to and cherished. Louis Waldman, my lawyer, assures me that the thing is so patently false, that I will have an excellent chance to sue both the Children's Society and thepaper.

But listen, Carl and Fania; I care nothing for anything anymore.

[2] *The charges were filed on behalf of three boys: Robert Lowrie, William Allen, and Jerry Whaley. Hurston was indicted along with one other adult, Rufus Cousar. Originally three other adults—Aracelia Irazarry, Frank Hardy, and Willie Richmond—were named in a separate indictment.*

[3] *Hurston had been in Rhinebeck, revising* Seraph on the Suwanee *at the home of Constance and William Seabrook.*

[4] *On October 23, 1948, the* Baltimore Afro-American *ran an incendiary front-page story titled "Boys, 10, Accuse Zora" with the subtitle "Novelist Arrested on Morals Charge. Reviewer of Author's Latest Book Notes Character is 'Hungry for Love.'"*

My country has failed me utterly. My race has seen fit to destroy me without reason, and with the vilest tools conceived of by man so far. A Society, eminently Christian, and supposedly devoted to super-decency has gone so far from it's announced purpose, not to protect children, but to exploit the gruesome fancies of a pathological case and do this thing to human decency. Please do not forget that this thing was not done in the South, but in the so-called liberal North. Where shall I look in this country for justice?

This has happened to me, who has always believed in the essential and eventual rightness of my country. I have been on my own since I was fourteen, scuffling my way through high school and college, and as you know, I have never lived an easy life, but struggled on and on to achieve my ideals. I have believed in America; I have fought the good fight; I have kept the faith. They talk of Russia and Madam Kasenkina,[5] but even Russia has never done a thing so foul.

124th St. is in a state of horror over the thing because they know tha it is not true. I find that various simple people have been running around trying to make themselves heard by officaldom, but they have no force, being ordinary colored people. The officials have stuck their necks out, Waldman says, and must try to make good on it, knowing the consequences, that is, if they fail, which they must. Two women of that 400 block hunted me up to express their indignation, and to tell me that this Mayme Allen,[6] was in love with a man, (married) whom she has been living with, and that he did not want the boy around, and that she had been trying for months to get him in some boarding school. He could not be placed because he is a mental defective. Then she began to seek some way to put him in an institution. She is quoted by Mrs. Davis and Mrs. Ryan[7] as saying that she saw her chance when one boy named Robert yelled across the street and called her william a fairy. She began to watch and a few days la[t]er, caught her son and a boy named Jerry [Whaley—co-complainant] in the act. She runs to

[5]Mrs. Oksana Stepanova Kasenkina, a Soviet teacher working with Russian children at the United Nations, sought asylum in an anti-communist camp in Nyack, New York, where she was seized by the Soviet consul, whose refusal to release her sparked a sensational incident during which Kasenkina tried to commit suicide by leaping from the Soviet consulate. The incident was largely responsible for the suspension of all U.S.–U.S.S.R. consular relations for the next twenty years.

[6]Hurston's former landlady and the mother of William Allen, one of the three boys listed as complainants. According to handwritten notes in the case file, Mayme Allen was a Columbia University employee from January 1947 to August 1948. The district attorney's case notes state that "Allen resented her [Hurston]" and that "Allen doesn't like Zora."

[7]Neighbors; both Ryan and Davis were interviewed by the attorneys investigating the case.

the Children's Society, but then, she does not wish to portray her son as a bad boy. He has been sinned against, not sinned himself, so she manufactures this horrible tale involving me, a man in the block named Rufus Cursair, a Puerto Rican woman who is married and keeps a candy store on La Salle St, and is the mother of four children [Aracelia Irazarry—not indicted in the case], saying that we all met this son of hers at 445 W. 124th St. at 4:30 every Sat. P.M. and all of us went with the boy. AND IN THE COAL-BIN! And all being present and participating at the same time. I have never seen any of these people, and they do not know me even by sight. It seems to me that if the Society really wanted to protect children, they would have made some sort of investigation of the home and the background of the boy. They did not know until I told them that I had urged the mother to take the boy to Bellevue back in the winter of 1946-7 for observation and treatment. The mother is herself a defective, and would not take the boy but a few times, stopping the observation, and trying to deceive me by telling me the doctors there said that William was of extraordinary intelligence, a prodigy, no less. So faced with the result of her foolishness, and wanting to be rid of William, this has come about. The Society now hates to admit that it has been victimized by a mental defective, and is passing the buck by saying that it is up to the D.A.[8] They have committed the foulest crime of the century. For leaving the havoc that they have wrought upon me as a public figure, think of what happens to that mother of four children, that poor building Supt. who is lying in jail because he cannot make bail and his job gone and his name ruined. What real estate agent will hire this poor man after this? AND I SWEAR TO YOU BY ALL THAT I HOLD SACRED THAT NOT ONE WORD OF THIS VILE CHARGE IS TRUE. I INVITE YOU, BECAUSE I VALUE YOUR TRUST, TO ASK QUESTIONS AND INVESTIGATE TO TEST MY INNOCENCE. DO THIS FOR THE SAKE OF MY MEMORY.

All that I have ever tried to [do, all—x-ed out] do has proved useless. All that I believed in has failed me. I have resolved to die. It will take a few days for me to set my affairs in order, and then I will go.

I thank you and Fania for your kindness. I had a word from Fanny Hurst too, and both touched me deeply. A similar note from Mary

---

[8]*Frank Hogan, district attorney; Aloysius J. Melia, deputy assistant district attorney. Melia recommended that the case be dismissed because the defendants contradicted themselves and one another.*

Margaret McBride,[9] though she did not mention it. Such tokens have held back this resolution for five days. But no acquital will persuade some people that I am innocent. I feel hurled down a filthy privy hole.

Most devotedly yours,

Zora

Zora Neale Hurston

TO FANNIE HURST

974 Ca[u]ldwell Ave.
New York, 53, N.Y.
fall/winter 1948

Dear My You:

Thanks for your magnificence of spirit. Your thrust of light reached me in my cave so dark and deep that it seems that all the suns of the universe cannot light it up.

I swear to you, by anything and all things that I hold sacred that not one word of this foul and vicious lie is true. It is against everything in my soul and nature. There is no excuse for this most horrible crime of the century.

However, both my race and my nation have seen fit to befoul me with no excuse whatsoever. Even Madam Kasenkina never suffered this much from Russia. And do no forget that this foul thing did not happen to me in the Deep South, but in enlightened New York City. So it seems that even here, there are those who care nothing about fairplay where a Negro is concerned. Nor can I look to christianity for justice, for this Children's Society purports to be governed by thos holy principles. I suppose that I could do a Kasenkina and take refuge in the Russian Embassy and fight my case from there, but now my soul is dead, and I care about nothing anymore. You must believe me when I say that I have ever, and do love my country. If it chooses to destroy me in so foul a manner, let the deed lie upon the city and the national conscience, for

---

[9]McBride, who was a friend of Fannie Hurst's, had a popular daytime NBC radio program on which Hurston was occasionally a guest.

the truth will certainly be known somehow. I believe in the unchange-able laws that govern the universe. Even if I am dead, the truth is bound to be known in time.

I thank you and thank you from the bottom of my soul, and pray that you hold an open mind and remember me kindly.

Most sincerely,

Zora

Zora Neale Hurston

I would never have known such people, but I was sent for to help out in the Republican campaign of 1946,[1] and had to have an address in the District, and to work with as many common people as possible. I honestly did all that I could and look what happens. Nor have I re-ceived a word from one of them.

TO MARJORIE KINNAN RAWLINGS

[fall/winter 1948]

Dear Mrs. Baskin[1]:

Mr. Scribner told me that he had sent you a copy of SERAPH ON THE SUWANEE. It is an anwser, or an attempt at an answer to your kind and loving letter of last Spring. In that letter you advised me to take care and do my best. I am not so sure that I have done my best, but I tried. I need not tell you that my goal still eludes me. I am in de-spair because it keeps ever ahead of me.

I hope that you and Mr. Baskin are feeling fine, and that I will see you when you head south again. I hope to be going down before snow flies myself. Carl Van Vechten says that he wants to give you a dinner when you come through.[2] He will be mighty outdone if you do not let him know when you get [t]o town. I want to see you too very much.

Naturally, I am praying that this book will have a big sale so that I can return the sum that you so generously loanded me. Oh, my dear, so

---

[1]*The Grant/Reynolds campaign.*

[1]*Rawlings was married to Norton Baskin.*

[2]*Rawlings and Van Vechten were distant cousins.*

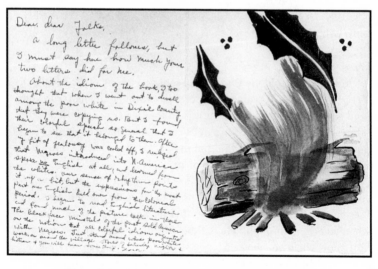

With ardor and fire I wish you a
Merry Qolde Christmas
and a
Happy New Year

Zora Neale Hurston

Had a lovely long letter from Mrs. Spessard Holland. Isn't she wonderful? I admire you two above all other women. — Love. Zora. Oh yes, I want to go back to Florida.

Dear, dear Folks,

a long letter follows, but I must say here how much your two letters did for me.

About the idiom of the book, I too thought that when I went out to dwell among the poor white in Dixie County that they were copying no. their colorful speech so general that I began to see that it belonged to them. After I fit of jealousy was cooled off, I realized that Negroes introduced into N. America spoke no English at all, and learned from the whites. Our sense of rhythm threw points it up a bit, but the expressions for the most part are English held over from the Colonial period. I began to read English literature and found much of the picture talk in those. The black-face minstrels of the past sold America with the notion that all colorful idiom originated with Negroes. Just steep your mind in villages where poor whites and you will hear such things.

Hurston's hand-drawn and hand-painted Christmas card to
Marjorie Kinnan Rawlings and her husband, Norton Baskin,
postmarked December 22, 1948.

much has happened to me since that time. I have had to go through a long, long, dark tunnel to come out to the light again. But I had the feeling all the time that you believed in me and that I had better git up and git or you would feel let down.

> With faithful feelings,
> Zora
> Zora Neale Hurston

I do hope that "Miss Mary" Holland likes the book too.

TO MARJORIE KINNAN RAWLINGS AND NORTON BASKIN

[postmarked December 22, 1948]
[Christmas card—"With ardor and fire I wish you a
Merry Oolde Christmas and a Happy New Year"]

[974 Cauldwell Avenue, New York N.Y.]

Dear, dear Folks,

A long letter follows, but I must say here how much your two letters did for me.

About the idiom of the book,[1] I too thought that when I went out to dwell among the poor white in Dixie County that they were copying us. But I found their colorful speech so general that I began to see that it belonged to them. After my fit of jealousy was cooled off, I realized that Negroes introduced into N. America spoke <u>no</u> English at all, and learned from the whites. Our sense of rhythm points it up a bit, but the expressions for the most part are English held over from the Colonial period. I began to read English literature and found much of the picture talk in there. The black face minstrels of the past sold America on the notion that all colorful idioms originated with Ne-

---

[1]Seraph on the Suwanee.

groes. Just stand around where poor whites work, or around the village stores of Saturday nights & listen & you will hear something. Zora.

[on back of envelope:]
"Tell My Horse"
"Dust Tracks in [sic] the Road"
"Seraph on the Swanee [sic]"
"Moses, Man of the Mountain"

[at bottom of card:] Had a lovely <u>long</u> letter from Mrs. Spessard Holland.[2] Isn't she <u>wonderful</u>? I admire you two above all other women.— Love, Zora. Oh, yes, I want to go back to Florida.

TO HELEN WORDEN ERSKINE

974 Cauldwell Ave.
New York, 56
Feb. 4, 1949

Dear Mrs. Erskine:

I have panged and pained over the fact that that conscienceless Rochester[1] called you up to expose his vile insides and drag you into something of his own making. I have suffered so because I have the impression that you blame me for it. I have searched myself and tried to see how I could have been in anyway responsible, but I have not been able to do so. I did <u>not</u> want him to call you, and that is why he did so. He has carried on a perfect campaign, intended by him to be one, of terror by slander, but still I have to refuse to perjure myself. As he threatened, he went to the Negro press with a story of my smoking marijuana and indecent exposure, but so far they have refused to print it. I have neither been guilty of any of these things, nor did I want him to call you up. This letter is just to put it in my own handwriting

[2]*Wife of Senator Spessard Holland; see glossary.*

[1]*Richard Rochester, the man Hurston felt was behind the false morals charge. Rochester's name is not mentioned in the court records of* People v. Hurston. *Rochester and Hurston were litigants in a simultaneous small-claims case for which court records were not archived. The small-claims case appears to have stemmed from a dispute over a used car.*

so that in some future year you may read it and by then, know that I
am truthful. He lies again when he says that my friends have turned
against me.

Respectfully yours,
Zora Neale Hurston

TO FANNIE HURST

974 Cauldwell Ave.
New York, 56
February 10, 1949

Dear Miss Hurst:

Please help me. You know that I can take it and would not cry out
for help unless I was really desperate.

I can see the end of my troubles as far as my case is concerned, so I
am reasonably calm on that score. In fact, I think that I have at last
ferreted out the source of the matter and know my enemy and whom
and how to fight. Things are now tangible, and my victory yesterday
in the Small Claims Court was a much more important step than it
might seem. I know that I am indebted to you and Mrs. Erskine and to
the Archangel James McGurrin for help in that. The Judge was right
in there defeating the unholy puropose of Richard D. Rochester at
every move. He helped me to prove himself that he did not come
there to collect any 20^{00} from me, but to use the court as a springboard
to scandalize my name. He had to admit that he had not even asked
Mr. Waldman[1] for the money when he talked with him on three different occasions, but had demanded that I perjure myself by swearing
that a man stole a car from Rochester so that he could put the man in
jail, when he knew so well that it was not true. I refused and then he
threatened me with a nation-wide bath of filthy publicity if I did not
agree and so forth. It was all pinned right on him yesterday, and he
could not deny it. From several things that I have learned in the last
two weeks, I know now that this Rochester is the source and founda-

---

[1]*Louis Waldman, Hurston's attorney in the morals case.*

tion of the whole business. He, a meglomaniac, felt so bucked up by what he considered the success of his first attack, that he came out to beat his breast and brag, and that will prove to be his undoing.

By the way, when I see you and give you all the details, you will have an even more powerful book than "Imitation of Life."

What I must have now is enough to keep me alive for two weeks. After that I can go to work. I owe room rent now and other things. I have used up every available resource before appealing to you—even to pawning my typewriter. I have counted up and find that I just must get hold of 76^{00} at once. You see, from my book, I have had to give my lawyer 1,000^{00} and that took care of all my ready cash. I am now strapped and most desperate in mind. I could have done things to help myself, even to going out and taking a job as a domestic, but I have had to keep on running down to court to answer this Rochester's spiteful and untruthful charges. It has been pretty awful. He boasts that he does not hope to win, but to harass me until I perjure myself by giving him that statement so he can jail Arnold Smith. If you were to invite Mrs. Mary Ryan of 425 W. 125th St., Apt. 3,[2] you could get quite a bit of material for your notebook.

Do, please help me, Miss Hurst. You know that I am rather self-sufficient and would not ask help if I could avoid it. I have left much unsaid until I see you.

Yours sincerely,
Zora.

TO WILLIAM CLIFFORD

[May 2, 1949—library dated]
974 Cauldwell Ave.
New York, 56.

Dear, dear Bill:

I have responded to your welcome greeting a thousand times since I got your card. My spirit waved and smiled at you, but my hands kept

---

[2] *Hurston's neighbor, interviewed by the district attorney in* People v. Hurston.

quiet. I had only the day before finished a hard stint at the behest of my literary agent,[1] and come down with a severe case of paper-poisoning, a disease which you will suffer from at times as you progress as an author. I loathed the very sight of writing material.

Sure and certainly, I will be only too happy to read what you have done, and will do all that is in my power to help you in case it requires it in any way possible.

You name the date for that peep at your garden and <u>I will be there.</u>

I want your help too. I want to write about Carl, but so far he has balked at it. You know so well of the magnificence of his nature and all, and add to that his tremendous influence on contemporary art. I would say that he was the greatest influence on American art trends of this century. He towers head and shoulders above all others. I think that he should be written about, a few articles scattered here and there in the best spots, then a book-length work. He and Fania make a team with plenty of color and drama and the world needs to know about them. And <u>I</u> want to be the one to ring up the curtain. See if he will consider it. They are filming the life-stories of far less important people.

I have no phone at present. What I want is a small apartment of my own to get back to hard work. Too many distractions where I am. I am terribly unhappy where I am situated, but until I hear from my agent, here I am, and no help for it.

Most Sincerely Yours,
Zora.

I want to pay Carl Van Vechten off for the marvelous things he has done, and the magnificent friendship he has shown me for 25 years. My heart aches to show him instead of just saying it.

Z

[1] *Jean Parker Waterbury; she worked first for the Ann Watkins agency and later for literary agents Mavis McIntosh and Elizabeth McKee.*

TO HELEN WORDEN ERSKINE

974 Cauldwell Ave.
New York 56, N.Y.
May 2, 1949.

Dear Mrs. Erskine:

On March 14 I was completely exonerated of the charges against me, and I want to thank you for your kind help in the matter. I thank you from the bottom of my soul.[1]

Rochester did everything that his twisted mind could conceive of to involve me on other charges—the same accusations he made to you—but on investigation the D.A. chose to disregard them. He has rushed ahead and proved himself the most unscrupulous of liars, while boasting around of his great cleverness. According to himself, he is brainier than the whole city government and Mr. Waldman[2] is a cretin compared to him, only things have not worked out that way. He was <u>so</u> eager to get me into court, but after his first defeat, he has been pleading for three months for delays on that car business that "his witnesses could not be present." At last, by poking around, he found that Arnold Smith[3] was graduating from the Police Academy on April 28. He asked for that date so that Smith could not be present. Then he boasted about it, and the news came to me, and I got in touch with my lawyer ten days ahead and it was changed to May 10. His chagrin was terrible. He had only a slim chance to win with Arnold Smith absent, and none with Smith there to testify that I had <u>nothing</u> to do with the deal that they made between themselves, which is the honest truth and Rochester so well knows it, Miss Worden. He made a charge of illegal voting against me, which fell flat. Nobody could be found to hear out his charge of my smoking marijuana. I was not even questioned about it. In truth, I have never even seen a marijuana cigarette in my

[1]*Hurston was exonerated of the sexual molestation charges on March 14, 1949. Assistant District Attorney Aloysius J. Melia reviewed the evidence and concluded that the Children's Society had not investigated the case carefully.*

[2]*Louis Waldman, Hurston's lawyer, was hired by Hurston's publisher. Waldman established the evidence—the passport showing Hurston's absence from the States during the alleged date of molestation—that proved Hurston was telling the truth.*

[3]*Police officer in the small-claims case.*

life to my knowledge. Mrs. Joy Ribiero, my former landlady——says that he called her and boasted to her that he was behind that sex charge for spite because I would not go along with him against Arnold Smith about that car. She says, my having lived [in] her house, she knew and he knew that it could <u>not</u> be true, and he laughed and said he didnt care so long as he got even with me for taking sides with Smith. The truth is, I was not taking sides with anyone. Merely sticking to the truth. My code would not allow me to swear that a person stole a car when I knew it to be a lie.

You must see how warped his mind is to do all that damage to himself for so little. I had been friendly to Rochester, and through me, he had met you and other famous people. On his own, he exposed himself as an extortionist, a black-mailer and a brazen perjurer. No one in their senses would trust him for a moment. He is through in New York as he was in Los Angeles, though I did not suspect the depths that he would dive until this car business came up. He merely told me then that his sister, whom he claims he helped to elect to the Board of Education in Los Angeles, had refused to give him authority to better himself "with her damned Methodist conscience." Now I know what he must have demanded of her. He boasted that nobody let him down and got away with it, and from what he has tried on me, I can imagine why he felt it better to place the width of the continent between him and Los Angeles. I fancy that when his sister is contacted, she will have a story to tell.

To show his lack of scruples, he told me that he only had the name of Sarah Speaks[4] when he arrived in New York. He called on her and she was kind to him in many ways. Yet, when he called me and began to make his threats, he boastfully involved her by saying that she was advising him in his campaign of slander. Remember she had been disbarred and was trying to be reinstated. You must know how my lawyer pricked up his ears when Rochester told him that Speaks was advising him. She hotly denied it to me. But even if she had done so, if he had been honorable, he would not have exposed her. Remember, it was Rochester, not I, who took your name in vain to my lawyer and others.

[4]Sarah Pelham Speaks was a black female politician and attorney. She was the head of the Republican National Committee Eastern Colored Division Women's Activities. Disbarred on July 1, 1948, for "a course of conduct which no member of the bar should pursue," she was found guilty of failing to perform legal services for which she had been paid, making false claims as to the status of matters in which she had been retained, and failing to return certain fees received without performance.

A prominent Republican told me that he had called her and used your name there too. You will never fully realize how badly I felt about it, but Mr. Waldman reminded me that it was he, <u>not I</u>, who dragged you in. Instead of influencing the lady against me, she was revolted and dismissed him without courtesy.

Now, May 10, Waldman says he will be handled as roughly as in that other action, and he will not permit another delay by Rochester. Rochester does not want to meet me there, because his weapon was taken from [him] when those sex charges were thrown out without even a trial. He had depended upon my fears to make me perjure myself against Smith and I had chosen to fight. He knew that the courts had already found that he had entered into an agreement with Smith, <u>not me,</u> concerning that car, found that Smith had carried out his part of the agreement promptly and fully, and ruled in Smith's favor. He never had a case against me, and he knew it. He thought that in my position (He said so) I could not afford to fight, and he could force me to make the statement and he could then extort $175^{00} more out of Smith. If I didnt, then he, with the aid of Sarah Speaks, was going to conduct a vicious campaign of slander against me.

I could not go away when you advised me, Miss Worden, because I had no money for transportation. Then I realized that I must stay and fight to the last or he would persuade you that I had something to flee from. I realize how you feared for me. Rochester being such a convincing liar. As terrible as things were for me at the time, I knew that the truth would prevail some day. I knew that time would prove that each and every thing he told you that he could prove on me would collapse for lack of fact. Mrs. Ribiero, my former landlady on 112th St. rushed to me, full of indignation at his charges that he had come there and found me walking naked before her two children and smoking marijuana. All she wanted was a chance to appear in court against him. She knew my habits only too well. All the people on 112th who knew me boil to get a whack at him. I did not tell you, but as early as October, my bail had been vacated, and my lawyer told that when the necessary number of courts had passed, he could apply for dismissal of the sex charges. On investigation, they proved too ridiculous.

Thanking you for your most loyal support in a horrible and trying time, I am

Most faithfully
Zora.

TO JOSEPHINE LEIGHTON

974 Cauldwell Ave.
New York, 56.
August 10, 1949.

Miss Josephine Leighton
John Simon Guggenheim Mem. Foundation
551 Fifth Ave.
New York City.

Dear Miss Leighton:

Yes, I am at the above address for the present, but a safer address will be my publishers, Charles Scribners Sons, 597 Fifth Ave, New York 17. I hope to return to Central America in the near future to try again to find the ancient temple of the Mayans which I believe is to be discovered when someone seeks it hard enough.

Thanks for the announcement of the 1950 awards.

Sincerely yours,
Zora Neale Hurston

TO HELGA EASON

[postmarked December 22, 1949, Miami, Fla.]
[printed greeting: "Best wishes for Christmas
and the New Year!" and "Holiday Wishes from Florida"]

On Board the Motor Vessel
Challenger, McArthur
Causeway, Miami, Florida.

Dear Mrs. Eason:

Your kind letter caught up with me at last right here in your own town.

Proud that you asked me. I will write out the material that you asked me for. I do wish, however, that I might see you face to face at some time.

I hurried down here at the invitation of Capt. R. Fred Irvine, owner of The Challenger, to go on a trip to Spanish Honduras, but it has not come off as yet. We have been out to the Bahamas though. It is a cargo boat and I am sort of super cargo on it, hoping to get some more material out of the tropics.

With faithful feelings,
Zora Neale Hurston

I think that the Challenger will have to move over to the commercial docks today to make room for pleasure craft where we are now. I think that is over on the Beach.

Z.

TO CARL VAN VECHTEN
AND FANIA MARINOFF

[December 22, 1949—library dated]
On board the M.V. CHALLENGER
Miami, Florida.
Box 772

Dear, dear Carl and Fania:

How warmly do I greet you! The warmth of my feeling is beyond the reach of the lead line of words.

I am on Fred's boat doing my book. We were supposed to have sailed for Central America weeks ago, but one thing and another has interfered. Been for a cruise to the Bahamas, though. Maybe back in New York any day now.

Ten million congratulations on your art gallery at Fisk.[1] Received

---

[1] *Van Vechten had established the George Gershwin Memorial Collection of Music and Musical Literature at Fisk in 1944 and the Georgia O'Keeffe Collection of the Work of Alfred Stieglitz at Fisk in November 1949.*

the announcement last week. You are <u>really</u> the greatest influence on American art of this generation. I do wish so much that you would allow me to write a book about you. It is a duty to the world that should be done.

I have regained my peace of mind and cheerfulness, all owing to you.

All my love and faithful feelings.

Zora.

"BEING 'DIFFERENT' HAS ITS DRAWBACKS"

The Fifties

Overleaf: Hurston with friends, late 1950s.

Hurston once told Claude Barnett, founder of one of the nation's most politicized black organizations, the Associated Negro Press, that she had "never been interested in politics."[1] Her apparent indifference to signal African American political events (Scottsboro, race riots, antilynching campaigns) incited the wrath of her activist friends. But as she turned sixty, Hurston increasingly focused on political controversy, ultimately devoting more energy to political writing than she did to anything else. She wrote a series of political essays, covered the highly charged murder trial of Ruby Mc-Collum, and worked on political campaigns. The work to which she devoted her greatest efforts, her biography of Herod the Great, was intended as a political allegory that would clarify contemporary politics. "The answer to what is going on in Europe, Asia, and America lies in that first century B.C.," she wrote her translator.[2]

Hurston's politics in this decade have often baffled her admirers, many of whom knew neither what led up to them nor that she entered the decade at fifty-nine years of age. Turning sharply to the Right and supporting white conservatives like George Smathers and Robert Taft while opposing the Supreme Court's 1954 anti-segregation ruling, Hurston alienated her contemporaries and seemed to move from an intriguing contrariness to an unpleasant bitterness, a near-total repudiation of everything she had once claimed. Consequently, critics write off this period of her life as a time of collapse and confusion, "a talent in ruins."[3]

[1]Hurston to Claude Barnett, [July 21–26, 1946].
[2]Hurston to Margrit de Sablonière, December 3, 1955.
[3]Robert E. Hemenway, Zora Neale Hurston: A Literary Biography (Urbana: University of Illinois Press, 1977), p. 345.

But the letters published here suggest something other than ruin or confusion. Hurston may not have been completely consistent, but there was an underlying logic to her thinking in this decade nonetheless. She became increasingly cantankerous, but her intolerance remained based in the fierce pride that had made her successful. And her wariness was not unearned.

Hurston felt betrayed, disappointed, and thwarted in her goals. At the start of the decade, she looked for a retreat, especially from the traumatic morals indictment of 1948. It was not easy, however, to recover her equilibrium after the nightmare of being falsely accused of molesting a young boy and, worse yet, having her name dragged through the mud by a black press unwilling to wait for the facts before composing their story. She turned her back on black New York, seeking refuge first with her friend Fred Irvine and second with her white Belle Glade friends the Creeches. "I feel that I have come to myself at last. I can even endure [t]he sight of a Negro, which I thought once I could never do again," she wrote Burroughs Mitchell from Irvine's boat.[4] When Irvine's boat was sold in January 1950, Hurston moved off the bay into Miami. She told Mitchell that she had "thought of returning to New York right away" but that she was not yet ready to do so. "'Baby, it's cold up there,'" she told him. Florida helped her regain her old energy. "Day by day in every way I'm getting human again," she wrote.[5] She promised Mitchell that she would return to New York in March for a final edit of her new novel, *The Lives of Barney Turk*, but she did not, in fact, make that trip until the fall. That brief stay in New York, from late September through early December 1950, was her last. From then on she remained in Florida.

Restlessness had always been a characteristic of Hurston's traveling, writing, and socializing. But this period was defined by a need for domesticity and peace. Above all (and for the first time) Hurston wanted a home. "I wait only on that possible check," she wrote her literary agent and friend Jean Parker Waterbury, "to . . . establish myself in housekeeping once more and again. Being under my own roof, and my personality not invaded by others makes a lot of difference in my outlook on life and everything. Oh, to be once more alone in a house!"[6] It would take months of effort and several moves to create that home, but in 1951, at

[4]*Hurston to Burroughs Mitchell, [winter 1950].*
[5]*Hurston to Burroughs Mitchell, January 24, 1950. She is parodying the popular credo of the era by Emile Caré: "Day by day, in every way, I'm getting better and better."*
[6]*Hurston to Jean Parker Waterbury, [March 6, 1951].*

sixty years of age (passing for much younger), Hurston finally settled down. "I am the happiest I have been in the last ten years," Hurston wrote Waterbury of returning to the run-down, one-room Eau Gallie cottage where she had written *Mules and Men* twenty years earlier. "Somehow, this one spot on earth feels like home to me. I have always intended to come back here," she wrote.[7] Hurston lived alone in the Eau Gallie cottage for six years, by far the longest period of time she had spent in any one place since her adolescence. She was penniless, and almost everything she wrote was rejected. But being able to garden, write, and take care of her pets, she insisted, brought her "definitely back from the dead."[8]

Hurston had come back to Florida to avoid the public. This made her relocation from Miami to Florida's Rivo Island in February 1950 a terrible miscalculation. On Rivo Island, Hurston took a job as a maid with the Burritt family. When her short story "Conscience of the Court" was published in the *Saturday Evening Post* in March,[9] Hurston's employers *and* the national wire services discovered what she was doing.[10] The resulting "publicity do-dad"[11] proved humiliating. Caught by the media, which she couldn't help but see as adversarial, Hurston claimed to be doing research on domestics. A letter written to Jean Parker Waterbury in July 1951 suggests that Hurston was in earnest, at least in part. "As soon as I can get some things in your hands to sell," she wrote, "I shall try to raise the cash for my newspaper devoted to those in domestic service. I really believe that the idea is sound and can makke [sic] money."[12]

It is particularly ironic that the short story that put Hurston back in the spotlight was "The Conscience of the Court," because this was one of the oddest pieces Hurston ever published. It is even odder when considered in light of "What White Publishers Won't Print," an essay that appeared shortly afterward. Published in *Negro Digest* in 1950, "What White Publishers Won't Print" is an important statement on race. It warns of "lack of knowledge about the internal emotions and behavior of the minorities . . . no demand for incisive and full-dress stories around Negroes above the servant class." The root of the problem,

[7]*Hurston to Jean Parker Waterbury, July 9, 1951.*

[8]*Hurston to Burroughs Mitchell, May 1, 1952.*

[9]*The* Post *paid Hurston $900 for the story, a fairly hefty sum for her at the time.*

[10]*James Lyons, "Famous Negro Author Working as a Maid Here Just 'to Live a Little,'"* Miami Herald, *March 27, 1950.*

[11]*Hurston to Burroughs Mitchell, [April 1950], cited by Hemenway,* Hurston, *p. 326. This letter is now missing from the Princeton archive of Burroughs Mitchell's papers.*

[12]*Hurston to Jean Parker Waterbury, July 9, 1951.*

Hurston wrote, had to do with what she called the "AMERICAN MU-SEUM OF UNNATURAL HISTORY": the assumption that "all non-Anglo-Saxons are uncomplicated stereotypes." This ideological museum, she noted, is only interested in the "typical" but never a "true picture." "Let there be light!" she concluded.[13]

"Conscience of the Court" is not very illuminating. It is stereotypical, sentimental, and bathetic and confirms some of the blindest assumptions about blacks. It is not only a story about a servant—exactly the subject matter Hurston decried in "What White Publishers Won't Print"—it is a story in which Laura Lee Kimble, a black female domestic, lives for her beloved white mistress, Celestine Clairborne. One day, when Mrs. Clairborne is away, a man comes to the door threatening to cart away all of Mrs. Clairborne's household goods. Laura Lee is, by her own description, an "unlearnt" and "common-clad" woman, but loyal to the core. She protects her mistress's household by beating the living daylights out of the intruder and then is surprised to find herself on trial for assault. Believing herself abandoned by her beloved mistress, Laura Lee experiences an anguish worse than death. "Even if the sentence was death, she didn't mind. Celestine Beaufort Clairborne had failed her." The court reveals that her mistress had been kept from knowledge of Laura Lee's troubles and that the intruder was taking advantage of Laura Lee's ignorance. Laura Lee is acquitted and released. Instead of feeling vindicated, Laura Lee feels profound guilt for having doubted "her Celestine." She goes back to her mistress's home and refuses to eat. Instead, she performs a "ritual of atonement" by polishing all of Celestine Clairborne's good silver. And here the story ends.[14] It is edited "some from the way I wrote it," Hurston told her librarian friend Helga Eason,[15] but Hurston does not suggest that this final "atonement" was intended as irony. Moreover, in a 1951 letter to Jean Parker Waterbury, Hurston wrote that what *Saturday Evening Post* editor Stuart Rose "did for THE CONSCIENCE OF THE COURT made it the successful story that it was."[16]

From the perspective of Hurston's trial experiences, "The Conscience of the Court" begins to make some sense. It is not just the story of a loyal maid. It uses a stereotypical frame to tell the story of a black woman who has been falsely accused and unfairly treated. Hurston's

[13]*Zora Neale Hurston, "What White Publishers Won't Print,"* Negro Digest, *April 1950.*

[14]*Zora Neale Hurston, "The Conscience of the Court,"* Saturday Evening Post, *March 18, 1950, pp. 22–23, 112–22.*

[15]*Hurston to Helga Eason, "St. Valentine's Day," 1950.*

[16]*Hurston to Jean Parker Waterbury, June 4, 1951.*

experiences in New York, her difficulties clearing her name in the courts, and the impossibility of clearing her name in the press may have drawn her to such a theme, particularly the wish-fulfillment plot of a court that vindicates her and clears her name. Hurston had used courtroom dramas to good symbolic effect before: in *Mule Bone, Their Eyes Were Watching God,* and *Dust Tracks,* they symbolize racism, sexism, and the difficulty of attaining public recognition.

Immediately after the publication of this story and the exposure of her maid's job on Rivo Island, Hurston became involved in another odd writing assignment. In the spring of 1950, she moved back to Miami, where, according to Sara Lee Creech, she stayed at the home of Senator George Smathers, working on his notorious 1950 Senate campaign. There she accepted the job of ghosting an autobiography for his father, Frank Smathers, who lived in an apartment over the garage. She also acted as nurse and aide to Frank, who suffered from arthritis so severe that, according to Creech, he was "crippled in every direction."[17] He was also a very difficult person. In the summer, Hurston wrote to Burroughs Mitchell that she had

> escaped at last from my job of editing, or ghosting that book for old Judge Smathers. I wanted the money, but never did I think I was taking on such a task. . . . he could not accept the reality that a descendent of slaves could do something in an intellectual way that he could not. . . . I let him have it with both barrels. . . . He stuck his crippled fingers in his ears finally, but I reached over and pulled them out and went on talking.[18]

The Smathers family had told her that she "could have ahome with them forever," in spite of her tussles with the elder Smathers.[19]

Hurston was always fiercely loyal to those who were generous with her. This may explain why Hurston supported George Smathers over Claude Pepper in a campaign that David Brinkley called "the dirtiest in the history of American politics."[20] Pepper was a liberal Democrat with the overwhelming support of black voters, as much

---

[17] *Personal interview with Sara Lee Creech. Frank Smathers's book,* It's Wonderful to Live Again, *was eventually published, by Glade House of Coral Gables in 1958. Hurston is not mentioned in it.*

[18] *Hurston to Burroughs Mitchell, July 21, 1950.*

[19] *Ibid.*

[20] *Claude Danson Pepper,* Pepper: Eyewitness to a Century *(New York: Harcourt Brace Jovanovich, 1987), p. 208.*

as 90 percent of the black vote according to some sources.[21] Throughout the South, the Democratic Party had been viewed by black voters
as the party of black disfranchisement, the poll tax, and racism. In
fact, throughout the South, those blacks who registered to vote prior
to the mid-1940s were virtually all registered as Republicans. In
Florida, the shift toward the Democratic Party, first evident in 1946,
has largely been attributed to a "concerted drive for Negro votes
made on behalf of Senator Pepper."[22] Whereas no blacks were registered Florida Democrats in 1944, by 1950 there were more than
100,000 registered black Democrats and only 9,000 registered black
Republicans. Smathers, on the other hand, began his career as a protégé of Pepper's, but then moved increasingly to the political right,
associating himself with such figures as Richard Nixon and Bebe
Rebozo.[23] The main strategy of his 1950 campaign was to Red-bait
Pepper.

Hurston was a passionate anti-communist, and this tactic may have
been effective with her, although the Smathers campaign's claim of
Pepper's communism was not very credible. Using the CIO's support of
Pepper to build a tale of a " 'spiraling web of the Red network,' "
Smathers billed his campaign as one of " 'the Free State against the Jail
State . . . Northern labor bosses, all the Communists, all the Socialists,
all the radicals and the fellow travelers.' " According to some sources, he
dubbed his former patron "Red Pepper" and insulted the intelligence of
his own constituency by assuming that uneducated southern voters
would associate all big words with an implied "great evil":

Are you aware that Claude Pepper is known all over Washington as
a shameless *extrovert*?

Not only that, but this man is reliably reported to practice
nepotism with his sister-in-law, and he has a sister who was once a
thespian in wicked New York.

---

[21]Hugh Douglas Price, "The Negro and Florida Politics, 1944–1954," in Harry A. Bailey, Jr., ed., Negro Politics in America (Columbus: Charles E. Merrill Books, 1967), pp. 260–61.
[22]Ibid., p. 261.
[23]"The Smathers Machine," Ramparts, 10, no. 7 (January 1972), p. 26.

Worst of all, it is an established fact that Mr. Pepper, before his marriage, habitually practiced *celibacy*.[24]

Perhaps the greatest irony of the campaign, however, is that on many crucial issues, the two candidates were not very different. Along with many white southerners, Pepper denounced the FEPC (Fair Employment Practices Commission). Smathers insisted that he was not a racist. Although he had a generally liberal record, Pepper had been a vigorous defender of the notorious white Florida primary—an effort to bar blacks, unilaterally, from voting in the party primary.

By the time of the election (which Smathers won), Hurston had already "escaped" working for Frank Smathers.[25] She went to a friend's house in Miami where she stayed a month or so before going to D.C. and then to New York, where she lived at 239 West 131st Street from September to early December 1950. Somehow, while working as a maid, a nurse, a ghostwriter, and a political campaigner, and moving from place to place, she managed to finish her novel *The Lives of Barney Turk*.

Hurston's only surviving letters from this period give little hint of why she had gone back to New York. Writing to Charles Johnson in December 1950, she stated that she was signing final papers "in the matter that brought me here." This may have been some final legal paperwork on the small-claims suit that had followed the morals charge. Or she may have gone north—as she had often done before—to meet with her editors and sign publishing contracts.

There is another possible reason. She had begun to work with her good friend Sara Lee Creech, a white woman from Belle Glade, Florida, on Creech's idea of an "anthropologically correct"—Hurston's phrase—black doll, and Hurston was instrumental in introducing Creech's project to influential, northern black intellectuals.[26] With Hurston's support and endorsement, Creech met with such black lead-

[24]*Pepper, pp. 198, 203–4. According to Bruce Smathers, Senator Smathers's son, the speech quoted above never took place and the press, not Smathers, created the "Red Pepper" appellation. In Smathers's view, such liberal myths have distorted both the historical record and Hurston's "integrity" in supporting Senator Smathers. In his view, "Zora could have easily supported the progressive segregationist she personally knew [Smathers], rather than the pro-Soviet progressive segregationist she did not know." (Bruce Smathers to Carla Kaplan, "Memorandum," August 29, 2000.)*

[25]*Hurston to Burroughs Mitchell, July 21, 1950.*

[26]*Personal interviews with Sara Lee Creech, May 6 and May 28, 2000. Creech does not believe that Hurston told either her or her mother exactly why she was going to New York, although the three were very close at the time. This suggests that the reason may have been lingering legal complications, about which Hurston was always very private.*

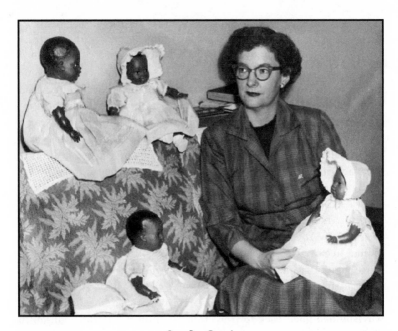

Sara Lee Creech.

ers as Mordecai Johnson, president of Howard University, Ralph Bunche, and Mary McLeod Bethune. All of these leaders attended a tea, sponsored by Eleanor Roosevelt, at which the precise color of the dolls was carefully chosen. The Ideal Toy Company manufactured a doll for Sears, Roebuck. Sears's gamble paid off when the doll proved a minor sensation upon its release in 1951.[27] Hurston was particularly impressed that Creech had sought to capture the beauty of black people. "The thing that pleased me most, Miss Creech[,] was that you, a White girl, should have seen into our hearts so clearly, and sought to meet our longing for understanding of us as we really are, and not as some would have us. That you have not insulted us by a grotesque caricature of Negro children, but conceived something of real Negro beauty."[28]

In the spring of 1950, when she was living with the Smathers family, Sara Lee Creech and her mother, Mary Araminta Young Creech, invited

[27]See, for example, "Realistic Negro Dolls," St. Louis Post Dispatch, November 11, 1951; "Doll for Negro Children," Life, December 17, 1951.

[28]Hurston to Sara Lee Creech, June 29, 1950.

Hurston to speak at Belle Glade's Interracial Council. When she arrived to address the racially mixed crowd at the Lakeshore Elementary School, on May 7, Hurston was carefully attired in what Sara Lee Creech describes as a "very severe white linen dress." She was nervous about her audience and did not relax until the end of her talk, when she acted out some of her characters and sang some of the folk songs she had collected. The second time she addressed the council, however, she "knew her audience." This time she arrived wearing what Sara Lee Creech describes as a slinky orange-red "rape drape" and a turban in the same flaming color. She spoke in both black dialect and "perfect English," performed railroad songs and spirituals, and told stories. She "had that audience," Ms. Creech remembers. "Zora was capable far beyond most to swing from one [world] to another and never miss a beat."[29]

Dressed in her fiery dress and offering what Creech remembers as spellbinding oratory, this flamboyant and flirtatious speaker was also a sixty-year-old woman exhausted from hellish ordeals, homeless, and broke. She was a writer facing a publishing climate inhospitable to black women writers and a celebrity from a movement long gone. Yet her friends remember her as high-spirited, youthful, and optimistic during this time. Hurston didn't like to admit when she was struggling. "Some of the economic kicks I have suffered in the last half year have reached my vitals," she once confided to Jean Parker Waterbury. "Just inching along like a stepped-on worm from day to day. Borrowing a little here and there."[30]

A lifetime of struggling and trying to keep it to herself began taking its toll. For the first time, her letters take a backward-looking stance, as if she was summing up her life, rather than planning ahead. "I have never expected to get rich, and if I have served this nation and the world by digging out a few of it's [sic] hidden treasures and thus enriched our culture, I have gained a great deal. I have had some influence on my time," she wrote to Carl Sandburg.[31] To her ex-husband Herbert Sheen, Hurston wrote: "It is interesting to see how far we both have come since we did our dreaming together in Washington, D.C. We struggled so hard to make our big dreams come true, didn't we? The world has gotten some benefits from us, though we had a swell time too. We lived!"[32]

[29]Personal interview with Sara Lee Creech, May 6, 2000.

[30]Hurston to Jean Parker Waterbury, March 7, 1951.

[31]Hurston to Carl Sandburg, June 12, 1950.

[32]Hurston to Herbert Sheen, March 13, 1953.

While Hurston put on a brave public face, her recuperation from the New York morals indictment was slow, and Sara Lee Creech felt it "scarred" her. She returned from her mysterious business in New York at the very end of 1950 and, at the urging of the Creeches, moved to Belle Glade, Florida, where she lived for six or seven months at the Roof Garden Hotel, which still stands today. During that time, she visited the Creech home daily. Sara Lee Creech remembers that her mother and Hurston sequestered themselves for hours at a time in the parlor, drinking tea and talking about Hurston's New York ordeal. Most of the time, Hurston and Mary Araminta researched Hurston's Herod book, reading the Bible or Josephus's history. Hurston frequently stayed for dinner at the Creeches', and they encouraged her to come and live in their home, but Hurston politely refused, preferring to keep her independence even though she did not enjoy living at the hotel. She kept her social world small—the Creeches and a group of young children who would gather in the hallway of the Roof Garden Hotel for storytelling sessions.[33]

The Creeches took an interest in Hurston's financial and physical health. "How very ill I have been," Hurston wrote to Waterbury. "Finally it came to the place where Sara Lee Creech, not seeing me, came here and found me only half conscious, and rushed me to the hospital. She got the second check out of the Post Office, got my signature at the hospital and paid off my car, income tax, and all the debts [f]or me, since she knew my affairs intimately. She just went ahead."[34]

Shortly after this illness and hospitalization, she moved from the Roof Garden Hotel into the Eau Gallie cabin where she had written *Mules and Men* and which she rented for five dollars a week until being evicted in March 1956. "I am fixing up my new home here," she wrote Waterbury in July. "It is a one-room house, but a large room, and set in two blocks of grounds with an artisan [sic] well. I have to do some pioneering, but I find that I like it. I am the happiest I have been in the last ten years. . . . I am up every morning at five oclock chopping down weeds and planting flowers and things. . . . I go to bed happily tired. . . . I still must remove tons of junk, old tin cans and bottles from the premises. Somehow, this one spot on earth feels like home to me. I

[33]*Personal interview with Cartheda Taylor Mann, June 11, 2000.*

[34]*Hurston to Jean Parker Waterbury, [April 9, 1951]. I read this letter to Sara Lee Creech, who did not remember actually taking Hurston to the hospital, although she said it was possible that she was the one to do so. She did remember that at this time Hurston was particularly low on funds and had asked for a $200 loan.*

have always intended to come back here."[35] Her gardens shortly became so lush that "tourists drive up to take pictures," she told Burroughs Mitchell.[36] Hurston's cabin has been moved from the corner of Guava and Aurora, and efforts are under way to restore it and mark its original site. Sara Lee Creech remembers it as comfortable and inviting, with a big front porch, rocking chairs, and a swing. The setting is still pleasant, with a good breeze coming off the Indian River only two short blocks away. Even today there are beautiful birds in the Indian River, and the area teems with plants and flowers. Hurston was so happy with this house that she made various attempts to buy it. The neighborhood had become mostly white over the years since she had last lived there, and her landlord, a Mr. Gleason, had to proceed cautiously. Nevertheless, Hurston was confident that she would eventually prevail.

The move to a home of her own gave Hurston the occasion to settle down to a great deal of writing. Much of it, however, never saw its way into publication. As Hemenway puts it, "she wrote constantly and without much success."[37] There were political articles penned primarily for money. There were two ghostwritten books, one for Frank Smathers and another that she undertook for a Colonel Lasher, whom she described to friends as "anti-women," a project she abandoned on the grounds that working on it "upset my digestive and elimination system to the extent of my serious illness . . . I gladly washed my hands of his book."[38] She also wrote many articles on Ruby McCollum's murder trial.

It has long been assumed that "Zora's last major literary undertaking was the story of Herod the Great, a story which obsessed her mind and took up most of her time."[39] Hurston described this book as a "great obsession."[40] For five years of this decade, she devoted a great deal of time to both writing the book and writing *about* it (in as many as ten very long letters to friends). Hurston felt that the Herod book was extremely important because it was "not really the story of a man, but of a movement which has ended up in Christianity on one hand, and as the basis of Western civilization on the other," as she wrote to her Scribner's editor Burroughs Mitchell. "Herod is THE connecting

[35]*Hurston to Jean Parker Waterbury, July 9, 1951.*

[36]*Hurston to Burroughs Mitchell, May 1, 1952.*

[37]*Hemenway, Hurston, p. 340.*

[38]*Hurston to "Keepers of the Sacred Spring" (reference librarians at the Miami Public Library), December 6, 1955.*

[39]*Lillie Howard, Zora Neale Hurston (Boston: Twayne, 1980), p. 52.*

[40]*Hurston to Burroughs Mitchell, October 2, 1953.*

personality between the old Judaism and Christianity," she told Mitchell. "Since nowhere else in Western literature is the picture of this century before Christ explained, I thought that I ought to do it by all means."[41] The "long and intense ideological war" between Jews and Christians stood, for Hurston, for much of what was transpiring in the modern world. She also felt the story was so filled with dramatic potential that it was perfect for Hollywood. Cecil B. DeMille, Orson Welles, or Winston Churchill should be approached about the project, she believed.[42] Not only was Herod greatly misunderstood in Hurston's view—"he never could have perpertrated [sic] the massacre of the innocents"—but the story, as she put it, "has EVERYTHING": political intrigue, adventure, romance, philosophy, religion, battles, national and international allegories.[43] As early as 1945, she wrote Carl Van Vechten that she was "burning to write" this "whale of a story."[44]

Scribner's rejected the manuscript in 1955, as did David McKay publishers in 1958 and Harper Brothers in 1959, shortly before Hurston's death. Only portions of the manuscript survived the fire that disposed of Hurston's personal effects, but even those fragments demonstrate why Hurston was unable to find a willing publisher. As Hemenway puts it, the "manuscript suffers from poor characterization, pedantic scholarship, and inconsistent style."[45] It is hard to imagine how Hurston could not have known there were problems with the Herod book. Even her letters about it seem dull compared to others. But evidently, she had lost touch with her audiences and with what they—and her publishers—wanted her to write.

Her letters reveal, however, that other writing projects, one in particular, may have been every bit as important to her as the Herod book. That project, of which no known manuscript survives,[46] was a book called *The Golden Bench of God*, based on the lives of hairdressing entrepreneur Sarah Breedlove Walker, known as Madame C. J. Walker, her daughter

[41]Hurston to Burroughs Mitchell, [July/August, 1951].

[42]See Hurston to Jean Parker Waterbury, July 9, 1951; Hurston to Miss Mousley, May 7, 1954; and Hurston to Mary Holland, June 13, 1955.

[43]Hurston to Burroughs Mitchell, October 2, 1953; Hurston to Max Eastman, August 2, 1955.

[44]Hurston to Carl Van Vechten, September 12, 1945; Hurston to Carl Van Vechten, July 30, 1947.

[45]Hemenway, Hurston, p. 345.

[46]Deputy Patrick Duvall, who salvaged most of Hurston's papers after her death and then stored them on his porch for over a year until he could persuade someone to take them, remembers that there were two manuscripts at the top of those papers and that one of Hurston's good friends in Fort Pierce took them away to read. It is altogether possible that those two manuscripts were Hurston's copies of The Lives of Barney Turk and The Golden Bench of God. Personal interviews with Margaret Benton and Patrick Duvall, June 12, 2000.

A'Lelia Walker, and Annie Pope Malone, also a hairdressing entrepreneur and one of Hurston's very early patrons and friends. Walker and Malone were two of the first black millionaires.[47] In fact, they were *the* first black American *women* to earn a million dollars. Both were flamboyant, dynamic, dramatic, and the focus of public fascination. There is much evidence that this book, unlike *Herod*, did have truly great potential.

Hurston was interested in Walker's and Malone's success and also, presumably, their role within the African American community. She discussed her book about them in more than fifteen known letters written in the early fifties, and she returned to the novel over and over, developing it variously as a novelette, a play, and a movie script. She was determined that this story see the light of day. "It is time that something is said about an industry so important to Negro millions," she wrote Waterbury.[48] "I have caught fire on the novel."[49]

The Golden Bench of God may have been the most racially conscious piece of writing Hurston ever did. One reason she was so fascinated with the hair-straightening business was that "there was no white man in it."[50] This book was also different from her other work because Hurston was determined that this one would be written for herself and for her black readers—no pandering to white popular or critical opinion. "You know," she wrote to Waterbury in a confidential mood, "never a truly indigenous Negro novel has been written so far. Punches have been pulled to 'keep things from the white folks' or angled politically, well to show our sufferings, rather than to tell a story as is. I have decided that the time has come to write truthfully from the inside. Imagine that no white audience is present to hear what is said."[51] Evidently, this was a liberating vision. "I feel more confident about this story," she wrote Waterbury, "than anything I have done since THEIR EYES WERE WATCHING GOD."[52]

Hurston was reluctant to work up the material as a novel, fearing another rejection. "The very mention of 'novel' gives me a shudder," she confided.[53] She was also afraid that the material was so rich and

---

[47] Each has been called, by various histories and sources, the "first" black woman millionaire. In all likelihood, they passed the million-dollar mark at roughly the same time.
[48] Hurston to Jean Parker Waterbury, [February 26, 1951].
[49] Hurston to Jean Parker Waterbury, March 18, 1951.
[50] Hurston to Jean Parker Waterbury, March 7, 1951.
[51] Hurston to Jean Parker Waterbury, [May 1, 1951].
[52] Hurston to Jean Parker Waterbury, March 18, 1951.
[53] Hurston to Jean Parker Waterbury, March 7, 1951.

original—so untouched by other black writers—that it would be stolen. "Since none of the others have thought to do anything with the hair-[s]traightening business, it might prove a temptation," she told Waterbury.[54]

Among other lost manuscripts from the fifties were short pieces on her dog, called "Spot" or "Miss Spot," an essay on intraracial black prejudice, one on gender, another on Ham's curse, and a story entitled "Spook Hill" (a version, presumably, of the Seminole legend about Florida chief Cufcowellax's fight against an enormous alligator that was tormenting his village and, in the process, creating a sacred basin, Spook Hill), and *The Lives of Barney Turk*. In the early winter of 1950, she had written to Burroughs Mitchell of her hope that he would find the novel "interesting."[55] In the fall, she sent him the completed manuscript. "Here's Barney Turk at last," she wrote. "I like the boy and wish him every success."[56] When Scribner's rejected the novel later that fall, Hurston was deeply disappointed—and also broke. "You have no idea what I have been through in the last six months," she wrote to Waterbury. "After using the money that I earned otherwise to buy the leisure to work on Barney Turk, I found myself with a year's work gone for nothing, and me cold in hand. That is a Negro way of saying penniless. And I do mean penniless."[57]

To follow such disappointment—over a novel she thought Scribner's would like—with one deliberately written "as if no white audience was present" was an act of extreme foolhardiness or bravery, or both. When Hurston believed in her material, as she did with both *The Golden Bench of God* and *Herod the Great*, she was capable of taking tremendous personal risk. She wrote regardless of the consequences, even when she could ill afford such a stance.

Probably no writing project had ever been as risky as the one she undertook in 1952 and 1953: coverage of the murder trial of Ruby McCollum, "perhaps the most sensational trial ever held in the South," Hurston wrote.[58] As white journalist William Bradford Huie put it, this case seemed more like fiction than reality: "in short, the richest and soberest Negro housewife in the county was murdering the biggest, most humane, and most ambitious white doctor-politician, on a Sunday

[54]*Hurston to Jean Parker Waterbury, July 9, 1951.*

[55]*Hurston to Burroughs Mitchell, [winter 1950].*

[56]*Hurston to Burroughs Mitchell, September 8, 1950.*

[57]*Hurston to Jean Parker Waterbury, March 7, 1951.*

[58]*Zora Neale Hurston, "Ruby McCollum Fights for Life,"* Pittsburgh Courier, *November 22, 1952, p. 1.*

morning, in tobacco season, in the shadow of the courthouse, the jail, and the church; and she was killing him while three other Negro women waited in his office."[59] Hurston covered Ruby McCollum's trial as a reporter for the *Pittsburgh Courier,* one of the nation's leading black weekly newspapers.[60] This assignment took her into the volcanic center of southern racial politics. Live Oak, Florida, the site of the murder, was a bastion of the Ku Klux Klan. Hurston, a fiercely autonomous and northern-educated, flamboyant African American author accustomed to fame and attention, could hardly have been more of a threat. In spite of her twenty years of experience getting blacks to open up to her, in Live Oak she found the black community closed to her. The Ruby McCollum case was simply too sensational.

Ruby McCollum, an attractive thirty-seven-year-old black mother, was easily the richest black woman in Live Oak, Florida. Her husband, Sam McCollum, ran the local bolita racket—a popular gambling game comprised of numbered balls in a "bolita bag" or numbers on a wheel—and had made a fortune from it. Sam's friend and bolita business partner was Dr. Clifford Leroy Adams, a man known as the poor people's doctor, and one of the most powerful white men in town. "He was a Big Man, powerful, a grandson of wealth and power."[61] He was also Ruby's lover. When Ruby McCollum shot him, he was in the process of parlaying his popular appeal into political and personal power with election to the Florida State Senate.

Adams, however, was anything but heroic. For one thing, he was not a good doctor. He was a man with a deep cruel streak, something of which his close friends were all too aware. " 'I have seen him veer three feet off the side of a road, risk wrecking his car at seventy-five miles an hour, in an effort to kill a dog. One of his favorite sayings was that he hated niggers, dogs, and Yankees—but he really hated almost everybody,' " a friend of Adams's told Huie.[62] In addition to a four-year relationship with McCollum, Adams had a longtime mistress, Evelyn Anderson, a woman twenty years his junior. He "gave" Anderson a house he did not own, a car that was not paid for, and a $50,000 life in-

[59]*William Bradford Huie,* Ruby McCollum: Woman in the Suwannee Jail *(New York: Dutton, 1956), p. 21.*

[60]*Hurston was to have been paid $1,000 for her extensive series of essays. She told Huie, however, that what she came to think of as the "dishonorable behavior of that Pittsburgh gang" resulted in her only being paid a fifth of what was owed her, with the consequence of losing both land and a car that she was in the process of buying. Hurston to William Bradford Huie, March 28, 1954.*

[61]*Huie, p. 20.*

[62]*Huie, p. 106.*

surance policy that did not exist (as Anderson learned after his death). Known for his great generosity to poor patients, Adams made much more money off them through insurance scams than he could have ever made by simply billing them for his services. " 'He was the crookedest sonofabitch I ever met,' " the head of Florida's Blue Cross told Huie.[63] Adams was also a member in good standing of the local Ku Klux Klan. " 'I think that this community ought to erect a monument to [Ruby],' " one former friend of Dr. Adams declared.[64]

Leroy Adams and Ruby McCollum began their affair in 1948. While some witnesses claimed that McCollum adored Adams, others were equally sure that she feared him and wanted out. She also insisted that the murder was committed in self-defense. " 'I think he hit her—he liked to hit women—and then she went for the gun,' " one of her defense lawyers stated.[65] In addition to beating her, some believed Adams was planning to kill Ruby McCollum. " 'If you'll look in the right places, you'll find evidence that he was arranging to kill Ruby, and she knew it,' " Dr. Adams's former nurse told Huie.[66]

During her trial, Ruby McCollum was denied the right to see or speak to any reporters or investigators. She suffered a miscarriage in jail, apparently from a botched abortion she did not want. She went from being a wealthy, robust woman of 145 pounds to a penniless, psychotic woman of 85 pounds who would not sleep on the prison mattress or eat the prison food, convinced that her jailers were trying to kill her.

The trial judge, Hal Adams (no relation to Leroy Adams), refused to allow any evidence in court that might malign Dr. Adams's reputation. This meant that no evidence of the sexual relationship between him and McCollum was admissable in court, including the fact that McCollum was pregnant by him at the time of the murder and had already given birth to a child of his, Loretta, who was then fifteen months old. The proceedings were notoriously irregular. Six of the jurors, for example, were later revealed to have been patients, or relatives of patients, of Dr. Adams. Yet it took more than twenty years and a Supreme Court ruling for her lawyers to have her released from the mental institution where she had been held.

[63] *Huie, p. 139.*
[64] *Ibid., p. 113.*
[65] *Ibid., p. 128.*
[66] *Ibid., p. 157.*

Hurston's coverage of the trial took three forms: a series of investigative articles for the *Pittsburgh Courier*, a section in Huie's book, and a ten-part biography of Ruby McCollum's life, serialized in the *Courier*. She also discussed the case in four letters to Huie, providing crucial hints about the case. Her attitude toward McCollum evolved over time. At first, she was critical of the woman and bent over backward to maintain her own journalistic objectivity, even according the clearly prejudicial judge every possible benefit of the doubt. Eventually, Hurston's view began to shift. While she never excused the murder, she began to sympathize with McCollum's position. She was especially taken with McCollum's stoicism, her refusal to let the courtroom turn her into a spectacle or stereotype of black womanhood. "Her powers of restraint were evident," Hurston commented approvingly. She noted that some blacks applauded McCollum's actions: "Something on the order of Jesse James."[67] "The discerning spectator could not avoid the conclusion that here was no ordinary mortal, no cringing victim inadequate to its fate. There sat an extraordinary personality. Here was a woman—a Negro woman with the courage to dare every fate. . . . She awaits her fate with courage and dignity."[68] Toward the end of the trial, Hurston became more and more sympathetic to Mc-Collum, especially as she uncovered information suggesting that Dr. Adams may have been planning her murder. "It is highly probable that Mrs. McCollum is a victim, instead of the cold, ruthless killer that the state claims her to be."[69] In one of her letters to Huie, Hurston confided sympathizing with McCollum as a scorned woman. "I was and am sorry for the poor thing," she wrote. "She was a woman terribly in love, and with us females, that makes strange and terrible creatures of us."[70]

While on the face of it Hurston and McCollum could hardly seem more different, Hurston may have been seeing points of identification in McCollum's "blanket of silence." Hurston had just completed *The Golden Bench of God*, a novel she felt was one of her best—one written as if "no white audience is present"—and it had been summarily rejected. She had been the victim of a court case in which her own voice was either silenced or not taken seriously, as if whatever a black

---

[67] Hurston, "Ruby McCollum Fights for Life."

[68] Zora Neale Hurston, "The Life Story of Mrs. Ruby J. McCollum!" (installment 1), Pittsburgh Courier, February 28, 1953.

[69] Hurston, "The Life Story of Mrs. Ruby J. McCollum!" (installment 10), Pittsburgh Courier, May 2, 1953.

[70] Hurston to William Bradford Huie, June 10, 1954.

woman might say in her own defense was of no consequence. By the fifties, Hurston was very much alone and, hence, may have identified with McCollum's jailhouse isolation. She certainly identified with the sexism and racism McCollum faced. Hurston's coverage of the trial makes frequent and pointed reminders that although she was a "Famous Novelist, Author, and Lecturer" (as stated in her *Courier* byline), she was still relegated to the upstairs gallery, with every other black spectator at the trial.

Another point of identification may have been McCollum's distrust of others. Throughout the fifties—though there had been glimmers of this earlier—Hurston became increasingly paranoid. She suspected her previous agent of being "after" both her and Jean Parker Waterbury.[71] She feared other writers, publishers, the government, journalists, and especially communists.

Hurston survived the morals charge of 1948, but her faith in others did not. She was depressed not just because she'd been falsely accused but because she now despaired of people ever being able to understand one another. She now despaired for the first time of communication.

One of the most astounding things about her coverage of Ruby McCollum is its word-for-word recycling of descriptions used almost twenty years before for Janie Crawford, heroine of *Their Eyes Were Watching God*, Hurston's most celebrated and autobiographical character. The metaphor used in that novel for personal—and sexual—fulfillment is a "blossoming pear tree." Janie lay under it and

> saw her life like a great tree in leaf . . . from barren brown stems to glistening leaf-buds; from the leaf-buds to the snowy virginity of bloom. It stirred her tremendously. . . . She was stretched on her back beneath the pear tree soaking in the alto chant of the visiting bees, the gold of the sun and the panting breath of the breeze when the inaudible voice of it all came to her. She saw a dust-bearing bee sink into the sanctum of a bloom. . . .[72]

In Hurston's account, Ruby McCollum "felt like a blossom on the bare limb of a pear tree in the spring . . . opening her gifts to the world, but

[71]*Hurston to Jean Parker Waterbury, July 15, 1951.*
[72]*Zora Neale Hurston,* Their Eyes Were Watching God *(New York: HarperCollins 1990), pp. 8, 10; first published by Lippincott in 1937.*

where was the bee for her blossom?"[73] Janie is described numerous times as setting out on "a journey to the horizons."[74] According to Hurston, Ruby McCollum "was ready to set out on her journey to the big horizon."[75] When Janie's second marriage fails, "something fell off the shelf inside her . . . it was her image of Jody tumbled down and shattered."[76] Describing the failure of Ruby and Sam McCollum's marriage, Hurston writes that "an image—something sacred and precious—had fallen off the shelf in Ruby's heart."[77] Only from a position of sympathy and identification could Ruby McCollum inhabit these thoughts and feelings of Hurston's much-loved Janie.

Janie's greatest search, like Hurston's, had been for "self revelation," something described in the novel as "the oldest human longing," which Janie finally satisfies with her best friend, Pheoby Watson.[78] McCollum's case, at this particular point in Hurston's life, came to mean the impossibility of such satisfaction, the complete absence of any possibility of a "kissin' friend" like Pheoby with whom one's life story could truly be shared.[79] Having worried in the forties that it *might* be "too hard to reveal one's self," Hurston now seemed *convinced* that it was impossible to do so. "The truth is that nobody, not even the closest blood relations, ever really knows anybody else. The greatest human travail has been in the attempt at self-revelation, but never, since the world began, has any one individual completely succeeded," she wrote about the Ruby McCollum case.[80] This theme is at the heart of "Conscience of the Court," her revisionary history of Herod, her political observations on figures such as Taft, Holland, and Smathers, and in declarations in her letters such as the claim that "being 'different' has its drawbacks."[81]

Perhaps this same despair explains why Hurston was never again to write about the black community that had been the source of her creative life for so many years. Instead, she turned increasingly to articles either

[73]Hurston, "The Life Story of Mrs. Ruby J. McCollum!" (installment 3), Pittsburgh Courier, March 14, 1953.
[74]Hurston, Their Eyes, p. 85.
[75]Hurston, "The Life Story of Mrs. Ruby J. McCollum!" (installment 4), Pittsburgh Courier, March 21, 1953.
[76]Hurston, Their Eyes, pp. 67–68.
[77]Hurston, "The Life Story of Mrs. Ruby J. McCollum!" (installment 6), Pittsburgh Courier, April 4, 1953.
[78]Hurston, Their Eyes, p. 6.
[79]Hurston, Their Eyes, p. 7.
[80]Hurston, "The Life Story of Mrs. Ruby J. McCollum!" (installment 1), Pittsburgh Courier, February 28, 1953.
[81]Hurston to Annie Nathan Meyer, October 17, 1925.

on politics or on small and uncontroversial topics such as her dog Spot. Does despair over "self-revelation" explain in any way her more controversial political writings of the decade? Resigned to being misunderstood, had Hurston become a hack? Or had depression over "being 'different'" and its effects on "self-revelation" finally freed her to state her true views? Unable to experience what it would be like to write as if "no white audience is present," did Hurston return to performing for various audiences, giving them what she felt they wanted to hear? Was she willing now to write just for the quick sale, the brief thrill of publication?

By 1954, Hurston had become terribly discouraged with her community. In May 1954, she wrote Huie that "<u>Negroes</u>, have played every vile trick upon me that can be imagined. . . . I want no parts of them, and if somebody were to set up a nation of American Negroes, I would be the very first person NOT to go there."[82] This disgust is evident in a 1950 essay published in the *American Legion Magazine*, a periodical with few black readers. This essay, entitled "I Saw Negro Votes Peddled," is a deliberately provocative and sensationalized account of what Hurston claimed was black vote-selling in the Smathers/Pepper campaign. Describing African Americans as sadly lacking in self-respect, Hurston questioned both their "integrity" and their "brains." The article treats the FEPC as a conspiracy, although she vigorously defended the FEPC just a few years later. Its inflammatory language describes the 1950s as a new "Reconstruction" era dominated by liberal northern "Carpet-baggers" and "Scalawag[s]." And it entirely ignores the fact that black voter registration was up markedly throughout the South that year in the wake of legal challenges to the formerly all-white southern primaries.[83] Lester Granger, executive director of the NAACP, was furious with Hurston. He challenged her representation of black voters as " 'childishly gullible' " and wrote that "so far as her [Hurston's] Negro public is concerned, when she has come out with a production it has been readily evident that she 'shoulda stood in bed.' "[84] Deputy Sheriff Patrick Duvall, a friend of Hurston's at the

---

[82]*Hurston to William Bradford Huie, May 14, 1954.*

[83]*Zora Neale Hurston, "I Saw Negro Votes Peddled,"* American Legion Magazine, *49 (November 1950), pp. 12–13; 59.*

[84]*Lester Granger,* California Eagle, *December 20, 1951, as quoted by Hemenway,* Hurston, *p. 329, and Howard, p. 42. Hemenway notes that there were numerous angry responses to this article, including "Negro Votes Sold Here, Author Says,"* Miami Herald, *October 25, 1950; "Negroes Heatedly Deny Votes Bought in Miami,"* Miami Herald, *October 26, 1950; and Bill Baggs, "Were Negro Votes Bought in Miami,"* Miami Herald, *clipping, Yale University.*

time, remembers trying to argue with her about this article. "You don't want to know the truth," Hurston told him. She had a way of arguing, Duvall remembers, that made it nearly impossible to "bite her back."[85]

The most controversial thing that Hurston ever wrote was a letter to the editor, published in the *Orlando Sentinel*, August 11, 1955, protesting the Supreme Court's 1954 decision in *Brown v. Board of Education*, one of the three or four most celebrated decisions in the history of American race relations. In the black press, the decision had been treated as a "clarion announcement" of "idealism and social morality" that neither "the atom bomb nor the hydrogen bomb" would be able to trump.[86] In the white southern press, the decision was also treated as a bomb, this time as one threatening to destroy society via inevitable "mongrelization of the human race."[87] In her letter, "Court Order Can't Make Races Mix," Hurston wrote that she knew she would be called a " 'handkerchief-head nigger' " for saying that the decision offended her integrity. "The whole matter revolves around the self-respect of my people. How much satisfaction can I get from a court order for somebody to associate with me who does not wish me near them? . . . I regard the ruling of the U.S. Supreme Court as insulting . . . I see no tragedy in being too dark to be invited to a white social affair."[88] As Hemenway notes, "she ignored the inescapable evidence that black schools were inadequately and unequally funded."[89] Yet her letter was not *absolutely* without foundation, particularly for someone as sensitive to racial slights as Hurston. The language of the ruling included the claim that separating black children from white "generates a feeling of inferiority." This would have been a red flag for Hurston. She was passionately opposed to any hint of white superiority. And she was violently opposed to anything she saw as "Govt by fiat."[90] Given both of these views, her letter can be seen as a sincere statement of outrage—however oversimplified—at what she saw as social condescension, legally imposed. "I have been astonished that my letter to *The Orlando Sentinel*

[85] *Personal interview with Patrick Duvall, June 12, 2000.*

[86] *"Will Stun Communists,"* Pittsburgh Courier, *May 18, 1954; "End of Dual Society,"* Chicago Defender, *May 18, 1954. While Hurston's views were decidedly in the minority, she was not the only one to communicate them. Black historian and professor Clennon King of Mississippi also "questioned the wisdom of 'advancement' based on forcing complete grade-school desegregation." Clennon King, "I Speak as a Southern Negro,"* American Mercury, *January 1958, pp. 23–33.*

[87] *"Bloodstains on White Marble Steps,"* Jackson (Miss.) Daily News, *May 18, 1954.*

[88] *Zora Neale Hurston, "Court Order Can't Make Races Mix," letter to the editor,* Orlando Sentinel, *August 11, 1955.*

[89] *Hemenway,* Hurston, *p. 336.*

[90] *Hurston, "Court Order."*

has caused such a sensation over the whole United States," she wrote to her friend and Dutch translator, Margrit de Sablonière: "I actually do feel insulted when a certain type of white person hastens to effuse to me how noble they are to grant me their presence." [91] To Sablonière she also wrote that "as a Negro, you know that I cannot be in favor of segregation, but I do deplore the way they go about ending it." [92]

Hurston had another reason for mistrusting the Supreme Court's decision. She associated it—rather idiosyncratically—with communism. Hurston had been suspicious of communists since witnessing opportunistic organizing efforts in New York during the Harlem Renaissance. By the fifties, she had become a rabid anti-communist. The worst crime of the Communist Party, in her eyes, was not its political position but its tactic—which she insisted was in common use—of recruiting blacks by promising them intimate association with whites. *Brown v. Board of Education*, to her, was old w(h)ine in a new bottle:

> It is most astonishing that this [the Supreme Court's decision] should be tried just when the nation is exerting itself to shake off the evils of Communist penetration. It is to be recalled that Moscow, being made aware of this folk belief [that blacks desire physical contact with whites above all else], made it the main plank in their campaign to win the American Negro from the 1920's on. It was the come-on stuff. . . . Seeing how flat that program fell, it is astonishing that it would be so soon revived. Politics does indeed make strange bedfellows. [93]

"I have witnessed some very stinky business in New York along that line," Hurston added in a letter. [94]

Hurston's own anti-communism wed her to such unlikely politicians as Robert "Mr. Republican" Taft [95] in his bid for the 1952 Republican presidential primary nomination. "A Negro Voter Sizes Up Taft" was published by the *Saturday Evening Post*, which paid Hurston a handsome $1,000 for the rambling and heavily edited article which, as Hemenway remarks, was "largely void of analysis." [96] Hurston wrote

[91] *Hurston to Margrit de Sablonière, December 3, 1955.*

[92] *Hurston to Margrit de Sablonière, March 15, 1956.*

[93] *Hurston, "Court Order."*

[94] *Hurston to William Bradford Huie, September 6, 1954.*

[95] *Duvall insists that the appellation "Mr. Republican" was invented by Hurston. Personal interview with Patrick Duvall, June 12, 2000.*

[96] *Hemenway, Hurston, p. 335.*

Jean Parker Waterbury that she did not "start out to be enthusia[s]tic about Senator Taft, but the more research I did on the man, the better I liked him."[97] In addition to what she called Taft's "open-faced Americanism," Hurston praised him for helping exclude Theodore Bilbo (a notorious racist) from the Senate, opposing the poll tax, supporting the FEPC (which Hurston claimed to oppose when convenient), supporting civil rights legislation, and opposing racial discrimination in housing and labor.[98] She credited him with having a watchful eye out for the communists and being more likely to rout them out of government than his opponent, Dwight D. Eisenhower, to whom Taft lost his bid for candidacy.

Hurston's attitude toward communism in the fifties is probably best seen in her June 1951 article, "Why The Negro Won't Buy Communism," published in the *American Legion Magazine*. Hurston's actual position that "nationality is stronger than race" and that American blacks would be Americans first and foremost[99] was not fundamentally askew of the view held by many other black anti-communists writing during this period. From the 1940s on, according to African American historian Wilson Record, "few criticisms of the Communist Party in this country, from whatever source, have equaled the NAACP's denunciation."[100] In 1950, the forty-first annual NAACP convention adopted a policy of prohibiting membership to communists by a resolution that passed by an "overwhelming vote" of 309 to 57.[101] A 1950 memo from Roy Wilkins, acting secretary of the NAACP, reminded the national branches that the "Association's Position" included a commitment to "condemn and actively oppose . . . [all] attempts of various groups, particularly Communists, either to secure control of our branches outright, or to use the branches as sounding boards for political and other ideas."[102] In arguing that the Communist Party was using blacks as "a dumb, but useful tool,"[103] Hurston echoed the NAACP's sentiment that "the Communists use the Negro merely as a pawn."[104] In arguing that

[97]*Hurston to Jean Parker Waterbury, June 4, 1951.*

[98]*Zora Neale Hurston, "A Negro Voter Sizes Up Taft," Saturday Evening Post, December 8, 1951, p. 150.*

[99]*Zora Neale Hurston, "Why The Negro Won't Buy Communism," American Legion Magazine, June 1951, p. 59.*

[100]*Wilson Record, Race & Radicalism: The NAACP and the Communist Party in Conflict (Ithaca: Cornell University Press, 1964), p. 160. For most of the research on which this paragraph is based, I am grateful for the assistance of William Jelani Cobb and his work on black anti-communism.*

[101]*Record, p. 146; Herbert Hill, "The Communist Party—Enemy of Negro Equality," Crisis, June–July 1951.*

[102]*Roy Wilkins, memo to NAACP branches, March 22, 1950, personal files of Herbert Hill, former field secretary, NAACP, citing resolution of March 8, 1947.*

[103]*Hurston, "Why The Negro Won't Buy Communism," p. 15.*

[104]*Roy Wilkins, foreword to Hill, "The Communist Party."*

the party was "patronizing," "insulting," and condescending, she echoed the NAACP's claim that the Communist Party's position on race was really a kind of "super-jim-crowism."[105] In asserting that few blacks were actually interested in the party, she echoed the NAACP and National Urban League position that "the Communist Party seeks to establish among Negroes and the rest of the world, the *illusion* of an influence they actually never hope to attain."[106]

Hurston deviated from many of her anti-communist peers, and deviated sharply, in her willingness to name names. She personally denounced African American leftists—who may or may not have been communists—who had once been her friends and allies: Wayland Rudd, William Patterson, Langston Hughes, Louise Thompson, Benjamin Davis, and W. E. B. Du Bois. Perhaps this was her way to get back—personally—at individuals from a community she felt had abandoned and betrayed her. Perhaps it was her way of signing off from any more writing about race.

When she was evicted from her Eau Gallie house in March 1956— "the house where I am living has been sold and I have been terribly distressed at the thought," she wrote Sablonière[107]—she seemed at loose ends and returned to the life of travel and temporary employment that had been her habit prior to the more settled Eau Gallie years. She left her cabin in early spring and worked briefly as a librarian at the Patrick Air Force Base in Cocoa Beach, Florida. Fired from this job on May 10, 1957, Hurston complained bitterly that she was a victim both of race discrimination and of personal animus for intending to blow the whistle on various forms of corruption she had uncovered. "It is a long and not-so-nice story," she wrote to Mary Holland. Hurston was so angry that she contacted both the President's Committee on Government Contracts (charged with enforcing the FEPC) and Vice President Richard Nixon.[108] At sixty-six years old, when many other people might be thinking of retirement, Hurston was being fired from a job that she detested and that paid her only $1.88 an hour, and she was prepared, if possible, to launch a national campaign of protest about it.

[105]Hill, "The Communist Party."

[106]Statement presented to and at the request of the House Committee on Un-American Activities (HUAC), by Lester Granger, Director, National Urban League, July 14, 1949, typescript. I am grateful to William Jelani Cobb for copies of this and other documents detailing the NAACP's position on communism.

[107]Hurston to Margrit de Sablonière, March 15, 1956.

[108]Hurston to Mary Holland, June 27, 1957.

She left Cocoa Beach and moved into a trailer on Merritt Island, where she worked on *Herod the Great*, lived on unemployment compensation (twenty-six dollars a week), wrote angry letters about her experience at Patrick Air Force Base, gathered up her papers and personal effects for donation to Yale, and began to anticipate her death. "If I happen to die without money, somebody will bury me, though I do not wish it to be that way."[109]

This is a prescient comment, given that Hurston *did* die without money and *was* buried by others. But she did *not* die *yet*. In fact, she showed extraordinary energy and perseverance for a woman of her age, health, and resources, cut off from her family, isolated from her friends, ostracized from the various communities that had sustained her. When she ran out of money in the fall, she applied for a job at the Air Force Missile Test Center back in Cocoa. When she failed to get the job, she accepted a job offer from C. E. Bolen, editor of the *Fort Pierce Chronicle*, a local black weekly, and moved to Fort Pierce, where she lived for the next two years. Even in her coverage of the Ruby McCollum case for the *Pittsburgh Courier*, Hurston had not worked as a regular journalist, so by accepting Bolen's offer she was also taking up the responsibility of starting a new career: in ill health, broke, and at sixty-six years of age. She was also taking a step down for a woman who had written for many nationally prominent magazines and papers, including the *Pittsburgh Courier, Opportunity*, the *Saturday Evening Post, Negro Digest, Story, American Mercury*, and the *Washington Tribune*.

Fort Pierce may have been a fortuitous choice for Hurston. According to N. Y. Nathiri, Eatonville historian, much of the community was migrant agricultural, a familiar setting for Hurston. Nathiri describes it as a "close-knit community" where people looked after one another.[110] In Fort Pierce, Hurston's last home was a twenty-eight-foot, two-room, green cinder-block house owned by her friend Dr. Clem C. Benton. Initially rented to Hurston for ten dollars a week, Benton gave her the house rent-free when she ran out of money. " 'I considered it an honor to sit and listen at her experiences as a writer,' " Benton told Nathiri.[111] In that house, according to Hurston's good friend Marjorie Adler, " 'she made a desk and bookshelves out of fruit boxes. We pro-

[109]*Hurston to Herbert Sheen, June 20, 1957.*
[110]*N. Y. Nathiri,* Zora!: A Woman and Her Community *(Orlando: Sentinel Communications, 1991).*
[111]*Ibid., p. 41.*

vided some furniture. The things that were precious to her were her typewriter, her trunkful of letters and her reference books. She spent her time at that typewriter.' "[112] The house is now a national landmark and has been moved from its original location, which has become part of an expansion of the Lincoln Park Academy. It is a small house, but pleasant, with many windows, two small rooms, built-in closets and shelves. It was part of a tight-knit community of many similar homes, and Hurston apparently had good friends right in the neighborhood.

In February 1958, Hurston took what would prove to be her last job: a teaching job at Lincoln Park Academy, just the sort of institution she had always mocked, though this school had "a reputation for excellence."[113] School authorities proved unsympathetic to Hurston's difficulties in becoming accredited. Howard University was slow to send her transcripts. The principal at Lincoln began to harass her. She felt herself discriminated against because of her overeducated background, which she had also experienced at her librarian's job. "This eternal harrassment appears to me to be a trifle unfair because I never applied to teach there," she complained to Mitchell Ferguson, coordinator of the state's Department of Education.[114] Unable to speed up the bureaucratic process, Hurston found herself dismissed from yet another job, a dismissal Patterson explains as having occurred in response to the intense external scrutiny being focused on the school as it struggled for accreditation by the Southern Association of Colleges and Secondary Schools.[115]

Freed from her teaching job, Hurston seemed to devote herself to her articles for the *Chronicle*. Her first piece for the paper is one of three essays she published on local issues, this one entitled "This Juvenile Delinquency," an argument that Jewish parents do a better job of instilling "good social behavior" in their children than black parents.[116] The other two local essays are entitled "The Tripson Story," on a local dairy and cattle ranch, and "The Farm Laborer at Home," an

[112] *Ibid., pp. 41–42.*

[113] Gordon Patterson, *"Zora Neale Hurston as English Teacher: A Lost Chapter Found,"* The Marjorie Kinnan Rawlings Journal of Florida Literature, 5 (1993), p. 52.

[114] *Hurston to Mitchell Ferguson, March 7, 1958.*

[115] *Patterson, p. 57.*

[116] *Zora Neale Hurston, "This Juvenile Delinquency,"* Fort Pierce Chronicle, *December 12, 1958. The* Chronicle *ceased publishing many years ago, and its back issues have not been archived. I am grateful to Robert Hemenway for supplying me with his copies of twenty of Hurston's articles for the paper, the bulk of the writing she did for the paper and, in all likelihood, some of the only surviving copies of these articles.*

uncharacteristically harsh treatment of migrant workers who, she suggested, were as likely as not to be "fugitives from justice . . . habitual and disgusting drunkards, petty thieves, knife-fighters and other miscreants who crowd our jail and in general, lower the moral tone of the city."[117]

Seventeen other articles she wrote are all part of a series entitled "Hoodoo and Black Magic." There is something of a mystery about this series. Hurston's first byline in the series appears in February 1959 and is part of a three-part story about the powerful "Ida" and her hoodoo revenge on her white employer for killing Ida's daughter. But this article, printed under the byline of "*Mrs.* Zora Neale Hurston," is not the first in this series. A number of articles in the series were published prior to Hurston's own under the byline of "Noel Siwell," a pseudonym for Leon Lewis (spelled backward), who also wrote for the *Chronicle* and who is probably Hurston, based on the language and style of the Siwell/Lewis essays. The articles in this series, sometimes recycling material from her folklore collection *Tell My Horse*, are notable for their complete inconsistency of attitude in regard to hoodoo. At times, she attacks it as a "black evil," "fraudulent claim," and "clever sales talk."[118] At other times, she not only defends it as an important source of pharmacological wisdom for treating such diseases as syphilis but also warns of its unknown and mysterious—but undeniable—powers. Her last essay for the series, written just six months before she died, reconfirms the power and validity of hoodoo.

As she was writing these last articles, Hurston was failing. In her small Fort Pierce home, she suffered increasingly from a weak heart, tropical diseases, gallbladder trouble, obesity, and a range of aches and pains. In early 1959, she suffered a stroke. At some point, she stayed in the home of friends and neighbors who spoon-fed her to keep her alive. In May 1959, she applied to the county welfare office for assistance, something she had not done since her days with the WPA in the thirties and which she had then felt compelled to keep secret. By October 1959, Hurston was forced to recognize that she was no longer able to look after herself.

[117]Zora Neale Hurston, "The Tripson Story," February 6, 1959; Zora Neale Hurston, "The Farm Laborer at Home," February 27, 1959.
[118]Zora Neale Hurston, "Sacrifices to Hoodoo," in series "Hoodoo and Black Magic," Fort Pierce Chronicle, August 7, 1959, p. 5; Zora Neale Hurston, untitled article in series "Hoodoo and Black Magic," Fort Pierce Chronicle, April 17, 1959, p. 5.

In late October 1959, at the age of sixty-eight, Hurston suffered another stroke, which finally forced her to enter Memorial Hospital in Fort Pierce, Florida. There she was visited regularly by friends, including journalists Marjorie Silver and Anne Wilder. She was "just very, very tired," Wilder remembers. "I had the feeling she'd packed it in." Wilder feels that Hurston was underappreciated and knew it. "Zora knew her own worth . . . I think that bothered some people," Wilder commented. "I respected her . . . a lot of us did. . . . She had a lot of hard luck but she always knew who she was."[119] After the stroke, Hurston returned home, where she had difficulty getting around and was attended by friends and neighbors. Eventually, she entered the St. Lucie County Welfare Home. Three months later, on January 28, 1960, she died.[120]

While most people believe that she died either in the welfare home or in the hospital—and legends about her death are legion—a woman who knew her at the time insists that she died at home. "J.H." (name withheld on request) and her sister were frequent visitors to Hurston's home and part of a coterie of children in the "Benton's Quarters" area whom Hurston mentored. She particularly liked to take them on walks, tell them stories, and encourage them to write. "Do you have a diary?" J.H. remembers Hurston asking. She showed them that "it could be done." J.H. vividly remembers Hurston's typewriter on the kitchen table and stacks of manuscripts and papers in the living room. Although Hurston's illness left her breathless, weak, and with badly swollen legs, she tried not to ask for help. So the children visited daily, almost as if their hostess were not ill.[121]

After her death, the papers and personal effects stored in her Fort Pierce home were taken out back and burned, a common practice at the time. Thankfully, Patrick Duvall, a local African American deputy

[119]Personal interview with Anne Wilder, June 2000.

[120]" 'You know, she didn't let anyone know she was sick,' Mrs. Clark [Hurston's niece, Winnifred Hurston Clark], recalls. 'I think Vivian's father [Clifford Joel], being close found out.' Clifford visited his sister in the St. Lucie County Welfare Home with two of his children shortly before her death and brought her gifts. Hurston refused them and handed them to the other patients. 'She didn't want them,' Mrs. Clark notes. And when the family members tried to get her to leave with them, Hurston refused. 'She said she was right where she wanted to be. She just didn't want anybody to take care of her or do anything for her.' " Pamela Bordelon, personal interview with Winnifred Hurston Clark, June 26, 1993, "New Tracks on Dust Tracks: Toward a Reassessment of the Life of Zora Neale Hurston," African American Review, 31, no. 1 (1997), p. 18. While other friends of Hurston's maintain that her family abandoned her, the family has maintained, in my interviews with them, that this simply was not so. Personal interviews with Vivian Bowden, Winnifred Hurston Clark, Dr. Lois Hurston Gaston, Zora Mack Goins, Dr. Clifford Hurston, Jr., Edgar Hurston, and Barbara Hurston Lewis, January 31, 1995.

[121]Personal interview with "J.H.," known as "Sunshine." Name and interview dates withheld by request.

sheriff (one of Florida's first black deputies) who knew Hurston (she affectionately called him a "devil"), saw the fire behind her house and stopped his car, even before he realized whose house it was, wondering if conditions weren't too dry for a bonfire. Realizing that the personal effects were Hurston's, he put out the flames. According to Duvall, the yardman had simply been told to clean out the house and was unaware of the value of what he was burning.

Patrick Duvall in 2000.

Duvall had met Hurston in the late thirties when he was a student at Lincoln Park Academy and his class went to Bethune-Cookman, where Hurston was teaching.[122] Duvall remembers Hurston's interest in showing the Lincoln Park Academy students the four-person boat she moored in Daytona Beach. Duvall kept up with Hurston's writing, although he often disagreed with her. And the two reconnected—often to argue politics—when she moved to Fort Pierce. She was clearly in poor health then, Duvall remembers, "looking her age" with a noticeably "unhealthy weight." But she was still feisty, doing things "*much* her own way" and being "quite a person." She "always" had to get the last word, Duvall remembers. "She was the kind of person who could cut you with a smile."

Duvall put the salvaged papers in the trunk and backseat of his Oldsmobile and took them home, where he set them on his porch. Then he began writing what he describes as "all sorts of letters" to her family and friends in Virginia, New Jersey, Eatonville, and elsewhere, regarding disposition of Hurston's papers. "I knew the writings were valuable," he said. None of his letters were answered, and Duvall eventually mentioned the situation to Silver and Wilder. After approximately two years—during which time Hurston's papers remained on Duvall's porch—Duvall, Silver, and Wilder arranged for them to be archived at the University of Florida, Gainesville, where, thanks to Duvall's prescience, they are available today.[123] Many of Hurston's un-

[122] Duvall remembers this as occurring in the late 1930s, but 1934 would be a more likely date.
[123] Personal interview with Patrick Duvall, June 12, 2000.

published manuscripts and much of her correspondence—saved by her on fragile carbon copies—were in that fire.[124] "He's a very modest hero," Anne Wilder says of Duvall.

Hurston's funeral was arranged by various friends and community members, including a number of people from the Lincoln Park Academy who joined together to raise over $600 for expenses. Scribner's and Lippincott's each sent $100. The funeral program from February 7, 1960, notes the participation of editor C. E. Bolen and principal Leroy Floyd of the Lincoln Park Academy, whose students served as the flower girls for the ceremony. The funeral was attended by a number of friends, including Sara Lee Creech, Margaret Paige of Lincoln Park Academy, Marjorie Adler, Anne Wilder, Marjorie Silver, and Theodore Pratt, who gave the eulogy, and approximately one hundred others. The local paper described it as "one of the nicest funerals ever in the St. Lucie County area."[125] There were multiple sermons, a solo, and songs sung by a chorus during the hour-long ceremony at a local funeral parlor. Hurston was buried in a bronze casket in an unmarked grave in the Garden of Heavenly Rest, Fort Pierce's designated black cemetery. After the funeral her brother John Hurston made efforts to collect information on his sister and pay the funeral expenses.[126] The cemetery is still used, though it is run-down and no longer clearly marked. Visitors to Hurston's grave will find various remembrances on the marker that was placed by Alice Walker in 1973: pennies, notes, rocks, candy, and flowers. The actual location of Hurston's body is unknown.

[124]*Those papers that could be salvaged, some of them partly burned and illegible, are carefully preserved in Mylar sheets at the University of Florida, Gainesville, library. I am grateful to Patrick Duvall and to librarian Jeffrey Barr for sharing with me their stories of the papers in the collection. Personal interview with Jeffrey Barr, Gainesville, Florida.*

[125]*"Final Rites Sunday for Author Zora Neale Hurston at Peek's,"* Fort Pierce Chronicle, *February 12, 1960.*

[126]*John C. Hurston to Theodore Pratt, February 12, 1960.*

TO BURROUGHS MITCHELL

[winter 1950]
On Board the Motor Vessel CHALLENGER
Box 772
Miami, Florida
MacArthur Causeway

Dear Burroughs:

I feel that I have come to myself at last. I can even endure [t]he sight of a Negro, which I thought once I could never do again.[1] The restoration of my peace and calm was delayed because of what I found when I arrived.

First, the boat[2] was nowhere near ready to sail as I had believed. It was in great disorder from bow to stern. It was that way because Fred Irvine was himself in an upset state, and wanted me to hurry down to aid him in settling his nerves, so you see, that was no great help to me who was seeking calm my ownself. But as he pointed out, friendship is stronger than love, and he needed my friendship because of his hectic love affairs which had soured on his soul. He has been a good friend to me in the past, so I took a long, tired breath and settled down. But it was impossible for me to write for the first two weeks. Then on later inspection, I had to tear up most of what I had written in that period.[3] Now, I am feeling fine and in a working mood.

Naturally, all is fish that comes into a writer's net. I am meeting a great number of characters down here on the waterfront, and the cross section of life that I am getting! It is really something. The rich and the poor and their ways and concepts.

The Challenger is berthed along the MacArthur Causeway, near the 13th St. Bridge and dead across the bay from Miami's well adver-

---

[1] *Hurston refers here to her terrible sense of betrayal following the coverage in the* Baltimore Afro-American *of the false morals charges made by a neighbor's son.*

[2] *Fred Irvine's boat, the* Challenger.

[3] The Lives of Barney Turk. *On January 10, Mitchell had written approvingly of the new draft of* The Lives of Barney Turk, *about a white youth from a Florida truck farm and his adventures in Central America and Hollywood. He cautioned Hurston not to idealize her main character and he urged her to keep writing and not go back over what she had been writing before her arrest.*

tised skyline. The traffic pouring to and from Miami Beach makes a steady drone from dawn till nearly dawn again. There is a little park that I can reach in a few steps ashore, and I stroll across and pick a coc[o]nut or two that falls during high winds, or pay a visit to the sapodilla tree and pick what I find ripe. I have a hard time of it because Miami does not prohibit the people from eating the fruits in the public parks, and everyday, some viper is around that sapodilla tree beating me to the ripe ones. There ought to be al <u>law</u>! The City representative who had to come aboard on business made me welcome to coconuts, all I could use, and being so hard to get at, I have no competition there.

And God keeps His appointment with Miami every sundown. Berthed on the east of Biscayne Bay, I can look to the western side, which I never fail to come top-side and do around sunset. Thus I get the benefit of His slashing paint brush all the way. It is just too marvelous, Burroughs. I do wish that our Darrow[4] could see it once. The show is changed every day, but every performance is superb.

From your letter, I decided to rewrite the beginning of the book.[5] You will see what changes I have made. The next fifty pages following what I am sending will deal with how Barney got to Honduras. The last part will of course detail what happened to him there. Naturally I hope that what I am sending you will prove interesting.

My love to your wife, Mr. Scribner,[6] Mr. Darrow, and all. My health is good and I am feeling fine and in the mood to work. I feel the d[e]epest gratitude for what the firm did for me last year,[7] and I yearn to repay you all by deeds.

With faithful feelings,
Zora (written on Saturday)

I cannot send the carbon copy to WATKINS[8] as I would like to do, for then I would have nothing to refer to in going ahead.

---

[4] *Editor Whitney Darrow; see glossary.*
[5] *The Lives of Barney Turk. Burroughs had been urging Hurston to keep Barney both likable and believable. He suggested she use less flashback in the opening chapters. He also made some detailed suggestions for minor revisions in the opening chapters, including which characters should have what information about one another.*
[6] *Editor Charles Scribner. Hurston had switched publishers from Lippincott to Scribner's in April 1947, working first with the legendary Maxwell Perkins and then, after Perkins's death, with Burroughs Mitchell.*
[7] *The publisher, and editor Burroughs Mitchell especially, had helped Hurston secure legal counsel and pay her legal expenses.*
[8] *Ann Watkins of the Watkins agency; Hurston's agent, Jean Parker Waterbury, worked for Watkins.*

It is a joke, Son, but here in Miami I have had to insist on remaining Colored. Somehow, everybody along the waterfront tries to make me out Cuban or Mexican. I suppose that started from the fact that two Argentine Vessels, the Don Guillermo and the Josefina Maria are berthed next to the Challenger, and both outfits used to come aboard to talk Spanish with me. Capt. Irvine and Capt. Hernandez had such a terrible fight two weeks ago that though they wave over at me when I go aft alone, there is no more Visiting.

Z.

TO BURROUGHS MITCHELL

3070 N.W. 23rd St.
Miami, Fla.
January 24, 1950.

Dear Burroughs:

First thing, note new address. Fred [Irvine] never succeeded in getting a paying cargo, and the boat has been sold. I thought of returning to New York right away, but to misquote a popular song, "Baby, it's cold up there." I do plan to be there in March, however, to do the repolish near my editor.[1]

Yesterday, I spoke at the Dade County Library meeting. Got a good reception and made some friends, I think.[2]

It is a curious thing, but everybody seems to want a copy of MULES ANS MEN. I suppose the two books that have come out on folklore in the last six weeks, and I am included in both, has aroused the interest.[3]

---

[1] *Of* The Lives of Barney Turk. *Hurston had edited the final version of* Seraph on the Suwanee *with Mitchell and, apparently, enjoyed working face-to-face with him.*

[2] *Librarian Helga Eason among them.*

[3] *In 1949, Hurston's friend Benjamin A. Botkin (see glossary) published* A Treasury of Southern Folklore *(New York: Crown), which included nine selections by Hurston: six from* Mules and Men, *one from* Dust Tracks on a Road, *one from her* American Mercury *essay "High John de Conquer," and one from the unpublished manuscripts collected for* The Florida Negro *project of the Federal Writers' Project. In 1950, Carl Sandburg published* New American Songbag *(New York: Broadcast Music) to update the earlier* American Songbag, *published in 1927.* New American Songbag *included Hurston's rendition of "Cold Rainy Day." In 1944, Bolkin had published* A Treasury of American Folklore *(New York: Crown), which included a preface by Sandburg and twenty-one pieces by Hurston: twenty from* Mules and Men *and one from "High John de Conquer."*

It will not be very long now before you have the rest of the book, and can point things out to me. Then I get down to reworking the job.

Your letter bucked me up a great deal. Day by day in every way I'm getting human again. I caught myself laughing fit to kill yesterday. Getting away from Fred is a help too, because his own affairs kept so complicated, and I had to hear about them all the time, kept me on edge. Maybe because he is a small guy and unsure of himself in other ways that he feels that he must promote all those meanigless "love" affairs to make him feel assured. Then when they get out of hand, calling on my so-called wisdom. I find him a fascinating study, but he does not fit in this book. He needs one all to himself, though I am not sure that I'll get around to using it soon.

Being lazy, and wanting to get back to the script, I throw myself on your mercy. Please phone the Watkins office of my change of address. The spirit is willing but the flesh is lazy as hell.

Sure appreciated that card from Whitney Darrow. My admiration of the man is boundless. When I get another pause from the book, I mean to write him a letter.

Jean Parker [Waterbury] is a darling. She wrote me a lovely letter. She tells me that Rawlins [Marjorie Kinman Rawlings] is working hard on her book.

Hope that you; the wife, the dog, the cat are all cutting big jim by the acre.

Most sincerely,
Zora

TO BURROUGHS MITCHELL

3070 N.W. 23rd Street
Moami, Fla.
Feb. 3, 1950

Dear Burroughs Mitchell:
Before I forget it, please see that the mailing clerk gets my new address. My mail is still arriving in Capt. Irvine's box. He now lives over

on the Beach, which is a long way from me. He has had to drive over three times to fetch my mail to me.

Here is the rest of the story. Do you want me to start back on the first part, or wait for your criticisms on the whole? But as soon as I typed that question, I remembered that you said for me to wait.[1]

Now, I shall put in to do some short pieces[2] right away. Please give my best love to all.

Most sincerely as ever,

Zora

TO HELGA EASON

3070 N.W. 23rd St.
Miami, Fla.
St. Valentines Day, 1950.

Dear Mrs. Eason:

How very happy I was to receive your letter today! It put me to singing on my silver-singing trumpet.

It will surprise you to know that my book is finished and already in New York.[1] You know what a free feeling that gives me. Of course, I will have to do some polishing later on, but the big, hard part is over, and I am no longer tied down. I feel justified in the decision I made. Instead of taking off for New York with the money that you, Mrs. Parsons[2] and others contrived for me, I decided to si[t] right down where I was and get the book off my hands. You see, moving around is upsetting, and it might be weeks before I could get

---

[1]*Revisions of* The Lives of Barney Turk. *Hurston was simultaneously revising the beginning and completing the story. The opening chapters had been revised a few times and Mitchell was urging her to finish.*
[2]*These might be "I Saw Negro Votes Peddled" and unpublished stories, including one on a Florida religious colony, one on turpentine workers, and a fable about Swiss cheese.*

---

[1]The Lives of Barney Turk, *later rejected by Scribner's.*
[2]*Frances G. Parsons, Director, Miami Public Library. Donations were collected by the Friends of the Miami Public Library and Miami Public Library employees who attended Hurston's speaking engagement at the library on January 23, 1950. I am grateful to Lynn Moylan for this information.*

back to work again after getting settled in some way in New York with the houseing shortage there and the weather and all. So now I have that off my hands and feel the deepest gratitude to you and to Mrs. Parsons, and to all the librarians who were so good and kind to me.

I have received word that a short story by me is appearing in the March 18 issue of THE SATURDAY EVENING POST.[3] It has been editied some from the way I wrote it, (they always do) but I hope that you will not be too disappointed in it.

So being free now, any time that you set for seeing me will be all right with me. You, your family and Mrs. Mizell can all come to my shabby little studio, or it can be arranged for me to meet you all somewhere that you like better. Anyway you fix it will be all right with me. Just so nobody don't come down with the laps.

For the past week I have been nursing a hope that I would have a better studio. I was tentatively offered an old schooner, 57 feet long and beamy, which I dreamed of fitting up for a house-boat as I had once before in Daytona Beach. It has no motor in it, and ne[e]ds painting, but then the man only asked $200. 00 for it, and I am very handy around a boat. But one of the ownership papers is missing, and the man is in the hospital, so things are dragging. If I can get it, I will tie it up somewhere along the river and have a good studio and not go North for a while yet.[4] Now that my book is in, I can talk advance royalties with Scribners as soon as I hear how much (or how little(they like the book. I have a feeling that my editor[5] will be reasonably pleased.

I tip my hat and make you a bow.

With faithful feelings,
Zora

---

[3] "The Conscience of the Court" was published on March 18, 1950.

[4] The purchase of this schooner did not take place; Hurston went to Washington, D.C., and then New York in the fall.

[5] Burroughs Mitchell.

TO BURROUGHS MITCHELL

[March 1950]
c/o Burritt
115 First Terrace
Rivo Alto Island
Miami Beach

Dear Burroughs:

Please send the script to me here as quickly as possible so that I can get back to work.[1] I am all set up in materials again—plenty of paper, etc. My working is causing a tremendous sensation in Miami. I tried to avoid the publicity but the paper <u>insisted</u>.[2] I am being lectured about at poetry & other literary clubs and there seems to be nothing that I can do about it. The announcer at the Copa devoted half his time to me over the air last week. Miami is certainly Hurston-conscious. I have offers now to do some "ghosting."[3] All I wanted was a little spending change when I took this job[4] but it certainly has turned out to be one slam of a publicity do-dad.

Do <u>please</u> send me 20 copies of Seraph as I am continually being asked so that they can be autographed.

Two more weeks and this job is over so far as I am concerned. $30.00 room and board and all the curiosity about me gives me no time to be bored.

Hurriedly with love,

Zora

---

[1]The Lives of Barney Turk. *In mid-March, Mitchell had sent Hurston a letter expressing concerns about the latest version of* The Lives of Barney Turk. *He felt that the novel was not living up to Hurston's design for it: the main character lacking interest, the plot—which involved a long digression about Honduras—not believable. He and Waterbury suggested drastic revisions which included scrapping everything after the first hundred pages and having the main character, white Barney Turk, fall in love with an "exotic" woman of color, perhaps from Cuba.*

[2]*The* Miami Herald *published an article entitled "Famous Negro Author Working as a Maid Here Just 'to Live a Little' " on March 27 after Hurston's story "The Conscience of the Court" was printed in the* Saturday Evening Post.

[3]*Hurston refers to two ghostwritten projects: one for Frank Smathers, published in 1958, and one for a Colonel Lasher which she had to abandon, uncompleted, in the winter of 1955–56.*

[4]*As a maid on Rivo Island.*

TO CARL SANDBURG

443 N.E. 39th St.
Miami, Fla.
June 12, 1950.

Dear Dr. Sandburg:

You need not send me anything for the use of Col' Rainy Day. I am highly honored that so great a soul as you could find use for it.[1]

Two years ago in New York at Dick Hucy's Aunt Dinah's Kitchen, Dick was teasing me about how so many people, Hall Johnson, Juanita Hall,[2] Rosamond Johnson, himself and others had made so much out of the material that I had collected while I had made so little. I replied honestly that I did not feel that way about it. I am an anthropologist and it is my job to see and to find and present to the world my findings. I have seen extracts from MULES AND MEN printed in many languages, proving that I did a fairly good job. I have never expected to get rich, and if I have served this nation and the world by digging out a few of it's hidden treasures and thus enriched our culture, I have gained a great deal. I have had some influence on my time.

Fred Koch is head of the Drama Dept. at Miami U. and he and I have been talking recently. It is proposed that we do a comprehensive folk festival next Fall in the stadium, and at once I thought of you and Alan Lomax. Between us four, I think we could turn out a very good job. What do you think of it? Koch was glad that I suggested it, and he thinks of it as a memorial to his late, great father with whom I have worked at Chapel Hill.[3]

Unless my plans change, I will be at Waynesville, N.C. by the middle of June, and if Flat Rock is within two hundred miles, I shall drive over to see you.[4] I have something very important to talk over with

---

[1] Hurston's song was published in his New American Songbag collection, published by Broadcast Music.

[2] Juanita Hall (1901–68), singer, actress, and choral director, best known for her portrayal of Bloody Mary in the 1949 Broadway production of South Pacific.

[3] Frederick Henry Koch (1877–1944) was a professor of dramatic literature and the director of the Carolina Playmakers.

[4] This trip does not appear to have taken place.

you. Nothing would give me greater pleasure than for you to join me in the project. No, not looking for financial aid on it. I hope to have cornered the necessary money for it by then. It would be too much for either of us to handle.

With faithful feelings,
Zora Neale Hurston

TO SARA LEE CREECH

443 E. 39th Street
Miami, Florida
June 29, 1950.

Miss Sara Creech
c/o Dr. Med Scott Brown
Emory University Hosp.
Emory University, Ga.

Dear Miss Creech:

Please allow me to say how pleased I am that you let me see the pictures of the Negro dolls that you plan to put on the market.[1] They are exquisitely designed, and magnificently executed in model.

The thing that pleased me most, Miss Creech was that you, a White girl, should have seen into our hearts so clearly, and sought to meet our longing for understanding of us as we really are, and not as some would have us. That you have not insulted us by a grotesque caricature of Negro children, but conceived something of real Negro beauty. Those dolls are adorable.

Out of our long friendship, may I suggest that you let the well-known and influential Negroes see the pictures that you showed me? I am certain that they will all feel as I do, and you can be assured of a tremendous sale when the SARALEE DOLLS appear on the market.

---

[1] *The Sara Lee doll was the first "anthropologically correct" (Hurston's phrase) black doll to be marketed nationally. It was designed by Creech, sculpted by Sheila Burlingame, produced by the Ideal Toy Company, and marketed by Sears, Roebuck.*

They will surely meet a long-felt need among us. It's a magnificently constructive thing that you are doing for the whole of America as well as for Negro children.

I suppose that I should not be surprised at the steps you have taken, for never was I more surprised and delighted than when I spoke at Belle Glade and found your extraordinary inter-racial organization.[2] It could be a model for the nation, and according to what I hear, you, Sara Creech are at the very heart of it. This follows a conclusion that I reached some years ago from observation. That is, that the so-called Race Problem will be solved in the South and by Southerners. I have noted that when a Southerner becomes convinced, he goes all out for correcting the situation. I need not cite the numerous examples to a well-informed person like you.

With every good wish for your success in this undertaking, I am

Most faithfully yours,
Zora Neale Hurston

TO BURROUGHS MITCHELL

1622 N.W. 63rd Street
Miami, Fla.
July 21, 1950.

Dear Burroughs Mitchell:

Please note change of address. I have escaped at last from my job of editing, or ghosting that book for old Judge Smathers.[1] I wanted the money, but never did I think I was taking on such a task. It did me good as an author for it gave me a better insight into human vanity. There was another enlightening angle too. I thought it a little

[2]*Hurston spoke at the Belle Glade Interracial Council twice, both times in the early 1950s. According to Creech, she was a smashing success.*

[1]*Frank Smathers, father of Senator George Smathers. The book was* It's Wonderful to Live Again, *published in 1958.*

tragic too. When a man has hired me to do what he admits he could not do himself, then from time to time going into revolt for a reason that he could not help by reason of his background and tradition. I could see at times that he could not accept the reality that a descendent of slaves could do something in an intellectual way that he could not. I do not feel bitter about it at all, just recognizing something very human.

I saw too that he valued me however, for being a hopeless invalid, he lacked intellectual contacts, as well as expressing his protest against his condition by fighting with everybody, and using his wealth to beat everybody down under his power. I do not beat down easily, and we fought like tigers—from day to day, and I came to see that he loved it. He had met at last a foeman worthy of his steel. I saw his wife and his two sons backing off him with bowed heads, but not your Topsy gal. I let him have it with both barrels time and time again. He has a habit of making the most preposterous accusations, and then not allowing the other person to say a word. "I don't want any answers. I don't want to hear a word from you" was his formula. I have seen his wife and sons bow down under that. In the presence of the Senator-elect, George Smathers and Mrs. Smathers, I told the old cuss that it did not matter to me what he wanted to hear or not hear. After he had accused me of something, he was going to liste[n]d anyhow. He stuck his crippled fingers in his ears finally, but I reached over and pulled them out and went on talking. George and Frank, Jr. told me afterwards that I was magnificent. They wished they had my nerve. The way I saw it, all he could do was to fire me, and I wouldn't mind that at all. I even told the old man he must have been a horrible example of a judge. His wife, oppressed as she was, seemed offended more than the Judge at my temerity. Traditions of the Old South, you know. She was more upset when he defended me agaisnt her. Said that I could have ahome with them forever. I don't want it because I could see she believed I had undue influence with the old man, and was possibly getting extra checks. All I wanted was <u>out</u> fromt there.

Getting along fast and well on the new writing of BARNEY TURK. I am glad now that I am doing it over. You will have it in your hands much sooner than you think.

I suppose Jean Parker told you that I have sold another article.[2]
My best to everybody and hope that you are not sweating as I am.

With faithful feelings,
Zora

1622 N.W. 63rd St.
Miami, Fla.
C/O Gomez.

TO BURROUGHS MITCHELL

[postcard postmarked August 23, 1950, Lake (word illegible), Fla.]

[Bant—x-ed out] Barney Turk in the mails to you before end of week.

Tried to loaf but work haunts me.

Best regards,
Zora

TO BURROUGHS MITCHELL

1461 S. Street N.W.
Washington, D.C.
September 8, 1950.

Dear Burroughs Mitchell:

Here's Barney Turk at last. I like the boy and wish him every success.[1]

---

[2] *Her next published article was "I Saw Negro Votes Peddled," which appeared in November 1950.*

---

[1] *On October 3, Mitchell wrote—with great regret—that they did not find the novel a "success" and would not be able to publish it. He suggested that Hurston set the book aside—not try another revision—and that she reconsider the second volume of her autobiography, which Mitchell had been urging her to write.*

I have given some space to the things or issues that so occupy the thoughts and conversation of his time and place, for he would have to be extra dumb for them not to have touched his life and thoughts. I remember how the South fairly erupted with the false story about the Eleanor Roosevelt Clubs.[2] It is still being mentioned in the South. The leading papers of the area took notice of it in editorials.

With the best of everything to you and yours, I am

With faithful feelings,
Zora

Note present address.

Please tell <u>dear</u> Jean Parker [Waterbury] that I am mailing the second copy to her as soon as I can go through & correct the typos.

TO CHARLES S. JOHNSON

239 West 131st Street
New York City, 27
December 5, 1950

Dear Dr. Johnson:

I have been in New York since late September. In a few days, however, I hope to return to sunny Florida. As soon as the final papers are signed in the matter that brought me here, I will be on my way. <u>I hate snow</u>! You could make a song out of that by just repeating it two thousand times, and that might give you an idea of how bare trees, cold winds, dirty snow under foot, no birds, no blooms, etc. get me down.

Was at Carl Van Vechten's Nov. 25 at a cocktail for Edith Sampson.[1] Several of our old crowd were there. Your name naturally was mentioned.

---

[2]*Rumors about these clubs launched an investigation during World War II. Named for Roosevelt in recognition of her opposition to segregation, they were purported to be comprised largely of disgruntled domestics planning subversive activities.*

---

[1]*Edith Sampson was a Chicago lawyer and judge. She was appointed to an alternate-delegate position with the United Nations by President Truman. Sampson was the only "ethnic" woman to graduate at that time from Loyola University in Chicago with a master's degree in law.*

I have, since adulthood, accepted the philosophy that Time is a great old fortune-teller. Once upon a time, when the "intellectuals" on the Left flourished like the green bay tree, Charles S. Johnson and Zora Neale Hurston were slurred plenty as leading chauvinists, reactionaries, fascists, and so on. I knew from common sense that the philosophy of the dictatorship of the proletariat could never work successfully. You just can't level people until you can level individual intelligence. Anyhow, who wants to be a peasant? What glory is in it, I ask you? What a dull, stupid level of life to establish! I am seeing the pay-off now. I am amused daily by the published plaints of our former "intellectuals" crying, "we was fooled and exploited!" Such a rat race to get back in with us! Please let this go no further, but Mrs. Bethune[2] told me last week that she is moving over as far as she can to the Right from now on. I have heard no sounds from our Number One echo, echo of whatever seems to be succeeding, Alain Locke for some time. He had critisized me in the New Republic by asking when was I ever going to become <u>socially conscious</u>? Because I openly expressed my scorn of them, they got up what they took to be an unbeatably wonderful scheme to kill me off for ever. Only these monumental "intellectuals", in their ecstacy, did not take the time to find out where I was when they stated the dates for things. It just happened that I was not even in the U.S. at the time. WHAM![3]

I assume that you will be taking a leading role in Civilian Defense, or/and organizing WAC units. It is possible that I shall do something of the kind too, since I am a chauvinist, and stupid enough to be patriotic.

I wish that it were possible for Miss Maxeda Von Hess [sic][4] to visit Fisk some time. As I told you, she and her mother teach Speech to many of the biggies of the nation, including Mrs. Roosevelt. They used to stay at the White House for weeks at a time, though they are conservative Republicans. She has many reminiscencies about their work. You will like her immensely.

Very grateful and faithful feelings,
Zora Neale Hurston

---

[2]Mary McLeod Bethune.

[3]A reference to the false morals charge and Hurston's vindication at trial.

[4]Maxeda Von Hesse (d. 1987) was a speech educator and good friend of Eleanor Roosevelt's; she became involved with the black doll project with Hurston and Sara Lee Creech.

TO JEAN PARKER WATERBURY

[telegram]

January 12, 1951
MRS JEAN PARKER WATERBURY, ATTN WATKINS INC

DELIGHTED WANTED TO DO IT[1] FOR YEARS LETTER FOLLOWS
ZORA NEALE HURSTON

TO JEAN PARKER WATERBURY

General Delivery
Belle Glade, Fla.
January 13, 1951.

Dear Jean Park[e]r:

Thanks for the letter about my brother. I have written him already. He owed me a letter for nearly a year.[1]

I switched to Gen. Del. because I found that the box at the house stands open. That letter of yours about the new article for AMERI-CAN LEGION reached my hands quite by accident.[2] A neighbors child was playing with [it] out on the corner when I passed and noted the color of the envelope. I just wrote a criticism for Irita Van Doren[3] at the Herald Tribune,[4] and I hope that her check has not been there and trrown away.

---

[1]*Waterbury had suggested Hurston's next article for the* American Legion Magazine—*on African Americans and communism.*

---

[1]*Hurston's brother Clifford Joel, principal of the Dallas County Training School in Selma, Alabama, had written Scribner's to order copies of* Seraph on the Suwanee *and ask for help in locating his sister's whereabouts.*

[2]*"Why The Negro Won't Buy Communism" was published in June.*

[3]*Irita Bradford Van Doren (1891–1966) was literary editor of the* New York Herald Tribune *from 1926 to 1963 and ran one of New York's toniest salons. She married writer Carl Van Doren in 1912 and they divorced in 1935. From 1937 to 1944 Van Doren's companion was Republican Wendell L. Willkie, who lost a 1940 presidential bid to Franklin Roosevelt.*

[4]*Review of* The Pencil of God, *by Pierre and Philippe Thoby Marcelin.*

I'm afraid that you and Burroughs Mitchell will lose your bet on them alphabet birds, according to the local folks. The Chamber of Commerce says they see you and raise you on that Q.

About the play, now.[5] Mr. Allen. script man at Whitehead Productions[6] advised me to first write it as a novelette as the author did THE MEMBER OF THE WEDDING,[7] then extract the play from that. He said that tere were two advantages in that. One, it would clarify the story line for me. Two, I can possibly sell the novelette. The story is written now. I must make another copy as you cannot offer a carbon to a publisher.

Sorry to have stuck you with that telegram, but I couldn't do any different. Already at work on the article. I assume about 3,000 words will be about right?

Back to the alphabet birds. Bob Creech, Commander of the Am. Leg. here and a local big shot[8] claims that they have special birds trained to form that tail of the Q.

Do you think any publication would ne interested in t[h]e farm labor recruited from the West Indies?[9] You remember that it was started by the Duke of Windsor for the Bahamas, then spread to Jamaica and Barbadoes. I was talking with a Jamican supervisor (under the powerful U.S. Sugar Corp.) and he said some interesting things.1. "We West Indians can no longer conside England our mother country, whwn we must look to the U.S. for everything."
2. The reaction of the American Negro laborer to the West Indians.
3. The advantage that the Bahaman workers have over the other West Indians by reason of the influence of the Duke, and his sharp bargaining for them.
4. The reaction of the West Indian worker to his work and his surroundings here.
5. The historic tour of inspection by the Duke accompanied by Eleanor Roosevelt.

> My best to you all with knobs on it.
> Zora

---

[5]The Golden Bench of God, *about hairdressing entrepreneurs Madame C. J. Walker and Annie Pope Malone; see both Walker and Malone in glossary.*

[6]*Robert Whitehead Productions, theatrical agents, founded by Robert Whitehead (b. 1916), producer.*

[7]The Member of the Wedding, *by Carson McCullers (1917–67), was produced on Broadway in 1950.*

[8]*Sara Lee Creech's brother.*

[9]*Hurston eventually did write on farm labor for the* Fort Pierce Chronicle.

TO MAXEDA VON HESSE

Box 613
Belle Glade, Fla.
January 23, 1951.

Dear Maxeda:

Just received a letter from my agents[1] saying that they can place the novelette of the play for me,[2] so I must make another first copy as quickly as I can. Do send along the copy that you have so I can rush it along to her.[3]

I do hope and earnestly pray that you and Sara Lee [Creech] have the world by the tail with a downhill pill on the dolls. I wait eagerly for the good news or you.

Hope that your mother continues to enjoy good health.

With deep and faithful feelings,

> Hurriedly yours,
> Zora

Will you please call the Robert Whitehead offices, ask for Miss Terry Fay, and ask if they have received the first copy. I have not heard a word from them as yet.

Robert Whitehead Productions
105 West 55th Street

Oh never mind about the call. They may be offended by my attempt to rush things—Z.

---

[1] *Ann Watkins and Jean Parker Waterbury.*

[2] The Golden Bench of God, *about hairdressing entrepreneurs Madame C. J. Walker and Annie Pope Malone; see both Walker and Malone in glossary.*

[3] *Waterbury had written that magazine editors were clamoring for novelettes—probably in response to Fannie Hurst's phenomenal success with them—but she had not promised that she could place Hurston's manuscript.*

TO JEAN PARKER WATERBURY

[late Jan./early Feb. 1951]

Dear Mrs. Waterbury:

Well, here is the article for THE AMERICAN LEGION. I do hope that it is good enough to sell and quickly. I am in my natural state of being broke. I started to name it, COMING THROUGH RELIGION ON THE COMMUNIST LINE, but thought it too long.[1]

SPOT will be on the way to you shortly now.[2]

Much love,
Zora

Maxeda Von Hesse lives at 36 Sutton Place South. Voice teacher to Eleanor Roosevelt and other biggies. She is an author besides being a swell person, and I do hope that you get to know each other. With her now for a few days is Sarilee Creech from Belle Glade, a young white woman who has invented some truly marvelous Negro dolls. They are supposed to go into production in the Spring. A real nice gal to know. I hear that Carl Van Vechten plans to get her a big spread in LIFE on those dolls.[3]

---

[1] Hurston's working title, "Mourner's Bench, Communist Line: Why The Negro Won't Buy Communism," was even longer.

[2] Essay about her dog, never published.

[3] Published December 17, 1951.

TO JEAN PARKER WATERBURY

[stamped: received February 9, 1951]

General Del.
Belle Glade, Fla.
Thursday.

Dear Jean Parker Waterbury:

No, I had no wish to turn hinckty[1] on you. I just noted that the steno always put (Mrs) before your name, and I decided it must be meant for a hint to me.

I am about through with the second writing of the novelette.[2] Set out to just re-copy, but you know how that it. Hope to mail it to you tomorrow.

Somebody stole Spot and I have almost been out of my head for the last two weeks, but I have located her now and will get her back tomorrow.

You must know how I hope and pray that The American Legion will like the article.[3] I am prepared to re-write it in a more dignified tone if they wish. <u>But</u> one observation I omitted. While the Communists are laying claim to everything, I should have pointed out that that is again old stuff. We negroes have been claiming that every important invention was made by Negroes and stolen by Whites ever since I could read. On top of that, we claim kin to half the big names of History. I even heard Dr. DuBois hinting that George Washington had a touch of the tar brush. The only claim that I will fight to prove is that Radio was invented by a Negro woman in the Georgia Insane Asylum. I believe that one—If it wasnt her then somebody in there done it.

Much love,
Zora.

---

[1] *Snobbish; pretentious; pompous.*
[2] The Golden Bench of God.
[3] *"Why The Negro Won't Buy Communism."*

I wonder if the Sat. Ev. Post would, (without prejudice) send along that 50 so I can pay my car note on February 18th.[4] If it's risky, please dont suggest it.

Z.

TO CARL SANDBURG

Belle Glade, Fla.
February 13, 1951.

Dear Carl Sandberg:

I received the copies of your new SONG BAG, and I cannot tell you how proud and glad I am of the association.[1]

Belle Glade, Florida, in the wake of the 1928 hurricane.

---

[4]*Perhaps money owed for "The Conscience of the Court." Hurston's next published article for them, on Robert Taft, appeared in December 1951.*

---

[1]*It included Hurston's rendition of the song "Cold Rainy Day."*

There is a fine ballad describing the 1928 hurricane,[2] and I am trying now to collect it for you. Somebody here has told me at last that they know a man who knows somebody who knows it.

If the offer is still open for your biography of Abraham Lincoln, I would love to accept. The reason that I did not ask for it before was because I had no place to keep it, moving around as I have been for over a year.[3] Now, there is a young white woman here whom I like very, very much, and she will keep the volumes for me until I call for them.[4] Born at Sparta, Georgia, and living here in the 'Glades since 1934, Sara Lee Creech is a phenomena. Perhaps the foremost individual of the area for better race relations, she does not come of the Southern aristocracy. Talented and balanced, she does force in such a quiet way that she moves things. Incidentally, she is a great admirer of yours, and of Lincoln. Her mother is extraordinary too. Never having got to school till she was twelve years old, she did learn to read and write and is now a great reader of serious books.[5] I pointed out one evening that Lincoln probably did more for the poor whites of the South by Emancipation, than he did for us, and she heartily agreed. When you think of the generations of individual talent among the poor whites that never got a hearing, it is truly tragic. I wish that some day you might know the Creeches. We have been talking over bringing you down to Palm Beach for a concert, and Sara Lee is seeing about it now.[6] Anyway, you ought to experience this geological freak that is the Everglades. And the raw, frontier atmosphere here would say something to you.

Let me thank you over and over again for the inclusion in your SONG BAG (I saw that two high schools got copies, and lectured on you) also gave Sara Lee a copy to her immense delight. Then I want to thank you in advance for your life of Lincoln. Sara Lee and her mother are looking forward excitedly to the reading of it.

With faithful feelings,

Zora

[2] *One of the worst disasters in the history of the United States. More than two thousand people—most of them African American—were killed in Belle Glade and nearby communities when a hurricane swept in off the Atlantic and gathered force over Lake Okeechobee. For years, farmers would plow up human remains in the area. Hurston wrote about the hurricane's devastation in* Their Eyes Were Watching God.

[3] *Sandburg's multivolume work on Lincoln was titled* Abraham Lincoln: The Prairie Years *(1926) and* Abraham Lincoln: The War Years *(1939).* Mary Lincoln: Wife and Widow *was published in the early 1930s.*

[4] *Hurston gave her copy to Mary Araminta Young Creech on Mother's Day in 1951; it is inscribed to Hurston by Carl Sandburg.*

[5] *Much of Hurston's research for* Herod the Great *was conducted with Mary Araminta Young Creech.*

[6] *This visit never took place.*

TO JEAN PARKER WATERBURY

Belle Glade, Fla.
February 13, 1951.

Dear Jean Parker:

Yesterday, Monday, the manuscript[1] and the check reached my hand, and I offer you my humble thanks for what you did for me. Then I offer my thanks to you again.

You will note that I am included in Carl Sandbergs [sic] new SONG BAG, for which I am duly grateful.

I go back to work on the article for THE AMERICAN LEGION MAGAZINE[2] with that peculiar joy that I suppose writers feel at getting another chance to polish. I know that I will have it off again by the end of the week.

You wonder what has become of the novelette.[3] It seems that I just can't help from revising it some more and then again. I am trying, for the sake of it's ultimate purpose, to keep a sharp eye out for characterization and sharp dialogue.[4]

My letter, which you must have received on Monday will clear up the matter of titles I hope. I certainly see no gain in having you call me "Miss", but from what I explained to you, I began to fear that I had been too previous with _you._

I do not know for certain what is going on at Whitehead's. I had a wire from them saying that I would hear from the immediately, but after two weeks still nothing. I assume that the script of the story[5] is being read around in the organization still. Anyway, I now wish that they wouldn't, because the revised version that I am sending you is tighter, I believe. I have about twenty pages of revision to go, which I think I shall finish in the next twenty-four hours.

My darling SPOT is back in my arms again, a g/rightened,

[1]_Probably "What White Publishers Won't Print."_

[2]_"Why The Negro Won't Buy Communism."_

[3]The Golden Bench of God.

[4]_Waterbury and Burroughs Mitchell had criticized Hurston's characterization in_ The Lives of Barney Turk.

[5]The Golden Bench of God.

heart-broken dog whom I am nursing back to mental health again.[6]
I am very glad that I have come through to a calm balance again so that
I can be of the best service to her, and also know just how she felt in
those ten terrible days away from me. She is thin, because she had refused to eat, and I never saw such tragic eyes on anybody. For her sake,
more than mine, I shall never let her get out of my sight again. You can
be sure that I am back to myself again at last. It was a very long journey
through a dark wilderness, but I have come home again. It is only in
these last weeks that I can see how lost I was. I am glad now that I did
not send SPOT's story along earlier. Now I feel that I can really write it.

    With an infinitely deeper appreciation of what you and Ann
[Watkins] have done and been to me,

Faithfully,

Zora

TO FREDERICK WOLTMAN

C/O General Delivery
Belle Glade, Fla.
February 22, 1951.

Dear Frederick Woltman:

    Somebody sent me your column of Feb. 17, I believe, I [in] which
you reveal the dodge of the Peace Center, involving Dr. W.E.B.
DuBois.[1] (On the quiet, George Schuyler pronounces it Dubious[2]) I
was not at all surprised at their slick change of name and location, nor
the indictment of DuBois and his associates.

    What did surprise me was your statement that Dr. Mordecai John-
son, President of Howard U. was to speak at this affair at the Essex

---

[6]*Her beloved dog, Spot, had disappeared for ten days. Hurston assumed she'd stolen. The dog lived with
her in the Roof Garden Hotel.*

---

[1]*Possibly published in the* New York World-Telegram. *The Peace Information Center was headed by W. E. B.
Du Bois from April 3, 1950, to October 12, 1950. On February 9, 1951, Du Bois and his associates were indicted
as "unregistered foreign agents" and charged under the Foreign Agents Registration Act of 1938.*

[2]*Harlem Renaissance writer, critic, parodist; see glossary; others attribute the apellation of "Dubious" for Du
Bois to Hurston.*

House on Feb. 23.[3] He was in this area two weeks ago and made a tremendous and favorable impression on white and clolred. Nobody wants to believe that Dr. Johnson has leftist leanings. So concerned were the two members of the Inter-Racial Committee that brought him to Belle Glade, that one of them called him at his office in Washington and asked him point-blank if it was true.[4]

Dr. Johnson replied that he had promised to speak at the birthday party of Dr. Dubois, who had been his teacher in college years ago. But when he found that it was not the simple birthday party as represented to him, he had asked that his name be withdrawn. Evidently, this was not done, as it was reported to you that he was to speak. The very next day, Feb. 21, your column stated that the Rabbi had withdrawn, and that Dr. Johnson was the principal speaker, with a member of his faculty, E. Franklin Frazier,[5] acting as MC.

This has some of his admirers here in a tizzy. They do not know what to believe, though earnestly wishing to give him the benefit of the doubt. Perhaps you have forgotten me, but I knew you in New York along in 1946–7. I suggested that if there was anything against Dr. Johnson, you would know, so I am writing you for that reason.

I quoted you briefly in an article on Negroes and Communism thet I am doing for the AMERICAN LEGION MAGAZINE.. I'll let you see the galleys when they come.[6] I think that you will agree with me that the commies have been deceived in thinking that if they capture a few Negro names, that the whole shooting-match will just fall into their arms. I notice rather, that this sets the "name" off from us. They take on a certain odor. "Sigsnifficant" to coin a word, though I did not use it in the article. I did tell one belligerent commie who saw me in a cafe in New York just before Christmas and came and stood glowering down at me, "Move back, Comrade. You smell significant."

Do drop me a line and settle the question of Dr. Johnson's political philosophy for these local people It will be a great favor. Then allow

---

[3]*Mordecai Johnson (1890–1976) was the first black president of Howard University (1926–60). He is credited with introducing Martin Luther King, Jr., to Mahatma Gandhi's philosophy of nonviolent resistance.*

[4]*Johnson was the council's first speaker; Hurston was the second. Johnson was a controversial president. In the early years of his presidency he was accused of running Howard in a dictatorial and unyielding fashion. In the 1950s, some of his opponents accused him of being a communist sympathizer, which he strongly denied.*

[5]*E. Franklin Frazier (1894–1962) was a sociologist at Howard University and head of the sociology department from 1934 to 1959. He was known for his numerous books on race, family, and Negro culture in the United States. In 1948, he was elected president of the American Sociological Society.*

[6]*"Why The Negro Won't Buy Communism."*

me to congratulate you on your noble Pulitzering[7] and things like that. May uou have a hundred more years and every one of them be award years. Then give my best to Helen Worden Erskine.

Sincerely yours,

Zora Neale Hurston

TO JEAN PARKER WATERBURY

[stamped: received February 26, 1951]

Dear Jeanie with the wavy hair:

It <u>would</u> be just my luck to finish off, shout with joy and dash off to the Post Office first thing in the morning to find that I can't send off the article[1] because it is George Washington's birthday. P.O. closed tight as a drum.

I was perfectly sincere about PENCIL OF GOD. It is just like Haiti. Spitting image. And so brightly written. It shows again that the U.S. is a wonderful place. If the Marcellins had not passed so much time here, I doubt if they would have achieved the objectivity that they did.[2] That goes for other expressions of Negro art. We Negroes here are out in front of others because there is something inherent on this continent that springs. Hence a new ingredient was given to our African material that gave it life and the element to reach people and endure. I am perfectly reconciled to slavery on that score. It had to be, or other things could not have happened.[3]

Please tell Redding how wonderful his book is.[4] He has done a magnificent, objective and comprehensive job. I have reccomended it

---

[7]*Woltman helped the* New York World-Telegram *win a Pulitzer Prize in 1931. He received an honorable mention Pulitzer Prize in 1946 and 1947. See Woltman in glossary.*

[1]*"Why The Negro Won't Buy Communism."*

[2]Pencil of God *was written by Philippe Thoby Marcelin (1904–75) in 1951. It was reviewed by Hurston in the* New York Herald Tribune Weekly Book Review, *February 4, 1951.*

[3]*This echoes a sentiment Hurston expressed in an early essay, "How It Feels to Be Colored Me," published in the* World Tomorrow, *May 1928.*

[4]*Writer Saunders J. Redding; see glossary. In 1951, he published* On Being Negro in America. *In 1950, he had published* They Came in Chains: Americans from Africa.

to white friends of mine, and they are reading it and being influenced.

I hope and pray that all goes well at THE AMERICAN LEGION MAGAZINE,[5] and that the novelette[6] can be placed. I think that it is a good job, and that it is time that something is said about an industry so important to Negro millions.[7]

Spot is quite herself again and sends her love. While I was not looking, she tooth-marked one page of the script, perhaps in an editorial spirit.

All my love,
Zora

TO JEAN PARKER WATERBURY

[stamped: received March 6, 1951]

Sunday Morning
Belle Glade, Fla.

Dear Jean P.:

I take it that MISS SPOT arrived safely to your hand. I suppose that what I needed was an inking-pad for Spot's signature. It turned out very poorly with ink.

Yesterday I had a note from Miss Brettner,[1] enclosing the royalty statement from Scribners as of Feb. 1. Also calling my attention to the fact that I owe the firm of Ann Watkins around five dollars. Yes, do please take it out of the first money that comes in.

The card acknowledging the receipt of THE MOURNER'S BENCH,[2] and the novelette[3] arrived and I noted that you would write me on Wednesday, but I know how that is. You get more rushed than

---

[5]*With "Why The Negro Won't Buy Communism."*
[6]The Golden Bench of God.
[7]*The hair-straightening business.*

---

[1]*Nancy Brettner, assistant to Jean Parker Waterbury.*

[2]*"Mourner's Bench, Communist Line: Why The Negro Won't Buy Communism," was Hurston's working title for "Why The Negro Won't Buy Communism," published in* American Legion Magazine, *June 1951.*

[3]The Golden Bench of God.

you expected, so you cannot take care of another letter. I do hope that the novelette will not disappoint you too much when you read it. I would pray that it get serialized in one of the big women's mags, but since I have paid no church dues in quite some time, Old Maker is under no obligation to me whatsoever. So I try to contain myself in patience, as a man said to me here the other day. His brother is a pushing go-getter, while this man just slopes along. He explained his viewpoint this way: "I figger that good luck got more chance to overtake me moving slow than he can run it down."

Now, I wait only on that possible check from AMERICAN LEGION to finish off with the car and establish myself in housekeeping once more and again. Being under my own roof, and my personality not invaded by others makes a lot of difference in my outlook on life and everything. Oh, to be once more alone in a house!

In your own home, I wish you many dishes and kisses and everything nice.

Faithful feelings,
Zora

TO JEAN PARKER WATERBURY

General Delivery
Belle Glade, Fla.
March 7, 1951.

Dear Jean Parker:

I take my machine on knee to write you a much-felt letter. I can see, that is, follow you and Ann [Watkins] about the material on Martha and Lola.[1] But the very mention of "novel" gives me a shudder. You have no idea what I have been through in the last six months. After using the money that I earned otherwise to buy the leisure to work on Barney Turk, I found myself with a year's work gone for nothing, and me cold in hand.[2] That is a Negro way of saying penni-

---

[1] *Characters in* The Golden Bench of God.
[2] *Rejected by Scribner's; this is one of Hurston's only expressions of bitterness at the rejection.*

less. And I do mean penniless. God! What I have been through. What I get for this article from THE AMERICAN LEGION will just about pull me even.[3] Just inching along like a stepped-on worm from day to day. Borrowing a little here and there.

Then add to that, I get a letter from Mr. [Whitney] Darrow saying that SERAPH ON THE SUWANNEE will be remaindered. Though it will bring me nothing financially, I feel grateful and write him a letter to that effect and get accused of trying to make him. Some day I am going to do a piece probing into why white men feel and believe that all females of darker hue are just dying to make them. It is astonishing. Maybe too much Kipling. AND so far, I have seen no sign of the remaindering.

About the gold piano on the Hudson, Madam Walker,[4] who pioneered the hair-straightening business really had one. The characters and plot are my own devising, but I have followed the history of the business pretty closely except that there was no white man in it to my knowing. I can see the expansion easily, and agree with you all down the line on the logical development. I had just tried not to write a novel. Some of the economic kicks I have suffered in the last half year have reached my vitals. But if you feel that it should be done, I will go ahead with it as soon as I can get me some permanent place to live.

SPOT was done much too hurriedly, and I am perfectly willing to lick the calf over again.

Otherwise, I feel fine and dandy. I know that Whitehead must be waiting for the first draft of the play, but I wanted your reaction on the story line.[5] If you want to show him the version that you have, okay, but he urged me to use my own judgment, and to submit what I myself believed was good. So I suppose that there is no need to show it to him. When you and Ann [Watkins] and I feel satisfied, you can just turn the play over to him.

Do prod that guy[6] because I am all too weary of going to the Post Office and turning away cold in hand and having to avoid folks who

---

[3]*The* American Legion *paid Hurston $600 for "Why The Negro Won't Buy Communism."*

[4]*Sarah Breedlove Walker, or Madame C. J. Walker (1867–1919), went from being a poverty-stricken washerwoman to a very wealthy businesswoman. At the height of her success, she had more than two thousand agents in the field selling her "preparations" and she grossed over $50,000 annually.*

[5]The Golden Bench of God.

[6]*At* American Legion.

have made me loans so that I could eat and sleep. The humiliation is getting to be much too much for my self respect, speaking from the inside of my soul. I have tried to keep it to myself and just wait. To look and look at the magnificent sweep of the Everglades, birds included and keep a smile on my face.

For the last two weeks, the weather here has really been hot and summery. Orange trees in bloom and that sort of thing. It is assumed here that summer has arrived.

My best to Ann [Watkins], Mike [Watkins], and you all. There is a lusty book to be done on the founding of Belle Glade and the Everglades in general. Regular old Wild West stuff and still some of it going on. The very next time that you fetch your husband down, try to find time to spend a few days down in the Glades. Tomorrow, nothing happening to prevent it, I am taking what they call my "Cracker pole" meaning a bamboo, and dipping a line in mighty Lake Okechobee. Wish that you and Ann could join me in a lazy day.

With faithful feelings,
Zora

TO JEAN PARKER WATERBURY

Belle Glade, Fla.
March 18, 1951.

Dear Jean Parker Waterbury:

Thanks for the $100. I had exactly four pennies when it arrived, and my landlord[1] was growing restless.

Anticipating what happened about that line, I returned the original script to you with the re-write. I thought that the editors of AMERICAN LEGION might want to make comparisons. It is there in your office.[2]

Irregardless, I have caught fire on the novel,[3] and I am back at work on it already. I do not know whether you ever went down to the Matanza river in your pig-tail days to fish and caught a toad fish. You

[1] *At the Roof Garden Hotel.*
[2] *"Why The Negro Won't Buy Communism."*
[3] The Golden Bench of God.

know if they are swallowed by a big fish, they will eat their way out
through the walls of it's stomach. That is like the call to write. You
must do it irregardless, or it will eat it's way out of you anyhow. So
come what may, I am back at it, keeping in mind your and Ann's suggestions. I do not conceive of Lola as really bad. To begin with, she is
stupid, and Martha with the best intentions in the world, creates what
she finally becomes out of the material she had on hand. After 25
years of indulgence, she can only see herself. She is willing to sacrifice
anything in the world, even her mother, her selfless mother, to what
she conceives of as her way of happiness. She cannot see the falsity of
it all as Martha can.[4] That is what I have to bring out more
de[f]initely. I feel more confident about this story than anything I
have done since THEIR EYES WERE WATCHING GOD.

  I thank you and I thank you in every way that I know how for that
advance check. You have no idea how it touched my heart, your concern for my distress.

Most sincerely,

Zora

TO MAXEDA VON HESSE

C/O General Delivery
Belle Glade, Fla.
April 7, 1951.

Dear, dear Friend:
  Belatedly, I thank you in the humblest way that I know how for
the loan of your most valuable notes. It is not because warm gratitude
and appreciation was not always present, but upon my soul, this has
been one of the most sombre winters of my whole life. All kind of
miseries camping on my tail. Financial worry, illness, and whatever
else you can think of, happened to me. The worst was a kind of disillusionment with some I thought steadfast.[1]

---

[4]*Characters in* The Golden Bench of God. *Lola is based on Hurston's critical view of the flamboyant Harlem
Renaissance figure A'Lelia Walker, daughter of Madame C. J. Walker.*

---

[1]*Possibly editor Whitney Darrow, among others; see Hurston to Jean Parker Waterbury, March 7, 1951.*

Mrs. Creech and Sara Lee did what they could, and it was a lot, to keep me feeling like keeping on living, but then sickness has dogged us all pretty closely since Christmas. First one and then the other of us was down. All we could do was hang together and groan. I do not know whether Sara Lee told you or not, but for a time she feared cancer and another operation. Happily, it turned out to be an encisted ovary, and the doctor is now trying to shock it back to activity. Of course she has been gloomy and difficult at times, but I made the mistake in saying to her that no one can be normal mentally when they are physically ill. She did not take to that kindly, pointing out that she has been illish all her born days. It took a few days for her to forgive me for that, though I know that it is true. I can gauge my own reactions to people and life by my physcial state. We did one thing which I think helped us both mightily by submerging our thoughts of our illness for the time. We painted her house. It looks simply swell now.[2] I suppose that she told you that she had done away with the tarpaulins now and replaced them with glass jalousies. The house looks <u>grand!</u> By the time that it was finished, I had a check from New York, and my circumstances are much improved. The next one will let me clear myself completely and have something over. And my literary reputation is steadily growing.

Do let me know how everything is with you, honey. I want to hear <u>everything</u>. Soon I hope to find that you see your way to get back to creative writing. You have so much to say. By the way, I wish that some textile firm would print a bedspread from your painting of the field here in the Everglades.[3] I never grow tired of looking at it, and wondering at your sure and subtle lighting. It is a grand piece, and I hope that you never give up painting.

My best to your mother. I had hoped that I would see her again before she went north, but fate was against me there. You will laugh yourself to death, but I had a most charming letter from Mrs. Smathers[4] last Friday.

I can understand your shock and fear at the Johnson incident.[5] The imminent peril to your dolls after all the time, money and anguish that you two have put into the undertaking. It would be utterly tragic

---

[2] *Sara Lee Creech remembers Hurston as a very good house painter.*
[3] *This lovely painting is still in the possession of Sara Lee Creech.*
[4] *Wife of Senator George Smathers, for whose father Hurston had worked as a ghostwriter.*
[5] *Mordecai Johnson, president of Howard University.*

for something to upset the apple-cart at this late date. But I knew all along that Dr. Johnson is too smart a guy to get mixed up in a thing like that. Further, I knew what you could not—that some faculty members and their alumni adherents have been trying to upset and overthrow the old boy for years and years. You can just imagine him sticking his neck out under such circumstances, couldn't you? Besides, he has great respect for established authority, a Baptist preacher from way back, and all that. No, he would not want that kind of a change <u>at all.</u> And he has tremendous prestige with both white and black in high places. Why kick it all to hell? Being a school under the government, and you know that under the New Deal, this leftist business was encouraged, so some members of his faculty like E. Franklin Frazier knew only too well that he dare not dismiss them. So even now, you see that he was defied. It is all very intricate. Some members of government still promote the radicals under other names, and since they wish to chase Johnson out and replace him with somebody of their own ilk, he must watch his step. But I would not be at all surprised if Frazier and a few others were not eased out by next year some how. The national wind is blowing from another direction now and strengthens Johnson's hand. Do write him.

Well, I plan to depart this muck now before long. If all goes well, I will take a little house at Eau Gallie, on the East Coast. A quiet, pretty town WITH NO MUCK.

SPOT wishes to be remembered to you in the kindest way. She is just as self-opinionated as ever, but as charming for her independence of spirit.

With all my love and faithful feelings,

Zora

Back to Dr. Johnson. I am certain that that goateed, egotistic, wishy-washy, W.E.B. DuBois had Johnson's name sent to the press with malice aforethought. He can endure no one being prominent but himself. He is the same man that spent nearly a generation trying to destroy Booker T. Washington. Then he was the haughty aristocrat. Now, his empty pretensions meeting the realities in his old age, and rejected elsewhere, he turns communist. I think his desire now is to become prexy at Howard. Of course, he'll never make it, but it is just like him to believe that he should have it. Hence his underhand lick at Johnson. He is utterly detestable. I went to the bat for Dr. Johnson with Woltman, thought Johnson does not know it. I knew that he was innocent, and I know the despicable tricks of certain prominent Negroes consumed with impotent jealousy.

ZNH

TO JEAN PARKER WATERBURY

[stamped: received April 9, 1951]

Dear Jean Parker:

Yesterday I returned from the hospital where I had been since March 24th. A case of that virus influenza, but with complications. One of the first things that met my eye was this letter addressed to you lying there catching dust. It gave me a queer feeling as if some evil magic had taken place, so sure was I that I had mailed it. But gradually I figured it out. I had occasion to write to Senator Taft, but being ill even then, I had considered the letter badly composed, and decided not to send it until I was myself again. So I thought that I laid it aside, and mailed only the one to you. Sure enough, there at the Post Office was a letter from Senator Taft, indicating that in my poor p[h]ysical condition, I had posted the wrong letter. It was like the folk tales of the changeling. I was crushed, because I had wanted the editors at AMERICAN LEGION to know that the old script was there immediately.[1] It only proves to me how very ill I have been. I tried for over a week to talk myself out of it, but finally it came to the place where Sara Lee Creech, not seeing me, came here and found me only half conscious, and rushed me to the hospital. She got the second check out of the Post Office, got my signature at the hospital and paid off my car, income tax, and all the debts [f]or me, since she knew my affairs intimately. She just went ahead.[2] Never have I been so ill since I have been grown.

---

[1] *"Why The Negro Won't Buy Communism."*
[2] *Creech does not recall this.*

If it is not too late, I would like to add enough words, perhaps no more than ten, to mention Frederick Woltman of the World-Telegram. I helped him with his research on Communism among Negroes, and since I do practically quout him once, would like to include his name. He would give the article extended notice.

Yes, I want a hundred copies of the November article.[3] I have use for them even if I have to pay for them. I'll be so very glad.

Do you think that THE SATURDAY EVENING POST would consider an article, A NEGRO VOTER LOOKS AT SENATOR ROBERT A TAFT?[4] I think that a great deal could be said there. I believe that Negro evaluation of a m man like Senator Taft depends on our political maturity. If we have gotten far enough from the dramatics of UNCLE TOM'S CABIN, the lore of the underground railway, general abolitionist sentiment and the pernicious "friends of the Negro" of Reconstruction, then we can take his measure for good or ill. See what he shapes up like as presidential timber. That would be my jumping off spot. Me, I have no political heroes. I can take them all or leave them. Even as pure and as wonderful and I am, (?) I am afraid that too much power would make a monster out of me too. Lincoln is great to me, not as the Emancipator, but as a man. His lack of fanatical hate all during the bitter struggle. His balance.

I have much more to say to you, but I am so weak and tired now. Another day or so and I will be back in harness. Right now, I do not know what day of the week nor month it is. I go to the Post Office for the first time in many days, and will buy a paper and catch up on the calendar.

All my love

Zora

[in left margin:] My thoughts are so scattered as yet. Thanks so much for everything you have done for me.

---

[3] *"I Saw Negro Votes Peddled."*

[4] *Published as "A Negro Voter Sizes Up Taft" in the* Saturday Evening Post, *December 8, 1951.*

TO JEAN PARKER WATERBURY

[added, probably by Waterbury: 5/1/51]

Sunday Night.

Dear Jean Parker:

I have been anguishing while trying to get hold of the data I want on Robert A. Taft.[1] No resources around here, so I have decided to run down to Miami and get into the morgue of the Miami Herald. What I want is his complete record on bills affecting minorities.

Already, he is being worked over down here, indicating his increasing importance. To the traditional and unchangeable Democrat, he is "That Taft! Always with his mouth gapped open and trying to tell everybody what to do." But you might be surprised to find what a large Republican party Florida has now. Even one in the State Senate. Then there are those who remain Democrats, but like Taft. "Smartest man in the whole Senate. Jeffersonian, I would say. Got too much sense and decency to run down the South. I would vote for him anyday before I would for that Truman."

Belle Glade is no place to look for a political opinion among Negroes. They just pick beans here.[2] But in West Palm Beach, forty miles directly to the east, there is a regular gale blowing around Taft. Traditionally, Negroes ask first, "But how does he feel about <u>us</u>? Is he a friend of the Negro?" You can readily see that that is not enough in a President these days.

I am sure to have my data in the next twenty-four hours, and can write the article in full. Otherwise, I am far along on that novel.[3] I think that I am doing much better on characterization on Lola and explaining her than before, leaving Martha as she is, but extended, as you suggested. You know, never a truly indigenous Negro novel has been written so far. Punches have been pulled to "keep things from the white folks" or angled politically, well to show our sufferings, rather than to tell a story as

---

[1] *For her article published in the* Saturday Evening Post, *December 8, 1951.*
[2] *Belle Glade was essentially a migrant agricultural community.*
[3] The Golden Bench of God.

is. I have decided that the time has come to write truthfully from the inside. Imagine that no white audience is present to hear what is said.

Hope that this outline on Taft is sufficient to sell Stuart Rose.[4] I hold no brief for Taft, nor one against him. I just want to take a good look at the man who might easily be our next prexy. I do think that the habit of the New Deal of whipping up racial antagonism has been very bad for the country. I stumble over the scars of it too often. For example, Britton Sayles, principal of the local Negro high school here had a job in Washington under the New Deal. He is so twisted now that he cannot bear to hear a favorable remark about a white person. Hate, hate, hate! And those eternal cliches on the matter. Eliza is still jumping ice cubes in his mind. The roar of the tractors in the bean fields are drwoned out for him by the baying of the hounds on her trail.[5] If he were the only one, it would not be important. They do nothing constructive. Just brood and talk. There is nothing in the world but racial angles. I lost his good will about two weeks ago by remarking, "But there are some good, fair-minded White people. You are doing just what you complain about in them, pre-judging people by their skincolor. Why not allow them to show what is in them before you make up your mind?" Wheweeee! Among other things, he told me that I am a special case, and that I cannot judge the sufferings of our people by what happens to me. I am a celebrity and all, etc. But left out that I was not born a celebrity, and must have known some white people before that. The joke is that the upper class whites here bend backwards being nice to him, never suspecting how he really feels about them. He likes to play that traditional trick of giving White people a dig on the sly. The tragedy is, those digs are always administered to the whites who favor better conditions for Negroes and come among us to help bring it about. One white man or woman at an inter-racial meeting, five hundred of us, and everyone who gets up to speak takes a poke at that one. Our press would scream to high heaven if that happened to us.

Well, off to the Post Office. Weather bright and clear, and your meek and humble servant feeling grand.

All my love
Zora

---

[4]*Stuart Rose (1899–1975) was an author and book and magazine editor. He was senior editor of the* Saturday Evening Post *for twenty-four years. He also worked for the* New Yorker, *the* Ladies' Home Journal, *Alfred A. Knopf, David McKay, and others.*

[5]*Hurston's allusion is to Eliza's melodramatic escape from slavery, across the partially frozen ice of the river, in Harriet Beecher Stowe's* Uncle Tom's Cabin.

TO JEAN PARKER WATERBURY

Thursday A.M. [added, probably by Waterbury: 5/10/51]

Dear Jean:

By this place being off the main line, your letter of May 2 just reached me yesterday after four oclock. I did not go to the P.O. in the morning as usual. I tried to figure out the quickest way to get in touch with you.

This business of the review, and trying to horn in on my idea about Taft gives you a slight idea.[1] The first thing too many Negroes do when they want to be writers and public characters in general is to grab something from me, and then hate me for being alive to make their pretensions out a lie. And then take all kinds of steps to head me off. "Block that Zora Neale Hurston!" is a regular slogan. I go in the out of the way places and collect and gather, and then they sit on their rumps in New York and filch from me. Someday I shall tell you some incidents that will astonish you, while disgusting you.

No, I do not want to stay with Ann Watkins, Inc. any more. A firm with no more honor than to make the ideas and work of one author available to another. It stinks like a million dead mules on a mile of manure. But at any rate, you must have known that I would go along with you. So here it is in writing. I finish the same day you do, May 31. Wish this article[2] was not hanging in the balance right now. The difficulty of getting congressional records has held me back, and depending on some one to get them for me, a hopee that failed. But I have a source in Miami now, and will have everything in your hands <u>at your home address</u> in a jiffy.

Most sincerely,

Zora

---

[1]*Hurston suspected someone at the* Saturday Evening Post *or the Watkins agency—or both—of stealing her ideas; see Hurston to Burroughs Mitchell, July 15, 1951.*
[2]*On Taft.*

TO MCINTOSH AND MCKEE

Belle Glade, Fla.
May 11, 1951.

McIntosh & McKee[1]
30 East 60th Street
New York, N.Y.

Dear Ladies:

Please tell Jean Parker Waterbury that I tried to phone her at home yesterday, but was told that she was out of town. I wrote her a letter to that address anyway. Hope to have the Taft article[2] to the office by Tuesday coming, and the script of the novel[3] to her home address.

With all good wishes,
Zora
Zora Neale Hurston

TO JEAN PARKER WATERBURY

[marked: received May 24, 1951]

Dear Jean:

Here is that article at last.[1] I was held back waiting on material from Taft's office. Then, bless me gawd, it laid here in theis Post Office ten days before they remembered to hand it to me.

Hope you made it back to New York all right, and that things go

---

[1] *Mavis McIntosh and Elizabeth McKee were literary agents for whom Waterbury worked when she left the Ann Watkins agency.*
[2] *"A Negro Voter Sizes Up Taft,"* Saturday Evening Post, *December 8, 1951.*
[3] The Golden Bench of God.

---

[1] *"A Negro Voter Sizes Up Taft,"* Saturday Evening Post, *December 8, 1951.*

well with you. I also hope and pray that Stuart Rose likes this piece
well enough to buy it.[2]

Love and stuff,

Zora

TO MCINTOSH AND MCKEE

Belle Glade, Fla.
May 28, 1951.

Dear McIntosh-McKee:

In case the wealth accumulated in the hair-straightening business by
the heroine of this story seems fantastic to you, be advised that Madame
C.J. Walker, [between lines: "(Indianapolis, Ind)"] the originator, was
said to have realized around two million dollars. The Poro System, that
came up (Madame Malone, St. Louis, Mo.) exceeded three million,[1] and
was then swamped in popularity by the Orchid System of Atlantic City,
N.J. It has become a permanent habit, and will continue to make great
fortunes, though there are so many "systems" now, that no one will
hardly make the large and quick fortunes realized by the earlier ones.

Respectfully submitted,

Zora Neale Hurston

---

[2] *At the bottom of the letter, someone (probably Waterbury) has written: "poor. Unorganized: diatribe against personal hate too often appears to be a side issue & something apart from discussion of Taft. If SEP rejects, try Amer Legion (Keeley) who has bought ZNH's earlier political article. (This more up his alley than Post's)."*

[1] *Fourteen million according to some accounts.*

TO JEAN PARKER WATERBURY

Belle Glade, Fla.
June 4, 1951.

Dear, dear Jean:

You are a salesman from way back! What I mean! I am so very happy that I am about to bust my britches. It is not the money, though you know, and I know and God knows I need it badly. It is the prestige of the thing that I admire so much.[1]

About the changes now. I would be the biggest chump on earth not to be glad to have Stuart Rose edit my few scattering remarks. What he did for THE CONSCIENCE OF THE COURT made it the successful story that it was. I even wish, should the novel be accepted, that he could work on that too. I know that such a thing is impossible, but I can wish all I please, can't I? So for my sake, treat Stuart Rose like a blue-bird that flew in the window. Pat him on the shoulder, kiss him good and then hug him around the neck. I am so grateful to him for everything.

I am writing ANN WATKINS, INC. by this same mail to have things out in the open and on the up-and-up. I enclose the carbon of my letter to her.

You know, I did not start out to be enthusia[s]tic about Senator Taft, but the more research I did on the man, the better I liked him. I admire Senators Russel [sic] of Georgia and Byrd of Virginia in the same fashion.[2] These men seem to see the United States as a whole and fight for what is good for the nation. Statesmen, in this poor day and age.

I felt real sorry to read about what happened to your old grove and everything. Three years before another crop of buds produce. It would be seven years if you fooled around with seedlings, though. We all get

---

[1] Her article on Taft was bought by the Saturday Evening Post.

[2] Richard Brevard Russell, Jr. (1897–1971), was a member of the Georgia State House of Representatives (1921–31), speaker of the Georgia State House (1927–31), governor of Georgia (1931–33), and U.S. senator from Georgia (1933–71). Harry Flood Byrd (1887–1966) was a member of the Virginia State Senate (1915–25), governor of Virginia (1926–30), U.S. senator from Virginia (1933–65), and states' rights candidate for president in 1956.

our lumps, but the talent and energy that got you there in the first place will take you back there again. In no time, your old bank roll will be putting on weight around the briskets. Hope that my work can contribute towards it. Me, I am penniless at the moment, but this time, no debts to speak of, thank God. I can save something this time. I am going to move up to Eau Gallie where I can pay $5.00 per week house rent and be on the coast where it is cooler and certainly cleaner than here. $10 is the cheapest I can pay here for a passably clean house, and then with garbage strowed around everywhere in the yards.

See you later and tell you straighter. Hope the novel does not disappoint.

Most sincerely,
Zora

TO ANN WATKINS

Belle Glade, Fla.
June 4, 1951.

Dear Ann Watkins:

In this mornings mail I got the information that Jean Parker Waterbury has a new business address, and while my relations with ANN WATKINS, INC. have been very pleasant to me, somehow I find that that the firm has come to connote Jean Parker Waterbury to me, so I want to go along with my state-mate.[1] So please consider that as of June 1, I look to Mrs. Jean Parker Waterbury as my literary representative.

With all good wishes, with deep gratitude and warm feelings, I am

Sincerely yours
Zora Neale Hurston

P.S. The breeze blew the carbon off the table and Spot pounced on it and ran out doors with it. By the time I got it back it was in three pieces.

Z.

---

[1] *Waterbury was a Floridian.*

TO JEAN PARKER WATERBURY

Eau Gallie, Fla.
General Delivery
July 9, 1951.

Dear Jean:

Thanks for the money. I am fixing up my new home here. It is a one-room house, but a large room, and set in two blocks of grounds with an artesian well. I have to do some pioneering, but I find that I like it. I am the happiest I have been in the last ten years, irregardles of whether Scribners likes the novel or not.[1]

I am up every morning at five oclock chopping down weeds and planting flowers and things. That is why I have been so long getting to my machine to write letters. I go to bed happily tired and swear that I will write you a letter first thing in the morning. But the birds, which I feed and who have begun to collect here already in large numbers, wake me up clamoring for their breakfast, and I dash out and place stale bread, etc. and watch the many colors and many behaviors of my feathered friends. Less than an hour ago, a male cardinal lit on the porch no more than five feet from me and complained that there was no more food outside, so I hurried to put some out. Then just as I opened up the machine, a great conclave of birds, led by two crows, screamed to me that some enemy was raiding a mocking-bird nest in a big oak tree, and I rushed over to find a lean and desperate cat climbing the tree, and chunked him clear off the place. Spot, and her daughter, Shag, love it here. They show it in many ways. They go hunting, and so far, have scared up a cat, two rabbits and an armadilla. It seems that t[h]ey are plentiful around here. From all that hoeing and what not, I am losing weight, God be praised![2]

This day, I take out my notes and go back to work with new vigor and a clean-swept mind. Two short pieces and back to the attempt at

---

[1] *Hurston had sent a draft of* Herod the Great *to Burroughs Mitchell and was awaiting word on* The Golden Bench of God.

[2] *Those who knew Hurston in the fifties describe her as becoming increasingly heavy, a weight gain that, in retrospect, seems tied to her high blood pressure and heart trouble. According to friends who knew her, this weight gain should have been an indication to her doctors that she needed serious treatment.*

drama. I believe that I can do it, and I'm giving it a very serious try this time. You will have assorted scripts in your hand very shortly.[3]

Now, you p[e]rhaps question why I am putting so much into this place where I now live. I have a chance to buy it. In this little house I wrote MULES AND MEN. Since that time, it has come to be in a White residential neighborhood. Eau Gallie has grown with the Jet Base, and not far away, near Cocoa, the Guided Missile Base, and many people stationed here are buying and building. Mr. W. Lansing Gleason, my landlord, is the mayor. He must go slow about selling it to me, waiting on public reaction. It is beginning to be favorable to me. Several of my neighbors have stopped in the last week and remarked on the improvements I have made. It looked like a jungle three weeks ago, and it took a strong heart and an eye on the future for me to move in when I arrived. The place had run down so badly. In what was meant to be a compliment, I have been told twice, "You don't live like the majority of your people. You like things clean and orderly around you." The manager of the local dairy, seeing me setting out flowers as I cleared, surprised me with a load of compost as a present Saturday. The grounds have great possibilities, and I really would love to own it. I still must remove tons of junk, old tin cans and bottles from the premises. Somehow, this one spot on earth feels like home to me. I have always intended to come back here. That is why I am doing so much to make a go of it. No house in a block of me four ways. No loud radios and record-playing to irritate me, and great oaks and palms around the place.

I do hope that other person that Burroughs Mitchell had reading my script[4] was not Roy [sic] Ottley.[5] You can see why I would not want a Negro writer to be handling it. Since none of the others have thought to do anything with the hair-[s]traightening business, it might prove a temptation to play my work down to Burroughs, then do something on it himself. Please check on that for me.

The Saturday Evening Post photographer has been here and took a lot of pictures. He caught me in my dungarees working outdoors, and

---

[3] *Hurston published nothing else until her coverage of the Ruby McCollum trial in 1952. She was working on* Herod the Great *(the "drama") and various pieces about her dog, Spot.*

[4] The Golden Bench of God.

[5] *Roi Ottley (1906–60) was an author, columnist, and war correspondent. His books include* New World A 'Coming *(1943),* Black Odyssey *(1948), and* Lonely Warrior *(1952).*

naturally insisted on photographing me like that. He told me that Ben Hibbs likes the article very much and it will be in an early issue.[6] I gather from reading the magazine that the SEP favors Taft, and so it probably falls right in with the plan. They never se[e]m to miss a chance recently to mention him favorably.

As soon as I can get some things in your hands to sell, I shall try to raise the cash for my newspaper devoted to those in domestic service. I really believe that the idea is sound and can makke money.

Have you an "in" with Cecil B. DeMille? I know that I sound ambitious, but nothing ventured, nothing gained. I plan to try the LIFE OF HEROD THE GREAT, as a drama, and it needs Hollywood. It is a great story, really, and needs to be done. The man had everything good, bad and indifferent. Handsome, dashing, a great soldier, a great statesman, a great lover. He dared everything, and usually won. He has both Henry VIII and Napoleon tied to a post. With a drama of an extra gang (r[a]ilroad) [a]nd the two short pieces in your hand, I'm tackling Herod before I [s]tart on the newspaper just as sure as you snore. Jack Kofoed, columnist in THE MIAMI HERALD, mentioned Orson Wells [sic][7] the other day, as moving from hotel to hotel, nearly all of his money gone, and doing nothing. I wished a great wish, that he could be induced to collaborate on Herod, but knowing him personally and his huge ego, I have been wondering whether to write him a letter. Yes I'm ambitious, but don't count me out too soon. I might make it. I remember so well Mike Watkins telling me that I could not write an article.

I paid up my sick and accident insurance for a year, $67.70, and spent so much getting the house wired and made more livable in other ways around the place, that I am almost broke already again. Bought an ice-box, and furniture too, so now, as badly as I hate to draw it, I need some cash to live on. For groceries and gas. And a pair of black slacks so that I can go downtown without messing up another dress which takes up my time to launder.

My best to you and yours, and pray that we make a lot of money this year, so that when/if I am told that I can buy this place, I can do it and build a comfortable little new house on it.

Love and faithful feelings,
Zora

---

[6]*On December 8, 1951, the* Saturday Evening Post *published "A Negro Voter Sizes Up Taft." The article was accompanied by a wonderful photo of Hurston in her beloved Eau Gallie home.*
[7]*Orson Welles, legendary Hollywood director.*

TO BURROUGHS MITCHELL

[July/August[?] 1951]

Dear Burroughs:

You have no idea how I have struggled to shorten this work,[1] and with a literary hop and jump place Herod on the throne and march on to the end of the work with no more than 80,000 words. But it just will not come out that way.

To begin with, as dynamic, as dramatic, as fascinating a character as Herod was within himself, his behavior and his place in history is unintelligible if he is torn out of the context of his time. Unless the reader gets some idea of the international situation of the First Century B.C., the renewed East-West struggle which began at Troy as it is renewed in our time, what was going on at Rome, Alexandria, Ctesiphon and Babylon (Parthia) at Petra in Arabia and Jerusalem, Herod has no true meaning. He is just a very handsome man astride an Arabian stallion. The Hellenization of Asia which also began with the siege of Troy, was stepped up and implemented by the invasion of Asia by Alexander the Great and it's impact upon Palestine. When the reader gets some idea of this prolonged and intense struggle in Jud[e]a, he can realize, as he must, that the LIFE OF HEROD THE GREAT is not really the story of a man, but of a movement which has ended up in Christianity on one hand, and as the basis of Western civilization on the other. Herod is seen then as merely the protagonist of this movement. This Hellenization of the then known world did not end with the overthrow of Greece by Rome. The right or privilege to disseminate Greek learing merely pas[s]ed from Athens to Rome. By birth, by education and inclination, Herod was for the West, and hence the conflict with that section of the Jewish priesthood which sought to maintain their rule by barring out Greek culture, or any foriegn influence as the Japanese were doing when Admiral Perry broke into Japan in 1853.

By accident of time and place, Herod is THE connecting personality between the old Judaism and Christianity. It seems to me that the story would be mutilated and practically worthless without the world

[1]Herod the Great.

background. So little has been written about that enormously important last century before the evolvement of Christianity, that people just say, "The Jew killed Christ" without having any conception of why it was done. They do not see the long and intense ideological war that brought it about, why and how it started, nor the steps that led to mental and spiritual revolution.

These are the elements that used up more pages than I wished to use. It seemed important to me that they should know that Jews were a minority in Galilee, that most northern province of Palestine and th[a]t Galilee was the cross-roads of the world, friendly to Gentiles, and more exposed than Judea to Greek and other foriegn culture, so that the shut-in Judeans regarded Galileans as outsiders and therefore the query in the New Testament when Judea heard of the works of Christ, "Can anything good come out of Galilee?" Herod, not being a Jew, loved Galilee and was loved by the inhabitants. They were of the same mind towards the temple crowd at Jerusalem. Hence his type of reign. Hence the tremendous success of his long reign, because Judea, even the priests and Pharisees were split down the middle over Greek culture. Therefore, Herod could toss the First Commandment out of the window with impunity. (No idols, no representation of anything) He brought in sculpture and other Western arts to say nothing of athletics, the theatre, and other forms of art.

Since nowhere else in Western literature is the picture of this century before Christ explained, I thought that I ought to do it by all means. Herod is tangled and mingled up in it to such an extent that you cannot see him without dealing with it. That called for the enotrmous amount of research that I have done on Herod. Naturally, I hope that it has been done well enough to please your eyes.

Nor do I wish to offend good taste by mentioning the almost universal custom of the men of wealth keeping "pretty boys" because it comes up in an important incident early in the reign of Herod involving Marc Antony and Herod's young brother-in-law. Antony was not considered a degenerate by his time for this practice. Starting in Greece, it had swept over Rome and been taken up by those who could afford it, even in Jerusalem. So now you know the wyhy of t hat. It is Plutarch, and not I who gives us a picture of Cleopatra first capturing the attention of Antony by a display of pretty boys and girls, so he could take whichever he wanted of her company, or both.

This leaves me well and in fine spirits, and I hope that it finds you and yours the same. You will perhaps be astonished to learn that both Caesar and Marc Antony began their letters in this style. "Marcus Antonius, imperator, to Herod, King of [t]he Jews, sendeth greetings. If you be in health, it is well; I also am in health and with the army." So you see that our grandparents were in good company.

Sincerely yours,
Zora Neale Hurston

I sent the manuscript by express this morning. Hope it arrives without delay.

TO BURROUGHS MITCHELL

Eau Gallie, Fla.
July 15, 1951.

Dear Burroughs Mitchell:

Digging in my garden, painting my house, planting seeds, and things like that, makes me lazy about getting to the Post Office, and so I did not get your letter until Friday P.M. So belatedly I thank you for your editorial comments, and the time you spent reading the book.[1]

In your last paragraph you asked to hear from me, so I am writing, though me putting in my nickle's worth with Scribners' justly celebrated editorial department looks silly on the face of it. I thank you for the compliment of asking me anyhow.

I am very happily located. Here in this little house I wrote MULES AND MEN years ago, and have always intended to come back here to live. So now I am back in my little house, and though facing a paved street, two blocks of trees around me on three sides. No neighbors radios and record-players to listen to. The place was quite shaggy when I arrived a month ago, but I have the joy of clearing it and arranging things like I please. About 15 cabbage palms and five shady oaks as a

---

[1] On July 9, Mitchell had written that he and Waterbury were "at a loss" about The Golden Bench of God, which they found neither publishable nor fixable. He wrote that they did not have suggestions for revision. While the center of the novel was apparently the character modeled on A'Lelia Walker, according to Mitchell, Hurston had not made her sympathetic or engaging.

background to start landscaping from. There is a flowing artesian well about fifty feet of the house, and already I have arranged a bit of or-namental water. I am planting butterfly ginger around it. My eastern limit is a low pile of stone 1 ft from an old ice-plant. Against the low line of stones I have planted pink verbena, and around the palms and the park-like ground west of the stones, I have scattered bright colored poppies. Going to let them run wild. The Indian river, touted as the world's most beautiful river, is two blocks to the east of me, and so there is ever a good breeze. As you know, it is not really a river at all, but a long arm of the sea cut off by sand-bars, at times less that a quarter mile wide from the Atlantic. The tropical water is so loaded with phosphorus, that standing on the bridge at night, every fish, crab, shrimp, etc. glows as it moves about in the water. When the surface is disturbed, it scintillates like every brilliant jewel you can mention. The so-called river begins with Lake Worth at Palm Beach and ex-tends to a few miles of Jacksonville. That gives the Florida East Coast a double exposure in the matter of water front; the river, a slight skip across "the peninsula" then the blue, blue open sea.

As you know, I left Ann Watkins, Inc. as of June 1 and went with Jean Parker Waterbury. I feel and believe that any author would have felt as I did about it. Quite independently of anybody in the Watkins office, I got the information that my outline of the article on Senator Taft, which I have recently sold tho the SATURDAY EVENING POST, had not only been handed to another Watkins author, but the firm was doing it's best to have that author beat me to the draw on it. MY OWN IDEA! I always assumed the relations between an author and agent was extrememly confidential and sacred. But what guarran-tee has an author when things like that happen? How can you ever know that any outline of work that seems attractive has not been passed along to somebody else; the publisher discouraged from accept-ing yours, and the other's given preference? It's a frightening picture, and no author wants to run the risk. Unfortunately for the scheme, the POST had information that it was my original idea, and would listen to nobody else.[2] I look with scorn upon an author who <u>wants</u> anything like that. I wouldn't, because it would belittle my own originality and inventiveness to <u>me</u>. Billy Rose[3] told me years ago, before I had ever

[2] "A Negro Voter Sizes Up Taft" was published December 8, 1951.
[3] Billy Rose (1899–1966) was a theatrical producer and syndicated columnist. He was the owner of the Billy Rose Theater in New York City.

written [t]he first book, that I was going to be the kind that was stolen
from, and then the thieves would hate me for being alive to make
their pretensions out a lie. But I have an unshakeable belief in the
mill of the gods. In the most terrible hours of my life, I have imagined a cosmic funeral, and se[e]n the bier of God pass by.

"So God Himself is dead", I have murmured through burning
tears, "and untruth and injustice is supreme."

"Ah, no", I am able to hear after a while. "An empty casket passes
you. He but gives opportunity for the proud and presumptious the
chance to destroy themselves. Be calm in your unchanging trust, and
truth shall be avenged."

Jean told me that you have a country place up at Croton-on-
Hudson with a steeply sloping lawn that makes it hard for you to
mow the grass. Even so, I know how you must love having land and
space around you. My sincere congratulations. My best to all your
family. Does your cat catch the birds? I chase them away from here
because I have a bird bath and feed the birds, and dozens are always
near the house. I know that they depend upon my protection, because the[y] set up a great clamor for me whwn a cat or a snake appears. I chase the cats, and on two occasions, had to catch oak snakes
and take them away. I do not kill them because they are good ratters,
and in this climate, there are plenty of woods-rats that will invade
the house if they get a chance. So I pick them up with a stick and
carry them about a mile from the house. It amuses me to see with
what satisfaction the birds watch the capture, and follow me for
awhile as I bear the enemy away. I notice that when the snake disap-
pears into the bag that it is dead so far as the birds are concerned,
and they burst into songs of joy, and go back to their business. The
cardinals seem to be the tamest of the lot, and a male, the most brilliant colored individual I have ever seen, lights on the porch while I
am sitting there. The mocking birds, being meat-eaters, and so not
dependent upon my grain, are stand-offish. The blue jays, eat like
hogs and then holler at me to get on out of the yard when they are
feeding. The wood-pecker is the only thing that can deal with a jay.
The war-like mockingbirds give the nest-raiding crows fits! You just
ought to see an attack.

The U.S. government makes great use of climate and terrain around
here. Her[e] at Eau Gallie is a Jet plane base. It is really something to
see something that looks like a silver barracuda tearing across the sky

ahead of it's own sound. As many as I have seen now, the thrill is still strong. At Cocoa, less that twenty miles away, is the guided missile base. I have glimpsed two way up in the blue seeminly faster than a comet.

Living the kind of life for which I was made, strenous and close to the soil, I am happier than I have been for at least ten years. I am up at five oclock and in bed around nine every night. I do hope and pray that you and yours and experiencing something like my delirium of joy.

Faithfully yours, Zora

TO JEAN PARKER WATERBURY

Eau Gallie, Fla.
July 15, 1951.

Dear Jean:

Being very busy, I did not go to the Post Office for two days, and so got your letter and the one from Burroughs Mitchell at the same time.

Let not your heart be troubled, honey. In bridge, this would amount to what is known as a psychic bid. On the night of July 8, I had a curious experience. In all the years that my mother has been dead, I have only dreamed of her three times, and this was the third. She appeared younger than I had known her, for she was twenty-nine when I was born, coming late in the litter, and in the dream, if I call it that, she was a girl in her late teens. A serene and happy aura was about her. She said nothing, just smiled and beamed on me, handed me a note written on the lined paper of a cheap tablet, and somehow was gone. I unfolded the note, written in lead pencil, and read, "The hidden enmity will come out into the open now, but do not be afraid. Thank them for the insincere advice given with cheerfulness. Make the new arrangements suggested to you, and see yourself go to greater heights."

I have interpreted it that Ann Watkins is after us both. The office has never acknowledged my letter of resignation.[1] Her husband is something at Scribners, isnt he?[2] Well, then we must expect for influence to

---

[1] See Hurston to Ann Watkins, June 4, 1951.
[2] Husband Mike Watkins was an editor, as Hurston knew.

be wielded. Burroughs' letter was subjective and on the defensive.[3] I am following the instructions of the dream, and shall answer pleasantly, but vague. Any move must be up to them. I shall not be helpful. I regret this behavior of Scribners only because we both need money, but otherwise, I really don't care. You are not dumb about the head, so you must know that Watkins is probably accusing us both of ingratitude, etc., me, in particular, and kidding herself that I am to be prevented from profiting by it, and you are not to succeed with your new firm if it can be helped. I am going to show her that she is not doodly-squat. Burroughs, unintentionally betrays conference with Watkins, as you can see from the last paragraph of his letter. I have never mentioned this story to him, so he had to learn about the shorter version from <u>somebody</u> who did know about it, thus indicating that he is not proceeding from what is in the script that he has, but from <u>conference.</u>[4]

My best to Tay Hohoff.[5] Tell her that THEIR EYES WERE WATCHING GOD has made me many friends in Scandinavia. I get letters inviting me to visit Denmark and Norway, and also the royalties every May are most welcome.

By the way, we might make a little something if THEIR EYES could be sold to a pocket-book edition firm.

Most sincerely,
Zora

P.S. Hold $75.00 and send me the rest. I am down hard at writing now, and I want to stock up with enough groceries to last me until I am through with what I have laid out. Thank you.

I have two pennies only now.

[along left side:] I cannot tell Burroughs about Watkins unethical behavior without letting on that you told me. But I hope that he finds out some way and some day. Anyway, I got my own in at Scribners. Max Perkins had asked me two years before, so she did not get me there.

---

[3]This letter was actually quite apologetic.

[4]The paragraph to which Hurston refers describes the novel as seeming more like a short story that had been "stretched" than like a novel in its own right. Burroughs might have learned of the earlier version through Waterbury.

[5]Therese von Hohoff Torrey (1898–1974), better known as Tay Hohoff, was an author, editor, and vice president of the J. B. Lippincott Company. She was the editor of To Kill a Mockingbird, by Harper Lee, which won the Pulitzer Prize in 1961. Her writings include A Ministry to Man, Cats and Other People, and The Cat Who Wanted Out.

TO JEAN PARKER WATERBURY

[marked "rec'd 8/8/51"]

Dear Jeanie. my Jean:

I haven't been out of my yard for five days, hard down at the machine, cooling and re-polishing SPOT.[1] I do hope that it meeets your, and some editor's approval. Personally, I think that it is a much better story than the first draft. Now, I turn back for another writing of SPOOK HILL.[2]

Don't think that I do not appreciate all that you say to me by way of advice. I have nothing against Burroughs Mitchell at all. I like him fine and dandy. In fact, I tried to find a nice crate of Hayden Mangoes to send him the very day that I wrote you, but found none in the area. I would need to go down to Fort Pierce for that, and I hadn't the leisure. What with my pionerring on this place and writing, I never get a moment of leisure these days. But I love it.

You remember that kind of decorative cane that grows down here? Well, there was a huge patch of it on this place, and I have had the devil's own time getting someone to grub it up for me. I can't put in my papaya crop until it is removed. At long last, I got a man and he has done the job for me, so now I buy my plants. That is what I saved the $75.00 for. I was afraid that it would slip through my hands and I find myself without the money for my plants. It is a safe and sure money crop, and not many are being produced in this area, so they bring high prices. Police Chief Sapp (and it fits him fine) was telling me Saturday what a bright idea it was. The fruit never falls below 10 cents a pound by reason of scarcity. I hope to be marketing them by Christmas. It takes ten months from the seed, but I am buying plants knee high.

---

[1]*Story about her dog.*

[2]*Seminole legend about Florida chief Cufcowellax's fight against an enormous alligator that was tormenting his village and, in the process, creating a sacred basin, named Spook Hill, which was known for directing horses and cars suddenly and inexplicably downhill.*

Well, heres hoping, heres, love, heres luck! Do, please mail the check right away so that I can pay the nursery man as soon as he sets the last plant. He starts to setting them out on Wednesday morning. He will be through by Friday at the latest.

Do you and your husband eat mangoes? I will send both you and Burroughs a box early next week.

With faithful feelings,
Zora

P.S. My neighbors are being very nice to me. I think that everything is going to be all right about buying this place. One by one they drop by now and compliment me on the improvements in the place. It is beginning to have a park-like sweep to it, and as the flowers and grass that I have planted grow, I think it is going to look very fine. They bring me plants and make suggestions. The City sent two men on it's truck to help me last Saturday and haul off more of the junk. It has been quite a task, and expensive for <u>me</u>, though not too much for a person who really had money.

TO JEAN PARKER WATERBURY

Eau Gallie, Fla.
August 19, 1951.

Dear J.P.W.:

I know that you have decided that I have abused even my ancestral rights and privileges of being trashy. All I can say is that now and then I am attacked by a spell of withdrawal. Something keeps me from communicating with the outside world. Perhaps I have told you that it used to come over me even as a child, and I would hide under the house all day at times, sneak into the garden and eat raw potatoes rather than go inside and eat warm meals. I wrote you everyday, and at length, in my mind, but could not bring myself to go to the machine and put words down. I have decided that it a sort of creative pregnancy period that makes me like that.

1. Shall I begin a re-write of SPOT?[1]

2. I feel to do three <u>short stories</u> out of dramatic stories in the Bible. A. What happened between Abraham, Sarah and Hagar. B. King Saul and Samuel, in his tragic championship of the will of the Hebrew people and his frustration by the Temple crowd. Not a preachment, but let the story speak for itself. C. HE LAUGHED TOO MUCH, the story of the expulsion of Ham by his father, Noah. D. I had a well-dreamed out story of David, Absalom and Bathsheba, but I see a movie has just been made on David and Bathsheba, so that'(s out, I suppose. Submit them to you <u>fully written</u>?[2]

3. I am half through with a tongue-in-cheek exhortation to career women to return to the home lest we lose our ascendancy over men. FRIEND DEVIL, NOW. "God is impartial, but Old Devil now, he always had his pets." His special pet being female woman, and he looks out for our interests. We have his expert guidance in handling men, if only we will stick to it.[3]

4. Article: DO NEGROES LIKE NEGROES? Behind the curtain of the lack of concerted action by the 15,000,000 of us in the U.S. The explosion from the center, driving us outward from each other. The will to destroy each other. a. In Africa. b. History here. c. Examples to prove the continuation and seeming inherent quality of the behavior. No moralizing, but presentation of picture. The eternal pacing of an invisible cage.[4]

The "farm" is coming along splendidly, but I had some news Saturday that upsets me some. It seems that this place is estate property and until the estate of the late George Gleason can be peacefully settled, there can be no sale. Not that I have the money to pay for it at present anyway. It seems that his nephew and namesake has put in a claim against W. Lansing Gleason, the son, and my landlord. It may take years to settle. However, I can live on here as long as I like.

Then, too, I have practically written through a short piece that might fit THE NEW YORKER or THE SATURDAY REVIEW OF LITERATURE. It is in the form of an advertisement for jobs for my

---

[1] *Waterbury has the "1" circled here.*

[2] *In left margin, Waterbury marked this with "good idea—try 1 and let's see."*

[3] *In left margin, Waterbury marked this "yup."*

[4] *In left margin, Waterbury marked this "yup."*

two dogs. Since only the best chairs, beds, and the like will do them to rest on, and since they turn up their noses at prepared dog food and demand only yhe best steaks, we argued it over, and I have told them that what they need is a job apiece and do their own shopping. I can't support them in the style that they demand.

SHAG: the female puppy would make an excellent maid and child-nurse. Vacuum cleaner tongue that would keep all dust under the carpet, and wash the baby ten times a day. Allow no weeds in yard nor garden, in fact, allow nothing whatever to grow. Great digger, and could be very serviceable to construction company as a bull-dozer or tractor. Etc.

SPOT: Make an excellent straw-boss or foreman. Takes no orders from anyone, but prepared to give out plenty. General Motors, Ford, and Standard Oil take notice, etc. Mind already made up on every subject in the world. Orders all ready to give out. Even orders guests to go home when she gets tired, and enforces her orders by going around and nipping each one on the heel. New hostess approach to guest-disposal. Prepared to teach it at a reasonable rate. (with snap-shots)

Hope that you and hubby are making a killing and fsat re-covery from what the unseemly winter did to you.

With faithful feelings,
Zora

Am going ahead writing just in case you approve of my submitted suggestions.

TO JEAN PARKER WATERBURY

Eau Gallie, Fla.
Sept. 13, 1951

Dear Jean:

You and Tay Hohoff do not need to handle me with kid gloves so. I feel all right about the refusal of the book.[1] I know that you mean me all the good in the world.

---

[1] The Golden Bench of God.

I am not quite satisfied about any of the three short things[2] I have done since you heard from me last, so I am cooling them and thinking how to polish them better. Something will be on the way to you soon. I feel creative and in addition I have to make some money. By you not saying anything, I assume that Spot is not clicking. And when I wanted it to sell so much.

Do tell Burroughs Mitchell that I plan to do as he suggested. I am bunching my muscles for the leap.[3] Give him my love and then give it to him again. My very best to you and yours.

Affectionately,
Zora

TO EDWARD EVERETT HURSTON

Eau Gallie, Fla.
Oct. 12, 1951

Dear Eddie:

No, I didn't mistake you for the Duke of Windsor, just thought I'd call you Eddie for a change. But dont let too many people get to calling you Eddie, they might get you and the Duke mixed up, as that is what all his friends call him.

Look, I got an idea. Since you and your dear friend want to come down together why dont you look around and see if you cant find a trailer? Hook it on to the back of your Buick and you got your hotel along with you all the time.[1] You can make as slow a trip as you like, stop along the road and rest when you please, a good place for your clothes. You can cook and eat, and make a very pleasant trip down. Please tell him that he will be most welcome here if he is a friend of yours, will you? Perhaps you can find a house-trailer not too expensive, and the two of you can pitch in and paint it up, etc. and have a lot of fun with it for a long time. Just don't pick up any <u>white</u> Janes on the

[2]In a previous letter, Hurston had spoken of a rewrite of her story on Spot; three short stories based on her Herod material; a parodic essay for women called "Friend Devil, Now," and an article called "Do Negroes Like Negroes?"

[3]Mitchell had been urging another volume of her autobiography.

[1]Hurston had bitter experiences of being denied accommodations while traveling in the Jim Crow South.

way. Let me know what you can find. You know of course, that you can't take curves at more than 40, (better slow to 35) pulling a trailer.

Now, Eddie, I do want you to come down <u>very</u> much. I look forward to a lot of fun out of you and your friend. Some school teachers are all whetting their teeth for you. All a few years older than you, but not much. They will do for a start until you get around and meet student girls, or whatever suits you the best.

Papayas are a kind of fruit, more like cantaloupes than anything I can think of off-hand, only they grow on trees. I have had a disappointment about my crop, however. I expected to buy this place, but it turns out that the title is not clear—may not be clear for years—until a lawsuit among heirs has been settled. So after I had ordered $75 worth of plants, I decided I had better not put them in on this property. I am looking around for a satisfactory place I can buy and have a clear title to, before I do anything so <u>permanent</u> as that. So dont look for the fancy lay-out I had planned. We can go to the football games, etc. fish, and have fun since the gardens I do have do not require so much work.

Your letter was very jolly and I loved it. Write me some more and let me know how you are making out financially to get down here. You must have had a swell time spending your 1500, but you are young and can make more than that again before long. Dont waste time and energy regretting that it is gone. Regret is the most useless emotion in the world. You had the experience of a free-spender for a while, so you know what it feels like now, and the next batch you get hold of, you wont need to buy <u>that</u> experience again. Hope you had one heck of a time!

Well, keep me posted on your plans, and do try to make it down here as soon as possible. Lets plan one whale of a Thanksgiving Day. Big games, dinner, dancing, etc.

My very best love to you, family and your friends and pals.

Most lovingly
Aunt Zora.

Keep in mind, Everett, that we dont have to make any fancy show about a house or furniture or anything, because a famous name gets you by and farther than things like that. All you need to be is Edward Everett Hurston, my nephew, and folks will stir themselves up to entertain <u>you</u>. You dont have to do much of that for them. When you are introduced, flash your good looks with confidence and go on from there.

TO JEAN PARKER WATERBURY

Eau Gallie, Fla.
October 25, 1951.

Dear Jean Park Waterbury:

My excuse is that I ran out of groceries and had to hock my machine. What is <u>yours</u> for igging (ignoring) me?

Now I have a borrowed machine and as soon as I can get a new ribbon for it tomorrow, I will be in the writing game again.

Ann Watkins sent me $11 for the reprint of the article on the Miami election.[1] This was what was coming after deducting what I owed her.

Let me hear from you, good, bad or indifferent news. As I told you in my last letter, (which I mistakenly sent to 624 Madison) that my nerves are in fine shape now. Keeping outdoors and raising a fine garden, both flowers and vegetablesl, has done me a world of good. As soon as I can get hold of money to get my machine out of hock, I will be in high spirits.

My best to Tay Hohoff. Same to Burroughs Mitchell, his heirs and assigns.

Faithful feelings,
Zora

I am sort of famished hungry for a word from you to keep up my courage. Drop me some kind of a line. You are my good luck piece as I am yours.

---

[1] *"I Saw Negro Votes Peddled," first published in* American Legion Magazine, *November 1950, and reprinted in* Negro Digest, *September 1951.*

TO HELEN WORDEN ERSKINE

C/O General Delivery
Eau Gallie, Fla.
November 15, 1951.

Dear, dear Mrs. Erskine:

You must know how happy it made me to hear from you! It seemed that the day had come around again in it's eternal circle. I hold the concept that God never made but one day, and the other spaces between dawn and dark are imperfect copies of it. Your feelings notify you when THE DAY has dawned again.

Too sorry I am to hear of your melancholy losses. It seems so trite to repeat about nature and we all must go, etc. That gives no comfort at all, but what can give solace at times like that? You know my worship of Dr. Erskine and so I felt a deep loss when I read of his passing too.[1]

I am in this little town, growing a garden when I get tired of the typewriter, and winning bak my health. Constipation and violent indigestion seem vanquished. That outdoors work has done me a world of good.

Apropos of that wretch[2] that made me all that ugly trouble, I found out something about him last year that seems an answer to some of his moves that I noted. Remember how much of a Republican he pretended to be? Well, he was one of the most enthusiastic workers for Dr, W.E.B. DuBois in his token run for the U.S. Senate. (Paul Robeson[3] is supposed to have financed the campaign) No wonder then that Marcantonio[4] knew so quickly that Sarah Speaks was

---

[1] John Erskine, Helen Worden Erskine's husband, died on June 2, 1951. Born in 1879, Erskine had a successful career as a literature professor at Columbia University, where he helped design the "Great Books" curriculum. Among his nearly two dozen novels was the controversial 1925 publication The Private Life of Helen of Troy.
[2] Richard Rochester.
[3] Actor, singer, athlete, and politician; see glossary.
[4] Vito Marcantonio (1902–54) became assistant U.S. attorney in 1930 but resigned to work for Fiorello La Guardia's campaign in 1933. In 1934, he took over La Guardia's seat in the U.S. House of Representatives to represent blacks, Puerto Ricans, and Italians. In 1936, Marcantonio joined the American Labor Party, and in 1942 became closely associated with the Communist Party, although he was not a communist. Paul Robeson described Marcantonio as "the foremost spokesman for the rights of man the Congress has produced in the twentieth century." Marcantonio was accused of being involved in the killing of Joseph Scottoriggio, the Republican elections captain. He was never completely cleared of his alleged involvement, although it was eventually disclosed that the murder was committed by members of the mob.

trying to get you information about that Scottiriggio [sic] killing and she was disbarred! There have been, and perhaps still are, a great number of secret leftists in the New York City official set-up. The reason that it was so hard to beat Marcantonio was that he had so many friends among the avowed Democrats. That was well known when he was in Congress. Someday I shall tell you about the terror campaign that was waged to keep me and the others quiet after they were forced to clear me.

I have an article in the SATURDAY EVENING POST Dec. 8 issue. A NEGRO VOTER SIZES UP TAFT. I take the position that he is an honest man, and being such, will not pretend any special love for us, but will be for justice for us for the reason that we are American citizens and due what our status implies just as other citizens, no more, no less.[5] That seems to me the only healthy viewpoint, Mrs. Erskine. I think that it is time that we Negroes came out of the Abolitionist propaganda, and the "pet" role of the Reconstruction. We have the same responsibilities as other citizens, as well as rights. We ought not to expect and require executives to make a special project of us.

Along the same lines, (though I do not digress to that extent in the article,) I think it is about the time that our "Race Champions" quit taking up valuable time at every session of congress on this Civil Rights farce. Sure, I don't want to be lynched, I want a an even break on everything, but lynching is nothing else but murder, and laws are already made and provided for that crime. Why is it another crime because the victim is a Negro? As for the other things, I contend that we are thoroughly covered under the Constitution. By the very admission that we <u>are</u> citizens, all protections due citizens are already ours. Now, it will be argued that we are denied these rights, but that merely strips the matter down to the bare facts. The fact is, that the trouble is not in the legislative branch of government, but in the executive. That being the case, (and it is) why encourage executives to evade their duty longer by passing more laws for them to evade? AND, who are we asking to execute these proposed new laws? The very men who are now, and have been for so long, flouting the Constitution. So what sense does these sashays mean at the opening of every Congress? Nothing

[5]*Hurston was not alone in pointing to Taft's progressive record on antilynching bills, the Fair Employment Practices Commission, and racial equality in education.*

more nor less than a game of kidding us. And that is not all on the part of the Whites. Negroes, whose only importance is "defending" us play yheir part in the game. Every year, for as long as I can remember, these bills are brought up, fillibustered and laid aside till the next time. The best proof that our so-called Negro leaders do not want them passed and done with is that they counsel the Negro masses to vote for the very party which is cure and certain NOT to pass it, the Democrats. The Northern Democrats can propose it, knowing full well that the Southerners will kill it off, then all the politicians, White and Black, can pose as great heroes, and save it for the next campaign. Why finish off a thing that has been good for so many Negro votes? All we need, all we have ever needed since the passing of the Four-teenth and Fifteenth Amendments[6] is for the fundamental law of the land to be enforced. The stupidity is on the part of the Negro voters. No more sense to it than Kelly of Chicago[7] running on a plank to keep King George out of Chicago. However, I could be wrong. I might be missing the fine points of the thing. Ask Fred Woltman and see if I am the one who is wrong, please. It seems to me that it all comes back to the fundamental fact that general public opinion is not quite ready as yet to accept the descendants of slaves as equals as yet, and national and state executives have not the courage as yet to buck that public opinion. The next question before our house is, could an executive suc-ceed in enforcing these things even if he tried? Maybe, yes, or maybe in a few years from now. God alone knows the answer. In some spots in the South, Georgia, South Carolina and Mississippi, for example, it would take a lot of enforcing, as can be seen from what is going on at this moment. Honey, I see by the papers that them folks is good and <u>mad!</u>

Again I thank you for your kind letter. All my best love to you and may God bless you!

With faithful feelings,
Zora

---

[6] *Enforcing equal citizenship and voting rights.*
[7] *Edward Joseph Kelly (1876–1950) was a Democrat and the thirty-seventh mayor of Chicago.*

TO JEAN PARKER WATERBURY

Eau Gallie, Fla.
March 6, 1952

Dear Jean:

I want to do the thing[1] very, very much and I thank you deeply for
arranging it for me. I can tell you just my difficulty in the matter. I
have no winter coat. You know that I do not need one down here. Even
when the mercury dips down in the thirties, by noon it is in the fifties
and by three oclock very comfortable. I have two sweaters and a short
jacket and that is all I need here, but Boston is something different
again. I have hung up heavy coats that I brought from the north to
have them eaten up by moths and roaches in a very short while, so I
have not invested in one this year.

For some time I have been the victim of some kind of tropical
virus that the doctors do not quite understand. Something they believe
that runs a cycle. They think th[a]t this last attack might be the end
and I will have no more trouble. It leaves me so weak that I can hardly
lift my hand, pains in the head and swellings in my groins and under
my arms. Some kind of a fluke that they think I picked up from im-
pure water in Central America. I am feeling better today than I have
in many weeks. I have been having something like this ever since I
came back from Honduras, but this last siege was really something,
and that is why they th8nk it is the end of the cycle for the organism.

I have some good material from the Sexton Ranch at Vero Beach.
He is breeding Ginny cows, a very small cow that finds her own keep,
makes small cuts of meat, and that he believes has a great future in
Florida beef cattle. I have pictures in color and a great mass of material on his experiments. I have sold the POST once on the cattle business in Florida and so I wonder if they will consider another on that
line even though from a different angle.[2] I wondered about TRUE.

Information Services, Government of India has written and offered
me any kind of material that they have. I have conceived of a piece, the

---

[1] *Participate in a debate in Boston over the upcoming election of 1952.*
[2] *"Lawrence of the River" had been published in the* Saturday Evening Post, *September 5, 1942.*

body of which is a statement from the head of every government in Asia, and that takes in the Near East, giving in brief the reason for the current antagonism to the U.S. We can no longer dodge it. The antagonism is there and it is not all due to Russia and communism. Russia is merely taking advantage of the known anti-Anglo-Saxon feeling in Asia and the Near East. I thought that a short statement from each government with an introduction by me and a summation, might help my own country to win away the masses of Asia from Russia. I have already written Mr. Moni Moulik, 3 East 64th Street, Government of India, Information Services, to see if I can get help from his office in such contacts. Do you approve of the idea? I know that it will provoke controversy, but that I do not mind if only my country can get the inside track with the asiatics and stop this senseless slaughter over there. You and I know that "race" is the all-important question, and now that they have learned the use of modern arms, just setting out to beat them down as in the Boxer Rebellion[3] is no longer feasible, as Korea has demonstrated. Colonialism and race is at the bottom of the whole thing. So long as we support France and England in their colonial policies in Asia, so long shall our young men die over there. Asia no longer intends to submit, and since we ourselves have no colonies there is no sense in trying to maintain it for others. Especially when we find England and France doing business with the very people who furnish the arms to kill our own boys. I have been mulling it over for several months, and here this week I see signs that others see the same thing that I do. Only, because of my race, I am in a favored position to get frank statements from the asiatics.

Finally, I do want to go to Boston, and I am willing to go at any time that you can arrange it. Now that you have settled the financial end of it, I shall drop Mr. Lewin a line and say that I am happy to come. Not touching on financial angles at all.

I have done a series of five folk concerts here in the last six weeks and picked up a little money that way. I could do more but it takes from my writing time. I had no intention of doing any, but people here discovering my reputation in that respect begged me to do it. Four concerts for white audiences and one for colored, and now I am being asked all over to keep it up. Too much work for too little money.

---

[3]*When Secretary of State John Hay attempted to strengthen foreign trading power in China by instituting an open-door policy, the empress Tsu Hsi advocated action and the Boxer Rebellion ensued in Shandong. Foreign powers assembled troops, and the open-door policy remained in effect until World War II.*

I already have a national reputation that way, so I do not need to work for one and ignore money.

It does not matter who my opponent might be in the debate, so long as he or she is of sufficient importance to be worth it. I hope that I shall not be confined to my own race entirely, for this is a matter of national, nut just racial importance. I feel ready to hold my own against all and sundry on Taft vs. Eisenhower.

Most lovingly yours,

Zora

TO BURROUGHS MITCHELL

Eau Gallie, Fla.
May 1, 1952

Dear Burroughs Mitchell:

Please do me a great kindness, (on top of the others that you have done me in the past and which have so sustained me). I have been be-seeched, and decided to become a contributor to a Negro newspaper, THE WEEKLY REVIEW, Augusta, Georgia. I think that it will in-crease my reading public for books, though the pay is necessarily small. The editor and owner has aked me for a picture of me to head my column, and I have no pictures of myself at present, and I am hop-ing that SCRIBNERS will give me one to send him quickly. I am send-ing him a letter in this mail with the biographical material requested, and telling him that the picture will follow shortly. This paper is very ethical, not even using ads like fortune-tellers, etc. The Editor got a Valley Forge award last year, so you can see what he aims at. So I have decided to accept his offer.

Well, I have started on the book at last.[1] One question I wanted to ask you was, should I take up where DUST TRACKS ON A ROAD left off, or loop back some?

My little shack has so many flowers around it now that tourists drive up to take pictures. I love flowers, but they mean more to me

---

[1] *A second volume of her autobiography; this project was never completed. It is possible that she is appeasing Mitchell here. No manuscript of this project survives.*

than just the colorful satisfaction. Getting out in the yard and growing things has been a marvelous release for me so that now I feel fine inwardly And receiving letters from the upper brackets of Negroes from all over the country letting me see that I stand high with them has been helpful too. So now you can consider me definitely back from the dead. Oh, I owe so very, very much to you!

How is your family feeling now? The wife, the cat, the dog? For the first time in my life I have a cat, though not because I chose one out. A tiny part-Maltese kitten marched up to my door one morning and out of pity, I took it in. Now, because I love her perhaps, I see in her a very intelligent animal. When I go out at dawn to work in the garden, all of us go together. It is amusing to see the kitty act like a dog. When Spot chases another dog off the premises, Kitty takes after him too. She trots along after me like a dog, and indoors, when I get the fly-swatter to kill a pest, both she and Spot help me catch it. I have read that domestic animals are not imitative, but I find the animal psychologists wrong in that respect. Spot, seeing me go out to get the paper every morning, now goes for it without coaching. The Kitty sits up on her haunches and claps her paws together trying to kill a mosquito or fly after seeing me do it. Yesterday, the cat, seeing that I compliment Spot for bringing me the paper, went across the street and got a small piece of paper and brought it to me too. I praised her and petted her, and she was as proud as punch. Seeing me and Spot in the car, now she gets in if I leave the door open too. I do not take her away from the house for fear she will leap out in some strange place and get lost. It is now my conviction that domestic animals would be much more imitative if encouraged by us, and understand what we are doing. Animals are much more like us (or we like them) than we grant. For instance, fondness for ecitement. A small female dog is in heat in my neighborhood. Three or four mornings lately, she and her band of hopefuls have arrived in front of my house. Thsi morning, the poor little dog was discouraging her suitors by tucking her tail between her legs. Spot, desiring the drama to proceed, went back of her and caught hold of her tail and raised it up. Never, [in left margin: "in animals,"] have I seen a thing like that before. I have seen humans egging on excitement in the same way.

So off to the Post Office and back to the typewriter again. Love and stuff to everybody at Scribners.

With faithful feelings,
Zora

TO JEAN PARKER WATERBURY

Eau Gallie, Fla.
May 6, 1952.

Dear Jeannie of the hair I wish I had:

I might as well admit to you that I am licked. I am licked on all the oceans of the universal world. I know what I know and the Orientals know that I know it, and I am sure and certain by now that my name has been mentioned in many capitols of Asia. It appears that I have spilled the beans. The article would make America aware of the real situation in a way, and before the Oriental powers that be are willing for us to know it. So I get no permission to name names.

But I want you to know that we have set off a violent chain reaction. Couriers are hastening from one Asian capitol to the other like mad. Things are being speeded up so that they will be in an advantageous position if and when our government does catch on and begin to meet things realistically. I suppose you saw that Madam Pandit, Nehru's sister has hurried off to Pieping and is now head-to-head with Chou En-Lai. A Pan-Asiatic Union is the object, so you can look for statements soon where one nation purports to speak for all. I said in the article, Asia, Africa and South America, and I mean just that, and our government might as well get ready to look facts in the face. Signs and symbols appear in our daily press confirming what I said, but they seem to make no impression at all. Note from an enclosed clipping what the Chilean Ambassador has to say. I hope you noted that Brazil has just decorated Eva Peron,[1] when once Brazil stuck with us against the Argentine. Things down there are jelling to put "the big bully ofthe North" in our place.

You will note through Drew Pearson's[2] disclosures that my presentation of Chiang Kai-Shek was also correct. He never was with us at heart. And from all sides comes confirmation that it is NOT commu-

---

[1]*Eva Perón (1919–52) ("Evita"). The wildly popular second wife of popular Argentine president Juan Perón was particularly influential as an unofficial—and controversial—spokeswoman for health, labor, education, and feminist issues. She died of cancer on July 26, 1952.*

[2]*Drew Pearson (1897–1969) was a well-known* Washington Post *reporter and columnist.*

nism which has turned Asia against us, but the backing up of the colonial powers in Asia and Africa.

Well, they will not hear me. But willful blindness will in no way
change what is going on on three continents. In my deep love of country, I yearn for it to get into a safe position, but it seems that they don't
want me to say it. So if you feel that it is useless, withdraw the article[3]
at your descretion.

With faithful feelings,

Zora

TO JEAN PARKER WATERBURY

Eau Gallie, Fla.
June 15, 1952

Dear JPW:

Oh, I am so delighted over the award! You look so ver dignified in
the picture receiving it for me. Why, bless my soul! I could not have
looked any prettier my ownself.

I am morbid right now because I have a bid to come to New York
and work in the CITIZENS FOR TAFT COMMITTEE[1] office, and I
have not money to get there with. The committee is headed by
Archibald B. Roosevelt,[2] Barclay Hotel, and this is the second letter I
have had to come on. It would be indelicate for me to ask him for advance money, you know how politics is, and so I sit here and fret and
stew. Oh, I do so wish that U.S.A. would take that article[3] and untie
my wings.

Here is an idea which I cannot use myself, but I think that Stuart
Rose might like it. Somebody ought to find ex-king Micjael of Rou-

[3]Probably on Hurston's view of Asia; unpublished.

[1]On May 5, 1952, the National Citizens for Taft was created as well as the New York City branch of Citizens for Taft.
[2]Archibald B. Roosevelt (1894–1979), son of Theodore Roosevelt, was a businessman and military officer. An active social critic, Roosevelt was a vocal anticommunist. In 1948, he accused President Truman of protecting communists and formed Alliance, Inc., a group dedicated to informing Congress about communist subversion.
[3]On Asia; no copies of this article have been found.

mania[4] and interview him now. You have no doubt read that Ana
Pauker[5] has recently gotten in bed with Stalin and been demoted. The
news accounts say she is stricken at her fall. Now, here is the drama of
the thing. During the war when Wild Bill Donovan[6] was pressuring
the young king to throw in with the Soviets, he did not like the idea.
Furthermore, Antonescu,[7] (or whatever his Prime Minister was
named) made a very moving speech warning and beseeching the King
not to throw in with Russia. Finally Donovan won and the Prime Minister was driven out of Roumania, I believe, in utter disgrace. You
know what followed. No sooner was the war won than Michael was
himself driven out, and Ana Paulker [sic] became the big shot. A
blow-by-blow account of what was said, and the ex-king's reactions
when he was told that he was through, and the behavior of the
Paulker at the moment ought to make dramatic reading right in now.
And after her triumph of trickery over Michael, it would be interesting to imagine her feelings now. It is her turn to be tricked and betrayed.

I try to get down to work but it is hard now when I worry about
money. I think tht at last I have arrived at a good piece on SPOT. You
have no idea how much animal psychology I have acquired in watching SPOT, her daughter, and the cat who adopted me. I had no idea
cats had so much intelligence. I have planned the piece out in a
jointed way. Each joint deals with some phase of my observation. For
example: 1. THE FELINE SENSE OF HUMOR. Yes, I find that cats
do have it. The entertainment angle is much more important to my
cat than food. Incidents to illustrate the point. 2. THE THROW-
BACK. Spot's daughter and her reversion to the wolf. 3. THE VAN-
ISHED PUPPY. Shag, Spot's daughter gave birth to seven puppies.
Two days later there were only six. The mystery of the vanished

[4]Michael (b. 1921), king of Romania (1927–30, 1940–47), overthrew Ion Antonescu in 1944 and concluded an
armistice with the Allies. He abdicated in 1947 because of conflicts with the communist-dominated government.
[5]Ana Pauker (1893–1960) was a Romanian communist politician. She served as Romania's minister of foreign
affairs (the first woman to do so) from 1947 to 1952. Along with her husband, Marcel Pauker, she founded the
Communist Party of Romania in 1921.
[6]William Joseph Donovan (1883–1959) was director of the Office of Strategic Services (OSS), later replaced by
the Central Intelligence Agency.
[7]Ion Antonescu (1882–1946) was a Romanian marshal and dictator. He fell out of favor with King Carol II
due to suspicions of his pro-Nazi sentiments, but was made premier with dictatorial powers in 1940 because of
Carol's fears of revolution. In September 1940, Antonescu forced Carol to abdicate the throne in favor of
Carol's son, Michael. In November, Antonescu gave Hitler control over Romanian economy and foreign policy. Antonescu was tried and executed in 1946 by King Michael.

puppy. Was Shag accusing Spot? The tense drama in the house between the two dogs for nearly two weeks. (I think Shag herself did
away with the puppy. Spot sensed that she was being accused, and
feared a murderous attack from her much larger and ferocious daughter. The scene when Spot, on the foot of the bed looked down into the
slant, killer eyes of her daughter and trembled for her life in every
fiber of her body. Me to the rescue. Myst[e]ry never solved.) Shag, the
Wild but affectionate bitch. Scolded, she goes off, kills two chickens
of a neighbor and brings them to me. 3. SPOT, THE MID-WIFE.
4) AMOROUS INCIDENTS. Observations on dog romance. I have proof
that it can go further than the mating period. Spot is in love with a
male dog, (owned by a city councilman) who has been castrated. Spot
cannot understand his difficulty, but her loyalty to him is unabated.
She will have no other. He lives a block up the street from us, and her
tension, when she expects to see him, is tremendous. When he barks,
day or night, she will run up there. She sits for hours in the drive
looking that way. She has not been in heat for nine months. Sort of
taken the veil in faithfulness to her eunuch. She will fight Shag or
any other femal dog who barks when her love barks. That is something that she alone must do with him. (Nobody can understand her
behavior. It can only be explained under a romance such as humans
feel.) 5. THE HOWLING KITTEN. A kitten, less than three months
old comes howling strangely out of the dawn to the door. Both dogs
and my own grown cat, name of Jean MacArthur Hurston, she is so
beautiful and seductive, draw back from the howling kitten in some
strange fear. All snarl at it, but none will get close enough to fight it.
6. THE IMITATIVE INSTINCT. Animal psychologists have stressed
the fact the domestic animals do not imitate humans, but this is not
true. Shag has tried to help me pick peas, tearing them off with her
mouth. She imitates a human smile perfectly. A doctor studied her
and said that it was not possible because dogs did not have the muscles at the mouth for it, but there it was. Both dogs and the cat help
me to catch and kill moths and roaches that get into the house. Shag
likes to lie on the window-sill. Seeing me run up the shade, she
caught the edge of it with her teeth and tried it too. Spot tries to help
me clean up by moving objects as she sees me do. Of course, she is
likely to take one shoe to where it belongs, but jump upon the bed
with the other one, or take it outdoors. 7. Puppy-Sitting. Both dogs
leave me in charge of puppies, and refusing to go out for a stroll un-

less I am there with the puppies. Evidences of perfect confidence, which they did not place in each other, of me left with their puppies. Indication of rapport and understanding. Jean MacArthur the same way. Has one kitten to which she is much devoted, but will leave it with me anytime. Allows me even to wash it. The humorous picture of the month-old kitten returning the favor, and attempting to give me a complete washing over with [her—x-ed out] his tiny tongue.

I plan to do this piece in about 4,000 words, divided as I have indicated, under topical headlines.

Cow material still interests me if I can only stop worrying about money and get back to work.

It is hot here! The fish are going up and down the Indian river washed down in sweat.

All my love,
Zora

TO HERBERT SHEEN

Eau Gallie, Fla.
March 4, 1953

Dear Herbert:

I have the chance of a lifetime to grab a fine piece of land for almost nothing, but I am $300 short of what it takes. If you could see your way to loan me that amount for ninety days, it would be the biggest favor in the world. Royalty checks are due in April and May,[1] and even if I did not sell anything before than I could still pay you back. Further, I would include your name as mortgagee so that if anything happened to me, it would go to you or your heirs and assigns. (By the way, the etymology of that word assigns must have

---

[1] *The* Pittsburgh Courier *had agreed to pay Hurston $1,000 for her coverage of the sensational Ruby McCollum case. Ruby McCollum was a black woman from Florida who killed her white lover, Dr. Adams. Hurston covered the McCollum case for the* Courier *and worked closely with William Bradford Huie, who wrote a book on the case called* Ruby McCollum: Woman in the Suwannee Jail. *Hurston's coverage of the case is included in Huie's book.*

once been spelled ass signs, for that it what it really amounts to, doesn't it?") The reason for my desperate hurry is that a big real estate firm wants the 7 and 7/10 tract for a new subdivision, and the [w]hite friend of mine is holding out to see if I can make the 1,100 down in a very few days.

Naturally, I do hope that your own affairs are going smoothly by now. I did not ask before because I felt that it was a painful affair that you would like to forget if you could until the edge were off. I declare, there is so much raw greed and dishonor in the world these days that it is simply appaling. Humanity has slid far back in the last decade or so. Now the ethics is, CAN I GET AWAY WITH IT? Decency and truth are out-moded. Naturally I want to hear when you feel like telling me. Jealousy and malice do not enter into what I feel about Q.[2] It is that my sense of justice is outraged. Blackmail, really. Cough up, or I will give you a name bad enough to destroy you.

You know very well that I would not ask this favor of you if things were not terribly pressing. I can see something really big coming from this land deal. I could get the cash I need from a big contracting outfit here, but I know that if they are in on the title, they will squeeze me out to quick to talk about it. I will deal with Van Werley, inc. when I hav th title in my own name. It is in an area that I am certain that no Negro could buy but me. Right on a good highway, but uncleared, which is fine, because the lumber on it is in itself a cash asset, and within the city limits where water, sewerage and electric lights are available. The people who own it have no intention to return south and want to get cash for it. Whether you can afford to loan $300 now or not, advise me by wire so that I can look elsewhere if you cannot afford it.

All my best to you and Prudence and the rest of the family.

                                        With faithful feelings,
                                        Zora

March 9 is the date I must meet.

[2]*Herbert Sheen's wife, Quinlock.*

TO HERBERT SHEEN

Eau Gallie, Fla.
March 13, 1953

Dear Young Lochinvar:[1] (And still in the west)

This letter leaves me crammed and glowing with the deepest gratitude of my life.[2] I was and still am up against a hard fight. That piece
of ground laid there for years without any local person showing the
least interest. When I saw the possibilities in it and mad[e] a move,
then the battle royal started. Two great big white real estate firms
woke up and went into action to head me off, and a hastily get-
together group of Negroes. "She's just come here and now she thinks
she can take over. Head her off." I do not fear the Negroes because I
know that they haven't got doodly-squat and will not hang together
because of our inherent genius for fighting each other—the individual forsaking the cause for personal advantage which is impossible the
moment that they cease to hang together which we never seem able to
understand. Both the Gleason[3] firm and the Harris–Van Bergen group
have too much money for me to buck, and my only chance was to get
title first. They are now pressuring Barr, (the owner) to repudiate his
contract with me. They offer to pay him more to do so than had been
agreed upon between us. You see, there is a tremendous burst of
growth in Eau Gallie now, which has been sleep for fifty years. The
Negroes are being forced out of where they have been living, even
property owners. There is now nowhere for them to go except the
place where I have jumped in. The Gleason idea was to force them to
move out of town all together. By my dipping in, not only can they
stay, but a lot of money can be made on the deal, and they cannot bear
the idea of a Negro making it. That is the picture. Another hitch is the
Van Werley firm is sticking with me to be in on the development of

---

[1]*Lochinvar is Sir Walter Scott's Marmion, a young medieval knight who kidnaps/rescues his love from marrying another.*
[2]*Sheen presumably did loan her the $300 requested in her previous letter.*
[3]*Probably the family of W. Lansing Gleason, Hurston's landlord.*

the tract, and Van Werley is the mayor, succeeding Gleason, and no good blood is between them. If they only cannot persuade Barr to try to break the agreement! If they don't offer him more than I can meet! Gleason's known stinginess and lack of imagination is my hope. His grandfather settled this town and named it, but the family has sat here all these years and done noting. Just held on. But in the last three years the U.S. has built Patrick Air Force Base and Guided Missils, and hundreds of new families have moved in. One Yankee, Leveridge, has built (where there was nothing but weeds) about 600 new, modern houses (Leveridge Heights) and the new folks are taking the old settlers just like Grant took Richmond. For the first time in the history of the city a Gleason is not mayor. He was voted out last year with a <u>bang</u>! Power has passed to the new order. Houses are going up on all sides. Gleason no longer has the power to hold things down to his own speed, which is that of a sauntering turtle. Some Negroes sent an ambassador to me to tell me that I just could not hold onto all that land for my backyard as they heard I was planning to do. They had to have somewhere to go. Mind you, it never occurred to them before, though they knew that they were being forced to move soon. So you see, the Hurston-Sheen combination is in the money if I cannot be squeezed out in the next week or so. If the ante does not go too high and Barr craw-fishes and makes me sue. Mumble a prayer for me, honey. I wish that you were here to help me out with thinking and planning. I know that I have literary ability, but that does not mean reasoning power. Talent and intelligence are not the same thing at all, you know. though the average person so believes. A person may be a genius in some way, and have no real intelligence at all.

And now to get personal. A letter from Prue came in the same mail with your letter and the check. What she did <u>not</u> say was eloquent. I can sense unhappiness between the lines. Please tell me what happened. She ssaid that she would write me fully from Chicago. She did say that Edwin and Roma made her feel so welcome. She also said that she is on the fence about returning to Los Angeles. I am certain that you have not intentionally hurt prue. I hope that you make her certain of that. I am writing her as soon as I finish this letter to you, hoping that it catches her before she leaves for Chi.

I am so very sorry to hear that the dark struggle cannot be avoided. The Negro press is so low. They will print any kind of a lie and distortion to sell a paper.[4] However, if you think it necessary, get in touch with T.W. Anderson, 913 You St. N.W. Washington, D.C. He is head of the Courier's Washington office and let him be your public relations man. That is, if you feel, after communications between you, that he will not sell you out. I have no faith in any of them, (big Negro papers) because I know that they care nothing about the truth.[5] Sensation is what they want. If it were not for our relationship, I would gladly handle all the stories for you, but as it is, I am barred from such a service for you.

About my being in Los Angeles in May, you must know that any excuse to be near you would delight me no end. But wouldn't Quinlock's lawyers try to make something out of it to your hurt? You can judge that better than I, you know. You know that I am not timid and that I would do anything I possibly could to help, or just to comfort you if I could, and certainly would want to do nothing to harm you. Your own mother has never loved you to the depth that I have, Herbert, though I know that there came a time when you did not believe it because I opposed certain tendencies in you which I knew would hurt you in the end. Like a mother hen, I tried to stand between you and all hurt, harm and danger, and learned that that is something nobody can do for another. You know that I have lied in print to mak it possible for you and Quinlock to be happy together. I loved you enough to give your children a chance to [be] happ[y] and proud of their name and their father. Frankly though, I never believed that it would work too well, because I had sized up Quinlock. Not only her methods and manner of roping you in, but when I was in Chicago (you and she were in St. Louis) Prue and Constance and all the family told me how she whined and complained and forever demanded things of you and her own way. Nothing could have made me happier than wh[e]n they told me how they regretted <u>our</u> separation. Prue told me another thing that made me happy. "We persuaded Herbie to marry Quinlock and give Tony a name, because Herbie would not have done so if we had not kept after him. Now, we wish that we had left him alone. We wanted children in the family and thought that after we did all that for Quinlock she would realize how fortunate she

was, but no! She seems to feel that she has done both Herbert and us a favor. Selfish as she can be, and her temper is something awful. All we can hope and pray for is some kind of happiness for poor Herbie."
Now it appears that I gave your children more consideration than thir own mother, for she would not have this public sensation if she considered their own welfare properly. Money and spite are too prominent in her calculations.

Thanks for the picture. I have one to send you so you can see how your battle-axe looks at present, but find that the enlarged snap-shot is too wide for this envelope. I should be as gray as you by all rights, but somehow I do not seem to grow gray easily. You can judge from the unretouched snap-shot otherwise.

Write me promptly about Prudence. She should be there with you at the crisis. I hate to think of you being alone with all the fury of attack of that spiteful woman.

Affectionatly and faithfully,
Zora

It is interesting to see how far we both have come since we did our dreaming together in Washington, D.C. We struggled so hard to make our big dreams come true, didn't we? The world has gotten some benefits from us, though we had as well time too. We lived!

TO HERBERT SHEEN

Eau Gallie, Fla.
March 31, 1953.

Dear Herbert:
The land deal is coming long famously. My fears of being scuttled were justified in a way, for there are those who certainly had the will and the means, but the former owner is a staunch Republican, had read my article on Taft in Readers Digest (says he missed it in the SSTURDAY EVENING POSTO) and is an ardent Hurston fan, and thought that the party owed me something. He wanted Zora Neale Hurston to have it if she wanted it. He had held onto it, planning to

develop the tract himself, but family trouble caused him to change his mind about any further expansion. That is why his decision caught the local real estate market by surprise and why the sudden scramble to get it away from me. One man told a friend the other day that he was just going to wait. My cash would run out and he would be there to pick up the pieces. But he's a slew-foot liar. I am not going to cut it up into lots at all and make a cheap Negro development out of it at all. I find that I can lease three acres for a white trailer park very readily as soon as the surveyor runs the lines. The rest is going into a home site and commercial horticulture. The legal papers are being fixed up now on the ownership, and I will send you a copy along as soon as I have them myself.

About coming to L.A. in May is a very troublesome matter. With all my heart I w[a]nt you to win out and secure and retain the devotion and trust of your children. I know tnhat is what you want and that is what I have been willing to help you in all that I might be able. The attitude of my publishers gives me concern. I do not know whether I should broach the subject again, attempt it without their knowledge, or just what to do.

I had a bright cheerful letter from Prudence from Chicago today. It seems that it has been a happy reunion and that all goes well with her there. She said that she had a fine letter from you. She is praying for your success. That was the gist of her letter so far as you are concerned. My heart was warmed by her saying that Constance considers paying me a visit down here. I truly hope that she does. Connie is so gentle and shy. She does kind things with such a bashful air. Elliot has something of that quality too.

If I may make a suggestion, is there a mutual frined that could go between you and Quinlock and affect some kind of working compromise? If you could be persuaded to do and say nothing that would rile each other until May 15 perhaps you can avoid the open conflict in court. You mentioned back in 1944 to me that Q was jealous of some younger woman. If that is the case now, can you avoid any public attentions to the young lady until the divorce papers are signed, sealed and delivered? That would be the smart thing for you to do, since you know that ols saw," Hell hath no fury like a woman scorned." Your hand is in the lion's mouth now. Play along until you can ease it out. You know that the American courts are stacked in favor of women and children. If she comes into court smartly dressed, drags her children along and gets up

on the stand and cries and acts pitiful, as her lawyers will certainly tell
her to do, you will have a very rough day in court. If Q can sort of get
the impression that you have fallen out with the other woman it will do
you a world of good. After you have the decree you can do as you please,
even though by California law you can get nothing more than an inter-
locutory decree which does not become final for a year. You will at least
be free to do as you like and appear with the young lady at any time and
place that you like without injuring your chances before the law. The
young lady will agree with me, I am sure, so that she may have you all
to herself in the end. And six weeks is not a very long time against a
lifetime together. I go on the assumption that there must be somebody
else in your life to place Quinlock in the position of the injured party.
You have practically told me that yourself and that is why I am making
the suggestion to placate her until you can carry your point. I am with
you to the last and want you to succeed. I will be in L.A. if I can without
having my contract voided.[1] You can count on that.

I think that this covers the ground except that I have not told you
again that you are the most loved man on earth no matter what happens. That does not mean that I hope or expect to thrust myself into
your life except as a friend. I am with you to the end. Just something
you can think about on a cloudy day when you might feel depressed.

With faithful feelings,

Zora

TO HERBERT SHEEN

Eau Gallie, Fla.
May 7, 1953.

Dear Herbert:

Oh I do thank you for the suggestion about the "anxiety" help.
How did you know that I needed something like that? Did you make
the diagnosis from my letters, or just probably thought that I might
need it? You are a wonderful doctor.

---

[1] *Her Scribner's contract.*

Your conclusions about the reactions of the church dignitaries is clearly analytical. Yes, they are very and only human after all. They could not admit that they might have been wrong years ago at Tyler Texas. "Authority" is very precious to the heirarchy and they will not abate one jot or tittle of it easily. The priest there has probably been convinced that yours is a King Henry VIII case, and is dealing with it accordingly. I hear that Quinlock accuses you of getting too big for your britches since financial success came to you, and bent on crushing any and all who dare to oppose you. She has no doubt wept that out to the church fathers. Just in case that it has not been expounded to you, the Rota in Rome, whose authority passes on divorce, take the stand that the only real grounds on which they can grant a divorce is that one party entered into the marriage with no intention of making it a real marriage, in other words, insincerely. For other reasons than a "holy" union. Keep that in mind when you approach Monsignor Fulton J. Sheen.[1] I have never met him, but Claire Boothe Luce[2] has discussed him to me. From what is said of him you have a better chance of being understood than with the small fry. He is abreast of the times instead of being ardently traditional.

Today Mr. Burch of the firm of Van G. Werley brought me the abstract to read, 41 pages going back to the time when Florida belonged to Spain and on down to 1953. The title is clear and there are no liens against the property except the taxes for 1953 which will not be due until November 1, 1953. $16.50. The contract has gone to Thomas R. Barr, Jr. at Fort Pierce[3] for his signature and I will have a copy in a week at the latest. Then I will send it along to you for your inspection. The firm is strong for me to develop it into a housing project, but at present I think that I would like it better to plant it to an acre of fancy mangoes and perhaps five acres of oranges. The demand for orange juice concentrates seems inexhaustable and the price is good. Since concentrates were discovered, they can be shipped so easily all over the nation and abroad without loss that fruit is really booming. The big companies lease your grove and take care of everything.

---

[1] *Fulton J. Sheen (1895–1979) was a U.S. Roman Catholic bishop. He was considered an outstanding orator and was a radio and television broadcaster. He wrote* The Cross and the Crisis *in 1938.*
[2] *Clare Boothe Luce (1903–87) was a journalist, playwright,* Vanity Fair *editor, a congressional representative from Connecticut, and U.S. ambassador to Italy. She was the wife of Henry Luce, publisher of* Time *and* Life.
[3] *Thomas R. Barr, Jr., was associated with the Van Werley firm in Eau Gallie.*

It's none of my business really, but if I were you, I would not be deterred by the ban of the church. I would go right ahead and get married if that is what you want. A ten-ton truck might run over Quinlock's head some day and then you could re-marry in the church. For my money, priests are only men and without your experience in the world and with women. They rule from theory, not practice and have no more intimate acquaintance with God than you have. I still believe that the Roman Catholic church is the greatest institution that <u>man</u> has ever invented for human spiritual comfort on the average, but I have never lost track of the fact that it is <u>human</u>. Priests have lectured me on my intellectual approach instead of trusting all and everything to faith which my mental set-up will not allow.

To me, Herbert, the concept of God being that He is both omnipotent and omniscient, that He should want humans to know certain things and to be guided by these principles and reveal it to <u>so few.</u> The sun shines fully upon us everyday. Why cannot His will be as freely revealed since it is so important? And why allow Himself to be so easily misconstrued? Why so many religions? Why "reveal" Himself to an Arab in one light and to a Caucasian in another? And to a Hindu in still another and to a Mongol in still another? No, I cannot go for that. To me these divergent views are evidence of humanity groping after the divine concept, each in his own way in the absence of any definite proof anywhere. I have no belief in any bearded divinity sitting on a cloud. That is an anthropomorphic concept entirely human. God made in man's own image. To me there is LAW to which all things in the universe must conform. What the explanation of it is, I do not know, though I would like to know. We are confusing human social arrangements with divinity. I cannot conceive of Law caring whether you "go forth and multiply" with Quinlock or with "the young lady". You cannot deny the command within your own body to commit the act of reproducing your kind., for that has not been obscured by human theories, (which to me proves my contention that LAW makes itself very clear and definite where it is concerned) and is not concerned with human social conveniences, for that is what it amounts to. Marriage and social laws were evolved primarily to protect children and the mothers of children, and that is that. Do not deny yourself the woman you want in this life in the belief that you will get her as a reward in Heaven. I have not been there, but somebody whispered to me that angels have no business in the marriage bed, having no sex organs. Maybe that is why cherubs are nothing but heads. See where that will bring you out? You and the "young lady" will meet as heads with wings under your chins in the hereafter. But what fun is that? The Moslem heaven is much more exciting where male spirits are surrounded by beautiful women. Houris.[4] But as you know, they do not even wait for that, but take full advantage of what is available here and now. That is a much more realistic religion. It goes along with nature instead of inventing sins to suffer for. Human beings invented sin, not God. Very religious people are either sadists or masochists, and sometimes both. They like to suffer and castigate themselves and know a horrid frenzy when you do not suffer likewise and set out to make you feel their vengeance, too. The famed affair of Heloise and Abelard is tragic to me only in that they were so chuckled-headed in spending all that time accusing themselves instead of her throwing off her veil and his stepping on out of that monastery and going about their business.[5] People waste too much time worrying about whether an affair will <u>last</u>. Enjoy it while it does last and then suffer no regrets later. That is the fundamental difference between Quinlock and myself. I look back upon my experience with you as a time of pleasure without regrets. She is full of bitterness and vengeance because it did not keep on lasting. Love <u>should not</u> last beyond the point where it is pleasurable. Ergo, she is not capable of love, but only a possessive frenzy. That passes for love with many people. "I killed him because I love him."

> Here's luck to your day of freedom!
> Sincerely,
> Zora

[along left side:] Guatamala City would be a wonderful place to get married in case you do not feel like waiting the year California requires. It is high, cool and very beautiful.

---

[4]In the Islamic tradition, houris are beautiful, virginal creatures living in paradise.

[5]The story of Heloise and Abelard is one of the most famous tragic love stories of all time. Peter Abelard (1079–1142) was a brilliant yet controversial philosopher. Heloise (1100–64) was his young pupil. Upon the discovery of their affair, it was revealed that Heloise had a son, Astrolabe, and the lovers were forced apart; Heloise was banished to a convent while Abelard was sent to a monastery. Heloise and Abelard, although separated for the rest of their lives, wrote letters to each other until Abelard's death. They are buried together in the Père-Lachaise in Paris.

TO WILLIAM G. NUNN

[fragment; remainder burned in fire]

Eau Gallie, Flori
May 28, 1953.

Mr. William G. Nunn,Man. Ed.
The Pittsburgh Courier
P.O. Box 1828
Pittsburgh 30, Pa.

My dear Mr. Nunn:

          I received another letter
moral statements in the Ruby McC
at all. I have been too occupied
keep up with the series, and so h
under my name.

          You must know that it is n
illegal to attribute statements to
not make. I had not given the matter
that you would do nothing that would
I have conducted myself with The Cou
work, I must turn aside to acquire a
extent you have injured me by puttin
build your circulation. A Republican
Cocoa two weeks ago to warn me about
a reader in California denouncing me
well that I never made. I have no fi
not even decently paid for what I did,
let myself be used as The Courier's w
did my utmost for you and feel that a
injure me for the sake of your circul

          A hint came to me from a sour
there is a chance of Ruby's being re
future on account of her mental st
and so have no idea how authenti
that she is ever going to the c
that I have heard whispered from a
know that certain angles which have
get to be public talk and that will
have been made on the quiet to meet t
if and when it comes, but would rathe
Collom case to head it off.

                              Sincerely y

                              Zora Nea

*Fragment of a burned letter from Hurston
to William G. Nunn, editor of the*
Pittsburgh Courier.

TO BURROUGHS MITCHELL

Eau Gallie, Florida
October 2, 1953.

Dear Burroughs Mitchell:
(Also wife, Kitty Cat and Dog)

No. I have not been asleep all this time. I have been passing
through the most formative period of my whole life. Under the spell
of a great obsession. The life story of HEROD THE GREAT. You have
no idea the great amount of research that I have done on this man.
Flavius Josephus, Titus Livius, Eusebius, Strabo, and Nicolaus of Damascus.[1] No matter who talks about him, friend or foe, Herod is a
magnificent character. I have hung back on offering him for years because I know what people generally think of him, his attempt to head
off competition by murdering all the babies in the hope of catching
the infant Jesus in the dragnet. Even after I had found that Herod was
dead four years before Christ was born, and even if Herod had been
alive, there were other reasons why he never could have perpertrated
[sic] the massacre of the innocents, I hesitated. Then it came to me
that a character does not have to be lovable to make good reading.
Some of the most popular books and plays have been built around detestable characters.

So, it is my wish to submit Herod for your inspection, and hope intensely for your approval. If I can only carve him out as I have conceived him, it cannot help from being a good book. The story, his actual
life, has EVERYTHING. He is set forth by all writers of his time as a
man of the greatest courage, of high intelligence, one of the handsomest men of his time, capable of thegreatest and most faithful
friendship, as exemplified by his friendship with Marc Anthony, one of

---

[1]*Flavius Josephus was a Jewish historian (A.D. 37–100); Titus Livius (Livy) was a writer and historian (59
B.C.–A.D. 17); Eusebius, the "father of church history," was a writer and historian (A.D. 260–340); Strabo was a
geographer (63–3 B.C.); and Nicholas (first century B.C.) wrote* Life of Augustus *and was a friend of Herod the
Great's.*

the truly great friendships in all history, and his equally famous love affair with his wife, Miriamne [sic], and his strength of character. Perils which would have de[s]troyed lesser men elevated Herod. "From his very dangers, Herod drew splendor." Herod, a non-Jew was easily the greatest king of the Hebrews, reigned a long time, was the friend of Julius Ceaser [sic], Anthony, Augustus Ceaser [sic], and with enemies within his own kingdom (thePharisees and the Sanhedrin) died peacefully in his bed and was borne to his tomb in splendor. He stands out for two other reasons. His handsome person, plus his intelligence and great courage attracted Cleopatra, but he is the one man who not only rejected her, but con[s]idered putting her to death as being unworthy of the love of his friend, Marc Anthony, and a bad influence in Anthony's life. The other reason is that Herod the Great, though unconscious of the fact since Christ was not born as yet, had a great influence in preparing the way for Him. He trampled upon the Pharisees and the corrupt Sanhedrin mercilessly, highly honored the sect of the Essenes, whom all Bible students acknowledge formed the early background of christianity. The Sanhedrin lost prestige under Herod and the Essenes gaines [sic], thereby forming a matrix for the growth of christianity. In fact, many Bible scholars state positively that what we know as christianity is nothing but the doctrine and practices of the Essenes.

I have several chapters written already. It came to me that I should go no further until I had a reaction from you.

The enclosed letter will indicate to you that others besides myself see Herod as an important literary subject. With this approval, it is possible to envision a large reading public from the start. I think that you will agree with me that Mngr. Fulton Sheen regrets that he did not think of doing Herod himself before I wrote him about it. His letter does not preclude the possibility of his still launching into it. I gain this impression by his telling me not to allow him to read what I write in manuscript. I call this to your attention so that in case he does, and [a second "and" crossed out] you feel that I do not quite make it, Scribners can grab his work. Of course, I would rather for it to be me who unveils Herod to the world. Not only a swell book is inherent in the theme, but a most magnificent movie.

With all the best kind of wishes to you and yours, I am

With faithful feelings,
Zora Neale Hurston

I have a cat now, the first cat that I have ever owned, and find them very intelligent and interesting creatures! Mine is a haughty hussy and full of engenuity. Whips every dog in the neighborhood, including Spot. Mama is the tyrant of the premises, and even talks. I cannot always interpret what she says when she comes before me and makes her speeches, and when I don't she makes with a groan of disgust and walks away. She emphasizes her disgust by getting up on something and sneers at my dumbness as she jumps down.

Sheen took around a month before answering my letters and I interpret that to mean that he read up on Herod before answering, and was surprised at what a wealth he found.

TO WILLIAM BRADFORD HUIE

Eau Gallie, Florida
March 28, 1954.

Dear William Bradford Huie:

Congratulations! It was not my intention to let you down as I have. When I wrote you I was at white heat, but things happened to me that just about rotted the marrow in my bones, so that by the time that your letter arrived I was possibly at life's lowest point. And foolishly, my pride restrained me from making explanations as I should have done. And strangely, my misfortunes came to me out of the Ruby McCollum case.

Briefly, I had paid down on an eight acre tract here with the notes at $50 per month.[1] I also owed on my car. When the Pittsburgh Courier both wired and wrote me urging me to report the case for them, I told them my fee would be $1,000. They put up a poor mouth, but finally agreed to pay it in installments. In the end and af-

---

[1] *Presumably out of her $300 loan from Herbert Sheen.*

ter many agonizing delays, I have received in small sums, a little over $200. I lost out on both my land and my car. As Mr. Cannon[2] could tell you, they even left me stranded in hostile Live Oak[3] for two days before the money was sent to enable me to get back to Eau Gallie. My earnings were down because I was then, and am not yet finished with a longish book, one that has called for a great amount of difficult research,[4] and as an author, you are aware that you are not making money at the writing stage of the game, but only when the job is done. The money I did get from the Courier was used up in the several trips that I made to Live Oak, and by the dishonorable behavior of that Pittsburgh gang, I was sunk. My nervous tension made both my sinus and my gall-bladder trouble come down on me with terrible force. I found myself without even the money for medical care. That was my situation when your letter arrived. I hated to confess to you that I had not even the cash to pay my bus fare to Live Oak nor Jacksonville. BUT last week, a local man came to me, (I happen to know that he is a kind of stooge for Theodore Pratt who suffers terribly from professional jealousy)[5] to warn me that I would get into trouble with the KKK if I dared to aid you in any way. (Pratt is probably suffering aches and pains from what he considers your "invasion" of Florida and getting all that publicity[.]) Then I knew that I must rise out of my melancholy fog and give you whatever aid I could on your book. I am not one bit intimidated by the threat. In fact, I am certain that the KKK knows nothing about what I believe Pratt sent Vergil Howard to tell me.

Now, I take for granted that you have access to the court records of the trial, but I have some notes which I took as I watched the thing go on which could not be in the stenographic records—impressions and significant little observations. You can have my notes, and in addition, I suggest that:

[2]Attorney Frank Cannon, a member of Ruby McCollum's defense team.

[3]Live Oak was active Klan territory.

[4]Herod the Great.

[5]Theodore Pratt (1901–69) was an author who wrote primarily about Florida. Among his thirty-five novels were many on Florida. Pratt attended Hurston's funeral, delivered her eulogy, wrote about her warmly, and tried to get her works reprinted.

1. trace down all you can about that incident where Ruby was within an hour of being set free on a fluke. SOMEBODY WITH POWER IN THE STATE LEGISLATURE HAD MADE CERTAIN MOVES WHICH, IF IT HAD NOT BEEN DISCOVERED BY [illegible] AND JUDGE ADAMS [illegible] TO FROM TALLAHASSEE, RUBY WOULD HAVE GONE FREE BY A LEGAL FLUKE. (Nobody can ever convince me either that Judge Adams was not wise to it himself. As Shakespeare said, "methinks he protested too much." I believe that some very damaging revelations were feared from Ruby on the stand, and it was decided to end it by a freak mistrial.) See Lawyer Crews on that.[6]

2. Perjury of jurymen who pretended to either not know Dr. Adams or scarcely know him when they were intimates of his.[7]

3. Judge Adams following the jury into the jury-room and being in there conferring with them for several minutes before they were locked up.

4. The dope angle, which I presume Cannon has discussed with you.[8]

5. The involvement of the father of Dr. Adams with Negro women. He himself had a family of children by a colored woman and had been run out of the area when Dr. Adams was a small boy. Perhaps his return was to vindicate his father.

6. The Negro undertaker who often drove Dr. Adams to Ruby's house.

7. It is my theory that the decision of Dr. Adams to enter political life and naturally to cover up his past brought on the killing. SEE ABOUT THAT LETTER TO SAM McCULLOM [Ruby's husband] FROM DR. ADAMS OF SATURDAY, THE DAY BEFORE THE MURDER. That was what provoked Ruby to shoot. I have my own idea of what was in it.[9]

8. See if you can find out who it was that Dr. Adams feared so much that he was trying to buy a gun. IT WAS NOT RUBY.[10]

---

[6]*McCollum's lawyer P. Guy Crews was on the point of being disbarred by the Supreme Court. Had the trial gone on just a few hours more, with Crews disbarred, McCollum's case would have had to be dismissed for lack of legal representation.*

[7]*Hurston was proved right on this, as she was on most of the other claims adduced in this letter. Judge Adams and Dr. Adams were not related.*

[8]*Defense lawyer Frank Cannon; there was some evidence that Dr. Adams was doping Ruby.*

[9]*This letter disappeared and was never recovered.*

[10]*A few days before his murder, Dr. Adams had purchased a pistol which would have been useless as a hunting weapon.*

Please understand that I am not trying to horn in on your book. You are doing all the work and spending all the money on research, etc. I am merely offering you any little help that I can. If you think that I might have any information which you could use, call on me for it. Nobody is going to try to scare me and get away with it.

With faithful feelings,
Zora Neale Hurston.

Dr. Adams furnished the money for Black's[11] campaign for Dist. atty.

TO MISS MOUSLEY

Eau Gallie, Fla.
May 7, 1954.

Dear Miss Mousley:

I am very happy to hear that I have some copies of SERAPH on hand. Many people here have asked me to sell them a copy, but I thought that they could not be had. It will be very kind of you to send them along to me here. Thanks and thanks.

Been working long and diligently on HEROD THE GREAT. Hope to have it in your hnds by the time that Mr. Mitchell returns from abroad. Perhaps it is crazy of me, but I do wish that some one versed in international relations of an empire like Sir Winston Churchill could (would) give at least an interpretation of the life and times of HEROD THE GREAT in an introduction. In fact, I suggested it to him (how brash!) in a recent letter, but have not heard from him yet, which I guess, puts me in my place. Yet and still, I am in no way discouraged believing as I do that it is a great theme. Ann Watkins wrote me after reading the rough copy that not only she thought that it was really something, but that the head of a very prominent publishing house agreed with her and let her see that he regretted deeply that one of <u>his</u> writers had not thought of it first. Frankly, I did not quite

[11]State's Attorney Keith Black.

like the idea of her showing it to him. But I did not complain to her for fear of making an enemy of her.[1]

Thanks again and all good wishes to all at Scribners.

With faithful feelings,
Zora Neale Hurston

TO WILLIAM BRADFORD HUIE

Eau Gallie, Florida
May 14, 1954.

Dear William Bradford Huie:

Congratulations for your magnificent accomplishment on your new book![1] I bought LOOK, and was deeply moved. Not only did you hold up to the light a thing which should have been illuminated, but your min-gling of words was superb.[2] I have a keen sense of justice and so natu-rally felt with that poor soldier. I await the copy of the book that you promised me, but acknowledge that I do not really deserve it because of my delay in getting this material on Ruby McCollom [sic] in your hands. Please overlook my sinful delay and endow me with it. I was bogged down in re-writing passages in HEROD THE GREAT and not too happy about it, fearing that I was not making it sufficiently lucid, and came to that place where you loathe the sight of paper and the very touch of a typewriter. I know that you must be familiar with that feeling.

BUT YES!! "My People" are definitely a bunch of stinkers.[3] I take it that you are familiar with that folk tale where the monkey beside the road shakes his head at some capers that Negroes are cutting and sighs, "my people, my people.' " But another story, sort of a sequel, has the monkey withdrawing from among us and sighing just as sadly, "Those people, those people.' " [sic] In spite of his long connection

---

[1]*Hurston refers to this in two previous letters: to Burroughs Mitchell, July 15, 1951, and to Jean Parker Water-bury, May 10, 1951.*

---

[1]The Execution of Private Slovik *(1954).*

[2]*"The Execution of Private Slovik," Look, May 4, 1954.*

[3]*Hurston could not get the Live Oak African American community to speak to her about the McCollum case.*

with the NAACP, James Weldon Johnson once complained to me sadly, "We are such a race of loud-mouthed cowards, such a collection of lying sychophants, such destroyers and reluctant builders, so innately brutal and cruel and envious of each other and haters of superiority, such bullies among the weak, that I despair of the future. The White man does not need to keep us down as we untruthfully complain in public, for we will do that ourselves effectively. In fact, if it were not for the deterrent pull of the White man, even in the Deep South, no Negro would ever get a chance to show ability. Certainly Negroes are not going to make opportunities for other Negroes, for fear of being surpassed. I confess that I feel that a great part of my life and a great part of my abilities have been wasted, and if I had it all over again, I would take a different course. You are young (I was at Barnard then) and obviously talented. I beg of you not to waste time on this so-called Race Problem. You will find it a thankless task." I have found this only too true. Not my supposed "White enemies", but <u>Negroes</u>, have played every vile trick upon me that can be imagined, without rhyme or reason except hating to see me reap any benefit from hard work. While they lounge around the bars of New York, I am out in the unglamorous places gathering material, and when it bursts on the world, "Zora Neale Hurston has been lucky again, and the White people have piled more honors upon her which she does not deserve." You guessed it. I want no parts of them, and if somebody were to set up a nation of American Negroes, I would be the very first person NOT to go there. I have found that ambition without talent is a terrible combination. It makes natural-born enemies of progress. Negro newspapers are loaded with would-be writers and naturally bloated with envy. They are the most brazen frauds on the American continent. Screaming about "Rights for Negroes" and lynching every Negro who shows any marked ability.

I am very glad for you to have this experience among us on the Ruby McCollom [sic] case so that you can see us from the inside. Knocking around Live Oak, you must have learned a great deal about our great "courage" and truthfulness. And the most disheartening thing is our cheapness. We will swear to ANYTHING for a dollar and a quarter. And not just the "ignorant niggers" either.

Enclosed you will find some of my pencilled notes taken on the spot in case some atmosphere, which you could never gain from the

court records might be there. I was so aware of the envy of Black towards Cannon.[4] In the first place, Black looked like a well-fed mule
beside a race horse with Cannon, then thrre was the lack of personality, so that, being a little man at heart, he got to behaving right
niggerish, the brotherhood of little folk existing under every color of
skin. As I think I said in my first letter to you, I would have no interest in defending Ruby because she is a Negro, my interest arose out of
the dramatics of the case, and the varied play of human emotions. I
repeatedly resisted the urgings of the COURIER to "angle" the stories. I have no interest in skin colors at all, but people, individuals as
they show themselves. And personally, I suspect that two ruthless individuals met and tangled in Ruby and Dr. Adams. Perhaps egotisti-
cal is a better word, or does it add up to the same thing?

Thanks for your kindness to me, and if there is anything further
that I can do for you, you must let me know. I was, and am not afraid
to appear in Live Oak, but wondered if you really wanted me there, or
just was being nice and polite. I was not invited to participate in the
Florida Folk Festival because of my reporting this case, but my reputation, national and international as a folk-lorist will not suffer because
of that.[5] I should worry. I did have to find homes for two cats which
had taken up around my house and find a boarding place for my dog
Spot, which took a few days, but that was all the preparations I had to
make for leaving here, but by then, Scribners was questioning me
about HEROD. So now you understand.

Why am I fascinated by the unpopular HEROD THE GREAT? Because he was an extremely talented and forceful and progressive rebel.
Naturally, he was Hellenized, and sought to encourage his nation away
from the primitive posture of the priesthood of his time. They feared
his influence, and therefore hated him. It is ironical that immediately
upon the death of Christ, His so-called followers, not understanding
Him, went back to the primitive fears and demonology, and looked
upon Herod as an enemy of religion, and concocted a bogeyman of
him, still, Christianity now follows Herod in advocating culture, and
the Vatican, as you know, has one of the world's finest collection of art,
consisting of the very "images" which he so aroused the priesthood by
introducing in his time. Protestantism also advocates art and athletic

---

[4]*State's Attorney Keith Black; Frank Cannon, defense attorney for Ruby.*
[5]*The Florida Folk Festival is the regional festival of the National Folk Festival.*

with a fine zeal now. Paradoxical, isn't it? While they still denounce him as a devil for favoring the same thing. The men who should be "blamed" for spreading Greek culture over Asia are Alexander the Great and his Aristotle, but they praise <u>them</u> for it. Human beings are funny people.

   With every good wish for your continued success, I

Most Sincerely yours,

[unsigned carbon]

TO WILLIAM BRADFORD HUIE

Eau Gallie, Fla.
June 10, 1954.

Dear W.B. Huie:

   Consider me in complete agreement all down the line. Already I am at work on the notes. You understand that when I first buzzed you on this case, it was my intention to collabotrate with you on the book, but I got so provoked at the treatment I got from the COURIER[1] in addition to other things that I blew my top and went as completely anti-Negro as is possible for a human being to be. I washed my hands and turned my back on everything that pertained to A'nt Hagar's chillun. I said that sometime or other, I ought to know when I have been sufficiently lynched.

   You don't know it, but there is a kind of kinship between us. Both of my parents were born in southern Alabama, Notasulga, Macon County, sort of straight west of Columbus, Ga.[2] If you shake the bushes in that vicinity Hurstons and Potts (my mother's family) will fall out by the hundreds. There is a white woman here who is from around Columbus, Ga. and when we meet, we call each other "cousin," she being of the Hurston clan, though she advises me that the real spelling is Hairston, and it has been handed down to her about the branch which moved west into Alabama a little more than a

---

[1] *Hurston claimed that of the $1,000 owed her by the* Pittsburgh Courier, *only $200 was ever paid.*
[2] *Hurston was born in Notasulga as well.*

generation before the Civil War. My father was a mulatto, but the Potts were all very dark. I am doing the old Southern thing of "scraping up kin" by common statehood through my parents.

In that same connection, I have in mind something that we could tackle together after your book on Ruby is out of the way. I plan to call it THE CRACKER CROP and let it run to series of amusing short stories loaded down with Southern idioms about a cracker who is always getting into trouble to the despair of his kin by stealing mules. He always comes up with a funny anecdote and bizarre explanations for the capers he cuts, and is so interesting that they forgive him until the next caper. Cousin Mule is all over the place in rural settlements of Alabama, Georgia and Florida, stealing mules, making love to widder women, stealing good hound-dogs and lying magnificently. He regains acceptance at his brother's house, where he has been forbidden to foot the place again after his last caper by dismounting from another stolen mule and approaching the porch where his scowling brother sits with an announcement that "I just found a baby angel, must of fell out the nest, didn't have hardly no feather on his wings at all." Dinner is being placed on the table, so before Cousin Mule gets through telling about the baby angel, dinner is announced and the brother, entertained in spite of himself, has to ask him in to eat. You have noted, I am certain, the magnificently colorful idiom of the southern cracker. Best in the USA. Like the body of folklore, it was once mistakenly attributed to the southern Negro, but I have found it to be sectional rather than racial, and now other folklorist[s] agree with me. It got attributed to the Negro because of the black-face minstrels.

Two days ago I also received your autographed copy of THE EXECUTION OF PRIVATE SLOVIK, and did not put it down until it was finished. I found it surpassingly fine. It is, and should be acclaimed an American classic. Because Patrick Air Force Base is near here, and numerous of the personnel live here, it is raising a fair fog in Eau Gallie. From LOOK MAGAZINE, and now the book, people are fighting it out to a finish. It is raising hell and rutting a chunk under it among the Republicans. The Eisenhower section resents the book as a reflection on the President, and the Taft section glory in it. You know that the bulk of the regular Republicans do not consider Ike a Republican at all, and hate all his works. They call him a Truman stooge, "that gang of shin-kickers" (from the saying that Dewey was kicking the Pennsylvania delegation under the table at the convention to make them go for his candidate, Eisenhower) So they find evil about Ike on every page. The "Shin-kickers" find Ike maliciously slandered, and one told me, "Why, poor Eisenhower knew nothing about this case. Don't you see that it says on one page that he never even saw that letter?" What with the McCarthy-Army hassle going on in Washington, SLOVIK is dumping fuel on the fire, for you must realize that the core of the e hearings is a tussle for control of the GOP between the original Republicans and the "Shin-Kickers." I am a Republican, but calm and cool about the split in the party, for I have realized for some time that both of the old parties are lying at the point of death and even perhaps 1956 may witness a new alignment.[3] The conservatives in both parties will get together, and the liberals of both parties get together in another new party. Truman as a Democrat and Ike and Dewey of the GOP merely hastened the process along. Trying to purge Joe McCarthy is merely a step in the war. All of the left of center Democrats are backing Dewey-Eisenhower, and all of the right of center Democrats are sticking up for Joe. Both parties are already split wide open. It only needs formal recognition. Ike, inexperienced in politics, was ill-advised to start this hassle of purging Joe, because the Taft branch, still boiling about the convention, was looking for trouble and only too happy to pick up the challenge. They are old heads at the game and know all the tricks. and know exactly how to make Ike look devious and dictatorial instead of themselves. And he keeps playing right into their hands. Somebody must have told him something, for I notice in the last few days he has not mentioned McCarthy, nor said anything that could be so construed. This is a wise move, for you notice how more and more commentators and columnists are going at the real quarrel, and more and more coupling Ike with Truman. Like a pine tree standing in water, Ike cannot stand that very long.

I will get the material to you on time regardless of the money. I wish that I had the cash to contribute to Ruby's new defense move. Though abhorring what she did, I was and am sorry for the poor thing. She was a woman terribly in love, and with us females, that makes strange and terrible creatures of us.

[3] Her prediction was not borne out. Eisenhower was reelected in 1956 by the largest margin of a Republican up to that time. He ran against Adlai Stevenson. Eisenhower remained conservative and upheld segregation.

Here's to our partnership for the future, and I solemnly swear to do anything I am able towards your career and be utterly faithful to this now.

With faithful feelings,
Zora Neale Hurston

TO WILLIAM BRADFORD HUIE

Eau Gallie, Florida
July 1, 1954.

Dear William Bradford Huie:

First let me set you straight about this "cousin" business. Don't think that I was really trying to scare up kin. With my tongue in my cheek, I was merely poking fun at an old Southern custom to make you laugh in spite of tussling with Judge Adams.[1]

And please do not conclude that I am seeking to muscle in as a collaborator on your book. That would neither be honest nor right. It is your book, but I stand ready to do any bits that you feel you want me to do. I predict that you are going past the million mark on it. The Negro population is going for it in a big way.

I will be there at the trial.[2] I know that it is going to be thrilling to see Adams upset. Honestly, I was filled with horror when I came to realize that they meant to kill this woman, and hustle her off without allowing her to tell the real story.[3] At the time I almost puked when I saw Judge Adams put on that hypocritical act of sniffling when he got ready to sentence Ruby to the chair. I do not object to acting, but when you do, make it good, brother. Make me like it. The Judge was the lousiest ham I ever witnessed. [Frank] Cannon hammed all over the place, but he was good at it, as I suppose all trial lawyers must be. Say! as a play, the guy who played Adams could be a scream.

---

[1] *Judge Hal Adams tried the Ruby McCollum case.*

[2] *It does not appear that she was able to attend.*

[3] *The trial judge placed a gag order on Ruby, denying her any access to the press.*

The central theme of this real-life drama, as I see it, is [Dr.] Adams and [Keith] Black, as hick-town Napoleons, set out to seize upon and conquer the State and the empire gets halted by four bullets before it can even get airborne. With your revelation that [Dr.] Adams intended to kill Ruby,[4] several loose bits of information fall into place. Trying to induce her to move out to his farm, for instance, where he probably intended to kill her. And other things. I take it that he and A. H. Black thunk it all up together. But I hold Ruby to be chuckle-headed too. The dumbest thing a woman can do is to refuse to fade out of the picture when the man is through with her. Certainly accounts for a lot of murders. I sensed this stubbornness in her by little things.[5]

Frankly, which is the only sensible course, I am not sure that I can get up there to the trial unless you send me at least transportation. I expect to have my book[6] in by then, but not enough time for Burroughs Mitchell to read it, I'm afraid. So there is the situation.

Wishing you a whole box of fire-crackers and two Roman candles for the Fourth, I am

Sincerely,
Zora N.

PREDICTIONS—

This: It will transpire that:

1. Dr. Adams, full of dreams of political success, sought to get rid of Ruby.
2. She refuses to be cast off
3. He and Black plot Ruby's murder out at Adams' farm.
4. Ruby wont step down from her social position and go.
5. It is then resolved to do away with her in some other way—drugs, etc.
6. Tried to make her get up on the operating table to force an abortion upon her.

---

[4]*Hurston's tip, corroborated by various interviewees in Huie's book.*
[5]*Ruby refused to eat or drink anything given to her in jail, convinced that she would be poisoned. She continued her refusal even when her weight dropped to eighty pounds.*
[6]Herod the Great.

TO WILLIAM BRADFORD HUIE

Eau Gallie, Florida
July 28, 1954.

Dear WBH:

I saw the granting of the new trial in THE MIAMI HERALD and
I'm all agog.[1] What is the date? I run to the Post Office every day looking for a letter from you. However, I know how busy you must be right
along in here.

I am in agreement with you on Ruby McCollom [sic] without your
inside information. I sensed a cold control in the woman, also a determination to keep control. Her brother, the barber, told me that she was
engaged to another fellow before Sam McCollom, but jilted him because "He was not getting ahead fast enough." Then she told her
lawyer, "I pick from the top. I had the top Negro man in the County
and then won the top White one." The killing came because Ruby was
not going to be outdone. Granting that Adams had jilted her, and that
he was on bad terms with her husband, what was to prevent her from
taking several thousand dollars and going North until the stink died
down? Or even permanently? I am certain that is the course I would
have followed. She could have easily laid her hands on $50,000[2] took
her small children and disappeared from Live Oak and had her
second child by Adams in peace and safety and let the whole affair be
forgotten.

I forgot to put in anything about myself, but if you think it necessary, I can furnish it when I see you at the trial.

My very best to you and yours. Have you talked to Dr. Hampton at
Ocala yet?[3] I interviewed him because he was Sam's closest friend. However, I warn you that he has no good opinion of Ruby. He, as some others had told me, had expected Ruby to kill Sam for something before

---

[1] *Ruby McCollum's defense team was able to get her a new trial, based on outside assessments of her sanity.*
[2] *Reportedly there was regularly that much in cash, and more, in the McCollum household.*
[3] *Huie did take Hurston's advice and interview numerous doctors, leading to some important revelations about Dr. Adams's questionable professional and personal behavior.*

August 3. I suppose you already know that Sam had taken his own gun away from the house weeks before. His brother would have told you that, I'm sure.

Faithful feelings,
Zora

TO THE *SATURDAY EVENING POST*

[fragment; remainder burned in fire]

Eau Gallie, Florida
September 2, 1954.

THE THRONE
SATURDAY EVENING POST
Independence Square
Philadelphia, Pa.

Dear Sir:

Believe me, it is with the utmost reluctance that I call your attention to the enclosed letter [not available]. I do so only because it came to me by air mail with a return of Editorial Rooms, of the SEP.

It makes no sense in a way, and since writers and other public characters receive so many crank letters, I would ordinarily toss it aside and forget it. But since it seems to have been sent jointly to the SEP and myself, I feel that I must give an account of it to you. On the face of it, it is absurd, for I have received no communications from anybody named Eric Eric Samuels of Nant . . . England at any time, that I can recall after a week of ha . . . ing, let alone discussed collaboration with him. Never . . . any communication with the Dell Publishing Corporation . . . It is indeed a very reluctant author who commits hi . . . to another author in a foreign land who has never a . . . letters with him and then wait eleven years to as . . . with his name unsigned to his demand. I could . . . absurdities and irregularities such as, CONSCIEN . . . ["Conscience of the Court"?] was not published until 1950, seven years after he . . . sent me his script SECRET FOG, via

Dell Publishing . . . he waits four years later to write me. Very, very . . . should suddenly become so concerned at <u>this</u> time . . . mice. It appears sinister, somehow.

As I said, I would toss it in the trash-can . . . but for all I know if Eric Samuels actually exists . . . lying tactics might be because he is a Communist or . . . or, as we find so often these days, both, and neither . . . shown any liking for me. In fact, all the unhappiness . . . have come from those quarters.

I got my first introduction to communism through just . . . a brazen claim. I had heard of communism, but it seemed something vague and distant to me. I met it personally through Langston Hughes. I had known him since I came to New York in 1925 and entered Barnard College. I thought him very innocent-like and full of simplicity and virtues. I was to discover later that his shy-looking mein covered a sly opportunism that was utterly revolting. I found out about communists from him.

As you know, I studied anthropology under Dr. Franz Boas. Skipping details, in 1929, Mrs. R. Osgood Mason gave me a fellowship for two years to continue research in Negro folk-lore. I did a very conscientious job. So much so, that the Library of Congress rates MULES AND MEN, the result of that work, as the most important single piece of work in the nation. Just before I returned to New York, Mrs. Mason, who wished me to call her Godmother, wrote me [Fragment ends here. On the back was typed: "Now is the time for all good men to come to the aid of the party."]

TO WILLIAM BRADFORD HUIE

Eau Gallie, Florida
September 6, 1954.

Dear William B:

I am indeed on the anxious seat, but not because of me, but for your sake, and I will keep on wringing and twisting until I know that you have the money pledged by the Courier and the Elks in hand. Anybody who has had any dealings with the Courier will tell you how trifling they are about keeping promises about cash.[1] [George] Schuyler can and will tell you in bitter words. Lord knows I have had my lumps.

I am certain that you are telling the truth about Ruby's guilt. The Courier and I had some words on that point. I stood out for factual reporting while Nunn[2] argued that I would leave her no reputation for them to fight on to save her life.

But that is not the real story and they know it and they know that I know it. No matter what the Emancipation Proclamation says, we are still slaves in spirit, lousy with inferiority complexes, and no matter how degrading the circumstances, see glory in the white-pulling[?]-sheets-with-black. Sometimes I feel like puking at the raptures in the Negro press at it. The success of STRANGE FRUIT, by Lillian Smith, NATIVE SON, Richard Wright, MULATTO, by LANGSTON HUGHES, and DEEP ARE MY ROOTS, authors names forgotten,[3] was due to this angle. No matter how trashy the writing, if you get that part in, you are sure of a large Negro sale. and most especially, IF THE HERO OR HEROINE KILLS A WHITE PERSON. In vain do you search for dignity and self-respect. No, the folklore prevails that all White people secretly yearn for Negro lovers (men in particular) and off they go on a wild spree of gloating. The Communists have discovered this, and their drive to gain the American Negro has been based on it. They offer to throw in a White wife or husband to Negro party members. I have witnessed some very stinky business in New York along that line. They confidently offer a highly cultivated Negro prospect some beat-up object that has been scraped up off a park bench—and who has joined the Party in order to eat—as a wife or husband. On the occasions when I was solicited to join up, with the usual bonus, I went right to the heart of the matter without beating around the bush and told them that I could get all the White men I wanted without any help from them and pick from a higher bush for a sweeter berry. Ruby would be lionized for what she has done if she were free and arrived in places like New York, Chicago, Washington, and Detroit, etc. So far as I am concerned, she stinks like a million mules on a mile of manure. Not so much because she crossed the line,

---

[1] *Out of $1,000 owed her by the* Pittsburgh Courier, *Hurston claimed to have received only $200.*
[2] *William G. Nunn,* Pittsburgh Courier *editor.*
[3] *Written by Arnaud d'Usseau and James Gow, this 1945 play featured an interracial love affair.*

as the circumstances surrounding her act, and because she is possessed of the poverty of soul to kill a man when she found she was not wanted. Never do I read of an individual who claims to have killed for love but I am revolted, knowing so well that it does not happen. They are just mean-spirited individuals who can't stand to lose.

I was in Washington when Langston Hughes MULATTO opened there as an opera with Lawrence Tibbetts [sic].[4] Despite the fact that we are no longer friends (he tried to [steal a play?] from me. and when I foiled him, he has been going about slandering me as taking his play away from him ever since, with the backing of the NAACP crowd) he sought me out to ask me why MULATTO was getting such a poor reception, I told him a) that it had succeeded on the stage because it was looked upon as good left-wing propaganda, anything to make the South look bad, since Dixie was the section putting up the stiffest resistance to left-wing penetration, and b) the theme was too low-down. On analysis, there was nothing about the hero to inspire admiration and induce sorrow at his lynching. In fact, one might be tempted to go forth and help do the job. What were the aims of the so-called hero? To squeeze more profit to himself out of his mother's degradation. His White father is giving him a college education which he has not sought. So home he comes from college, gets off the train, and instead of getting into the car which his father has sent to meet him, he jumps in the car and goes off on a spree. (Indicating great bravery in defying White folks. Then makes a great to-do about coming in the front door) Both things trivial and playing up the nigger-rich approach of the ignorant Negro. Both the car and the door were the property of his White father. He could dispose of them as he pleased. Now, if he had come home and demanded that his mother and sister leave the place an allow him to support them, he would have been getting somewhere, but killing his father over using the father's front door was too low and despicable to mention. Quit looking for his mother's backside to support him in degradation and stand on his won [sic] feet. If he had had to kill his father in order to remove his mother and sister from their shameful position, then THAT would have been worth looking at. Needless to say, neither Hughes nor the half dozen Negroes, all upper-class, agreed with me. The theme was noble, they

[4]*Lawrence Tibbett (1896–1960) was a baritone who worked primarily for the Metropolitan Opera. His first major role was in 1925 as Ford in Verdi's* Falstaff. *For this performance, he received the longest ovation ever recorded (fifteen minutes). He sang more than seventy roles before leaving the Met in 1950.*

said. He had demanded to come in the front door, and killed that nasty White man for not letting him do it. Great hero.

That brings us to a fundamental which will interpret Poston[5] and the rest to you. In spite of centuries in the USA and the Anglo-Saxon attitude towards women, I am afraid that we are still orientals that way. In Africa, according to what I have learned through study in anthropology and otherwise, women do all the hard work and support the men. Too many American Negro men, high and low, still see it that way. HOWEVER SHE GETS HOLD OF THE MONEY IS ALL RIGHT, SO LONG AS SHE GIVES IT TO HIM. There is a proud gloat, "Let her go on with that White man and get his money. Some nigger will be living on it and having himself a ball, hee, hee, hee.' " No, in many ways, Negroes do not have the same attitude towards women that White Americans do. They cringe before the power of the White man over them and exercise tremendous cruelty over those, say women, children, and domestic animals, that they can. Even educated men will double-teen a Negro woman who surpasses them in achievement with utmost skullduggery and think nothing of it. IT IS SAFE. Anyway, you can hear a Negro man say, "I don't allow no woman to cuss me." A man can cuss him because he has a harder fist. In other words, we have not as yet absorbed the principle of protection for the weak. So you see, in Ruby McCollom's case and others similar, they want to believe that she was irresistable to Dr. Adams and they are secretly glorying in the fact that a Negro killed a White man, something none of them have the courage to do themselves. They love to read about it, even in fiction such as in the stories I mentioned. You remember Paul Robeson's long run in Othello. An educated Negro man in New York gloated to me, "I have been to see it four times. I love to see Paul Robeson choking that white woman to death. White folks have killed enough Negroes." Hence the rush at the box-office.

And turning away from Ruby's case for a paragraph, I know that Robeson's heart was in that scene, for knowing him as intimately as I do, I know that he became a Communist because, like Ruby, he left his wife, Eslanda, for a titled English woman, and she turned from him and went back to her own after a long affair that became the scandal

---

[5]*Hurston probably refers here to journalist Ted (Theodore Roosevelt Augustus Major) Poston, who wrote for the* New York Amsterdam News *and the* New York Post *as well as for the* Pittsburgh Courier. *Poston was a dedicated leftist, and his older brothers, Robert and Ulysses Poston, were both officials in Marcus Garvey's back-to-Africa organization, the UNIA (United Negro Improvement Association).*

of two continents.[6] He felt that she had let him down in the clinches because of race, and his bloated ego was ripped and torn and he came to hate the English and American Whites with an unbelievable fury. It was hard for me to understand at first, Paul, because of his talents as an athlete, had been supported through high school, a scholarship to college, every letter at Rutgers that could be given, honor speaker at his graduation, scholarship to Columbia law school, and a partnership in a White law firm on graduation with high honors, and other things which I will not take up your time to enumerate, that he could become so bitter. Finally, I recognized that his ego had become so distended that he thought a cousin of the king of England was none too high for him and his self-conceit, like Ruby's, couldn't take it. Off he hied to Russia and came back to overthrow the White race. Same as Ruby, only he did not shoot the lady. He meant to get the whole kit and biling come that day. Both cases are the same in my estimation. They went into something on their own, then couldn't stand failure. No doubt if Ruby had had Paul's education and contacts, she would have joined the Party too, to overthrow the Nordic. If Paul had been as limited as Ruby, he would have made a momuck [?] out of Lady Mount-batten. Too drunk with self-esteem to take it.

I will be very happy if some newspaper commissions me to do the story for three reasons. 1) To put a more rational and self-respecting version before the public. 2) More advertising for the book. 3) To make a piece of change so that I can work on my book[7] without worrying about money to live on.

But please, please bear in mind that you owe me nothing in the world. I am rather concerned that I got you into this, and I have the weak-trembles lest the Courier and the Elks play it shabby and let you down. In frustration and anger, I don't want you raking over my ancestry and discovering that my damn mammy was a two-bumpted camel and my pappy was a mule. I know of no group on the earth greater masters of the invective than the Southern American, and you are likely to come up with some such analysis of my ancestors as that or worse. My house is only two blocks from the White Elementary

---

[6]Hurston refers here to the scandal caused by widespread but thoroughly discredited rumors that Robeson was leaving his wife for Lady Edwina Mountbatten, who successfully sued British press sources for libel. Although Robeson and his wife had indeed separated for some time during this scandal, the separation had mostly to do with Robeson's affair with another British woman, Yolande Jackson, and, as Hurston probably knew from mutual friends, Paul and Essie Robeson ultimately reconciled.

[7]Herod the Great.

School, and a lot of the children have to pass my door every day. Friday came, I heard Jimmy Cannon tell Butch Gray, "Your damn pappy wasn't nothing but a rusty [illegible word] rhinoceros and your good-for-nothing [illegible word]-eyed mammy wasn't nothing but a rusty-throwed-away tomato can that was low enough to have your pappy. Don't like it, don't take it. Here's my collar, come & shake it." Butch retaliated by observing that the buzzards laid Jimmy and the sun hatched him. Further, Jimmy had better think well before he risked a fight with him since a streak of lightning had struck him one time [?]he went off through [three words illegible]. (Then seeing me, he dashed up on my porch to [two words illegible] off of him)

You have my sympathy and understanding. I have been through the [four words illegible], too many tasks at hand and some uncertainties. My very best to you and yours.

[written on back of last page:] My interest in the case has never been that Ruby was a heroine that should be saved at all costs, but but that of a writer in that it is a good story by the time you analyze all the characters concerned, and as you point-out, the reactions of the community to the scandal. I see Ruby & Dr. Adams of the same essential human-types—success had persuaded both that they were above and beyond the laws that govern the ordinary mortals. Notice how she went home after the murder tossed the gun in the hedge and went about fixing the baby's formula [next four lines illegible] their bolita gone. Did you talk with the telephone operator and find out how she called Dr. Adams about 40 times on Saturday, the day before the murder?

[unsigned carbon]

TO WILLIAM BRADFORD HUIE

[1954/1955]

Dear <u>Huie</u>:

Please forgive me. My typewriter had developed trouble, and being told that I would not get it back for four days, I took off for Vero Beach in search of a rare type of geranium which I had been told could be found there. Hence the delay.

You wonder why I deleted the words "and works" but I was afraid it might be misinterpreted by the ever-present and envious literary would-bes among my own race. I point out the lack of drinking water in the Courthouse for Negroes. You can make the change or not as you see fit.

I am very eager to talk with you and looking forward to the visit. If there is anything that I can do to stir up interest & <u>boost sales</u>, you must tell me what you want done.

You are a great artist, as your sentences flow past my inner mind, I am impressed by both the happy choice of words and the rhythm of sentence-passage. Your foreword makes you a great <u>man</u>. If you do not get the Nobel literary award on this work, I shall be surprised.

How does your wife fancy her new role of "passing for white"? I hope that she can still laugh. You see I <u>know</u> my West Florida. There is eternal conflict between that backward area and peninsular Florida. Those Crackers up there are "agin" <u>every</u>thing that smells like progress. You have seen their unreasonable attitudes, their stubborn bitterness when opposed Because I wrote you about this case, the prominent ladies who run the Foster Memorial & state folk festival bar <u>me</u>—held to be if not the #1 folklorist of America, among the highest bracket, certainly #1 in Florida, from the festival <u>and</u> the dear lady feels justified in not returning my only copy of "Mules and Men." They would certainly have accused us of not flying right if I had shown up.

I'll be so glad to see you that I'll kill that lil' red rooster when you come. So much to talk about.

With faithful feelings.

Zora

TO HERBERT SHEEN

Eau Gallie, Florida
January 7, 1955.

Dear Herbert:

If you are well and happy, you can ignore this letter. I had a spiritual experience which forced me to drop my hard and continous grind on my book[1] and write you.

---

[1] Herod the Great.

Last night, I had something between a dream and a vision in which you were with me and you were very playful, happy and affectionate as you were in our salad days. The dread prohibition to love you was removed, and I was excruciating happy as I used to be whenever you came in sight. This last sentence brings me to a matter which I do not think I have ever mentioned to you. That is, that I am the subject of the as yet unexplainable to psichiatrists, recurrent dreams. I keep mum about it because I fear people might look on me as being "tetched in the head." However, science knows about this phenomena, but has found no explanation, since no basis can be found in past experience, memory, etc. but evolves on future happenings which never fail to come. They usually begin in early childhood, and cease when the thing dreamed of comes to pass, often far into adulthood.

Mine, a series of about a dozen scenes began when I was around six or seven, and all have come and passed except the last where I see myself approaching a huge building in two parts. Iam expected, and there are a great many people about. There appear to be shops on the first floor of one part of the building, which is of stone. A series of rooms upstairs that might be class-rooms or offices with many people in them. A diningroom. There is a sort of passage with stairs that lead to the other building, and that I cannot see as yet. I keep trying to find the way there, where some pleasant experience waits for me, but somehow I get mixed up about the stairs and the passage. There is a railroad with a junction somewhere near at hand. The entire scene indicates that I am reaching some much-desired goal. But on the way to this big establishment, there is a body of water, not very large, and lying in a deep basin like a lagoon. I walk around it and come to the railroad, and in some myterious way, I am at the building. [in left margin:] I was not allowed to see details of the first building until recently.

Now, in last night's dream, for the first time, you met me near the water, and we ran up the hill playing and very happy. Then you lifted me and carried me part of the way to the building where all the people were and we mingled with them. Then you said that you had a pain in your side low down as in your pelvic region and we walked along hand in hand and very happy.

Once before I had a vision-dream about you. It was the night before you arrived in Florida to marry me. This was not a happy one and cast a dark shadow over me for years. A dark barrier kept falling between us, and I sat up with the voice of your [s]ister Mildred calling my name in most unfriendly terms commanding me to leave you alone. Leave you alone or suffer severe penalties. It was as vivid as noon, and it haunted me for a very long time. It made me forever fearful that you would escape out of my life. It all seemed unreal in a way, I mean our union. We appeared like shadowy figures seen through an opal. It was terrible. Therefore, I was not surprised when something came between us. Remembering the dream, I looked upon it as fate.

Of course, it can be argued that both experiences came out of my sub-conscious according to Frued [sic], the hidden fear in the first case and the wish-fulfillment in the second. I do not think so. Neither floowed [sic] the regular dream pattern. Too vivid and a half wakefull plane of consciousness which is always present in such experiences with me. I even read, word for word, a letter being written to me on one occasion which I received two days later. I have had many experiences of that kind, but almost never speak of them for fear of being thought queer, to say the least. But I did submit the information to the Dept. of Psychology at Columbia, and was taken very seriously, to my surprise and r[e]lief, for the Dept. had numerous cases on record and I was told that the answer was being sought, but as yet unsuccessfully. I was allowed to read case histories and some were very interesting. In every instance, the dream or dreams, end with the fulfillment. Both Kipling and Mark Twain had them. You remember that Kipling uses this as the basis of his story, THE PHANTOM RICKSHAW.[2] The physicists now attempt to explain it through time. Einstein maintains that time has folds, or something like that, and occasionally an individual gets a glimpse of wh[a]t is in front. In short, time as we think of it conventionally, does not exist. Not knowing any physics, I do not explain it very well. They maintain that such as I am is not dreaming it at all, but with the conscious mind at rest, we are actually <u>seeing</u> it. Of course, Freud would say that you had merely escaped from the walls of the subconscious which I had built around you—a hidden wish.

Your Christmas gift is being sent under separate cover. I bought it fully six months ago, but when Christmas approached, I was deep in creative mood and did not emerge until I realized that the day was here. It is a Seminole Indian shirt of the Cypress clan. There are two

[2]*In Rudyard Kipling's "The Phantom Rickshaw" (1885,* Quartette Magazine*), the narrator has an affair with Agnes Keith-Wessington, whom he shortly thereafter discards for a younger girl. Agnes dies of a broken heart, and her ghost, riding in a rickshaw, haunts the narrator to madness.*

clans among the Seminoles, Tiger and Cypress. I wanted a Tiger Clan shirt for you, but Sally Tiger-tail, daughter of the chief gave me a Cypress shirt and a Tiger skirt. They are very expensive, and you will see why when you examine it. The tourists who crave them pay $15 and up for them when they can get them from the Indians. Mine were a gift from a friend, and so I could not squawk about the shirt I wanted. When I get a chance to return to the Everglades, I will send you the other. The enclosed clipping shows you how it is worn. Merely fastened at the belt as a rule. When the men button them up, they wear a flowing tie. I could not resist wearing yours a couple of times and then laundered it. But the Indians wash them first to mellow th colors down a bit. The clipping shows you how the shirts are worn. X marks Tiger clan shirt. Arrow marks Cypress clan. All the Osceolas are Tiger clan.[3] I considered sending Constance the skirt, but feared she would be too shy to wear it. I am sending them a hamper of fruit after Jan. 15, when the oranges will be fully sweet.

All my love,

Zora

TO WILLIAM BRADFORD HUIE

Jan. 28, 1955

Dear W.B.H:

What happens? I have been watching the papers to see what our "Jedge" [Judge Adams] pulled off, but not a word in the Orlando Sentinel, and except for your Christmas card, no word from you.

The article in the Negro magazine was <u>splendid.</u> It really packed a punch. I came to believe it backed him off.

Best Regards,

Zora

Zora Neale Hurston

Eau Gallie, Fla.

[3]The name "Osceola" was taken by Seminoles in memory of a famous Seminole rebel who refused to sign treaties with the United States.

TO BURROUGHS MITCHELL

[postcard postmarked May 24, 1955, Eau Gallie, Fla.]

Dear Burroughs:

Have completed two-thirds of new version of HEROD after exten-sive additional research. Shall I send it along for your scrutiny or hold until all is complete?

My best to you and family. Thanks for holiday card, etc.

Most sincerely,

Zora

TO MARY HOLLAND

Eau Gallie, Florida
June 13, 1955.

Dear, dear, dear Miss Mary:

You will never know how happy the arrival of your delayed letter made me! My soul was reaching out to you. I was so depressed by the death of Marjorie Kinnan Rawlings, first because I am deprived of the warmth of the association, and secondly because I feel that I failed her in her last extremity. She wrote me, and Burroughs Mitchell, who was editor to us both at Scribners, wrote me that she was ill. I wrote her that I would be there as soon as I could, but everything went bad for me at that time. My car. like the old one-horse shay, just fell to pieces, and there I was with no transportation, and no means to replace it, and could not bear to admit it to her lest she feel sorry for me. Next thing I knew was the announcement of her death.

You know that recently Mary Bethune died, and though I was never as close to her as I was to MKR [Rawlings] (which in all hon-esty, I feel to be her fault in that she suffered from megolomania, and could not bear success in anyone but herself and wanted only inferior people close to her so as not to diminish her own shine) we were friends of a sort, and she too had written urging me to come to Daytona Beach (when no distinguished guests would be around who might admire me also, thought she did not say it in those words, but she never wanted me present when anything big was going on) but I was too busy with my own work to go there. I do not feel the same way about not going as I did about Cross Creek[1] for I knew Bethune too well. Whenever she got urgent about seeing me it was something I could not do like taking a swipe in print at somebody who aroused her jealousy, or submitting a list of wealthy White people she could solicit for money, or soliciting them for her. As I do not trouble my friends like that for my own sake, I have no intention of doing it for others. Especially when I knew that her son, Bert, was always up to his elbows in the school treasury. Her well known, "My people," meant her son and grandson, both heavy spenders, more than it did the Negro race.

However, her death brought home to me the sad fact that while we once were four, we are now only two. The thought made me feel desolate sort of. I was unspeakably happy to receive a word from you.

I came here to Eau Gallie, a quiet little spot to sit down and do a work that I had had in contemplation for some years, a LIFE OF HEROD THE GREAT. I know that you will be startled at my choice of subject, for being bred and born to Sunday School as I was, you think of him immediately as the fiend who slaughtered the babies around Bethlehem in an attempt to do away with the Infant Jesus. I first became interested in Herod when casually looking up another matter, and came across his name in it, and the statement, "However, scholars state that there is no historical basis for the legend of the slaughter of the innocents by Herod." Then it went on to point out that the dates of Herod the Great were definitely established historically, 72–4 B.C. while no one can say when Christ was born, since He had no biographer, and there was no interest in the matter until generations later when Christianity was an established religion. The synoptic Gospels, Matthew, Mark and Luke were all written so long after His death that legend crept in, so that even they differ on events of

[1]Rawlings's home.

the life of Christ. Nobody can be sure of even their authorship. Then from Titus Livius, fragments extant of Herod's authorized biographer, Nicolaus of Damascus, Plutarch, Strabo Flavius Josephus (who follows Nicolaus closely except for his added opinions) presented this man I had always thought of as nothing but a mean little butcher, as a highly cultivated, Hellenized non-Jew, the handsomest man of his time, the greatest soldier of Southwest Asia, and ablest administrator, generous both of spirit and materially, "Herod the Over-bold," ["]Herod of the sun-like splendor" and other such epithets, and my interest and curiosity was aroused. And as I read, I perceived why the priestly scribes detested him. You know how bound the Jewish priesthood was by tradition. On returning from the Babylonian captivity, they had shut Judea in. The stranger, Gentile was absolutely taboo. For the same reason as Russia of today. The only wa[y] that Ezra and Nehemiah could maintain the absolute priestly rule that they set up, was to keep out knowledge. The 70 years in the highly civilized Persian country had shown them that. So they put up a curtain of their own.

When they accuse Herod of having brought in customs of the Gentiles and "caused the nation to sin," they are blaming the wrong man. Greek culture in Asia was given it's tremendous impetus by Alexander the Great when he crossed the Hellespont with his great army and his scholars in 326 B.C. I will not bore you with detail, but Greek culture had been working like a yeast in Palestine as well as all Asia ever since. Herod's family was of ducal status in Idumea, (northern Arab, really) highly educated for many generations, and the wealthies of all in Celesyria (Which embraced Syria, Palestine and Arabia) except for one Syrian, Saramella. They were cosmopolitan, international bankers, and even Herod's grandfather was known from Babylon to Alexandria as the "friend of kings." Herod's father was a close friend to Julius Caesar, Pompey and Marc Antony. Now place this over against a priesthood bent on maintaining their ancient rule over the nation, and you see the conflict. You can imagine the reaction of the Pharisees and priests to a king who was not only not descended from Aaron, but not even a Jew. The Jews had developed no arts except religious music, not even a style of architecture, and here comes this Herod bringing in the arts of Greece, sculpture, paintings, drama, architecture, universal education, and even athletics and built amphitheatres for the Olympic games. And the nation took to these things like ducks to water. They loved Herod, threw garlands at him when he appeared in the streets. Contrary to what I had been led to believe all along, he was beloved by the nation. Even many Pharisees and priests went over to him. You can see the feelings of the traditionalist minority, who happened, however to be setting down records. They fought a senseless and losing battle "Geography warring with time and history." After 37 years on the throne, Herod died peacefully in his bed. Flavius Josephus, the Jewish historian, a traditionalist, who boasted that he belonged to the first of the 22 courses of the priesthood, a Pharisee, and distantly related to the Jewish royal house which Herod succeeded, though he regarded Herdo [sic] as a sort of sacrilege, admits of Herod's glorious deeds, but you can see that he hates like the devil to admit of Herod's popularity with the people. He says at one place, "The people loved Herod, but it was only because of his splendid appearance," and then even more reluctantly, "and because he took such good care of them." As to Herod's reputed harshness, he says, "Herod was the first man of the world in excusing offenses against himself. When seditious men were brought before him, he gave them a talk and dismissed them. Yet he was the first man in the world to punish unfaithfulness in his own family."

That is not hard for me to understand for I think that all of us expect greater fidelity out of our own than others. If a stranger made public attacks on Senator Spessard, he would take it as no more [than] to be expected in political life, but if one of his sons was found plotting with his political enemies, not only to drive him from office but to take his life, he would react vastly different. Herod's two sons by the Jewish princess.[,] and naturally daughter of the high priest who repeatedly plotted against him, he had strangled, a very hard thing for a father to do, but as the Encyclopedia Brittinnaci [sic] observes, "Herod but outdid those who sought to do the same thing to him." Josephus, traditionalist and bent on the restoration of absolute power to the priesthood, seem[ed] to take it very hard that Herod did not allow the family of his wife to put him to death. It is not difficult to understand when we remember the tenacity of the Bourbons of modern times. The divine right to rule whether they had the ability for it or not, and whether it benefitted the nation.

Though Herod was an extraordinarily handsome figure of a man, celebrated lover (though very faithful in marriage,) brilliant and very daring soldier, so able an administrator that Augustus Caesar when his Roman governors had trouble in Asia got into the habit of writing them, "turn that province over to Herod," so that he came to rule from the Delta of the Nile to the Euphrates and Caesar still said that the territory Herod ruled was too small for his abilities, had wider and more exciting experiences than any man who has yet appeared in history, his chief interest for me is that Herod holds the unique distinction of being THE transition figure between the old Judaism and Christianity, and his influence on the trend by his attitude. Being a non-Jew in Palestine at this crucial time, a man of vast culture and favoring the culture and outlook of the West, he was invaluable in that tense renewal of the struggle for Asia which began with the siege of Troy, and is going on (again with bitter intensity) in our own time. In Herod's day, Parthia was the leader of the Asia-for-the-Asiatics, and a touch [sic] customer, as both Crassus and Marc Antony found out, and Herod threw his weight to the West. His counterpart today is Romulo of the Phillipines[2] or Chiang Kai-Shek.[3] There is another interesting parallel, for as far as it can be determined, the Parthians originally migrated into Persia, (and later overwhelmed it) from the Steppes of Russia. They are the progenitors of our modern Turks. These Parthians, from all accounts were a barbarous, unwashed gang who lived in tents and having killed off the arts of Persia, developed none of their own. Superstitious and priest-ridden (the Magi, which correspond very closely to the Jewish sanhedrin) I could understand Herod's choice. If I had to choose between the USA and any of those Asiatic nations, with the possible exception of Japan, do you suppose that I would want those unwashed, ignorant, lice-bitten barbarous Parthians messing over me? Celesyria was in a position where it had to be Rome or Parthia over them. I too would have chosen Rome. It is interesting to observe how those Parthians loved to gain their ends by lies and treachery just like modern Russia.

As to the philosophical side, Herod lent his aid to the movement out of which Christianity evolved. Thus it is ironical that he should be be the boogerman of our religion. When you review the tenets of the Essenes, that third philosophical sect in Palestine, you will find that everything Christ did or said, according to the Four Gospels was straight from it. Other things tend to confirm that both Jesus Christ

---

[2]*Carlos Peña Romulo (1899–1985) was the resident commissioner to the U.S. Congress from the Philippines (1944–46), the permanent delegate to the United Nations from the Philippines, and ambassador to the United States (1952–53, 1955–62).*
[3]*Chiang Kai-shek was expelled from China in 1949 and fled to Taiwan.*

and John the Baptist were Essenes. Of Herod's attitude towards the Essenes, Josephus complains, "Herod paid the Essenes a reverence greater than their mortal nature required." They were scattered all over Palestine, but their stronghold was Galilee, and that was Herod's favorite province, though as you know, both Essenes and Galileans were held in low esteem by the powers in Jerusalem. "The Fringes," (Pharisees), Scribes and priests in general could not lay a finger on Herod's pets while he was alive. So the doctrine of brotherly love, God the father of all mankind equally, and not just the Jews, gained ground in his reign. Not only would Christ never have been put to death under Herod, but the sanhedrin would not have dared to even start the commotion. As we Negroes say, Herod would have been all over them just like gravy over rice. It is possible that our American leftists borrowed that habit of getting up a rabble and "demonstrating" from the Jewish priesthood, for it was a favorite maneuver of theirs, Only one occurred during Herod's reign, and that was when he was on his death-bed, and they therefore thought it was safe. But the old boy (68) sprung out of bed, polished them off and went on back to bed with his ulcers.

These are my reasons for choosing Herod the Great as a subject. I have spent five years on it, three years of research alone. It is a hard, tough, assignment, but I think that it should be done. Nobody has thrown sufficient light on that First century B.C. with it's all-important implications for present-day Western civilization. Humanitarian Greek civilization sweeping the then known world; new concepts seeping into Judea and being transmuted into a new religion for though Greece had fallen before Rome, the sweep of Greek culture was rather accelerated than destroyed. Triumphant Rome had merely won the right to disseminate it. Logos, The Word, (see prologue to St. John) had come into Palestine from India and taken hold of Jewish thought. A new and greater concept of God. Then there was the dynamic personality of Herod, the soldier, the statesman, seeing friendship as a religion, and far from being the mere stooge of Rome as pictured by his detractors, "Allow me to be a realist and a rationalist: it is history and history alone, which without involving us in actual danger, will mature our judgment and prepare us to take the right views, whatever may be the crisis or the posture of affairs. Rome will be the center of history and the world for the next thousand years." So the handsome six-footer on his Palomina stallion (One authority insists that his family was Aryan from Pheonicia) became King of the Jews and so stamped his personality upon Asia that the first three-quarters of the First century of Christianity cannot be disassociated from him or his descendants. His boyhood was touched by Pompey, Julius Caeser, and his early manhood by Cassius, Marc Antony, Cleopatra, (she fell in love with him but was rebuffed) Augustus Caesar, Agrippa (the Roman Commander-in-chief under Augustus) and all the famous men of his age and was on intimate terms with thwm. Caesar offered to take Herod two sons as his houseguests during their years of study at Rome, but Pollio, the Consul grabbed them. Such a tragic waste of time money and opportunity on conceited stupidity!

I am more than two-thirds done with the final writing, and hope and pray that Scribners will be pleased with it. Please do not laugh at me. but I think that the subject is so important that I broached Sir Winston Churchill to do a running comment on the political implications of each chapter. He wrote graciously that he would do it if it were not for the fact that he had refused several other writers who asked him to colaborate, and would thus give offense if he did it for me. Besides, his health was not too good now. Maybe he was only giving me a quick brush-off, but he was very nice about it. I wish some scholar like Senator Spessard would do it, but having escaped with my life from bra[s]hing Sir Winston, maybe I ought to be thankful and keep my big mouth shut. Senator Spessard is plenty spry and does not have to cross any ocean to get to me.

The witholding of your letter for five years burns me up. That address is Fred Irvine at Miami. I was on his boat with the idea of returning to Honduras to write some articles. Irvine said he would bring back lobsters. He kept me waiting for over five months expecting to sail any day. It was his mother who revealed to me that he never had any intention of going at all, that he had lured me to Miami for the use of my name on his boat. It seems that he had a very poor character with folks along the waterfront, and I had a good one and he was using me for a cover to hide some shady deals. He actually beat his mother for exposing him to me, and I left the boat and spent several months ghosting a book for Judge Smathers, father of the Senator. I had wasted so much money while I was vainly expecting to go to Central America. I suppose when he found your letter in the box, he was scared to forward it, lest I sick you on him. The rat! He is now an

American citizen, but English born, and just like Charlie Chaplin. Always messing around with some young girl. He has had five wives and none over 16 when he got hold of them, to say nothing of some of his other activities. His mother said, and he said the same thing himself, that he respected me more than any individual he had ever met, and that is why he was so furious when his mother let me know about certain of his "deals." For example, picking up boys in their late teens allegedly to work on his boat, then sending them out to steal things off of other boats which Irvine then sold. Notice his cunning in writing on your envelope, "Not at this address." He knew only too well that I was at the Smathers. So very sorry that I missed the scarf. I'll bet you it was pretty and red. Having vegetated here so long on this book, I'd love to dress up for a change. Having spent so much on research, you know that I cannot afford to buy new clothes, but please consider that this is a statement of fact and not a "touch."

God love and bless you and all your house, and I am certainly coming to Bartow when you come home.[4]

I know that you do not mess with politics, but I'm wondering out loud to Senator Spessard if the USA is not getting a Minister of Propaganda on the quiet. I am a Republican, but I cannot avoid noting how Dr. Gallup,[5] by timing, by selection of subject, and by the way it is put, manages to forever make Eisenhower sound invincible so as to discourage other aspirants of both parties. Then I read somewhere that he holds a position under Eisenhower on the Voice of America or something like that. If so, he cannot but be prejudiced. Next thing we know we will have a dictatorship on our hands. Further, I note Ike's fondness for publishers. If he hires them all up, where will be public opinion in the USA? He's got the majority of the big ones on his payroll already. It has been noted that it is almost impossible to get in a word edgeways about this segregation mess right now. NONE OF THE BIG MAGAZINES WILL ALLOW A WORD SAID AGAINST IT. I have tried. In fear of my freedom, I am voting Democratic next time.

With loving and faithful feelings,
Zora

---

[4] *Bartow, Florida, Senator Holland's home and birthplace.*
[5] *George H. Gallup (1901–84) founded the Gallup Poll in 1935, originally called America Speaks.*

TO MRS. THOMAS MARTIN [1]

Eau Gallie, Fla.
June 20, 1955.

Thanks so much for the clippings. Some among them I had never seen. There is a matter that has me worried now. I sent the Mss of Herod The Great to Mr. Burroughs Mitchell by Express on June 3, but have not had a card saying it arrived as yet.

Most sincerely,
Zora Neale Hurston

TO MAX EASTMAN

Eau Gallie, Fla.
August 2, 1955.

Dear Max Eastman:

I seek your advice on a very serious matter. Nearly ten years ago I fell in love with the story of the life of Herod the Great. I have done enormous research on it, and now it is almost all written. I think that Scribners is a little timid about it on account of the possible opposition of the Catholic church. Bishop Fulton Sheen advised me to do "as a good Catholic" which means that I must do the man an injustice in order not to disturb the established Feast of the Innocents.

That is all very well and good for the Catholic church, but I have a keen sense of justice by nature, and having been grossly slandered myself by a group of homosexuals, I am even more careful about the truth.[1] I have consulted every possible source, religious as well as other-

---

[1] *Barbara M. Martin worked as an assistant to Burroughs Mitchell.*

[1] *Hurston presumably refers here to Richard Rochester and the group behind the spurious story in the* Baltimore Afro-American. *There is no evidence that they were homosexuals; elsewhere Hurston accuses them of being communists. Given that many leading figures of the Harlem Renaissance were purportedly homosexual or bisexual, it is also possible that Hurston refers here to earlier disappointments, including her difficulties with Locke—who indeed favored his male protégés—over Charlotte Osgood Mason, her patron.*

wise, and there is NO historical background for the story in Matthew 2, that Herod butchered those children. <u>He died in 4 B.C.</u> There are other facts which show that it is impossible for Herod to have done such a thing. I do not plan to argue the matter, just ignore it.

Outside of his life being perhaps the most dramatic of any ruler that ever lived, there are two other reasons why I think that it is important to be done. 1. It throws light on the First Century B.C. when so m[u]ch was happening that influences our times—rise of Rome, East-West struggle for Asia, emergence of new religious philosophy, etc. 2. New concept of God and His relationship to man which had been working like a yeast in Palestine for 300 years emerging, formulated at last as what is now known as Christianity. It was a movement totally within the Jewish people NOT A SUDDEN AND MIRACU-LOUS HAPPENING AS IS TOLD IN THE NEW TESTAMENT. The church is not willing for that to be dwelt upon either, as being destructive to the divinity of Christ. I think that it <u>should</u> be told to dispel the common belief that Christianity is and was a non-Jewish affair that the Jews tried to stifle by murdering Christ. The first 100 years was almost purely Jewish, even after the death of Christ. It might tend to a better understanding of the Jews. The error lies in the fact that the church heads keep on holding up a picture of the Jews in that First century B.C. as if they were the same people who came out of Egypt, as if they did not evolve philosophically like other peoples, which is far from true. 3. Herod the Great is truly a heroic figure of a man. He dared like hell. The intimate friend of both Marc Antony and Augustus Caesar and Cleopatra, he held his own among them. He was not a Jew by blood, but, like many of immigrant stock in the USA, his patriotism was more flaming than those of the blood. In spirit, Herod was Jew of the Jews, for which the nation adored him. When he, in company with Sosius, the Roman general in 37 B.C. he offered to fight Rome if one Roman pushed his way into the Holy of Holies, or plundered a single house in Jerusalem or violated one Jewish woman. There are other and even more dramatic instances of his love of country. As to his personal life, it might have been plotted by Hollywood itself.

Now, would you dare to do the book if you were in my place? If so, as busy as you are, would you glance over the manuscript to see if I have gone wrong anywhere in spirit so far? I am fairly certain of my facts. You must realize how important I think the account is, outside of

it's story-quality. There, it is tops. I wonder what an intellectual like
Eugene Lyons would think of it's appearance.

My very best to you and yours and for any minute you might give
Herod the Great. It is almost dawn and sleep is coming down over
my eyes.

With sincerity,
Zora Neale Hurston

TO THE *ORLANDO SENTINEL*

[August 11, 1955]

Editor:

I promised God and some other responsible characters, including a
bench of bishops, that I was not going to part my lips concerning the
U.S. Supreme Court decision on ending segregation in the public
schools of the South. But since a lot of time has passed and no one
seems to touch on what to me appears to be the most important point
in the hassle, I break my silence just this once. Consider me as just
thinking out loud.

The whole matter revolves around the self-respect of my people.
How much satisfaction can I get from a court order for somebody to
associate with me who does not wish me near them? The American
Indian has never been spoken of as a minority and chiefly because
there is no whine in the Indian. Certainly he fought, and valiantly for
his lands, and rightfully so, but it is inconceivable of an Indian to seek
forcible association with anyone. His well known pride and self-
respect would save him from that. I take the Indian position.

Now a great clamor will arise in certain quarters that I seek to
deny the Negro children of the South their rights, and therefore I am
one of those "handkerchief-head niggers" who bow low before the
white man and sell out my own people out of cowardice. However an
analytical glance will show that that is not the case.

If there are not adequate Negro schools in Florida, and there is some
residual, some inherent and unchangeable quality in white schools, impossible to duplicate anywhere else, then I am the first to insist that Ne-

gro children of Florida be allowed to share this boon. But if there are adequate Negro schools and prepared instructors and instructions, then there is nothing different except the presence of white people.

For this reason, I regard the ruling of the U.S. Supreme Court as insulting rather than honoring my race. Since the days of the never-to-be-sufficiently deplored Reconstruction, there has been current the belief that there is no great[er] delight to Negroes than physical association with whites. The doctrine of the white mare. Those familiar with the habits of mules are aware that any mule, if not restrained, will automatically follow a white mare. Dishonest mule-traders made money out of this knowledge in the old days.

Lead a white mare along a country road and slyly open the gate and the mules in the lot would run out and follow this mare. This ruling being conceived and brought forth in a sly political medium with eyes on '56, and brought forth in the same spirit and for the same purpose, it is clear that they have taken the old notion to heart and acted upon it. It is a cunning opening of the barnyard gate wit[h] the white mare ambling past. We are expected to hasten pell-mell after her.

It is most astonishing that this should be tried just when the nation is exerting itself to shake off the evils of Communist penetration. It is to be recalled that Moscow, being made aware of this folk belief, made it the main plank in their campaign to win the American Negro from the 1920's on. It was the come-on stuff. Join the party and get yourself a white wife or husband. To supply the expected demand, the party had scraped up this-and-that off of park benches and skid rows and held them in stock for us. The highest types of Negroes were held to be just panting to get hold of one of these objects. Seeing how flat that program fell, it is astonishing that it would be so soon revived. Politics does indeed make strange bedfellows.

But the South had better beware in another direction. While it is being frantic over the segregation ruling, it had better keep its eyes open for more important things. One instance of Govt by fiat has been rammed down its throat. It is possible that the end of segregation is not here and never meant to be here at present, but the attention of the South directed on what was calculated to keep us busy while more ominous things were brought to pass. The stubborn South and the Midwest kept this nation from being dragged farther to the left than it was during the New Deal.

But what if it is contemplated to do away with the two-party system and arrive at Govt by administrative decree? No questions allowed and no information given out from the administrative dept? We could get more rulings on the same subject and more far-reaching any day. It pays to weigh every saving and action, however trivial as indicating a trend.

In the ruling on segregation, the unsuspecting nation might have witnessed a trial-balloon. A relatively safe one, since it is sectional and on a matter not likely to arouse other sections of the nation to the support of the South. If it goes off fairly well, a precedent has been established. Govt by fiat can replace the Constitution. You don't have to credit me with too much intelligence and penetration, just so you watch carefully and think.

Meanwhile, personally, I am not delighted. I am not persuaded and elevated by the white mare technique. Negro schools in the state are in very good shape and on the improve. We are fortunate in having Dr. D.E. Williams as head and driving force of Negro instruction.[1] Dr. Williams is relentless in his drive to improve both physical equipment and teacher-quality. He has accomplished wonder[s] in the 20 years past and it is to be expected that he will double that in the future.

It is well known that I have no sympathy nor respect for the 'tragedy of color' school of thought among us, whose fountain-head is the pressure group concerned in this court ruling. I can see no tragedy in being too dark to be invited to a white school social affair. The Supreme Court would have pleased me more if they had concerned themselves about enforcing the compulsory education provisions for Negroes in the South as is done for white children. The next 10 years would be better spent in appointing truant officers and looking after conditions in the homes from which the children come. Use to the limit what we already have.

Thems my sentiments and I am sticking by them. Growth from within. Ethical and cultural desegregation. It is a contradiction in terms to scream race pride and equality while at the same time spurning Negro teachers and self-association. That old white mare business can go racking on down the road for all I care.

Zora Neale Hurston
Eau Gallie

---

[1] *D. E. Williams was the Florida state supervisor of Rural Negro Schools for almost fifty years.*

TO BURROUGHS MITCHELL

Eau Gallie, Florida
August 12, 1955.

Dear Burroughs Mitchell:

I have been off on a speaking tour and found both your kind letter
and the manuscript waiting here for me on my return. Naturally, I am
sorry that you found HEROD THE GREAT disappointing, but do not
feel concerned about the refusal upon me. I am my old self and can
take it easily.[1]

However, I cannot understand the criticism that the work does not
represent that first century B.C. That was where I spent so much time
in research. My conclusion is this: it does not represent the accepted
traditions of the period, but it does set forth the <u>facts.</u> I checked with
various well known historians AND churchmen on that score. Even a
casual study will reveal that more fables and fictions have been concocted and sanctified by church tradition than can be imagined, and
there is no wish to have them disturbed. One churchman told me that
frankly. The enormous distortions rose from the fact that His disciples
were simple, unlearned men who never understood what He was saying. On his death, Peter, the most influential of them, immediately returned to the old Jewish way though calling it Christianity. He broke
with Paul who did have some concept of the philosophy of Christ. The
early churches followed Peter so that for nearly 300 years, what we
know as the New Testament had practically no standing. The result is
that whatever was rejected by the Jewish leaders has been rejected by
the church. The Jewish leaders were resistting Greek culture and naturally not only condemned it, but all those who [s]ponsored it. Origen,
St. Augustine nad Justin, the most influential church fathers in the
formation of christianity, followed suit. Their findings followed tradition and the church has followed them. I know that you are far too
busy to go through the studies that I did, but all you need read is the

---

[1]*On July 21, Mitchell had written that though they had read* Herod the Great *numerous times and were
"truly sorry" to say so, they were rejecting the manuscript, which seemed to them unengaging and "difficult"
reading.*

article CANON Encyclopedia Brittanica, and you will gain some idea of what went on. (I have the Ninth edition) I know that the church did not exist in B.C., but the suppressions and distortions of the period were later perpetrated by churchmen to fit thier position. The historians do not agree with them. It is preposterous to pretend that the world of that time was not in flux and turmoil. Old philosophies were dying and the new was being born; Rome was on the march; the old struggle for Asia was flaming with Parthia as the new champion of Asia-for the Asiatics Judea was torn between Greek culture and thr [sic] old Judaism. That is the picture of the First Century B.C. and nobody can get away from it. What other picture can you offer? That is, without violating history? It really would be interesting to know who your adviser was.[2]

But please, please do not think that I feel badly about the rejection. I was astonished myself how easily I felt. Perhaps it is because I have such faith in the material and now my conviction that I can handle it. All is well.

Right now, the weather here is awful. Atmosphere of hurricane when there is a peculiar, striking-down kind of heat that characterizes the approach of a hurricane. Perhaps Diane will hit us in a day or so, or possibly pas[s] us by, but we feel her presence just the same. It is like living and moving in a furnace where the fires have just been banked and gusts of hot air flow about you. A threatening kind of feeling.[3]

I hope that all goes well with you and family. Have you succeeded in adopting a baby as yet? At times I have wished that I might have one of those from Japan where the mothers were unwed by American fathers. Then again, I am glad that I have none to tie me down.

All my love, sincere love and gratitude to you and Mrs. Mitchell.

> With faithful feelings,
> Zora
> Zora Neale Hurston

---

[2]*Mitchell had written only that the story was not "vivid." His letter did not challenge Hurston's accuracy; in fact, he complimented her command of the material.*

[3]*Hurricane Diane indeed bypassed Florida but caused massive flooding in New England between August 17 and August 20.*

TO MARGRIT DE SABLONIÈRE

ROUTE 1, BOX 86-E
EAU GALLIE, FLORIDA, U.S.A.
DEC. 3, 1955.

Dear Madam Sablonière:

Please excuse my writing you by hand, but no sooner did I get the envelope addressed to you than my typewriter go out of order. I am conscious that my handwriting is not very good.

A million thanks for your kind and understanding letter. I have been astonished that my letter to The Orlando Sentinel has caused such a sensation over the whole United States. But when I realized the intense and bitter contention among some Negroes for physical contact with the Whites, I can see why the astonishment that one (myself) should hold that physical contact means nothing unless the spirit is also there, and therefore see small value in it. I actually do feel insulted when a certain type of white person hastens to effuse to me how noble they are to grant me their presence. But unfortunately, many who call themselves "leaders" of Negroes in America actually are unaware of the insulting patronage and rejoice in it. It is not that I have any race prejudice, for it is well known that I have numerous white friends, but they are <u>friends</u>, not merely some who seek to earn a spurious "merit" by patronizing Negroes, or by seeking political advancement through our votes.

I am getting DUST TRACKS ON A ROAD to you, and also THEIR EYES WERE WATCHING GOD, which has had several foreign translations. I hope that they will please you. At any rate, whether anything comes of it or not, my heart is warmed by your magnificent generosity of soul.[1]

I have been ill with gall-bladder trouble for two years, but now recovering nicely and back to work.[2] I am trying something more diffi-

---

[1] *Some of Hurston's works were translated into Japanese, Spanish, French, Swedish, Italian, Korean, and German. Sablonière's translations were either unpublished or simply unfinished.*

[2] *Hurston suffered from chronic health problems, including an ulcer, high blood pressure, intestinal and stomach ailments, gallbladder infection, and an irritated colon. Some of these were the result of her travel in Honduras.*

cult than ever before. I am attempting a LIFE OF HEROD THE GREAT. You will wonder about my choice, but he was a great and influential character of his time, and the answer to what is going on in Europe, Asia, and America lies in that first century B.C. Besides he was dynamic, the handsomest man of his time, a great lover, courageous to reckless, and I do not believe that any other man in public life anywhere ever lived such a dramatic life so that the epithet was applied to him "Herod of the sun-like splendor." Pray for my success, please.

With faithful feelings
Zora Neale Hurston

TO THE REFERENCE LIBRARIANS, MIAMI PUBLIC LIBRARY

Box 86-E, Route #1
Eau Gallie, Florida
December 6, 1955.

Dear KEEPERS OF THE SACRED SPRING:

Or Vestal Virgins of the Shrine of Knowledge, I salute you and hastily state that I do not wish you to send me any books.[1] What I want is really the address where I can buy the books, DUST TRACKS ON A ROAD, THEIR EYES WERE WATCHING GOD to send to a translator in Holland, a Madame Margrit de Sabloniere, who urges me to get them for her.

It appears that having read a recent short article by me, she is convinced that a publisher in Holland, WERELDBIBLIOTHEEK AND MEULENHOFF will be interested in doing especially DUST TRACKS and possibly both.

My excuse or explanation for having disturbed you so unreasonably was that on the reception of the letter from Mme. Sabloniere I was really ill, what the illiterate Negroes would call ill-sick which means very bad, approaching the worst degree starting off with "poorly." I

---

[1] *On December 13, 1955, Edna H. Savoya wrote Hurston to say that, as asked, she would not be sending her books.*

had a gall-bladder infection, to say nothing of being harrassed with ghosting a book (anti-women) for Col. Lasher.[2] My Physician here is of the opinion that being bothered with Lasher was what upset my digestive and elimination system to the extent of my serious illness—Lasher being so emotionally off-balance himself, so I gladly washed my hands of his book. I had such a high temperature and was so off-normal in every way, that I mumbled on receoiving the letter from Holland that I did not have the books at hand and wished you could take care of it for me. That was very bad of me, because that was all his megalomania required to give him opportunity to introduce himself to you. Recently, he had to return to New York in connection with his domestic affairs answering the numerous suits his wife has brought against him, and lost no time in going to Scribners, my publishers and telling my editor that I was collaborating on his book (a sales talk) and to Harpers also. I had to write and make corrections, explaining that I was merely ghosting. So please forgive me any disturbance you have had.

Now that I am free of ghosting an impossible book and regaining my health and sanity, I am deep in my own book and a couple of short pieces.[3] I send you all my deep love and gratitude and all the finest and shiniest wishes that this world can afford.

With most faithful feelings,
Zora Neale Hurston

Madame Margrit de Sablonière
Maredijk 23,
Leiden, Holland.

---

[2]According to Robert Hemenway, Hurston abandoned this project when it became apparent that Lasher was interested in little more than a personal attack on his wife.

[3]Hurston was still working on her Herod book at this time, which Scribner's rejected.

TO BURROUGHS MITCHELL

[1955]
Route 1, Box 86E.
Eau Gallie, Fla.

Dear Burroughs:

A hurried note to you because I had a letter from Col. Lasher informing me that he had seen you and told you that the book I am ghosting for him "was the best book that I had ever written." You must realize that the statement makes no sense because it is <u>not</u> my book. I am merely doing the best I can with his ideas. It is not that I am knocking Crowing Hen, but you can see that it is impossible to make comparisons when it is not really my work in full. He should have asked my permission before using my name under the circumstances. Let him accept responsibility for his own planning.

My best goodest wishes to you all.

Sincerely,
Zora

TO MARGRIT DE SABLONIÈRE

Box 86-C, Route #1
Eau Gallie, Florida
March 15, 1956.

Beloved Margrit:

You have done nor said anything except being your incomparable and soulful self. The fault is all mine. I told you that I had been seriously ill, but just as I got to feeling fine and down to work again, the house where I am living has been sold and I have been terribly distressed at the thought and necessity of stopping everything to pack up my numerous papers and books to find another location.

I have found the books at last through a book-hunting agency, and DUST TRACK[S] ON A ROAD should reach you in a few days now. Soon THEIR EYES WERE WATCHING GOD will come to you also through the same agency.

This segregation affair is a mess! (I employ a colloquism here) Both sides are going all out of bounds in the search for sensationalism. It is sickening. My nature would not permit me to go through what Authorine [sic] Lucy[1] undertook. I could not bear to be so rejected. I am a sensitive soul, so I would rather go on to some school where I would be welcome. What they do not say is that there are two magnificent Negro institutions of learning in the state of Alabama which she could attend easily. 1. Tuskegee, 2. Talladega, both with the same library course which she says she wants. At the same time, the University of Alabama is supported by state funds, and so any resident of the state is entitled to attend. I give yiu [sic] the facts in the case. O course, the NAACP is using her to make a test case and force the issue, but their choice of a contestant could have been much better. She is 26, already a college graduate, and thus obviously not acting in good faith. And their paying her $300 per month to contest does not make it look any better. They should have chosen some person just out of high school and prepared for a college entrance for the test.

Naturally, I hope that some publisher will consider publishing my book in your country. Do you think that you could sell a few articles by me on the segregation situation here over there? As a Negro, you know that I cannot be in favor of segregation, but I do deplore the way they go about ending it. It will be understandable there bexause of the Dutch experiences in Indonesia and other places. If it can be arranged, you get your percentage as an agent.

With most admiring and faithful feelings,
Zora
Zora Neale Hurston

---

[1]*Autherine Lucy was the first black student admitted to the University of Alabama.*

RECIPIENT UNKNOWN

(probably Margrit de Sablonière)

May 9, 1956.
Eau Gallie, Florida.

Dear, dear Friend:

I have been made very unhappy. Only yesterday your parcel was delivered to me, but it had been opened and robbed. The containers were still there, but everything you sent had been removed except three post cards, 1. Woman's head of bronze, Benin, 2, Mask used at funerals, 3 woman and child. I am enraged at the brazen theft of the things you sent me. I am demanding an investigation by the Federal Bureau of Investigation. It occurred at either the Customs Inspection or at the Post Office.

I am writing to Martin Anderson, owner-publisher of the OR-LANDO SENTINEL-STAR, Orlando, Florida, to send you a photo of me. He has some on hand for that purpose. Perhaps it will be well if you made the request also and make him realize the urgency and get it to you quickly. My book seems to have been delayed a whole month in transit. It should have come to you about March 16. I do not know if Lippincott has still some copies of a sketch by the noted artist Schrieber[1] of me.

My hope is to leave Eau Gallie by the end of this week. Possibly I shall go to Miami, Florida. I will advise you immediately.

May you have every success for yourself in the articles on me. I am trying to promote a tour of Europe by me with a concert group, and if I get the assent, I shall write you at once so that if there is any way that you can share in it, you can profit by it.

> Devotedly yours,
> Zora Neale Hurston

---

[1]*Probably Belgian artist Georges Schreiber (1904–77), whose drawings of writers and celebrities appeared in* Fortune, Saturday Review, *and the* Nation.

TO MARGRIT DE SABLONIÈRE

516½ King Street
Cocoa, Florida
November 7, 1956

Dear Sister Artist:

My long silence can be explained by the unsettling things growing out of this race disturbance here.[1] I will write you in detail later when I get this confounded sputtering ribbon off my typewriter which the mechanic put on when I had it overhauled.

Things began to stir unhappily in this area just about the time that your magnificent article appeared. No physical violence touched me, but the surliness, the unthinking soul of the mob prowled the state. I was too unhappy for any normal activity. I pray that you can understand and forgive me.

June 18, I accepted the post as librarian at the Technical Library (PAN AMERICAN WORLD AIRWAYS, INC) at the Patrick Air Force Base, Guided Missiles Division near here. I get no great salary, $325 per month, and that keeps me from worrying about money as I strive now to finish my book.[2] In six more weeks, I can get reduced rates for travel by air, and circumstances being favorable, hope to peep in on you in the Spring.

Naturally, I join you in prayer that the publisher accepts the book.

Be assured that now, each day my soul emerges more from it's hiding place. I am returning to a normal outlook on life. To you, Margrit de Sabloniere, I send my deepest respect as an artist, my regards as a friend, and my hopes for your future success.

With faithful feelings,
Zora

My ball-point pen is playing one of it's nasty tricks on me tonight. No ink will come from it, so I sign with pencil.

---

[1] *The NAACP was particularly active at this time, organizing sit-ins at Kress and Woolworth stores and supermarket and bus boycotts in nearby Orange County.*
[2] Herod the Great.

TO EDWARD EVERETT HURSTON

[postcard postmarked December 3, 1956, Cocoa, Fla.]

Plenty welcome waiting here for you from me, and plenty jobs at Patrick Air Force Base.

Love
Aunt Zora

TO EVERETT AND IVY HURSTON

516½ King St.
Cocoa, Fla.
Jan. 8, 1957

Dear Everett & Ivy:

So very glad to have any kind of a word from <u>you</u>. Never doubt that I love you and stand <u>forever</u> in your corner. I am glad that you have found love and you must send me snapshots of your wife and yourself.

I have told your father 100 times that you are a genius and therefore cannot be like average people. Have no fear, you will come out OK in the end.

There is a debt of $200^{00} that I have to pay off on my jaloppy, then I will help you on yours. Your fruit will be shipped on Sat. [illegible]. I am tempted to quit this job so those who [?] did not love me so before can go back to their old ways.[1] I am not fooled one bit. You know what I mean. If you want to know the truth, I don't care a hang about anybody but you.

All my love
Aunt Zora.

---

[1] *Hurston had begun working at the Patrick Air Force Base as a librarian in June 1956. She was fired from the job in May 1957.*

TO EVERETT EDWARD HURSTON

516½ King Street
Cocoa, Florida
March 31, 1957

Dear E. Jr.

Now, look what you went and done? Here I had me a pet stomach ulcer which I had raised from a pup, and you go and make me laugh out loud and scare it off. In the first place, nobody is supposed to have ulcers but rich folks loaded down with responsibilities for taking care of their loot. You know that I'm not guilty of the millions of bucks. Second, ulcers are very rare in females. Therefore you can see how hard it was for me to get hold of a baby ulcer and raise it up. Then you have to up and run it off from home. However, there is a local acquaintance with $3,000,000 who had not an ulcer to his name and therefore was looked down upon by other millionaires. He was very glad to take out a five-year lease on my fugitive ulcer and give it a good home. Poor thing! But I guess it will get along all right in its new home. That frantic hand you drew grabbing after the fleeting buck was a killer! I laugh and laugh everytime I look at it. It goes to prove my contention that you have the talent you just do not believe in yourself enough. Chalk up another score against Myrtis. After I saw what she was like I never could understand how your father could take it!

Maybe he really means to do something about it now for he told me 2 months ago that he was determined about it. It has always been my impression that he had ceased to care for her. It was the financial angle that bothered him.

Now as to your own marriage—I think that you are too much like me to be tied up when you are not happy regardless of the good qualities of the other party. So do not count on my kicking the bucket if you call it a day. In fact, artistic people just dont go for much tying down even for the economic safety angle. Your father was terribly distressed at first, but then he wrote that it was something you had to work out for yourself, even though he felt that your wife was a fine person & good for you. Your own happiness came first with him.

Thems my sentiments also. That goes for both of you E.E's. You dont live but once and you might as well be as happy as possible on this one trip on earth. He should have shucked off Myrtis years ago and been a contented and self-respecting man. As you harked—take off at the dropping of a hat—in fact, drop the hat yourself.

The variety of oranges you got was pineapples and temples with very thin skin like a tangerine. I will send some more next week but this time it will be Valencias, because it is too late for anything else. Oh yes, you got navels last time too. Valencias make a pretty show and are the most profitable to grow, but to me the [illegible]

Since your father is going to buy property down here & no doubt put in a few fruit trees, I will tell you the names of the most popular oranges & grapefruits

1. Parson Browns = [larg oranges—x-ed out]
1. Parson Brown = the first orange ready for the market in the Fall. Start picking in late October or early November. Skin a little thick, fairly good favor
2. Pineapple = Mid-November on. Excellent flavor when allowed to ripen on tree. Floridians seldom eat <u>any</u> orange until after Christmas. We sell 'em to the Yankees before Christmas.
3. King Orange = flat bud-end like a tangerine & loose rough skin like a tangerine. Pinkish-yellow meat like a bitter-sweet. Top of all oranges in quality & price.
4. Temple = resembles King in shape & color. Very fine in quality. I prefer temples to Kings.
5. Navels = large, sweet when allowed to fully ripen on tree. little navel at bud-end.
6. Satsuma = late orange, appears to be a cross with tangerine
7. Valencias = latest crop matures from March on. Brings high prices because there is no competition & it makes a fine show in a package.

Grapefruit
1. Marsh Seedless = "white" meat, large & sweet
2. Pink = best variety has dark pink meat very popular with Yankees, but I think that a white meat grapefruit with seeds top all for flavor.

It has been my dream for years that you would illustrate a book of mine. I <u>know</u> that the stuff is there. You just do not as yet recognize your own talents. But again like me, through spiritual upset in youth. You are a late bloomer. That is to the good in a way. You will appear on the scene with more maturity & finish in your work. We will discuss the whole thing at length at the first opportunity.

Right now, I am overcome with happiness over you & your father finding the good & the glorious in each other. I was afraid at my last writing that your marital woes might hurt you with him.

> See you later, Alligator—
> With all my love,
> Aunt Zora

2 more payments on the Willys Station wagon & I will be free. I am going to save the tough old jaloppy for you, me & [remainder illegible]

TO JOSEPHINE LEIGHTON [1]

[typed addition to letter from Leighton dated June 18, 1957, inquiring about Hurston's address]

Hello Folks:

The new address is Box 75, Route #2, Merritt Island, Fla. I am living in a house-trailer now for privacy to work and like it very much.

> Best regards to all.
> Zora Neale Hurston

---

[1] *Administrative assistant, Guggenheim Memorial Foundation.*

TO HERBERT SHEEN

Box 75, Route #2
Merritt Island, Florida
June 28, 1957.

Dear Herbert:

My, but you made a conquest of Fulcher! You overwhelmed her like Alexander the Great did Darius. This is no deprecation of your charms, but the fact is, she has never come into contact with upper-class Negroes before you and myself. Only servants. She had a poor backgraound herself lacking the things that money and education bring, but now they are making some money. She was carried away with you as I knew she would be. She is only now beginning to be conscious of the power of background; that wealth is only a part of social acceptance. I saw the bewilderment in her eyes when she and I were at the home of Mrs. Stewart, a multi-millionaire widow here on the Island. Mrs. Stewart is originally from Mississippi, but she and I have both travelled and in some in[s]tances, to the same places; she is an educated woman, knows some of the big familily names in New York that I do, and so we find plenty ground to meet on. Also, from association, I know good social usage, which always hepls.

Congratulations on your Ethel![1] I am so glad that you have come into a calm, safe harbor at last. I am very, very happy for you. I suffered for you while you floundered out of your natural waters. Therefore now I feel calm and happy for you too. You deserve all that you get from her. God balances the sheet in time.

Likewise, conjure up no sense of guilt about your children. You did the best you could. Bob, my oldest and M.D. brother died in great disappointment over his, after doing everything he could to point them along a scholarly course and earning honors for themselves in life. It did not come off. Perhaps too much ease and money in their childhood. My brother Everett who owns 8 apartment hpuses in Brooklyn has not been able to induce his only child to show any desire to follow

---

[1]Probably the "young lady" to whom Hurston refers earlier. See Hurston to Herbert Sheen, March 31, 1953.

in his steps. However, I blame my brother in this case for trying to twist nature. Everett, Jr. showed marked artistic talents from an early age. His father is very clever mechanically, and has hounded him to be like that. His son is mightly skilled with a drawing-pencil or brush, and I tried to persuade him to let him go his own way, which I am certain he will do eventually. He was born the same year as your Tony. Do any of yours show the bent for music as you do? It is very important to select a mother for your children for you must remember that the mother is with the children more than the father and gives them their direction in life.

As for myself, I have gone through a period that might appear outwardly unprofitable, but in reality extremely important. A taking-in period like the gestation of a prospective mother. Now, I am ready to give forth again. I feel that I have made phenominal growth as a creative artist. Yes, I am doing a book as well as some [s]hort stuff.

I am very pleased that you are now enriching your life by travel. You and Ethel must go somewhere as often as you can. All you can take with you is the experiences of your life. You can't take your bank account. Travel broadens and educates. It maketh the full man.

I live in a house-trailer here on Merritt Island which is only across the river from Cocoa, Florida. I have a station-wagon which I call "the truck" because I haul so much in it. After certain things are accomplished, I plan to go back to New York in the Spring, but not to live permanently. That is suicide for a creative artist. You know about the literary parties, etc. that sap everything out of you. Ernest Hemmingway [sic], also a Scribners author beats me hopping around and living informally. He suggested that I run over to the Isles of Pines [sic], an island belonging to Cuba and buy a spot. It is not so well built up an[d] one can find quiet there to work. He did his last book there and is going back. I have no sentimental involvements. I have no talent for business nor finance, but I do not mind that as Mrs. Fulcher thinks. I am not materialistic. I do take a certain satisfaction in knowing that my writing are used in many of the great universities both here and abroad, both literary and anthropological. If I happen to die without money, somebody will bury me, though I do not wish it to be that way.

Again, my very best to you and your Ethel. May every good and beautiful thing be yours.

Devotedly,
Zora Neale Hurston

P.S. All of my papers, letters, etc. that are not already in the Library at Yale are pledged to the Library of the U of Florida at Gainesville. My correspondence with you goes too unless you object.[1]

Zora

TO MARY HOLLAND

Box 75, Route #2
Merritt Island, Florida
June 27, 1957.

Dear Miz' Mary:

I am living in a house-trailer out here on the Island, which I am sure you know all about. It's peculiar climate so tropical for this far north in Florida and it's plentiful mosquitoes have gotten much publicity.

So glad to hear from you. Perhaps it is only a coincidence and not really Extra Sensory Perception, but I was contemplating writing you myself. I see by the papers that Ex-Senator Claude Pepper is beginning to circulate around which arouses the suspicion in me that he hopes to get the nomination to oppose your husband. As was proved during his campaign against Senator Smathers, the man is abstiffically a fraud. Just another of those opportunist[s] who go for "liberal" (the word ought really to be spelled "liperal" or just "lipper") so far as this race business is concerned. I worked hard and effectively agaisnt Pepper in Miami, where he would naturally pull a heavy Negro vote. I pointed out that he was nothing but talk. Spicy to listen to, but no substance to the thing, and finally boiled it down to the slogan, "You cant make a meal off of Pepper." The NAACP is quite annoyed with me because I continue to insist that they are working on the wrong end of the Negro. All their fights boil down to a matter of <u>seats</u>. Knowing conditions as I do, I clamor that improvements should start on the other end. Let us learn more about a better, a higher and cleaner way of life and all other things will follow. Let us not concern ourselves so

---

[1]*This correspondence did not go to Gainesville.*

much about wherev we are going to sit, but rather what we are going to DO to contribute to the welfare of this nation. Be givers and not receivers only. That is the only answer, and eventually we will be driven to it whether we will or not.

I have been concerned in another matter of which race plays only a minor part. From June 18, 1956-May 10, 1957 I was a librarian at Technical Library at Patrick Air Force Base. There was a peculiar situation there which put me on the spot almost immediately. The Government has said that there must bo [sic] no discrimination in hiring on government contracts. I was hired without any trouble. What gave me trouble was not my race so much as the average education which I have. More and more the educational standards slumped which made me with an A.B. from Columbia U. stick out like a sore thumb. Mrs. Eva Lynd, a Southerner, who is now employed in California, highly appreciated my abilities. They were after her already, she being a graduate of California Tech. The excuse for firing her was shameful. They knew that I was her friend, and then went after me. The Supervisor when I went to work was Melvin Bennett. Mrs. Lyn reported a breach of security on his part. The investigation turned up that he was not only guilty of destroying classified papers without the required witness, but more than 800 classified documents were unaccounted for. The Air Force finally went over the head of Pan American and fired him. It is a long and not-so-nice story of why it was necesary for the AF to do so. That came about early in October, 1956. Believe it or not, a man named Robert Allen, who not only knew nothing about library science, but was merely a high school graduate, and a poor sample of that, was now made Supervisor of Technical Library. All of these poorly educated folk in the library who rated first under Mrs. Lynd and then under myself, were in a rage. Not with Allen, since he was one with them in every way, but against Mrs. Lynd for reporting the breach of security, which slogans all over the Base urges every loyal American employee to do. All around I could hear that Mrs. Lynd was "not to be trusted." So I asked one day what was tis—a branch of the U.S. government or a Communist cell or the Black Hand society? What was there to hide from government officials? Further, Mrs. Lynd had not gotten Bennet fired. If the breach had not been proved, if those classified documents could be accounted for, nothing that Mrs. Lynd had said would have mattered. I first got hold of the information from the Secretary of Addiscott that Mrs. Lynd was going to be done away with. It was already being set up in Flemming's office. (Vice President of Pan Am.) Sur[e] enough, Allen came to Mrs. Lynd later and told her that he wanted her to re-catalog all the books in the library according to a way that "we" like better. "We" meant Maria Dussich, a woman of Italian birth, who complained to me that even history was to hard for her in high school, but who had gotten in the Library on the lowest classification and was put on as receptionist. An ignorant Machivelli [sic] and Lucrezia Borgia rolled into one. Mrs. Lynd was naturally both astonished and outraged to be ordered to re-catalog a library to their specifications, and indignantly refused. HA! Mission accomplished. Mr. Addiscott sent for her to come to his office and fired her for refusing to obey her supervisor. All this foolishness on government money. Now, I could either knuckle under, be loud in my denunciation of Mrs. Lynd, or suffer the same fate. I stood by my guns. I thought of myself as the thin gray line of the Confederacy of the last two years of the struggle. 1. This was government money being cynically diverted to a purpose never intended. The Air Base was not esteblished to provide salaries and advancement to the unprepared merely because they helped along unclean doings. 2. The U.S. government never contemplated sectional discrimination. There I soon found a sly latter-day Reconstruction program of crying down southerners, of putting in most poorly educated northerners before prepared sout[h]erners. The intimidation had reached the point where people from North Carolina, Virginia, Maryland and Kentucky were loudly insisting on being called Yankees. Can you beat it. Miss Mary? But the point is the pressure that made them cower like that. So I made a point of keeping everybody in mind that I was a Floridian, the implication being that as far south as I came from, I stood there the best educated and most cultivated person among them. They had to forever be running to them to explain things and find things for those RCA technicians. In fact, the technicians would pass them by and come to my desk of themselves. 2. [sic] The waste of government money in hiring so many inferior, incapable people, not only in the library, but all over. Pan American at Patrick is notorious for this. The local people make jokes about it. Naturally, a training period before they are any use is too long to be economically good, and the turn-over is terrific. So I asked myself, why such a policy? Saving of funds by reporting to the government one sum when a much lower one is actually the figure?

And since Pan Am was being investigated for holding out on the government on moneys from it's subsidiaries, I saw that such was possible at the Base. 3. [sic] I was determined to test if The President's Committee on Government Contracts really guarranteed equal opportunity for work or was some more political hog-wash. (b) If it worked where the violator was a heavy contributor to Eisenhower's political campaign as Pan Am was. So I kept the Committee posted from January 18 on until I was terminated on May 10. I called it to the attention of Vice-President Nixon himself, so that come 1958, he could not pretend that he was not aware of what was going on. Come 1960, it would stare him, as Eisenhower's successor stark in the face.

May 10, 1957, I was terminated, believe it or not, for "being too well educated for the job." William J. McKay, head of Office Services which the Library is under, came up with that one. In reality, I was being punished for continuing to be friendly with Mrs. Lynd, who had reported Bennet justly, and second though a married man, he had a girl friend whom he wanted to repay for her favors at the expense of Pan Am, which is really dispensing government funds there. Allen and compny were only too glad to play footsie by finding a place for his girl and one for a girl said to belong to Mitchell, Pres. of Pan Am at Patrick. The matter had become notorious on the Base. Possibly assuming the heavy contributions to the GOP campaign chest, it was assumed that nothing would be done about such a flagrant breach.

I do not tell you this because I hope for Senator Holland to do anything to get back my job. I do not care one way or another about it. I have been through months of really sadistic persecution from November 1956 on. There is something about Armed Services Technical Information Agency documents which I shall [not?] go into here because it is not under any Committees on which the Senator serves. I assure you that I have had it. ALL I WANT IS FOR YOU to KNOW IF THE MATTER BECOMES PUBLIC THAT IT HAS NO RACIAL SIGNIF-ICANCE FOR ME, NO NAACP WHOOPING AND HOLLERING AT ALL. It is a matter of loyalty to the United States and due process.

I look forward with great eagerness to your letter. I want to hear all about the family and everything.

With faithful feeling,
Zora
Zora Neale Hurston

This intimidation and low-rating of southerners on the Base can readily be traced to all this lurid literature showing us to be practically uncivilized and under-privileged down here. I dont mean Negroes. <u>All</u> southerners. Ignorant Northerners not only expect us to eat missionaries, but eat them raw. But why place such ignorance at a Missile Base?

TO MARY HOLLAND

Route #2, Box 75
Merritt Island, Florida
July 2, 1957.

Oh, Miz' Mary!

I thank you for your most generous birthday gift in every way that I know how. It so happens that I began my cradle days on January 7 when I tumbled into this sin-sick world (as a good old stomp-foot Baptist preacher like my father would phrase it) The very gift itself gives cause for celebration for now I will put this typewriter in the shop for a slight but necessary repair.

A book I m writing and a very difficult one,too, on which I have done a good six years of research.[1] I am conscious of a a greater competence with the tools of my trade than formerly. I would tell you all about it, but there is a superstition of the writing craft that to do so is like prying open a womb to take a peep at the embryo. You will have no success with the book if you talk it while in preparation.[2]

My eyes flung wide open in dismay when I saw the announcement of the series THE SOUTH SAYS NEVER, by John Bartlow Martin. It is not that he is failing to do a good and objective job, but I had laid out an article for the SATURDAY EVENING POST which I planned to call, TAKE FOR INSTANCE SPESSARD HOLLAND, in which I

---

[1] Herod the Great.
[2] *Ironically, Hurston wrote a great many letters about this book, more than any other of her works.*

am attempting to show the plight of the Southern law-maker.[3] The general impress[i]on in the North is that a Southern Senator is a lay figure, activated only by racial stimuli. I yearn to show the inevitable prolonged thought, speculation and pondering in the mind of a cultivated man like Spessard L. Holland. My startling and unhappy experiences at Technical Library was a good thing, for it pointed up to me the vast ignorance of that gang of latter-day carpet-baggers. In their great emptiness, they have become assured that mere geography constitutes intellect and information, i.e. a Northerner, <u>any</u> Northerner, is per se superior mentally to any Southerner regardless of background and training. They look at the pictures in LIFE AND LOOK and are convinced of it. Therefore when their sectional religion is disturbed, they set out to beat down the disturbance so they can return to their smugness. I am by no means the only one who has recognized this. A White girl, Carolyn Sutton of Warm Springs, Georgia, who was induc[ted] on the same day that I was—we got to talking as we sat waiting for the next step in the processing—and when she heard my name she recognized it and we did a lot of talking. She has done three years at Emory and is highly intelligent by nature. She is stuck down in Base Supply as a Clerk-typist while a waitress from the lower East side of New York and who admits that she has never even heard of David Lawrence[4] nor Dorothy Thompson[5] is in the Library, and saying openly, "Everybody knows that Southerners dont know nothing." They have taken this northern-flattering propaganda to their hearts and when their pretensions meet the realities, they are moved to to fury and consider that honor and deceny must be thrown overboard to defend their ingrained beliefs. As you know, there is is NOTHING that a man knows which is half so precious as what he <u>wants to believe.</u> To let them know that I saw through their crude mechanisms, I

---

[3]*John Bartlow Martin's book-length account of anti-integration southern sentiment,* The Deep South Says "Never," *was published in 1957 (New York: Ballantine). Known principally as a journalist, Martin was the author of* Why Did They Kill? *and* Break Down the Walls, *among other works. According to Arthur Schlesinger, Jr., who wrote the foreword to Martin's book, Martin wanted people to be aware that anti-integration feeling had "hardened ominously in the Deep South."*

[4]*David Lawrence (1888–1973) was the founder, president, and editor of* US News & World Report. *Although Lawrence had a home in Sarasota, Florida, he was originally a northerner, born in Pennsylvania.*

[5]*Also a northerner, journalist Dorothy Thompson (1893–1961), sometimes called the first lady of American journalism, was a columnist in the thirties, a journalist and activist (she founded Ring of Freedom in 1941) in the forties, and an anti-Zionist activist and journalist in the fifties. She was married to writer Sinclair Lewis from 1928 to 1942.*

said one day, "There may come a Gettysburg for me one day here, but
first, I assure you xshall come for you a Chancellorville." And not a
one of them understood what I meant. That shows you the point I am
making. Maybe they have found out now because I have been told that
from Mitchell, Pres. of Pan Am at Patrick Air Force Base on down,
they are having the screaming heebie-jeebies at the investigation
which the Air Force is giving them. Before they were aware that it was
being done, they got so lordly in what they considered their unchal-
lenged power that they sought to influence the Florida Industrial
Commission office here at Cocoa not to allow me to have the Unemployment money due me. The first week that I went in to make my
application, the [g]irl at Desk 4 was most cordial. But t[h]e following
Wednesday when I was supposed to get a check for $26.00, she was
very, very nasty and told me that she could not guarrantee that I could
draw the $416 due me. "The money belongs to the company (Pan
American) and you can only get it if they allow you to have it." The
next week she said that my check had not come from Tallahassee.
Anyway, there was a meeting to be held on me, and then it would be
be decided whether I could get it. I merely asked why such special attention to me when I was due it? and like Pilate, I walked out without
waiting for an an[s]wer. BUT, Miz' Mary, you should have seen her
when I showed up the fourth Wednesday. I knew then that the blow
had fallen from Washington. Everything is back to fair and warm. I
knew all along that the Florida Industrial Commission had no idea of
what she had been persuaded to do by gross misrepresentaion from the
department of Office Services at the Base. Nor will I ever tell on her.
She was lied to.

Therefore, you can see the grave necessity to give the world some
idea of the real conditions in the South and the men who represent
the South in Congress assembled. This is not the South of say, 1900.
Most of our law-makers are no mere bigotted jumping-jacks. They
see the problems, economic and sociological and ponder them seriously and intelligently, seeking the answers infinitely more earnestly
than the on-lookers from above the Mason-Dixon line. We are
blessed with two Senators of good family and education, given to
broad reading and gathering information. I remember only too well
the most extensive Library which Spessard Holland has and know
that the books are really read. He has books on the Negro from way
back before the war between the states. I saw them and envied him.

A man of such information is not inclined to be brash and mouthy.
He can see too much. I have in memory the earnest attack which
Holland, as Governor, made upon the solution of the race question in
Florida. He began at the only realistic place to begin, the foundation,
by stepping up the educational program among us. He is of the Herbert Hoover type, sticks to fundamentals and leaves the flashy gestures to the demagogues. LOOK and LIFE will not camp on his
doorsteps, but time will show the value of his deeds. This is the kind
of article I have laid out. I shall still se[e] what I can do at SATUR-
DAY EVENING POST through Stuart Rose as a follow up to the current series by Martin. If they do not take it, there are others.
AMERICAN LEGION MAGAZINE likes me very much.

How well do I remember meeting you! Never can I forget your
jaunty little tam and the way you wore it. How swell you became your
clothes; your trim figure topped by a face of lively intelligence and
good will towards all mankind glistening up your face. I hoard the
memory of your generous offer to allow me to read in your husband's
[overwritten: library and his interview . . . showed his calm and gra-
ciousness . . . in which he] library at the Executive Mansion, and when
I arrived, how gracious and kind he was in confirming your assent.
And was he stuffed with information! Not in a showy and pedantic
fashion, the knowledge just seeped out where it fitted in the conversation. In a few minutes it was evident that that traditional Southern
question, "Who's your folks, honey?" was already answered. It does
not take much discernment to tell big wood from brush. Dozens of
times I have said to Negroes that Spessard Holland was my ideal of a
Southern statesman. For the identical reason I prefer a Herbert
Hoover to a FRD; I favored Robert A. Taft over Dwight Eisenhower
for the same reason. The Northern Negroes bitterly opposed Taft because he stated when asked by a group of NAACPers at Durham,
whether if he became president he would force desegregation of the
schools in the South, "No. The President of the United States is an executive, elected to carry out the laws made and provided, not to make
laws himself. There is nothing in the Constitution that would give me
the power to interfere and I would not do so. If it was there, I would
follow the law." This stand certainly helped to lose Taft the nomination, but I do not believe that he ever regretted it. It won him my
deepest respect, trust and admiration. The rabid ones failed to grasp
the significance of his words. I saw that if you turn an executive loose

to go outside the law in your favor on Monday, you have also given him the power to go outside the law on Thursday against you. No country is safe from tyranny unless the chief executive is kept within the bounds of law made and provided. Now, they can see what a mess the country is in from Eisenhower's too susceptibility to pressure. Neither White nor Black know where they are except in a hate-filled, stinking mess. There is an old Southern proverb which says, "Never let your head start more than your rear-end can stand," but in this caper they have cut, the rear-end (this seating business) has started more than the head can figger what to do with. Where do we go from here? Well, when the loud-mouths on both sides have hollered themselves to death, then the quiet, prepared Southern statesman will have to step in and restore order. Like Napoleon amid the excesses of the French revolution. TAKE SPESSARD L. HOLLAND FOR INSTANCE. And Mary Holland is his voice of gentleness speaking from out of the whirlwind.

Therefore I am very glad to get the family information you sent along. With your permission, I shall exert myself mightily to sell this article on the Senator. I have the handicap of some national magazines refusing anything favorable to the South, but I am not discouraged. Something will <u>have</u> to give.

Most faithfully, most lovingly,
Zora

TO JOSEPHINE LEIGHTON

[handwritten addition to letter from Leighton dated July 1, 1957, inquiring about Hurston's address]

1. Route 2, Box 75 is my permanent address as far as I can see at present.

2. Work: (a) Librarian at Pan American World Airways, Inc. Technical Library at Patrick Air Force Base, but where I can receive no personal mail. (b) Hard at work on a new novel which I think, because of central character and scope to be a very important work. If I can set it down as I see it, it bears upon the state of the entire world at present—

ideological, racial & political—without sounding didactic and
"smelling of the lamp." (labored)[1]

Zora Neale Hurston

Began work at Technical Library June 18, 1956

TO MITCHELL FERGUSON

NOTE: This machine refuses to single-space today somehow.

Lincoln Park Academy
Fort Pierce, Florida
March 7, 1958
Mr. M. Mitchell Ferguson, Coordinator
State Department of Education
Tallahassee, Florida

Dear Mr. Ferguson:

Your office and Dr. D. E. Williams have been most kind and cooperative that I dislike to burden you further. However, I am puzzled
about things here.

The Assistant Principal, informing me that she spoke for the Lincoln Park Academy administration, came to my house on Feb. 8th and
reminding me that she had asked me two months before if I cared to
teach, urged me to be on hand the next morning to fill a vacancy in
the English department.

I told Mrs. Paige then that I had no Florida certificate, that I had
taught in college and none had been required of me, that I had never
taught in a public school system. I was assured that they would not
only wait for me to get a certificate, but aid me in getting it. Then I
said I would try it.

Ten days later, she came to my room and asked if I had sent for my
transcripts from Howard U., Washington D.C. and Barnard College of
Columbia U. where I took my B.A. and I told her that I had. I had also

[1]Herod the Great.

written to the General Extension Division at U. of F. to inquire about the teaching methods courses that I would nee[d]. I knew that I had sufficient English credits, but had nothing of the methods so popular now. They replied immediately offering suggestions. I had also written to Dr. D. E. Williams as to wht [sic] steps I should take, and you know his reaction.

Now, about tendays ago, Mr. Leroy Floyd, the principal here, began to be very urgent that I get my transcript to submit an application for certification, seeming to think that I had done nothing along that line. I assured him that I had, and showed him the letter from Dr. Williams. I said that all I could do was wait on the transcript from Barnard for which I had applied. Further, my mail was directed to the school office here, and he could easily find out whether a letter had come for me or not. I had received the transcript from Howard U., but I received my degree from Barnard, and I was waiting on that to apply.

He met me in the corridor on the very afternoon that I received your instructions, and so I showed your letter to prove that I was trying, but still had heard no word from Barnard. I was very glad when he called Barnard long-distance, and he was told that my request was there and that they had sent me a card saying that it would be sent on receipt of $1.00 from me. The call was made on March 3. The enclosed card tells its own story. It reached me on March 5th.

Principal Floyd impressed me that if I did not have the certificate by Monday, March 10, he could not allow me to teach. When I left school today at 4 oclock, the transcript from Barnard still had not appeared in my mailbox.

This eternal harrassment appears to me to be a trifle unfair because I never applied to teach there. I was urged, and assurances given. Further, I know my English both by college courses, and practical application as an author, as you know. In addition, he has seen the evidence that the transcript is being sent. I teach six hours a day, and I can do it. I get on well with my classes as any other teacher here.

I have an explanation in two clauses, which Dr. Williams in his long years of contact with Negro education will readily grasp, though you might not be aware. My name as an author is too big to be tolerated, lest it gather to itself the "glory" of the school here. I have met that before. But perhaps it is natural. The mediocre have no importance except through appointment. They feel invaded and defeated by the presence of creative folk among them. As Gray, who first was president at Florida Normal, then by some freak of fate at FA & AMU, told me after he begged me to teach English at St. Augustine. The third day of my stay there, THE ST. AUGUSTINE RECORD found out I was there and sent reporter with camera. Gray rushed out on the grounds where I was about to be photographed and objected that he was the president, and if any pictures were taken, they should be of himself as the president. Later he told me angrily, "You have no business among us little folks. You are too big."

The second clause of this complex sentence is discipline at Lincoln Park Academy. It is terrible. Too many over-age students. Most students from what you might call under-privileged homes. There are—as in all Negro schools—some "old heads" who manage by hook and crook to dominate whoever is principal. I was told how they managed to get quiet in the schoolroom. Impossible otherwise, I was warned. It was admitted that 10C, my homeroom class was the worst on the campus. I admit that I have not resorted to their methods because it is a sad fact that Negroes are given to too much violence. I cannot see where more violence will persuade them to decent behavior. I said in faculty meeting that instead of the goal being to merely get silence by force, the responsibility of good conduct should be placed on the individual student by reasoning, since they had known nothing but violence all their lives with such poor results, to the end that when they arrived at the physical size where corporal punishment could no longer be administered, NOTHING could be done with them, as was the case with numerous students there. To the dismay of the "old heads" 10C is actually being tamed. They admit it themselves, but it does not go down so well. I am attempting to wean the students from the habit of toting knives. No teacher could detect and take away knives by watching, as you must see. A boy was stabbed last week. My aim is to show them that there is no need to own one, and no need to settle their differences with weapons. FROM THEIR PARENTS AND ASSOCIATES, IT IS FELT THAT ONE MUST BE READY WITH A DANGEROUS WEAPON FOR THE LEAST DIFFERENCE. They must be disabused of this concept. But is [sic] cannot be done by using more force in the schoolroom. That merely fortyfies the student in his persuasion that force is the thing. Further, it has come out that even the "terrors" have no better discipline than I, though they pretended differently.

Now, Principal Floyd knows that my transcript has been applied for, and Barnard informed him that it was being sent, so I cannot see why the urgency. He implies that he might lose his job if it is found out at Tallahassee that I am teaching without a certificate. I do not know whether he is really frightened, or being yanked around by the old heads. But he knew that I did not have a certificate when he urged me to teach there.

This I want to say: I do not wish to be the center of one of those school fights which are so common in every Florida county that I have been in. So prevalent are they that I quip that the first greeting when you enter a new town should be, "How's your principal?"[1] If Floyd is sincere in his fright, the arrival of my transcript from Barnard should calm him. I told him today that it cannot be more than a day or two in coming now. Bear this in mind that I can live without teaching. I did not ask for the job. It was urged upon me. None here can say, not truthfully, that I do not know my subject.

I found discipline terrible when I came here. Some boys bring their dice to class.

As I said, I have made my living without teaching mostly since I left college.[2] But since I started to teach here, I am reminded of something I observed in my years of gathering folklore. That is the element of attention, so closely joined with intelligence and learning. You already know that the world is divided between visual and aural-minded people. I find Negroes prdominantly aural-minded. I conceived the notion that based on that, some means could be devised for teaching Negro children faster. To hold attention for as you know, intelligence measurements rests on the quantity and the quality of attention. This factor sets humanity apart from the lower animals. I have found so far that the holding of attention is brief. Like the line from Rigoletto "Like a plume in the summer wind." I did wish to see if I could work something out along that line that would be useful in education below the college level.

So, I have told you truthfully about my peculiar position here. There is nothing else for me to say. Since I had never taught in a secondary school, I naturally had no certificate, and getting my transcript is implicit in the process. He knows that your office knows that.

Most sincerely yours,
Zora Neale Hurston

---

[1]*Hurston expresses similar sentiments in her essay "The Rise of the Begging Joints," American Mercury, March 1945.*
[2]*Hurston always insisted that she hated teaching.*

TO SARA LEE CREECH

Fort Pierce, Florida
October 20, 1958

Dear, dear Sarah [sic] Creech,

A very nice lady who works at the local CHAMBER OF COM-MERCE told me that you wanted to find out if I were really here, and so I write to assure you that this is me, but heartily ashamed that I have allow3ed you to have to inquire. I do wish that I could see you, and hope that a kindly impulse will turn the wheel of your car this-away soon. Outside of the natural pleasure of seeing you, we have so much to talk about.

1. What goes on in inter-racial circles here. I am afraid that I am being very annoying to the "Race Champions" among us by suggest-ing that the meetings should be something more than a re-hashing of the wrongs done to Negroes in the past, and a begging expedition for what wwe want instead of presenting a program of our own efforts to help ourselves. I keep pointing out that you cannot hang around the backdoor for a handout, and expect to be invited in as an equal. The champions look upon me as a traitor to my race for taking such a posi-tion, but I have no intention of changing. I have offended the NAACP underground here by going so far as to set up what I call a DO-IT-YOURSELF playground for Negroes in which we choose the type of game we want, then somehow get up the equipment ourselves. IT IS AROUSING GREAT enthusiasm among the citizenry, for as you know, man is so constituted that there is nothing he loves so much as the work of his own hands. The kids love the beat-up toys they botch up infinite[ly] more than the expensive store-bought ones. The Mayor anf City Manager both agree that I have hit upon something, are h[e]lp-ing me, and say it should be expanded, it being the essence of personal initiative which has made America the great productive nation that it is, but the Champions are furious, charging that I am instrumental in depriving the Negroes of their due. that the City can and should be forced to provide all recreational facilities for us. Naturally the City is not buying, not having as yet provided the first tennis-racket nor

croquet set for the Whites. And the young Negroes are having a won-
drerful time setting up their own swings, base-ball diamond, etc.
I have ab ambitious plan to bring down ROY CAMPanella[1] to inspire
the young soon and keep right on advocating personal initiative till
I am bombed out.

2. Still crazy about growing things, I am about to get hold of a plat
of ground of my own,[2] which if I get the green light from the florists
in this area of FLORIDA, I SHALL grow greens for them and do my
own flocking. this all depends upon whether the trade in this area is
still ina[d]equately supplied and must send a great distance to get
greens. Just in case, where would one start to look for a flocking machine? MY whole heart is in the matter, and I think that I can manage
financially about slat-houses, flocking equiptment and the like if you
tyink [sic] it would be needed. Please give me your frank opinion.

I was ill a month ago but okay now, All my love to yourself and
mother.

> Affectionately,
> Zora
> Zora Neale Hurston

TO MARY HOLLAND

1734 School Court
Fort Pierce, FLORIDA
October 21, 1958.

Dear Mrs. Holland,
My friend Marjory [sic] Silver came yesterday to tell me she had
seen you at the Homecoming at Gainesville, and I was very happy.[1]
I did not try to publish anything concerning the Senator[2] before

---

[1]*Legendary black baseball player who began his career in the Negro League, played for Brooklyn, and was
inducted into the Baseball Hall of Fame.*
[2]*This did not take place.*

---

[1]*Marjorie Silver was a journalist and friend of Hurston's who was instrumental in her funeral and in helping
to preserve her papers and send them to the University of Florida.*
[2]*George Smathers was a Democrat in the U.S. House of Representatives (1947–51) and the U.S. Senate
(1951–69). Smathers labeled Claude Pepper as "Red Pepper," accusing him of having pro-Soviet sentiments.*

no[r] during the campaign, for I soon learned that Pepper[3] wanted to pin the label og [sic] Nigger-lover on the Senator, and so I would harm instead of helping as I So much wanted to. but I did speak before small groups of Nwgroes [sic] reminding them that Senator Holland was the father of Negro education in Florida, and that it is always preferable to see a promise any day than to hear about one, and that Pepper had not[h]ing to show but words and weasley words at that. I could point to his quick switch in the Smathers campaign, showing his lack of [sin]cerity. Naturally I was delighted at the overwhelming victory. But as Mrs. Silver can tell you, I had gathered some stuff to knock him cold at the last minute, his receiving inter-racial couples socially in New YORK ans [sic] was headed for your local headquarters to turn it in when she stopped me, saying that it was unnecessary that you would not lose.

All my best love to you and yours,
Zora
Zora Neale Hurston

TO HARPER BROTHERS PUBLISHERS

1734 School Court
Fort Pierce, Florida
Jan. 16, 1959.
Editorial Department
Harper Brothers, Publishers
New York, N.Y.

Dear Sirs:

This is to query you if you would have any interest in the book I am laboring upon at present—a life of Herod the Great. One reason I approach you is because you will realize that any publisher who offers a life of Herod as it really was, and naturally different from the groundless legends which have been built up around his name has to have courage.

Sincerely Yours,
Zora Neale Hurston

[3]Claude Pepper (1900–89) was in the Florida House of Representatives (1929) and the U.S. Senate (1936–50). He sponsored bills for national health care, equal pay for women, heart disease programs, and the minimum wage. In 1962, he was elected to the U.S. House of Representatives.

> 1734 School Court
> Fort Pierce, Florida
> Jan. 16, 1959.
>
> Editorial Department
> Harper Brothers, Publishers.
> New York, N. Y.
>
> Dear Sirs:
>   This is to query you if you would have
> any interest in the book I am laboring upon
> at present — a life of Herod the Great.
> One reason I approach you is because
> you will realize that any publisher who
> offers a life of Herod as it really was, and
> naturally different from the groundless legends
> which have been built up around his name
> has to have courage.
>
>   Sincerely yours,
>   Zora Neale Hurston

One of the last letters Hurston sent to a publisher,
Harper Brothers, Jan. 16, 1959.

CHRONOLOGY

1891-According to the Hurston family Bible, Zora Lee Hurston is born January 15, in Notasulga, Alabama, to John Hurston (born 1861) and Lucy Potts Hurston (born 1865). Notasulga, in Macon County, was mostly an agricultural community, comprised largely of sharecroppers and tenant farmers. The Notasulga family home is near Tuskegee Institute, founded by Booker T. Washington and dedicated at that time to vocational training of African Americans.

1892-The Hurston family moves to Eatonville, Florida, where Zora Hurston's father, John, begins work as pastor of the Zion Hope Baptist Church in Sanford. The Hurstons build an eight-room house and a barn on a multi-acre plot that includes a garden, citrus grove, and livestock.

1897-John Hurston is elected mayor of Eatonville.

1900-Hurston attends Eatonville's Hungerford School, founded in 1889 on the Tuskegee model with land donated by white benefactor Edward C. Hungerford.

1904-On September 19, Zora Hurston's mother, Lucy, dies, and Hurston attends school in Jacksonville.

1905-On February 14, John Hurston marries Mattie Moge, twenty years old. Hurston returns home briefly, but she and Moge quarrel bitterly, and Hurston leaves home again. She is fourteen. Some of the ensuing years are spent at the Florida Baptist Academy, a boarding school in Jacksonville, Florida, and some with other members of her family who had already left the Hurston family home in Eatonville. Little is known about the years 1905–12, and no known letters survive that period.

1912-John Hurston is again elected mayor of Eatonville. Hurston spends time with her brother, Dr. Robert Hurston, his wife, Wilhelmina, and their son, Robert, Jr., in Jacksonville, Florida, and with her brother Dick in Sanford.

1914-Hurston lives with her brother John and his wife, Blanche, in Jacksonville.

1915-Hurston moves to Memphis, Tennessee, where her brother Robert and his wife, Wilhelmina, have moved. She helps care for their three children.

1916-Hurston leaves Memphis and her brother's home to work as a maid with a Gilbert and Sullivan troupe. When she becomes ill in Baltimore, where her sister Sarah lives, she decides to stay. Her appendix is removed in the free ward of the Maryland General Hospital. A white woman for whom she is working tries to arrange for Hurston to attend high school.

1917-Hurston finds work as a waitress in Baltimore while attending night school. On September 17, she enters Morgan Academy, working as a maid in the home of a white trustee to support her studies.

1918-Hurston's father, John, is killed in a car accident on August 10. Upon graduation from Morgan Academy, Hurston moves to Washington, D.C. That summer she works as a waitress at the Cosmos Club and as a manicurist in a D.C. barbershop. In September, she enters Howard University's preparatory school.

1920–24-Hurston receives her associate degree from Howard in 1920. While at Howard, she works with linguists Lorenzo Dow Turner and Dwight O. W. Holmes and begins to work on her writing, pursuing a number of different genres, and she joins the Zeta Phi Beta sorority. Her only extant poetry dates from this period. Through Alain Locke and Georgia Douglas Johnson, Hurston meets Bruce Nugent, Jean Toomer, W. E. B. Du Bois, Marita Bonner, Alice Dunbar-Nelson, Jessie Fauset, and Angelina Grimké. She corresponds with Charles S. Johnson, who encourages her to come to New York.

1925-Hurston moves to New York City in January, living first at 163 West 131st Street, in Harlem. In May, she wins second place in the *Opportunity* awards and meets white writers Annie Nathan Meyer, Fannie Hurst, and others. In June she moves downtown briefly, writing from 23rd Street. She leaves Manhattan for New Jersey, living first at 1014 Rivington Street in Roselle and then at 624 West 4th Street in Plainfield. By late September, Hurston is back in Harlem, living at 260 West 139th Street. She moves briefly to 27 West 67th Street, in November. In December, she is back on 131st Street, living at 108, a few doors from her previous address at 163 West 131st. She works briefly as a secretary for Hurst and meets expenses with other jobs, including domestic work. With help from Meyer and Barnard dean Virginia G. Gildersleeve, Hurston is accepted into Barnard College and offered a scholarship. Study begins in September. Hurston majors in English but also begins work with renowned Columbia anthropologist Franz Boas. She sends poems to Annie Nathan Meyer's husband and to other friends. She works on her French.

1926-In the summer, Hurston moves again from Harlem, this time to the Upper West Side of Manhattan, taking an apartment at 43 West 66th Street. Although she travels to the South in 1927, she holds on to this apartment for most of the rest of the decade, subletting it sometimes to strangers and sometimes to friends. Still at Barnard and taking classes at Columbia as well, Hurston does fieldwork in early anthropometry, boldly measuring heads in Harlem. In conjunction with Wallace Thurman, Langston Hughes, Aaron Douglas, Gwendolyn Bennett, and Bruce Nugent, she begins work on the journal *Fire!!* She contacts theater manager Frank Shay and works on magazine articles. She looks for authentic spiritual singers.

1927-Hurston receives a fellowship for $1,400 from Carter Woodson's Association for the Study of Negro Life and History and goes south to collect folklore in Florida in February. She marries Herbert Sheen on May 19, 1927, in St. Augustine, Florida. She returns to New York by car with Langston Hughes. They stop along the way to visit Dorothy Hunt Harris's parents in Fort Valley, Georgia; to attend a Bessie Smith concert in Macon (where Hurston and Smith become friends); and to lecture to summer students at Tuskegee Institute. Back in New York, Hurston spends some time at Columbia organizing her material and seeks financing for a folk opera. There she meets Charlotte Osgood Mason, who is supporting Alain Locke and Langston Hughes. Hurston signs a one-year contract with Mason on December 8, which is eventually renewed until 1931 and which establishes Mason as Hurston's patron and, officially, her "employer." She publishes her first anthropological pieces, including one that is largely plagiarized, and begins a book-length study (which she calls, variously, *Kossula* and *Barracoon*) of Cudjo Lewis, purportedly the last survivor of the last slave ship, the *Chlotilde*. She works with Annie Nathan Meyer to turn Meyer's play *Black Souls* into a novel. On December 14, she takes a train to Mobile, Alabama, to complete her interviews with Lewis. Copies of *Fire!!* are destroyed in a house fire.

1928-In January, Hurston and Sheen split up, presumably through correspondence. Hurston continues folklore collecting, moving to Polk County, Florida, in March, where she spends time in the turpentine camp near Loughman and travels to Mulberry, Pierce, and Lakeland, Florida. She describes the folklore she is collecting as being so rich that she does not even have time to take good notes. She receives her B.A. degree from Barnard in May and that month publishes "How It Feels to Be Colored Me," an essay that offends Mason. In the spring, she collects fossils for Alain Locke. In the summer, she moves to New Orleans to begin research on hoodoo, conjure, and legendary hoodoo priestess Marie Laveau. She tells Hughes that she has been suffering from writer's block. In November, she sends him money. While traveling, she offers poetry readings of Hughes's work, testing its effect on small-town, illiterate blacks.

1929-In April, Hurston organizes her folklore field notes while staying with her brother John in Jacksonville. That month she moves to Eau Gallie, Florida, where she rents a house near the Indian River. She attempts to purchase land.

In the summer, she is hospitalized at Flagler Hospital in St. Augustine, Florida, with liver problems. She moves to Miami, where she revises the folklore manuscript multiple times and works on theater scripts. The manuscript is originally titled *Negro Folk-Tales from the Gulf States.* Portions of it will eventually be published as *Mules and Men.* In October, she travels to the Bahamas, where she spends two weeks on research, films dances, returns to Miami for lack of funds, then back to New Orleans, where she assists anthropologist Otto Klineberg with research, against Mason's insistence that she return to her own work. A violent hurricane in the Bahamas in October makes travel difficult and provides later inspiration for *Their Eyes Were Watching God.*

1930-Hurston spends January and February finishing her fieldwork in the Bahamas. She returns to New York and, through arrangements Mason makes, spends the spring in a Westfield, New Jersey, rooming house. In June, she returns south, from where she publishes "Dance Songs and Tales from the Bahamas" in the July–September edition of the *Journal of American Folklore.* She measures heads with Melville Herskovits in Louisiana. In addition to assembling materials for *Negro Folk-Tales from the Gulf States,* later to become *Mules and Men,* Hurston begins to work with Hughes on *Mule Bone: A Comedy of Negro Life,* dictating much of the play to Louise Thompson, whom Mason hires. During this same period, Hurston is consulting Franz Boas on her field notes, working with him in secret. In November, she visits her sister Sarah in Asbury Park, New Jersey, and tries, unsuccessfully, to sell her car. In December, she tries to persuade Ruth Benedict to join her in Honduras.

1931-Hurston returns to 43 West 66th Street in Manhattan and engages Elisabeth Marbury as her agent. In January, Hurston visits Carl Van Vechten, after hearing from Hughes that he is angry that she has sent *Mule Bone* to Jelliffe. That month, Hurston files for copyright for *Mule Bone* in both her name and Hughes's, but also writes Hughes that the play is hers alone. The Samuel French Agency denies the Gilpin Players permission to use the play, but Hurston changes her mind and gives her permission. In February, on Hughes's birthday, Hurston arrives in Cleveland to discuss the *Mule Bone* production with him, the Jelliffes, and the Gilpin Players. She cancels permission for the next day's production. In March, Hurston's contract with Mason ends, although Mason continues some support through September 1932. Hurston finishes *Barracoon* in April. It is rejected by Harper and Covici-Friede. In early April, she takes a weekend trip to Washington, D.C. In June, she retreats to Pleasantville, New York, and Ontario to edit *Mules and Men* in quiet. In August, she hires Wallace Thurman to revise *Mule Bone,* which enrages Hughes. In September, she appears in the Broadway review *Fast and Furious,* which opens and closes in one week, after which she works on *Jungle Scandals,* another unsuccessful production. In October, she forms a theater troupe to perform her play *The Great Day,* collaborating with Hall Johnson. The collaboration soon breaks down. Hurston finishes revisions on *Barracoon,* sending it and *Mules and Men* to editor Harry Block.

1932-*The Great Day* is produced at the John Golden Theater in New York City. It is a critical success, but a financial failure, accruing more than $600 in debt to Mason, for which Hurston signs another contract. In January, her brother John entertains Langston Hughes in Jacksonville. In March, she produces *The Great Day* at the New School for Social Research. In April, it opens at the Vanderbilt Hotel under the auspices of the Folk Dance Society. Then Hurston's stomach problems recur. That same month, Hurston is chastised by Alain Locke, acting as Mason's emissary. Mason agrees to buy Hurston new shoes and sends her fare to Florida. She addresses the Barnard Alumnae, meets Faustin Workus and Max Eastman, moves out of her 66th Street apartment, and stores her belongings in Brooklyn. In May, Walter White invites her to participate with himself, Paul Robeson, and others in *Batouala*, an opera based on René Maran's popular novel. She meets Hamilton Holt, president of Rollins College, and Professors Edwin O. Grover and Robert Wunsch. At Rollins that fall, she works with Wunsch to train a local cast for *The Great Day*. Hurston begins her search for a publisher for *Mules and Men,* which continues until 1934. She has troubles with one of her drummers, problems with her wrist, problems with her teeth, and her garden is destroyed by drought.

1933-Stomach troubles persist and worsen. Mason cuts off funding. In January, a version of *The Great Day,* retitled *From Sun to Sun,* is performed in a small auditorium at Rollins. Because the production is a success, it is restaged in February in the college's main auditorium. Hurston lobbies without success for the performances to be opened to blacks, but a special performance open to blacks is, instead, given in Eatonville. Throughout the winter and early spring, she takes *From Sun to Sun* to various Florida cities, including Mary McLeod Bethune College in Daytona Beach, and a performance at Daytona Beach's segregated public auditorium. For three days in the spring, Hurston exhibits *From Sun to Sun* at the National Folk Festival in St. Louis, Missouri. She gives Robert Wunsch a copy of "The Gilded Six-Bits," which he sends to *Story* magazine. It is published in August. Impressed by the story, Bertram Lippincott asks Hurston if she has a novel. Although she does not, Hurston immediately replies yes. She moves to Sanford, Florida, in July to write *Jonah's Gourd Vine,* completed in nine weeks and mailed to Lippincott in early October. His acceptance and $200 advance arrive coincidentally with an eviction notice. In December, Hurston is invited to start a school of drama at Bethune-Cookman College.

1934-In January, Hurston moves to Daytona Beach to teach at Bethune-Cookman. She finds the school without facilities and the students lacking energy. She stages no productions while she is there but does acquire one of her first boats, of which she is very proud. In early May, Hurston takes a Bethune-Cookman dance troupe to the National Folk Festival in St. Louis, where they are billed as a "Primitive Negro Folklore Group." *Jonah's Gourd Vine* appears in May. Lippincott accepts *Mules and Men* but asks for substantial revisions. The Book-of-the-Month Club recommends *Jonah's Gourd Vine* as one of its titles. In the summer, Hurston rents a cabin in the turpentine camp of Loughman, Florida, and continues revising *Mules and Men* and travels to New York, staying at the Dewey Square Hotel. In the fall, she goes to Fisk University to talk to President Thomas Jones about starting a drama school there and gives a performance of *The Great Day*. She then goes to Chicago, where she performs two versions of *The Great Day*, retitled *Singing Steel*, in late November. She is paid $500 and stays at the YWCA. Also in November, she plans a trip to Asia with Nora Holt (they don't go) and is invited to apply for Rosenwald Foundation money for doctoral study with Boas. The Rosenwald initially offers $3,000 but then reduces its funding by increments. Boas protests unsuccessfully. When it is clear that the Rosenwald money is insufficient for serious study, Hurston attends classes only sporadically through the winter and the spring of 1935, devoting her time instead to a variety of theater and writing projects. She makes contact with organizers of the National Folk Festival and fights with Walter White. At year's end she is back in New York, staying with Harold Jackman.

1935-A love affair goes bad in the winter, adding to disappointments. Although Boas approves her plan of study at Columbia, the Rosenwald Foundation cuts her funding down to $700, and by year's end, Hurston loses interest in doctoral study, declaring her lack of interest in teaching. Annie Nathan Meyer has a tea for Hurston with Pearl Buck, Fannie Hurst, Bertram Lippincott, and others, in February. In June, Hurston goes south with folklorists Alan Lomax and Mary Elizabeth Barnicle to collect folk music for the Music Division of the Library of Congress. In August, she returns to New York. In September, she visits the Huberts in the country. She joins the Harlem unit of the Federal Theater Project, a division of the Works Progress Administration (WPA), working with Orson Welles, John Houseman, and others as a drama coach, for which she is paid $23.36 a week. *Mules and Men* appears in October and is well reviewed. She makes contact with Julia Peterkin and Miguel Covarrubias.

1936-In March, Hurston is awarded a Guggenheim Fellowship and subsequently resigns from the Federal Theater Project. She throws a party for Harold Palmer Davis. She goes to Kingston, Jamaica, in April, where she spends time living and studying with the Maroons (descendants of escaped slaves) until September, although Herskovits is urging her to leave for the Bahamas. She loses her purse and a letter of credit in May and cables Henry Allen Moe of the Guggenheim Foundation that she is "penniless." Moe sends emergency funds. She travels to Haiti in late August, staying there for the rest of the year. From early November through the third week of December, she writes *Their Eyes Were Watching God*, completing it in only seven weeks.

1937-In March, Hurston goes back to the United States. That same month, she begins work on *Tell My Horse*. Her niece Wilhelmina, daughter of her brother Bob, comes to live with her in Eatonville, where Wilhelmina stays until her marriage in August 1938. Hurston's Guggenheim Fellowship is renewed in

April. She returns to Haiti in May. In the spring, she arranges a lecture tour through the Colston Leigh Bureau. In June, very ill with stomach troubles and convinced that she is dying (perhaps as a consequence of her research into the "terrible" Petro gods), Hurston goes to the American consulate for help. She travels to the south end of Haiti in July, spends August recovering and sight-seeing, and returns to the United States in September. *Their Eyes Were Watching God* appears in September and is mostly well received, although Richard Wright, Sterling Brown, and Alain Locke are harsh. She contacts Edna St. Vincent Millay and plans, then cancels, a folk concert at the Ambassador Theater.

1938-Hurston finishes the manuscript of *Tell My Horse* in February or March (it appears in October and is not well received). She is enraged by Alain Locke's review of *Their Eyes Were Watching God.* She joins the Federal Writers' Project (FWP) of the WPA, working on *The Florida Negro,* a long-delayed Florida guidebook, and collecting and recording Florida folklore and songs. Initially, Hurston is hired as a relief worker earning $67.50 a month, although writers with her credentials were usually hired as editors or supervisors and paid more than twice that amount. In the spring, she goes to Washington, D.C., with the Rollins College folklore group, to perform for the National Folk Festival. Henry Alsberg, national director of the FWP, meets with Hurston in D.C. and suggests to her supervisor, Carita Doggett Corse, that Hurston be promoted to editor. Corse declines, but raises Hurston's salary and changes her title to "Supervisor of the Negro Unit." While working with the FWP, Hurston initiates fieldwork with her friend and fellow anthropologist Jane Belo, on "sanctified" church practices in South Carolina. In July, Hurston records folk music in the Everglades. Throughout this period, she is also working on *Moses, Man of the Mountain.* Hurston's niece Winifred comes to Eatonville to live with her in her house by the lake at "Tuxedo Junction," on the edge of town. She writes few letters from June to December.

1939-In January and February, Hurston stages two productions of folklore from *The Great Day* in Orlando in association with the FWP, under the title *The Fire Dance,* and travels to Cincinnati to do a radio series. Morgan State Academy awards her an honorary doctorate in June. She accepts a position as drama instructor at North Carolina College for Negroes in Durham. In June, she also spends time in Florida, collecting songs and stories for the Library of Congress and the Folk Arts Committee of the WPA. On June 27, 1939, Hurston marries Albert Price, III, a young man from Jacksonville's well-connected Sugar Hill society who is also working for the WPA, in its Recreation Division. Price was the grandson of one of the cofounders of the Afro-American Life Insurance Company, the first insurance company—black or white—in Florida. He is twenty-three; she is forty-eight. (She gives her birth date as 1910, which would have made her twenty-nine). The marriage is unsuccessful, and they do not live together for more than a few weeks at a time. In September, she is hired by James Shepard at North Carolina College to build a drama program. Unhappy there, she attends a weekly playwriting seminar at playwright Paul Green's home, discusses collaborating with him on a drama to be called *John de Conqueror*, makes connections with the Carolina Players, and speaks in October at the Carolina Dramatic Association. In October, *Tell My Horse* is published in London as *Voodoo Gods* and meets with success. In November, *Moses, Man of the Mountain* appears to uneven reviews. Hurston participates in the Boston Book Fair.

1940-In February, Hurston files for divorce from Price, but the two then reconcile. She resigns her teaching position at North Carolina College for Negroes. During the summer, Hurston goes to Beaufort, South Carolina, to research religious trances in "sanctified" churches for a project of Jane Belo's. In late summer, Hurston returns to New York City. She and Price are once again separated. She falls ill with malaria.

1941-Hurston relocates to Los Angeles in late spring at the invitation of Katharane Mershon. *Dust Tracks on a Road* is drafted by mid-July, and Hurston spends the rest of the year revising it. In October, she serves as a consultant at Paramount Pictures, where she attempts, unsuccessfully, to interest the studio in filming her work. She leaves Paramount in January 1942.

1942-Hurston travels the black college lecture circuit, then settles in St. Augustine, Florida, in April to live on her savings and further revise *Dust Tracks on a Road*. In early spring, she contracts pneumonia and tonsilitis. She tells Van Vechten she has malaria. She travels throughout Florida during the summer, collecting folklore. She teaches part-time at the local black college, Florida Normal, where she clashes with the administration. She collects material on the Seminole Indians. She strikes up a friendship with local novelist Marjorie Kinnan Rawlings. In November, *Dust Tracks on a Road* is published to good reviews, and Hurston plans but does not complete travel to New York to attend a James Weldon Johnson Literary Guild dinner in honor of Carl Van Vechten on the twenty-eighth. The dinner is attended by Walter White, Margaret Walker, Marian Anderson, Stephen Vincent Benet, W. C. Handy, and Blanche and Alfred Knopf.

1943-Early in the year, Hurston purchases the *Wanago*, a twenty-year-old, thirty-two-foot houseboat. She develops an interest in the slave ship, the *Chlotilde*. She leaves St. Augustine for Daytona Beach. In February, *Dust Tracks on a Road* is awarded the $1,000 Anisfield-Wolf award for the best book in race relations and is featured on the February 20 cover of *Saturday Review*. She tells Hamilton Holt that the book was not as she wanted it. Hurston is quoted in a February article in the *New York World-Telegram*, "When Negro Succeeds, South Is Proud," as saying that "the Jim Crow system works." Later that month the NAACP's Roy Wilkins responds angrily in the *New York Amsterdam News*, calling Hurston an opportunist. Hurston insists she was misquoted. In March, she accepts Howard University's Distinguished Alumni Award. She speaks at a Zeta Phi Beta meeting during her trip to Washington, D.C. She joins the Florida Negro Defense

Committee. She serves the Recreation in War project, speaking to segregated groups of GIs stationed around the state. On November 9, 1943, her divorce from Price is finalized. She tells Marjorie Kinnan Rawlings that she is getting fat and takes care of Rawlings for a week in the fall when Rawlings becomes ill.

1944-The February 5 edition of the *New York Amsterdam News* announces Hurston's engagement to James Howell Pitts of Cleveland. Pitts and Hurston had married, however, in Duval County, Florida, on January 18, 1944, and they divorced on October 31, 1944. On the marriage certificate, Hurston lists her birthplace as Eatonville and her age as forty (she is fifty-three). Hurston returns to New York in the spring, staying at the Hotel Theresa in Harlem, to collaborate with Dorothy Waring on a musical comedy script based loosely on "High John de Conquer," *Mules and Men*, and *Mule Bone*. The play is eventually titled *Polk County*. In the summer, she declines interest in radio programs that perpetuate stereotypes. She returns to Florida and in the fall is contacted by English gold miner Reginald Brett, who interests her in secret, unexplored Mayan ruins in British Honduras, along the Patuca River. In October, she applies, unsuccessfully, to the Guggenheim Foundation and the Library of Congress for grants to do fieldwork there, and witnesses a hurricane. In November, she sails the *Wanago* to New York to secure funding for *Polk County*.

1945-Hurston spends most of the year attempting to fund the Honduras trip and her writing. Back in Daytona Beach, she buys a new houseboat, the *Sun Tan*. She attempts to involve Miami adventurer Fred Irvine, a friend with a twenty-seven-ton schooner, in her plans for Honduras. The Honduras trip is postponed. During the summer, she is sick once again with various stomach and intestinal ailments. In June, she suggests to W. E. B. Du Bois that a Negro cemetery be constructed for the "illustrious Negro dead." In September, Lippincott rejects *Mrs. Doctor*, her novel about wealthy African Americans. She begins her next novel, set in Eatonville and using material from *Mule Bone* and *Polk County;* it is later rejected. In the fall, she begins work on the story of Herod the Great and prepares encyclopedia entries on "Negroes" to replace those written by Du Bois.

1946-In February, she goes on a shrimping boat as research for her novel, *Seraph on the Suwanee*. Tracy L'Engle visits on her houseboat in May. She becomes interested in the political career of John S. Knight. Hurston returns to New York in the fall, living on 55th Street. She works on Republican Grant Reynolds's congressional campaign against Adam Clayton Powell, Jr., and puts together a community child-care program in Harlem. She is generally unhappy and socially isolated. In November, she rents a room on 124th Street.

1947-In April, Hurston switches from Lippincott to Scribner's, acquiring renowned editor Maxwell Perkins, who passes away in June. With her $500 Scribner's advance for *Seraph on the Suwanee,* she sails for Honduras on May 4, settling on the north coast at Puerto Cortés, where she stays at the Hotel Cosenza. She concentrates on writing her new novel and traveling. In September, she sends the draft of the novel to New York and works on the revisions until December. She suggests a book on Carl Van Vechten and continues work on Herod.

1948-Hurston leaves Honduras on February 20 to do final rewrites of *Seraph on the Suwanee*. The manuscript is completed on March 17, with the title *Sign of the Sun*. She stays with Constance Seabrook in Rhinebeck, New York, during the summer, then rents a room at 140 West 112th Street, in Harlem, in the fall. In September, she is arrested on the false charge of molesting a ten-year-old boy, the son of a former landlady. She moves to the Bronx. Her new editor at Scribner's, Burroughs Mitchell, helps her retain Louis Waldman as counsel. The scandalous arrest story is leaked to the *Baltimore Afro-American* by a black court employee, and on October 23, the paper runs a sensational front-page article on the case. Demoralized, Hurston considers suicide. *Seraph on the Suwanee* is published on October 11 to good reviews.

1949-In March, the indictment against Hurston, whose passport proves she was in Honduras at the time of the allegations, is dismissed. Sales of *Seraph on the Suwanee* are impressive. By July, she has rejoined her friend Fred Irvine to travel to the Bahamas on his boat, the *Challenger*. For the next five months, Hurston lives on Irvine's boat and makes plans to return to Honduras. Her depression lessens. She works on a new novel, *The Lives of Barney Turk*, for Scribner's. The *Saturday Evening Post* buys the short story "The Conscience of the Court" for $900.

1950-In January, Hurston speaks at the Dade County Library, then takes a job as a maid on Miami's Rivo Island. Her work is published by Benjamin Botkin and Carl Sandburg. When "The Conscience of the Court" is published, the *Miami Herald* runs an article with the headline "Famous Negro Author Working as a Maid Here Just 'to Live a Little,' " attracting unwanted attention. Hurston continues work on her next novel, *The Lives of Barney Turk*, the story of a white Floridian's adventures in Central America and Hollywood (eventually rejected by Scribner's). Hurston leaves Rivo Island to work for conservative George Smathers on his successful Democratic Senate primary campaign against the liberal Claude Pepper, and to help his father, Frank Smathers, write an autobiography, *It's Wonderful to Live Again*. Hurston lives briefly at the Smathers home at 443 N.E. 39th Street in Miami. The *American Legion Magazine* publishes "I Saw Negro Votes Peddled," an article many blacks consider objectionable. In the fall, Hurston travels to D.C., staying at 1461 S Street, then to New York, staying at 239 West 131st Street from late September to early December. In December, she moves to Belle Glade, Florida, visiting her friends the Creeches, taking up residence at the Roof Garden Hotel, and exploring the Everglades by car.

1951-Hurston works on the novel *The Golden Bench of God*, about hairdressing entrepreneurs Annie Pope Malone and Madame C. J. Walker. In February, her dog is lost for nearly two weeks, causing Hurston great anxiety. In March and April, she is hospitalized with influenza. In June, the *American Legion Magazine* publishes "Why The Negro Won't Buy Communism," also considered objectionable by some of Hurston's old friends. In mid-June, Hurston moves back into the Eau Gallie cabin where she wrote *Mules and Men* twenty years earlier and embarks on ambitious home repairs and gardening. Scribner's rejects *The Golden Bench of God.* Her favorable profile of Ohio senator Robert Taft, candidate for the Republican presidential nomination, is published in the December 8 issue of the *Saturday Evening Post.* She switches from Ann Watkins to Jean Parker Waterbury as her exclusive literary agent. She believes the Watkins Agency is giving away her ideas. She begins reviewing books.

1952-Hurston lives in Eau Gallie, tending her gardens and caring for her pets. She starts a sequel to *Dust Tracks* (never completed) and pursues other smaller projects. She barely gets by on fees for speaking engagements, reprint fees from Lippincott, and translation rights. She suffers from various health problems. In June, Waterbury accepts an award on Hurston's behalf. In October, she is hired by the *Pittsburgh Courier* to cover the Ruby McCollum trial, a sensational case about a black woman charged with the murder of her lover, a prominent white doctor. Hurston works with journalist and anti-segregationist William Bradford Huie during the trial. (His book on the case, *Ruby McCollum: Woman in the Suwannee Jail,* includes a section on the case by Hurston.) Hurston's stories on McCollum appear in the *Courier* from October 1952 to May 1953.

1953-Hurston works on her biography of Herod the Great. She consults the works of Josephus, Livy, Eusebius, and Nicholas of Damascus. Believing Herod to have been a great leader and a dramatic, appealing figure, she tries to interest Cecil B. DeMille in producing and/or directing the story. She returns to the idea of buying Florida land. She advises ex-husband Herbert Sheen on marital problems.

1954-Hurston works on the Herod project to the exclusion of all other work. The book is half completed at midyear. Efforts to purchase land collapse when expected monies fail to materialize. She advises Huie on his Ruby McCollum book.

1955-By June, the Herod manuscript is nearly finished. Hurston is advised by Scribner's that the work has to be cut, but she is unable to part with any of her extensive research. She goes on a speaking tour in the late summer. In August, Scribner's rejects it as "disappointing." Hurston takes the rejection well and continues her work. She writes a controversial letter to the *Orlando Sentinel* criticizing the Supreme Court's landmark *Brown v. Board of Education* decision on segregation. The letter thrusts her into the political spotlight, which Hurston finds unpleasant. In December, she suffers a gall-bladder infection.

1956-Evicted from her cabin in March, Hurston moves out in May. In late May, she receives an award for "education and human relations" at the Bethune-

Cookman College graduation ceremony. In June, she begins work as a librarian at Patrick Air Force Base in Cocoa Beach, Florida, where she is paid $1.88 per hour ($325 a month). She begins to assemble her papers for donation to Yale University and the University of Florida. She continues to defend her position on racial integration.

1957-She encourages her nephew to visit. Troubles with her ulcer lessen. On May 10, Hurston is fired from her library job. She receives $26 per week in unemployment. She moves to Merritt Island across the Indian River and lives in a trailer. She continues to work on *Herod*. In October, she applies unsuccessfully for a job at the Air Force Missile Test Center in Cocoa. In December, C. E. Bolen invites her to write for his *Fort Pierce Chronicle*, a local black weekly. Hurston moves to Fort Pierce and contributes a series of columns called "Hoodoo and Black Magic," with most of the work recycled from earlier research. She writes a number of other articles. She tells Herbert Sheen that the disposition of her papers has been settled.

1958-In February, she starts substitute teaching at Lincoln Park Academy, a black school near her house in Fort Pierce. In September, she writes to the David McKay Company to solicit interest in her *Herod* manuscript, which they decline. In October, she works on establishing a Negro playground in Fort Pierce. Her health deteriorates: high blood pressure, obesity, gallbladder troubles, an ulcer, and various other ailments continue to plague her.

1959-Hurston suffers a stroke, leaving her weak and unable to concentrate. In May, she applies for welfare to cover her medicines; in June, she begins receiving food vouchers. She writes for the *Fort Pierce Chronicle* when she feels able. She suffers a series of strokes and is looked after by friends in Fort Pierce. On October 29, she enters the St. Lucie County Welfare Home. She does not communicate with her family. She spends time in Memorial Hospital. Friends also help care for her at home.

1960-Hurston dies on January 28, of "hypertensive heart disease." Her name is misspelled Zora Neil Hurston on her death certificate. The February 7 funeral is financed by donations from local acquaintances, friends, and publishers and is attended by approximately one hundred people. Hurston is buried in the Garden of Heavenly Rest, a segregated cemetery, in an unmarked grave (marked by Alice Walker in 1973).

GLOSSARY

Associated Negro Press. Established in 1919 by **Claude A. Barnett,** the ANP was a cooperative whose members—mostly black weeklies—supplied news through the mail and also shared expenses. In 1945, the ANP's peak period, there were 112 domestic subscribers to its news service. More than two hundred papers in Africa received the ANP wire services, which were translated into numerous languages. At times, nearly 90 percent of all black newspapers subscribed to the ANP's wire service. At its sale in 1964, a news service agency called the Negro Press International was established by some of the ANP staff. In 1969, its name was changed to the Black Press International and its ownership came under the Chicago offices of the Muslim paper *Muhammed Speaks.*

Claude A. Barnett (1889–1967). Born in Sanford, Florida, Claude Barnett attended public school in Oak Park, Illinois, and went to the Tuskegee Institute, where he earned an engineering degree. After college he worked for the Chicago post office for nine years and also worked as an advertising salesman for *The Chicago Defender,* which convinced him that black publications lacked sufficient news of black people. To expand black news, he founded and served as director of the **Associated Negro Press,** an international black wire service, in 1919. Barnett continued to head the ANP until 1964, when it ceased functioning. During his career, Barnett worked as special assistant to the secretary of agriculture in the Roosevelt and Truman administrations, directed the Supreme Life Insurance Company, and traveled often to Africa, from which, after World War II, he was able to add one hundred publications to the ANP subscribers. Barnett married Etta Moten in 1934.

Etta Moten Barnett (1902–). Born in San Antonio, Texas, singer, actress, community worker, and arts patron Etta Moten was a film and concert artist who had movie roles in *Flying Down to Rio* (1933) and *Gold Diggers* (1933) and theater roles in *Zombie, Fast and Furious* (the ill-fated 1931 revue produced by Hurston, **Porter Grainger, J. Rosamond Johnson,** and others), and *Sugar Hill* (also an unsuccessful black musical comedy). Moten performed in concert halls and on radio throughout the thirties. She was the first African American to sing at the White House. She represented the

U.S. government in Africa and served on the National Women's Conference Committee in the eighties. She married **Claude A. Barnett** in 1934.

Mary Elizabeth Barnicle (1891–1978). A musicologist and professor from New York University, Mary Elizabeth Barnicle worked with Hurston and **Alan Lomax** during a collecting trip in Belle Glade, Florida. Upon Hurston's suggestion, Lomax and Barnicle put on blackface in order not to be disturbed by whites during their trip. Hurston left the expedition after arguments with Barnicle. Most of Barnicle's work focused on Appalachia.

Richmond Barthé (1901–89). Perhaps the most famous sculptor of the Harlem Renaissance, Richmond Barthé is primarily known for his African and primitive motifs in works such as *Flute Boy, African Dancer,* and *Feral Benga,* all of which portray freedom and/or sensuality. Barthé's artistry was discovered at an early age (he began selling his portraits at the age of twelve) in Louisiana. During his residency at the Chicago Art Institute (1924–29), he developed a love of sculpting. In 1928, he received the Harmon Award and a Rosenwald Fellowship. In 1938, he was commissioned by the Harlem River Houses in New York City. He was also commissioned to make a bronze monument of **James Weldon Johnson**'s "black and unknown bards" but was not able to complete the project. Barthé was introduced to the patron **Charlotte Osgood Mason** by **Alain Locke.**

Mr. and **Mrs. Norton Baskin**: see **Marjorie Kinnan Rawlings.**

Jane Belo (Tannenbaum) (1904–68). Jane Belo's interest in anthropology began after a trip to Egypt, the Middle East, and Sudan. She studied at Barnard College, then took courses at the Sorbonne in 1934. She traveled to Haiti and Cuba with her first husband, George Biddle, a painter, and began to paint. In 1930, she traveled to the Dutch East Indies with her second husband, musicologist Colin McPhee, and researched Balinese life and art. While there she cultivated relationships with other Bali enthusiasts, including **Katharane Edson Mershon** and Margaret Mead. Belo and Hurston worked together in South Carolina studying religious trances in the "sanctified" church, and together they later produced anthropological films. Belo's photographs and films of Balinese religious ceremonies are particularly valuable. Belo's publications include *Trance in Bali* and *Traditional Balinese Culture* (ed.). In 1940, Belo married Frank Tannenbaum.

Ruth Benedict (1887–1948). Cultural anthropologist and poet Ruth Fulton Benedict was educated at Vassar, at the New School for Social Research, and at Columbia University under **Franz Boas.** She received her doctorate in 1923. Hurston started studying under Boas in 1925. In *Patterns of Culture* (1934) and *The Chrysanthemum and the Sword* (1946), she contended that the anthropologist should seek to understand, not judge, the cultural practices she documents. Her 1943 pamphlet, "The Races of Mankind," argued that given equal economic and educational opportunities, blacks and whites would achieve equally; this popular work was banned in army recreation centers.

Gwendolyn Bennett (1902–81). Born in Giddings, Texas, Gwendolyn Bennett was a poet, artist, teacher, journalist, and editor who became closely involved with Harlem Renaissance circles in the early twenties. In 1924, she graduated from the Pratt Institute with a degree in fine arts and accepted a teaching position with Howard University's fine arts department. Bennett's work came to the attention of Harlem Renaissance writers and artists in 1923 when her poem "Heritage" was published by *Opportunity*, and *Crisis* carried a cover illustrated by her. Along with **Langston Hughes, Countee Cullen, Eric Walrond, Helene Johnson, Wallace Thurman, Richard Bruce Nugent,** and Alta and **Aaron Douglas,** Bennett was a member of the Harlem Writers' Guild. She married Alfred Joseph Jackson in 1927 and accompanied her husband to Florida. After her husband's death in 1932, she returned to New York, working with the **Federal Writers' Project** and Federal Art Project of the Works Progress Administration and eventually marrying Richard Crosscup.

Mary McLeod Bethune (1875–1955). A pioneering African American educator, Mary McLeod Bethune founded the Daytona Normal and Industrial School for Negro Girls. This school eventually merged with the Cookman Institute to become Bethune-Cookman College. Bethune presided as president between 1922 and 1942. She was also a vice president of the **NAACP,** president of the National Council of Negro Women, and received the **Spingarn Medal** in 1935. In addition to several honorary degrees, she was given the African Star of Liberia and the Haitian Order of Honor and Merit. She married Albertus Bethune (d. 1919) in 1898. Her motto was "Be calm, be steadfast, be courageous."

Franz Boas (1858–1942). Often called the father of American anthropology, Franz Boas received his Ph.D. in physics from the University of Kiel in 1881, then undertook anthropological fieldwork among the Baffin Land Eskimos. He worked as an associate editor for the journal *Science* and supervised anthropological exhibits at the Chicago world's fair from 1892 to 1895. He joined the faculty of Columbia University in 1899 and taught there until 1937; also on the faculty at that time was **Ruth Benedict.** Hurston began her work with "Papa Franz" in 1925 while she attended Barnard. Throughout his career, Boas sought to demonstrate that the foundations of culture were social and environmental rather than biological, thus rejecting contemporary mythologies of racial or ethnic superiority. Boas was generally opposed to the trend in his field toward producing anthropological works for popular consumption, though his own widely read *Anthropology and Modern Life* (1928) was clearly written for a nonprofessional audience.

Arna Bontemps (1902–73). Writer, librarian, and educator Arna Bontemps was born in Louisiana and educated at Pacific Union College in Los Angeles and the University of Chicago. He was the recipient of a Rosenwald Fellowship for writing and work in the Caribbean in 1938. From 1943 to 1965, he served as head librarian at **Fisk University.** Among his many publications are *Black Thunder, God Sends Sunday,* and *The Harlem Renaissance Remembered* (ed.). From 1969 to 1972, he served as curator of the **James Weldon Johnson Collection** at Yale University. He married Alberta Johnson in 1926.

Benjamin A. Botkin (1901–75). Benjamin Botkin was hired in 1938 as the first full-time director of the **Federal Writers' Project**'s folklore program. Hurston probably came to know him when she went to work for **Carita Doggett Corse** that year. Later she would be in touch with him again in his role at the Archive of American Folksong in the Library of Congress's Folklore Division. Botkin was the recipient of Rosenwald and Guggenheim fellowships. He edited over a dozen books on folklore and was the author of *The American Play-Party Song*, published in 1937.

Herschel Brickell (1889–1952). Henry Herschel Brickell, born in Mississippi, was a reporter, editor, translator, journalist, and Latin Americanist who wrote for *The New York Times, New York Post, New York Herald Tribune,* and *Saturday Review,* and edited the *O. Henry Stories* from 1941 to 1951. He served as cultural relations assistant to U.S. ambassador Spruille Braden and as chief of the State Department's Division of Cultural Cooperation for Latin America. He was married to Norma Brickell.

Sterling Brown (1901–89). Poet and critic Sterling Brown was educated at Dunbar High School under Angelina Grimké and Jessie Fauset, at Williams College, and at Harvard University under Bliss Perry and F. O. Matthiessen. Brown taught at Virginia Seminary and College in Lynchburg, Lincoln University in Missouri, and **Fisk University** before joining the faculty of Howard University in 1929. His first volume of poetry, *Southern Road* (1932), powerfully conveys his extensive knowledge of folklore and folk vernacular. In *The Negro in American Fiction* (1937), Brown identified the stereotypical roles of American blacks as literary subjects, including the tragic mulatto, the contented slave, and the exotic primitive. *Negro Poetry and Drama* (1927) argued for the rich history of black cultural aesthetics. Brown served as national editor of Negro Affairs for the **Federal Writers' Project** from 1936 to 1939, was literary editor of *Opportunity,* and taught at Howard University for forty years.

Whit Burnett (1901–73). Author, editor, and Columbia University writing teacher Whit Burnett founded *Story* magazine in 1931 with his wife, Martha Foley, and served as its editor until 1953. He was the author or editor of dozens of books and anthologies, including many collections of stories culled from the magazine. His 1933 publication of Hurston's story "The Gilded Six-Bits" drew the attention of Bertram Lippincott and led to Hurston's first book contract.

Challenge (1934–37). In 1934, novelist and short-story writer **Dorothy West** used forty dollars of her own money to create the little magazine *Challenge,* a forum for both the old and the new guard of the Harlem Renaissance. Contributors included Hurston, **Langston Hughes, Arna Bontemps, Countee Cullen, Helene Johnson,** and **Claude McKay.** "We would like to print more articles and stories of protest," she wrote in the June 1936 issue. Financial problems and lack of quality submissions caused the publication to fold in 1937. West's *New Challenge* appeared in 1937, with Richard Wright as associate editor; it survived for only one issue. Hurston's "The Fire and the Cloud" was published in the September 1934 issue.

William Clifford (1924–). Travel, food, and wine writer William Clifford met Hurston through **Carl Van Vechten** and was friends with her in the late forties and early fifties. At the time he knew Hurston, Clifford was interested in writing on Indian history and philosophy, which Hurston encouraged. He lives in Morris, Connecticut.

Carita Doggett Corse (1891–1978). Carita Corse was Hurston's supervisor during 1938–39 when Hurston worked for the **Federal Writers' Project** in the Negro Unit, on the *Florida Negro* and a long-delayed Florida guidebook. Corse studied in the North, receiving her undergraduate degree from Vassar in 1913 and her master's degree from Columbia in 1916. She returned to the South and worked in Florida tourism and as a writer on Florida and early Spanish history. She received an honorary degree from the University of the South in 1932. Her works include *Dr. Andrew Turnbull and the New Smyrna Colony of Florida* (1919) and *Florida, Empire of the Sun* (1930). Corse and her husband, Herbert, had four children.

Miguel Covarrubias (1904–57). In 1923, Mexican painter, anthropologist, and writer Miguel Covarrubias left Mexico City and traveled to New York City, where his satiric portraits of jazz age celebrities for *Vanity Fair, The New Yorker,* and *Vogue* quickly gained him a national reputation. He shared a studio with caricaturist Al Hirschfeld and was, like Hurston, supported by wealthy patron **Charlotte Osgood Mason.** A collection of his early caricatures, *The Prince of Wales and Other Famous Americans,* was published in 1925. In Mexico he taught art history and wrote anthropological works on the native peoples of Bali and North and Central America. He was married to Rose Rolanda.

Sara Lee Creech (1916–). Born to Mary Araminta Young Creech, dean of girls at a small college, and Lewis Thomas, Sr., a merchant, Sara Lee Creech was raised in Sparta, Georgia. She moved to Belle Glade, Florida, in the early thirties and graduated from Pahokee High School in 1935. In Florida, Creech worked as a businesswoman, starting her own insurance agency in 1938, as an activist for civil rights and education, and as a florist. Creech helped found Belle Glade's Inter-Racial Council in 1947 and served as president of the Business and Professional Women's Club. In the late 1940s, with the help of Maxeda Von Hesse and Sheila Burlingame, and the support of Eleanor Roosevelt and Ralph Bunche, she created the Sara Lee doll, the nation's first high-quality black doll. In the fifties and sixties, Creech helped develop the Wee Care Child Development Center in Belle Glade, one of the nation's first daycare centers designed for migrant workers. She worked at Palm Beach Community College until her retirement in 1985. She lives in Lake Worth.

Crisis. The official publication of the **NAACP,** the *Crisis,* founded in 1910, was first edited by **W. E. B. Du Bois.** The monthly magazine reached a circulation of 116,000 and became the most significant publication in black America. Du Bois contended that the mission of the *Crisis* was to "set forth those facts and arguments which show the danger of race prejudice." The publication included articles on race relations, editorials arguing a vigorous antilynching and anti–Jim Crow stand, reports of the NAACP, and literary works.

Countee Cullen (1903–46). Orphaned as a child, Countee Leroy Porter was informally adopted by the Reverend and Mrs. Frederick Cullen in 1918. While attending DeWitt Clinton High School in New York City, Cullen published "I Have a Rendezvous with Life" for *Magpie,* the school's literary magazine. Cullen's success continued while he attended New York University, publishing in such popular magazines as *Opportunity, Crisis,* and *Harper's* as well as winning numerous poetry contests. His 1925 publication of *Color* (while a graduate student at Harvard) was followed by *The Ballad of the Brown Girl* and *Copper Sun* (both published in 1927), earning him the title of Harlem's poet laureate, which he shared with **Langston Hughes.** At the height of his literary popularity, in 1928 Cullen married Nina Yolande Du Bois, daughter of **W. E. B. Du Bois.** Many believed that the two-year marriage was cut short by Cullen's relationship with **Harold Jackman** (they were known to friends as "David and Jonathan"), who accompanied Cullen to France shortly after the wedding. He and his wife divorced soon after his return to the States. From 1932 to 1945, he taught at Frederick Douglass Junior High School in New York City. In 1940, he married Ida Mae Roberson.

Nancy Cunard (1897–1965). Heiress to the Cunard cruise line fortune, poet, writer, and editor Nancy Cunard was enough of a rebel to be disowned by the family. She was married briefly, in 1916, and moved to Paris, where she wrote and worked as an artistic and literary model for such modernists as Brancusi, Wyndham Lewis, Man Ray, T. S. Eliot, and Aldous Huxley (one of Cunard's many lovers). She became a communist, worked actively on the Scottsboro case (over which she fell out with **W. E. B. Du Bois** and the **NAACP**), lived openly with her black lover, composer and musician Henry Crowder, and devoted herself both to the modernist avant-garde and to black culture and arts. She and Crowder founded the Hours Press in Paris, publishing the work of Samuel Beckett, Ezra Pound, and others. Cunard edited her massive *Negro: An Anthology* in 1934. Like **Carl Van Vechten,** Cunard was thoroughly associated with black culture. Hurston's contributions to Cunard's *Negro,* the often reprinted "Characteristics of Negro Expression" and "Spirituals and Neo-Spirituals," are among her most important early statements on the beauty of vernacular black culture. Unfortunately, no correspondence between Hurston and Cunard has been found.

Whitney Darrow (1881–1970). Editor Whitney Darrow founded Princeton University Press and served as its director from 1905 until 1917, when he moved to Scribner's, from which he retired in 1956, having served as executive vice president. He published *A Child's Guide to Freud* in 1963.

Aaron Douglas (1899–1979). Painter, muralist, sculptor, and educator Aaron Douglas was educated at the University of Nebraska, the University of Kansas, Columbia University Teachers College, and the Académie de la Grande Chaumière in Paris. In 1924, Douglas moved to Harlem, where he studied with German artist Winold Reiss.

In 1926, Douglas was, like Hurston, one of the many coeditors of *Fire!!*. Hurston and **Langston Hughes** introduced Douglas to **Charlotte Osgood Mason,** who became his patron. Mason disapproved of formal study for Douglas, fearing it would blunt what she saw as his natural primitivism; he eventually broke with her. Douglas's work appeared widely and his murals were commissioned for Harlem's Club Ebony and the Countee Cullen Branch of the New York Public Library. He later taught and became professor emeritus at **Fisk University.** He was married to Alta Sawyer.

W. E. B. Du Bois (1868–1963). Sociologist, scholar, pacifist, activist, anti-imperialist, historian, editor, and writer W. E. B. Du Bois was one of the leading intellectuals of the twentieth century and one of the most influential senior figures of the Harlem Renaissance. Born in Great Barrington, Massachusetts, Du Bois was educated at **Fisk University,** Harvard, and the University of Berlin. He received his Ph.D. from Harvard. Deeply resented by Hurston for his idea of the "talented tenth," his political opposition to the policies of Booker T. Washington, his prominent role as a "race man," and his socialism, Du Bois was known both for personal aloofness and for constant attention to race and racial inequality. Du Bois helped to found the **NAACP,** served as its director of publicity and research from 1910 to 1934, and founded and edited the organization's magazine, the *Crisis.* He also founded the Niagara Movement and organized the influential Pan-African Congress as well as the Krigwa Players, a black theater troupe started in Harlem in 1927. In 1934, Du Bois went to Atlanta University, where he served as chairman of the sociology department and edited *Phylon.* He joined the Socialist Party in 1911 (which he left a year later), traveled to Russia in 1927, was ousted from the NAACP for his radical views in 1948, visited Russia and China in 1958 and 1959, and joined the Communist Party in 1961, when he moved permanently to Ghana. Among his many books are *The Philadelphia Negro, The Souls of Black Folk, Dark Princess, Darkwater,* and *Black Reconstruction.*

Max Eastman (1883–1969). Editor, writer, and activist Max Eastman founded the influential radical journal the *Masses* in 1913, which was banned by the U.S. government in 1917. He then founded the *Liberator,* which he edited from 1918 to 1922. These journals published a range of radical writers, including John Reed, Floyd Dell, Louis Untermeyer, Mary Heaton Vorse, Walter Lippmann, **Carl Sandburg,** Amy Lowell, and Sherwood Anderson. Eastman was twice tried for sedition under the Espionage Act but was not found guilty. He authored more than three dozen books, including *The Literary Mind, Artists in Uniform,* and *Marxism: Is It Science?* Eastman's socialism might seem to make him an unusual friend for the strongly anti-communist Hurston. But Eastman's disillusionment with Stalin led him to attack Marxism late in his life and even to support Senator Joseph McCarthy; this may have endeared him to her. Eastman worked as a reporter for *Reader's Digest* from 1941 to 1969. He married three times: to Ida Rauh, Eliena Krylenko, and Yvette Szekely.

Edwin Rogers Embree (1883–1950). Trained as a sociologist and descended from abolitionists Elihu Embree on his father's side and John G. Fee on his mother's, Edwin Embree devoted much of his life to race relations and public service. He served as secretary and vice president of the Rockefeller Foundation, president of the **Rosenwald Foundation,** and, in 1948, president of the Liberian Foundation. Embree received his B.A. in philosophy in 1906 and his master's in 1913, both from Yale University, and worked from 1906 to 1913 as a reporter, editor, alumni registrar, and secretary of appointments at Yale. In 1907, he married Kate Scott Clark. They had three children (John Fee, Edwina, and Catherine). As secretary of the Rockefeller Foundation from 1917 to 1923 and director of its division of studies from 1923 to 1927, Embree traveled widely, promoting the foundation's work in medicine, biology, anthropology, and public health. He served as vice president for a year before leaving the Rockefeller Foundation to assume the presidency of the Rosenwald Foundation, which he held from 1927 until the foundation's funds were exhausted in 1948. Embree's publications include *Brown America: The Story of a New Race, American Negroes: A Handbook, Brown Americans: The Story of a Tenth of a Nation,* and *Negroes in America.*

Helen Worden Erskine (Cranmer) (1896–1984). Helen Worden Erskine was a writer, editor, correspondent, and columnist whom Hurston came to know during the late forties and early fifties, perhaps through writing reviews for the same papers for which Worden was writing or, more likely, through Hurston's employment with the Republican congressional campaign of Grant Reynolds (who ran against Adam Clayton Powell, Jr.), a campaign to which Worden contributed. Worden worked for the *New York World* from 1926 to 1931 and for the *New York World-Telegram* from 1931 to 1944. From 1944 to 1947, she wrote for *Reader's Digest* and *Liberty* magazine. From 1947 to 1949, when Hurston came to know her, she was working as a columnist for the *New York Herald Tribune.* Worden was associate editor of *Collier's* magazine from 1951 to 1956.

Fast and Furious. On September 15, 1931, this "colored revue in thirty-seven scenes" opened at the New York Theater and closed in one week after poor reviews. Hurston wrote three scenes, appeared in two, and assisted with direction. **J. Rosamond Johnson** and **Porter Grainger** worked on the show. The cast included Hurston, Jackie "Moms" Mabley, **Etta Moten Barnett,** Tim Moore, and Juano Hernandez.

Federal Writers' Project (1935–43). Part of the New Deal's Works Progress Administration (WPA), the Federal Writers' Project (FWP) sought to provide work for unemployed writers during and after the Depression. The FWP employed more than three hundred writers, including Hurston, John Cheever, Ralph Ellison, Richard Wright, and Saul Bellow. Hurston was first involved in the Harlem Unit of the Federal Theater Project in 1935. In 1939, she joined the FWP in Jacksonville and became head of the Florida FWP's Negro Unit. Hurston's supervisor was **Carita Doggett Corse,** Florida director of the organization.

Fire!! Published in November 1926, and "devoted to the Younger Negro Artists," *Fire!!* was a high-quality literary quarterly founded by **Wallace Thurman** (editor), **Langston Hughes** and Hurston (coeditors), John P. Davis (business manager), **Richard Bruce Nugent** (distribution), **Gwendolyn Bennett,** and **Aaron Douglas.**

Announcing its intent to "burn up a lot of old, dead conventional Negro-white ideas of the past," *Fire!!* was deliberately controversial. A publicity letter of Thurman's expressed the group's desire to "be provocative—[we] want it to provide the shocks necessary to encourage new types of artistic interest and new types of artistic energy." Responses in the black press were mixed. **W. E. B. Du Bois** and **Alain Locke** offered cautious praise for *Fire!!*'s "striking" illustrations, "beautiful printing," "literary revolt," and "left-wing literary modernism," and called for "wide support" for its efforts. Others excoriated the journal: "I have just tossed the first issue of *Fire!!*—into the fire and watched the crackling flames leap and snarl as though they were trying to swallow some repulsive dose," *The Afro-American* wrote. Ironically, most of the copies of *Fire!!* were destroyed in a fire in the basement of Thurman's apartment building. Only one issue was ever published.

Fisk University. Fisk University, founded as an elementary and normal school in 1865 on the grounds of a former Union hospital in Nashville, Tennessee, as the Fisk Free Colored School, is a private, coeducational liberal arts university and one of the most highly regarded among the historically black colleges. Fisk's goal, unlike that of many other vocationally and industrially oriented black colleges, such as Hampton and Tuskegee, was to provide a "first-class college" of instruction in classics, the liberal arts, and the natural and social sciences. In 1871, Fisk's treasurer and music instructor, George L. White, formed the famous Jubilee Singers and took them on the first of many successful fund-raising tours of spirituals. During the 1920s, controversy raged at Fisk over long-standing policies of a strict disciplinary code for blacks, segregated concerts and other school functions, and lack of support for student government and the student paper. Among Fisk's illustrious alumni are **W. E. B. Du Bois,** Mrs. Booker T. Washington, the son of Booker T. Washington, Congressman William Levi Dawson, novelist Frank Yerby, and Roland Hayes. Fisk faculty included **Charles S. Johnson** (president of Fisk, 1947–56), **James Weldon Johnson, Aaron Douglas,** and **Arthur A. Schomburg.**

Lewis Gannett (1891–1966). As a journalist and author, Lewis Gannett wrote for such newspapers as the *New York World,* the *Survey,* the *Nation,* the *Manchester Guardian,* and eventually the *New York Herald Tribune,* where he was the book review columnist for "Books and Things" from 1930 to 1956. As the author of more than six thousand columns, Gannett was awarded the Best Book Reviewer award by the American Writers Congress in 1939. He also wrote books himself, including *Young China, Sweet Land,* and *Cream Hill.* Along with others, Gannett circulated a petition in 1922 protesting Harvard's ban on African American dormitory residency.

Porter Grainger (birth and death dates unknown). Porter Grainger was a lyricist, musician, composer, writer, actor, and accompanist. He appeared in and contributed to numerous shows of the 1920s, including *Get Set* (1923), featuring Ethel Waters, *Lucky Sambo* (1925), *De Board Meeting* (1925), and *Brown Buddies* (1930). He is known to have accompanied Bessie Smith and Clara Smith during their Columbia recording sessions. Along with Bob Pickett, Grainger published "How to Play and

Sing the Blues Like the Phonograph and Stage Artists," an instructional pamphlet for fans of blues music who could learn how "to play the role of the oppressed and depressed." After the 1920s, Grainger virtually disappeared.

Paul Green (1894–1981). Interested in the dramatization of black American folklore, Paul Green was one of the first white playwrights in America to write for black actors. He attended the University of North Carolina and taught there before going to Cornell for graduate study. In 1927, he won the Pulitzer Prize for *In Abraham's Bosom*, a drama of black life set in his native North Carolina. Hurston attended Green's weekly playwriting seminar at Chapel Hill in 1939, and they talked of collaborating on a play called *John de Conqueror*. Green worked with Orson Welles and Richard Wright to adapt *Native Son* in 1941; he also wrote the screenplay for *State Fair*.

Edwin Osgood Grover: see **Rollins College.**

Guggenheim Foundation. The John Simon Guggenheim Memorial Foundation was founded in 1925 by former Colorado senator Simon Guggenheim and his wife in memory of John Simon Guggenheim, their son, who died on April 26, 1922. A broad-minded man from a Jewish family that had gone from poverty to great wealth, Simon Guggenheim ran a purportedly corrupt political campaign, determined to buy his way into office, if necessary. The Guggenheim Foundation, one of the most far-sighted foundations in the history of philanthropy, was modeled on the Rhodes Foundation and had, as initial advisers, Cecil Rhodes and **Henry Allen Moe.** The idea behind the Guggenheim Fellowship, unique in its day, was that its recipients would be "selected by juries of experts in their fields" and that their fellowship money would free them up to do whatever they wished in order to advance their work— paint, write, read, or travel. The Guggenheim Foundation was especially interested in funding the creative work of blacks, a policy that was aggressively and positively pursued to the benefit of Hurston, **Langston Hughes,** and others.

Melville Herskovits (1895–1963). Cultural anthropologist and Africanist Melville Herskovits studied at Columbia University under **Franz Boas.** In 1927, Herskovits began working at Northwestern University, where he founded the first African studies program in the United States, focusing on the ethnography of the African diaspora. *The Myth of a Negro Past* (1942) examined African antecedents in African American culture. Other major works by Herskovits are *The American Negro: A Study in Racial Crossing, Suriname Folk-Lore,* and *Man and His Works: The Science of Cultural Anthropology.* He was married to anthropologist Frances Shapiro Herskovits.

Spessard Lindsey Holland (1892–1971). Conservative Democratic senator Spessard Holland was born in Polk County, Florida, and raised in Atlanta, Georgia. He graduated from Emory College in 1912 and the University of Florida College of Law at Gainesville in 1916. After World War I, Holland became prosecuting attorney then county judge of Polk County. He was a member of the Florida State Senate from

1932 to 1940. While governor of Florida, from 1941 to 1945, Holland placed labor unions under state regulation and negotiated the establishment of the Everglades National Park. As United States senator from Florida from 1946 to 1971, Holland participated in filibusters against civil rights legislation, arguing that civil rights were a state, not a federal, issue. Holland did, however, sponsor the Twenty-fourth Amendment to the Constitution, which outlawed the poll tax in federal elections. Hurston publicly endorsed Senator Holland over his liberal Senate rival, Claude Pepper.

Hamilton Holt (1872–1951). Hamilton Holt graduated from Yale University in 1894 and began to work on the *Independent,* a New York religious weekly his grandfather owned, in the same year. Holt started graduate work at Columbia University but did not finish, deciding instead to devote himself to journalism. In 1912, he became editor of the *Independent,* which he secularized and broadened. After a failed 1924 bid to become U.S. senator from Connecticut, Holt assumed the presidency of Florida's all-white **Rollins College.** He served as president from 1924 to 1949.

Nora Holt (1890–1974). Nora Holt is one of the more intriguing and mysterious figures of the Harlem Renaissance. Born Lena Douglas in Kansas City to Grace Brown Douglas and the Reverend Calvin N. Douglas, an African Methodist Episcopal minister, Nora Holt was a stunning beauty who married six times and whose love life was avidly reported by the news media. A serious composer and music critic, Holt was the first black woman to receive a master of music degree (from Chicago Musical College in 1918). She also performed as a nightclub singer in Chicago. She studied at Western University in Kansas, Columbia University, and the University of Southern California, also serving on the board of education for the city of Los Angeles. She founded the National Association of Negro Musicians and had a radio show, from 1953 to 1964, called *The Nora Holt Showcase.* A wealthy woman by the time she was thirty, Nora Holt was tagged with the line "she can't behave." The character of Lasca Sartoris in **Carl Van Vechten**'s infamous novel *Nigger Heaven* is based on Nora Holt, as is a character in **Countee Cullen**'s novel *One Way to Heaven.* Holt and Hurston were friends and corresponded, but no letters between them survive. Nora Holt died in a Los Angeles nursing home.

William Stanley Hoole (1903–90). Librarian, teacher, and author William Stanley Hoole was educated at Wofford College, North Texas University, Columbia University, the University of Chicago Graduate Library School, and Duke University. Hoole worked in numerous government capacities and became university librarian and dean of the libraries at the University of Alabama in 1944, where he organized the university's special collections department. The special collections division of the library was named in his honor in 1977. Among Hoole's many publications are articles and monographs on the Civil War, Reconstruction, South America, Alabama history, Florida history, Native Americans, military history, southern theater, southern folklore, and higher education. In 1936 when Hoole knew Hurston, he was working as a librarian at Birmingham College.

Langston Hughes (1902–67). Born in Joplin, Missouri, Langston Hughes grew up in Lawrence, Kansas, and Cleveland, Ohio. He attended Columbia University briefly in 1921–22 and graduated from Lincoln University in 1929. Hughes's career as a writer of poetry, fiction, essays, drama, opera, gospel, history, biography, autobiography, humor, anthologies, and translations began in the twenties with poetry publications in the *Crisis* and radical black weeklies such as the *Messenger*. Throughout the twenties, Hughes lived in Harlem and Washington, D.C. He traveled to Africa and Paris in the twenties and to Haiti, Cuba, and the Soviet Union in the thirties. Hughes came from a radical family, which included a grandmother whose first husband was killed at Harpers Ferry, and throughout his life he worked for many progressive causes. Like Hurston, Hughes published in *The New Negro* (edited by **Alain Locke**) in 1925, worked on *Fire!!,* and was a protégé of **Charlotte Osgood Mason** (from 1928 to 1930). Hughes received awards from *Opportunity* and the *Crisis* and won the Harmon Award in 1930. He traveled with Hurston in the South collecting folklore and worked with her on *Mule Bone,* the collaboration that many believe destroyed their relationship. *The Weary Blues* and *Fine Clothes to the Jew* were published by Knopf in 1926 and 1927, establishing his reputation, along with Countee Cullen, as one of the two poet laureates of the Harlem Renaissance. *Not Without Laughter* was published in 1930. Other publications include *A Negro Looks at Soviet Central Asia, The Big Sea, Fields of Wonder, Street Scene, One Way Ticket, Montage of a Dream Deferred, Ask Your Mama,* and *The Panther and the Lash.*

William Bradford Huie (1910–86). Controversial writer William Bradford Huie wrote twenty-one books and hundreds of essays, articles, and short stories, often focusing on violent, sensational stories of race relations. Throughout his career he faced criticism for "checkbook journalism." When Hurston was denied permission to interview Ruby McCollum in 1952, she urged Huie to cover the sensational murder trial. Four years later, Huie published *Ruby McCollum: Woman in the Suwannee Jail,* which contained a section by Hurston. Huie would later pay James Earl Ray $40,000 for the story of the assassination of Martin Luther King, Jr.

Fannie Hurst (1889–1968). Fannie Hurst was one of the most famous and most highly paid writers of the 1920s and 1930s. Born in Hamilton, Ohio, of German-Jewish descent and raised in St. Louis, Hurst began her writing career in her early teens. After thirty-five rejections from the *Saturday Evening Post,* Hurst's "Power and Horse Power" was finally published in 1912. In 1914, she married classical pianist Jacques S. Danielson, a marriage she kept secret until 1920. During her career, she published more than eighteen novels (*Imitation of Life* was one) and hundreds of short stories, plays, and other writings. Hurst formed close friendships with Hurston, **Carl Van Vechten,** Blanche and Alfred Knopf, the Roosevelts, and many others. Her political activity included membership on the Committee on Workman's Compensation for Household Employees, the Heckscher Foundation, the Russell Sage Foundation, the Mayor's Committee on Unity in New York, the New York Urban League, and United Neighborhood Houses. She supported public health, advocated birth control, and demanded rights for homosexuals, Jews, and African Americans.

Harold Jackman (1900–60). Born in London, raised in Harlem, Harold Jackman was friends with **Countee Cullen, Carl Van Vechten,** Hurston, and others. He was caricatured in both *Nigger Heaven* by Van Vechten and *Infants of the Spring* by **Wallace Thurman.** Jackman was a schoolteacher in Harlem and founded the Countee Cullen Memorial Collection at Atlanta University in 1947. Many believe that Jackman's intimate relationship with Cullen broke up Cullen's first marriage.

Charles S. Johnson (1893–1956). As a sociologist, editor and founder of *Opportunity,* advocate of racial equality, and the first black president of **Fisk University,** Charles S. Johnson was, according to **Langston Hughes,** one of the three "midwives" of the Harlem Renaissance (the other two were Jessie Fauset and **Alain Locke**). Born in Bristol, Virginia, to a middle-class family, Johnson graduated from Wayland Academy, Virginia Union University, and the University of Chicago, where he studied with Robert E. Park, who influenced Johnson's assimilationist philosophy of race relations. The 1922 publication of *The Negro in Chicago: A Study of Race Relations and a Race Riot,* as well as his consequent position with the National Urban League, helped to establish him as one of the most important figures in the study of race relations. While an editor for *Opportunity,* Johnson emphasized the importance of black literary production and sponsored numerous literary contests (some winners were Hurston, Langston Hughes, **Countee Cullen,** and **Sterling Brown**). In 1928, Johnson became chair of the department of social science at Fisk University. Some of his major works are *Shadow of the Plantation, Growing Up in the Black Belt: Negro Youth in the Rural South,* and *Patterns of Negro Segregation.* Johnson became Fisk's first black president in 1947, determined to make it "the Harvard of Negro colleges." Johnson married Marie Antoinette Burgette on November 6, 1920.

Georgia Douglas Johnson (1886–1966). Born in Atlanta, Georgia Douglas Johnson graduated from Atlanta University's normal school and studied at Oberlin's Conservatory of Music. Johnson opened her home in Washington, D.C., as a weekly literary salon, nicknamed the "Half-way House." Visitors included Jean Toomer, **Langston Hughes,** and William Stanley Braithwaite. Johnson was the recipient of two *Opportunity* prizes and, in 1965, was awarded an honorary doctorate from Atlanta University. She married Henry Lincoln Johnson in 1903. She published poems in *Crisis, Voice of the Negro, Opportunity,* and elsewhere. Her books of poems include *The Heart of a Woman, Bronze: A Book of Verse, An Autumn Love Cycle,* and *Share My World.*

Grace Mott Johnson (1882–1967). A sculptor and civil rights activist who studied in Paris and with Gutzon Borglum in the United States, Johnson grew up on a farm in New York and was educated at home. She and her husband, cubist Andrew Dasburg (m. 1909, d. 1922), both exhibited in New York City, including at the Armory Show and the Whitney Studio show. Johnson was particularly well known for her animal sculptures and her 1930s series of sculptures of black children and adults.

(Francis) Hall Johnson (1888–1970). African American composer, choral director, and playwright Francis Hall Johnson studied music at Knoxville's Knox Institute, Atlanta University, Columbia's Allen University, Philadelphia's Hahn School, the University of Pennsylvania, and the University of Southern California. He played violin in Will Marion Cook's New York Syncopated Orchestra in 1918, in the orchestra of the smash musical comedy *Shuffle Along* in 1921, and in the Negro String Quartet, which he began in 1923. In 1925, he founded the Hall Johnson Choir, which performed with prominent orchestras for radio, film, and theater. In 1930, he was choral director for Marc Connelly's successful musical *The Green Pastures*. Johnson wrote and produced the successful folk opera *Run Little Chillun*, which ran on Broadway for 126 performances in 1933 and was revived in Los Angeles in 1935. Hurston attempted to collaborate with Johnson on her own show *The Great Day*; she later claimed that Johnson's *Chillun* stole material from this work.

Helene Johnson (1908–95). Born in Boston to a professional, literary, middle-class, Brookline family which included her cousin **Dorothy West,** Johnson traveled frequently between Boston and Oak Bluffs, Massachusetts, on Martha's Vineyard. Helene Johnson graduated from Girls' Latin High School and in 1927 moved to New York, living at 44 West 66th Street, a building in which Hurston also had an apartment. In 1925, Johnson won first prize in a *Boston Chronicle* short-story contest, then her poem "Trees of Night" received an honorable mention in that year's *Opportunity* literary contest, and her poem "Fulfillment" received an honorable mention the subsequent year. Between 1925 and 1930, Johnson's poetry appeared frequently in such publications as *The Messenger, Vanity Fair,* the *Saturday Evening Quill,* and *Challenge.* Her work was anthologized in **James Weldon Johnson**'s *Book of American Negro Poetry* (1922) and **Countee Cullen**'s *Caroling Dusk* (1927). Johnson married William Warner Hubbell in the thirties and worked, along with **Gwendolyn Bennett,** at the Consumers' Union in Mount Vernon, New York.

J(ohn). Rosamond Johnson (1873–1954). A classical pianist, J. Rosamond Johnson was trained at the New England Conservatory of Music in Boston but moved quickly into popular music, beginning in 1897 with *Oriental America,* the first African American Broadway show to move away from burlesque. In 1899, Johnson began collaborating with his brother, **James Weldon Johnson,** on theater productions, beginning with *Toloso,* a satire of American imperialism. The two brothers also worked with Bob Cole, and the threesome wrote more than two hundred songs, including the Negro National Anthem—"Lift Every Voice and Sing"—and "Under the Bamboo Tree." With Bob Cole, J. Rosamond Johnson had an extremely successful career as a vaudevillian and theatrical producer. Johnson was the first African American to conduct an all-white orchestra in New York, which he did in 1911 for the production *Hello Paris.* In 1912, he became musical director of the Grand Opera House in London. He married Nora Floyd in 1913.

James Weldon Johnson (1871–1938). Born in Jacksonville, Florida, James Weldon Johnson studied at Atlanta University, was principal of Jacksonville's black grammar school, and was admitted to the Florida bar in 1897. He served as U.S. consul to

Venezuela (1906–8) and to Nicaragua (1909–12). In 1914, he began work as a writer and translator. In 1916, he accepted the post of field secretary for the **NAACP**, was promoted to secretary in 1920, and remained with the NAACP until 1930. Toward the end of his life, Johnson accepted a teaching post at **Fisk University. Carl Van Vechten** named his Collection of Negro Arts and Letters at Yale University in Johnson's honor. Among Johnson's many publications are *The Autobiography of an Ex-Colored Man, The Book of American Negro Poetry, God's Trombones: Seven Negro Sermons in Verse, Black Manhattan, Along This Way,* and *Negro Americans: What Now.* Johnson married Grace Nail in 1910.

Thomas Elsa Jones (1888–1973). Born in Fairmount, Indiana, Thomas Elsa Jones was president of **Fisk University** from 1926 to 1946. During his presidency, Fisk's programs, faculty, endowment, and buildings grew, and Fisk was accredited by national organizations such as the Association of American Universities. Jones was able to attract significant support for Fisk from the **Rosenwald Foundation** and the Carnegie Corporation, as well as from the General Education Board of Tennessee. Upon leaving Fisk, he assumed the presidency of Earlham College, his alma mater, in Richmond, Indiana, which he held until retirement in 1958. Jones was a founder in 1944 of the United Negro College Fund. Among his publications are *Letters to a College President* and his autobiography, *Light on the Horizon.*

Stetson Kennedy (1916–). Born in Jacksonville, Florida, Stetson Kennedy is an activist, writer, investigative reporter, lecturer, and folklorist. Kennedy studied at the University of Florida but left in 1937 to join the WPA. There he served as Hurston's supervisor on *The Florida Negro.* As a reporter, Kennedy went undercover into the Klan, which he exposed in his 1954 book, *I Rode with the Klan.* He ran as a write-in candidate for the State Senate in 1950, inspiring a campaign song by Woody Guthrie. He is a founding member and past president of the Florida Folklore Society. Among his publications are *Palmetto Country, Southern Exposure, The Jim Crow Guide to the South, After Appomattox: How the South Won the War,* and *South Florida Folklife,* which he edited. Kennedy has been featured on radio, television, and in various histories of labor, the South, and civil rights.

Otto Klineberg (1899–1992). Born in Quebec and educated at McGill, Harvard, and Columbia Universities, social psychologist Otto Klineberg's work demonstrated the effects of substandard schools on blacks. His work on race and intelligence testing was influential in the 1954 Supreme Court case of *Brown v. Board of Education* and was helpful in overturning the "separate but equal" laws. Along with **Melville Herskovits** and Margaret Mead, Klineberg was the recipient of a fellowship from the National Research Council through which Klineberg first began his studies of migration, education, race, and intelligence. Like anthropologists Hurston, Herskovits, and Boas, Klineberg repudiated notions of rigid racial difference. In 1961, he went to Paris, where he served as director of the International Center for Intergroup Relations at the University of Paris until 1982, when he returned to New York to teach at the City University of New York. Among Klineberg's publications are *Race Differ-*

ences, Diversity Within National Unity, Children's Views of Foreign Peoples: A Cross-National Study, and *Students, Values, and Politics: A Cross Cultural Comparison.*

Marie Laveau (1794?–1881). A free New Orleans woman of African, Indian, French, and Spanish descent and a onetime devout Catholic, Marie Laveau, the self-proclaimed "Pope of Voodoo," became the most powerful voodoo priestess in the world during the 1800s. Voodoo, Hurston wrote understatedly in *Mules and Men,* "has its thousands of secret adherents. . . . Nobody knows for sure how many thousands in America are warmed by the fire of hoodoo, because the worship is bound in secrecy." In 1928 in New Orleans, Hurston served as an apprentice to a number of hoodoo priests and priestesses, most of whom were followers of Laveau and some of whom claimed to be her descendants. As a novitiate, Hurston was "crowned" by a grandnephew of Laveau's after an elaborate rite of passage that required her to lie facedown and naked for nearly seventy hours, without food or water. For Laveau, hoodoo was a way for black women to gain power in a racist and sexist world. Laveau was married to Jacques Paris, a free black man, in 1819. Marie Laveau continues to have followers.

Katherine Tracy L'Engle (1892–1986). Born in Atlanta, Katherine Tracy L'Engle was a Broadway actress, writer, radio broadcaster, little theater director, editor, and lecturer on women's fashions. She was educated at Columbia University, where she received her M.A. She worked as a YMCA volunteer with the American Expeditionary Force and the Army of the Occupation in France and Germany. In the twenties and thirties, she worked as a radio broadcaster in New York, under the name of Winifred Carter. In 1955, she married William Mack Angas. She died in Jacksonville, Florida.

J. B. Lippincott Company. One of the oldest publishing firms in the United States, Lippincott was first established in Philadelphia in 1836 as a publisher of Bibles and other religious literature. It was particularly well known for medical, religious, and educational textbooks. Known as willing to risk controversy, Lippincott published the scandalous novels *The Quick and the Dead* (1889) and *The Woman Thou Gavest Me* (1913). When Hurston signed with Lippincott in the 1930s, the company was one of the biggest trade publishers in the nation and had moved its offices to New York. The company was bought by Harper & Row in 1977.

Alain Locke (1886–1954). In 1907, educator and critic Alain Locke became the first black recipient of a Rhodes scholarship. He had previously distinguished himself at Harvard University, where he received his B.A. Locke began work as an assistant professor of education and philosophy at Howard University in 1912, stayed for four years, then returned to Harvard for his Ph.D. in philosophy. He chaired the department of philosophy at Howard from 1918 to 1953. Hurston was a student of Locke's at Howard and a member of his literary club, the Stylus. His influential anthology *The New Negro* was considered by many to be the definitive collection of Harlem Renaissance writings. Locke wrote many critical works for *Opportunity,* including a qualified review of *Their Eyes Were Watching God* in 1938. Like Hurston and

Langston Hughes, Locke was for a time supported by **Charlotte Osgood Mason.** Among his many writings are *Four Negro Poets, Plays of Negro Life: A Source Book, The Negro in American Literature, The Negro in America, Frederick Douglass: A Biography of Anti-Slavery, The Negro and His Music, Negro Art: Past and Present,* and *Race Contacts and Interracial Relations.*

John Lomax (1867–1948) and **Alan Lomax** (1915–2002). Folklorists, musicologists, and anthropologists John and Alan Lomax are known for bringing folk music to wide American appreciation. John Lomax was born in Mississippi and grew up in Texas. He received his B.A. in English from the University of Texas and his M.A. from Harvard. He served as president of the American Folklore Society and then curator of the Archive of American Folksong at the Library of Congress. His first wife, Bess, died in 1932; he remarried in 1934 and moved to Washington, D.C. Together, he and his son, Alan Lomax, traveled more than sixteen thousand miles in one four-month collecting trip alone. Among folksingers they fostered were Huddie "Leadbelly" Ledbetter and Woody Guthrie. John Lomax's publications include *Cowboy Songs and Ballads, Songs of the Cattle Trail and Cow Camp,* and *Adventures of a Ballad Hunter.* Alan Lomax was born in Texas and also lived in Illinois. He received his B.A. in English from the University of Texas. He worked in Haiti as well as the United States and began a weekly radio show in 1939. He started at the Library of Congress as assistant to his father in the Archive of American Folksong and took over as its director in 1940 when his father partially retired. He has also served as the director of folk music for Decca Records and directs the *American Patchwork* series for PBS. He developed a multimedia database called "The Global Jukebox." Among his many publications are *The Land Where the Blues Began* and, with his father, *American Ballads and Folksongs, Our Singing Country,* and *Folksong USA.*

Annie Turnbo Pope Malone (1869–1957). Born into a family of eleven children in Illinois and considered the first black female millionaire, Annie Malone invented hair-straightening techniques—including the pressing iron and comb—that were marketed across the nation. Her Poro system earned her millions of dollars, much of which she poured back into the African American community, at one time reportedly supporting at least two full-time students at every black college in the nation. Malone was especially generous to the St. Louis community, which housed her business. She founded Poro College, which offered education and employment to African Americans. At its height, the Poro system employed 75,000 agents across the country and earned Malone in excess of $14 million. Malone was active in such organizations as the National Association of Colored Women, through which she made prominent friends, including **Mary McLeod Bethune.** Among Malone's students was **Sarah Breedlove Walker,** known as Madame C. J. Walker, who went on to become a millionaire as well. Malone's 1927 divorce from Aaron Malone became a public battle which divided black leaders.

Elisabeth Marbury (1856–1933). Born in New York City, Marbury became a literary and theatrical agent in 1887 when she went to Europe after having run a poultry business on Long Island. Among her first clients were Oscar Wilde, W. Somerset Maugham, and George Bernard Shaw. In 1914, she began a second career as a Broadway producer. Marbury opposed both women's suffrage and Prohibition. From 1887 until her death, she lived with Elsie de Wolfe, an actress and interior decorator. Marbury published *Manners: A Handbook of Social Customs* and *My Crystal Ball*, an autobiography. Hurston probably met Marbury through **Fannie Hurst,** whom Marbury also represented.

Fania Marinoff (1887–1971). Fania Marinoff was a Russian émigré, an actress, and **Carl Van Vechten's** wife of more than fifty years. Marinoff began her acting career at eight years old and worked on the stage and screen until the 1920s. She and Van Vechten hosted numerous parties that mingled the most prominent black and white artists and intellectuals of their day. **Walter White** dubbed their house "the midtown office of the **NAACP.**"

Charlotte Osgood Mason (1854–1946). Charlotte Osgood Mason was a wealthy Park Avenue patron of the arts who became fascinated with "primitivism" and black arts during the twenties. Her interests included American Indian as well as African American culture. Among those she supported were Hurston, **Langston Hughes, Aaron Douglas, Hall Johnson, Claude McKay, Miguel Covarrubias,** and **Alain Locke.** According to some stories, Mason had constructed a throne and footstools in her apartment and would sit on her throne with her protégés at her feet; at times she would have them dance for her at home. She insisted that they call her "Godmother." During Hurston's tenure as a protégée of Mason, Hurston was not allowed to reveal Mason's identity, nor was she allowed to make career or publication decisions on her own. Mason supported Hurston from 1927 to 1932. "Mrs. Mason," Robert Hemenway writes, "born Charlotte van der Veer Quick, is one of the mysteries of the Harlem Renaissance, a patron who had such a powerful hold on Langston Hughes that breaking with her made him physically ill, a woman who would become a spiritual godmother to Zora Hurston, a figure of such charisma that a sophisticated intellectual like Alain Locke could become deferential in her presence." As a widow, Mason had received much of her money from the estate of her late husband Dr. Rufus Osgood Mason (1830–1903), a leading New York surgeon. Dr. Mason published on parapsychology and hypnotism, and Mason shared his views that "primitive" people were repositories of the spiritual force missing from civilization.

Claude McKay (1889–1948). Born in Sunny Ville, Jamaica, to peasant farmers, Claude McKay was the youngest of eleven children. As a published poet (*Songs of Jamaica* and *Constab Ballads* in 1912) and a recipient of the Jamaica Institute of Arts and Science award, McKay left Jamaica for Tuskegee Institute in 1912 to pursue a scientific agricultural education. Determined to be a writer, however, McKay moved to Harlem in 1914 and shortly thereafter married Eulalie Imelda Edwards. They were divorced six months later. Under the pseudonym of Eli Edwards, McKay published "The Harlem Dancer" and "Invocation" in *Seven Arts*. Shortly afterward McKay published one of his most radical and militant pieces, "To the White Fiends," in *Pearson's Magazine*. In response to the Chicago race riots of 1919, McKay published "If We Must Die" in **Max Eastman's** *Liberator*. McKay left America for Europe in 1923, where he became interested in Marx and Lenin. Upon returning to the States, he joined the *Liberator* as associate editor. Following his eventual disillusionment with communism, McKay moved to Berlin, France, and North Africa. During this time, he wrote *Color Scheme* (1925), which was not published, and *Home to Harlem* (1928), which became a best-seller. Within the next few years, he published *Banjo* (1929), *Gingertown* (1932), and *Banana Bottom* (1933). Upon returning to the United States in 1934, McKay completed his autobiography, *A Long Way from Home*, which was published in 1937. In 1938, he met Ellen Tarry, a Catholic author of children's books, who was probably the biggest influence in McKay's conversion to Catholicism in 1944.

Katharane Edson Mershon (1892–1986). Feminist, activist, dancer, public speaker, and labor organizer Katharane Mershon also worked as an anthropologist in the 1920s and 1930s, when she presumably met Hurston. Her book on Bali, *Seven Plus Seven*, published in 1971, was based on research done during that period. Mershon's fieldwork in Bali was conducted with other anthropologists, including **Jane Belo,** Colin McPhee, Gregory Bateson, Mershon's husband, Jack Mershon, and Margaret Mead, who wrote a short foreword to Mershon's book. **Miguel Covarrubias** was also involved in work on Bali. It is likely that Hurston and Mershon met through Belo, or vice versa, but it is also possible that all met through Margaret Mead.

Annie Nathan Meyer (1867–1951). Born into a distinguished family of New York Jews, Annie Nathan Meyer devoted her life to writing and activism. She attended Columbia University but dropped out to marry her cousin Alfred Meyer, a doctor. Meyer began organizing a women's college at Columbia, named after F. A. P. Barnard, Columbia's recently deceased president (1809–89). Barnard College opened in 1889, and Meyer served as a trustee from 1889 to 1951. Among Meyer's many publications are twenty-six plays, including *Black Souls;* three novels, including *Helen Brent, M.D.;* two books of nonfiction; an edited volume of essays, *Women's Work in America;* an autobiography, *It's Been Fun;* and many articles on culture and politics, including anti-suffrage essays, which advocated domesticity as women's proper sphere. In an era when many colleges limited their enrollment of Jewish students (institutionally sanctioned anti-Semitism that ended only recently at schools like Harvard, Princeton, and Yale), Meyer's Jewishness may have spurred her involvement with black organizations such as the **NAACP.** Hurston met Meyer at the May 1925 *Opportunity* awards dinner, and Meyer arranged for Hurston's Barnard scholarship to begin in the fall of that year, making Hurston Barnard's first black student.

Burroughs Mitchell (1914–1979). After the death of **Maxwell Perkins** in June 1947, Hurston's editor at Scribner's became Burroughs Mitchell, who saw *Seraph on the Suwanee* through to publication and became a good friend of Hurston's, arranging for her release from custody in 1948 after she had been falsely charged with a morals crime and securing her attorney in the case, Louis Waldman. Although Scribner's never published another of Hurston's books, her relationship with Mitchell remained close. "One of the first writers I inherited was the black novelist Zora Neale Hurston," Mitchell wrote in his autobiography. "By the time Zora came to Scribner's, in 1947, she had lived through as many tribulations as triumphs. She was unforgettable; everything she did was arresting, stimulating, and usually improvident. . . . Our first meeting left me delighted and dazed." Mitchell was educated at Bowdoin College, served in the U.S. Navy, and married Jean Carse. He began at Scribner's in 1946 and left, as editor in chief, in 1977, when he retired. He is the author of *Education of an Editor*, posthumously published in 1980.

Henry Allen Moe (1894–1974). One of the original advisers to the creation of the **Guggenheim Foundation,** mathematician, lawyer, and journalist Henry Allen Moe served as secretary-general of the foundation from 1938 to 1954 and later as trustee and president. Hurston was by no means the only Guggenheim fellow to develop a deep and personal affection for Moe. "During his term as secretary-general," John H. Davis writes in *The Guggenheims: An American Epic*, "he presided over a renaissance in art and learning comparable to that which flourished in some of the courts of central Italy during the fifteenth and sixteenth centuries. Hardworking, highly intelligent, sensitive, yet tough, Moe gave of himself unsparingly in his passionate and relentless quest for excellence."

Mule Bone. Written collaboratively by Hurston and **Langston Hughes,** *Mule Bone* has been called "the most notorious literary quarrel in African-American cultural history." Set in Eatonville, Florida, *Mule Bone* was designed to highlight the riches of southern black culture, especially forms of southern black speech. The play was mostly written in 1930 when Hurston and Hughes were living in New Jersey. Hurston gave a draft of it to **Carl Van Vechten,** who, unbeknownst to her, gave it to the Theater Guild, which sent it to the African American theater troupe the Gilpin Players. They sought to produce the play, but by then it was too late—Hurston and Hughes each suspected the other of marketing the play as his/her own work, and each felt betrayed by the other. The play was never produced in their lifetimes, and many sources feel that it caused their falling-out.

NAACP (National Association for the Advancement of Colored People). In 1909, to honor the hundredth anniversary of Abraham Lincoln's birth, the National Negro Congress called for a new era in the struggle for civil liberties. This led to the formation of the NAACP, whose membership grew to over ninety thousand in ten years, despite attempts to outlaw the association in some areas. The black and white founders of the NAACP included Ida Wells-Barnett, Mary White Ovington, Henry Moscowitz, Oswald Garrison Villard, William English Walling, and **W. E. B. Du Bois,** who edited the association's monthly publication, the ***Crisis.*** Moorfield Storey was the organization's first president, succeeded by **Joel Spingarn** in 1929. **James Weldon Johnson** served as field secretary in 1916 and national secretary in 1920; he was succeeded by **Walter White** in 1928. In its first three decades, the NAACP documented racial injustice in publications, such as *Thirty Years of Lynching*, represented black citizens (including the Scottsboro Boys) through its Legal Committee, and pleaded the cause of civil rights to state and federal governments. Through the **Spingarn Medal** and the publication opportunities provided by the *Crisis,* the association also fostered black achievement in the arts and sciences.

National Folk Festival. Founded by Sarah Gertrude Knott (1895–1984) in 1934, the National Folk Festival is the oldest folk festival in the United States. The purpose of the National Folk Festival was twofold: to share folk songs, folk dances, and handcrafts among different regional and multicultural folk groups, and to educate the nation about the influence of folk culture on early American life. Migrating from city to city, the festival has opened in New York, Philadelphia, Chicago, Cleveland, and elsewhere. During Hurston's time, its headquarters was in Nashville, Tennessee, and its chairman was **Paul Green.**

Negro: An Anthology. Edited by **Nancy Cunard** in 1934, this 855-page anthology contained 150 contributors, 300 pieces, half a million words, and 385 illustrations. It offered articles on history, slavery, slave revolts, black leaders, politics, language, education, colonialism, art history, journalism, fiction, poetry, short stories, and more. It contained more than 150 English, European, African, and American contributors, including Hurston, Cunard, Pauli Murray, William Carlos Williams, V. F. Calverton, Henry Crowder, Michael Gold, Josephine Herbst, Theodore Dreiser, Samuel Beckett, Nicolás Guillén, Louis Zukofsky, Ezra Pound, George Padmore, **Alain Locke, Langston Hughes, W. E. B. Du Bois, Walter White, Sterling Brown, Countee Cullen,** and **Georgia Douglas Johnson.** It was controversial because of its size, expense, dedication by Cunard to her black lover Henry Crowder, and its inclusion of a number of controversial pieces such as an essay by William Carlos Williams touting the physical attractiveness of black maids. The anthology was not well reviewed and received little notice, and its original plates were destroyed. A nearly complete edition was published in 1969 by Negro Universities Press. Hugh Ford published an abridged version with Ungar in 1970.

The New Negro. Perhaps the most influential and widely read publication to emerge from the Harlem Renaissance, *The New Negro* anthology, edited by **Alain Locke** and published by Boni in 1925, was based on a shorter collection of writings that Locke assembled for the March 1925 special issue of *Survey Graphic* magazine. Hurston contributed the short story "Spunk," and there were also contributions from Locke, Rudolph Fisher, Jean Toomer, Jessie Fauset, **Richard Bruce Nugent, Eric Walrond, Countee Cullen, Claude McKay, James Weldon Johnson, Langston Hughes, Arna Bontemps, Charles S. Johnson, Helene Johnson, Melville Herskovits, Walter White,** and **W. E. B. Du Bois.**

Niggerati. Hurston's ironic and oft-cited name for the intellectual elite of the Harlem Renaissance: the inner circle composed of herself, **Langston Hughes, Wallace Thurman, Richard Bruce Nugent, Countee Cullen, Aaron Douglas, Gwendolyn Bennett, Arna Bontemps,** and **Helene Johnson.**

Richard Bruce Nugent (1906–87). Born into a middle-class Washington, D.C., family that valued the arts, writer, artist, and actor Richard Bruce Nugent, also known as Bruce Nugent and Richard Bruce, contributed poems, stories, and musicals to many publications, including *The New Negro.* Known for his highly stylized, modernist work as well as for his open expressions of homosexuality, Nugent was a controversial, charismatic figure represented by his fellow writers as passionate and bohemian. In **Wallace Thurman**'s novel *Infants of the Spring* (1932), the character of the bisexual painter, Paul Arbian, is based on Nugent. Nugent spent several years on the touring cast of DuBose Heyward's *Porgy,* worked with the Federal Art Project, the **Federal Writers' Project,** and the Federal Theater Project during the Depression, wrote homosexual romances in the forties that were never published, helped to found the Harlem Cultural Council in the sixties, and continued to publish and give interviews through the seventies and eighties.

Opportunity. The official publication of the National Urban League, *Opportunity: A Journal of Negro Life* ran from 1923 to 1949. Edited by **Charles S. Johnson** until 1928, the quarterly included news of the national league and its local affiliates, business opportunities, and results of sociological research into race relations. Under Johnson, *Opportunity* regularly published poems, short stories, and book reviews. It also sponsored the Harlem Writers' Guild and held literary competitions. Hurston and **Dorothy West** tied for second place in its 1926 short-story contest.

Maxwell Perkins (1884–1947). Famed editor at Scribner's from 1914 until his death, Maxwell Perkins is particularly well known for discovering writers such as Thomas Wolfe. Hurston's connection to Scribner's and to Perkins came about through her friendship with **Marjorie Kinnan Rawlings.** Perkins died just after Scribner's accepted *Seraph on the Suwanee.* Perkins was succeeded by **Burroughs Mitchell,** and in spite of the fact that Scribner's did not accept another manuscript of Hurston's for publication, her relationship with the company remained friendly.

Julia Peterkin (1880–1961). White writer Julia Peterkin was born on a plantation in South Carolina called Lang Syne and was fascinated with the lives of Gullah natives and the history of black plantation life. While her work was controversial, it was mostly well regarded by black contemporaries such as **W. E. B. Du Bois** and **Walter White.** It was also well regarded by progressive whites such as **Carl Sandburg** and H. L. Mencken, editor of *American Mercury.* Among her works are *Green Thursday, Black April, Scarlet Sister Mary* (which won a Pulitzer Prize), *Bright Skin,* and *Roll, Jordan, Roll.*

Dorothy Peterson (1897–1978). Teacher, librarian, and actress Dorothy Peterson was active in little theater in Harlem. She also appeared in the 1930 play *Green Pastures.* A lead character in **Carl Van Vechten**'s controversial novel *Nigger Heaven* is based on Peterson. She worked as a librarian at the Harlem branch of the New York Public Library and taught at Wadleigh High School, the first public high school for girls in

Manhattan. She was centrally involved in establishing the **James Weldon Johnson** Memorial Collection at Yale University.

William Pickens (1881–1954). William Pickens was an educator, orator, editor, and civil rights leader. Educated at Talladega College and Yale University (he received his degree in classics in 1904), Pickens taught classics, sociology, and foreign languages for almost two decades at Talladega, Wiley University, and Morgan College, where he became the first black dean and then vice president. In 1920, Pickens became field secretary for the **NAACP,** a position he held for the next twenty years. Pickens's criticism of **Walter White**'s "Two Front" policies during World War II led to his dismissal from the NAACP in 1942. Amid public accusations of his association with Communism, Pickens raised almost $1 billion in bonds while working for the Treasury Department. His publications include his autobiography, *Bursting Bonds* (1923).

Burton Rascoe (1892–1957). Drama critic, journalist, editor, and author Burton Rascoe served as a literary and drama editor at the *Chicago Tribune, McCall's,* and the *New York Tribune.* His syndicated column, "The Daybook of a New Yorker," ran from 1924 to 1928. He was a member of the editorial board of the Literary Guild of America in 1928 and became general editorial adviser to Doubleday, Doran & Company in 1934.

Marjorie Kinnan Rawlings (1896–1953). Marjorie Kinnan Rawlings was a Pulitzer Prize–winning writer known principally for her children's novel *The Yearling* (1938). Rawlings began winning writing contests by the age of fifteen. She received her B.A. from the University of Wisconsin. After her marriage to writer Charles A. Rawlings, she moved to Cross Creek, Florida. Marjorie Rawlings was fascinated with the Florida wilderness and was often praised for her authentic portrayals of "cracker" life. In 1933, *South Moon Under* was honored by the Book-of-the-Month Club. This year also marked the end of her marriage to Charles Rawlings. In 1941, she married Norton Sanford Baskin. Hurston and Rawlings became friends in 1942.

Nora Holt Ray: See **Nora Holt.**

Jay Saunders Redding (1906–88). Professor, critic, and writer Jay Saunders Redding was educated at Brown and Lincoln Universities. He taught at Morehouse College, Louisville Municipal College, Southern University, the State Teachers College of North Carolina, Brown University, Hampton Institute (1943–66), George Washington University, and Cornell University, where he was the Ernest I. White Professor of American Studies from 1971 until 1975. He is said to have taught the first American literature course on black writers. Among his writings are *To Make a Poet Black, No Day of Triumph, Stranger and Alone, They Came in Chains,* and *On Being Negro in America.* Redding received numerous awards, including grants from the Rockefeller and Guggenheim foundations and the Distinguished Service Award of the National Urban League in 1945.

Gladys Reichard (1893–1955). Gladys Reichard received her Ph.D. in anthropology from Columbia University in 1923, where she studied with **Franz Boas.** A specialist in Navajo society, she published works on Navajo religion, linguistics, weaving, women in Navajo culture, and Navajo social organization. Reichard was a full professor of anthropology at Barnard and was secretary of the American Ethnological Society, the American Folklore Society, and the New York Linguistic Circle.

Eslanda Robeson (1896–1965). Trained as a chemist at Columbia University, Eslanda Robeson was the first black staff member of New York's Presbyterian Hospital, where she ran the Surgical Pathological Laboratory. After she married **Paul Robeson** in 1921, she resigned her job at the hospital and in 1925 became his business manager, a role that she continued to play throughout his career.

Paul Robeson (1898–1976). Athlete, actor, singer, and political activist Paul Robeson was the most famous black male actor and singer of his day. As a student at Rutgers University, Robeson received renown for both his athleticism and his scholarship. After Rutgers, he went to Columbia University, where he studied law. He practiced law briefly in New York before switching to theater in 1921. Robeson was highly successful in such plays as Eugene O'Neill's *All God's Chillun Got Wings* and *The Emperor Jones.* In 1929, Robeson went on a European tour after two wildly successful concerts in Carnegie Hall. He was a smash hit in *Othello,* first in London in 1930 and then in New York in 1943, where the play ran for a record-breaking 296 performances. Among his many successful films were *King Solomon's Mines, Show Boat,* and *Tales of Manhattan.* The son of a runaway slave, Robeson was a socialist and visited the Soviet Union in 1934. He offered his talents for many political causes and benefits, including those of striking workers. In 1938, he traveled to Spain in support of the antifascists and became a leader in many civil rights and progressive causes. In the fifties, Robeson had his passport revoked and was subject to extensive harassment by the government, resulting in his being blacklisted from the entertainment industry for much of the decade. He married Eslanda Cardoza Goode (see **Eslanda Robeson**) in 1921.

Rollins College. During Hurston's time, Rollins College was an all-white coeducational college in Winter Park, Florida. In 1932, Hurston met Rollins president **Hamilton Holt** and professor Edwin Osgood Grover, who encouraged her to come to the campus. That same year, Hurston received financial support from the college to stage a performance of *The Great Day* on campus. The successful show, produced with the help of Rollins professor Robert Wunsch, used players from Eatonville, Florida. In spite of Hurston's protests, tickets were not sold to blacks. In 1933, Wunsch sent Hurston's story "The Gilded Six-Bits" to *Story* magazine; its publication eventually earned Hurston the attention of publisher **J. B. Lippincott.** In 1938, the Rollins College Folklore Group sponsored a choir led by Hurston at the **National Folk Festival** in Washington, D.C.

Rosenwald Foundation. Incorporated in Chicago on October 30, 1917, by Julius Rosenwald and headed by **Edwin Rogers Embree** with income from the Sears, Roebuck company, the Rosenwald Foundation was designed to benefit black life and black-white relations through an array of programs that supported rural schools, farmers, conferences, publications, and grants to individuals working in literature, the arts, and social sciences to promote "the well-being of mankind." During its twenty-one-year operation, the fund allocated approximately half a million dollars a year. Some of the recipients of the fund were James Baldwin, **Arna Bontemps, Sterling Brown, W. E. B. Du Bois, Aaron Douglas,** and William S. Braithwaite. The Rosenwald Foundation was terminated in 1948 after disbursing $22 million.

Margrit de Sablonière (1905–79). Margrit de Sablonière was the pseudonym of Dutch writer and translator Margaretha Catherina Bicker Caarten, born in Leiden, Netherlands. A writer with particular interests in African American culture and African apartheid, which she strongly opposed, Sablonière published books and journalistic essays on Africa, African history, black folklore, and the artists Vincent van Gogh and Paul Gauguin. Among her many translations of African American writings were essays by Martin Luther King, Jr., and five books by Richard Wright. Her planned translations of Hurston's work did not come to fruition. Sablonière, whose full name after her marriage was Margaretha Catherina Bicker Caarten Stigter, died in Meepel, Netherlands. Her last book, published in 1966, was *Staphorst,* a study of the social life and customs of the Netherlands.

Carl Sandburg (1878–1967). Known as a socialist, free-verse poet Carl Sandburg wrote a two-volume biography of Abraham Lincoln, *Abraham Lincoln: The Prairie Years* (1926), and a four-volume sequel, *Abraham Lincoln: The War Years* (1939), which was awarded the Pulitzer Prize in history in 1940. Sandburg was also a folklorist, journalist, novelist, social activist, and politician. His poetry first appeared nationally in 1914 in Harriet Monroe's *Poetry,* followed by *Chicago Poems* in 1916 and *Cornhuskers,* which launched his career. Sandburg was awarded the Pulitzer Prize in poetry in 1951 for his *Complete Poems* and was named the poet laureate of Illinois in 1962. In 1908, Sandburg married fellow socialist Lilian Steichen, sister of photographer Edward Steichen, and they had three children.

Saturday Evening Post. Established in 1728, the foundering *Saturday Evening Post* was purchased by Cyrus Curtis in 1897 and saved with his profits from the *Ladies' Home Journal.* Curtis appointed George Horace Lorimer, a racial conservative, as editor. The *Post* boasted a circulation of 2 million by 1922 and 3 million by 1937. It focused on interesting personalities in business, public affairs, romance, sports, humor, science, and literature. Hurston's "Lawrence of the River," "The Conscience of the Court," and "A Negro Voter Sizes Up Taft" appeared in the *Post* in the 1940s and early 1950s.

Augusta Savage (1892–1962). Born in Florida, sculptor Augusta Savage attended Tallahassee State Normal School and then moved to New York City in 1921, where she studied at Cooper Union. In 1923, after being denied an arts scholarship because of her color, then granted it on appeal, Savage turned the money down, an act that drew a storm of coverage in the press and may have inspired a similar story in Jessie Fauset's novel *Plum Bun*. Savage was known for her work in bronze, wood, and plaster, for her busts of **W. E. B. Du Bois,** Marcus Garvey, **James Weldon Johnson,** and others, for her work as a teacher, for the Savage Studio of Arts and Crafts, which she founded in New York in 1932, for her work with the Harlem Arts Guild, which she organized, and for her statue *Lift Every Voice and Sing,* based on the popular black anthem (written by James Weldon Johnson and his brother, **J. Rosamond Johnson**) and created for the 1939 New York world's fair. Savage studied in Paris from 1929 to 1932 with the aid of the **Rosenwald Foundation,** worked for the WPA, and directed the Harlem Community Center. She was married three times: to John T. Moore, James Savage, and Robert L. Poston.

Arthur A. Schomburg (1874–1938). Bibliophile Arthur Schomburg was born in San Juan, Puerto Rico, to a white father and a black mother. He moved to New York in 1891, became an activist in the Cuban and Puerto Rican independence movements, and started collecting texts related to the history of blacks throughout the world. Elected president of the Negro Academy in 1922, Schomburg served as curator of the Negro Collection at **Fisk University** from 1930 to 1932. He was curator of the Division of Negro Literature, History, and Prints at the New York Public Library from 1932 to 1938. Schomburg helped to establish the Negro Society for Historical Research. The New York Public Library's Schomburg Center for Research in Black Culture is named in his honor.

George Samuel Schuyler (1895–1977). Black journalist, novelist, and satirist George Schuyler began working on the radical magazine the *Messenger* and the black weekly the *Pittsburgh Courier* in the mid-1920s. His essays also appeared in the *Nation, American Mercury,* **Crisis,** and *New York Evening Post. Black No More* (1931), his first novel, lampooned major Harlem Renaissance figures, satirizing racial politics. Schuyler's other writings included pulp science-fiction serials and investigations into Liberia's modern slave trade. He was at one time a member of the Socialist Party, but in later years Schuyler became a militant anti-communist and conservative, opposed to the Nobel Peace Prize's bestowal on Martin Luther King, Jr.

James Edward Shepherd (1875–1947). Educator James Shepherd worked as a pharmacist, a clerk, and a deputy collector for the Internal Revenue Service before becoming the International Sunday School Association's superintendent of fieldwork among blacks. Shepherd helped to establish the National Religious Training School and Chautauqua of Durham, which became first the National Training School and then North Carolina Central University and, finally, the North Carolina College for Negroes. Shepherd received three honorary degrees and served as president of the university from 1910 until his death.

Amy Spingarn (1883–?). Together with her husband, **Joel Spingarn,** artist and activist Amy Einstein Spingarn gave generously of her time and money to the **NAACP,** supporting its national headquarters, its Legal Defense Fund, and the growth of its twentieth-anniversary fund drive in 1929. She sponsored an antilynching art display in 1933 as part of the NAACP's Writers' League Against Lynching. The prizes for literature she established were awarded to many Harlem Renaissance writers, including **Langston Hughes** and **Countee Cullen.** She was elected to serve out her husband's unexpired NAACP presidential term after his death in 1939.

Arthur B. Spingarn (1878–1971). Lawyer and **NAACP** official Arthur Spingarn was born in New York to Austrian Jewish parents. Both he and his older brother, **Joel Spingarn,** were active in the NAACP from its founding. A graduate of Columbia Law School, Arthur Spingarn offered his services as the association's legal counsel without cost. In his first case before the Supreme Court, Spingarn successfully argued for the right of black citizens to participate in primary elections in Texas. He served as chairman of the NAACP's Legal Committee from 1911 to 1940 and as president of the association from 1940 to 1966, succeeding his brother, Joel, and sister-in-law, Amy. A bibliophile, Spingarn amassed a significant collection of literature by and about African Americans, which he donated to Howard University in 1948.

Joel Spingarn (1875–1939). Deeply committed to the new civil rights movement, Joel Elias Spingarn was a founding member and official of the **NAACP.** He received his doctorate from Columbia University in 1899, publishing his dissertation on literary criticism in the Renaissance that year. In 1903, he established the *Journal for Comparative Literature.* He was unsuccessful in a bid for a congressional seat in 1908 but was appointed professor of comparative literature at Columbia the next year. Fired from this position for defending a dismissed colleague, Spingarn turned his attention to editing the *Amenia Times,* a suffragist newspaper. Spingarn served as chairman of the board of the NAACP from 1913 to 1919, as treasurer from 1919 to 1930, and as president from 1930 until his death in 1939. During his tenure, Spingarn drafted anti-lynching legislation, investigated and protested Jim Crow discrimination, and established and endowed the annual **Spingarn Medal.**

Spingarn Medal. In 1914, **Joel Spingarn** established the Spingarn Medal, a gold medallion bestowed yearly for the "highest and noblest achievement of an American Negro" in public service, the sciences, or the arts. Spingarn believed that blacks were particularly gifted in the arts—"rich by inheritance and by temperament, but willing to share [their] gifts with [their] poor, cold, uninspired brothers of white blood." Spingarn bequeathed $20,000 in his will to endow the prize in perpetuity, with the instructions that the medal be awarded by the president of Howard University should the **NAACP** cease to exist. Recipients include **W. E. B. Du Bois, James Weldon Johnson,** Charles W. Chesnutt, **Mary McLeod Bethune, Walter White, Paul Robeson,** and **Langston Hughes.**

Louise Thompson (1901–99). Educator, cultural critic, civil rights activist, and radical, Louise Thompson was born in Chicago and educated at the University of California at Berkeley, the University of Chicago, and the New School for Social Research with support from an Urban League fellowship. Thompson was a protégée, briefly, of

Charlotte Osgood Mason's, and presumably through Mason, she worked as secretary for **Langston Hughes** and Hurston while they were working on the ill-fated play *Mule Bone.* Thompson was briefly married to Harlem Renaissance writer **Wallace Thurman.** She was active in a number of social causes, including the Scottsboro case. Along with **Augusta Savage,** she formed a left-wing group called the Vanguard Club. Thompson traveled to the Soviet Union with Langston Hughes and others in 1932 and became secretary of the Friends of the Soviet Union. She joined the Communist Party in 1934 and worked as a full-time organizer for the International Workers' Order for many years. Thompson was married in 1940 to William L. Patterson, a Communist Party leader and lawyer for the Scottsboro Boys.

Wallace Thurman (1902–54). Born in Salt Lake City, Wallace Thurman was an active member of the Harlem Renaissance and of "the **Niggerati.**" Prior to coming to New York City in 1924, Thurman studied at the University of Utah, then lived and worked in Los Angeles, where he attended the University of Southern California. In New York, he shared a rooming house at 267 West 137th Street with **Langston Hughes.** Thurman worked for the *Messenger* and *World Tomorrow,* became a senior editor for *Macaulay's* (the first African American to hold such a position), published in venues such as the *Crisis,* attempted screenwriting in Hollywood, and ghostwrote for *True Story.* He assumed primary editorial as well as financial liability for *Fire!!* and spent four years paying off its $1,000 printing bill. His contribution to *Fire!!,* "Cordelia the Crude," was a deliberately shocking piece about a prostitute, written in an attempt to get the issue banned in Boston. Before *Fire!!,* Thurman had tried another journal, the *Outlet,* which also failed. After *Fire!!,* he tried again, with the journal *Harlem,* yet another failure. Although he was reportedly homosexual, Thurman attempted a brief marriage to **Louise Thompson.** He was described by Langston Hughes as "brilliant," "bitter," and cynical in the extreme. Thurman was the author of *Negro Life in New York's Harlem, The Blacker the Berry, Infants of the Spring, The Interne,* and *Harlem.*

Lorenzo Dow Turner (1895–1972). Educated at Howard University, Harvard University, and the University of Chicago (Ph.D., 1926), African American linguist Lorenzo Dow Turner was a specialist on African and Gullah languages and the first African American linguist. He taught at Howard University, **Fisk University,** and Roosevelt College, in Chicago. Among his many publications are *Anti-Slavery Sentiment in American Literature Prior to 1865, Africanisms in the Gullah Dialect, An Anthology of Krio Folklore and Literature,* and *Readings from Negro Authors for Schools and Colleges.*

Carl Van Vechten (1880–1964). No white person's name appears more often in conjunction with the people and events of the Harlem Renaissance than Carl Van Vechten's. Born in Cedar Rapids, Iowa, Van Vechten would eventually become a consummate urban sophisticate, providing entrée into New York's culture, music, art, and writing for scores of other white intellectuals. A photographer, writer, and patron of the arts, African American arts especially, Van Vechten promoted the careers of many black artists, musicians, and writers, including Nella Larsen, Rudolph Fisher,

Eric Walrond, Langston Hughes, Countee Cullen, Wallace Thurman, James Weldon Johnson, Paul Robeson, Bessie Smith, Ethel Waters, Aaron Douglas, and Hurston, with whom he was very close. Also friends with prominent white publishers such as Alfred and Blanche Knopf, and with white modernists such as Gertrude Stein and Mabel Dodge, Van Vechten worked hard to bring black writers to public attention. Informally, he brought many blacks and whites together through his lavish and famous interracial parties. Formally, he acted as a patron to introduce blacks to white publishers and performance venues. Van Vechten also established important collections at Yale University, **Fisk University,** and Howard University. In his own words, Van Vechten was "violently interested in Negroes." Van Vechten's 1926 novel, *Nigger Heaven*, a love story set among blacks in Harlem that featured scenes of sexuality, violence, and cabaret life, but that was also a serious attempt to expose racial divides, was extremely controversial, winning both ardent support and furious condemnation for what some saw as a sensationalization and exploitation of black life. A bisexual whose scrapbooks at Yale University have recently been opened, Van Vechten married Russian-born actress **Fania Marinoff.** Many of his writings about black America are collected in *Keep A-Inchin' Along* (1979).

Sarah Breedlove (Madame C. J.) Walker (1867–1919). A former washerwoman who worked as a Poro agent for hair-straightening entrepreneur **Annie Turnbo Pope Malone,** Sarah Breedlove was the child of poor Louisiana parents, orphaned at the age of six, and married at fourteen to C. J. Walker. Known popularly as the first black female millionaire (see **Malone**), Walker's hair care business was highly successful, allowing her a lavish lifestyle that included a limestone mansion in New York City and another mansion, Villa Lewaro, on the Hudson River. Her estate was valued at $2 million when she died. Her daughter, A'Lelia Walker, used much of the money to further African American arts and culture, throwing parties and setting up a literary salon in 1928, known as the Dark Tower, in her home on 136th Street.

Eric Walrond (1898–1966). A writer of essays and short stories, Eric Walrond was an important figure in the Harlem Renaissance. Walrond was born in Georgetown, British Guyana, and began his journalistic career in New York City in 1921. In 1923, he worked with Marcus Garvey and the UNIA (Universal Negro Improvement Association), whose house organ, *Negro World,* Walrond edited. Shortly thereafter he began to work for ***Opportunity.*** His collection of stories, *Tropic Death,* was published in 1926. That same year, he left the United States for Europe, a decision of which Hurston was particularly critical.

Jean Parker Waterbury (1915–). Author and literary agent Waterbury worked for the Ann Watkins Agency and the McIntosh, McKee Agency. She is the author of a number of books on Florida history, including *Coquina; Markland; The Oldest City, St. Augustine: Saga of Survival* (ed.); *The Oldest House; Where Artillery Lane Crosses Aviles Street;* and *The Ximenez-Fatio House: Long Forgotten, Now Restored.* She lives in St. Augustine, Florida.

Ethel Waters (1896–1977). Blues singer and actress Ethel Waters mesmerized audiences from the 1920s through the 1950s. Nicknamed "Sweet Mama Stringbean," Waters performed in theater and on television and film in many highly successful productions. Her first autobiography, *His Eye Is on the Sparrow*, a best-seller, was published in 1951, and her second, *To Me, It's Wonderful*, in 1972. Readers were fascinated with Waters's rise from poverty to celebrity. Although she earned a reported $1 million during her career, by the time of her death she was impoverished and living on Social Security. From 1957 until her death, Waters was associated with Billy Graham's evangelical ministry.

Dorothy West (1907–98). West was a writer, editor, and journalist who, along with her lesser-known cousin **Helene Johnson,** was an early member of the Harlem Renaissance. Her father, Isaac Christopher West, a successful produce dealer, was known as "Boston's banana king." Born in Boston, Dorothy graduated from Girls' Latin High School in 1923 and studied journalism in Boston and at Columbia University. She began writing stories when she was only seven years old. In 1926, her short story "The Typewriter" received a second-place award in that year's *Opportunity* literary contest, an award that she shared with Hurston, into whose apartment (at 44 West 66th Street) West moved when she came to New York. West acted in the touring company of *Porgy* in 1927 and traveled to the Soviet Union, where she lived for one year, during the thirties. She founded *Challenge* in 1934 and *New Challenge* in 1937. West worked as a welfare investigator in the thirties and with the **Federal Writers' Project** into the forties. She was a regular columnist for the *Boston Globe*, the *New York Daily News* (1940–60), and, after moving to Martha's Vineyard permanently in 1945, for the *Martha's Vineyard Gazette*. Her books include *The Living Is Easy*, *The Wedding*, and *The Richer, the Poorer*.

Walter White (1893–1955). An important writer and advocate for black civil rights, Walter White was often noted for his insistence on his blackness when, given his blond, blue-eyed, fair-skinned appearance, he could easily have passed for white. Born in Atlanta, Georgia, White was educated at Atlanta University and Howard University. He began working with the **NAACP** in 1918 as secretary to **James Weldon Johnson** and became executive director in 1931. In his many years at the NAACP, White worked on laws relating to lynching, taxes, and civil rights. White was the recipient of many awards, including the **Spingarn Medal** in 1937. Among his many close friends in Harlem Renaissance circles were **Carl Van Vechten** and **Fania Marinoff, Langston Hughes, Alain Locke,** Rudolph Fisher, and Hurston. White encouraged Hurston to participate in the opera *Batouala*, based on René Maran's novel and starring **Paul Robeson.** Later, White and Hurston fell out over her allegations that he had stolen dramatic properties—costumes and drums—from her. In 1922, White married Gladys Powell. In 1949, he and Powell divorced and he married white food writer Poppy Cannon. Among White's publications are *The Fire in the Flint, Flight, Rope and Faggot: A Biography of Judge Lynch,* and *A Man Called White: The Autobiography of Walter White.*

Frederick Enos Woltman (1905–70). Born in York, Pennsylvania, Frederick Woltman was particularly well known as a journalist whose 1940s articles on communism won him a Pulitzer Prize as well as the reputation as a "Red-baiter." Woltman studied at the University of Pittsburgh. His long association with the *New York World-Telegram*, for which he investigated Tammany Hall, the real estate mortgage bond racket, union and labor issues, and communism, began in 1929.

Carter Godwin Woodson (1875–1950). Considered the father of modern black history, Carter Woodson was born in Virginia to former slaves and received little formal education until he was twenty years old. Eight years later, he had received a high school diploma, a teaching certificate, and a Litt.B. degree from Kentucky's Berea College. He taught English in the Philippines, then returned to the United States to earn a master's degree from the University of Chicago in 1908 and a Ph.D. from Harvard in 1912. In 1915, Woodson formed the Association for the Study of Negro Life and History. One year later, the *Journal of Negro History* became the association's official quarterly. To generate enthusiasm for black history, Woodson created the *Negro History Bulletin* for high school students in 1921 and Negro History Week in 1926. It was through the Association for the Study of Negro Life and History that Hurston received her first grant, for $1,400, for folklore research in Florida.

Robert Wunsch: see Rollins College.

BIBLIOGRAPHY OF
THE WORKS OF ZORA
NEALE HURSTON

BOOKS

Jonah's Gourd Vine. Philadelphia: J. B. Lippincott, 1934. Reprinted, with an introduction by Larry Neal, Philadelphia: J. B. Lippincott, 1971. Reprinted, New York: HarperCollins, 1990.

Mules and Men. Philadelphia: J. B. Lippincott, 1935. Reprinted, London: Kegan Paul & Co., 1936. Reprinted, New York: Negro Universities Press, 1969. Reprinted, with an introduction by Darwin Turner, New York: Harper & Row, 1970. Reprinted, Urbana: University of Illinois Press, 1978. Reprinted, New York: HarperCollins, 1990. Reprinted, San Bernardino, Calif.: Borgo Press, 1990.

Their Eyes Were Watching God. Philadelphia: J. B. Lippincott, 1937. Reprinted, London: J. M. Dent & Sons, 1937. Reprinted, Greenwich, Conn.: Fawcett Publications, 1965. Reprinted, New York: Negro Universities Press, 1969. Reprinted, Westport, Conn.: Greenwood Publishing Group, 1970. Reprinted, Urbana: University of Illinois Press, 1978. Reprinted, with a foreword by Mary Helen Washington, New York: HarperCollins, 1990. Reprinted, San Bernardino, Calif.: Borgo Press, 1990. Reprinted, with an introduction by Sherley Anne Williams, Urbana: University of Illinois Press, 1991. Reprinted, Reading, Mass.: Addison-Wesley, 1995.

Tell My Horse. Philadelphia: J. B. Lippincott, 1938. Published as *Voodoo Gods: An Inquiry into Native Myths and Magic in Jamaica and Haiti:* London: J. M. Dent & Sons, 1939. Reprinted, with an introduction by Bob Callahan, as *Voodoo Gods: An Inquiry into Native Myths and Magic in Jamaica and Haiti,* Berkeley, Calif.: Turtle Island Foundation, 1981. Reprinted, with a new foreword by Ishmael Reed, New York: HarperPerennial, 1990.

Moses, Man of the Mountain. Philadelphia: J. B. Lippincott, 1939. Reprinted, London: J. M. Dent & Sons, 1941. Reprinted, Chatham, N.J.: Chatham Bookseller, 1974. Reprinted, with an introduction by Blyden Jackson, as *The Man of the Mountain*, Urbana: University of Illinois Press, 1984. Reprinted, San Bernardino, Calif.: Borgo Press, 1991.

Dust Tracks on a Road. Philadelphia: J. B. Lippincott, 1942. Reprinted, London: Hutchinson & Co., 1944. Reprinted, with an introduction by Darwin Turner, New York: Arno Press, 1969. Reprinted, with an introduction by Larry Neal, New York: J. B. Lippincott, 1971. Reprinted (with additional original chapters), edited and with an introduction by Robert Hemenway, Urbana: University of Illinois Press, 1984. Reprinted, New York: HarperCollins, 1996. Reprinted, San Bernardino, Calif.: Borgo Press, 1996.

Seraph on the Suwanee. New York: Charles Scribner's Sons, 1948. Reprinted, Ann Arbor: University Microfilms, 1971. Reprinted, New York: AMS Press, 1974. Reprinted, San Bernardino, Calif.: Borgo Press, 1991. Reprinted, New York: HarperCollins, 1991.

OTHER PUBLICATIONS

"John Redding Goes to Sea." *Stylus,* 1 (May 1921): 11–22. Reprinted in *Opportunity,* 4 (January 1926): 16–21.

"O Night." *Stylus,* 1 (May 1921): 42.

"Poem." *Howard University Record,* 16 (February 1922): 236.

"Night," "Journey's End," and "Passion." *Negro World,* 1922.

"Drenched in Light." *Opportunity,* 2 (December 1924): 371–74.

"Spunk." *Opportunity,* 3 (June 1925): 171–73. Reprinted in *The New Negro,* ed. Alain Locke (New York: Albert & Charles Boni, 1925), pp. 105–11.

"Magnolia Flower." *Spokesman,* July 1925, pp. 26–29.

"The Hue and Cry About Howard University." *Messenger,* September 1925, pp. 315–19, 338.

"Under The Bridge." *X-Ray: Journal of the Zeta Phi Beta Sorority,* December 1925.

"The Ten Commandments of Charm." *X-Ray: Journal of the Zeta Phi Beta Sorority,* December 1925.

"On Noses." *X-Ray: Journal of the Zeta Phi Beta Sorority,* December 1925.

"Muttsy." *Opportunity,* 4 (August 1926): 246–50.

"Possum or Pig." *Forum,* 76 (September 1926): 465.

"The Eatonville Anthology." *Messenger,* September–November 1926, pp. 261–62, 297, 319, 332.

Color Struck: A Play. In *Fire!!,* 1 (November 1926): 7–15.

"Sweat." *Fire!!,* 1 (November 1926): 40–45.

"Spears: A Play." *X-Ray: Journal of the Zeta Phi Beta Sorority,* December 1926.

The First One: A Play. In *Ebony and Topaz,* ed. Charles S. Johnson (New York: National Urban League, 1927), pp. 53–57.

"Cudjo's Own Story of the Last African Slaver." *Journal of Negro History,* 12 (October 1927): 648–63.

"Communication." *Journal of Negro History,* 12 (October 1927): 664–67.

"How It Feels to Be Colored Me." *World Tomorrow,* 11 (May 1928): 215–16.

"Dance Songs and Tales from the Bahamas." *Journal of American Folklore,* 43 (July–September 1930): 294–312.

"Hoodoo in America." *Journal of American Folklore,* 44 (October–December 1931): 317–418.

"The Gilded Six-Bits." *Story,* 3 (August 1933): 60–70.

In *Negro: An Anthology,* ed. Nancy Cunard (London: Wishart, 1934):

"Characteristics of Negro Expression," 39–46.

"Conversions and Visions," 47–49.

"Mother Catharine," 54–57.

"The Sermon," 50–54.

"Shouting," 49–50.

"Spirituals and Neo-Spirituals," 359–61.

"Uncle Monday," 57–61.

"The Fire and the Cloud." *Challenge,* 1 (September 1934): 10–14.

"Race Cannot Become Great Until It Recognizes Its Talent." *Washington Tribune,* December 29, 1934.

"Full of Mud, Sweat and Blood." Review of *God Shakes Creation,* by David Cohn. *New York Herald Tribune Books,* November 3, 1935, pp. 15–16.

"Fannie Hurst by Her Ex-Amanuensis." *Saturday Review*, October 9, 1937.

"Star-Wrassling Sons-of-the-Universe." Review of *The Hurricane's Children*, by Carl Cramer. *New York Herald Tribune Books*, December 26, 1937, p. 4.

"Rural Schools for Negroes." Review of *The Jeanes Teacher in the United States*, by Lance G. E. Jones. *New York Herald Tribune Books*, February 20, 1938, p. 24.

"Stories of Conflict." Review of *Uncle Tom's Children*, by Richard Wright. *Saturday Review*, April 2, 1938, p. 32.

"Now Take Noses." In *Cordially Yours*, ed. Boston Herald Book Fair Committee (Philadelphia: J. B. Lippincott, 1939), pp. 25–27.

Cold Rainy Day: Musical composition with words from Hurston's *Mules and Men*. Date of publication: January 27, 1939.

John Henry. Musical composition with words from Hurston's *Mules and Men*. Date of publication: January 27, 1939.

"Cock Robin, Beale Street." *Southern Literary Messenger*, 3 (July 1941): 321–23.

"Story in Harlem Slang." *American Mercury*, 55 (July 1942): 84–96.

"Lawrence of the River." *Saturday Evening Post*, September 5, 1942, pp. 18, 55–57. Condensed in *Negro Digest*, 1 (March 1943): 47–49.

"The 'Pet Negro' System." *American Mercury*, 56 (May 1943): 593–600. Condensed in *Negro Digest*, 1 (June 1943): 37–40.

"High John de Conquer." *American Mercury*, 57 (October 1943): 450–58.

"Negroes Without Self-Pity." *American Mercury*, 57 (November 1943): 601–3.

"The Last Slave Ship." *American Mercury*, 58 (March 1944): 351–58. Condensed in *Negro Digest*, 2 (May 1944): 11–16.

"My Most Humiliating Jim Crow Experience." *Negro Digest*, 2 (June 1944): 25–26.

"Negroes." *The New International Year Book, 1945*. New York: Funk & Wagnalls, 1946.

"The Rise of the Begging Joints." *American Mercury*, 60 (March 1945): 288–94. Condensed in *Negro Digest*, 3 (May 1945).

"Crazy for This Democracy." *Negro Digest*, 4 (December 1945): 45–48.

"Bible, Played by Ear in Africa." Review of *How God Fix Jonah*, by Lorenz Graham. *New York Herald Tribune Weekly Book Review*, November 24, 1946, p. 5.

"Jazz Regarded as Social Achievement." Review of *Shining Trumpets*, by Rudi Blesh. *New York Herald Tribune Weekly Book Review*, December 22, 1946, p. 8.

"The Negro in the United States." *Encyclopedia Americana*, 1947 edition.

"Thirty Days Among Maroons." Review of *Journey to Accompong*, by Katharine Dunham. *New York Herald Tribune Weekly Book Review*, January 12, 1947, p. 8.

"The Transplanted Negro." Review of *Trinidad Village*, by Melville Herskovits and Frances Herskovits. *New York Herald Tribune Weekly Book Review*, March 9, 1947, p. 20.

Carribbean Melodies for Chorus of Mixed Voices and Soloists. With accompaniment for piano and percussion instruments. Arranged by William Grant Still. Philadelphia: Oliver Ditson, 1947.

Review of *Voodoo in New Orleans*, by Robert Tallant. *Journal of American Folklore*, 60 (October–December, 1947): 436–38.

"At the Sound of the Conch Shell." Review of *New Day*, by Victor Stafford Reid. *New York Herald Tribune Weekly Book Review*, March 20, 1949, p. 4.

"The Conscience of the Court." *Saturday Evening Post*, March 18, 1950, pp. 22–23, 112–22.

"I Saw Negro Votes Peddled." *American Legion Magazine*, 49 (November 1950): 12–13, 54–57, 59–60. Condensed in *Negro Digest*, 9 (September 1951): 77–85.

"Some Fabulous Caribbean Riches Revealed." Review of *The Pencil of God*, by Pierre Marcelin and Philippe Thoby Marcelin. *New York Herald Tribune Weekly Book Review*, February 4, 1951, p. 5.

"What White Publishers Won't Print." *Negro Digest*, 8 (April 1950): 85–89.

"Why The Negro Won't Buy Communism." *American Legion Magazine*, 50 (June 1951): 14–15, 55–60.

"A Negro Voter Sizes Up Taft." *Saturday Evening Post*, December 8, 1951, pp. 29, 150.

"Zora's Revealing Story of Ruby's First Day in Court." *Pittsburgh Courier,* October 11, 1952.

"Victim of Fate." *Pittsburgh Courier,* October 11, 1952.

"Ruby Sane." *Pittsburgh Courier,* October 19, 1952.

"Ruby McCollum Fights for Life." *Pittsburgh Courier,* November 22, 1952.

"Bare Plot Against Ruby." *Pittsburgh Courier,* November 29, 1952.

"Trial Highlights." *Pittsburgh Courier,* November 29, 1952.

"McCollum-Adams Trial Highlights." *Pittsburgh Courier,* December 27, 1952.

"Ruby Bares Her Love." *Pittsburgh Courier,* January 3, 1953.

"Doctor's Threats, Tussle over Gun Led to Slaying." *Pittsburgh Courier,* January 10, 1953.

"Ruby's Troubles Mount." *Pittsburgh Courier,* January 17, 1953.

"The Life Story of Mrs. Ruby J. McCollum!" *Pittsburgh Courier,* February 28, March 7, 14, 21, 28, April 4, 11, 18, 25, May 2, 1953.

"The Trial of Ruby McCollum." In *Ruby McCollum: Woman in the Suwannee Jail,* by William Bradford Huie (New York: E. P. Dutton, 1956), pp. 89–101.

"This Juvenile Delinquency." *Fort Pierce Chronicle,* December 12, 1958.

"The Tripson Story." *Fort Pierce Chronicle,* February 6, 1959.

"The Farm Laborer at Home." *Fort Pierce Chronicle,* February 27, 1959.

"Hoodoo and Black Magic." *Fort Pierce Chronicle,* July 11, 1958–August 7, 1959.

UNPUBLISHED WORKS

"Art and Such." January 1938. Printed for the first time in *Reading Black, Reading Feminist: A Critical Anthology,* ed. Henry Louis Gates, Jr. (New York: Meridian Books, 1990), p. 27.

"Back to the Middle Ages, or: How to Become a Peasant in the United States." Essay.

Bama. Date of copyright registration: May 14, 1931. Musical compositions by Hurston and Grace Randolph Wood.

Barracoon. 1931. Biography of Cudjo Lewis.

"Black Death." Short story submitted to 1925 *Opportunity* contest.

Blue Bird. Date of copyright registration: May 14, 1931. Musical compositions by Hurston and Grace Randolph Wood.

"The Bone of Contention." Short story.

"Book of Harlem." Short story.

"The Chick with One Hen." Character sketch.

Cold Keener. Date of copyright registration: November 4, 1930. Dramatic work.

Cold Rainy Day. Date of copyright registration: May 14, 1931. Musical compositions by Hurston and Grace Randolph Wood.

"Contentment." Poem.

"The Conversion of Sam." Essay.

De Turkey and de Law. Date of copyright registration: October 29, 1930. Dramatic work.

"Eatonville." Essay

"Eatonville When You Look at It." In *The Florida Negro.*

"The Elusive Goal—Brotherhood of Mankind." Essay.

"The Emperor Effaces Himself." Character sketch.

"The Enemy." Personal experience.

The Fiery Chariot. A play in one act.

Fire and Sweat. Play.

"The Florida Expedition." Essay.

The Florida Negro. Manuscript prepared by Hurston and others for the Florida Federal Writers' Project.

"Folklore." In *The Florida Negro.*

Forty Yards. Date of copyright registration: August 6, 1931. Dramatic work.

Gointer See My Long-Haired Babe. Date of copyright registration: May 14, 1931. Musical composition by Hurston and Grace Randolph Wood.

The Golden Bench of God. Novel.

"Goldsborough." In *The Florida Negro.*

"Harlem Slanguage." Essay.

Herod the Great. Biography.

"Home." Poem.

"Joe Wiley of Magazine Point." Folklore.

"Just Like Us." Essay.

Lawing and Jawing. Date of copyright registration: July 21, 1931. Dramatic work.

The Lives of Barney Turk. Novel.

"Longin'." Poem.

"The Lost Keys of Glory." Story.

"Love." Poem.

"Maitland." In *The Florida Negro.*

Meet the Momma. Date of copyright registration: June 12, 1935. Dramatic work.

"The Migrant Worker in Florida." Journalism.

Mister Frog. Date of copyright registration: May 14, 1931. Musical compositions by Hurston and Grace Randolph Wood.

Mrs. Doctor. Novel.

Mule Bone: A Comedy of Negro Life. Play in three acts written with Langston Hughes. Act 3 published in *Drama Critique,* spring 1964, pp. 103–7. Play edited by George Houston Bass and Henry Louis Gates, Jr. (New York: HarperCollins, 1991).

"Negro Folk Tales." Folklore.

Negro Folk-Tales from the Gulf States. Folklore. Edited by Carla Kaplan (New York: HarperCollins, 2001).

"Negro Legends." Folklore.

"Negro Mythical Places." In *The Florida Negro.*

"Negro Religious Customs: The Sanctified Church." Folklore.

"Negro Work Songs." Folklore.

Poker. Date of copyright registration: July 21, 1931. Dramatic work.

Polk County: A Comedy of Negro Life on a Sawmill Camp, with Authentic Negro Music. Date of copyright registration: December 9, 1944. Play in three acts written by Hurston and Dorothy Waring (Mrs. Stephen Kelen d'Oxylion).

"Ritualistic Expression from the Lips of the Communicants of the Seventh Day Church of God, Beaufort, South Carolina." 1940. Essay.

The Sanctified Church. Anthropology. Edited by the Netzahualcoyotl Historical Society (Berkeley: Turtle Island Press, 1983).

"The Seventh Veil." Short story.

"The South Was Had." Essay.

Spunk. Date of copyright registration: June 15, 1935. Dramatic work.

"Take for Instance Spessard Holland." Essay.

There Stands a Blue Bird. Date of copyright registration: May 14, 1931. Musical compositions by Hurston and Grace Randolph Wood.

"Thou Art Mine." Poem.

"Turpentine." In *The Florida Negro.*

"Uncle Monday." In *The Florida Negro.*

"Unique Personal Experience." Essay.

"Which Way the NAACP." Essay.

"The Woman in Gaul." Short story.

Woofing. Play.

"You Don't Know Us Negroes." Essay.

You May Go. Date of copyright registration: July 2, 1931. Musical compositions by Hurston and Grace Randolph Wood.

SELECTED
BIBLIOGRAPHY

Anderson, Jervis. *This Was Harlem: A Cultural Portrait, 1900–1950.* New York: Farrar, Straus & Giroux, 1982.

Ayers, Edward L. *The Promise of the New South: Life After Reconstruction.* New York: Oxford University Press, 1992.

Bailey, Harry A., Jr., ed. *Negro Politics in America.* Columbus: Charles E. Merrill Books, 1967.

Bass, George Houston, and Henry Louis Gates, Jr., eds. *Mule Bone: A Comedy of Negro Life by Langston Hughes and Zora Neale Hurston.* New York: HarperCollins, 1991.

Berman, William C. *The Politics of Civil Rights in the Truman Administration.* Columbus: Ohio State University Press, 1970.

Bernard, Emily, ed. *Remember Me to Harlem: The Letters of Langston Hughes and Carl Van Vechten.* New York: Alfred A. Knopf, 1991.

Bigelow, Gordon. *Frontier Eden: The Literary Career of Marjorie Kinnan Rawlings.* Gainesville: University Press of Florida, 1966.

Bigelow, Gordon, and Laura V. Monti. *Selected Letters of Marjorie Kinnan Rawlings.* Gainesville: University Press of Florida, 1983.

Boas, Franz. *Anthropology and Modern Life.* New York: W. W. Norton, 1986.

Bordelon, Pamela, ed. *Go Gator and Muddy the Water: Writings by Zora Neale Hurston from the Federal Writers' Project.* New York: W. W. Norton, 1999.

Boston Herald Book Fair Committee. *Cordially Yours . . . A Selection of Original Short Stories and Essays by America's Leading Authors.* Boston, 1939.

Boylan, James. *The New Deal Coalition and the Election of 1946.* New York: Garland, 1981.

Brown, Canter, Jr. *Florida's Black Public Officials, 1867–1924.* Tuscaloosa: University of Alabama Press, 1998.

Buhle, Mari Jo, Paul Buhle, and Dan Georgakas, eds. *Encyclopedia of the American Left.* 2nd ed. New York: Oxford University Press, 1998.

Bunche, Ralph J. *The Political Status of the Negro in the Age of FDR.* Chicago: University of Chicago Press, 1973.

Burke, Virginia M. "Zora Neale Hurston and Fannie Hurst as They Saw Each Other." *CLA Journal: A Quarterly,* 20, no. 4 (June 1977), pp. 435–47.

Cobb, James C., and Michael Namorato. *The New Deal and the South*. Jackson: University of Mississippi Press, 1984.

Cronin, Gloria L., ed. *Critical Essays on Zora Neale Hurston*. New York: G. K. Hall, 1998.

Cruse, Harold. *The Crisis of the Negro Intellectual: A Historical Analysis of the Failure of Black Leadership*. New York: Quill, 1984.

Davis, John H. *The Guggenheims: An American Epic*. New York: William Morrow & Co., 1978.

Davis, Rose Parkman. *Zora Neale Hurston: An Annotated Bibliography and Reference Guide*. Westport, Conn.: Greenwood Press, 1997.

Davis, Thadious M. *Nella Larsen, Novelist of the Harlem Renaissance: A Woman's Life Unveiled*. Baton Rouge: Louisiana State University Press, 1994.

"Doll for Negro Children." *Life*, December 17, 1951, pp. 61–62.

Douglas, Ann. *Terrible Honesty: Mongrel Manhattan in the 1920's*. New York: Farrar, Straus & Giroux, 1995.

Duberman, Martin. *Paul Robeson: A Biography*. New York: New Press, 1989.

Du Bois, W. E. B. *Writings*. New York: Library of America, 1986.

Erskine, Helen Worden. *Out of This World: A Collection of Hermits and Recluses*. London: Bodley Head, 1954.

Favor, Martin J. *Authentic Blackness: The Folk in the New Negro Renaissance*. Durham: Duke University Press, 1999.

Gabbin, Joanne V. *Sterling Brown: Building the Black Aesthetic Tradition*. Charlottesville: University Press of Virginia, 1985.

Gambrell, Alice. *Women Intellectuals, Modernism, and Difference: Transatlantic Culture, 1919–1945*. Cambridge: Cambridge University Press, 1997.

Gates, Henry Louis, Jr., and Kwame Anthony Appiah. *Zora Neale Hurston: Critical Perspectives Past and Present*. New York: Amistad, 1993.

Glassman, Steve, and Kathryn Lee Seidel, eds. *Zora in Florida*. Orlando: University of Central Florida Press, 1991.

Goggin, Jacqueline. *Carter G. Woodson: A Life in Black History*. Baton Rouge: Louisiana State University Press, 1993.

Grant, Michael. *Herod the Great*. New York: American Heritage Press, 1971.

Green, Ben. *Before His Time: The Untold Story of Harry T. Moore, America's First Civil Rights Martyr*. New York: Free Press, 1991.

Griffin, Farah Jasmine. *Beloved Sisters and Loving Friends: Letters from Rebecca Primus of Royal Oak, Maryland, and Addie Brown of Hartford, Connecticut, 1854–1868*. New York: Knopf, 1999.

Grover, Edwin Osgood, ed. *Animal Lover's Knapsack*. New York: Thomas Y. Crowell, 1929.

Haygood, Wil. *King of the Cats: The Life and Times of Adam Clayton Powell, Jr.* Boston: Houghton Mifflin, 1993.

Hemenway, Robert. *Zora Neale Hurston: A Literary Biography*. Urbana: University of Illinois Press, 1977.

———. "Zora Neale Hurston and the Eatonville Anthropology." In Arna Bontemps, ed., *The Harlem Renaissance Remembered*. New York: Dodd, 1972.

——, ed. "Folklore Field Notes from Zora Neale Hurston." *Black Scholar,* April 1976, pp. 39–46.

Hill, Herbert. "The Communist Party—Enemy of Negro Equality." *Crisis,* August 1951.

Hine, Darlene Clark, and Kathleen Thompson. *A Shining Thread of Hope: The History of Black Women in America.* New York: Broadway Books, 1998.

Holt, Hamilton, ed. *The Life Stories of Distinguished Americans, as Told by Themselves.* New York: Routledge, 1990.

Howard, Lillie P. *Zora Neale Hurston.* Boston: Twayne, 1980.

Huggins, Nathan Irvin. *Harlem Renaissance.* New York: Oxford University Press, 1973.

——, ed. *Voices from the Harlem Renaissance.* New York: Oxford University Press, 1976.

Hughes, Langston. *The Big Sea.* New York: Knopf, 1940.

——. *Five Plays.* Bloomington: Indiana University Press, 1963.

Huie, William Bradford. *Ruby McCollum: Woman in the Suwannee Jail.* New York: E. P. Dutton and Company, 1956.

Hutchinson, George. *The Harlem Renaissance in Black and White.* Cambridge: Harvard University Press, 1995.

Jackson, Kenneth T., ed. *The Encyclopedia of New York City.* New Haven: Yale University Press, 1995.

Johnson, Abby Arthur, and Ronald Maberry Johnson. *Propaganda & Aesthetics: The Literary Politics of African-American Magazines in the Twentieth Century.* Amherst: University of Massachusetts Press, 1979.

Johnson, James Weldon. *Black Manhattan.* New York: Arno Press, 1968.

Jordan, June. "On Richard Wright and Zora Neale Hurston: Notes Toward a Balancing of Love and Hatred." *Black World,* 23 (August 1974).

Kaplan, Carla. *The Erotics of Talk: Women's Writing and Feminist Paradigms.* New York: Oxford, 1996.

——, ed. *Negro Folk-Tales from the Gulf States.* By Zora Neale Hurston. New York: HarperCollins, 2001.

Kellner, Bruce. *Carl Van Vechten and the Irreverent Decades.* Oklahoma: Oklahoma University Press, 1968.

——. *The Harlem Renaissance: A Historical Dictionary for the Era.* New York: Methuen, 1987.

——, ed. *Letters of Carl Van Vechten.* New Haven: Yale University Press, 1987.

Kirby, John B. *Black Americans in the Roosevelt Era.* Knoxville: University of Tennessee Press, 1980.

Kroeger, Brooke. *Fannie: The Talent for Success of Writer Fannie Hurst.* New York: Times Books, 1999.

Kuehl, Warren F. *Hamilton Holt: Journalist, Internationalist, Educator.* Gainesville: University of Florida Press, 1960.

Laville, Helen, and Scott Lucas. "The American Way: Edith Sampson, the NAACP, and African American Identity in the Cold War." *Democratic History,* 20, no. 4 (fall 1996), pp. 565–90.

Lewinson, Edwin R. *Black Politics in New York City.* New York: Twayne, 1974.

Lewis, David Levering, ed. *The Portable Harlem Renaissance Reader*. New York: Viking Penguin, 1994.

———. *When Harlem Was in Vogue*. New York: Oxford University Press, 1979.

Locke, Alain Leroy. *The New Negro: Voices of the Harlem Renaissance*. New York: Atheneum, 1992.

———. *Race Contacts and Interracial Relations*. Washington, D.C.: Howard University Press, 1992.

Lueders, Edward. *Carl Van Vechten and the Twenties*. Albuquerque: University of New Mexico Press, 1955.

Major, Clarence. *Juba to Jive: A Dictionary of African-American Slang*. New York: Penguin, 1994.

Mangione, Jerre. *The Dream and the Deal: The Federal Writers' Project, 1935–1943*. Syracuse: Syracuse University Press, 1996.

Maran, René. *Batouala*. Reprint, London: Heinemann, 1973.

Maxwell, William J. *New Negro, Old Left: African-American Writing and Communism Between the Wars*. New York: Columbia University Press, 1999.

McAuliffe, Mary Sperling. *Crisis on the Left: Cold War Politics and American Liberals, 1947–1954*. Amherst: University of Massachusetts Press, 1978.

McKay, Claude. *A Long Way from Home*. New York: Harcourt Brace Jovanovich, 1970.

Mershon, Katharane Edson. *Seven Plus Seven: Mysterious Life-Rituals in Bali*. New York: Vintage, 1971.

Naison, Mark. *Communists in Harlem During the Depression*. New York: Grove, 1983.

Nathiri, N. Y. *Zora!: A Woman and Her Community*. Orlando: Sentinel Communications, 1991.

Nichols, Charles H., ed. *Arna Bontemps–Langston Hughes: Letters*. New York: Paragon House, 1990.

Orser, Frank. "Tracy L'Engle Angas and Zora Neale Hurston: Correspondence and Friendship." Special issue "Zora Neale Hurston," ed. Anna Lillios. *Southern Quarterly: A Journal of the Arts in the South*, 36, no. 3 (spring 1998), pp. 61–67.

Osofsky, Gilbert. *Harlem: The Making of a Ghetto: Negro New York, 1890–1930*. 2nd ed. New York: Harper & Row, 1971.

Otey, Frank. *Eatonville, Florida: A Brief History*. Winter Park, Fla.: Four-G Publishers, 1989.

Ottley, Roi, and William Weatherby, eds. *The Negro in New York: An Informal Social History*. New York: New York Public Library, 1967.

Parker, Idella, with Mary Keating. *Idella: Marjorie Rawlings' "Perfect Maid."* Gainesville: University Press of Florida, 1992.

Parker, Idella, with Bud and Liz Crussell. *Idella Parker: From Reddick to Cross Creek*. Gainesville: University Press of Florida, 1999.

Patterson, T. James. *Mr. Republican: A Biography of Robert A. Taft*. New York: Houghton Mifflin, 1972.

Pepper, Claude Danson. *Pepper: Eyewitness to a Century*. New York: Harcourt Brace Jovanovich, 1987.

Perowne, Stewart. *The Life and Times of Herod the Great.* London: Hodder & Stoughton, 1956.

Perry, Margaret. *The Harlem Renaissance: An Annotated Bibliography and Commentary.* New York: Garland, 1982.

Price, H. D. *The Negro and Southern Politics: A Chapter of Florida History.* New York: New York University Press, 1957.

Rampersad, Arnold. *The Life of Langston Hughes,* vol. 1, *1902–1941, I, Too, Sing America.* New York: Oxford University Press, 1986.

———. *The Life of Langston Hughes,* vol. 2, *1941–1967, I Dream a World.* New York: Oxford University Press, 1988.

"Realistic Negro Dolls." *St. Louis Post Dispatch,* November 11, 1951.

Record, Wilson. *Race and Radicalism: The NAACP and the Communist Party in Conflict.* Ithaca: Cornell University Press, 1964.

Robbins, Richard. *Sidelines Activist: Charles S. Johnson and the Struggle for Civil Rights.* Jackson: University Press of Mississippi, 1996.

Ross, Joyce B. *J. E. Spingarn and the Rise of the NAACP, 1911–1939.* New York: Atheneum, 1972.

Rymer, Russ. *American Beach: How "Progress" Robbed a Black Town—and Nation— of History, Wealth, and Power.* New York: HarperPerennial, 2000.

Sandburg, Carl. *New American Songbag.* New York: Broadcast Music, 1950.

Scally, Sister Anthony. *Carter G. Woodson: A Bio-Bibliography.* Westport, Conn.: Greenwood Press, 1985.

Scheiner, Seth M. *Negro Mecca: A History of the Negro in New York City, 1865–1920.* New York: New York University Press, 1965.

Silverthorne, Elizabeth. *Marjorie Kinnan Rawlings: Sojourner at Cross Creek.* Woodstock, N.Y.: Overlook Press, 1988.

Simpson, George Eaton. *Melville J. Herskovits.* New York: Columbia University Press, 1973.

Smitherman, Geneva. *Black Talk: Words and Phrases from the Hood to the Amen Corner.* Boston: Houghton Mifflin, 1994.

Stocking, George W. *Race, Culture, and Evolution: Essays in the History of Anthropology.* New York: Free Press, 1968.

Sullivan, Patricia. *Days of Hope: Race and Democracy in the New Deal Era.* Chapel Hill: University of North Carolina Press, 1996.

Talalay, Kathryn. *Composition in Black and White: The Life of Philippa Schuyler.* New York: Oxford University Press, 1995.

Vincent, Theodore G., ed. *Voices of a Black Nation: Political Journalism in the Harlem Renaissance.* Trenton: Africa World Press, n.d.

Von Eschen, Penny M. *Race Against Empire: Black Americans and Anticolonialism, 1937–1957.* Ithaca: Cornell University Press, 1997.

Walker, Alice. "In Search of Zora Neale Hurston." *MS.* 3 (March), pp. 74–79, 85–87.

Walker, Alice, ed. *I Love Myself When I Am Laughing . . .* New York: Feminist Press, 1979.

Wall, Cheryl A., ed. *Zora Neale Hurston: Folklore, Memoirs, and Other Writings.* New York: Library of America, 1995.

Wall, Cheryl A., ed. *Zora Neale Hurston: Novels and Stories.* New York: Library of America, 1995.

Watson, Steven. *The Harlem Renaissance: Hub of African-American Culture, 1920–1930.* New York: Pantheon Books, 1995.

White, William S. *The Taft Story.* New York: Harper & Row, 1954.

Wiesen Cook, Blanche. *Eleanor Roosevelt,* vol. 1, *1884–1933.* New York: Penguin, 1992.

———. *Eleanor Roosevelt,* vol. 2, *The Defining Years, 1933–1938.* New York: Penguin, 1999.

Williams, Susan Miller. *A Devil and a Good Woman Too: The Lives of Julia Peterkin.* Athens: University of Georgia Press, 1997.

Wirkus, Faustin. *The White King of La Gonave.* New York: Doubleday, 1931.

Wolf, Charles, and Kip Lornell. *The Life and Legend of Leadbelly.* New York: HarperCollins, 1992.

Wolseley, Roland E. *The Black Press, U.S.A.* 2nd ed. Ames: Iowa State University Press, 1990.

Zinn, Howard. *A People's History of the United States: 1942–Present.* New York: HarperCollins, 1999.

ACKNOWLEDGMENTS

In the course of editing a volume such as this, one incurs many debts. This book could not have been completed without the generous assistance of scholars, librarians, colleagues, friends, family, and students. It is a pleasure to acknowledge the remarkable generosity I encountered while working on this book.

Some of the earliest work on this project began at the Schomburg Center for Research in Black Culture; I gratefully acknowledge the support of the Aaron Diamond Fund of the National Endowment for the Humanities. The University of Southern California supported this project in the form of Faculty Development Grants and an Undergraduate Research Program Award, which allowed me to involve some of my undergraduate students in research. I thank deans Joseph Aoun and Beth Meyerowitz for a study leave, which allowed me to both complete the book and to recuperate from it.

I had the privilege of giving talks on Hurston's letters at the Center for Feminist Research, University of Southern California; the Los Angeles Humanities Institute; the International Conference on Narrative Theory, Dartmouth College; the University of Washington; Mt. Holyoke College; New York University; Princeton University; Antioch College, Los Angeles Campus; and the Modern Language Association. I am grateful to all of these audiences for their feedback and to my graduate students in Hurston seminars at Yale University and the University of Southern California.

Deep gratitude is owed to those who I interviewed: Margaret Benton; Norman Chalfin; Sara Lee Creech; Patrick Duvall; Jean Parker Waterbury; William Clifford; Cartheda Taylor Mann; Michael Silver; and Bruce Smathers.

I owe an enormous debt to the librarians and archivists who answered innumerable questions and filled endless requests for materials: Alison Lewis at the American Philosophical Society; Brenda Phillips Square and Rebecca Hankins at the Amistad Center; Karen Jefferson at Atlanta University; Jane Lowenthal and Donald Glassman at Barnard; Susan McElrath at Bethune-Cookman; Susan C. Pyzynski at Brandeis; Jean Ashton at Columbia University; Linda McCurty at Duke; Nancine Thompson and Craig Tuttle at Florida Atlantic University; G. Thomas Tanselle at the Guggenheim Foundation; Leslie A. Morris at the Houghton Library, Harvard University; Becky Cape and Saundra Taylor at Indiana University; Alice Birney, Deborah Ann Evans, and Mary Wolfskill at the Library of Congress; Ed Gibson at Lincoln University; Sam Boldrick at the Miami-Dade Public Library; Thomas Verich at the University of Mississippi; JoEllen ElBashir at Moorland-Spingram; Jason D. Stratman at the Missouri Historical Society; Walter B. Hill, Jr., and Heather Mcrae at the National Archives; P. J. Brownlee at the National Council for the Traditional Arts; Janet C. Olson at Northwestern University; Anna Lee Pauls, Margaret Sherry, and Don Skemer at Princeton; Sylvia McDowell at the Radcliffe Institute, Harvard University; Paulette Delahoussaye, Kathy Henderson, and Tara Wenger at the Harry Ransom Humanities Research Center; Kate Reich and Trudy Laframboise at Rollins College; Anne Engelhart and Marie-Helene Gold at the Schlesinger Library; Diana Lachatenere and Mary Yearwood at the Schomburg Center for Research in Black Culture; Wendy Chmielewski at Swarthmore; Terry Keenan at Syracuse University; Nancy Beard at Western Kentucky University; Georgia de la Garzia, Ricardo Villegas Tovar, and the Miguel Covarrubias Collection at the University of the Americas in Puebla, Mexico; Jeffrey Barr at the University of Florida, Gainesville; Eileen Brady at the University of North Florida; Linda Seidman at the University of Massachusetts; Laura C. Brown and Rachel Canada at the University of North Carolina; Debra T. Wynne at the University of South Florida; Mary Mackechnie at Special Collections, Vassar College; Elaine McIlroy at the Wellfleet Public Library; Marlayna Gates, Alfred Mueller, Ellen Cordes, Patricia Willis, and all the Beinecke librarians at Yale University. Very special appreciation goes to Frank Orser at Gainesville, Ruth Wallach and Yolanda Retter ("research goddess"), both at USC.

I am deeply grateful to my crackerjack research assistants for excellent research and much-appreciated moral support on the footnotes and glossary: Silvia Aviles, Elizabeth Binggeli, Beth Callaghan, Russell Dahlquist, Joanna Davis, Lissa Fetter, Anthony Foy, Caitlin Goddard, Eric B. Grant, Jinny Huh, Jake Milstein, Tanynya Patterson, Jennifer Rosenhaft, Kathy Strong, and Devi Zinzuvadia. I am especially grateful for "dramastic" last-minute help with the galleys from Beth Callaghan and Kathy Strong.

Indispensable help, material and nonmaterial, was offered by many. I am grateful to Hugo Achugar, Michael Anania, Nellie Ayala-Reyes, Kristy Anderson, Jocelyn Baltzell, Nancy Berg, Kate Chandler, Amy Cherry, Gaye Clock, William Jelani Cobb, John C. Conlon, John Doggett Corse, Toisan Craigg, Kathie and Stewart Dalzell, Roxanne Davis, Alice Echols, Percival Everett, Lynn Enterline, Joanna Fabris, Robert Finch, Lynn Fleischer, Henry Louis Gates, Jr., Gerald Graff, Alice Morgan Grant, Laura Green, Shocky Greenberg, Margaret Homans, the late Lee Howell, Lynne Huffer, Robin Hultgren, Selena James, Claudia Johnson, Delores Hogan Johnson, Rosalyn Kaplan, Caledonia Kearns, Bruce Kellner, Stetson Kennedy, Rob Knaack, Lindy Seidner Lohmann, Susan Lurie, Liz Maguire, Peter Manning, Jane Marcus, Susan McCabe, Nina Miller, Lynn Moylan, N. Y. Nathiri, Marilyn Neimark, Cory Nohl, Gordon Patterson, Carla Peterson, Donald Pease, Paul Robeson, Jr., Lisa Rood, Rosalind Rosenberg, Jennifer Rosenhaft, Flora Ruiz, Meg Russett, Russ Rymer, Victoria Sanders, Mo Sila, Michael Silver, Alisa Solomon, Roberta Spivak, Judith Stacey, David Sternbach, David Kaplan-Taylor, Brenda Kay Watson, Imani Wilson, Jamie Wolf, and Louise Yelin. Special thanks to Steve Larsen, my magnificent light at the end of a long tunnel—gratitude always.

Friends and colleagues who read portions of the manuscript include: Jonathan Arac, Lois Banner, Joe Boone, Hazel Carby, John C. Conlon, Erin Cramer, Michael Denning, Judith Jackson Fossett, Alice Gambrell, Farah Jasmine Griffin, Bruce Kellner, Kathleen McHugh, Brooke Kroeger, Tara McPherson, Tania Modleski, Douglas Payne, Kathy Shorr, and Robert Stepto. I am profoundly grateful for their feedback.

An enormous debt is owed to the family, friends, and colleagues who read all of the manuscript, sometimes in multiple versions: Russell Dahlquist, Bernard Kaplan, Clair Kaplan, and Amy Kaplan, who now knows more about Hurston than she ever imagined possible.

A very special thank-you is due to two scholars who were unwavering in their openness to my questions and invaluable, always, in their replies: Robert Hemenway, who opened his file cabinets to me one hot August and who supported this work from the very first, and Emily Bernard, who has been a true friend and a terrific reader at every stage. Both set an extraordinary model for me.

The community of Hurston scholars was gracious and generous. I am particularly grateful to Pamela Bordelon, Valerie Boyd, C. Arthur Ellis, Jr. (*The Trial of Ruby McCollum*), Claudia Johnson, Brooke Kroeger, and, especially, Lynn Moylan.

This book would not have existed without the support of the Hurston family, especially Lucy Ann Hurston and Lois Gaston; my agents, John Taylor Williams and Brettne Bloom; and my generous and insightful editor, Janet Hill; all of whom saw the value of this project from the very start and invested their trust in me throughout a process which turned out to be more complex than any of us could have predicted. My terrific team at Doubleday included Roberta Spivak, Toisan Craigg, Katia Nelson, Vanessa Weeks Page, Charlee Trantino, Lawrence Krauser, and Nancy Clements, and I gratefully acknowledge all their help and attention. I was also lucky in having the assistance of those I worked with at Anchor, and I would especially like to thank Alice van Straalen.

The following archives provided copies of Hurston's letters and other assistance for which I am grateful: the Annie Nathan Meyer Papers, American Jewish Archives; Charles S. Johnson and Countee Cullen Papers, Amistad Research Center; Franz Boas Papers, American Philosophical Society (Courtesy of the American Philosophical Society); Barnard College Archives; Langston Hughes Papers, Zora Neale Hurston Papers, Harold Jackman Papers, James Weldon Johnson Papers, Thomas E. Jones Papers, Carl Van Vechten Papers, and Walter White Papers, the James Weldon Johnson Memorial Collection of African American Arts and Letters, Beinecke Rare Book and Manuscript Library, Yale University; Dorothy West Papers, Boston University; Fannie Hurst Papers, the Robert D. Farber University Archives and Special Collections Department, Brandeis University Libraries; Claude A. Barnett Papers, Chicago Historical Society; Helen Worden Erskine Papers, Rare Book and Manuscript Library, Columbia University; Rosenwald Papers, Fisk University Library, Special Collections; the Archives of the John Simon Guggenheim Memorial Foundation; Lewis Gannett Papers, Houghton Library, Harvard University; NAACP Papers, Margaret Mead Papers, Carter Woodson Papers, and the General Collections of the Manuscript and Folklore Divisions, Library of Congress; Benjamin Botkin Papers, American Folklife Center, Library of Congress; Florida Authors Collection, Miami-Dade Public Library; Max Eastman Papers, The Lilly Library, Indiana University (Courtesy, Lilly Library, Indiana University, Bloomington, Indiana); Alain Locke Papers, Moorland-Spingarn Research Center, Howard University; the Records of the Works Projects Administration, the Records of the Federal Writers Project, National Archives; the Melville J. Herskovits Papers, Northwestern University; Archives of Charles Scribner's Sons, Manuscript Division, Department of Rare Books and Special Collections, Princeton University Library; Fannie Hurst Papers, Harry Ransom Research Center, University of Texas at Austin; John Avery Papers, Center for American History, Harry Ransom Research Center, University of Texas at Austin; Department of College Archives, Special Collections, Rollins College; Carl Sandburg Papers, Rare Books and Special Collections Library, University of Illinois, Urbana-Champaign; Dorothy West Papers, Schlesinger Library, Radcliffe Institute, Harvard University; Zora Neale Hurston Collection, Manuscripts, Archives, and Rare Books Division, Schomburg Center for Research in Black Culture, the New York Public Library, Astor, Lenox and Tilden Foundations; the W. E. B. Du Bois Papers, Special Collections and Archives, W. E. B. Du Bois Library, University of Massachusetts; Paul Green Papers, Southern Historical Collection, Wilson Library, University of North Carolina at Chapel Hill; Zora Neale Hurston Papers, George A. Smathers Libraries, University of Florida, Special Collections; Miguel Covarrubias Papers, Puebla Biblioteca, Universidad de Las Americas; Herschel Brickell Papers, Williams Library, Williams College; Ruth Benedict Papers, Special Collections, Vassar College Library.

2.

to add to the store of human Knowledge and permanent literature. So don't bother about me. You could never understand me.

Cordially yours

Dr. Zora Neale Hurston Lit. D.

Undated letter fragment.

INDEX OF
RECIPIENTS

June 4, 1931
July 23, 1931
August 14, 1931
September 15, [1931]
September 25, 1931
October 10, 1931
October 15, 1931
October 26, 1931
December 16, 1931
December 21, 1931
January 14, 1932
January 21, 1932
February 29, 1932
March 19, 1932

March 27, 1932
April 4, 1932
April 16, 1932
April 27, 1932
May 8, 1932
May 17, 1932
May 26, 1932
July 6, 1932
July 20, 1932
July 29, 1932
August 11, 1932
September 16, 1932
September 28, 1932
January 6, 1933

EGON MATHIESON
January 22, 1948

MCINTOSH AND MCKEE
May 11, 1951

May 28, 1951

ANNIE NATHAN MEYER
May 12, 1925
June 23, 1923[5]
July 18, 1925
September 15, 1925
September 28, 1925
October 12, 1925
October 17, 1925
November 10, 1925
December 6, 1925
December 13, 1925
December 17, [1925]
[1925]

[winter 1925/26]
[January 1926]
January 15, [1926]
January 31, 1926
February 22, [1926?]
[spring 1926?]
March 7, 1927
May 22, 1927
October 7, 1927
April 25, 1935
[spring 1937]
[Jan. 15, 1941]

MIAMI PUBLIC LIBRARY REFERENCE
LIBRARIANS
December 6, 1955

BURROUGHS MITCHELL
July 31, 1947
September 3, 1947
[September 1947]
October 2, 1947
October 1947
December 5, 1947

January 14, 1948
February 3, 1948
February 14, [1948]
August 5, 1948
[winter 1950]
January 24, 1950
February 3, 1950

INDEX

Numbers in italics refer to photographs and drawings; ZNH refers to Zora Neale Hurston